*Death
Without
Weeping*

Death
Without
Weeping

*The Violence
of Everyday Life
in Brazil*

NANCY SCHEPER-HUGHES

University of California Press

BERKELEY   LOS ANGELES   LONDON

University of California Press
Berkeley and Los Angeles, California

University of California Press, Ltd.
London, England

© 1992 by
The Regents of the University of California

First Paperback Printing 1993

Library of Congress Cataloging-in-Publication Data

Scheper-Hughes, Nancy.
    Death without weeping : the violence of everyday life in Brazil /
Nancy Scheper-Hughes.
        p.   cm.
    "A Centennial book."
    Includes bibliographical references and index.
    ISBN 0-520-07537-4 (ppb.)
    1. Poor women—Brazil, Northeast. 2. Mother and infant—
Brazil, Northeast. 3. Infants—Brazil, Northeast—Death.
4. Violence—Brazil, Northeast. 5. Brazil, Northeast—Social
conditions. 6. Brazil, Northeast—Social life and customs.
I. Title.
HV1448.B72N677   1992
303.6'0981—dc20   91-12829
                                                CIP

Printed in the United States of America

08   07   06   05   04   03   02   01   00
12   11   10   9   8   7   6

To George Louis and Anne Znojemsky Scheper,
for the gift of life,
and to Michael, Jennifer, Sarah, and Nathanael,
for making that life worth living.
And to Seu Jacques, wherever you are . . .

Contents

I have seen death without weeping.
The destiny of the Northeast is death.
Cattle they kill,
but to the people they do something worse.

Geraldo Vandre, *Disparada*

Prologue
Sugar House

And our faces, my heart
brief as photos
   John Berger (1984:5)

Connections

There was, however improbably, an artist living on our block, on South
Third Street in the Williamsburg section of Brooklyn. He inhabited a
basement apartment, the kind below street level with iron bars across the
windows, so that when one looked out all that could be seen were amputated
legs and feet scurrying across pavement. How he painted in that dark, dank,
cold-water flat I'll never know, but it obviously required great powers of
imagination. We didn't have a clue that the funny little man—Morris Kish
was his name—was anything at all until he invited several neighbors to a
"showing" in his flat. We children sat together, in the front, on straight-
backed kitchen chairs, half expecting we would have to suppress giggles and
then gales of laughter. For what could Morris Kish ever think to paint?

   Morris Kish could think to paint a great deal, indeed, and I remember
being lost in a swirl of colors and vivid impressions and impish magic, as he
showed us what *we* never thought to see in the rundown, workaday world of
Williamsburg. There was the bridge, of course, but a bridge teeming with
humanity crossing and recrossing, bundled in long coats and sweaters, each
face revealing a different story. There was the Saints Peter and Paul Church
carnival, not the dowdy one with dull paint-chipped carousel horses and
abusive "carneys" that we knew but rather the carnival when, just before
dawn and after the crowds had left, the carousel horses came alive and
danced and played cards with each other. But what I remember most of all in
those huge surprise canvases were the men of Berry Street and South First
and South Second all rushing and converging together on the front gates of
the black monster that dominated our landscape, the DOMINO SUGAR
refining factory, which we knew only as the "Sugar House." Those of us who
grew up at the foot of the factory—adults and children, workers and not—

all responded to the movements of the beast. We woke to its shrill whistles, its humming and clangings were a permanent backdrop to all our conversations, we breathed its foul fumes, and finally we went to bed to the comforting sound of foghorns guiding ships and their precious cargo to its docks. The crude block of brown sugar coming from the tropics (darkest Africa, we imagined, for what did we on South Third Street in Brooklyn know?) would be purified and whitened, while our flats were dirtied and darkened by the damnable Sugar House soot. How, we wondered, could something so sweet and delectable come out of that noisy, smelly, dirty place? It was, I supposed, a mystery rather like the Holy Trinity, puzzling and a bit paradoxical but accepted, unquestioningly, on faith.

This book takes me full circle from childhood to midlife, for it is, I think, no coincidence that my anthropology finally brought me "home" to Northeast Brazil and to those verdant but cloying fields of sugarcane (more akin, Claude Levi-Strauss was to write, to "open-air factories, than to a landscape" [1961:99]) to work with people who invariably describe themselves as having grown up "at the foot" of the cane. Foot of the factory, foot of the cane, we are all implicated (as workers and as consumers) in the vicious sugar cycle and in the *miséria morta*, "deadly misery," it leaves in its wake. As a child of the Williamsburg Eastern European (later Puerto Rican) slum, I was marked by the image of the Sugar House, and in writing about the cane cutters and their families of Bom Jesus da Mata, I am also trying to reach out and touch the fading images of those sugar workers I knew as a child and whose faces I remember but only, as it turns out, in the vivid and impressionistic paintings of Morris Kish.

The ethnographer, like the artist, is engaged in a special kind of vision quest through which a specific interpretation of the human condition, an entire sensibility, is forged. Our medium, our canvas, is "the field," a place both proximate and intimate (because we have lived some part of our lives there) as well as forever distant and unknowably "other" (because our own destinies lie elsewhere). In the act of "writing culture," what emerges is always a highly subjective, partial, and fragmentary—but also deeply felt and personal—record of human lives based on eyewitness and testimony. The act of witnessing is what lends our work its moral (at times its almost theological) character. So-called participant observation has a way of drawing the ethnographer into spaces of human life where she or he might really prefer not to go at all and once there doesn't know how to go about getting out except through writing, which draws others there as well, making them party to the act of witnessing.

These are not ordinary lives that I am about to describe. Rather, they are short, violent, and hungry lives. I am offering here a glimpse into *Nor-*

destino society through a glass darkly. It entails a descent into a Brazilian heart of darkness, and as it begins to touch on and to evoke some of our worst fears and unconscious dreads about "human nature," and about mothers and infants in particular, one may experience righteous indignation. Why am I being served this? Death is never an easy topic, not for science, not for art. It is not surprising that Edvard Munch's most famous expressionist painting, *Death of a Child*, was also the one that most outraged and offended his sophisticated cosmopolitan audience.

But lest we forget: the reading, the reflecting, and the writing are as nothing in comparison with the cost to those who have lived the stories told here. And these lives, these faces, although pained and as fleeting as photos, have also been touched with beauty and grace. I trust I have done them no further violence in the rough and impressionistic strokes I have left on this canvas.

My story begins, then, in a specific relationship to the community, one generally thought of today in critical and enlightened anthropological circles as something of a stigma, just one step removed, perhaps, from having been a Christian missionary: I was a twenty-year-old public health/community development worker with the Peace Corps. (Because stigma and stigmata are generative themes of this book, my own stigmatizing origins in the field seem appropriate.)

Ours was the first group sent into the northeastern (*Nordestino*) state of Pernambuco, and we arrived on the coattails of a "bloodless" and "peaceful" military coup in the spring of 1964 that turned out to be not so bloodless or blameless as time wore on. Contracted to work as rural health extension agents for the Pernambucan Health Department, we were assigned to health posts in the "interior" of the state, the women to work as *visitadoras*, the men as "sanitary engineers." *Visitadoras* were door-to-door frontline health workers in poor and marginalized communities, a concept not too far removed from Chairman Mao's "barefoot doctors." The engineers were "backyard" health workers mainly employed in digging pit latrines, although monitoring trash disposal and water supplies was also part of the job description.

My first assignment, however, was not to a community per se but to a large public hospital in a town that I call Belem do Nordeste, located in the sugarcane plantation zone, the so-called *zona da mata*. The hospital served the impoverished cane workers (and their families) of the region. For the first few weeks I slept on a fold-up cot in the emergency rehydration clinic, where small babies mortally sick with diarrhea/dehydration were brought for treatment when it was usually too late to save them. That first encounter with child death left its mark on me, indelibly so.

The hospital in Belem do Nordeste functioned without a qualified medical staff (and often without running water as well) for most hours of the day and night, and the patients, both young and adult, were treated largely by untrained practical nurses with the assistance of hospital orderlies, who, when they were not washing floors, helped to deliver babies and suture wounds. My one lasting contribution to that first assignment, before leaving in a state of considerable ignominy, was to organize in February of that year a fated *carnaval* ball in the back wards of the hospital where the terminally ill, the highly contagious, and the stigmatized ill were isolated from other patients. When a hospital administrator arrived unexpectedly to find some of the more "animated" back-ward patients dancing in the halls and spilling out into the enclosed courtyard dressed in borrowed surgical garb and masks for their *carnaval* costumes, he was not pleased.

My next assignment was to a more lively town in the extreme north of

Hospital *carnaval*.

the sugarcane region, one bordering the state of Paraíba. This town, which I call (and not without a hint of irony) Bom Jesus da Mata, is the locus of this book. After living for a few weeks in the home of the laboratory technician of the state health post, I moved into a small *quarto* (room) of a mud-walled hut near the top of a hillside "invasion" *bairro* that had annexed itself to the town. The shantytown of some five thousand rural workers was called the Alto do Cruzeiro, or simply O Cruzeiro, a reference to the large crucifix that dominated the top of the hill.

The hillside was first "occupied" in the 1930s but began to grow rapidly in the late 1950s when many rural workers in the *canavieira*, the sugarcane region, were forced off their traditional small holdings, where they had lived for generations as "conditional squatters" (*moradores de condição*) on marginal plantation lands. Shantytowns sprung up throughout the plantation zone during this particularly accelerated phase in the "modernization" of the sugar industry. The couple with whom I lived, Nailza and her husband, Zé Antônio, had just returned from the state of Mato Grosso, where they had migrated following word that new lands were available to those willing to "colonize" them. But it had not been a successful venture, and Zé

Panorama: Bom Jesus da Mata.

Antônio was happy to return to his native Nordeste. But Nailza, a part Tupi-Guarani Indian *cabocla* from Mato Grosso, despised the Nordeste and the "spineless dependency" (as she saw it) of the sugarcane workers. And she longed to return again to her native region.

There on the Alto do Cruzeiro I was able, finally, to actualize my work as a *visitadora* and as an *animadora do bairro* (community organizer). I was ridiculously proud of my official uniform—a black skirt, white nylon blouse, thick cotton stockings, and large brown handbag that contained the essential paraphernalia of the *visitadora:* a single glass syringe and a few hypodermic needles, with a pumice stone to sharpen the blunt points from time to time; a portable sterilization mess kit; a bottle of alcohol; a pair of surgical scissors; gauze; a bar of yellow soap and a roll of extra-strength toilet paper. *Visitadoras* were expected to pick up various vaccines (against smallpox, diphtheria, tetanus, whooping cough, and tuberculosis) as well as a small array of basic medications (piperizine, aralan, antibiotics, painkillers, and so on) from the local health posts to which they were assigned. Often these medical supplies were lacking.

During daylight hours I "walked the Alto" immunizing infants and babies, giving glucose shots to all the "weak" and dispirited adults who wanted them, and administering penicillin injections to the dozens of *mora-*

dores with active cases of tuberculosis. I was, in effect, a kind of "injection doctor" and a popular one among the young mothers of the Alto who particularly appreciated the care I took in swabbing every infant backside with alcohol and with my swab marking the upper right quadrant where it was safest to apply the injection. "*Oh, chê!*" the women exclaimed. "What a *doutora santa*—she makes the sign of the cross on every baby's behind!" In addition, I took feces samples from children whose bellies were particularly pregnant with parasites and blood samples from the *mulheres da vida* (prostitutes), and I established a record system whereby each prostitute was registered with the local health post and her health status periodically monitored. Each bore a card that certified, where appropriate, a clean bill of health. Finally, I dressed wounds, rubbed down the bodies of those tormented with tropical fevers, and very occasionally (and reluctantly) delivered babies if one of the local midwives could not be found. Not infrequently, *visitadoras* were called on to assist in preparing the bodies of dead children for burial.

In some localities *visitadoras* also worked as community organizers. In rural Pernambuco the model for community organization, before the penetration of the military presence into every nook and cranny of social life, was Paulo Freire's method of *conscientização* (critical consciousness) through literacy training (see Freire 1970, 1973). And so my evenings were often spent in small "cultural circles," as they were called, where by the light of smoky and flickering kerosene lamps, residents and squatters of the Alto learned to read while simultaneously organizing around the founding of a shantytown association, which was known by the acronym UPAC (União para o Progresso do Alto do Cruzeiro, or the Union for the Progress of the Alto do Cruzeiro). I served as a founding member and *orientadora política* of UPAC, and I worked with members in the collective construction of a headquarters for "local action," a child care center that also served at nights and on weekends when the creche was closed as an adult literacy school, a game room, a dance hall, a house of Afro-Brazilian spiritism, and a large meeting room for the boisterous "general assemblies" of the shantytown association. Often I groped blindly to understand and act within a context of radical, sometimes opaque, cultural difference as well as within a situation of economic misery and political repression in which my own country played a contributing and supporting role.

In 1964–1966 about a third of the residents of the Alto do Cruzeiro lived in straw huts, the remainder in small homes constructed of wattle and daub. The mayor of Bom Jesus (the long-reigning *prefeito*, whom I refer to as Seu Félix), had gradually come to understand that the urban squatters of the Alto were now permanent residents of the town, and he began to extend certain minimal public services to the shantytown. Municipal street lamps were provided along the two main roads, front and back of the hill, and those *moradores* living close enough to them to do so "pirated" electricity to their homes. But the vast majority of residents relied on kerosene lamps, which resulted in frequent fires that were particularly catastrophic to the simplest homes made of straw. Many older residents today carry serious burn scars that resulted from such accidents in childhood. There was a single source of running water, a public spigot, a *chafariz*, installed at the base of the hill, and Alto women lined up twice a day (between 4:00 and 6:00 in the morning and again at night) to fill five-gallon tin cans and then carry them home gracefully on their heads. Those who arrived late, or at the end of the long line, often went home empty-handed and were forced to fetch water at the banks of the chemically and industrially polluted Capibaribe River, which ran through the town carrying debris from the sugar factories as well as from the local hospital and the tanning factories of Bom Jesus. For those *moradores* who lived near the top of the Alto, the burden of carrying heavy cans of water up the hill was a daily source of misery. It was what people most often had on their minds when they referred to the everyday *luta* (struggle) that was life.

Most Alto men and boys worked as seasonal sugarcane cutters for various plantations during the harvest season and were unemployed in the interim. Some men and a few women worked in the municipal slaughterhouse on the eves of the large open-air market (*feira*) held in Bom Jesus on Wednesdays and Saturdays. The *feira* of Bom Jesus served the entire *município*, the town and its rural surrounds (including several large sugar plantations and mills), and scores of rural workers and their families arrived by truckloads to do their marketing or to buy, sell, or trade horses and jackasses. Some Alto men were employed by the *município* to sweep the streets following market days. In an early journal entry in 1965 I described the *feira* of Bom Jesus. It has hardly changed since that time.

> There is a steady, manic beat to the market, and one must learn how to fall in with the crush of humanity and with the din of street cries, whistles, catcalls, and beggars' laments. Today, however, the winter rains, pounding off the tops of the canvas stalls, all but muffled the usual sounds, so I was caught unaware by a hand attached to a long, thin arm that tugged at my skirt. It was a tall, skinny, sallow-faced boy with eye rims and fingernails that were morbidly white. "Dona Nancí," he rasped in an eerie, faraway voice, "*estou morrendo* [I'm dying]." He repeated this several times with no other intent than announcing his obvious condition. I escaped this ghost in the crowd only to have a strange vendor thrust a large

wedge of ripe farmer's cheese in my face. "Here, *moça* [girl, but also virgin], have a smell of my pungent cheese," he said with a hint of malicious mischief. I quickly elbowed my way into the indoor municipal market, trying not to breathe while passing the stalls with their coils of entrails and slightly rotting, fresh beef. From their overhead perch the *urubus* [vultures] flexed their greasy, black wings, slowly and deliberately casting their ominous shadows on the stands below. Were I a butcher, I wouldn't tempt the birds by wearing the same blood-soaked apron day after day.

Alto workers earned little, about forty or fifty cents a day in the mid-1960s, not nearly enough to feed, house, and clothe a family. What saved many Alto households were the rented garden plots, their small *roçados*, often a few kilometers outside of town, where women and men cultivated basic foodstuffs to feed their families. In addition to tending their *roçados*, most Alto women with large families had to work outside the home for wages. Some were domestics in the "big houses" (*casas grandes*) of the wealthy on country estates and in town. Many more women, such as Tonieta and Nailza, worked as *lavadeiras*, taking in the dirty laundry of middle-class, and even working-class, families able to pay a pittance for the grueling work. Without public washstands, the only recourse was to wash clothes in the schistosome-infested river, dry them on the sand or over bushes, and carry the bundle home for starching and ironing with heavy cast-iron irons filled with burning charcoal.

Whether they worked on the plantations or in the homes of the rich, Alto women had to leave their babies (even newborns) at home unattended or watched over by siblings, sometimes barely more than babies themselves. These constraints on infant tending, imposed by the economic realities of Alto life, contributed to an exceedingly high infant and child mortality. To a young and naive North American, the situation was frightening, as can be seen in this journal passage: "Smoky, fly-infested huts, hungry toddlers, and hungry goats competing for leftovers served in tin plates on the dirt floor. Men stripped to their sunken chests, sucking on pipes to quiet the raging within. Women squatting by their twig or charcoal fires, stoop shouldered and sagging in toward the middle where, inevitably, another tongue lay coiled, waiting to be born and to strike. Each descending circle of the Alto, like Dante's *Inferno*, worse than the last."

It was this confrontation with sickness, hunger, and death (especially child death) that most assaulted the sensibilities and the conscience of a comfortable-enough outsider and that shaped first my community development work and, many years later, my anthropological research. In the early conversations with Alto women in their homes and in the first open and

Mutirão: building the creche of UPAC, 1965.

chaotic meetings of the shantytown association held in various "public" houses on the Alto (in the little *barracas*, or dry goods shops, that served the hill and in the homes that also served as *terreiros*, centers for the practice of Afro-Brazilian possession religion), the idea for a permanent meeting center, and for a creche, a cooperative day nursery for the vulnerable babies of working mothers, was born.

After eighteen months of collective and participatory action (see chapter 12), the construction of a creche, which also served as a community center, and the installation of water pipes, a water pump, a storage tank, and a community-owned *chafariz* for the Alto were actualized, despite the open hostility of the local power elite—the traditional planter families—to the projects. Accusations of Marxist subversion and infiltration, however, led to a six-month-long military police investigation of UPAC and to the arrest and questioning of several leaders of the shantytown association, myself included. Although the military could never substantiate the accusations, the shantytown association was effectively crippled. Large meetings were prohibited.

Nonetheless, the creche opened on July 16, 1966, with some thirty infants, babies, and toddlers and some twenty Alto women participating in the cooperative. The women elected Dona Biu de Hollanda as their leader and as the director of the creche, a position she held for nearly three years. Eventually, Biu de Hollanda was paid a small "subvention" from the *município* in recog-

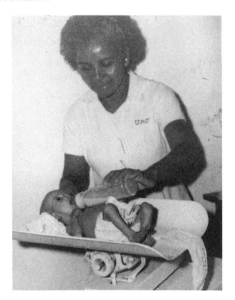

Mother and one of the first UPAC creche
babies, 1966.

nition of her pivotal role in the day-to-day operations of the cooperative, the
only one of its kind in Bom Jesus. Several months later the town council
awarded small subsidies allowing the creche to maintain a part-time practical
nurse, a traditional midwife from the Alto, and a kindergarten teacher for the
oldest creche children. But the creche was mainly dependent on the mothers
themselves, each of whom contributed one day of work at the creche each
week. And until the completion of the UPAC water project, each creche
mother had to bring a five-gallon can of water to the center each morning.

Infant *mingaus*, milky gruels similar to pap, were made from donated
Food for Peace powdered skimmed milk that we fortified as best we could
with vitamin A drops. Very sickly infants were fed *mingaus* made from fresh
goat's milk donated by Alto women who kept the animals in their little
backyard *quintals*. The midday meal for the older babies and toddlers was an
eclectic "stew" made from Food for Peace bulgar and flavored with as many
onions, carrots, potatoes, and squash as mothers could contribute from their
roçados. Occasionally, local meat vendors donated scraps of beef and entrails,
and these were relished by the toddlers and older creche babies.

Alto babies "thrived" in the creche. Most arrived sickly and malnourished, and all were tested and treated for parasites. Many, like little Zezinho
(see chapter 8), had to be coaxed into eating. Younger Alto mothers learned
new methods of infant care from older and more experienced mothers, and
all learned from the attempts of the nurse-midwife to introduce basic,

hygienic practices to the creche so as to prevent infant diarrheas and other infectious diseases from spreading wildly among the babies and toddlers. Moreover, communal child care was fun, and many "prestigious" elites of Bom Jesus climbed the stigmatized hillside for the first time in their lives to witness, with their own eyes, "the miracle" that had seemingly transformed the shantytown. For a brief period at least, the people of Alto came to be seen by townspeople as full of vitality, creativity, and initiative.

My Alto friends have never been able to agree on the exact nature of the events that brought about the closure of the creche and the final dissolution of the shantytown association in the late 1960s, a few years after I left the community. But malicious interference from the outside was largely responsible. Essential Food for Peace foodstuffs were diverted from the creche by the underhanded maneuvers of a powerful right-wing faction in Bom Jesus. When the "opposition" gained control of the *prefeitura* (town hall) and town council, and Seu Félix was temporarily removed from office, the small subventions for Dona Biu, the nurse-midwife, and the teacher were discontinued. After the military investigations of UPAC, open meetings of the shantytown association were no longer possible. Consequently, dissension resurfaced among the creche mothers and between the active women leaders of the creche and those Alto males who had once been active in the outlawed *diretoria* (governing board) of UPAC. In the absence of the open community meetings of UPAC, which had served as an important vehicle for airing complaints and mediating differences, there was no way for the men to express themselves and address their anger at their loss of power, voice, and "face" on the Alto. The men no longer had a function in UPAC, and they were jealous of the women and expressed it in destructive ways. They refused, for example, to "police" the creche at night; eventually thieves broke into the building and stole equipment and food supplies. Before long, homeless men and youths began to occupy parts of the creche building, sleeping there at night, building fires to cook their meals, and generally making the premises dirty and unsafe.

Seu Teto de Hollanda, who had taken over the installation of the water project after Valdimar hung himself, was left without a role or a say in the activities of the creche, which was all that remained of UPAC. Meanwhile, his wife, Dona Biu, as creche director, grew in prestige and influence in her own quiet and efficient way. The couple began to fight, and Dona Biu accused her husband of stealing flour from the creche storeroom and selling it to a bakery in town. The couple split up acrimoniously, and Dona Biu suffered many reprisals from those who sided with Seu Teto and felt that she had been unfair to her husband. The malicious gossip surrounding the very "public" separation of a once "model" Alto couple forced Dona Biu to leave the creche and move off the Alto and away from Bom Jesus altogether. When she did so, the creche collapsed, and she herself was never seen nor heard from again. Her husband, Seu Teto, died several years later of alcoholism, loneliness, depression, and severe malnutrition.

I introduce this brief history of my first encounter with the people of the Alto to show what these people, struggling constantly against almost impossible odds, are capable of and to indicate some of the political sources of their despair and their seeming paralysis of will. It should serve as something of a corrective to the very different picture of shantytown life that emerges in the following pages, more than twenty years later and following just as many years of political repression and economic madness in Brazil. I am referring to the great *folia/delírio* (mad folly) of the "economic miracle" years and to the disastrous consequences of Brazil's current $112 billion external debt and its effects on working-class *bairros* and rural and urban shantytowns in Brazil.

During this first encounter with Brazil and with the people of the Alto do Cruzeiro, I confess to viewing the occasional anthropologists I ran into as remote intellectuals, overly preoccupied with esoterica and largely out of touch with the practical realities of everyday life in Brazil. It was a humbling experience to read, many years later, Shepard Forman's *Raft Fishermen* (1970) and *The Brazilian Peasantry* (1975) and to discover how very much I had failed to see and understand about the society and culture of Northeast Brazil when, in Bom Jesus, I was so totally immersed in practical activities. Nevertheless, by the time I returned to Bom Jesus and the Alto do Cruzeiro more than fifteen years had elapsed, and it was anthropology, not political or community activism, that was the vehicle of my return. I came back not as Dona Nancí, *companheira*, but as Doutora Nancí, *antropóloga*. As for Lordes, Biu, and Tonieta, they joined my other former neighbors and coworkers in UPAC to become—and I fear there is no good word for it—key "informants," research "subjects," and assistants . . . at least initially.

I had postponed my appointment with Brazil because of conflicts that were both external and internal. Throughout the late 1960s and the 1970s Brazil became daily more steeped in a military dictatorship that came to rely on torture and threats of torture, imprisonment, and exile to coerce an appearance of popular consensus and to rid the country of its "dangerous" democrats and "subversives" (see Amnesty International 1988, 1990). Meanwhile, the United States maintained (with the exception of the Carter years) courteous and open relations with the brutal dictators, who were described to the U.S. public as enemies of communism and therefore friends of the United States. There was no way I would (or could) return under those conditions. It would not have been safe for the people of the Alto or for me or my family. I was also concerned about exposing my three then very young children to the considerable health hazards of fieldwork in an impoverished shantytown. Moreover, I squirmed at the thought of returning to a place where I had been so actively and politically engaged as one of the remote intellectuals I had arrogantly dismissed years before. Could one be both *antropóloga* and *companheira?* I doubted that this was possible, and I wondered about its ethical and political implications as well.

Instead of Northeast Brazil, then, I began my anthropological career in a tiny mountain community of peasant farmers in western Ireland, a place that could not be more removed in spirit and in tempo from the Alto do Cruzeiro. My fascination with the Irish (and with madness) led to further research among Irish-Americans in south Boston interspersed with brief periods of fieldwork among Spanish-Americans and Pueblo Indians in Taos, New Mexico. But all the while I continued to puzzle over crucial questions about human nature, ethics, and social relations, especially as these are affected by chronic scarcity and loss, questions and issues that had emerged within the specific context of Northeast Brazil and among the people I felt that I knew best of all on the Alto do Cruzeiro.

In 1982, with the Brazilian government's announcement of its commitment to a new politics of *abertura*—a democratic "opening" and political "awakening"—I was convinced by a Brazilian colleague to return, and quickly, for no one knew just how long the *abertura* would last. I did so, accompanied by my husband and children, for the first of four field expeditions to Bom Jesus between 1982 and 1989, a total of fourteen months of anthropological fieldwork.

The original, and in many respects still the central, thesis of my research and of this book is love and death on the Alto do Cruzeiro and specifically mother love and child death. It is about culture and scarcity, both material and psychological, and their effects on moral thinking and practice, particularly on "maternal thinking," a term I have borrowed from Sara Ruddick (1980, 1989). What, I wondered, were the effects of chronic hunger, sickness, death, and loss on the ability to love, trust, have faith, and keep it in the broadest senses of these terms? If mother love is, as some bioevolutionary and developmental psychologists as well as some cultural feminists believe, a "natural," or at least an expectable, womanly script, what does it mean for women for whom scarcity and death have made that love frantic?

This research agenda was set during those earlier years, when immediately following the Brazilian military coup, I witnessed a wholesale "die out" of Alto infants and babies. More than three hundred babies died during 1965 alone, and for each one that did the bells of Nossa Senhora das Dores in Bom Jesus da Mata tolled. Many of the deaths from hunger, thirst, and neglect were senseless and unnecessary. Had I not been so traumatized then, I might not have written this book today. At the time and with the gentle coaching of my Alto friends, I eventually learned to "distance" myself from the deaths and to pick up and continue, as they did, with the strands of my life and work in the shantytown. I learned, as they did, to "conform" and to tell myself that, after all, perhaps it was "meant" to be so. (Or had God deserted the Alto do Cruzeiro altogether?) In all, those years provided a powerful experience of cultural shaping, and it was only after I returned "home" again that I recovered my sensibilities and moral outrage at "the horror, the horror" of what I had experienced. The horror was the routinization of human suffering in so much of impoverished Northeast Brazil and the "normal" violence of everyday life.

In 1982 my initial goal was to reacquaint myself with the people of O Cruzeiro. We had lost contact with each other for many years. Letter writing was complicated by my friends' illiteracy, and after a few years both sides desisted. And if many of my Alto friends were peripatetic rural migrants, I was even more so during the early years of life "in the academy," when my family and I constantly moved back and forth across the country. Nonetheless, prior to my return in 1982 I sent dozens of letters to everyone I could think of . . . and received no response. I feared returning to a social void and felt that I might as well begin my research anywhere at all as in Bom Jesus da Mata, for clearly the social world I once knew had evaporated. But curiosity and my *saudades*, as Brazilians call the pull of nostalgic longings, led me to persist in the plan to return to Bom Jesus. In my letters I had mentioned the approximate date of my arrival in the capital city of Recife but had given no other details. Yet when we stepped off the plane, there in the crowd waving madly to us was my old friend and sometime adversary, Seu Félix, still the reigning *prefeito* and "boss" of Bom Jesus. "Did I forget to send you a reply?" Félix asked in his usual distracted way. I had indeed come home.

A small but neat hut near the base of the Alto was waiting for us, as were many of my old friends from the days of the creche and UPAC. I need not go into the details of those touching reunions. Time was short and precious. At a community meeting held in the now abandoned and dilapidated creche, I introduced my family and explained why and how I had managed to return. As I had always worked closely with women and children on the Alto, it came as no surprise that I wanted to learn more about the lives of women and of mothers in particular. With the help of an old friend and creche mother, Irene Lopes da Silva, one of the few semiliterate residents of the Alto, I was able to interview close to a hundred women of O Cruzeiro. I gathered essential information on their family and reproductive histories, migration and work histories, domestic and conjugal arrangements, many loves and almost as many losses, and hopes and wishes for themselves, their husbands or companions, and their children. I learned how essential long-term research was for understanding lives that looked like roller-coaster rides with great peaks and dips, ups and downs, as women struggled valiantly at times (less valiantly at others) to do the greatest good for the greatest number and manage to stay alive themselves.

What of my personal relations with the people of the Alto? The sixteen-year hiatus between the time I left Bom Jesus at the close of 1966 and the initial return in 1982 meant that all of us had changed, some almost unrecognizably so, and there were many instances of mistaken identities before I could eventually sort everyone out. Meanwhile, Dona Nancí, the *moça*, was now both a mother and an anthropologist. Even though my old friends were gracious and willing "informants," they soon became restless with the interviews and with the monotony and repetitiveness of fieldwork. When I observed something once in a clinic or a home, asked Irene, or when I learned something in an interview, why did I have to repeat the experience again and again before I was satisfied? And so I tried to explain the rudiments of the anthropological method to Irene and several other women who worked with me as assistants.

Most of my old neighbors and friends were anxious to be interviewed, and they were fearful of being the only ones "left out" of my research. They understood the basic lines of inquiry, and they did not consider the questions I asked irrelevant. But they wanted to know what else I was going to do while I was with them again. Shouldn't we have UPAC meetings again, they asked, now that grass-roots organizations and squatters' associations were no longer outlawed or seen as a subversive threat to the democratizing social order? What about the old cultural circles and literacy groups? Shouldn't they be revived now? Many adults had forgotten the basics of the alphabet that they had learned years before. And what about the creche? Even more women, they said, were working than in years previously, and the need for a child day care center was more pressing than ever. Finally, the old headquarters of UPAC and the creche was in a dangerous state of disrepair, its roof tiles broken, its wooden crossbeams rotting, its bricks beginning to crumble. Shouldn't we organize a *mutirão* (collective work force) as in the old days to get the building back into shape as a first step toward reviving UPAC? But each time the women approached me with their requests, I backed away saying, "This work is cut out for you. My work is different now. I cannot be an anthropologist and a *companheira* at the same time." I shared my new reservations about the propriety of an outsider taking an active role in the life of a Brazilian community. But my argument fell on deaf ears.

On the day before my departure in 1982, a fight broke out among Irene

Lopes and several women waiting outside the creche where I was conducting interviews and gathering reproductive histories. When I emerged to see what the commotion was about, the women were ready to turn their anger against me. Why had I refused to work with them when they had been so willing to work with me? Didn't I care about them personally anymore, their lives, their suffering, their struggle? Why was I so passive, so indifferent, so resigned, to the end of UPAC and of creche, the community meetings, and the *festas?* The women gave me an ultimatum: the next time I came back to the Alto I would have to "be" with them—"accompany them" was the expression they used—in their *luta,* and not just "sit idly by" taking field-notes. "What is this anthropology anyway to us?" they taunted.

And so, true to their word and mine, when I returned again five years later, for a longer period of fieldwork, a newly revived UPAC was waiting, and I assumed willy-nilly the role of anthropologist-*companheira,* dividing my time, not always equally, between fieldwork and community work, as it was defined and dictated to me by the activist women and men of the Alto. If they were "my" informants, I was very much "their" *despachante* (an intermediary who expedites or hastens projects along) and remained very much "at their disposal." They turned me back into their image of "Dona Nancí." I have had to occupy a dual role ever since 1985, and it has remained a difficult balance, rarely free of conflict. The tensions and strains between reflection and action can be felt throughout the pages of this book.

But more positively, as my *companheiras* and *companheiros* of the Alto pulled me toward the "public" world of Bom Jesus, into the marketplace, to the *prefeitura,* to the ecclesiastical base community and rural syndicate meetings, the more my understandings of the community were enriched and my theoretical horizons and political orientations expanded. The everyday violence of shantytown life, and the madness of hunger, in particular, became the focus of my study, of which the specific case of mother love and child death was one instance. And so although this book treats the "pragmatics" and the "poetics" of motherhood, it concerns a good deal more than that. To understand women as mothers, I needed to understand them as daughters, sisters, wives, workers, and politically engaged beings. My original questions gradually brought me out of the private sphere of wretched huts and into the cane fields and the modern sugar refineries, and from the mayor's chambers to the state assembly of Pernambuco, and from the local pharmacies, clinics, and hospital of Bom Jesus to the pauper graves of the municipal cemetery and even to the public morgue at the Institute of Forensic Medicine in Recife. In all, I simply followed the women and men of the Alto in their everyday struggle to survive by means of hard work, cunning, trickery, and triage, but, above all, by means of their resilience, their refusal to be negated.

Chapter 1 traces the colonial history of the local plantation economy of the Brazilian Northeast and that bittersweet commodity, sugar, up through its cultivation on the *engenhos* and *usinas* (sugar plantations and mills) of the present time. The chapter culminates in an ethnographic tour of the largest sugar plantation and mill in the cane region of Pernambuco, Usina Agua Prêta outside Bom Jesus da Mata. Chapter 2 looks at the meaning of thirst as a generative metaphor for people inhabiting a region, O Nordeste, continually plagued by threat of drought, the *seca*. Chapter 3 introduces the market town of Bom Jesus and the shantytown of Alto do Cruzeiro as a complex social world dominated by the multiple social realities of three separate but intersecting realms: the *casa* (the house), by which I mean the remaining feudal world of the plantation "big house," the *casa grande*; the *rua* (the street), by which I mean the new world of industrial commerce and capitalism found on the streets and in the factories and *supermercados* (supermarkets) of Bom Jesus; and the *mata* (the forest, the countryside), by which I mean the precapitalist, rural world of the traditional squatters who have come to live on the Alto do Cruzeiro as stigmatized *matutos*, or "backward country people."

Bom Jesus da Mata is a pseudonym, although anyone with more than a passing interest in the Pernambucan *zona da mata* will be able to identify this town. The Alto do Cruzeiro, however, is not a pseudonym, and it appears here very much as itself. Like most shantytowns the world over, the Alto do Cruzeiro is anonymous enough as it is; most of its tangle of streets and dirt paths cannot be located on the official maps of the *município*. Likewise, while I have disguised the names and, to some extent, even the personalities of key public figures in Bom Jesus who would easily be recognized, I use the actual first names and nicknames of the *moradores* of the Alto and for similar reasons. Their social invisibility in Bom Jesus da Mata diminishes *and* protects them. Moreover, the women and men of the Alto have enjoyed seeing their names in print in the obviously irrelevant scholarly journals where I have previously published fragments of their narratives.

Chapters 4 and 5 treat the explosive subject of hunger in O Nordeste, tracing the gradual transformation of nervous hunger from the popular idiom *delírio de fome*, the "madness of hunger," into the ethnomedical idiom *nervos*, "nervous frenzy," a condition that is now treated with tranquilizers and sleeping pills. Chapter 6 explores the political tactic of "disappearance," which, originating in the military years, continues to this day in a new and even more disturbing form. Death squad "disappearances" form the backdrop of everyday life and everyday violence on the Alto do Cruzeiro, thereby confirming people's worst fears and anxieties: that of losing themselves, their ownership of their bodies, to the random forces and institutionalized violence of the modern, even democratizing, state.

These first chapters, constituting the first part of the book, situate the people of the Alto do Cruzeiro in their larger context—O Nordeste—land of sugar and hunger, thirst and penance, messianism and madness. But this strong interpretation of the *miséria morta* of the Northeast is not solely my own. Ethnographers, like historians, do not write on a blank page. There is a long and deep history to the study of the Northeast emerging from a specific Brazilian literary tradition and sensibility to the troubles of that region. I have learned, and been enriched by, a generation of Brazilian writers from Euclides da Cunha, Gilberto Freyre, Graciliano Ramos, the early Jorge Amado, through to Josué de Castro, and their presence can be felt in these pages. I have had the good fortune of being able to stand on their shoulders, especially because, like the people of the Alto, I am rather small myself, and without their help I might not have had a broad perspective of the lay of the parched land I am trying to survey.

The remaining chapters (7 through 12) treat the central thesis of the book as well as the subject of resistance. I argue that in the absence of a firm grounding for the expectancy of child survival, maternal thinking and practice are grounded in a set of assumptions (e.g., that infants and babies are easily replaceable or that some infants are born "wanting" to die) that contribute even further to an environment that is dangerous, even antagonistic, to new life.

Chapter 7 treats the routinization of infant death in the creation of what I call an average expectable environment of child death, meaning a set of conditions that place infants at high risk, accompanied by a normalization of this state of affairs in both the private and public life of Bom Jesus da Mata. What is created is an environment in which death is understood as the most ordinary and most expected outcome for the children of poor families. Chapter 8 explores the various meanings of motherhood, the poetics and the pragmatics of maternal thinking. It also treats the subject of women's morality by examining close up the triage-based choices that women of the Alto must make; these choices lead to the mortal neglect of certain presumed-to-be-doomed babies. Chapter 9 looks at the role of disappointment in shaping the reaction to child death, specifically the failure to mourn. It also reveals the spaces where attachment and grief are "appropriate" and where they may be expressed.

Chapter 10 poses the question of resilience to adversity and follows the life histories of the half-sisters Biu and Antonieta. Chapter 11 traces the attempts of one sister, at least, to try "forgetting" herself and her difficulties in the celebration of Brazilian *carnaval*. Chapter 12, the conclusion, reflects on the everyday tactics for "getting by" and "making do" in the shantytown that are occasionally punctuated by religious rituals and dramas of resistance and celebration that enhance the lives of the *moradores* and that hint at the possibilities of a new world, one free of hunger, social injustice, and violence.

Moral Relativism and the Primacy of the Ethical

Everyday violence, political and domestic horror, and madness—these are strong words and themes for an anthropologist. Although this book is not for the faint of heart, it returns anthropology to its origins by reopening— though in no way claiming to resolve—vexing questions of moral and ethical relativism.

For much of this century anthropological relativism has been taken up with the issue of divergent rationalities—with how and why people, very different from ourselves, think and reason as they do (see Tambiah 1990 for an excellent summary of this history). The study of magic and witchcraft provided a springboard for anthropological analyses designed to reveal the internal logic that made magical thinking and practice a *reasonable*, rather than an irrational, human activity. E. E. Evans-Pritchard's 1937 book on Azande witchcraft as an alternative explanation of unfortunate events is a classic in this regard. But his functionalist interpretation of sorcery and countersorcery in Azande society sidesteps entirely the question of the ethical. How might one even begin to evaluate witchcraft as a moral or an ethical system? What does witchcraft presuppose in its relations between self and other—"the other" as the bewitched but also "the other" as the accused bewitcher? The "othering" of others takes place within (not only across) societies and cultures. But these questions have generally been disallowed in contemporary anthropology, where "reason" and "the ethical" are often collapsed into each other, thereby producing an untenable sort of "cultural relativism" for which our discipline has often been criticized (see Mohanty 1989 for a critical review of cultural relativism and its political consequences). Moreover, the anthropological obsession with reason, ratio-nality, and "primitive" versus "rational" thought, as these bear on questions of cultural relativism, reveals largely androcentric concerns.

A more "womanly" anthropology might be concerned not only with how we humans "reason" and think but also with how we act toward each other, thus engaging questions of human relationship and of ethics. If we cannot begin to think about cultural institutions and practices in moral or ethical terms, then anthropology strikes me as quite weak and useless. The problem is, of course, how to articulate a standard, or divergent standards, for the

f a moral and an ethical reflection on cultural practices that
ɩunt but does not privilege our own cultural presuppositions.
.ɩtic instance that I treat in the following pages, the relations of
ɩntytown women toward some of their small babies, *is* troubling. It
disturbs. One wonders, following Martin Buber, whether there are extraordinary situations that not only signal a kind of moral collapse but that
actually warrant a "suspension of the ethical" (1952:147–156). He referred
to the Old Testament story in which God commands Abraham to sacrifice his
only, and beloved, son, Isaac, clearly a brutal and unethical act. But Abraham
submits and obeys the Divine command because Yahweh alone may break or
suspend the ethical order that He Himself ordained. For Buber the dilemma
of the modern world (a world in which "God has gone into hiding") is how
men and women can distinguish the voice of the Divine from the false
prophets, who imitate the voice of God and continually demand that humans
make various kinds of human sacrifices.

The theologian Buber confronted the "suspension of the ethical" in
accordance with the will and purpose of something "higher," the Divine;
here the anthropologist confronts a "suspension of the ethical" in accordance
with a will and duty to self-survive, as it were. There are many analogues in
the moral dilemmas of those victimized in wartime, famine, slavery, or
drought or incarcerated in prisons and detention camps. I have stumbled on
a situation in which shantytown mothers appear to have "suspended the
ethical"—compassion, empathic love, and care—toward some of their weak
and sickly infants. The "reasonableness" and the "inner logic" of their
actions are patently obvious and are not up for question. But the moral and
ethical dimensions of the practices disturb, give reason to pause . . . and to
doubt.

How are we to understand their actions, make sense of them, and respond
ethically ourselves—that is, with compassion toward the others, Alto
women and their vulnerable infants and small children? The practices described here are not autonomously, culturally produced. They have a social
history and must be understood within the economic and political context of
a larger state and world (moral) order that have suspended the ethical in
their relations toward these same women and within the religious order (or
disorder) of a Catholic church that is torn in Brazil, as elsewhere, with moral
ambivalence about female reproduction.

Anthropologists (myself included) have tended to understand morality as
always contingent on, and embedded within, specific cultural assumptions
about human life. But there is another, an existential philosophical position
that posits the inverse by suggesting that the ethical is always prior to
culture because the ethical presupposes all sense and meaning and therefore

makes culture possible. "Morality," wrote the phenomenologist Emmanuel Levinas "does not belong to culture: it enables one to judge it" (1987:100). Accountability, answerability to "the other"—the ethical as I am defining it here—is "precultural" in that human existence always presupposes the presence of another. That I have been "thrown" into human existence at all presupposes a given, moral relationship to an original (m)other and she to me.

A Note on Method

"Methodologists, get to work!"
  C. Wright Mills (1959:123)

This book, and the research on which it is based, obviously departs from traditional or classic ethnography in a number of ways. The first concerns the way the self, other, and scientific objectivity are handled. Another concerns the explicit values and sympathies of the anthropologist herself. For generations ethnographers based their work on a myth and a pretense. They pretended that there was no ethnographer in the field. In treating the self as if "it" were an invisible and permeable screen through which pure data, "facts," could be objectively filtered and recorded, the traditional ethnographer could exaggerate "his" claims to an authoritative science of "man" and of human nature. And in so doing, the ethnographer did not have to examine critically the subjective bases of the questions he asked (and of those he *failed* to ask), the kinds of data he collected, and the theories he brought to bear on those assorted "facts" to assemble and "make sense" of them, to make them *presentable*, as it were.

I do not wish to get into a tortured discussion of facticity, empiricism, positivism, and so on. Our work as anthropologists is by its very nature empirical; otherwise we would not bother to go into the "field." Obviously, some events are "factual." Either 150 or 350 children died of hunger and dehydration on the Alto do Cruzeiro in 1965; here the ethnographer has a professional and a moral obligation to get the "facts" as accurately as possible. This is not even debatable. But all facts are necessarily selected and interpreted from the moment we decide to count one thing and ignore another, or attend this ritual but not another, so that anthropological understanding is necessarily partial and is always hermeneutic.

Nevertheless, though empirical, our work need not be empiricist. It need not entail a philosophical commitment to Enlightenment notions of reason and truth. The history of Western philosophy, thought, and science has been characterized by a "refusal of engagement" with the other or, worse, by an "indifference" to the other—to alterity, to difference, to polyvocality, all of which are leveled out or pummeled into a form compatible with a discourse that promotes the Western project. And so the "Enlightenment," with its universal and absolute notions of truth and reason, may be seen as a grand pretext for exploitation and violence and for the expansion of Western culture ("our ideas," "our truths"). Ideally, anthropology should try to liberate truth from its Western cultural presuppositions.

A new generation of ethnographers (see Clifford & Marcus 1986; Marcus & Cushman 1982; Rabinow 1977; Crapanzano 1977, 1985) has suggested alternative ways of dealing with the self in the field. One of these is to document the fumbling path of the ethnographer in her own gradual process of misunderstanding and misrecognition, occasionally illuminated by small beacons of recognition and clarification, of cultural translation. But far more difficult and vexing questions concern the ethnographer's ways of dealing with the "other" in the field.

If theology entails a "leap of faith" of oneself toward an invisible, unknowable Divine Other, anthropology implies an "outside-of-myself" leap toward an equally unknown and opaque other-than-myself, and a similar sort of reverential awe before the unknown one is called for. Following from the theologically driven phenomenology of Levinas, the "work" of anthropology entails, at base, the working out of an ethical orientation to the other-than-oneself: "*A work conceived radically is a movement of the Same toward the Other which never returns to the Same*" (Levinas 1987:91). Anthropological work, if it is to be in the nature of an ethical and a radical project, is one that is transformative of the self but not (and here is the rub) transformative of the other. It demands a "relationship with the other, who is reached *without showing itself touched*" (Levinas 1987:92) . . . or altered, violated, fragmented, dismembered.

But how can such a utopian premise be translated into a real "work" of anthropology, especially an *antropologia-pé-no-chão?* We cannot (nor would we want to, I think) deceive ourselves into believing that our presence leaves no trace, no impact on those on whose lives we dare to intrude. We are, after all, human, and we can hardly help becoming involved in the lives of the people we have chosen to be our teachers. As Seu Fabiano, the local journalist of Bom Jesus, once said with a wicked grin (referring to my "unsavory" political leanings): "We'll forgive you, Nancí. After all, *no one* here is innocent" (i.e., indifferent to politics and power). So although I reject as "unreasonable," perhaps, the monastic demand that ethnographers leave the sands on which they tred without a trace of their sandals, what may never be compromised are our personal accountability and answerability to the other.

This work, then, is of a specific nature, both active and committed. Anthropology exists both as a field of knowledge (a *disciplinary* field) and as a field of action (a *force* field). Anthropological writing can be a site of resistance. This approach bears resemblances to what Michael Taussig (1989b) and others called "writing against terror," what Franco Basaglia (1987b) referred to as becoming a "negative worker,"[1] and what Michel de Certeau (1984) meant by "making a *perruque*" of scientific research. The latter tactic refers to diverting the time owed to the factory or, in this case, to the academic institution into more human activities. We can, offered de Certeau, make "textual objects" (i.e., books) that "write against the grain" and that signify solidarity. We can disrupt expected roles and statuses in the spirit of the *carnavelsco*, the carnivalesque (see chapter 11). And we can exchange gifts based on our labors and so finally subvert the law that puts our work at the service of the machine in the scientific, academic factory.

My particular sympathies are transparent; I do not try to disguise them behind the role of an invisible and omniscient third-person narrator. Rather, I enter freely into dialogues and sometimes into conflicts and disagreements with the people of the Alto, challenging them just as they challenge me on my definitions of the reality in which I live. To use a metaphor from Mikhail Bakhtin (1981), the ethnographic interview here becomes more dialogic than monologic, and anthropological knowledge may be seen as something produced in human interaction, not merely "extracted" from naive informants who are unaware of the hidden agendas coming from the outsider.

Even though I make no claims to a privileged scientific neutrality, I do try to offer a fair and true description and analysis of events and relationships as I have perceived and sometimes participated in them. By showing, as I go along, the ways that I work in the field, offering glimpses behind the scenes, I hope to give the reader a deeper appreciation of the way in which ethnographic "facts" are built up in the course of everyday participation in the life of the community. In this way the reader should be in a better position to evaluate the claims made and the conclusions drawn.

As a woman and a feminist, although not a conventional one, I am drawn (but I won't say "naturally") to the experiences of women, and their lives were initially more open to me than the private worlds of Brazilian men of the Alto. This ethnography, then, is woman centered, as is everyday life in a shantytown marginalized by poverty and set on edge by what I describe in chapter 5 as "nervous hunger." Mothers and children dominate these pages even as they dominate, numerically and symbolically, Alto life (a feature of the shantytown recognized ruefully by Alto men). I turn to the fragility and "dangerousness" of the mother-infant relationship as the most immediate and visible index of scarcity and unmet needs. Hence in the following chapters I return again and again to the lives of Lordes, Biu, Antonieta, and their neighbors on the Alto do Cruzeiro to illustrate in a graphic way the consequences of hunger, death, abandonment, and loss on ways of thinking, feeling, acting, and being in the world.

Finally, as a "critical medical anthropologist," I may be seen as something of a pathologist of human nature who is drawn to illness, both individual and collective, as these shed light on culture, society, and their discontents. The view through this lens is skewed, for I am slicing, dissecting, and holding up to the light the diseased tissues of the social body gone awry. The anthropologist-diviner names ills and speaks of taboos broken, of deadly words spoken, of human passions and weaknesses, of distortions in human relations, all of which can produce suffering, sickness, and death. The anthropological "hand trembler" points to the troubled organs, individual and social, while the healing itself lies outside her sphere and in the collective will and good faith of the larger community. Nonetheless, with an eye toward social healing, I conclude the book with a search for the paths of resistance, healing, and liberation in Bom Jesus da Mata today.

Fraternity and Recognition: The Anthropologist as Clerk of the Records

The mood of contemporary anthropology, and not just of this book, is somber, its poetics guided by a complex form of modern pessimism rooted in anthropology's own tortured relationship to the colonial world and that world's ruthless destruction of native peoples. This remains so even as anthropologists branch out to study the lives of peasant and urban peoples more like "ourselves." Because of its origins as mediatrix in the clash of cultures and competing civilizations in the colonial world, nineteenth-century anthropological thinking was guided by a particular metaphysical premise governed by the priority of keeping, conserving, maintaining, and valuing what was at hand. This fundamentally "conservative" position looks glumly on the ravagings enacted in the names of "progress," "development," "modernization," and the like, slogans that have been used against those traditional, nonsecular, and communal people who have stood in the way of various Western colonial and postcolonial projects.

In a book critically evaluating the nature of ethnographic authority, James Clifford (1988a and b) questioned the alienated nostalgia of traditional anthropologists pursuing lost worlds in an anxious, fragmented, postmodern age. This theme was taken up again by Renato Rosaldo (1989) in his book *Culture and Truth*. Although I agree with their perceptions of the ethnographic "mood" as one of intense longing, *saudades*, after an unspoiled, primitive world, a world now hopelessly "on the wane" (Levi-Strauss 1961), to dismiss the ethnographer's malaise as originating in a personal sort of existential, postmodernist alienation misses the mark. The longing and sense of loss also derive from the perceptions of what Western imperialism (including the checkered history of their own discipline) has extracted from the bodies and the communities of the peoples that anthropologists study. Herein lies the dilemma of the *tristeza antropologá*, the "anthropological melancholy." One need only read Levi-Strauss's poignant reflections on urban blight amid the monumental beauty of the natural forests of coastal Brazil to grasp the source of the anthropological malaise.

When Levi-Strauss went to Brazil in the 1930s, he did so to carry out the overdetermined "mission" of the twentieth-century ethnographer: to study the natives "before they disappeared." For Levi-Strauss, the lifeways of Brazilian tribal peoples—of the Bororo, Nambiquara, the Tupi-Kawahib, and the Caduveo—were as precious and as intricate as the geometrical designs they painted on each other's faces and bodies. Against the natural order and beauty of primitive thought, aesthetics, and social life, Levi-Strauss reflected on the dirt, disorder, and decay of Brazil's modern cities. By the time Levi-Strauss arrived among the Nambiquara Indians in 1935, less than two thousand of the original twenty thousand remained, and these were a fairly miserable group, reduced and disfigured by tuberculosis, syphilis, and malnutrition. Their nomadic way of life was over, and they were reduced to a humiliating dependency on the fringes of "Western civilization." No wonder the Brazilian tropics were, for Levi-Strauss, so mordantly sad. But Levi-Strauss also idealized the tropics in his writings on the elegance and beauty of "primitive thought" and mythologies (see C. Geertz 1988).

I find no comparable beauty to celebrate in another part of the Brazilian "tropics," in the sugar plantation zone near the coast where the history of Brazil begins. In the *zona da mata*, a doomed plantation economy, one born of one kind of slavery and maintained to the present through slavery of another form, the tropics are also "sad." And, as with the Amazonian rain forests, the old plantation world almost tenderly described by Gilberto Freyre is on the wane in response to the vagaries of a ruthless world economic order. But in the passing of this tropical world, what is there to lament, save what might come next, the fire next time?

What is the value of ethnography in such a sad contemporary context? Many young anthropologists today, sensitized by the writings of Michel Foucault (1975, 1980, 1982) on "power/knowledge," have come to think of ethnography and fieldwork as unwarranted intrusions in the lives of vulnerable, threatened peoples. The anthropological interview has been likened to the medieval "inquisitional confession" (Ginsberg 1988) through which church examiners extracted "truth" from their naive and naturally "heretical" peasant flocks. We hear of anthropological observation as a hostile act that reduces our "subjects" to mere "objects" of our discriminating, incriminating, scientific gaze. Consequently, some young anthropologists have given up the practice of descriptive ethnography altogether in preference for distanced and highly formalized methods of discourse analysis or purely quantitative models. Others concern themselves with macrolevel analyses of world economic systems in which the experiential and subjective experience of human lives is left aside. Still others engage in an obsessive, self-reflexive hermeneutics in which the self, not the other, becomes the subject of anthropological inquiry.

I grow weary of these postmodernist critiques, and given the perilous times in which we and our subjects live, I am inclined toward a compromise that calls for the practice of a "good enough" ethnography. The anthropologist is an instrument of cultural translation that is necessarily flawed and biased. We cannot rid ourselves of the cultural self we bring with us into the field any more than we can disown the eyes, ears, and skin through which we take in our intuitive perceptions about the new and strange world we have entered. Nonetheless, like every other master artisan (and I dare say that at our best we are this), we struggle to do the best we can with the limited resources we have at hand—our ability to listen and observe carefully, empathically, and compassionately.

I think of some of the subjects of this book for whom anthropology is *not* a hostile gaze but rather an opportunity to tell a part of their life story. And though I can hear the dissonant voices in the background protesting *just this* choice of words, I believe there is still a role for the ethnographer-writer in giving voice, as best she can, to those who have been silenced, as have the people of the Alto by political and economic oppression and illiteracy and as have their children by hunger and premature death. So despite the mockery that Clifford Geertz (1988) made of anthropological "I-witnessing," I believe there is still value in attempting to "speak truth to power." I recall how my Alto friends grabbed and pushed and pulled, jostling for attention, saying, "Don't forget me; I want *my* turn to speak. That one has had your attention long enough!" Or saying, *"Tá vendo? Tá ouvindo?"*—"Are you listening, *really* understanding me?" Or taking my hand and placing it on their abdomens and demanding, *"Touch me, feel me,* here. Did you ever feel anything so swollen?" Or "Write that down in your notes, *now.* I don't want you to forget it." Seeing, listening, touching, recording, can be, if done with care and sensitivity, acts of fraternity and sisterhood, acts of solidarity. Above all, they are the work of recognition. Not to look, not to touch, not to record, can be the hostile act, the act of indifference and of turning away.

If I did not believe that ethnography could be used as a tool for critical reflection *and* as a tool for human liberation, what kind of perverse cynicism would keep me returning again and again to disturb the waters of Bom Jesus da Mata? What draws me back to these people are just those small spaces of convergence, recognition, and empathy that we do share. Not everything can be dissolved into the vapor of absolute cultural difference and radical otherness. There are ways, for example, in which we are not so indefinably "other" to one another, my friends of the Alto and I. Like them, I instinctively make the sign of the cross when I sense danger or misfortune coming. But also, like some of them, I sit in the back of the church and mock the visiting bishop of nearby Belem do Nordeste when he arrives outrageously decked out in scarlet silk and lace, calling him a parrot, a peacock, and a transvestite *baiana* (an exotically dressed Afro-Brazilian food vendor). But when the same bishop-shepherd raises the staff in his perfumed hands, I'm on my feet with the rest; head bowed, fingers crossed, I take on Pascal's wager . . . with the rest. In other words, I share the faith with the people of the Alto and of Bom Jesus da Mata in all its richness, complexity, contradiction, and absurdity. And so I am not afraid to speak and engage my Brazilian *companheiras* on matters of faith (in the broadest sense), morals, and values where these are at least partially shared.

There is another way to think about fieldwork. I am taken with a particular image of the modern ethnographer, one borrowed from John Berger in his book *A Fortunate Man: The Story of a Country Doctor* (Berger & Mohr 1976). Berger described John Sassall, general practitioner to the "foresters" of an isolated and impoverished English countryside, as the "clerk of the records." The clerk, or the "keeper," of the records is the one who listens, observes, records, and tries to interpret human lives, as does the traditional country doctor. The clerk can be counted on to remember key events in the personal lives and in the life history of the parish and to "keep trust," not betray confidences shared in private—that is, the clerk can be counted on to know the difference between public and private, between *casa* and *rua.*

The ethnographer, like the country doctor, knows the personal history of the community. She is their genealogist, and because of her privileged presence at births and deaths and other life cycle events, she can readily call to mind the fragile web of human relations that binds people together into a collectivity. Both ethnographer and country doctor should know when to speak and when to keep silent. Although class and upbringing separate the country doctor from his "disadvantaged" patients, like the ethnographer, the perennial stranger and friend, the physician is sometimes shocked by his recognition and almost intuitive understanding of lives so very different from his own. "I know, I know . . . ," they nod in empathy and recognition with their subjects' stories. This is the image I suggest for the ethnographer-anthropologist: like John Sassall, a keeper of the records, a minor historian of ordinary lives of people often presumed to have no history (Wolf 1982). In the context of Bom Jesus da Mata, there are many lives and even more deaths to keep track of, numbering the bones of a people whom the state hardly thinks worth counting at all.

The answer, then, is not a retreat from ethnography altogether or ethnography written only by native sons and daughters (who often turn out to be equally distanced from the people they study in terms of class, education, and experience); rather, the answer is an ethnography that is open-ended and that allows for multiple readings and alternative conclusions. In literary criticism this is called the search for multiple voices in the text, including the dissident voices that threaten to deconstruct the notion of a single, controlled, third-person narrator. Some of these "dissident voices" are my own as I move back and forth between third-person narrator and first-person participant, now as Dona Nancí engaging her Alto friends in a political debate on *nervos* at a base community meeting, later as the quirky anthropologist, Scheper-Hughes, engaging her colleagues in a theoretical discussion or debate. Just as the dissident and multiple voices of Lordes, Antonieta, Biu, Black Irene, Terezinha, Amor, and others show little agreement and consensus about what it means to be *bem brasileiro*, "really Brazilian," in Bom Jesus, the narrator is not always in agreement with them or with herself throughout a work that has tried to keep the cuts and sutures of the research process openly visible and suppress the urge to smooth over the bumps with a lathe. This hopefully good-enough ethnography is presented as close to the bone as it was experienced, hairline fractures and all.

Like all modern ethnographies, this one may be read at various, sometimes "mutually interfering" levels (Clifford 1988b:117): as a book of voyage and discovery, as a moral reflection on a human society forced to the margins, as a political text (or as a Christian passion play) that indicts a political economic order that reproduces sickness and death at its very base. Finally, it may be read as a quest story, a search for a communal grail and for a roundtable here envisioned as a great Bakhtinian banquet where everyone can find a place at the table and a share in the feasting.

1 O Nordeste
Sweetness and Death

A people that entrusts its subsistence to one product alone
commits suicide.
                                                    José Martí (1975:356)

We begin, then, with the context, the "600,000 square miles of suffering,"
as Josué de Castro (1969) described them, that constitute the pockmarked
face of the Brazilian Northeast. Land of sugar and sweetness but also of
leather and darkness, O Nordeste is, as Roger Bastide (1964) noted, a *terra de
contrastes*, a land of cloying sugarcane fields amid hunger and disease, of
periodic droughts and deadly floods, of authoritarian landowners and primitive rebels, of penitential Christianity, ecstatic messianic movements, and
liberation theology coexisting with Afro-Brazilian spirit possession.

Despite numerous "developmental" projects launched to rescue the
Northeast since the 1930s,[1] its widespread affliction still justifies Brazilian
intellectuals' wry description of their country as "Bel-India"—half (the
Southeast) Belgium and half (O Nordeste) India. At present 47.2 percent of
the population of 40 million people spread among the nine states that
constitute the region remain illiterate (W.H.O. 1991; PAHO 1990). Ten of
every twenty childhood deaths in Latin America are of Brazilians and five
are *Nordestinos*. In other words, the Nordeste contributes a quarter to all
Latin American child mortality (Aguiar 1987).

Throughout the 1980s diseases once thought to be safely under control in
Brazil—typhoid, dengue, malaria, Chagas' disease, polio, tuberculosis, leprosy, and bubonic plague—resurfaced to claim new victims, many of them
children, especially in the Northeast.[2] Although we tend to think of these
pestilences as tropical diseases arising from the more or less "natural"
interactions of climate, geography, and human ecology, we might do better
to think of them as poverty diseases or as diseases of "disorderly development" (Doyal 1981) in which the social relations that produce rural to urban
migration, unemployment, *favelas*, illiteracy, and malnutrition are the primary culprits behind the epidemics.[3]

During the late 1960s and 1970s Brazil's military dictatorship propelled the nation toward a rapid industrial growth that made it the Western world's eighth largest economy and one of its most enterprising nations. But this now-tarnished "Brazilian economic miracle" failed to filter down to the millions of workers and migrants of the Nordeste, for whom the only economic miracle was that they managed to stay alive at all. Eduardo Galeano chose an unsettling metaphor in writing that the political economy of the Nordeste had turned that region into a "concentration camp for more than thirty million people" (1975:75).

The social, political, agrarian, and health problems of the Northeast extend back to the earliest days of colonization, when the complex formed by the interactions among *latifúndio*, *monocultura*, and *paternalismo* was first established (see Freyre 1986a). I am referring to the consolidation of land-holdings into large plantations dominated by a single export crop (sugar, cotton, or coffee) at the expense of diversified and subsistence farming and to the cultivation in exploited rural workers of a humbling set of economic and psychosocial dependencies on their essentially feudal landlords, lords in the truest sense of the term.

In the *zona da mata* of Pernambuco (the fertile strip of what was originally natural woodlands), sugar is "king," as it has been since the arrival of the first Portuguese colonists in the sixteenth century. Sugarcane is a particularly predatory crop, which has dominated both the natural and social landscape. In every generation sugarcane preempts more and more land; it consumes the humus in the soil, annihilates competing food crops, and ultimately feeds on the human capital on which its production is based. Not only have the peasants' subsistence gardens been "eaten up" by cane, but so has the once dense and luxurious vegetation that gave the region its name, so that the "forest zone" is today virtually without forest. The plantation workers and cane cutters who now reside on the Alto do Cruzeiro complain bitterly that they must travel farther and farther to find *lenha*, the kindling wood they once used to cook their garden crops: beans, sweet manioc, yams, and corn. Now that both the *roçados* (garden plots) and kindling have disappeared, these recently proletarianized rural workers must purchase virtually everything they need to survive. A growing dependency on wages and the loss of their gardens were what brought these plantation workers to the Alto do Cruzeiro and to the market town of Bom Jesus da Mata in the 1950s and 1960s during a transformation of the sugar industry. These changes in the traditional relations of production are understood by some elders of the Alto as a curse or as a *castigo*, a "punishment" from God. Norinha, a midwife of the Alto, explained the curse of Bom Jesus: "I am seeing things in the world today that I never saw before in all my seventy years. I am seeing healthy women with only two or three living children. In days past they would have had eight or ten children. And before this time we always had good winters with lots of rain, and everyone's house was filled with fresh vegetables from their *roçados* to 'kill' their hunger. No one went as hungry then as they are suffering today."

She paused to look out her window and cast her eyes sorrowfully over the green hills surrounding Bom Jesus, and then she said, "In these times we are living in, all you can see in the middle of the world is cane, cane, *cana de açúcar*. That is our curse. The *roçados* and *sítios* [small traditional peasant holdings] are gone, and we have been chased away. Our lands have been 'eaten up' by sugar. This is a *castigo* [punishment] from God."

"A punishment for what?" I inquired.

She replied, "For the evils that women have invented and forced on the doctors—abortions and tubal ligations."

Here Norinha links the "sterility" of women to the "sterility" of the cane fields for a hungry rural population. But what other links exist among hunger, drought, and sugar? What other sources are there for the curse that hangs over Bom Jesus da Mata? For this we must go back to the history of Portuguese colonization and to the origins of the social and cultural institutions that grew up around sugar production, the "sugarocracy" described by Manuel Moreno Fraginals in 1976 with particular reference to Cuba and the *bagaceira* described by Gilberto Freyre in his monumental work *The Masters and the Slaves* (1986a:xxix) as the "general life and atmosphere of the sugar plantation." Fraginals dealt with the political economy of sugar monoculture from a Marxist perspective; Freyre dealt with the culture and social institutions of the plantation from an anthropological as well as a personal and nostalgic perspective. Each contributed something of value to the picture of the new world that the plantation masters made (Genovese 1971), its totality and globality defining almost every aspect of life for slave and freeman, wage laborer, sharecropper, and migrant worker from the seventeenth century through the present day.

Evocative of this total world of the plantation is Freyre's metaphorical use of the term *bagaceira*, which in its original meaning referred to the shed where *bagaço*, the residue fiber spewed out by the crushing of the cane stalks, was stored in huge mounds. Freyre used the same term to refer to the plantation "culture" likewise spewed out as a by-product and residue of sugar cultivation in Northeast Brazil. But in colloquial Brazilian Portuguese the term carries yet another meaning, the one I wish to appropriate for my brief and cursory discussion of the history of the sugar plantation. People of the Alto do Cruzeiro use the word *bagaceira* to refer to any junk, garbage, riff-raff, or marginalized, "low-life" person, such as a prostitute or a drug addict. For me, then, *bagaceira* evokes the social and human *waste* produced under sugar plantation monoculture, a whoring social and economic formation if ever there was one. But what is most remarkable, perhaps, about the history of Northeast Brazilian sugar plantation society is its remarkable resilience throughout nearly four centuries and in the face of radical changes in the value and fortunes of that bittersweet commodity, cane sugar.

Sugar

The story of a lump of sugar is a whole lesson in political
economy, politics, and morality.
            Auguste Cochin (cited in Fraginals 1976:45)

In his ambitious monograph *Sweetness and Power*, Sidney Mintz (1985) traced the world history of that "favored child of capitalism," sucrose, as it moved in trading vessels among Western Europe, Africa, the Caribbean, and Brazil, marking the transition from one type of society (mercantile) to another (industrial capitalist). He narrated a history of the perversity of capitalist relations of production and consumption, including the production of new "tastes," especially for these products of the colonized tropics: sugar, tobacco, and rum. In the beginning it was the cultivation of a taste for sugar (and later for sugar *in* tea, coffee, and cocoa, compounding the assault on the tropics) among European aristocrats that propelled the slave trade and slave labor necessary to cultivate the damnable sweet in the sickening humidity of the coastal tropical plantations of the New World. But in a mere two centuries, Mintz pointed out, sugar passed from being an expensive luxury of the rich to being a cheap necessity of the poor, so that it was the deadly overconsumption of sugar by the English working classes that was to maintain the tropical sugarocracies up through the twentieth century. He concluded his discussion with the following observation:

> The first sweetened cup of hot tea to be drunk by an English worker was a significant historical event, because it prefigured the transformation of an entire society, a total remaking of its economic and social basis. . . . [And so] was erected an entirely different conception of the relationship between producers and consumers, of the meaning of work, of the definition of the self, of the nature of things. What commodities are and what commodities mean . . . [as well as] what persons are, and what being a person means, changed accordingly. (1985:214)

Obviously, the "case" of sugar is a strategic one in understanding the links between field and factory, between rural and urban populations, both of which consume an inordinate amount of sugar. Consumption is the flip side

"There has to be more to sugar than its good taste."

of production, as people learn to relish what is made available to them, whether it is lumps of *rapadura* (brown sugar candy that has been a special treat in the Northeast since the beginnings of sugar cultivation there) or artificially sweetened soft drinks. Mintz later admitted that he was unable to "comfortably or confidently attribute this [historical] transformation [in taste] to some single cause or even series of causes . . . such as 'malnutrition,' or 'advertising,' or 'sweet tooth' " (1987:8). Clearly, he said, there *must* be more to the success of sugar than its good taste.[4]

Taussig suggested looking at the practices of everyday life that make, for example, "a cup of tea, a Bex [an analgesic], and a good lie down" (1987:159) the meaning of pleasure among working-class women in Sydney, Australia, and he cited the marvelous dialogue from James Joyce's *Ulysses* that focuses on the meaning of a good, strong, sweet cup of tea. And so I recall the gloom and panic that struck the little mountain parish of "Ballybran" in western

Ireland (see Scheper-Hughes 1979) during the hard winter of 1975, when the otherwise lean and ascetic farmers, shepherds, and fishermen were confronted with an intolerable sugar shortage generated by various confusions and adjustments within the European Economic Community, which Ireland had then just recently joined. Villagers young and old cajoled, begged, borrowed, and stockpiled large plastic bags of sugar so as to not be without the minimum household ration of sixteen pounds of sugar per week. The Irish government finally intervened in the interim with the distribution of five-pound "pots" of strawberry jam to every schoolchild.

In short, sugar is a powerful metaphor and its fatal attractions, its power and danger, are located in its deep-seated associations with sex and pleasure and with the dark-skinned people who to this day are primarily responsible for the brute labor required for its cultivation and milling. "Brazil is sugar, and sugar is the Negro," wrote Gilberto Freyre (1986a:277), but how much suffering is concealed by these only partly conscious associations! Even as dry and arcane a social scientist as Roger Bastide could wax poetic on the fantasized sensuality and sexuality of the mulatto sugar-plantation culture of the Northeast, against which he contrasted the lean, "leathery," and ascetic culture of the dry *sertão*. Bastide, too, fell into the "sticky web of sugared metaphor" (Taussig 1987b:154) when he wrote that "the baroqueness of funeral processions in the plantation zone is sweetened by contact with black mothers, mulatto lovers, humid vegetation, and the heavy odor of sugar" (1964:62).

Bastide's incidental juxtaposition of death and sugar is apropos of the thesis of this chapter—had I gotten there before Mintz, I would have titled the book not *Sweetness and Power* but rather *Sweetness and Death*. The history of the *Nordestino* sugar plantation is a history of violence and destruction planted in the ruthless occupation of lands and bodies. Fortunes were made in sugar and in black bodies. Like Bastide, I can never smell the rotting fermentation of cut sugarcane without smelling death, an association further etched in memory by the *Nordestino* custom of covering the tiny bodies of dead babies with cloyingly sweet, tiny white flowers.

The World That the Plantation Masters Made

The Old World, gorged with gold, began to hunger after
sugar; and sugar took a lot of slaves.
Claude Levi-Strauss (1961:95)

By the time that Duarte Coelho disembarked on the coast of Pernambuco in 1535 to claim his *sesmaria* of "sixty leagues of [coastal] land granted him by the Portuguese crown" (Burns 1966:45), sugar was already worth, pound for pound, almost as much as gold on European markets. Soon after his arrival Coelho founded two colonies, Olinda and Iguaraçu, and by subdividing his land grant into large parcels of virgin forest (never mind that these were already inhabited by the native Tabajara and Caetés Indians) and awarding them to his companions, he was able to supervise the establishment of five sugar plantation-mills (*engenhos*) in the first fifteen years of colonization. These mills and their accompanying plantation lands multiplied rapidly along riverbanks and near the coast, extending both north and south so that by 1630 there were 144 sugar plantations in Pernambuco.

Historians have argued whether the colonial land-grant system that was established in Pernambuco shared more features with feudalism (which had all but vanished from Portugal itself by the sixteenth century) or with mercantile capitalism. Certainly, the captaincy system established from the first a landed aristocracy that transferred wealth and property within family lines through the traditional feudal principle of primogeniture. Hence by 1575 Duarte Coelho's son was the richest man in Pernambuco.

Initially, the colonial sugar mills of Pernambuco were scattered and separated from each other by dense forest, and their growth was inhibited by a chronic labor shortage and by the limited capacity of the small, animal-powered mills to crush the cane. In addition, the transportation of cut cane from the fields to the mill remained an obstacle to growth. Primitive wooden ox carts were in use on *engenhos* in Pernambuco until the mid-nineteenth century. One of the ways in which particularly enterprising plantation owners overcame these obstacles was to create a number of small mills, one just ahead of or below the other, and each with its own surrounding fields of sugarcane. Hence, it was not uncommon for one *senhor de engenho* to be the owner of four or five small *engenhos* (Galloway 1968:291).

The labor shortage for the many tasks of sugar cultivation and production—clearing land, planting, weeding, harvesting, transporting, crushing, and boiling cane in the mills—was acute from the start. The original Portuguese colonists were an indolent and syphilitic lot with an aversion to manual labor. Meanwhile, many of the indigenous Indians of the coast made themselves scarce by escaping into the interior of Pernambuco once they realized what the colonists had in mind for them. Of course, some stayed behind, and others were hunted and trapped like wild animals. Those caught were impressed into service. But the indigenous Indians made very unsatisfactory plantation slaves. As traditional hunting and gathering peoples, they were unfamiliar with, and unaccustomed to, the discipline of agricultural and milling tasks. Many sickened and died, some by their own hands. Consequently, from the very beginning of the Portuguese sugar colony in

Pernambuco, African slaves were imported in large numbers. Duarte Coelho received permission from the king of Portugal (and later from Queen Catarina) to import as many as 120 blacks for every *engenho* owner under Coelho's jurisdiction (Burns 1966). The average *engenho* in the *zona da mata* during the eighteenth century had between 100 and 200 black slaves. Nonetheless, African and Indian slavery coexisted on these plantations (although in greatly disproportionate numbers) until *Indian* slavery was finally prohibited by law in 1831.[5] It would take another fifty-seven years for the abolition of black slavery.[6]

The colonial *engenho* was built around the master's *casa grande*, or "big house," in which resided his large extended family, called the *parentela*. These early *senhores de engenho* were prodigious reproducers, and their power and authority were so absolute that they openly took up second wives and live-in slave concubines, sometimes recognizing the resulting illegitimate and mulatto children. Each *engenho* had its residential Catholic priest, a "bought" cleric who tended not to interfere (if he knew what was good for him) in the sexual behavior of the *engenho* master or his sons.

In the southern and coastal regions of Pernambuco, the *casa grande* was a veritable mansion of stone or brick, fully appointed with the most elegant furnishings and silver. Freyre noted that

> the Brazilian aristocrat of the Pernambucan littoral and of the Recôncavo immediately began enjoying such advantages as only the refined courts of Europe could offer in the sixteenth century. . . . The stories that are told of the opulence and luxury of the Bahian and Pernambucan plantation-owners in the sixteenth and seventeenth centuries impress us as being, at times, friars' tales. . . . But if we stop to think that many of the luxuries of the table, the house, the personal attire, had been brought from the Orient, it will not be hard to understand this display of wealth and the appearance in the new land of unlooked for refinements. After all, Pernambuco and Bahia speedily became ports of call for ships returning from the East with heavy cargoes of valuable merchandise, vessels that made their way across the sea. (1986a:273–274)

But as sugar production gradually spread inland from the coast and north toward the edge of the *agreste* (the intermediate semiarid zone between the *zona da mata* and the *sertão*) displacing grazing and cotton production there, these *casas grandes* were more like overgrown mud-walled ranch houses than European mansions.

At some distance from the traditional big house stood the *senzala*, the row of connected one-room huts that served as semicommunal slave quarters. In addition, the colonial *engenho* generally had a small chapel where the women and children of the extended family assisted at mass and received the sacraments, the priest's blessing, and the benefits of his "sugar-coated" theology. Slaves were permitted to assist at mass by congregating outside on the patio or verandas of the chapel.

Finally, there was the mill complex: the various buildings and lean-tos for crushing the cane, boiling and clarifying the juice, and purifying the sugar crystals. Surrounding the mill buildings and the *casa grande* were the outlying fields of sugarcane.

Gilberto Freyre, Brazil's first native anthropologist and social historian, and until his death in 1987 one of its dominant intellectual voices, introduced a rather soft and almost nostalgic, sympathetic portrait of *Nordestino* plantation society from slavery to the present day, owing perhaps to his own origins within that society. His was a deeply personal social history in which it was "our Mammy who rocked us to sleep. Who suckled us. Who fed us, mashing our food with her own hands . . . (and) who initiated us into physical love and, to the creaking of a cot, gave us our first complete sensation of being a man" (1986a:278).

In various of his publications Freyre seemed to be defending Brazilian slavery as a more benign and humane institution than elsewhere in the New World. "The slave on the Brazilian plantation," he told an American audience in 1945 during a lecture series at Indiana University, "was generally well treated and his lot was really less wretched than many European laborers who were not called slaves" (1945:49). To explain, Freyre invoked the argument that Portuguese Catholicism and its social institutions were less dehumanizing than the religion and institutions of the Anglo-Protestant colonial world. Brazilian slaveowners never thought of their charges as any less valuable than themselves before the eyes of God, and this, Freyre maintained, protected slaves against the worst forms of maltreatment.

The main thrust of his argument, however, concerned the "positive" effects of the customary practice of miscegenation between master and slave, openly in the bedrooms of the *casa grande* and more covertly and furtively in the *senzala*. Under the Law of the Free Womb (enacted in 1871), the issue from such interracial couplings were freemen and women. The presence of these brown-skinned offsprings reduced, Freyre argued, the social distance between the *casa grande* and the *mata* and between the big house and the slave quarters. What the colonial plantation society created in terms of aristocratization, dividing Brazilian society into extremes of masters and slaves, was contradicted in large part, maintained Freyre, by the social effects of miscegenation. First the Indian woman and then the black woman, followed by the *mulata,* the *cabrocha* (dark-skinned mestiza), the *quadrona* (one-fourth black), and the *oitava* (one-eighth black), entered the big house as domestics, concubines, and then later as wives of their white masters. And so miscegenation acted powerfully toward social democratization in Brazil (Freyre 1986a:xi, xiv, xvi, xix–xx). The Brazilian sociologist made the proud boast that

> the social relations between the two races, the conquering and the conquered [never] reached that point of sharp antipathy or hatred the grating sound of which reaches our ears from all the countries that have been colonized by Anglo-Saxon Protestants. The racial friction [in Brazil] was smoothed by the lubricating oil of a deep-seated miscegenation, whether in the form of a free union damned by the [Catholic] clergy or that of a regular Christian marriage with the blessing of the padres. (1986a:181–182)

And so was born the great myth of Brazil's racial democracy that was to remain unchallenged until very recently.

As if adding insult to injury, Freyre went so far as to derive virtually all contemporary human and cultural values in Brazil from plantation and slave society. Out of the institution of the *casa grande,* with its slavery, concubinage, and even with its admittedly "sadomasochistic" sexual relations between master and slave emerged the "best expression" of the Brazilian character:

> The social history of the plantation manor house is the intimate history of practically everything Brazilian: of its domestic, conjugal life, under a polygamous and slave-holding regime; of the life of the child; of its Christianity reduced to a family religion and influenced by the superstitions of the slave quarters. The study of the intimate history of a people contains something of a Proustian introspection. It is as if one were meeting oneself. . . . It is in the plantation manor house that Brazilian character achieved its best expression down to our days: our social continuity is in its story. In this story the political and military part is minimized, and instead of the striking things it offers us, we are given the routine of life; but it is in routine that one can best feel the character of a people. (1986a:xliii)

What Freyre neglected in his monumental analysis of the *casa grande* was an accompanying sociological analysis of the *senzala.* The world that the Brazilian slave master fashioned consisted of more than the bedroom and the nursery: it also encompassed the sugar fields and the boiling house where both Indian and African slaves (as well as wage-earning freemen) sickened and died in great numbers. Manoel Correia de Andrade pointed out

(1980:47) that two factors made the investment of capital in African slaves a perilous venture: first, their exceedingly high mortality from overwork, exposure to accident and to excessive heat in the fields as well as in the mills, inadequate diets, and poor and overcrowded living conditions in the *senzalas*;[7] and second, the tendency of slaves to escape and form their own runaway slave settlements (called *quilombos*) in the interior of Pernambuco.

The late nineteenth century marked a transition—really a rupture—in the political economy of plantation society in Pernambuco, as slave labor gradually gave way to wage labor and as the traditional mill was replaced by the modern, industrialized sugar factory, the *usina* (see Galloway 1989). At the same time the Brazilian sugar industry faced strong competition from European beet sugar. Nonetheless, the industry managed to meet these challenges and to survive, if not, however, to prosper.

Up through the mid-nineteenth century, sugar cultivation and processing remained primitive in Pernambuco. Only one species of cane, Creole cane, was cultivated, and it was grown from cuttings planted in rows of shallow holes dug with crude hoes. Shoots sprouted after several weeks and were harvested when they were fully grown (reaching two and one-half meters) a year or more later. After several harvests, old fields were abandoned for newer ones, with no attention to preserving or replenishing the fertility of the soil.

The milling process was likewise wasteful and inefficient. The majority of the mills were powered by horses and oxen, but the Sugar Museum of Recife displays a harness that was used for slaves as well. The cane had to be passed several times through the presses, and the bagasse, the husks left after the sugar juice had been extracted from the stalks, was not used as fuel, as it was in the Caribbean, for example, during the same period (Fraginals 1976:32); it was simply left in huge rotting piles near the mill. To make matters worse, fuel was obtained by cutting down trees, which further reduced the forest zone in Pernambuco until in the late nineteenth century the *zona da mata* took on the totally deforested appearance it has today. The *senhores de engenho* had secured the right to dispose of trees on their lands without any legal-juridical restraint. There was never an argument or discourse concerning the rational use of forest land but only one regarding who had the right to fell, raze, and destroy. Without a trace of guilt or self-consciousness, the plantation masters frequently named their *engenhos queimados*, or "burned."

In describing the lush countryside along the coastline from Rio de Janeiro to Santos, where coffee, rather than sugar, has reigned as king crop since the seventeenth century, Levi-Strauss was moved to lament the destruction of "virgin" forest lands by a rapacious pioneer population:

Erosion has done much to ravage the country before me; but above all it was Man who was responsible for its chaotic appearance. Originally it had been dug and cultivated; but after the few years continual rain and the exhaustion of the soil made it impossible to keep the coffee-plantations in being. They were therefore moved to an area where the soil was fresher and more fertile. The relationship between Man and the soil had never [in Brazil] been marked by the reciprocity of attentions which, in the Old World, has existed for thousands of years and been the basis of our prosperity. Here in Brazil the soil has been first violated, then destroyed. Agriculture has been a matter of looting for quick profits. . . . [In the New World] I became familiar with a Nature which, though more savage than our own, because less populated and less under cultivation, had yet lost all its original freshness: a Nature not so much "wild" as degraded. (1961:97–98, 99)

The availability and abundance of land led to other wasteful patterns. When an *engenho* became run down and dilapidated, it was common for its owner to simply abandon that site for a new one. Consequently, sugar production was lower in Pernambuco than in other sugar-producing areas of the Americas. Gradually, however, in the face of competition from these other sugar colonies, some changes were made: new, higher yielding species of cane were introduced; manuring fields became more common; and heavier and more efficient horizontal presses replaced the old vertical rollers. The first steam-powered mills appeared in the 1820s, but these were expensive and spare parts were difficult to obtain, so they were not widely adopted.

The abolition of slavery in 1888 (making Brazil the last Western nation to free its slaves) should have thrown the sugar plantation economy into crisis. That it did not, and that sugar production remained virtually unaffected in the years following abolition, needs some explanation. Beginning in the early nineteenth century, slave labor came into competition with wage labor. Virtually every *engenho* had large numbers of poor squatters, impoverished freemen (acculturated Indians, mulattos, and free blacks) who, in exchange for the right to clear a small piece of land, build a hut, and cultivate a garden or orchard, worked certain days for the *senhor de engenho* for free or for a nominal wage (de Andrade 1980:76; Galloway 1968:298–299). These *moradores de condição* (bonded or indentured squatters) represented a huge rural reserve labor force, and they turned out to be crucial in the transition from slave to wage labor.

On the eve of abolition in the late 1870s (when statistics on agricultural wage laborers in Pernambuco first became available), free workers already outnumbered slaves in every *município* of the *zona da mata*. After abolition the newly freed slaves simply became indentured squatters and share-croppers, "replacing the discipline of slavery with the discipline of hunger," as Mintz (1985:70) described the emancipation of plantation slaves in the Caribbean. As squatters, the ex-slaves continued to live in the converted *senzalas* or more commonly in mud and straw huts in small clearings near the sugar fields. Their diet remained scanty and limited: manioc meal, dried meat, and whatever they managed to cultivate in their small gardens or to poach from the *engenho* property. Impoverished, illiterate, and dependent on the whims of their *senhor de engenho*, who could have them removed at any time, such was the "racial democracy" enjoyed by the dark-skinned rural workers from emancipation through the present day. A mid-nineteenth-century newspaper in Pernambuco described the compromised situation of the "free" workers. It might just as easily describe that of the contemporary plantation worker and his or her family: "Dry meat, salted—and many times spoiled—fish, flour without manioc, bad food, a hard bed, an uncomfortable house, ragged clothing are the products which the poor use. Even these come in limited amounts in order not to exceed the budget" (quoted in Burns 1966:235).

The Rise of the Modern Sugar Factory

Just before the turn of the twentieth century the first central mills were established with the help of government incentives and foreign investors and capital. The Brazilian government had hoped that these central mills, fully mechanized with the most up-to-date technology, would render the traditional *engenho* as a mixed agricultural and industrial institution obsolete. The separation of the *cultivation* of cane and the *production* of refined sugar was deemed essential to the modernization of the sugar industry.

For a variety of reasons—including general mismanagement, a lack of skilled technicians, and shoddy construction—these first centralized mills fared poorly, and by 1886 the British-owned Central Factories of Brazil Ltd. and the North Brazilian Sugar Factories Ltd., the two companies that introduced the new sugar factory system into Pernambuco, had gone bankrupt (Galloway 1968:300). Nevertheless, these first attempts paved the way for a second, more successful wave of industrialization in the early twentieth century, financed by Brazilian, German, French, and British capital.

The modern sugar factories, the *usinas*, first appeared along the railway system that crossed the southern part of Pernambuco. Here they replaced the traditional plantations and turned the feudal sugar barons, the *senhores de engenho*, into a new social type, the *fornecedor de cana*, or "supplier of cane." Although the new *usina* fought to dominate the *zona da mata*, the traditional *engenhos* resisted the onslaught for nearly a half century more.

Finally, however, the smaller mills were confined to the more remote and hilliest northern regions of the *zona da mata*, such as the area surrounding Bom Jesus da Mata. By the end of the 1950s these last holdouts of the old-style *engenho* system disappeared from the landscape, leaving behind only the dilapidated *casas grandes* and their abandoned mill buildings, several of which are within walking distance of Bom Jesus.

Those *senhores de engenho* who did not wish to become just the suppliers of a raw product for the new sugar industrialists, called *usineiros*, left the land and their rural homesteads behind and moved to Recife, Rio, or São Paulo, where they invested their dwindling fortunes in new commercial ventures. Others, however, graciously accepted the new set of structural relations and set out to exploit the possibilities inherent in the role of modern suppliers of sugarcane. Some consolidated their landholdings by purchasing the lands of those *senhores de engenho* who had opted out of the new system.

Seu Reinaldo of Bom Jesus is one such modern supplier of cane. Today he owns thousands of hectares of plantation land spread among three states: Pernambuco, Paraíba, and Rio Grande do Norte. He supplies cane to several *usinas*, and he employs more than five hundred rural laborers to cultivate, cut, and transport his product. Although Seu Reinaldo, as a *fornecedor de cana*, is no longer at the pinnacle of the social-political-economic hierarchy of the region, he does not resent his "displacement" by the new class of corporate *usineiros*, and he has adjusted well to the role of a wealthy agricultural businessman. In many ways he is more independent and autonomous than the *usineiro*, who is generally a member of a larger corporation and whose economic activities are closely monitored and curtailed by governmental regulations regarding production quotas and the distribution of sales and markets both domestically and internationally. Moreover, in terms of local power and prestige in Bom Jesus, Seu Reinaldo has maintained his paternalistic status and his clout over the working and rural populations to which he is still *o senhor de engenho* and their "boss" and patron.

By contrast, the owners of the five surrounding *usinas* are more distant figures who generally reside in the city, leaving their opulent country mansions empty save for domestic help and occasional visitors. Their power is less well articulated in traditional "personalistic" terms. So one could say that although everything has changed, actually very little has changed. The new *fornecedores de cana* have simply stepped into the gap left by the *senhor de engenho* in the local popular and political culture of Bom Jesus da Mata.

The *fornecedores* supply about half the cane that is cultivated and milled in Pernambuco today. The rest grows on the often extensive landholdings of the modern *usinas*. The division between the cultivation of cane and the production of sugar, thought so necessary to the modernization of the industry, was never really accomplished. Although there are two *usinas* within the radius of Bom Jesus that cultivate only a small percentage of the cane that they mill, the general tendency throughout the *zona da mata* is the consolidation of landholdings—*latifúndios*—by *usineiros* as well as by *fornecedores de cana*.

The transformation of the plantation economy, completed by the mid-twentieth century, had a disastrous effect on the traditional peasant class of the *zona da mata:* the tenants, sharecroppers, and conditional squatters (see Forman 1975:chap. 3). Of these, the most common arrangement was that of the *morador de condição,* who lived on the *engenho* and kept his cottage and *roçado* in exchange for one or more days of "conditional" labor for the *senhor de engenho.* Some peasants had nothing but disdain for *moradores de condição,* saying they had made themselves "slaves" to the *senhor de engenho. Posseiros,* by contrast, were peasants who had been squatters on patches of marginal and unused *engenho* lands for such a long time that they were thought of as having tenure there (they had *posse*). Today this traditional relationship is contested by the *latifundiários* who are now taking violent measures to rid their lands of *posseiros.*

The process of evictions began in the 1950s when many *usineiros* and cane suppliers began to eye even the smallest and least accessible subsistence-based *roçados* as more land for sugar cultivation. Because of the pressures of new competition from the south of Brazil, as a highly mechanized sugar industry emerged there in the state of São Paulo, plantation owners in Pernambuco also recognized a need to "modernize" the rural labor force. A general trend toward wage labor made older arrangements such as sharecropping and conditional tenancy inconvenient and obsolete. It spelled the end of a semiautonomous peasantry living in the crevices of plantation society.

In addition to straightforward evictions, some traditional peasants and sharecroppers were simply starved off their small *sítios* and *roçados* when their landlords increasingly awarded them only the most useless, inaccessible, or exhausted plots of land or assigned them very temporary fields that they were allowed to use only between sugar harvesting and recultivation. Landlords began to increase the number of days that *moradores de condição* had to work on the plantation, leaving them little time for tending their own gardens. Finally, landlords forced many peasants to leave the land by restricting the crops they could cultivate, including such basic necessities as sweet manioc, beans, and bananas, and by forcing peasants to grow sugarcane to be sold to or shared with the landowners.

It was during this period that many older residents of the Alto do

Cruzeiro were forced to leave the surrounding countryside to try their luck in town. Bom Jesus da Mata, centrally located within commuting distance of five large *usinas* and many smaller plantations, was a magnet for evicted or otherwise displaced peasant-workers. Cut loose from paternalistic bonds to a particular landowner, plantation, or sugar mill, these workers became "free agents" who sold their labor for wages on a temporary basis. In effect, they formed a ready reserve army of rural day laborers.

From September through January, the sugarcane harvesting and milling season, a parade of rickety but brightly painted wooden trucks arrives at the base of the Alto each morning before dawn to recruit and collect workers. Individual "contracts" are negotiated for periods of time ranging from a few days to an entire season. Since the late 1960s registered and "carded" rural laborers have been protected by a minimum wage, but between 1987 and 1989 this averaged only forty dollars a month. Although the cost of housing is minimal on the Alto do Cruzeiro, food is expensive. To fill a basic, weekly *cesta* basket to feed a family of six requires four times the minimum wage. The net result is misery and a constant scramble among all household members, including children, to find supplementary wages. In recent years some residents of the Alto do Cruzeiro have made arrangements with small plantation owners allowing them to plant small gardens on "idle" lands between sugar harvests in exchange for clearing those lands in preparation for replanting with cane. This form of barter is a great gamble, however, for all too frequently the workers are unable to harvest their produce before being ordered to clear the fields to make way for sugar production.

Not all peasant-workers left the plantations and sugar mills, however. Those who remained were likewise transformed into a proletarianized labor force. The price they paid was a required move into concentrated workers' *vilas*, those for the cane cutters built in clearings amid the cane fields, those for the mill workers in attached cement block cubicles within walking distance of the sugar milling plant. Both seemed very much like "modernized" equivalents of the old *senzalas*. At the start of this transformative process, the peasants of Pernambuco mobilized in an effort to protect their fragile, indeed their endangered, interests.

The Peasant Leagues, 1954–1964

If the years 1910–1950 marked the transformation of sugar cultivation and production into a "modern" industry based on wage labor, the decade 1954–1964 marked a transition in peasant consciousness, as rural workers in Pernambuco organized into peasant leagues that challenged the evictions of tenants as well as the definitions of work relations and terms of labor on the *latifúndio* of the *zona da mata*.

The movement began in 1954 on the lands of the *engenho* Galiléia, located in the *município* of Vitória de Santo Antão, some sixty kilometers from Recife in a transitional zone between the *mata* and the *agreste*. In that year a *foreiro*—a peasant renting marginal lands from a plantation to plant subsistence crops—named José Hortêncio was unable to pay his high rents and was ordered to leave his land. Hortêncio sought the help of a member of the Brazilian Communist Party (PCB), José dos Prazeres, who suggested to Hortêncio that his situation was far from unique and that the best way to proceed might be to form a society among his *companheiros* with the goal of eventually forming their own cooperatively owned and operated *engenho*. In this way all could be free of rents and the constant threats of expulsion (Bastos 1984:19).

By the end of that year a group of peasants from *engenho* Galiléia had formed their society with the advice and guidance of José dos Prazeres. The association, awkwardly named the Farming and Stock-Raisers Society of Planters of Pernambuco (SAPP), was registered as a traditional beneficiary society; its modest goal was to "improve the lives of its members" through the building of a primary school and through the acquisition of seeds, insecticides, farm tools, and small government subsidies. These, however, were long-term goals, and the first project of the peasants' organization had nothing to do with rents, education, or general economic or political complaints. Rather, the society initially mobilized to found a traditional rural funeral society that would provide each member and his family with a proper burial, i.e., "six feet under and a coffin" (de Castro 1966:12–13), and so spare them the considerable humiliation of a pauper funeral (see chapter 6).

The irony of a peasant mobilization centered on land and a proper home for the dead (while the living were without the same) could not have been lost on those who first lent their support to the peasants' beneficiary society. Among these was the owner of the Galiléia plantation himself, Oscar de Arruda Beltrão, who (following the tradition of *paternalismo*) was invited by the peasants to serve as a patron of the society and its "honorary" president for life, a title and position that the landlord accepted. José Francisco de Souza, known as Zeze de Galiléia, was elected the first actual president of the peasants' society. Zeze was both a peasant and a manager of the mill employed by the plantation.

The early mobilization of the rural workers at Galiléia made other landlords in the sugarcane region nervous, and they quickly put pressure on Beltrão to withdraw his support from the society and to refuse to serve as *padrinho* (godfather) to an organization that they feared might eventually lead to the undoing of the planter class (Bastos 1984:19). Pressured as well by his son and heir to the Galiléia plantation, Beltrão did try to put an end to the organization, and he began to use the courts to evict peasant leaders he now perceived as troublesome and dangerous influences on the life of the plantation. Local landlords began referring to the peasants' society as the "peasant league," so as to link the apparently innocuous activities at Galiléia with the communist-inspired Peasant Leagues that had been active throughout the Northeast in the 1940s and had sought such benefits as legal aid, education, health care, and funeral benefits for peasants and other rural workers. During the earlier period the use of the term *Ligas Camponesas* was intentional and meant to evoke the Peasant Leagues of the Middle Ages, when European serfs organized against their feudal landlords. But the movement at Galiléia was initially without any conscious political ideology other than the rhetoric of "self-improvement" until the retaliatory wave of evictions of activist peasants turned the beneficiary and funeral society into a class-based mobilization.

The evicted peasants and their worried *companheiros* sought outside help, first petitioning the governor, General Cordeiro de Farias, to prevent further evictions, but he turned them away. After exhausting the possibilities for help and support from local "strongmen" and wealthy "patrons" and "godfathers," they finally sought legal redress and were directed to a young lawyer in Recife, Francisco Julião, with a reputation for being fair and for representing rural workers in eviction suits. Julião, in addition to being a sympathetic lawyer, was a state deputy (assemblyman) representing the Socialist Party in Pernambuco (see Horowitz 1964:chaps. 2–3; Forman 1975:186–188). Although Julião had handled many similar cases on an individual basis, he quickly perceived the opportunity for a class action suit at Galiléia. In addition to legal maneuvers, Julião used the state assembly to publicly denounce the situation at Galiléia and at other plantations in the *zona da mata* and the *agreste*. In so doing, Julião generated broad public support for evicted peasants (see Julião 1962, 1963, 1964a, 1964b).

The fight over Galiléia lasted until 1959 when, by an act of the legislature (rather than through the courts), the *engenho* Galiléia was expropriated from its owners and its lands distributed among the peasant-worker tenants. This extraordinary action immediately catapulted the mobilization at Galiléia to national and international preeminence; soon after, other groups of dispossessed peasants in the Northeast began to organize, and other expropriations of plantation lands followed. These peasants now appropriated for *themselves* the name of the Peasant Leagues, and they adopted Julião as their charismatic leader and emblem of the movement. The strength and numbers of the Peasant League movement increased with the election in 1963 of a leftist, populist governor in Pernambuco, Miguel Arraes, and by the end of that year the movement claimed some forty thousand members

(Palmeira 1979:72). As the movement to expropriate plantations mushroomed, the media (especially in the United States) described the Peasant Leagues as a frightening and subversive "communist-led" mobilization (see Szulc 1960, 1961).[8] In fact, however, the actual relations between the Peasant Leagues and the PCB were tenuous, as the PCB leaders feared that the increasingly radical demands, actions, and impassioned rhetoric of Julião might push the nation toward a conservative backlash.[9] And, indeed, this was the case. The military coup in the spring of 1964 invoked, as one of its rationales, the need to stop the revolutionary activities of the Peasant League movement. In a matter of months the entire movement was crushed, activists and leaders were imprisoned and tortured or forced (like Julião) into exile, and the rank-and-file membership was frightened into disbanding.

Nevertheless, the memory of the Peasant League movement and of the new forms of social and political consciousness that they awakened in the peasants and rural workers of the interior of Pernambuco have been kept alive in the form of small "cultural circles" where literacy and Paulo Freire's method of *conscientização* (critical consciousness) are taught within popular organizations and shantytown associations and in the Catholic church–founded ecclesiastical base communities (CEBs) (see chapter 12). Meanwhile, the church-initiated rural syndicate movement (aimed more at the proletarianized wage workers than at the vestigial peasant population of the sugar plantations) survived the period of the military dictatorship, although it hardly thrived given the harassment and death squadron killings of several syndicate leaders during this period (see Amnesty International 1988).

Female Workers in the Cane

The transformation of rural labor in the plantation zone of Pernambuco affected women as well as men. Although women in the *zona da mata— norte* were hard workers who labored side by side with their husbands and sons tending small gardens, fishing in the river, weaving baskets from rushes, and selling small bits of excess produce in the marketplace, women did not work in sugar cultivation on *engenhos*, nor did they work in the *usinas*. That was men's work, although women and children might assist by carrying lunch pails and water buckets back and forth the many miles between home and fields. Now, with the dislocations and disruptions caused by the modernization of the sugar industry and the proletarianization of labor, women and children have entered the rural industrial labor force in great numbers, especially in the past ten years.[10]

Although it is the rare woman indeed who would be caught cutting sugarcane, the most proletarian and masculine of all rural labors, it is not uncommon today to come across large rural work crews composed wholly of

Woman working at the foot of the cane.

women and children clearing fields in preparation for planting or engaged in the endless task of weeding. The large increase of women and children in wage labor on *engenho* and *usina* lands in the surrounding *mata* of Bom Jesus constitutes a well-guarded "community secret." In this traditionally male-dominant society, men are still expected to do the heavy and dirty paid agricultural work; women (even very poor women) are expected to confine their work and activities to the home and household *roçado*. Men do not want their daughters and wives to shoulder a *foice* (scythe) and join strangers in mixed rural work teams. This would be a *vergonha* (humiliation) for the husband, the traditional head of the household, a suggestion that he is not man enough to care for his wife and children.

At a rural workers' syndicate meeting held in Bom Jesus, the topic of female agricultural labor was discussed heatedly by both women and men.

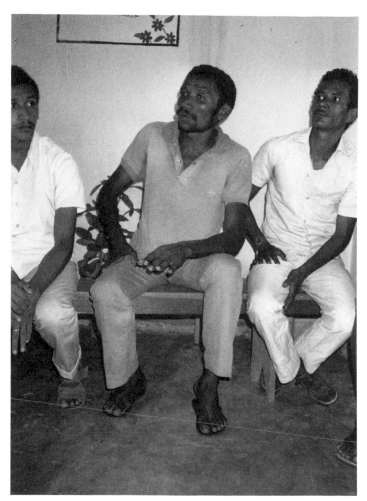

"I'd rather kill myself first before I see my woman working in the cane."
Rural syndicate meeting, Bom Jesus, 1987.

The men were univocal in condemning this new practice, saying, as did one weather-beaten and work-battered elderly man, "We are seventeen in my house. I have fifteen children to feed. But I would rather see them all die of hunger before I would let my woman work in the cane." Another jumped to his feet in the crowded, boisterous syndicate hall to state with passion: "The man who earns but 483 cruzados and 2 centavos [about $10.75 in 1987] a week doesn't have enough to feed a family of thirteen. But he has pride, and he will strike, or he will *pedir esmola* [beg in the street], or he will steal, but *he* and *he* alone will feed his family."

As things began to get out of hand (the topic is incendiary), the syndicate representative tried to return some order to the hall by asking why the workers and peasants present felt so strongly about what is apparently a fact of life for many rural families today, proven by the number of *companheiras* who had traveled from great distances to attend the meeting. An intense-looking young man asked to be recognized to deliver this moving homage to the rural women in the *zona da mata—norte:* "Look here. Some men say that their wives are lazy, but look at the work they do to sustain us. We leave the house early in the morning, and when we come home at one we are angry because the beans are not ready for us. But do you know what she has been doing all morning? She has been looking for water, searching for *lenha*, making the fire, washing the clothes, feeding the children, tending to the animals and the garden. The work of our *companheiras* is endless. And on top of that she is often a captive of her *companheiro* as well." The few, rather timid women present applauded. Most of the men were silent; some appeared abashed. The discussion ended on this note.

Later, and in private, the syndicate leader revealed another reason for the heated emotion surrounding the entry of women (and children) into the wage labor force: the majority are *clandestinas,* women working without the official "working papers" that are meant to ensure rural workers their basic rights and benefits.[11] As clandestine workers (hired by plantations and *usinas* through middlemen), women and children are willing to accept even lower wages than the miserable minimum wage, and *clandestinas* naturally avoid participation in the new mobilizations of the rural workers' unions. In short, they are viewed as scabs. Some are suspected of treachery, of spying and reporting on the political activities of organized workers. The fact is that most female workers in the cane are abandoned or otherwise stranded women—mothers of often large families who have been left by their husbands or lovers and are therefore forced to assume his place to survive. Their desperate straits make them vulnerable to exploitation and to manipulation by their bosses.

Biu, the hapless sister of Lordes and Antonieta, was one such clandestine worker. When Oscar deserted her with five hungry and often sick children in 1987, Biu wrapped a cloth around her head, borrowed long pants and a man's shirt, and returned to the hard labor that she had known as a young girl (when her own mother was similarly abandoned). Biu preferred to negotiate brief contracts (rarely more than a week or two at a time) and to find work relatively close to home so that she could return to her children no later than 3 or 4 P.M. "Carded" workers do not have this kind of flexibility. As both a woman worker and a *clandestina,* Biu is doubly exploited. At age forty-four, following some fifteen pregnancies, she is no longer physically strong. She is slight of build and severely anemic. It is rare that she can complete the

Fearless, hardworking Biu.

agreed-on work in exchange for her negotiated wage. Often, Biu brings her nine-year-old son along with her to supplement her productivity. Yet Biu does not blame her boss for the minuscule wages she brings home at the end of the week (often only about five dollars). "I'm finished, washed up," she explains, without a trace of self-pity. "My body's not worth anything." As a *clandestina*, Biu is not eligible for free medical care or other social benefits that might bolster her deteriorated health. (This situation changed in Brazil in 1989 when nationalized health care was extended to all Brazilians.) All too frequently, her meager wages are spent on expensive tonics and useless medications purchased without prescription from a local pharmacy.

Being a female worker in the cane confers other disadvantages as well.[12] Biu prefers to walk to her assigned fields rather than suffer the "rudeness," sexual overtures, and vulgarities of male workers in the communal truck rides provided by the *usina*. On a normal workday Biu must leave her hut at the top of the Alto do Cruzeiro and begin her long trek to often very distant fields as early as 3 or 4 A.M. One morning Biu instructed her thirteen-year-old daughter, Xoxa, to walk me to a nearby plantation where Biu was clearing fields with a large group of women and children. "Nearby" turned into a demanding hour-and-a-half trek along muddy roads with cane rising on either side obscuring any view. Finally, Xoxa pointed excitedly to a distant hill, where I could barely see tiny figures working halfway up the incline. "There they are!" she exclaimed. As we approached the hill it became apparent that we would have to wade through a shallow but filthy river to reach the workers. I balked at the thought of exposure to the snail-born schistosomes (a blood fluke that is a major cause of death and misery in this region), but Biu, who had already caught sight of us, strode boldly across the river while rolling herself a cigarette.

Once across, she pulled up some rushes and used them to rub her legs and feet vigorously to rid herself of the parasites. Then, sitting down at the bank of the river, Biu took a break from her morning's work to engage in some uncharacteristic complaining. She explained that she was paid by the *quadro* (square) of land and that she suspected the *cabo* (boss of the work team) of mismeasuring the legally determined lot size to the advantage of the planta-tion owner.[13] In the "old days" a man or a strong woman could clear a *quadro* in a single day; now it took workers (especially women) two and sometimes three days to finish the same task. Biu was aware that her boss was getting free labor out of many of the women's young sons, who should be in school, but she shrugged her shoulders and concluded with the unarguable, "*É um jeito, não é?*"—"It's a way of getting by, isn't it?"

Not everyone makes her peace with the new conditions of rural labor. Some, like Nailza de Arruda, with whom (and her husband, Zé Antônio) I lived for a year in 1964–1965, could never forget what it was like to cultivate one's own *sítio* and to be in more control of one's life. During the time I shared her tiny hut on the Alto do Cruzeiro, Nailza never ceased to pine after her childhood home in rural Mato Grosso, where land was free for the asking, or so it seemed. Nailza had migrated to the Northeast, following her husband, whom she first met while he was a temporary migrant laborer working on an extension of the railroad into the interior of her state. Nailza found her new life in Bom Jesus greatly wanting. Zé Antônio worked at several jobs (some of them simultaneously)—clearing fields, cutting cane, doing construction, making bricks—but none was sufficient to provide a decent life for the couple. Nailza's health failed (a failure she attributed to the polluted drinking water of Bom Jesus), and she suffered a painful succession of reproductive failures—spontaneous abortions, stillbirths, and infant deaths—which she blamed on the hardness and barrenness of the Brazilian Northeast. She complained, "The people here think that *caboclos* [people of mixed white and Indian ancestry] are savages, but our lives in Mato Grosso are more civilized than this *porcaria* [rubbish heap]."

Despite the protests (and some sorcery) on the part of her mother-in-law, Nailza finally succeeded in convincing her husband to return with her to Mato Grosso. And there they have prospered, proving Nailza correct. The family photo that Zé Antônio sent his disconsolate mother in 1986 is hanging on her crumbling *taipa* wall. It shows a healthy and stout, now middle-aged couple surrounded by eight tanned and robust dark-eyed children, one of them already an adult and holding a daughter of his own. "They look like wild Indians to me," Dona Carminha said sourly of her distant but healthy grandchildren.

Into the Belly of the Beast: Usina Água Preta

In September 1987 I made a two-day visit into the bowels of one of the largest and more distant *usinas* in the region of Bom Jesus da Mata, accompanied by Seu Severino, a local syndicate leader traveling incognito. It was the start of the milling season, and the giant machines had just begun to heave and roll and gyrate. We were cordially received by Dr. Alfonso, the general manager of Usina Água Preta, to whom I introduced myself as a visiting North American social scientist with an interest in the modern sugar plant. Dr. Alfonso was employed by a large, family-based "corporation" of brothers who showed little inclination to bother with the day-to-day operations of the plantation and refinery. Alfonso decided that my first day should be spent surveying the widely dispersed lands in cultivation and observing the organization of rural work teams in the company of Seu Jaime, an *usina* agronomist.

First, however, we were taken on a brief tour of *usina*-related institutions: the laboratories where the quality of the cane brought in by the suppliers was tested; the small plant that produced the soybean milk distributed to all workers and schoolchildren on the *usina*; the medical, dental, and social services building; the central primary school and middle school (*ginásio*) for the professional, technical, and factory workers of the central complex. We passed by but did not enter the plantation owners' modern *casa grande* complex, with its many patios, sculptured gardens, pool, and tennis courts. The owner and his family were away (as they often were) in the south of Brazil, leaving the *casa grande* sadly empty and the management of house, factory, and plantation lands in the hands of a large and competent technical and professional staff.

At some distance from the *casa grande* was the *vila dos técnicos*, the residential compound for two strata of *usina* management: the professionals and "scientists" (engineers, chemists, agronomists, doctors, industrial psychologist); and the technicians/managers (those who supervised and managed mill workers and machinery inside the plant). All were housed in rent-free, modern, ranch-style homes "with every convenience." The *vila dos técnicos* had its own private social club, swimming pool, restaurant, and gardens, all modeled after the *casa grande* complex. A few miles from the technicians' villa stood the far more modest *vila dos operários*, the factory workers' villa, several rows of small, square, cement-block homes. The paved roads gave way here to muddy paths, but the workers' villa did boast a large soccer field and an open-air pavilion that served as a poor man's country club for weekend dances, the annual *carnaval* ball, and São João's Day festivities.

Following the local tour of facilities, Dr. Alfonso introduced us to Seu Jaime, and we were settled into a comfortable four-wheel drive luxury car for a rather long and uncomfortable ride along rutted and muddy roads and through cane fields that spanned two states, Pernambuco and Paraíba. Jaime seemed intent on emphasizing that all twenty thousand hectares of land owned by the *usina* were in full production. After some time we encountered the first of several clearings in the cane where the *vilas dos trabalhadores* (rural workers' villas) were scattered. The one we visited was a newly constructed "model" villa, an "experiment," Seu Jaime called it, albeit one that was less than successful. Jaime described the row of tiny attached stucco cubicles as a great "improvement" over the traditional, dispersed mud huts in clearings and on hillsides that they replaced. It was more "convenient," he said, for the rural workers to be "concentrated" in villas where each cubicle had electric power and running water. But the residents themselves pointed out that both electricity and water were unpredictable, and most often they went without either. At the end of the rows of cubicles stood a public washstand in a great state of disrepair. Seu Jaime used this to illustrate the difficulties involved in the effort taken by the *usina* to raise the standard of living of rural people not yet ready for "progress." The women, he said, still preferred to wash clothes at the banks of the polluted river that ran through plantation lands. Similarly, the rural workers were not sufficiently "motivated" to keep up the communal garden reserved for each *vila*. A woman standing nearby interrupted to say that the men were too tired from their fieldwork to come home to tend a *roçado* at the end of the day, while the women had their hands full doing other work and trying to control the many villa children, who were *mal criadas* and who stole from or destroyed the gardens the women did try to plant.

I thought back to the Sunday I had spent not long before in the home and *sítio* of my old friend Seu Milton, a traditional peasant, on the plantation Votas, just a few kilometers walk from Bom Jesus. His large and pleasant mud hut was built on the top of a hillside with a panoramic view of the surrounding cane fields and part of the town of Bom Jesus. Milton, his second wife, and their five children lived, Milton said, "freely—like goats!" In exchange for the right to build his hut and plant his garden of corn, beans, squash, manioc, and potatoes, Milton gave two days' labor (for minimum wage) to his landlord. It seemed an ideal situation, and he agreed. All were relatively healthy and more than well fed. What they lacked, offered Milton, were the "conveniences" of town life: electricity, the public *chafariz*, school for the children (his attended only sporadically because of the distance and the help they gave their mother at home and in the garden), store-bought clothes and shoes (his own wore cloth sacking shorts, and he and his children were barefoot). After lunch we lay down in the doorway of the hut as cool breezes circulated around our bodies. The difficult part was still to come, however, for Milton insisted that before we leave we collect, and carry back to town across our shoulders, sacks of garden produce for his "poor" kin living on the Alto do Cruzeiro, including his ex-wife, Lordes, and his much loved sister-in-law, Biu. These images of abundance were hard to reconcile with Jaime's portrayal of "traditional" life in squalid mud huts in the *mata*, over which the new workers' villas were offered as a great experiment in progress and modernization.

As we left the villa and again negotiated the rough roads in search of a team of workers cutting cane, Jaime told us a little about the history of the *usina* and its transformation from a small, central *engenho* that in 1927 produced only 6,000 sacks of sugar into an agroindustrial giant producing 1.2 million tons of sugar each year. Usina Água Preta is a leader in the sugar producing region, Jaime said, because of its progressive management. For example, there were (he boasted) no clandestine workers, not even among the class of temporary day workers, the *bóias-frias* (cold lunch workers). All workers on Água Preta were officially registered and received the same minimum wage (about ten dollars a week), which was tied to a minimum work requirement calculated in kilos of cane cut or *quadros* of land cleared. Cane cutters were expected to cut at least 200 kilos per workday, a task, Jaime offered, they should be able to complete by midday, assuming they arrived at work just before or at dawn. Workers could double their income by "managing" their day efficiently and returning to work for a second shift following lunch and rest during the hottest hours of the day.

Seu Jaime described the *usina* as a large "beneficiary society" that looked after and provided for its workers needs. Of the 2,300 regular workers employed by the usina, 1,300 were rural workers, and in one sense, said Jaime, they represented the *usina*'s most important resource. Therefore, it was the duty of the company to take care of them by providing free or subsidized housing, health and dental care, medicine, psychological counseling, education, social services, and recreation. The managers of Usina Água Preta thought of the plantation-mill as a "social utopia," Jaime said. And so, for example, the sale of intoxicating drinks was strictly prohibited and there were no bars on *usina* property.[14] Instead, each worker was given a free glass of sugar-sweetened and fruit-flavored soybean milk, a drink workers initially rejected but now fought over. In addition, each rural worker was supplied with all the tools he needed: a *foice* and sharpening stone, protective clothing against the sharp stalks of cane, plastic masks to guard against pesticides, plastic water bottles, and shoes. Jaime added, "The focus of the *usina* is organization; we want to offer the most modern technical services available so that we can solve small problems on a daily, personal basis before they turn into large and unmanageable grievances. I myself always treat workers as well as I can within the prescribed conditions."

"Which are?"

"Nothing is more unfair than treating inferiors as if they were one's equals. Why give a VCR to a rural worker? He won't even know what it is, and he would only destroy it. It would be better to give him a transistor radio, something he understands and knows how to use and enjoy. Similarly, we considered installing electric stoves in the workers' villas, but after a small experiment that failed, we decided to let the workers cook with charcoal or kindling the way they are accustomed. Bitter experience has taught us that you can treat a poor man like a rich man, but it is a waste of time and money. What is important is knowing how to treat people according to their abilities, giving them neither more nor less than they can handle. This is a basic principle of modern management. For our part, we are well organized, and we never miss a payday. This creates psychological security and trust in our workers, and it makes it easier for us to demand efficiency and loyalty from them."

Jaime further explained that the *usina* had hired technical experts to teach the workers how to organize their time and labor and how to conserve their calories. The workers were shown new methods of cutting cane: how to hold the *foice*; how to bend; how to make large, sweeping cuts; how to sharpen their knives using the fewest strokes; even—and here Jaime begged my pardon—the best way to urinate while working. He concluded with some passion, "We are doing our share for the nation. If the sugar industry in Pernambuco were to fail, at least 250,000 men would be out of work. We have to cooperate, learn to work together—owners, management, technicians, mill workers, and cane cutters—to build our industry and build our nation. If those on the very top were to fall, the others would follow suit like a line of dominoes."

Finally, we approached a work team, but many workers were already beginning to leave the fields for lunch. A few were still chopping at stalks that stood about ten feet high. Many were stripped to the waist, and all were without protective clothing and shoes. Jaime noted this, and he pointed out, disgustedly, that the men were not cutting the cane according to the instructions of the management technicians: "Their strokes are too short and choppy, they're bending over more than they need to, and their legs are too far apart. A man could double his productivity if he paid some attention to 'method.' " Provoked by this challenge and insult to the common sense of the workers, my traveling companion, Severino, could contain himself no longer, and he leapt into the middle of the workers. Grabbing a large machete out of the hands of one of the workers, he began a savage attack on the sharp, tall stalks of cane, cutting them down quickly like so many enemies arrayed for battle. "This," he said proudly, "is how I began my life as a boy, a true *menino de engenho* [child of the plantation]."

The incident called to mind E. P. Thompson's (1967) evocative descriptions of the subversions of the body, its natural time and rhythms and synchronized movements, to the regimentation and discipline of the machine through industrial capitalism. The labor of peasants, Thomas Belmonte wrote, is a "slow, pained ballet of bending, bowing, and praying to earth and to divine and secular masters. The work of factory laborers is a stiff military drill, a regiment of arms welded to metal bars and wheels" (1979:138–139). In the fields and the factory of Usina Água Preta I was to see both agricultural and industrial work disciplines welded to the massive agroindustrial machine that is the "modern" sugar plantation and mill, the "open-air factory" described by Levi-Strauss.

The next day we arrived at the main, locked gates of the *usina* at 8 A.M., and the military guard, perhaps recognizing Seu Severino as a union organizer, took awhile to approve our papers and let us through. As the gates crashed closed behind us, I was reminded once again of the total and enclosed world the *usina* represented. On viewing the multiple buildings of the *usina*—many of them little more than huge lean-tos with iron catwalks connecting belching vats, compressors, and the monstrous wheels, pulleys, conveyer belts, and gears that one associates with a primitive form of early industrialization—I was immediately struck by the contradiction of a modern industrial plant gouged out of the face of a lush, tropical countryside.

We were introduced to Seu João, the chief engineer of the *usina*, who, although dressed in blue workshirt, boots, and hard hat, spoke with the soft and cultured accents of an educated Paulista (from São Paulo). On our way to the main buildings, João filled us in on the various details of production. Of the primary products of Água Preta—brown sugar, molasses, alcohol, and animal feed—about 45 percent was exported. Up to 65 percent of all the sugar produced was exported, but 100 percent of the alcohol and animal feed was used domestically. Unlike other *usinas* in the vicinity and in the south of Brazil, Água Preta did not operate a refinery; it exported large blocks of crude brown sugar and reserved a quantity of unattractive grayish-white large-crystalled sugar for local consumption. The sugar industry was under tight governmental controls, and it was the government, not the *usineiro*,

Inside the monster: taking notes from Seu João, Usina Água Preta.

that set production quotas and regulated markets. In addition to processing these primary products, the *usina* also maintained subsidiary interests in an ice cream conglomerate and in the Pernambucan textile industry.

Our tour began at the laboratory (a small prefabricated temporary building), where chemists were engaged in testing the quality of the cane that arrived daily from some 400 local suppliers. Água Preta cultivated only a third of the sugarcane it processed; the remainder was supplied by roughly 350 small plantation owners (one hundred to one thousand hectares) and by 50 large *latifundiários* (two thousand to twenty thousand hectares). The government set the quotas so that the *usina* could not favor certain suppliers of cane at the expense of others, although the *usina* was free to set prices according to the quality of the cane delivered.

Once the cane entered the factory, it was washed to remove the sand and pebbles that were a by-product of stacking and loading the cane onto trucks. Inside the main buildings of the *usina* the cane was crushed, and its tough fibers were removed. The remaining juice was boiled and reduced to crystals. As we moved inside the factory, we were immediately assaulted by a beastly heat, the tropics magnified, and as specks of cinder stung our eyes, I was keenly aware that the visitors (unlike João himself) were unprotected by boots and hard hats. The tour required us to climb along rusted iron catwalks a few hundred feet in the air past vats of boiling cane juice. Taking fieldnotes

Sugarcane: trapped in the jaws of the *usina*.

was complicated by the sweat that poured into my eyes, while interviewing amid the crashing din was all but impossible, although we continued to yell back and forth at each other. The workers, standing at the wheels and the vats, were amused.

Outside we passed the mounds of bagasse, part of which would be used for fuel, another part mixed with protein and sold as animal foods, and the remainder dumped into the river to contribute to the water problems of the region. Toxins from the milling process were also disposed of in the river, and I inquired about water pollution in Bom Jesus and surrounding rural towns of the *zona da mata*. João vehemently denied that the *usinas* were responsible for the contamination, and he insisted that we walk to the water treatment plant where *usina* water was purified and fed back into the factory system. As we walked around the reservoir and surveyed the water treatment plant (not in operation), João explained that state workers arrived periodically to sample the water, and if it was unclean, the *usina* was fined. Furthermore, the water used by the factory was recirculated within the factory itself—it was, he insisted, a completely closed-circuit system. Finally, we discussed the reservoir at Água Preta and the refusal of the *usina* family to allow its use for public consumption despite a severe water shortage in the region. The engineer defended the property rights of his *usineiro*, saying that the reservoir could not possibly solve the water problems of Bom

Jesus and the other interior towns. The state, he said, had to assume that responsibility. With that the tour was over, and we were left once again with Dr. Alfonso, the general manager of the *usina*, for a final interview.

Like the agronomist and the engineer, Dr. Alfonso wanted us to carry away a positive image of the *usina* as social utopia, and he continually referred to "this social universe of the *usina*," or to this "social experiment." "On the *usina*," he explained, "we are engaged in a kind of social revolution, implementing radical programs to improve the well-being of our workers and their families. We believe that healthy and well-adjusted workers will be more productive." Therefore, the *usina* employed three doctors, three dentists, four nurses, and dozens of medical assistants, some of whom worked full time vaccinating children in the rural villas. Social workers and a resident psychologist supervised "creative work" and "creative living" classes to put into operation "the most modern scientific technologies."

In answer to my question about widespread malnutrition and child mortality among rural workers in the *zona da mata*, Dr. Alfonso replied heatedly, "There is no hunger in the Nordeste. That is just the propaganda of the radical politicians and of the Catholic church—excuse me if you are a Catholic, I am a Catholic myself—but I am referring to the clerics and the bishops who profit from preaching the idea of misery."

"How is that?"

"The Catholic church is losing its hold over the Brazilian people; the Protestant Evangelicals are gaining new members every day. The Protestants are preaching a message of hard work and self-discipline. And that is good. To compete with them, many priests and a few bishops are turning to Marxist propaganda as a way of reaching the popular classes."

"You would deny the existence of misery and malnutrition?"

"There is no hunger, no *real* hunger in Brazil. But the people eat poorly. They have bad dietary habits. For instance, the rural workers don't have the custom of eating fresh vegetables, fresh meat, fresh poultry, or even fresh fruits. Their diet is all carbohydrates—manioc, *farinha*, beans, bread, spaghetti, cornmeal. Meat and fish are only 'residuals' in their diet. Workers need more bodybuilding protein. So our job is to educate the workers to improve the way they eat."

"What about infant and child mortality?"

"There is no child mortality on the *usina*. We have reduced child mortality to 2 percent through immunizations and supplementary food programs for mothers and children."

But when I asked for access to the data on mortality, Dr. Alfonso immediately recoiled, saying that the figures he gave me were not "scientific" but only estimates based on the observations of his medical and social work staff.

Moreover, the *usina* did not keep records of births and deaths among rural workers, which were recorded at the civil registry office, the *cartório civil*, of the *município* of Bom Jesus da Mata.

With respect to his opinion on the agrarian reform proposals then being debated for inclusion in Brazil's new constitution, Dr. Alfonso became impatient: "This is a polemical question. Everybody has his mind on land reform today, and nobody is thinking about production. Without increasing production people will still be hungry; tables and food baskets will still be empty. Yes, agrarian reform is necessary, but it is not sufficient by itself to eradicate human misery. That requires education, orientation, nutrition, machinery, and credit. I am not opposed to land reform, especially if the land in question is not being exploited or developed. Every bit of land in this country should be put into use. What I am opposed to are old prejudices against the *latifundista*. Where would the Brazilian sugar industry be without him? The important thing is not how much land one owns, but how productive one is. It is often overlooked that small landholders—*minifundistas*—waste land, too. Look at our Indians, for example, the way they waste so much land for so few people. And they leave the lands they have totally unchanged and undeveloped."

After a pause he continued, "The government is, after all, the largest *latifundista* in Brazil, and the state needs to explain to the people why, when it controls 112 million hectares of empty and unexploited land, it goes after private lands that are already in production. Too many people see agrarian reform as a magic wand that can solve Brazil's problems: poverty, crime, violence, illiteracy, hunger, and sickness. All this by moving people out of urban slums and shantytowns and into the country. But these urban poor have no 'vocation' for the land. If the government takes an entire *favela* and moves it into the countryside, what you will get is a rural *favela*. Don't make the *latifundista* into the 'enemy' of society."

"Who is the real enemy of society?"

"The state when it is corrupt and when it forces those who are paying taxes, and who are shouldering the costs of economic development, to curtail their activities."

"What if the state could effect changes that could reduce the social cost of poverty in Brazil?"

"There is not so much poverty in Brazil as there is poverty of spirit, which is worse. Poverty of spirit—which you find among the rural workers—means that one is unwilling to improve one's condition. It means that one does not hunger after the better, the finer things in life, that one is content to live and let live. The *matuto* is soft; he doesn't like to work hard. He is not ashamed to ask for things, to beg."

"Gilberto Freyre writes that *paternalismo*, which encourages dependency, is the cultural heritage of the sugar plantation economy."

"I'm not talking about *paternalismo;* that is bad, very bad. Here on Usina Água Preta we don't *give* anything away. We make sure that people pay something, even if only a pittance, for whatever they receive."

As we cordially shook hands and exchanged business cards and mutual invitations to visit each other again, Dr. Alfonso concluded with intensity, "Every man should be the *dono*, the owner of his own self." It was a phrase that would be repeated again and again in many different contexts.

2 Bom Jesus
One Hundred Years Without Water

Tô com sede
I thirst
Popular graffito in Bom Jesus da Mata

The cars, motorbikes, and brightly painted wooden trucks with their sugary cargo were backed up for at least two blocks waiting for the tail end of the parade—the two sanitary engineers of the state health post—to wind through the main street of Bom Jesus da Mata. The single traffic light had never in the memory of any residents functioned since its much celebrated installation ten years earlier in 1972 and hence was of no help on this day either. Meanwhile, in the sad little plaza named after Euclides da Cunha, the twenty-four-piece Seventh of September band dressed in workaday tan uniforms had positioned its tiny stools. Once seated, band members began to blast the first discordant notes of a Sousa march, to the dismay of the irritable crowd crushed in below the bandstand. Seu Floriano, the touchy maestro, realizing his mistake, frowned and brought the march to such an abrupt conclusion that it unseated tall Seu João in the back row. But as soon as the band, urged on by maestro Floriano, struck up the more familiar chords of a wild *Nordestino frevo*, the crowd cheered appreciatively. Quickly warming, people began to sway until, despite the oppressive heat and the jostling for space, a few managed to jump, throwing themselves into the air with the ease and abandon characteristic of *Nordestinos*, delighted to "play" *carnaval* even in the decidedly off-season of late May.

The *frevo*, too, however, came to an abrupt halt as a line of somber male dignitaries was sighted making its way to the bandstand and as the crowd reluctantly parted, making way for the "big men," the "somebodies," to pass. The Barbosa family, which has controlled Bom Jesus since the revolution of the 1930s, was well represented for the day's festivities marking the centenary of the *município*. There was Seu Félix, of course, the small, volatile mayor, the *prefeito* of Bom Jesus, uncomfortable in his ill-fitting, off-white formal suit. Close behind the *prefeito imperfeito*, as he was affectionately called by friends and foes alike, came the real chief, the real *dono* of the *município* and of the entire region of the *zona da mata*, Dr. Urbano Barbosa Neto, state senator and speaker of the Pernambucan House of Representatives. The firstborn grandson of the original Coronel Barbosa and the older brother of Seu Félix, Dr. Urbano was as cool and polished as his younger brother was crumpled and hotheaded. Where Dr. Urbano was known for his oratorical style, sprinkled with allusions to Cicero and Phaedrus, Seu Félix was fond of telling his constituency, composed primarily of the "humble" population of Bom Jesus, that he, like them, was mostly illiterate. Of his many boasts this one, at least, went unchallenged even by his sharpest critics, of whom there were a good many, yet never *so* many as to loosen the firm hold of the "first family" over the *município*.

Before climbing the rickety steps to the makeshift bandstand, Dr. Urbano dropped his protective hand from his younger brother's shoulder to turn and give an affectionate *abraço* to his second cousin once removed, Dr. Gustavo, the federal senator who had flown in from Brasilia in a generous display of family solidarity. Dr. Gustavo, however, unprepared for the enthusiastic bear hug, stepped back quickly onto the toes of Dr. Francisco, the currently out of favor secretary of health of the *município*, who suppressed a cry of pain and turned away to make small talk with Fabiano, the flush-faced and eager-to-please editor of the local newspaper, the *Diário de Bom Jesus*.

The decorous silence was short-lived, however. Impatient rustling and chatter in the crowd reflected the political chiefs' uncertainty about when and how to initiate the formal ceremonies in the glaring absence of the parish priest. In the "old days" Monsenhor Marcos would have been counted on to open the events with a Latin benediction followed by a few kind words honoring the leading family of Bom Jesus. But times had changed since the arrival in 1981 of the young Padre Agostino Leal, who was given to "making politics" from the altar of Nossa Senhora das Dores. He preached to the now almost entirely poor and rural congregation that agrarian reform was the New Jerusalem, the first step on the road toward the Kingdom of God on earth.

Consequently, relations between the secular and the religious authorities of Bom Jesus were strained. Public ceremonies such as this one were vastly more secular than in the old days, save for the recognition always extended to Madre Elfriede, the frail and ancient German nun who had come to Bom Jesus with a half dozen permanently dazed and culture-shocked young postulants to build the Colégio Santa Lúcia in the 1940s. The Colégio, founded as a finishing school for the daughters of the landed aristocracy of Bom Jesus, was sustained through foreign mission collections in Stuttgart and through the unwavering moral support of the Barbosa family.

Nevertheless, even in 1982 nuns could not be called on to speak on behalf of Holy Mother the Church, so the ceremonies would have to begin with a few mumbled and inarticulate words from the *prefeito*. But before even his first sentence was completed, Seu Félix was interrupted by shouts that sounded alarmingly like "WATER!" The *prefeito* looked about quickly. Was there a fire on the old bandstand? But no. Meanwhile, more in the crowd began to raise their voices in what now sounded like a chant calling for "água, água," so that Seu Félix was quite drowned out by the din. Then he spotted two rather tall figures standing on a park bench in the plaza. They had unfurled a large red banner with the legend:

BOM JESUS DA MATA
CEM ANOS E SEM ÁGUA
Bom Jesus da Mata, One Hundred Years Without Water

"Bull's sperm!" spewed the *prefeito* under his breath, for he very rarely cursed. "What next?"

"It's those two commie-faggots again, João Mariano and Chico," hissed the partisan journalist, Fabiano, with a slight lisp. Very red in the face, he turned to the hefty but soft-looking young men standing behind the older family members. "*Do something,*" he demanded between clenched teeth.

The crowd was abuzz with the commotion in the plaza and on the bandstand, and as the word spread from one to the other—from those who could barely read to those who could not read at all—and as the meaning of the banner was grasped, the crowd convulsed in a riot of unrestrained laughter. It would take the maestro another impromptu *frevo* while the young Barbosa sons and nephews descended into the crowd to disperse the irreverent "radical agitators" before it was safe enough for Dr. Urbano Neto to begin his prepared and eloquent oration on "Bom Jesus—the first hundred years." But by then most people had already gone home to escape the heat of midday. Besides, the party was over.

Vidas Secas

Chegariam a uma terra distante, esqueceriam a catinga onde
havia montes baixos, cascalhos, rios secos, espinhos, urubus,
bichos morrendo, gente morrendo. Não voltariam nunca mais,
resistiriam a saudade que ataca os sertanejos na mata. Então
eles era bois para morrer tristes por falta de espinhos?

They would arrive at a distant land where they would forget
the stunted, sparse forest [of the *sertão*] with its low hills,
rocks, dry riverbeds, thorns, vultures, dying beasts, dying

people. They would *never* return; they would resist the
nostalgia that preys upon the *sertanejo* who has been forced
into the *mata*. Were they dumb oxen to die of sadness, longing
thirstily after thistles?

Gracíliano Ramos (1984:122)

If there is one raw and vital nerve among *Nordestinos*, rich and poor alike, it
is their horror of drought (*seca*) and thirst. Drought images loom large
among people with a collective memory of the droughts of 1744, 1790, 1846,
1877, and 1932 and personal recollections of the droughts of 1958, 1965, and
1987. Many of the original residents of the Alto do Cruzeiro came to Bom
Jesus from the dry *agreste* and the *sertão* in search of water, food, and work.
They were *retirantes* (driven or expulsed ones) and *flagelados* (the afflicted),
who crossed barren wastelands that even birds and small mammals had
deserted only to find when they arrived finally at the sugar plantations of
Bom Jesus that the local waters were "spoiled": brackish, salty, putrid, and
contaminated by microbes and chemical pollutants. Their response has been
angry. Graffiti lambasting the inadequate and contaminated water supply
cover the walls of public buildings:

> *Água? Não, suco de micróbios.*
> Water? No, amoeba juice.
> *Nossa água mata sêde mas também mata gente.*
> Our water kills thirst, but it also kills people.
> *Bom Jesus, onde água é veneno.*
> Bom Jesus, where water is poison.

The people of Bom Jesus worry constantly about their drinking and
bathing water, its quantity as well as its quality. Water is a key word, a Paulo
Freirian "generative theme." It animates social life in Bom Jesus and both
divides and unites the social classes of this interior town. Water, like sex,
forms the backdrop of daily discourse in Bom Jesus so that any conversation,
any discussion, has a way of veering back to the subject. Even a simple "How
are you?" is as likely to elicit a litany of water complaints as a litany of one's
bodily symptoms. Everything, it seems, relates to water.

And yet the paradox is that Bom Jesus is not located in the parched
badlands of the *sertão* or even in the dry *agreste* but in the fertile *zona da
mata*, where rainfall is adequate during a well-defined "winter" (April to
August), when the fear of drought is replaced briefly by the fear of floods.
But there is, as well, a long, hot, dry season from September to February,
and it is the "dry," not the "wet," that has impressed itself on the populace.
The people of the Alto approach each dry season with something akin to
dread, as if it were an annual drought. And the rural migrants who came

finally to settle on the slippery ledges of the Alto do Cruzeiro interpret their lives as doubly cursed—by fears of a *seca* that carries deep psychological resonances and of a *fome* (famine) that is symbolized by the ever-encroaching fields of sugarcane.

The image of drought is formidable, capturing the imagination of people who are inclined to describe all that is bad in terms of dryness and who sometimes project the image of the drought onto their own bodies. Hence a woman of the Alto will describe her body as worn out, as *dried up*, her breasts as withered as two peas rattling about in a sun-dried pod, and her "scanty" milk (if there is any at all) as "dirty" and "contaminated" as the polluted waters of the Capibaribe River. Babies are "born thirsty," say Alto mothers, "their blackened tongues hanging out of their mouths," too thirsty even to grab hold and suck on a nipple. Likewise, hunger is described not as an empty stomach but as a *barriga seca*, a "dry stomach." And to eat beans, yams, manioc, or *farinha* without a little meat or a few sardines is described as eating it "dry," without flavor or enjoyment. "It is like eating *mata* [dry weeds]," offers Dona Dalina.

Hunger cannot compete with thirst for sheer human misery. As one rural worker explains, "You know what I think? As horrible as hunger is, thirst is even worse. Have you ever been so thirsty you thought that you could kill for a drink of water? Last year I was walking home from [Engenho] Bela Vista, and I had forgotten to carry a jar of water. By the time I finally reached the river I said, 'I don't care if that water is as salty as the sea or as filthy as a cesspool, I'm going to drink it.' So I jumped down on my belly and I lapped it up like a poor animal. I gulped it down without paying any attention to the taste because if I had let myself taste that nauseating, filthy water, I surely would have vomited."

Water anxiety is general in the population, although it is the poor whose health is most compromised by the scarcity and poor quality of the public water supply. The thirst and the *seca* of Bom Jesus are real enough, but they have their origins in history and political economy, not in a cruel geography. Up through the 1970s the water supply of Bom Jesus was a large reservoir. The quality was good, although shortages and interruptions in supply increased with modernization as indoor plumbing became the norm for all but the poorest *bairros* of Bom Jesus. In the marginal *bairros* residents are dependent on several public water spigots (*chafarizes*), some municipal, some state owned, others privately owned and operated. Only the Alto do Cruzeiro boasts its own community-owned and operated *chafariz*, built through the collective efforts of the members of UPAC, its shantytown association.

Nonetheless, there is still scarcity. In the most populous and disadvantaged *bairros* residents form long lines twice a day, at dawn and in late

Queuing up for water at the *chafariz*, Alto do Cruzeiro.

afternoon, when the *chafariz* is turned on and when they can fill their five-gallon tin cans at prices varying from a half cent to two cents a can. The *município* provides free water to the poorest residents of the Alto da Santa Terezinha, but it is rationed at two gallons per household. For this reason, the people of the Alto do Cruzeiro have resisted the mayor's offer to assume responsibility for their community-owned and -operated water spigot. The average poor household of the Alto do Cruzeiro (with approximately eight members) uses ten gallons of water a day, and a two-gallon rationing program would penalize them excessively. By comparison, the voluntary water-rationing scheme proposed for northern California single-family households during the drought of 1988 was four hundred gallons of water per day per household. The poor of Bom Jesus *do*, then, experience a chronic water shortage that feels very much like a perennial drought, and it is little wonder that tempers are so often short at the public *chafariz* and that malicious gossip, accusations, disputes, brawls, and knife fights do erupt around the daily distribution of water.

A poorly conceived and drastic attempt to alleviate the water shortages of Bom Jesus made matters considerably worse. In 1982 COMPESA (the state water utility company) made the decision to supplement reservoir water with water from the local Capibaribe River. Additional chemicals were used to render the contaminated water "potable." To avoid public outrage and panic, the public was not informed, and officials in power tended to deny the rumors (many of them erroneous) accounting for the strange taste and bad smell of the public water supply. Once the new practice *was* admitted, however, public officials denied that the treated river water posed any threat to

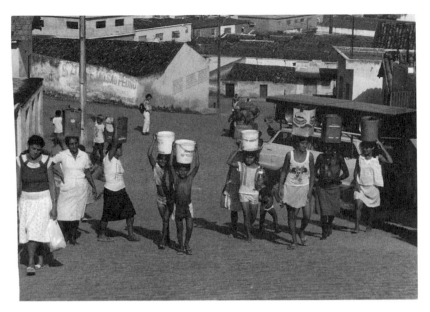

Precious water.

the health of the community. These denials threw the *município* into confusion and contradiction. It was quite simply a denial of basic common sense.

The mere thought of drinking polluted river water nauseated most residents of Bom Jesus, rich and poor alike, who have long treated the local river as a cesspool and a dump and who consider it a major source of sickness and infection in the *município*. In addition to the chemical pollution of the river by the sugar industry, local shoe factories dispose of animal carcasses in the river, and the local hospital disposes of many contaminated medical and human wastes there as well. The desperately poor residents of the Campo de Sete and the Bico de Urubu (Vulture's Path), who live in squalid encampments along the banks of the Capibaribe River, dispose of all their wastes (including dead animals) in the shallow river.

And so even as elected officials declare the public water supply potable, in the privacy of their own homes, all of them drink bottled mineral water, and many have installed elaborate electrical filter systems to purify common bath- and dishwater. Meanwhile, federal health workers representing SUCAM (the federal public health agency) have targeted Bom Jesus for a universal schistosomiasis treatment campaign, based on their separate evaluation of the Capibaribe River as "teeming" with schistosomes and other harmful microbes.

By 1986, 70 percent of the municipal water supply was being provided by the local river during the dry season. The tolerance of the community was fast approaching the breaking point. In response to growing unrest about the water crisis of Bom Jesus, the rarely critical and politically partisan family newspaper of Bom Jesus published the following editorial on July 15, 1987:

> We have reached the limit of our tolerance. Our running waters are polluted by the sugar factories and by other local industries. The problem has reached crisis proportions now that it has become common knowledge that most of our drinking water comes from the Capibaribe River. When the sugar mills dump their chemical refuse into the river, the water is not even safe for washing dishes. In short, our river is dead. Its fish are gone. The oxygen content is disappearing. Yet this is the water we are being asked to drink.

Although the poor are by far the most disadvantaged class (their only filter system consists of a cheesecloth rag over the mouth of the large clay pot into which the *chafariz* water is poured and stored), the middle class and wealthy residents of Bom Jesus cannot create a private oasis for themselves. The water that harms one class harms the others as well. When the front page of the *Diário de Pernambuco* (published in the capital city of Recife) carried the story on July 2, 1987, that the two most common brands of bottled mineral water distributed in the Northeast, Itaparica and Indiana, were contaminated with bacteria and were judged unfit to drink, many affluent residents of Bom Jesus began to experience a sense of their shared destiny with the poor and humble population. Their frustration was expressed in both classist and racist terms: the water crisis had reduced them to the status of *pobre-pretos* (poor blacks) in Bom Jesus. This sentiment was captured in a cartoon that appeared on January 30, 1988, in the "radical" and alternative (mimeographed) newspaper of Bom Jesus, called *O Grito*, "The Shout."

And so three years after the centenary of Bom Jesus, Padre Agostino Leal organized the largest mass demonstration in the recent history of Bom Jesus: a communitywide protest that attracted rich and poor. The demand was clear: clean water—NOW! For a precious brief moment Bom Jesus was united by a common fate, a collectively shared human need. The words *Tô com sede* (I thirst), scribbled across handmade placards and painted on crumbling walls, became the slogan that united the victims of a drought as much man-made as geographic. Only such a concerted collective effort was capable of staving off the more anomic forms of anarchism threatening to topple a social consensus that was, at best, fragile and "troubled."

Cartoon appearing in *O Grito*, January 30, 1988. The caption reads, "Who are you?" "I'm yourself after you've taken a shower in the water of Bom Jesus da Mata."

The First Hundred Years

In the beginning, a plantation, a chapel and a sovereign lord.
Master of everything, lands, water, and men.
Owner of their bodies, but not of their minds.
And so, one day a man thought, and with his own hands
freed himself of the despot's yoke!
In the rushing waters of the Capibaribe River
he washed the hands and feet of Our Lady of Sorrows
He made the sign of the cross and so was born
the proud people of Bom Jesus.

These words, written by a local poet to commemorate the *centenário* of Bom Jesus, are carved on a stone monument (in the shape of a one-cruzeiro note) standing in the center of the open-air yam market. By day the monument provides a seat for tired yam vendors; by night it offers shelter to the many homeless street children of Bom Jesus. Few can read the words, with their terse rendering of the sacred charter of the community, a history of colonialist greed, exploitation, and explosive and purifying retaliation. It is a history similar to that of many other plantation societies in the New World.

Originally, Bom Jesus was part of a large land grant awarded by the Portuguese crown to a sixteenth-century colonist. By the early nineteenth century the *latifúndio* fell into the hands of a ruthless *fazendeiro* named Antônio José Guimarães, who eventually came to control the *mata—norte* of Pernambuco. A cotton and a sugar planter, slaveowner, and (later) textile merchant, the founding father of Bom Jesus was described by a local historian as an "impudent, bold, and consuming landowner, a man who stopped at nothing to increase his wealth and power." Guimarães dominated the production and marketing of cash crops in the region, even succeeding in moving the large open-air market of a neighboring *vila* to the patio of his own plantation home. Consequently, the once thriving little village sank into economic and population decline (from which it has never fully recuperated, although it survives still), while a new and vital community sprang up around the Guimarães plantation, slave quarters, and marketplace. Eventually this complex became Bom Jesus da Mata.

The slaves, peasants, and conditional squatters lived under the tyranny of their oppressive master and landlord until 1847, when a small *posse* of freemen invaded the *casa grande* of the despised "Portuguese" and murdered him, thus (according to the local historian) "demonstrating the noble sentiment of liberty that characterizes our people." The widow of Guimarães was spared assassination, however, and in deep gratitude she sponsored the building of a chapel dedicated to the patroness of the plantation (later of the *município*), Nossa Senhora das Dores. On her death in 1870 the devoutly religious widow returned her husband's *patrimônio* to the state to be used for the future growth of a *município*.[1] Twelve years later, in 1882, Bom Jesus da Mata incorporated as that *município* with Nossa Senhora das Dores as its parish church. Six years later slavery was abolished in Brazil, but as elsewhere abolition left intact the feudal structures of *coronelismo*, *latifúndio*, and *paternalismo* (see Lewin 1987). The murder of one despot allowed for a multiplication of other, smaller despots. Some of these local *coronels* were good and some bad (in the local parlance), but all of them dominated the lives of the rural workers.

In the early decades of the twentieth century the *região canavieira*, the "cane-cultivating region," crept further north into the *município* of Bom Jesus, displacing cotton production altogether. Today, the *município*, centered in the town of Bom Jesus, contains within its outlying rural area three large *usinas* (two others are within commuting distance), and more than seventy small *engenhos* for the cultivation of sugarcane. Despite the growth of a large and vital shoe industry in Bom Jesus in the early twentieth century, and of banking and commerce (there are seven major bank branches in Bom Jesus, two hundred large and medium-sized commercial ventures, and three hundred small stalls and bars functioning at the weekly open-air *feira*), the political economy of the *município* remains founded on sugar. In

income and in wealth, in family power and in prestige, in political influence
and in local popular culture, the dominant ethos and the "feel" of Bom Jesus
are still that of an agrarian, semifeudal, traditional society; that is, once the
more surface forms of modernity are peeled away.

Other businesses come and go in Bom Jesus, but sugar is forever—or so it
seems. The shoe and textile industries of Bom Jesus are a case in point. At
their height in the mid-1960s there were thirty-six small shoe factories in
Bom Jesus in addition to many more cottage shoe industries based on a
single sewing machine and family labor. Together, these provided employment to several thousand residents, many of them small boys and teenage
women. By 1989 the shoe industry in Bom Jesus was practically moribund,
with only two large factories still in operation and the cottage industries
gone. In the decade of the 1980s shoe production declined from twenty-five
thousand to four thousand pairs per day. Similarly, the local cotton textile
industry, founded by Guimarães, followed the fate of cotton production
generally, moving west into the *agreste*. By the late 1980s only one small
textile factory remained to produce cotton string for the local hammock
cooperatives and gauze for the local hospital.

Over the decades the dominance of the sugar monoculture has caused
distortions in the production and marketing of foodstuffs. As a result of the
destruction of a peasant-producer base in the *zona da mata*, the quantity,
variety, and quality of vegetables and fruits sold in the weekly *feira* have
declined precipitously. Moreover, the majority of vegetable and fruit vendors today are not small producers themselves but rather middlemen selling
produce grown in other regions of the Northeast and even in other states of
Brazil. In 1987 almost 80 percent of all food consumed in Bom Jesus was
produced outside the *município*. Even the brown beans that are the staple
food of workers are imported from the south of Brazil rather than cultivated
locally, testimony to the disastrous side effects of the sugar monoculture.

For the poor, the illiterate, the rural migrants living in the hillside *bairros*
of Bom Jesus, and those for whom almost any work is preferable to cutting
sugarcane, there are few options. As one embittered young father put it,
"Sure I love sugarcane—to suck on or to drink [i.e., as rum]. Damned if I
have to work in it! But for most of us there's no choice. It's a matter of cut
sugarcane or die."

Population growth in the *município* of Bom Jesus has been slow. In 1890,
the first year of census taking, the population of the *município* was 28,250;
by 1980, at 54,588, the population had not even doubled. What *has* changed,
and dramatically, however, is the distribution of that population from the
rural to the urban sectors of the *município*. In every decade since the 1950s a
greater proportion of the *município*'s population has come in from the rural

communities and from the *usinas* and *engenhos* to live in the town of Bom Jesus itself. Consequently, the borders of the town have been pushed outward to include the chaotic, disorganized, and crowded shantytown "occupations" on each of the three municipally owned hills surrounding the downtown and those camped along the margins of the polluted and "toxic" Capibaribe River. By 1980 the poor and marginal *bairros* of Bom Jesus contained more than half the town's population, overtaxing the already limited water, energy, sanitation, health, and educational resources. Meanwhile, the juxtaposition in one small, dense, and congested locale of a powerful traditional landed aristocracy; a striving and aggressive commercial and professional class, modern in both its aspirations and its frustrations; and a large sprawling underclass of displaced and "thirsty" rural workers and their families makes for a highly charged social and political environment.

Casa, Rua, *and* Mata

At first encounter Bom Jesus appears to be a typical "developing" town in the "interior" (as Brazilians refer to every community more than ten miles inland from the seacoast) of an aggressively and self-consciously modernizing nation. It is an active, busy community very much "on the go." Its residents take pride in the dynamic rhythms of its *movimento*, exaggerated by the constant din of sound trucks and public speakers tuned to the municipal radio station, with its frenzied DJs, public announcements, and relentless and crude advertisements. Until the early 1970s the public speaker system was turned on at 5:30 A.M. and went off precisely at 9 P.M. with the playing of "Silent Night," which during the military years signaled the start of curfew. Lights went out on the main street, and kerosene lamps were lit on the three hillside Altos, giving the town its nickname, "the mountain princess." The candle-lit Altos were the jewels of the crown, and from a safe distance one could hardly fault that lilting description.

Bom Jesus has all the trappings of modernity. Its single, long main street was newly paved in 1989, replacing its more picturesque cobblestones, and cars, trucks, and motorbikes whiz by in disdainful contempt of pedestrians. Some of those on foot carry heavy or painful cargoes in their arms, across their shoulders, or on their heads: a dozen or more hammocks neatly folded and precariously balanced; a TV set to be delivered to an elegant home; *feira* baskets filled with sweet manioc, mangoes, and bananas; a deathly sick infant carefully wrapped and hidden in stone-washed sugar sacking.

In the main plaza, loudspeakers announce a Saturday night "Festival of Blue Jeans" at the local social club. All patrons of the dance must come appropriately attired in acid-washed designer jeans. A group of middle-class "trendy" teenagers gathers in front of the newly opened videocassette rental

Bom Jesus postmodern.

store in the minimall called the Galeria. Here the talk is all music, films, clothing, style, and sex. The teens are cosmopolitan, very savvy. Several are self-consciously gay or bisexual, flaunting their challenge to the old patriarchal sex-gender system of the "interior" (see Freyre 1986b; Fry 1982; Parker 1990). They stop me to ask about AIDS in California, about the fortunes of various rock (pronounced "hocky") musicians, and then (the clincher) whether people in the United States know how to "play" *carnaval.* This last question is disingenuous; it is a critique that requires no answer, for "only *Brasileiros* know how to 'play' *carnaval.*" I will be told again that North Americans may be rich, but Brazilians are sexy. Just then a little boy, a homeless "street kid" (*menino da rua*), approaches asking for a handout. He is ignored. His requests increase in their persistence until he is chased away with threats, and the talk returns to sex and to *carnaval*, which is only several weeks away.

Walking down the main street one hears the sounds of an early morning aerobics or "jazzercise" class from the open windows and verandahs of a gracious old Portuguese colonial home, its exterior walls decorated with exquisitely hand-painted and inlaid tiles imported from Holland or Portugal. The home is an urban version of the rural *casa grande*. Inside, the small group of meticulously groomed and bored wives of local businessmen and bankers gather to exercise and complain about their husbands' professions, which require them to move hither and yon, from coast to interior and to "sweet" but "pathetic" little towns like Bom Jesus. At precisely 10 A.M. the mulatto maid enters the large and airy front room carrying a silver coffee service and small bowls of diced tropical fruit salad topped with an excessively sweet caramel sauce. The women protest, but not one refuses a second serving. The maid remains in the room to brush away the flies from each visitor's dessert dish and to quickly retrieve the demitasse cups that are a magnet for the persistent pests. The maid is dressed in her own store-bought cotton dress, a size too small and its print unbecoming, but she will use a hand-embroidered, spotless, white linen towel to chase away the insects.

Dona Zélia is the center of attention this morning. She just returned the day before from Recife, where she scheduled her first major plastic surgery. Although only thirty-seven years old, the telltale lines around the corners of her eyes and mouth have not escaped her notice or, more importantly, that of Seu Alexandre, her dashing husband and man-about-town. "I want to keep up his interest," Zélia explains to her approving and sympathetic friends. Helena, older and wiser, assuages the younger woman's lingering doubts and anxieties, pulling back her carefully arranged, tinted hair to show the tiny, "almost perfect" scars resulting from her first surgery two years earlier. "Women have to be courageous;" Helena says, "we really are the stronger sex."

Just outside the brand new Banco do Brasil building, a bank vice-president and officer of the local Lions Club and one of Bom Jesus's "most outstanding and respected Negro citizens," Dr. Eduardo, is supervising the hanging of a large banner announcing that club's campaign on behalf of the famine victims of Mozambique. Dr. Eduardo smiles his approval and nods graciously to a town councillor who passes him to enter the bank. Inside the heavy glass doors of the bank, a guard in military uniform checks out each person who enters. I am startled when he thrusts himself between me and Dona Beatrice, preventing the terrified woman from taking another step. He took note immediately of her plastic sandals and her wiry hair, despite the care she took in dressing for the occasion. "She's with me," I state firmly, and reluctantly he allows Beatrice to take her place on the short line. Here, at least, it is quiet and cool. It could be a modern bank in any city. The tellers are distant, officious, and efficient. Both men and women have nails that are carefully manicured and polished and of which they are quite vain. The bills are all newly minted and colorful cruzados novos in first-issue CR $500 and CR $1,000 denominations. The teller counts them out, snapping each one with an impressive flourish. (When later, at home, I try to do the same, the bills refuse to cooperate.) A very dark young man, dressed in the workday uniform of the bank servant, steps up to each of the patrons in line to offer a tiny cup, a "shot" really (for that is how the drink is taken), of dark, sweet *cafezinho*. The "boy" is thirty-year-old Zezinho from the Rua dos Magos of the Alto do Cruzeiro. He nods his head almost imperceptibly, as if he were not "family," for Zezinho is my eldest godson.

A few blocks away and down a cobblestoned and shaded side street, the "city" disappears into the beginnings of the countryside, the *mata*. I stop for lunch at a beautiful old *fazenda* that has recently been converted into a *churrascaria*, a restaurant specializing in meats slowly roasted over live coals—steaks, ribs, whole chickens, pork, strips of dried beef, and savory sausage. At one table sit several well-dressed businessmen, speaking quietly and sipping Cinzanos with ice and a twist of lemon. At another table sits a more rumpled and animated group of local "big men," *políticos*, including the somewhat drunk *vice-prefeito*, Duarte Vasconcelos, a small-time *senhor de engenho*. At this table the talk is not "business" in the commercial sense but rather the business of politics and power, the rise and fall of old families in the current transition from military to "democratic" rule in the country. Vice-prefeito Duarte calls for another bottle of Pitu (a local brand of *cachaça*, sugarcane rum). Much banter and thinly disguised hostility are tossed back and forth between the two tables, one representing the "old" and the other the "new," emerging Bom Jesus.

In the back room of the restaurant several engineers from Usina Novo Século gather around Roy, a business consultant from South Africa who spreads out his design for a sugar harvesting machine able to negotiate the local hilly terrain and guaranteed to put a quarter of the town's population out of work. "Doctor" Simão, a main shareholder in the *usina*, debates the cost of the machines over cheap manual labor, but the South African emphasizes the continual annoyance and threat of strikes by the local syndicate of cane cutters and rural laborers. The local engineers squirm, however, when the foreigner tosses a wad of cruzado notes at a waiter, asking him loudly to take out what he needs from the "play money, the Monopoly money." "Monopoly money, indeed," comments my friend João Mariano in a stage whisper from our table. Indeed, we are all "on stage" in this small and tense theater where disputes can suddenly rumble across tables like a Texas thundercloud, although the clouds are just as often dispersed by the skillful use of an absurdist, mocking humor. Only "fanatics" would take these issues too seriously. In the Northeast one learns to live with contradiction and with deeply submerged angers and resentments.

This is "front stage" Bom Jesus—the *rua*, the public face of the town as it is seen and known by the *donos*, *fildalgos*, and *gente fina* of Bom Jesus, the owners and bosses, the somebodies and the big people, those with names like Andrade, Cavalcanti, Lima, and Vasconcelos, heavy with the history of sugar and cotton plantations and cattle *fazendas*, and "newer" names like Galvão, Carvalho, and Monteiro, associated with banks, car dealerships, the textile and shoe industries. The somebodies of Bom Jesus are literate and modern. They operate in a world of commercial ventures, finance, interest, travel, newspapers, documents, legality, bureaucracy, rationality. They are the *patrões*, the bosses in a wealthy, highly stratified interior town. The *fildalgos* include the traditional landed gentry, the old families who have replicated in town many of the architectural and social rural structures that served them on the plantations while simultaneously adopting certain urban norms and standards when these better serve their interests. The somebodies also include the aggressive commercial and industrial middle class holding the new wealth and power, those who would transform Bom Jesus from a traditional, patriarchal town of patrons and clients into a thoroughly modern, more open, and "republican" but still class-, gender-, and race-stratified society.

Hierarchy and dualism characterize social life in the interior of Northeast Brazil. At the top of the social pyramid remain the sugar barons, the *usineiros* and the large cane producers and suppliers. Within this class, power is articulated in a sometimes extravagant display of wealth, conspicuous consumption, gentlemanly leisure, and political clout. The sugar barons are the real *donos* and bosses of Bom Jesus. There is high agreement about who "the rich" are in Bom Jesus. "The rich," volunteers one resident of the Alto do Cruzeiro "are the owners of the city. They are the people who don't have to work for a living, who are 'excused' from the daily struggle that is life. For the rich, living in their mansions and big houses, nothing is ever wanting. Every wish is satisfied. They are our bosses, our *patrões*. They don't owe anything to anybody. Everybody owes them."

Despite petty jealousies and competitiveness, and political differences that had divided some of the "first families" of Bom Jesus into pro- and antimilitary rule during the 1960s and 1970s, the local aristocracy unites to defend its class-based interests against any incursions into its privilege by church and state. The power elite protects its power and wealth through traditional forms of familism: class endogamy, including first-cousin marriage, early marriages, and large families (see Lewin 1987; de Melo Filho 1984). The poor of Bom Jesus observe the cohesiveness of the ruling, dynastic families of the region in the saying (while rubbing together two index fingers) "In the end, the rich team up with the rich."

Although the headquarters, the *patrimônio*, of the old dynastic families is still the traditional plantation house, the *casa grande*, most wealthy families today also maintain a residence in the town of Bom Jesus as well as a house or an apartment in the nearby capital city of Recife. If they do not go abroad to Europe to study, the older children of the wealthy families generally take up residence in the family home or beach apartment in a fashionable section of Recife under the pretext, at least, of being university students. Although the general rule for males in the "old wealth" families is a great deal of gentlemanly leisure, some sons do involve themselves in the management of the *usinas*, and others enjoy "playing" at being ranchers and *fazendeiros*, sometimes whipping into town on horseback, with guns protruding from only partly concealed holsters. Other sons may pursue politics, law, or medicine. "Some of the rich work," offers a poor resident of Bom Jesus, "but only for the sport of it."

Seu Reinaldo is the eldest son of a branch of the Cavalcanti family, which is one of the most powerful landed families in the *zona da mata—norte*. Reinaldo evidenced early in life a true "vocation" for the land, and as soon as he came of age he was managing both *engenho* and *fazenda* lands. One of the wealthiest, most popular, and well-liked men in Bom Jesus, Seu Reinaldo is at best functionally literate. He describes himself as a "cowboy" and a *matuto* (sometimes as a "farmer"), although admittedly a wealthy one. He avoids pretensions of all kinds. In his younger years he cut a flamboyant figure in Bom Jesus as one who kept a permanent and "exotic" (so they say) mistress in the *zona* and who had a dangerous reputation as a "spoiler" of the virtue of other planters' aristocratic daughters, especially those "irresistible ones" in childish middy blouses and blue uniforms who studied at the Colégio Santa Lúcia under the watchful hawk-eye of Madre Elfriede. At the age of forty, Reinaldo married a *colégio* girl of fifteen, a favorite daughter of the *prefeito*, and although it was a match across tense and politically oppositional family lines, the marriage was a good one that produced five heirs. Reinaldo further consolidated his holdings to become one of the largest *latifundiários* in the cane-producing region. Nonetheless, his manner remained rough and unassuming, and he was little impressed by his brief travels to Europe and the United States, where he underwent complicated surgery for the repair of organs long since damaged by chronic schistosomiasis.

All of his children were educated at the local *colégio* (i.e., private secondary school), but rather than send them off to Europe or even Recife for a higher education, Reinaldo presented each with a package tour to Miami Beach and Disney World. Following this local version of the Grand Tour, each was expected to settle down into the ill-defined roles of the contemporary leisured rural class. The oldest son, Junior, was at sixteen, like his father, a notorious rogue and a "playboy" who spent his weekly allowance at the local "sex motel" just outside of town, presumably "ruining the virtue" of his generation's plantation daughters. "Don't you worry about Junior's behavior? Won't it get you into hot water with the girls' fathers or brothers?" I ask. Reinaldo hoots and replies, "I tie up my own female goats, and their fathers should do the same. But my males are free to graze where they can!" The eldest daughter, at her own insistence, was engaged at fourteen to an indolent and sulky first cousin who was rarely seen sober. She was married immediately following her fifteenth birthday and debutante party.

Reinaldo works and plays hard, but only because he has a "taste" for it. He likes the outdoors and tends to be ill at ease at home in Bom Jesus, where he walks about the spacious rooms, open patios, and poolside in an undershirt and shorts and with a frosted glass of local Antarctica beer always near at hand. As soon as dinner is over he is relieved to be out the door again. Reinaldo is a believer in the future of plantation mechanization, and he freely expresses the opinion that the kind of "peon labor" (his words) that the current system supports is both wasteful and "backward." On a trip to the state of São Paulo he was impressed with what he saw of a thoroughly modernized sugar industry, complete with "modern" and well-paid workers who arrived at work by bus, dressed in new jeans and stylish shirts, and carried lunch boxes while discussing the previous night's TV soap operas. Reinaldo has heard of the new harvesting machines under production by the South African Implenol Company, and he says that he would invest in them immediately if it were not for the lives and well-being of more than five hundred rural workers on his plantation lands. "What would become of them?" he asks, adding, "Sometimes I feel as though I am *their* captive!"

Reinaldo attributes his own stunning financial success to the "firm hand" of the Brazilian military through the "growth and crisis years." He believes, however, that democratization is necessary, and in the months before the presidential election of 1989 he spoke evasively of supporting any candidate who was sensitive to the needs of all Brazil's independent "farmers," small as well as large, and all those who had a stake in the land and the economy. "I have no other politics than this," Reinaldo says disarmingly. When the time came he voted in 1989 for the presidency of Fernando Collor de Mello of the center–right wing National Reconstruction Party.

The old wealth of Bom Jesus (as exemplified in Seu Reinaldo) is resented by the "new wealth" of the town, the small class of enterprising indus-trialists, successful large businessmen, and bankers. These substantial men of commerce and industry privately criticize the older families as self-indulgent and socially backward, men who impede progress and the path of modernization in Northeast Brazil. Meanwhile, the middle class of Bra-zil—including some of the professionals, teachers, state and municipal administrators, and smaller businesspeople and shop owners—feels itself squeezed by both a predatory wealthy class from above and a desperate and "parasitical" mass of poor people from below.

The middle class is in a particularly unstable social position in Bom Jesus. A great deal of energy, vigilance, and resourcefulness is required to maintain one's social standing, which hinges on such symbols of relative affluence as a new home (preferably two stories), a luxury car, a staff of at least two domestic servants, membership in one of the better social clubs in town, and a versatile and stylish wardrobe. Consequently, a favorite genre of malicious gossip in Bom Jesus concerns signs that one or another middle-class person or family is slipping down into the great, undistinguished mass of common people, into the "popular classes."

The maintenance of so high a standard of living is, needless to say, a challenge to middle-class people lacking inherited wealth and living on wages or on professional salaries during years of high inflation, contin-ual devaluation of the currency, and frequent government-mandated price freezes, which most especially affect small businesses. The middle class is indeed always scrambling, trying to find a *jeitinho* (a clever way out of one's problems), selling a piece of land here or a few cows there, adding on another shift in another clinic, or teaching a course in accounting or science in a commercial night school in Bom Jesus.

Claudinho, a thirty-one-year-old dentist, typifies the struggling bour-geois professional in Bom Jesus da Mata. Born into a working-class family in town, Claudinho was educated in state schools and on scholarships, manag-ing to work his way through dental school in another, larger interior town. He returned to Bom Jesus where he worked first in a municipal clinic, later at the state health post. In three years he was able to add on a small private practice in a rented office and to begin building a home for his wife and baby. To make ends meet, he teaches biology at a local secondary school two nights a week. In all, his monthly income (in 1988) is about seven hundred dollars. His entire worth, says Claudinho grumpily, including his house under construction, his car and motorcycle, his furniture and office equipment, is about three million cruzados (in 1987), or about sixty-two thousand dollars. He is considering selling his car to cover some unanticipated house con-struction costs. Claudinho is bitter about the vagaries of the Brazilian economy, is critical of the PMDB (the Brazilian Democratic Movement Party, the ruling coalition in Brazil and in Pernambuco between 1982 and 1988), and supports the return of a "limited" military rule in Brazil. Above all, Claudinho despises the Catholic church for its "self-serving" about-face on behalf of the "unwashed and barefoot marginals." Consequently, he has recently left the church and joined a spiritist center in Bom Jesus. In 1989 Claudinho (like Seu Reinaldo) welcomed the presidential candidacy of Fernando Collor de Mello, whose political platform supporting free-market policies and the removal of all barriers to foreign and domestic investments struck the young bourgeois dentist as "formidable." Perhaps, Claudinho hoped, Collor could finally do something about inflation.

The dentist complains about the cost of basic foodstuffs in the markets and *feira* of Bom Jesus. He blames the old sugar barons for their failure to "modernize" and diversify cultivation and so free the *município* from its dependency on other regions and states to feed its large population. Each week Claudinho spends about $14 for fresh fruit and vegetables and another $35 for meat and other "staples." Extras like beer and cigarettes and the daily purchase of bread, milk, butter, cheese, and eggs brings his monthly grocery bill up to about $250, or more than five times the minimum wage earned by 80 percent of the town's population. Claudinho maintains that even though he and his wife eat well, entertain somewhat, and have a small staff of domestic servants to feed, they eat "simply"—*nada de luxo*—and he wonders how, given these expenses, he is expected to maintain a middle-class standard of living. Rather than wondering how the rest of Bom Jesus manages to feed itself at all, Claudinho asks whether he would be considered "poor" in the context of the United States. Like many middle-class professionals in Bom Jesus, Claudinho greatly exaggerates the North American standard of living, and he does not believe me when I tell him that he would be considered quite well-to-do in California and that his domestic staff (live-in maid, part-time cook, gardener, chauffeur, and nursemaid for the baby) would be out of the reach of all but very wealthy Californians. He thinks I am either flattering or patronizing him, although he does understand that hired help is a luxury in the United States.

Finally, at the bottom of the social hierarchy of Bom Jesus is the undifferentiated mass known politely as the "humble" population or simply as *os pobres*, "the poor." Legally, these people are referred to as the *analfabetos*, the "illiterates," who (until recently) were unable to vote and therefore for all practical purposes did not count, were nonentities. Yet among themselves the poor make finer distinctions, subdividing themselves into the working classes, the respectable and the disreputable poor, and the "beyond the pale" under-underclass. Antonieta explains the social hierarchy this way: "There are three classes among us: *os pobres, os pobrezinhos,* and *os pobretões.* We can begin with the poor (*os pobres*), which is my class. We *pobres* always have to work very hard to get what we need. In fact, we have to work at least twice as hard as everyone else. The whole family has to cooperate, we all have to find work, but in many ways we are better off than the middle class because we are more independent."

Antonieta goes on to explain that respectable poor people of Bom Jesus do not have checkbooks or savings accounts. They do not borrow money. They strive to pay cash for every purchase, although they often buy large items on the installment plan. Antonieta notes, for example, her eldest daughter's wedding trousseau piling up in the bedroom: linens, towels, dishes, and silverware. And just as Tonieta and Severino built their own home, first on the Alto do Cruzeiro and later at the base of Santa Terezinha, the most upwardly mobile of the town's hillside shantytowns, they are helping their daughter and future son-in-law to build a small house near the outskirts of town. "Luckily," she adds, "as poor folk we don't yet have to spend money just to keep up appearances or to be 'in style.' We are not dependent on maintaining a particular standard of living. And we are a self-respecting class with a social conscience, which the middle classes cannot afford. We are able to distribute charity to those worse off than ourselves. And so we are respected by those above us and in our own class, and we are loved by those beneath us."

Beneath Tonieta and Severino are the *pobrezinhos,* the "truly poor," described as the "struggling souls" who may own or rent a little hovel on one of the Altos. Whereas the respectable poor have regular employment, through the city or state, and social security and medical insurance, the *pobrezinhos* are seasonal workers without any benefits or security. Their fortunes rise and fall because they are dependent on temporary work: clearing fields; weeding, cutting, and stacking cane; milling; and so on. The women have to wash clothes or work in the homes of the rich. When they fall sick they must rely on charity of one kind or another, and when they die they are buried in pauper's coffins and graves. The only way they can succeed, explains Antonieta, is through a powerful patron. "My sister, Lordes, and her husband, Dejalmer, are in this situation. It is where Severino and I started from, but God is good, and we are now where we are."

At the very bottom of the social ranks in Bom Jesus are what Antonieta calls the *pobretões,* the "truly wretched" ones, those who have nothing, who live from hand to mouth, who are chased from hovel to hovel, who sometimes have to beg for a living. These include the disabled, the *doido* (crazy), and the "walking corpses" of the sick-poor.

Antonieta's politics is complicated, and her loyalties are divided. Like many of the poor and self-respecting poor, her fortunes (whether she likes to admit it) are tied to certain benefactors or "patrons" from the wealthier classes. And so from the time of the military coup in 1964 Antonieta and Severino supported a promilitary political family and faction in Bom Jesus. They did so following the lead of the director of a large elementary school in Bom Jesus who favored them and was responsible for their gradual climb out of grinding poverty (see chapter 10). In 1989 Antonieta and her husband split their votes in Brazil's first presidential election in twenty years. Antonieta voted for a right-wing extremist candidate that her present boss and patron favored, out of respect for his efforts in arranging her eldest son a secure job with the state water company and one of her middle sons a place in the military. Severino, however, as a devout Catholic and an active member of a local CEB, voted for the staunchly leftist labor leader, Luís Ignacio da Silva (Lula), whom the CEBs and the radical wing of the Brazilian Catholic clergy were supporting.

As we can see from the foregoing, social life in the Brazilian Nordeste occurs in a diversity of realms and spaces, each with its own ecological and economic niche and each operating within its own set of norms, values, assumptions, and ethics. Often these realms and ethics stand in flagrant opposition to each other, colliding head on, as it were, given the density and the complexity of a social arena as small and compact as Bom Jesus. Foremost of these is the dynamic tension between the old sugar plantation economy and the new bourgeois economy of a modernizing, industrializing interior town. Gilberto Freyre (1986b) and, later, Roberto da Matta (1983, 1987), located this tension in the dialectic between *casa* and *rua*, or "house" and "street," each with a slightly different interpretive slant.

For da Matta, the terms *casa* and *rua* evoke a clash of unassimilable *mentalités*, one that governs *private* behavior and morality, the ethic of the *casa*, and one that governs impersonal and *public* behavior and morality in the street and marketplace, the ethic of the *rua*. Whereas one is a *person*, a "somebody," at home, where one is embedded in ongoing and inalienable relationships, rights, and duties based on birth and family, as these are mediated by the "natural" hierarchies of age and gender, one is an *individual*, but really an "anybody," in the street, where, technically speaking at least, all men are equal before the law and in commercial transactions. At home one is a "super"-citizen; in the street one is a "universal" and quite ordinary citizen, a situation (da Matta argued) that is intolerable and irksome to most Brazilians of all social classes, who apply various interactional strategies, bluffs, and power plays (see da Matta 1979:chap. 4) to "personalize," hierarchize, and so "domesticate" the impersonal and alien world of the street.

For Gilberto Freyre, the term *casa* evokes not so much a *mentalité* of domestic, private life in modern Brazil as it does the social history of Brazilian personalism and familism as these are represented in the archaic symbol of the planter class: the *casa grande*. Here the *casa* evokes the feudal structure and history of slavery, patriarchy, and patronage and the political system of *coronelismo*, a premodern form of chieftainship or leadership by big men, the heads of large, extended households protected by privately owned police forces. In stark contrast to the history of the *casa grande* in Northeast Brazil stands the competing social space of the *rua*, a generative metaphor symbolizing the growth of town and city life in nineteenth-century Brazil. The *rua* is at once a more open, democratic, and modern space, representing the ethos of a tentative equality in contention with the hierarchy of the *casa grande*.

As the sugar plantation society gradually moved from the *casas grandes* of the traditional rural *engenhos* into town (corresponding in Bom Jesus with the rise of the sugar *usina*), this social formation did not immediately accommodate itself to the newer, republican, more egalitarian, and less personalistic urban world. "Brazilian patriarchalism," wrote Freyre, "when it moved from the plantation to the town house, did not at once come to terms with the street; for a long time they were almost enemies, the house and the street" (1986b:30). And so one notes, in Bom Jesus, for example, the tendency of the old wealthy plantation families to wall themselves off from the *rua* by building large mansions in town with enclosed gardens surrounded by high walls menacingly decorated with shards of broken Coca-Cola bottles to discourage the curious "public." The urban mansion remains a closed and total world in which the *rua* exists for the rich only as a path between the houses of the wealthy, or even worse, as a place to discard one's garbage and drain one's dirty water and other sewage. Within their mansions-as-fortresses the landed aristocrats, the "old" families of Bom Jesus, appear to live isolated and independent lives. They seem to enjoy a law unto themselves, the ultimate privilege of the dying gasps of a feudal patriarchy, a personalistic social order in which "who" a person is—one's name—determines power, esteem, and moral worth.

As da Matta pointed out, however, the tensions involved in the "double ethic" of a modern individualism versus a feudal and familistic personalism in Brazil have not really been resolved. Instead, the ethics and the rules of democracy and hierarchy coexist in perpetual conflict and contradiction, lending themselves to the common perception of Brazilian social life as chaotic, disorderly, divided, anarchistic—as anything *other* than the "order and progress" of its national standard.

In addition, however, to the tensions between *casa* and *rua*, which I reinterpret here in more class-based terms as the conflict between old and new wealth and between feudalism and capitalism, is another dialectic. This I call the dynamic tension between *rua* and *mata*. It concerns the relationship between the street and the forest, between the somebodies and the nobodies, between the big people and the little people of Bom Jesus.

Although the people of the forest, the *matutos*, came to Bom Jesus to partake of a better life, a life in the *rua*, they are not really of the street. They are the little people, the no-account people, those whose features, clothing, gait, and posture mark them as anachronisms in modern Bom Jesus. The somebodies, the *fildalgos* and *gente fina* of Bom Jesus, are sometimes simply referred to, quite unconsciously and in common daily conversations, as the *gente*, the "people" of Bom Jesus. And so it is said, for example, that "nobody" goes to mass anymore, although the church may be packed with poor "country" people. Similarly, it is said that "everyone" left town for *carnaval* last year and that the town was completely "deserted," even though the town plaza was crowded with barefoot people in rag-tag, makeshift costumes beating handmade drums and blowing on whistles fashioned out of discarded tin cans. The *gente* are quite blind to the world behind their movie set (and the one that by and large sustains their privilege and fortunes), oblivious to the "second city" where a different social reality is daily constructed, played, and lived. This double exists as a reverse image, the underside and backside of modern Bom Jesus. It is the *bagaceira*, the world bequeathed by the old plantation society.

If one veers off the main street, takes the dusty, and sometimes muddy footpaths that crisscross the town from beneath and behind, and follows the railroad tracks or the outlines of the old *engenhos* just outside town, the images of modernity vanish. One is immediately plunged into this other world and into another tempo, another chronicity altogether. If one descends into the dried-fish market or into the small *zona* (the red-light district), or if one climbs the Altos, the trucks and cars give way to horses, donkeys, and stray goats, and designer jeans give way to drawstring pants made from old pieces of sacking, softened by beatings against rocks in the river. Here the Galeria shopping mall bows to the "fair," the open-air market with its canvas stalls, where rural buyers and sellers can, on two mornings a week, take over the *rua* (reversing the normative social order) with their crates of squawking chickens, ropes of black tobacco, sacks of corn and manioc meal, and rows of medicinal herbs, amulets, cheap perfumes, and incense to counteract sorcery, cure the evil eye, stimulate a lover, call back to its grave a wandering spirit, weaken an enemy. At night on each of the hillside Altos the entertainment is provided not by television sets and stereos, even less by VCRs, but rather by African circle dances, *cirandas*, and

Returning from market.

by bawdy troubadours, called *repentista* singers, whose witty verses tumble the mighty and exalt the lowly and the weak.

Here we enter a rural world, an extension into the city, into the *rua*, of the *mata*—the country, the woods, the forest. It is ironic that the word *mata* remains strongly marked in the vocabulary of the *Nordestinos*, despite the disappearance of the woodlands. What remains of the *mata* today are its former inhabitants, the rural people, the country people, disparagingly called *matutos* by the *fildalgos* of Bom Jesus.[2] It is a term used to label the poor, the illiterate, the humble, the devout, the "backward" and rural, especially the cane cutters and other rural workers who have taken up residence on the backside of the Alto do Cruzeiro, the side that faces toward the *mata*. *Matuto* is a term used by some of the migrants themselves, but only in the negative and to refer to everything and everyone they left behind so as to carve out a new life, a "life on city streets," as they say.

The compelling image of the *rua* as an open, democratizing space is as alive and meaningful to the rural workers of Bom Jesus as it is for Freyre and da Matta. The *rua* stirs their imaginings of a life free of enormous obligations to "bad" *patrões* and mean-spirited *senhores de engenho*. "Those who live on plantations are slaves," says Black Irene. "Life in the *mata* is a kind of slavery because one always has obligations to the *senhor de engenho*. Here I hope to live freely and work *a vontade* [as I please]." The liberating image and promise of the *rua* quite literally "move" these people. Offers Tereza Gomes: "My husband and I left the Engenho Xica—my God, what a *buraco feio da nada* [dark little hole] in the *mata*—to come to the *rua* because we didn't want our children to grow up in ignorance and so far away from everything modern."

And yet these rural migrants live imperfectly in, and sometimes much at odds with, the world of the *rua*. Its promise of autonomy and equality eludes them, and freedom from personal obligations is a sham or comes only at the price of a negating, depersonalized anonymity. The democracy of the *rua* is not meant to extend to the likes of them.

The people of the *mata* who have come to reside in the hillside crevices of Bom Jesus look very different from the bronzed Europeans who are their bosses and *donos*. The *matutos'* faces are browner; their bodies are smaller and slighter. One might see them as tough and sinewy, but that would be at variance with their own image of themselves as weak, wasted, and worn-out. One can see both the Amerindian and the African in their eyes, cheekbones, hair, and skin, although it is the African that predominates. Their feet are wide and splayed from toting other people's loads and from walking great distances through the *mata*.

These people are the descendants of a slave and runaway slave–Indian (*caboclo*) population. Yet they do not think to link their current difficulties to a history of slavery and race exploitation. Racism is a disallowed and submerged discourse in Northeast Brazil, so that every bit as much as Wolf's (1982) European peasants, these are a people "without a history." They call themselves simply *os pobres*, and they describe themselves as *moreno* (brown), almost never as *preto* or *negro* (black).[3] They are "brown," then, as *all* Brazilians, rich and poor, are said to be "brown." In this way the ideology of "racial democracy," as pernicious as the American ideology of "equality of opportunity," goes unchallenged, uncontested, into another generation.

I seize on the term *matuto*, and despite its negative connotations, I refashion it according to my needs to throw into bold relief the competing worlds of *rua* and *mata*. So allow me to refer momentarily to the people of the Alto do Cruzeiro as the "foresters," if nothing else a quaint rendering of *matutos* that lends a feudal, almost medieval, but also dignified character to the term. In so doing I want to link these rural migrants to a not-so-distant, yet almost mythological, past when these "good country people" did indeed live in small clearings in dense woodlands as "conditional squatters," as peasant-workers on peripheral lands of sugar plantations, before these marginal lands, too, were claimed for sugar.

But just as the *zona da mata* is today without *mata*, so are the *matutos* stripped of their fields and woodlands and forced into life in the shantytowns and *mocambos* on the edges of urban life. But the culture of the foresters, the ethos and the ethic that define and guide their actions, is still largely that of the *mata*. Meanwhile, to the somebodies of Bom Jesus the foresters are the little people, the João Pequeno of Bom Jesus, the humble people, those without names, possessions, and family connections, in short, the nobodies. Worse still, their very names betray them, linking them inexorably back to the forest. Among the people of the Alto the most common surnames are da Silva and Nascimento. Da Silva (from *selva* for forest or woods, and *selvagem*, for savage, untamed, uncivilized) resonates with the wild. Nascimento (by birth) was a surname commonly given to the natural, or birth, children of the slave women on the sugar plantations.

Rural and illiterate, the foresters operate in a world of gifts and favors, barter and cunning, loyalties and dependencies, rumor and reputation. They live by their wits, not by the book. In the world of the *rua* they are anathema—neither modern individuals with rights protected by universal laws and jural processes (see da Matta 1984:233) nor yet persons, people "of family," reputation, substance and influence, respected and cherished because they are the children of somebody within the traditional system of feudal patriarchal familism that coexists in Bom Jesus with more modern and democratic forms. Consequently, the foresters have created an alternative community in the margins of urban life; they attempt to minimize their contacts with the formal social and legal institutions, the *burocracia*, as even they call it. Meanwhile, the formal institutions of Bom Jesus are more than happy to consign the foresters to obscurity and marginality. And so the foresters are all too often dismissed and negatively labeled as "marginals," a word that in local usage confers almost outlaw status on all those seen as posing an inexact and unnamed threat to the social order, the status quo.

In describing the people of the Alto, who are the primary subjects of this book, as foresters, I am searching for a more intimate, less alienating way to talk about social class formation in Bom Jesus, one that takes into account cultural forms and meanings as well as the political economy. Although the foresters could be described as a "displaced rural proletariat" or even as a newly formed "urban underclass," they are both of these and yet a good deal more. They are poor and exploited workers, but theirs is not simply a "culture of poverty," nor do they suffer from a poverty of culture. Theirs is a rich and varied system of signs, symbols, and meanings. The *matutos* have brought with them into the urban environment ways of seeing, knowing, and reacting to the world around them that bear traces of their former lives in the *mata*.

Anomic Anarchism

The double ethic of Bom Jesus is maintained at a high social cost. One of these is the climate of cynicism, pessimism, and desperation that is fanning a spirit of anomic anarchism resulting from the convergence of several factors.[4] The people of Bom Jesus endured the long, ugly period of military rule (1964–1985) stoically and fearfully as a staunchly "opposition" community. The Barbosa family, which has controlled the *município* and much of the region of the *mata—norte* since the 1930s, refused throughout the military years to recognize the legitimacy of the military dictatorship. Consequently, the community suffered a kind of intentional economic neglect from both state and federal government.

Expectations were high, beginning with the *abertura* (the democratic awakening) and culminating in the election and return to office of the populist governor, Miguel Arraes (who was forced from office by the 1964 coup), that now things would change for the better in Bom Jesus da Mata. People trusted that the new democratic state government (elected with a huge outpouring of enthusiasm and popular support) would finally begin to attend to the long neglected and pressing needs of the *município* for a clean and adequate water supply, improved health services, public housing, jobs, and a generally raised standard of living. But the years from 1984 to 1988 saw only a worsening of the crisis brought about in part by a severe drought and in part by the financial chaos resulting from Brazil's international debt. Escalating inflation, the cruzeiro–cruzado–new cruzado monetary fiasco, price freezes followed by consumer shortages, hoarding, stockpiling, and various kinds of price fixing contributed to a state of near panic that led to explosions of protest and of urban violence throughout the troubled Nordeste.

Although black humor and a kind of reckless, absurdist abandon have always seemed to me a dimension of the "social personality" of *Nordestinos*, rich and poor alike, what I have been seeing and hearing in recent years is of a wholly different, more desperate quality that must give pause. Accompanying the positive spirit of the *abertura* is an unchecked license to express antisocial, anarchist, and racist sentiments that were previously disallowed, at least publicly. The declared "anarchism" of a small but visible group of upper-middle-class and middle-class professionals has become a new political force with which to be reckoned. In the plazas, restaurants, bars, and shops of Bom Jesus one hears the rumblings of a discontent that blames not only the government (federal and state) and political parties but also the masses of the poor (and more recently, one hears, "the blacks") for the vast problems of the community and the region. Savage racist jokes abound, and caricatures of one's "ugly" black maid or washerwoman are "playfully" engaged in by both children and adults in some wealthy households. *Pobre e preto só dão problemas, preocupação, e prejuízo* is a popular saying that is often repeated: "The poor and the blacks have brought us only problems, worry, and misfortune." This is followed by various "creative" solutions for "getting rid" of them. Inevitably someone will suggest that nothing need be done, that nature itself is on the side of the well-to-do, for eventually the "natural laws" of famine, sickness, and death will cure Bom Jesus of its problem populations. These are jokes, to be sure, and the mood is cavalier, but the emotions underlying them are passionate, and what begins as a joke can rapidly turn into a heated political discussion or an argument. Allow me to illustrate.

While I was standing in line at a local hardware store, a respected physician rushed in with the architectural plans for his new home, which was under construction. He began to complain to the owner of the shop, an old crony of his, about the slipshod work of the contractor, the poor quality of the building materials, the thievery of the work crew, and the corruption of the local *políticos*, who required bribes to process various building permits. "It is," he said, "a total demoralization. Everything is falling apart. There is no structure, no standard, no core." Then, recognizing me and pointing to my association with the poor of the Alto do Cruzeiro, the doctor jested loudly, "Nancí, *querida*. Do us a favor. Can't you call Mr. Bush and arrange a *jeitinho* [a little solution] for the Alto do Cruzeiro? Just a little 'project' will do, nothing quite as big as Hiroshima or Nagasaki, just a *bombazinho* [little bomb]. Phet! [he snaps his fingers]. Like that and it will all be over. Then we can have a fresh start." Then he added in utter seriousness, "I mean it. The only solution left for us now is total destruction. Understand? Total."

Similarly, while stranded with several others on a park bench in the town *praça* during a long anticipated downpour, we stood up as the fast-rising water rushed past us. Suddenly someone "prayed" aloud, "O Lord, let this little flood solve the problems still left over in the Campo de Sete!" The Campo de Sete, a poor community built on the margins of the river, almost washed away during the floods of 1978. Many people from that community died; their bodies swept into the river, polluting the drinking water (some complained). Survivors found temporary shelter in the makeshift stables of a state animal exhibition center that had been built near the *bairro*. They caused a public scandal when five years after the flood, the flood victims refused to leave the exhibition quarters to make way for a rodeo and animal exhibition planned by the state. The flood of 1978 is sometimes referred to cynically as nature's "beautification project" for Bom Jesus.

On yet another occasion a physical therapist began to complain about a phone call he had just received from a poor (nonpaying) client who was in great pain with a very probably dislocated hip. The therapist told the boy to lie quietly until the morning (because the therapist had more pressing matters to attend to until then). When I asked if he had contacted anyone else to look in on the boy, Luciano replied, "Yes, indeed. I called the local funeral service and made a deal with them in advance, in case anything goes wrong during the night."

The jokes unmask widely shared sentiments about which residents are both ashamed and troubled. Beneath the exterior of callousness is a good deal of pain and quiet desperation. And so, noting my discomfort, Luciano turned to make a poignant aside: "There is so much misery here, I have to joke. I have to horse around. What else can I do? Wring my hands and weep?"

Nonetheless, the impoverished rural migrants who have taken up permanent residence in Bom Jesus are seen as a kind of modern-day plague, an unruly cancerous growth, an infectious epidemic inflicted on the once healthy and sound social body of the community. And plagues require aggressive interventions: social sanitation. And here I am using these metaphors advisedly, for the threat that the squatters of the Altos pose to the town is often described in medical terms. The poor are said to be making Bom Jesus a risky, unhealthy place to live. Wealthy residents refer to the return of "old" diseases once thought to be safely under control: dengue, tuberculosis, schistosomiasis, Chagas' disease, polio, typhoid fever, and rabies. These highly infectious diseases cannot be contained within the shantytowns. All residents share the risk of contamination, especially as carried in the water supply, through the open and inadequate public drains, and in the exposed garbage dumps.

Shock and anger surface when a local teacher is suddenly struck with typhoid fever, when the child of a middle-class family almost dies of diarrhea and dehydration, when a ten-year-old from a wealthy household comes home from a doctor's exam in Recife with evidence of "schistomes" in her blood. The wife of a local *fazendeiro* is beside herself when she learns that her husband is infected with amoebas: "How can this have happened? In our house everything is clean, sterilized; I have trained the maids so well. A fly never rests on anything that goes into our mouths. We drink only bottled mineral water. We don't mix with anyone; our lives are private, very clean."

But attempts to keep the sick and the poor at bay, as it were, are of course thwarted by the long-established patterns of mutual dependency among the social classes. The maintenance of the average upper-middle-class to wealthy household of Bom Jesus is dependent on a large staff of servants, nannies, cooks, washerwomen, chauffeurs, and gardeners, who are recruited from the unhealthy, infected, and "contaminating" populations living in the marginal *bairros* of Bom Jesus. These employers prefer not to know where their help come from or the kinds of homes and outhouses they return to at night or on the weekends. Potential employees are interviewed in the homes of the wealthy, and when they are perfunctorily asked if they are "clean," the workers invariably answer with a polite, "Yes, ma'am." I am thinking, for example, of Nia, the twenty-year-old daughter of the old sorceress Célia, who borrowed a dress from me to "pass" an interview with a wealthy matron, while at home her mother was mortally ill and covered with infected sores and two of Nia's four children were racked with fever, explosive diarrheas, and vomiting. Nia, as neat as a pin when she went for her job interview, was hired on the spot as a cook. "What goes around, comes around" was all I could think of at the time, plus the irony that nature's "poetic justice," invoked by the rich, might be turned against them first.

I refer to sentiments of anomic anarchism, for often these are accompanied by a detachment from the formal political process and from public life and by a withdrawal into a selfish cocoon of private domesticity that Brazilians sometimes refer to as *egoismo*. As one self-described "anarchist" of Bom Jesus explains his social philosophy: "I have inherited my politics from my father, who was an anarchist like me. He taught me the following rule: me in the first place, me in the second place, and me in the third and fourth places. *Maybe* others in the fifth place."

This cult of domesticity and privatization is pursued by those who try to insulate themselves from the more disturbing aspects of community life. Many wealthy households are protected by round-the-clock, armed guard surveillance. Even the cloistered nuns of the Colégio Santa Lúcia keep ferocious German shepherds in their enclosed courtyard to protect the convent from pilfering by homeless street children. There is little confidence in local institutions, including medical services, so that when they are ill, members of the upper class of Bom Jesus fly to the United States for diagnostic tests and treatment. In preparation for a medical emergency some of the wealthy keep a private blood supply to eliminate the possibility of contamination in a hospital with AIDS-infected blood.

The malaise is shared by the poor, the rag-tag proletariat so feared and despised by the anomic wealthy class. But should the people of the *morros* and the river margins of Bom Jesus ever mobilize around their anarchistic sentiments, the young doctor quoted earlier might well live to experience the total destruction that he viewed as cleansing.

I am reminded of a conversation with Ramona, an unemployed factory worker from the stigmatized Campo de Sete. After enumerating the general problems of Brazil and of the *município* in particular (the closure of shoe factories that put so many, herself included, out of work; the crisis of the *roçados;* the scarcity and high cost of foodstuffs; the pollution of drinking water), Ramona concluded, "The PMDB was the hope of the people. For twenty years we waited to be liberated from the military. During the state and municipal elections of 1982, how the people prayed, how they begged God and the Virgin for the PMDB to win. Some of us did penances; we fasted and went without shoes to church, all to bring the PMDB into power and so to end our years of suffering. And here we are; we have arrived! The 'people' are in power again, and . . . *nada feito* [nothing accomplished]. We are disillusioned, deceived, fooled. . . .

"What can be worse than hunger? And we are still hungry. What is worse than sickness? And we are still sick. If anything, we appear to be sicker than before. We have no strength left. They say that Brazilians are *mole* [soft]. That we are dying like flies, *a toa* [for no reason at all]. That we are weak, without energy. But if we are weak, it isn't because we are soft. It's only because we are hungry. Food is the source of the weakness of the poor . . . and money. Most men make only about twelve dollars a week. That isn't enough to make *feira* [to do the shopping]. We need a government that will take care of the people, but I have begun to think now that this doesn't exist; that it is another *engano* [deceit]. The poor work like donkeys and asses cutting cane, cleaning streets, washing clothes, butchering animals—all the dirty work there is, we do it, and we still don't make enough to buy a kilo of fresh meat at the end of the week."

"And what would be the solution?"

"Solution? There is no solution, but one. Only a total strike. Nothing less than that. We need to organize the people to refuse to vote in the next election. [Ramona was referring to the coming local elections for *prefeito* and town councillors in 1988, not to the presidential elections of 1989.[5]] To refuse to vote, that is also the right of the people. We should not participate in any elections or work for any of the candidates or support any political party. They all lied to us and fooled us. Now it is our turn to show them. We will engage in *desordem* [chaos]. We will steal and kill until we have reached a general and total paralysis that will stop everything. We have been passive for too long. The rich and powerful have been so accustomed to violating our lives, our persons, and our bodies that everyone takes it for granted. A poor person is murdered or is made to disappear, and who cries out in his defense? Where is there justice for him or for his family?"

"What do you hope will come out of this chaos, this disorder?"

Her answer was immediate and spontaneous: "*Água, terra, e remédios;* Water, land, and medicines." The *Nordestino* equivalent of Rosa Luxemburg's "bread and roses." Thus far, water seems to be the one issue capable of uniting and igniting the people of Bom Jesus in sustained political action, even if only in the somewhat carnivalesque incident with which I began this chapter. To understand life in Bom Jesus da Mata is to understand the ambiguity and contradictions of dominance and dependency and to develop a keen sensitivity to thirst as a generative metaphor of frustrated longings and unmet human needs.

3   Reciprocity
and Dependency

The Double Ethic of Bom Jesus

The people of the Alto act, because they must, within a dual ethic, one egalitarian and collectivist, the other hierarchical and dyadic. One guides behavior toward family, kin, *compadres,* coworkers, and friends who are *pobres* like themselves. The other guides behavior toward *patrões,* bosses, *donos,* superiors, and benefactors. Whereas the first siphons off the most minimal surplus to redistribute it among those even worse off, the other locks the foresters into relations of servility, dependency, and loyalty to those who oppress and exploit them. The one enhances class solidarity; the other contains within it the seeds of class betrayal. The first is the ethic of open and balanced reciprocity. It is the ethic of the *mata.* The other is the ethic of patronage, of *paternalismo,* of misplaced loyalties and self-colonizing dependencies. It is the ethic of the *casa grande,* of the big house and the sugar barons, the *senhores de engenho.* Both ethics coexist in a tense dialectic on and around the sugar plantations; both are transformed when the foresters come to reside as *moradores,* as squatters, along the muddy paths of the Alto do Cruzeiro. The foresters' double ethic sets them apart and sometimes on edge in their relations with the "big people" of the *rua.*

More has been written about the ethic of patronage among rural workers, their "dyadic contracts" with bosses, their fawning humility in the presence of social superiors, their tendency to look for "strong leaders" and "good patrons" and to make sure they align themselves with the winners, the strong, and the powerful, whoever these may be.[1] But this ethic obtains in a delimited social space regulating only vertical relations. Outside this domain and in the *moradores'* relations to one another, there are competing loyalties to their own kind and a generosity of spirit that lends them a sense of almost self-righteous moral superiority when they contrast their behavior to that of the greedy bosses and patrons they are forced to endure.

Among the *moradores* of the Alto do Cruzeiro, money, food, medicines, and relatives (but most especially children) circulate continually in a ring of exchange that links the *mata* to the *rua* and the impoverished households of the Alto to one another. On the Alto do Cruzeiro there is no household so wretched that it will refuse hospitality to visiting or migrating kin from the *mata* or deny help to a neighbor whose *feira* basket is completely empty, even though migration and hunger are constant and ordinary, rather than occasional and extraordinary, events.

Because of the implicit rule of reciprocity among the foresters (whom henceforth I refer to interchangeably as *moradores*, residents, or squatters), household composition shifts radically even over very brief periods of time. Among the more than one hundred households of the Alto on which I have been keeping records, the "actors" shift continually, so that a good deal of my time is taken up on each field visit adjusting the household censuses. For example, in July 1987 Dona Maria d'Água (as the old water carrier is called) seemed quite overwhelmed by a household very nearly splitting at the seams. Into two and a half tiny rooms were crammed Dona Maria, her two adult daughters, their children, an adult son, his child, and two other grandchildren sent home by a daughter working in São Paulo. In addition, there was the occasional visiting father, mother, or boyfriend.

When I returned in February of the next year, I felt as though I were visiting an entirely different household. True, Dona Maria remained the immobile fixture, "one of the oldest 'rocks' of the Alto," as she referred to herself. But living with her in 1988 were only one of her adult daughters (who, sick and disabled, had sent *her* children to live with their father's mother); Juliana, the severely neglected and malnourished two-year-old daughter abandoned to the indifferent care of her grandmother by Dona Maria's misbehaving and errant younger daughter, Gorete, who had run off to Recife; and an eleven-year-old grandniece sent up alone by bus from São Paulo. "Where are the others"? I asked. Dona Maria looked perplexed. "Who *was* here last Santana [i.e., July, the month of Santa Ana]?" she asked me. There is no "bookkeeping" regarding the transfer of people and goods on the Alto. It is an open system. As Dona Maria explained, "That's just the way it is. Sometimes I have a crowd; sometimes I am all alone."

Actually, one is never really alone on the Alto. Should a person suddenly become totally bereft of household members, a neighbor will send someone to live with that "poor, solitary creature." I have been the recipient of live-in "company" on more than one occasion. When Nailza and Zé Antônio decided, virtually overnight, in December 1965 to pack up their few belongings and migrate across Brazil to Mato Grosso, no sooner had they begun their descent of the Alto than a nine-year-old daughter of Dona Dalina knocked on my door, thumb stuck in her mouth and ratty plaid hammock over her shoulder, saying, "My mother sent me to keep you from being lonely." "It never crossed my mind," I replied, but I welcomed the child, who lived with me for the next several months. Anything else would have struck the *moradores* as most "disagreeable" behavior on my part.

Although petitioning is a standard feature of Alto residents' interactions with their social "superiors," no self-respecting *morador* of the Alto wants to *ask* a neighbor, or any other equal, for what she desperately needs. These needs should be anticipated by those nearby. When Dona Célia (see chapter 5) fell desperately ill, the victim of putative witchcraft, leprosy, or both, and took to her hammock, her body fat virtually dissolving before her neighbors' eyes, she never stooped to ask for help. Although ostracized by some, her few faithful neighbors came by daily, each carrying a small offering discreetly wrapped in brown paper and tied with a string: cooked beans, mangoes, bananas, medications, holy relics, folded one-hundred-cruzado notes, and so on. As each entered the tiny hut and approached the once-powerful old woman, they asked a parting blessing of their *comadre*, who, sorceress or not, headed for heaven or hell, was still *gente* like themselves. As Célia approached her final crisis, the same neighbors formed a human chair, carrying the old woman like a fallen queen down the slippery slopes of the Alto do Cruzeiro to a charity ward of the local hospital. This is archetypal forester behavior, and it illustrates certain traits that are far removed from the usual description of *Nordestino* plantation workers.

Alto women especially keep themselves apprised of each other's situation, and they respond according to a kind of triage that diverts attention and resources to the most "deserving" cases. Moreover, the women of the Alto suspect that experiencing want and hunger has made them "selfish," "jealous," and "greedy," and so they actively struggle with themselves so that those who are even *more* desperate are not totally abandoned. For example, the amount of control exercised during the rare distribution of free clothes by Franciscan nuns following community meetings on the Alto is quite remarkable. The women, among themselves, monitor the painful distribution according to publicly and collectively negotiated decisions regarding perceived need and misery. "No," the women may correct Sister Clara, "give that suit to Dona Nalva. She can use it to bring her husband home from the hospital in Recife." Or, "Maria da Ana first. She has that bunch of babies in her house." Consequently, some have to go home empty-handed and dissatisfied, as the old spinster Maria do Carmel did on one occasion. She wiped a tear from the corner of her eye, commenting, "*Só quem não ganhou fui eu!* The only one left out was me!" But almost certainly, the slight will be remembered and corrected at the next giveaway: "Don't forget Dona Carmel," someone will be sure to say. "She didn't get anything the last two times." One can feel comfortably observed among the community of Alto women.

Alto women readily take up and contribute to collections for various worthy causes on the Alto: bus fare to send Little Irene's daughter to São Paulo so she can be reunited with her husband; the last few sacks of cement needed to help *comadre* Teresa Gomes finish the outhouse she has always wanted; a coffin for Black Irene's mother so she will not have to go into the ground a pauper. Although these collections will also be taken up in the *rua* and among various wealthy patrons and bosses, Alto people say that one does best looking for help among neighbors and kin.

Alto women with just a bit of literacy, schooling, or know-how serve their friends and neighbors as informal *despachantes*, a Brazilian social role for which there is no easy translation. A *despachante* is a paid or a voluntary "intermediary" who helps those without power, especially the illiterate, negotiate the Kafkaesque municipal and state bureaucracies that serve largely to prevent those in need from gaining access to the health care, work benefits, educational programs, subsidies, legal rights, and basic public and social welfare services to which they are entitled. A *despachante*, then, is anyone with the *jeito*, the chutzpah, personal charm, political clout, or familial influence necessary to cut through the discouraging lines; the endless, nonsensical paperwork in quadruplicate; the officious "functionaries" and arrogant secretaries who collectively prevent a client's request from being heard and attended to by the appropriate authorities (see Pereira 1986). My clever research assistant, Little Irene, frequently served her friends and neighbors on the Alto as a bold *despachante* who was not ashamed to "go right to the top" to make her client's request heard. In "repayment" she demanded and expected little, except that her neighbors overlook her occasional problems with *cachaça* (the local rum) and with "difficult" and quarrelsome men.

As an outsider who was literate, formally detached from local political parties and struggles, and "related" to Little Irene, I was an obvious target and a natural for the role of *despachante* on the Alto. I came to accept the role, if somewhat reluctantly, as an "organic" one in the community, a burden that was shared with many other local people, poor as well as wealthy.[2] Accepting the role was a sign of my "good faith" with the people of the Alto and evidence of my willingness to participate in the reciprocal exchanges that were expected. But even this role was controlled and distributed as a scarce commodity and "limited good" by the women leaders of the Alto, who would intervene by telling me to honor certain requests and to postpone or disregard others. The women made it easier for me to turn down requests that they judged among themselves to be noncritical, totally hopeless and beyond repair, or simply "undeserving." Then I would sometimes be taken by the hand and led down a tricky, slippery path into a situation that was considered truly *péssimo* (wretched) or simply more worthy. Triage is an essential component of the squatters' moral reasoning and the practical underpinning of their sense of social justice, a theme that I take up later in considering the allocation of scarce resources within the family.

The sharing of responsibility for the welfare of "widows" again illustrates the *moradores'* traditional ethic of reciprocity. Alto women frequently find themselves alone, abandoned, widowed, and desperately needy. Given the predominance of female-headed households on the Alto, it is curious that particular attention is still paid to the plight of the "widow." The majority of Alto women are unmarried in the eyes of church and state, but most strive to maintain permanent relations with men they love and to whom they expect to be married someday. About a fifth of the women live in less regular arrangements, frequently changing partners and mothering children by two or more different men. These "loose" arrangements are not condoned by the women of the Alto, who continue to draw firm distinctions between "moral" and "immoral" sexual behavior. Although economic difficulties often delay formal marriage for many years, Alto women expect one another to live "in friendship" with the man who is the father of their children and to do so honorably. That is, man and woman should act toward each other as if they were, for all practical purposes, a married couple. Promiscuity and prostitution, both of them facts of Alto existence for a substantial minority of Alto women who survive by formally or informally trading in sex, are nonetheless strongly disapproved. A prostitute or a woman perceived to be "promiscuous" can never claim for herself the social status of an "abandoned" or "widowed" woman. And she cannot make claims on her neighbors for help as a right, although she may "beg" for the charity due a miserable sinner. More often than not such "bad" women are forced back onto the *rua* as common beggars when they are stranded or otherwise in bad straits.

This distinction is illustrated by the community reactions to two widows of the Alto do Cruzeiro, Maria José and Maria Luiza, both of whom found themselves homeless following the winter rains of 1987. Although neither widow had been married to the father of her children, Maria Luiza was a quiet, sober little woman who had left the *sertão* following her "husband," Seu Sebastião, an elderly widower and carpenter, by whom she had four children (two living) before he died of malpractice in a charity ward of a teaching hospital in Recife (see chapter 6). In contrast, Maria José was (in local parlance) a "wild woman," a *doida*, who had been seduced and raped by age thirteen and who had lived with several men, the last of whom she

The "good widow" looking into her demolished hut.

followed to São Paulo, where he was murdered in a barroom brawl. Maria José returned to Bom Jesus and the Alto do Cruzeiro as a widow, pregnant and with three pretty but dirty and malnourished children. She carried a mean scar over her eye, the badge of her brave attempt to stop the fight that claimed her husband's life. When the two women appeared at the same UPAC community meeting to ask members to organize a *mutirão* (a collective work force) to help rebuild their mud huts, the Alto community responded favorably to Maria Luiza's request but negatively to that of the *doida*. Moreover, henceforth, Maria Luiza was referred to as "the widow,"

Collective house raising.

and her little house was raised in one happy outpouring of collective effort, largely by the older women of the Alto, many of whom were widows themselves.

Evidence of the *moradores'* system of reciprocity is also found in the patterns of fictive kinship, both godparenthood (*compadrio*) and the informal fosterage of children, *filhos de criação* (children by rearing). Both patterns extend outward the definition of family, household, and kin obligations by turning distant relations into closer kin and making kin of friends or mere acquaintances. Both institutions stress already limited material and emotional resources, spreading them ever more thinly among a larger network of people. The rescue of vulnerable sick, neglected, or abandoned children by other poor women, sometimes relatives, sometimes strangers, who then raise them for a period of time, is understood as an unremarkable and wholly expected act of kindness and mercy on the Alto do Cruzeiro. It is also very common.

In a random survey of every other house along several main roads and paths of the Alto do Cruzeiro in 1988 and 1989, I found that in 38 percent of the more than fifty households sampled, an adult woman had at one time or another helped to rear a child who was not her own for periods ranging from several weeks to several years or more. The most common arrangement was for a grandmother to take care of her grandchildren when their mother was away from home working or was simply too sick, poor, or discouraged to care for the children herself. Godmothers often assumed this same responsibility for their godchildren. But neighbors, usually older women, sometimes intervened, uninvited, in a desperately poor situation and might "demand" to take a child whose life or whose safety seemed threatened. "Give me that child," the older woman might say to a young mother, "for I can see as plain as day that the baby has no future [i.e., that she or he will die] in your home." Sometimes she might add, "I ought to know. Didn't I lose [sometimes she might even say 'kill'] several of my own infants when I was as young and poor and foolish as yourself?"

Less frequently, but common enough, is fosterage through abandonment. Antonieta, Black Irene, Maria José, Nailza de Arruda, and Dona Amor, among many others on the Alto do Cruzeiro, acquired one or more children this way. Tonieta found a prettily cared for newborn in a plastic basket on her doorstep in 1982. The infant had a note pinned to her little shirt begging Antonieta to adopt the little one out of the goodness of her heart, and she readily did so (see chapter 10). Maria José, the "bad widow" of the Alto, explained how she came to mother the flaxen-haired little tyke who was the envy of the Alto. Maria was walking through the *mata* of a sugar plantation in Paraíba when she heard the sound of an infant crying in the sugarcane. "You are mad," her husband told her, but when Maria went into the cane she found a newborn left on the ground "all bloody with the birth matter still on it." She carried the child to the police and then, as directed, to the office of the justice, where she was asked if she had the "resources" to care for an infant such as this. "Resources we don't have, your Honor," she replied, "but our will [*vondade*] to raise the infant as our own is very strong." And so the judge allowed the couple to register the infant in her husband's name. Soon after, however, Maria José found herself widowed.

Informal fosterage is the usual pattern, but when a child is taken at a very young age or raised for many years, the foster parents often try to register the child in their own names or to "clean up" (*limpar*) an old birth certificate by substituting their names for those of the birth mother and father. Black Irene, for example, agreed to care for two of her godchildren after their mother died in a car accident. Their father agreed to pay Irene what amounted to a few dollars a month to cover the cost of the children's meals and clothing. But after several years passed and the stipend had long since stopped coming, Irene came to think of her godchildren as her own. When out of the blue one of the children's maternal aunts appeared asking to take the now nearly grown children home with her, Irene suffered a severe *susto*, a "deadly shock." She now wanted to register the children, retroactively, in her name. But the children's baptismal certificates clearly showed Irene to be their godmother. "Whatever will I do?" worried Irene. "One cannot be *both* godmother and natural mother. Do you think I could have them baptized again, with you serving as their godmother, so that I can be free to claim them as my natural children?" It was quite a conundrum in kinship relations and one that, luckily, did not need to be resolved, as the children's aunt left town.

Similarly, when Nailza de Arruda and I went to the Barbosa hospital to adopt a newborn that had been abandoned by its fourteen-year-old mother, we both signed the informal copybook kept in the nursery for just this purpose. We agreed to name the beautiful little boy Marcelinho, but we delayed having the sickly infant baptized for neither of us would agree to serve as the boy's godparent and thus surrender our rights to maternity. The jealous competition was finally resolved when Nailza, who had lost an infant of her own a few months earlier, began to lactate, stimulated by Marcelo's hungry cries. Once she began to breast-feed him, I surrendered and became Marcelo's godmother.[3]

But it is in the story of Dona Amor's rescue of an abandoned and severely stigmatized little girl that the compassion and beauty of the foresters' traditional system of fosterage really come to the fore. "It was like this," Amor began. "I was living with my old mother, who was almost ninety years old, when one morning as I was going to work a neighbor woman called out to me from her front door, 'Oh, Dona Narcí, be good and come here for a minute.'"

Amor was reluctant to go there knowing that she was going to be asked a favor, but she gave in out of curiosity. "What is it you want?" she asked.

"Nothing more than for you to carry this poor abandoned child home with you. She's just arrived from the *mata*, sent here by her poor, distracted father, who can no longer care for her. The child is hopeless, *sem jeito*. I gave her to my sister, and her husband said, 'Nothing doing. You'll have to chose between the brat and me.' And so she sent the creature back. I can't keep her here with me. For the great love of God that you have, take her, or else the girl will surely die."

Amor asked to have a look at the child, and she was shocked because the ten-year-old girl was so ill-kempt and ill-treated. Worse, Amor could see right off that the child was damaged, "not right" in the head.

"Her head was weak; she was a crazy child. The poor creature had one of 'those terrible diseases' [i.e., child attack; see chapter 8]. Her head was covered with scabs and pus. Her clothes were ripped and filthy. She had the smell of the river about her. She was completely *podre* [decaying, rotting]."

"God help me!" said Amor. "Let me go home and ask my mother."

But when Amor went home the first thing she did was to light a candle to the Sacred Heart and to pray for advice: "Dear God, why did you bring a child like this in from the *mata?* What was Your plan in bringing her to me?" After completing her prayers, Amor returned to get the child, who resisted and refused to move. Half carrying, half dragging the wild child, Amor brought her home. Meanwhile, Amor's neighbors expressed their disgust and displeasure at what she was doing. The child was ravenously hungry, and Amor sat her down at the table before a plate piled high with beans, rice, and manioc. But the child did not know how to hold a spoon, and she ate by using her hands and putting her face into the food like a dog. Amor held a spoon in the girl's hand and tried to show how to eat like a proper human. "I cried; I had such pity for her."

"Do you want more?" Amor asked.

"*Não,*" the creature growled.

"That's fine, *senhora,*" replied Amor.

When the girl heard Amor call her so politely, so gently, *senhora,* she covered her face with her hands. She was filled with shame.

"As she did so, boff! Jesus first entered her head."

This marked, for Amor, the beginning of her foster child's long and difficult recovery, which terminated in the crowning moment of Mariazinha's (for so she was named) baptism and holy communion.

"The girl may be *boba* [dumb], but she learned many things: how to help in the house and to go to market with me and even how to cook. The only thing she never learned was how to read and write, and that made me sad because I always hoped that one day there would be someone in our house who could understand the alphabet. But it was not to be. Still, when I take her to mass on Sunday, I am as proud as any mother. She sits so still, and when Padre Agostino raises the host, she is totally transformed. It is the most sacred thing you ever saw. I feel myself blessed to be in her presence, and I thank God for bringing His little dumb saint into my life."

But even so, the neighbors continued to taunt and torment Amor. Each time she descended the hill with Mariazinha at her side, they laughed and called out, "*Olha a doida!* Look at the crazy kid!" This went on until finally one day a *posse* of neighbors came to confront Amor saying, "Are you still keeping that crazy child in your house? Get rid of her! Why would you want to raise a child without any sense? A child like that is not human [not *gente*]. She is going to be the death of your poor old mother. How can you take food from your old saint's mouth and put it into the mouth of that devil of a child?"

"Devil nothing! Hold your tongues! Do you want me just to throw her away? Wasn't it Jesus who told us to love the blind and the lame and the sick?

What kind of love is it that would throw a poor creature like this into the street to live like an animal hunting for scraps in garbage heaps? Be ashamed of yourselves!"

The women were silenced and went home thinking over her words. They knew them to be just and from that day on, Dona Narcí became known on the Alto do Cruzeiro as Dona Amor, Dona Love. And Amor's little girl grew in beauty, if not in wisdom.

The Mirage of Care: Patron-Client Relations

We have to push the notion of hegemony into the lived space of realities in social relationships, in the give and take of social life, as in the sweaty, warm space between the arse of him who rides the back of him who carries.

Michael Taussig (1987b:288)

With respect to relations across class, between the foresters and their variously described bosses, patrons, and owners, an altogether different image of the impoverished *morador* emerges, that of a fawning, "humble" man or woman, hat in hand, eyes cast downward, as unctuous and dishonest and conniving as Dickens's Uriah Heep. The history of the sugar plantation, slavery, peonage, paternalism, and *coronelismo* can weigh heavily on the demeanor and the behavior of the rural workers, who throughout their lives put up with humiliating gestures and postures and with unequal exchanges that obligate them to people who would only take further advantage of them. The squatters behave toward their bosses in ways that end up angering and disgusting themselves, so that later and in private they rain forth invectives on the head of their bad boss or greedy patron, vowing never again to trust the man (or woman) whom only hours before they had endearingly referred to as *meu branco* (my white one) or *meu careca* (my bald one).

Although when disillusioned the people of the Alto will and do "give up" on one or even on a whole series of bad bosses and disappointing patrons, they do not give up on the idea of patronage and the persistent belief that there are good bosses to be had: kind, just, noble, generous, caring, strong, and charismatic. A good boss is a rescuer and a savior, one who will swoop down at a precarious moment and snatch a dependent worker and his or her family from the clutches of disease, penury, death, or other forms of destruction. For people who live their lives so close to the margins of survival, the idea of a benefactor is soothing. To admit the opposite, to entertain the idea that patronage itself is exploitative, is to admit that there is no structural safety net at all and that the poor are adrift within an amoral social and economic system that is utterly indifferent to their well-being and survival.

It is to suggest that hope is absurd and that "good fortune" is an illusion. Occasionally such insights break through in a throwaway comment, a cynical remark, but they are then quickly buried and followed by an unlikely or contradictory disclaimer, such as "Well, but my *patrão* really *does* care about me. Didn't he pay for the *mortalha*, the funeral supplies, for my [deceased] children?"

To visualize how the system of unequal exchanges and dependencies operates, let us put ourselves for the moment in the sandals of Dona Irene, the one known on the Rua da Cruz of the Alto do Cruzeiro as Black Irene. Let us say it is a Saturday morning in Bom Jesus da Mata, and Dona Irene wakes up in considerable pain. Her bad leg is acting up again; the old wound has opened, and pus is oozing from the nasty sore. She first noticed it on Friday on her return from washing clothes in the river. Over the weekend she went to the private hospital in town that bears the name of Dr. Urbano Barbosa Neto, elder brother of the *prefeito*. After several hours of waiting, she was looked at perfunctorily by an untrained nurse, who handed her a prescription for an antibiotic, which Irene learned at the pharmacy across the street would cost her many times what she earns washing clothes each week. She can go to the *prefeito*'s municipal dispensary, but that means waiting until Monday morning and another long negotiation to get the mayor's signature on a voucher to be used at the pharmacy. Irene detests having to beg from a man she does not like or respect, but what other *jeito* (solution) is there, she asks, "for a poor black like me?" (Irene is one of very few *moradores* who interprets her misery in terms of pernicious race-caste relations.)

After waiting almost two hours on Monday morning, Irene is finally allowed to enter the mayor's chambers. The room is high ceilinged, large, and airy; its huge windows open onto the street, where Seu Félix can see the long line of sick men, women, and children waiting with their endless petitions for money, drugs, sacks of cement, eyeglasses, false teeth, jobs, ambulance rides, school books, pens and pencils, and so on. Several men stand around the *prefeito*'s desk. Some appear to be humble petitioners like herself who, although dismissed, are still hoping for a change of heart that may solve their problems. The others are the mayor's cadre of personal and political friends, all of them "hail fellows well met," exchanging gossip and jokes, passing the time before lunch. They provide an audience for Seu Félix, one that he often delights in playing to. The *prefeito* is in one of his more relaxed and expansive moods, and he waves Black Irene toward him, calling out, "What is it, Tia [Auntie]?" Irene explains by modestly lifting up the hem of her long skirt just high enough to expose the wound, putrid and weeping pus. Félix looks away quickly and raises an eyebrow toward Seu

Seu Félix: the *prefeito imperfeito* of Bom Jesus.

João, the functionary who dispenses tonics, vitamins, painkillers, elixirs, and, occasionally, antibiotics from his cabinet-sized room to the rear of the municipal chambers.

"Ampicillin is out of stock," Seu João says, shaking his head. Irene then asks for help in purchasing the *remédio* at a local pharmacy. "Dona Maria," the *prefeito* addresses Irene, with some impatience in his voice. "Do you really think that I can foot the medical bills for the whole *município?*" Irene does not raise her eyes but waits, standing her ground. The mayor gets up and pushes his small hands deep into his pockets, turning them inside out. They are quite empty. He whistles through his teeth and then adds, "What shall I do? Do you want me to ring up Dona Emília [his wife] and see if she can lend me some cruzados? But I do think she's gone off to Recife this morning."

Dona Irene is being toyed with, and she knows it. But she stands her ground until the laughter subsides around her. Then she is gently but firmly led to the door. From the *prefeitura* Irene goes directly to the home of Dona Carminha, her *patroa* of more than forty years. She asks for a three-week advance on her washing to purchase the expensive medication. Her *patroa* is annoyed and moody. She tells Irene that she isn't worth the trouble, that

Irene is "exploiting" her *patroa*'s goodwill. Irene takes the abuse silently and stoically, saying that in any event she cannot put her leg back into the polluted river to do the washing until it has been treated. Finally, the *patroa* digs into her purse and pulls out several bills, adding up to about two dollars toward the purchase of the drug. Irene picks up the crumpled bills from the table and walks directly out the back door, her mouth set in a straight line. "She didn't even thank me," comments Dona Carminha to Irene's broad back.

Scenes like this one are commonplace in Bom Jesus da Mata, occasioned by a social hierarchy based on competing claims, "entitlements," and obligations between patrons and their clients. As an almost palpable vestige of plantation slavery and feudalism to this day, the rural workers of the *zona da mata* labor not so much to receive wages but to maintain a relationship with one or more "strong" or wealthy bosses. The *morador* of the Alto does not evaluate his bosses and patrons exclusively in terms of wages per hour or unit of work, of sugar cut or basket of laundry washed, starched, and ironed. One's boss is also judged by the "gifts" he or she has bestowed over the duration of the relationship: meats, poultry, baskets of vegetables, corn, fruit; used clothing for the family; the payment of various registration fees, medical bills, prescription drugs, eyeglasses; and most important perhaps, contributions toward a marriage, a birth, a baptism, the schooling of a child, or the burial of a family member. These relationships to patrons are based on a kind of bartering for existence. Hence, to say that one's boss is good because she paid for the burial of one's (sick and hungry) children can be understood as a straightforward, rather than an ironic or critical, comment.

The relationship between a *senhor de engenho* or a *dona da casa* (head of a large, wealthy household) and a poor worker sets into motion a series of mutual responsibilities, debts, and dependencies concerning the "person" of each: patron and protégée. Nothing is less "simple" than the hiring of a temporary cane cutter, a woman to clear *mata*, a cook, a washerwoman, a driver, a gardener, or a *babá* (nursemaid). The implicit rules of the contract obligate the *dono* to a considerable responsibility toward the life of that worker *and* his or her dependents. The wages delivered to the worker may be a pittance, but the *patrão*'s obligations do not end there. If the client is reduced, by the terms of her labor, to an unremitting vulnerability and to a clutching dependency upon her *patroa*, the boss, on her part, is morally bound to rescue her client from starvation, sickness, prison, and other chronic troubles associated with destitution. This is a vicious cycle and a relationship in which both parties can feel themselves ill-served and exploited, for what is being hidden in this "bad faith" economy (Bourdieu 1977:176) is the true nature of the relations governing the transactions, where desperation can be called loyalty and exploitation can masquerade as care and nurturance. Francisco Julião referred to this particular charade as the "cunning" of the *patrão*, the *fazendeiro*, and the *latifundista*. Julião told the rural workers to beware of the patron's false benevolence, the proverbial wolf in sheep's clothing: "[He will enter] your home as tame as a lamb. With claws concealed. With poison kept under wraps. His cunning consists in offering you a flask of medicine and the jeep to take your wife to the hospital, or lending you a little money. . . . It is only to catch you unaware" (1964b:47).

Let us now look back in on the discredited widow, Maria José, whose household is at the present moment in considerable disarray. Her partly reconstructed mud-walled hut lacks a door and windows, and the smoke building up from her charcoal and twig fire is suffocating. Her little foster son is sitting nude in mud, playing with a squawking chicken whose foot is tied to a rope attached to a shaky table leg. The young widow is savagely combing (although perhaps "pulling" is a better word) large knots from her matted, bushy hair. She is rushed and irritable, explaining to me that she is "adjusting herself" in preparation for talking to a future *patrão*. She goes through the heap of dirty, ragged clothing in a corner of the hut, and she pulls out a halfway presentable cotton skirt and a tight blouse, wrinkled and none too clean but showing off to advantage her still attractive figure. She splashes cheap cologne on her neck, arms, and legs and skillfully applies lipstick without a mirror. "Where are you off to?" I ask.

Maria points to distant green hills to the west of town. "Engenho Votas," she replies. It is a good ninety-minute trek each way.

"What will you do with the children?"

"They're safe enough here." If she is successful in getting a short-term contract to clear fields in Votas, it is likely that her seven-year-old daughter will be kept out of school to "keep house" in her mother's place.

"Are you meeting with the owner of the Votas?"

"No, just with his field boss," she replies.

With the care she takes, it almost seems as if Maria is going off to meet a lover, but another agenda is at work. "People say that God will punish me for wearing bright colors [i.e., as a recent widow], but I have to look nice to get a job," she explains. Single women, abandoned or widowed, are, as we have seen, a recent entry into the rural labor force on the plantations of the *mata—norte*, and the field crew managers are reluctant to hire them. They are not considered reliable or dependable workers. Often they are not strong and cannot do the work assigned them in the allotted time. Not infrequently they are concealing a pregnancy, and on occasion there are miscarriages or messy abortions in the fields. (Maria once had to deliver herself of a stillborn child while clearing a field on a plantation to the north.) Women take time off, without notice, to care for sick children or to bury dead ones. Maria's care with her appearance is designed, then, not so much to signal sexual allure but rather to show the crew boss that she is still young and strong; and her revealing, tight blouse, tucked neatly into her waistband, is to demonstrate that she is not pregnant, or not noticeably so. Maria remarks that she is thankful that women field workers do not have to produce medical documentation of sterilization, as is now required by the managers of female workers in the local textile and shoe factories of Bom Jesus.

Nonetheless, as survival strategists, women like Maria exercise one power: to walk off a job or away from a *patrão* who does not please them and in so doing to generate a critique that erodes the social standing of that particular employer as a *bom patrão* (see Forman 1975:76–83). A *patrão* without honor, no matter how wealthy, loses face, charisma, and authority in the local community.

Good Boss / Bad Boss

The life and work histories of the people of the Alto are strewn with references to their "good" and "bad" bosses. These references make up a key theme in a kind of Alto morality tale, one pointing to the tensions between the ethos of *casa, rua,* and *mata* and the underlying dynamic of class conflict. The narratives of Alto women resonate with accusations of injustice at the hands of their bad *patroas* and with praise for rescue and redemption at the hands of their good ones. The *bom patrão* is represented as a nurturant protector, as the good parent in this familistic, patriarchal world.[4]

Black Irene complains, for example, that she has been "bound" almost like a slave to her *patroa* Carminha ever since Irene's mother sent her from the *mata* at the age of nine to live and work as a domestic in exchange for her keep and ten "old cruzeiros" (i.e., a few pennies) a week. Although Irene worked as an unpaid apprentice in the home of Carminha, she was allowed, indeed even encouraged, to attend night school for five years, and she is one of the few semiliterate women of the Alto. Consequently, she is highly respected among her peers. There were a number of "in-between" months when Irene left Carminha's household to work in the fields clearing mata and working in her mother's rented *sítio*. At the age of fourteen Irene left Bom Jesus for Recife, where she spent ten years working as an *empregada* (maid) for a more humane *patroa*, a good boss. When Irene met a decent young man in the city, she asked her boss, following custom, for permission to marry. Her *patroa* agreed and even sponsored the wedding festivities, but when Irene left her husband soon after the birth of a son, the patron was angry and fired her. Irene was then forced to return to Bom Jesus, and lacking other alternatives, she went back to work in the house of Dona Carminha.

"Was anything good about this arrangement?"

"Yes," replies Irene, "she gave me food and fresh milk for my infant son. She was like a *madrinha* [godmother] to him."

"What was bad?"

"That I earned nothing. Today it's not too different. I wash, dry, starch, and iron her clothes for only fifty cruzados a week [in 1987 the equivalent of about one dollar for a full week's wash]. There were times during these past forty years of working for Carminha that I have experienced great misery, and I would write her a note asking for her help, but the notes would remain unopened on her bureau. 'If your message is about money,' she would say later, 'I'm not interested.' Is a *patroa* like that worth anything?"

Irene now has six adult children still living at home in addition to the two godchildren whom she is rearing. Her husband was shot by a neighbor in 1986, and a year later her favorite son De was "disappeared" before her eyes and later found slain and mutilated in a cane field (see chapter 6). During these hard times Irene felt particularly abandoned. Sometimes she was hungry, but her pride and resentment prevented her from eating the solitary meal that her *patroa* would leave out for her on a tin plate. Irene felt that Carminha should have provided food for her children and grandchildren as well: "I have no courage to eat, to fill my own belly when I know my children are at home hungry." But the expected *feira* basket was never forthcoming.

"Did you ever let Dona Carminha know how you felt?"

"Only once. It was after she had cut my wage to twenty cruzados for a week's wash and I complained, and my *patroa* said that this was already more than I deserved. So I didn't wash her clothes for a year after that. But necessity has driven me back to her, and I fear that I will never see the end of this bad boss. I will wash her clothes until I keel over at the margins of the river."

Of all the many bad boss stories I heard, perhaps none captures the conflict between the *moradores*' ethic of sharing and the *casa grande*'s ethic of consuming more directly than Lordes's tale, stimulated by her husband's memory of the day their son's arm was broken. Although he had worked more than twenty-five years as a servant and a construction worker for the *município*, Dejalmer was reduced to begging on his knees in front of Seu Félix to get an order for the municipal ambulance to carry the boy to a "decent" hospital in Recife. Dejalmer asked rhetorically, "Why should we be made to beg for what is our right?" And then Lordes began her story.

"I worked for Dona Rita [the wealthy wife of a local *fazendeiro*] for three years and six months, and in all that time she offered me a meal only five times. I would arrive at her house at daybreak, often with an empty stomach, and I would have to clean up the last day's dirty dishes before I could even begin my own chore of washing clothes. There would be piles of dirty clothes, organdy dresses her daughters had worn for only a few minutes mixed together with mud-caked jeans from the *fazenda*, and school clothes from the [college-age] children living in Recife. There would be no end to the dirty clothes. I would scrub until my knuckles bled, and all the time I wouldn't be offered so much as a piece of dry bread or a cup of black coffee. My pay in those days was twenty-five mil reis [and she laughs at the absurdity], but I never even got all of it at once. Always there would be something owing, 'toward next week.' I think now that this is how she kept me coming back! After three years of working myself like this, I began to cough and vomit blood.

"Dona Rita caught me spitting blood in the *quintal* [backyard], and she ordered me out of the household immediately. She said, 'Get away from us. You are contagious with tuberculosis.' I replied, 'I'll leave your service and gladly, Dona Rita, but you should know that if I am coughing up blood, it's because I've been made to work all these years on an empty stomach.'"

And so Lordes left that household but soon took up a position with the adult daughter of Dona Rita, where she fared no better. The structural and psychological hold of patron-client relations is such that a break with a particularly bad boss often leaves the client stranded so that she is virtually forced to take up where she left off, sometimes (as in this instance) going to work for another member of the same family. In addition, there is the "lure" of even marginal involvement in the lives of the wealthy. The rise and fall of fortunes in the *patroa's* extended household and family often provide the "high drama" missing in one's own seemingly impoverished and lackluster life. These affective ties and points of reference and identification are difficult to sever. But at the end of the following "morality tale," for once Lordes is vindicated and her bad *patroa* is punished and humiliated.

"After Dona Rita I went to work in the house of her daughter, Dona Fátima, and her husband, Seu Teto [one of the largest *fazendeiros* in the *município*]. Whenever Seu Teto would leave the house for the day, he would give his wife orders for what meats were to be prepared for dinner. One day he told Fátima to have three large chickens killed and to divide the innards between the *empregada* and me. The liver, the heart, the tripe, the head, and the feet were to be our share. When my service was done and I was about to leave for home, the maid [who was Lordes's friend] asked Fátima for my share of the chicken parts, but Fátima said, 'No, I've decided to toast those innards for our dinner tonight. Go and start the charcoal.' You see, Fátima was even too cheap to use the gas stove. The maid did as she was told, but she knew there was an injustice done.

"When Seu Teto came home, my friend told him straight off what had happened, and Seu Teto exploded and said to his wife, 'Stop being a cheapskate in my house. You are to do what I say. I'm the one who brings the meat into this house, and I'm the one who will decide how it is to be used.' But it didn't help because of the way that Fátima had been raised: she knew only how to be stingy.

"One day a sugar harvester ploughed into a cow on Seu Teto's lands, and he ordered the carcass to be carried home, butchered, and divided into shares. There was going to be so much for Seu Teto's parents and his brothers and sisters, and so much for Dona Rita and Seu Antônio, and some for the local hospital to feed the charity cases. But before Seu Teto went back to work, he told Dona Fátima to make sure to reserve a package of beef for me. Fátima agreed, but once again when the time came for me to leave, it was my friend, the maid, who had to stand up for me and ask for my share. I was such a *matuta* in those days, I could never speak up for myself! But that maid, she was little but tough! Fátima replied that there was no meat left to share, but the maid said, 'How can you say that when there's so much meat packed into the refrigerator that it will spoil if we don't give it away?' But Fátima still wouldn't give in, so that the maid had to make me a package in secret, and I left happily enough with it!

"When Seu Teto came home that night and the maid told him that Fátima had again refused to share any of the beef with me, he really blew his stack. He grabbed Fátima by the shoulder and shook her like a three-year-old, saying, 'Didn't I tell you that I'm the one who runs this place? Why didn't you give the washerwoman her share?' Fátima began to cry, and she begged her husband to lower his voice, which was carrying into the street outside, but the more she pleaded with him, the louder he yelled. In the midst of all this confusion Fátima's mother and father arrived. Seu Teto stopped screaming, and Dona Rita told her daughter that her husband was right and that as long as she was living in *his* household, she had to follow her husband's orders. But in the kitchen we all agreed that Fátima had learned her mean ways from her own mother and that it was probably too late to change her."

I asked Lordes if she ever had had a *boa patroa*, and she answered immediately. "Oh yes, there was Dona Júlia. She was like a mother to me: she took care of me, gave me good clothes to wear, sheets for my beds, and cloth so I could make school clothes for my children. She once even gave me three new straw mattresses so we could all have something to sleep on. But I had to sell them. At the end of every week she would send me home with a big basket of food—beans, macaroni, *farinha*, rice. I remember one day when she brought me into the kitchen and she said, 'Look, I've got three whole chickens. I want you to pick out and take home the biggest and the fattest and leave me the other two.'

"When I would get sick, Dona Júlia would always insist that I stop working and go right to the clinic, and she would buy all the medicines for me. Sometimes I would go to see the doctor, but I would be ashamed to run up my *patroa*'s account at the pharmacy. But she would catch me and ask, 'Did you buy the medicine?' and I would reply, 'How can I? I'm too ashamed to do that. You have already spent so much on me, and I'm still not well enough to go back to work for you.' Then she would go right out herself and buy me the medicine.

"Mind you, this *patroa* of mine wasn't a grand lady; she wasn't even rich. She was from a small business family, not a rich *fazendeiro* family. And yet she knew how to treat her help like *gente*. Dona Júlia was the only boss I ever had who insisted that I bring my children to work with me, even the babies. She would say, 'Hang him up in his little hammock next to your wash where he'll be safe.' Most *patroas* want us to leave the children at home locked up in the house where they can burn to death while we are out working in their fields or in their kitchens working and worried to death. But Dona Júlia would say that crying babies bring *alegria* [happiness] into a home. Now she was a *boa patroa, mesmo.*"

But a *boa patroa* is hard to find, and most patron-client relations in Bom Jesus are tinged with resentment, disappointment, disillusionment, and bitterness. These sentiments are dynamic aspects of all relations built on mutual dependencies and entitlements (see Memmi 1984). In Bom Jesus the rich and poor eye each other with longing, as potential sources of material and psychological gratification, and with suspicion and mistrust. In the eyes of the *patroa*, the dependent always demands, always asks for too much. From the point of view of the dependent, the benefactor is almost never generous enough, has never provided sufficient help, moral support, material goods, or protection. Each class behaves, in its own realm, as a group to whom things are entitled: service, homage, loyalty, on the one hand, and the basic necessities of life, on the other. Each can appear insatiable to the other.

Dona Emília, the now deceased wife of the *prefeito*, who was known widely throughout the region as a *boa patroa*, often expressed in private her doubts about the rural tradition of *paternalismo* that brought a long line of petitioners to her courtyard every day: "I wonder whether all this charity is worth anything? The more I distribute, the more the people return. There is no end to the requests. They ask me for everything under the sun! But there is only so much I can do, and it is so tiresome." Yet a gracious noblesse oblige prevented this grand woman from publicly showing her annoyance and displeasure, so that virtually to the eve of her death she could be seen seated in her rocking chair behind the gate of her garden, in full view of the people of the *rua* to whom she would attend one by one with courtesy and a soft-spoken gentility. Consequently, since her death, Dona Emília's image has gone up on the walls of many of the *moradores'* huts, joining the likes of other "great patrons" of the region such as Padre Cícero and Frei Damião.

The Catholic church also participates in the ethic of paternalist dependencies that so characterizes class relations in the region. And so for the past three decades Madre Elfriede, the founder of the German Colégio, has likewise held "open court" to the poor of the hillside shantytowns of Bom Jesus, to whom she distributes food baskets, powdered milk, medications, small amounts of cash, various favors, and a good deal of advice.

Madre Elfriede, despite almost a half century of living in the community, has been miraculously preserved from any political education, and she remains utterly confused and naive about the sources and causes of poverty in the plantation zone. She does not understand where "all these poor" come from or why they are so poor, although she accepts that ministering to their spiritual (and material) needs is part of her Christian duty. She is frustrated by the poor's sense of entitlement, their expectation of perpetual help, their failure to somehow "bootstrap" themselves out of their misery, and their refusal to take command of their lives. When annoyed by an "inappropriate" request, Madre Elfriede has been known to call the women (less often the men) who approach the huge locked gate that separates the *rua* from the cloister "common beggars," and she sometimes sends home a petitioner with the stinging reprimand "Where is your pride?" Forty-five years in Northeast Brazil have had no effect on the Germanic cast of Madre Elfriede's character. For their part, the poor of Bom Jesus defend their petitioning behavior as righteous in light of their destitution. One woman, turned away by Madre Elfriede, remarked, "Begging is ugly, and no one would do it unless they were forced to do it."

One evening I met Biu (Lordes and Antonieta's half-sister) walking the *rua* late at night looking for her children, whom she had sent out earlier in the day to get help to purchase medication for her desperately sick baby from her various patrons in the town. When they didn't come home to eat supper, she became distraught, worried that some harm might have come to one or the other. There was a rumor circulating among the *moradores* that men in station wagons were kidnapping poor children to sell to medical schools in Recife. "Now we have this new thing to worry about; not even our children's insides are safe from vultures." And she continued her nervous soliloquy:

"I know I should keep my daughters safely locked in at home. But what

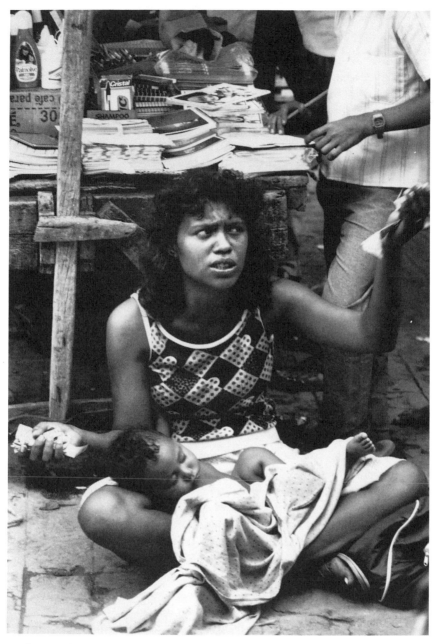

"Shame is for those who steal, not for those who have to beg to feed their children, Nancí."

can I do? I have to send them out in times of sickness or emergency. You are a mother yourself. Could you stand by and watch your baby burning with fever and do nothing about it? I *hate* this begging for money, for medicines, for food, this scavenging everywhere for tiny handouts so that I can somehow embroider one day to the next. I am a *mulher trabalhadora;* I've worked all my life. There's practically no job I can't do. I've worked in the fields, in the river, in the factories, in the *feira.* I do whatever is necessary. Do you think I *like* asking for money? You who have half a conscience for the misery of the poor, tell me, Nancí, *what else* am I supposed to do?"

Sweet Charity: Child Saving from Mata to Casa

A good boss is described by these women as a man who is "like a father" or a woman who is "like a mother" to them. This notion goes back to the earliest days of the large, extended families (the *parentela*) of the sugar plantations, where house slaves or servants were on occasion treated like family members by their master and mistress. Children born of unions between slaves and their masters were sometimes reared within the bosom of the *casa grande* in the status of *filhos de criação.* But unlike the pattern of fosterage in the families of the *moradores* described previously, foster children reared in the *casa grande* occupied a liminal status somewhere between that of slave and free servant but certainly not equal to their legitimate and white half-brothers and half-sisters. Similarly today, the "charity" that motivates the fosterage of poor children by the wealthy families of Bom Jesus contrasts sharply with the fosterage practiced among the *moradores* of the Alto do Cruzeiro.

Of twenty-three wealthy and middle-class households surveyed in 1987 (and these were drawn from the membership roster of an elite social club in Bom Jesus), eight of the adult women, *donas da casa,* had at one time taken in a *filho de criação,* often a child rescued from dire poverty, need, and neglect. This "Christian practice," as it was described in reverential tones by well-to-do women of Bom Jesus, demonstrates the sharp contours of semifeudal class distinctions in the plantation zone of Pernambuco today. Felipa, the wife of José Costa, a wealthy Bom Jesus businessman, is a devoutly Catholic mother of three children. She explained how it happened that at the age of thirty-seven (she was forty-one at the time), she came to rear and foster (but not adopt) an unwanted child, Maria Erva da Santa.

Leaning back on a comfortable cushion and lighting up a cigarette, Felipa settled into her story, which took the better part of a morning. It was a middle-class morality tale in which the virtues of charity, responsibility, and discipline were emphasized. There was also a magical aura surrounding the events narrated and a sense of personal destiny.

"It began in a strange way," Felipa explained. "When my first child was born, I dedicated her to Saint Francis, the saint of poverty, and I believe this marked her. I taught her to pray as soon as she could speak. Every night before bed I would ask her whom she wanted to remember in her prayers, and she would always say, 'Mama, Papa, Grandma, and Grandpa.' But one day she added something new. She said, 'My mother, I want to pray for the children of the *rua* who live begging *esmolas* [alms].' And so began her custom of asking Jesus to look after the little children who had no home, no clothing, no food to eat. When she got older, she would always ask me to give change to the beggar children, and when they came to our door, she would never let them leave empty-handed.

"When the second and third children came along, she taught them to pray for the abandoned children of the street. Soon it became a family custom. Still, I never thought in those early years that I would come to rear one of them myself. I never *looked* to foster a child. It just happened to me.

"My husband was working in a branch office of his business in Aliança [a small town near Bom Jesus], and during this period I had my hands full and I needed an extra maid. I asked José Costa [it is customary for middle-class women to refer to their husbands by their full names] to find me a young girl from the rural area near Aliança. And so he drove to a villa during his lunch hour, and he knocked on the door of a woman to whom he had been referred. The woman was black, black, and her house was filled with black children. The woman was sick with a tumor in her belly, and she was crazy to get rid of one of the children, a six-year-old niece whom she had been raising since the death of her sister. The woman pleaded with my José, saying, 'I have too many children of my own. I can't raise this little pickaninny, too, and if you don't take her from me, I am going to have to go out into the fields and give her to anyone who will take her off my hands.'

" 'Well, let me see the child,' José Costa said doubtfully. He was surprised when the little girl was called into the front room because she was so fair, white like flour, and delicate, although she was filthy, ill-kept, and skinny. She looked like *gente* [i.e., meaning in this instance white, like one of the rich]. He asked her her name and if she was happy living there. The child shook her head.

" 'Take her,' the old *preta* urged José Costa.

" 'No, I can't. I'm looking for an older child to help my wife in the house. She's much too little and too young.'

"And so he left the house just as the woman was calling all the children to the table. There were only black beans and *farinha* to eat and little enough of these. José Costa had turned on the motor of the car, and he was about to drive away when he was struck by a Divine message. It was a *toco interior* [kind of inspiration]. He thought about the misery of that table and of the abundance of our own. He was paralyzed. Then he turned off the motor and let his feet carry him back inside the poor hovel. He asked the woman to give him the girl's birth registration papers, and he asked Erva if she would come with him. She nodded her head and in a few minutes was ready with a paper sack containing all her possessions: two torn and dirty dresses, a broken comb, and a worn, plastic pacifier.

"Zé Costa left her in the car while he came inside to break the news to me. I was totally unprepared; it came as a great shock to me. I said, 'Bring her in and let me have a look at her.' As soon as I saw how *white* she was, I thought to myself, 'This is a mean trick. Here is the daughter of Zé Costa by some woman he arranged for himself in the rural zone, and now he's trying to trick me into raising his bastard child. But he swore to me that his story was true, and after I questioned the child alone, I believed him.

"I resolved to keep her. But I made it clear to the child right away that I was not, and would never be, her mother. I said that I would be like a 'fairy godmother' to her, that I was the luck that God had decided to give her in her life. I told her that until she grew up and was on her own, we would provide for all her necessities. She would never go to bed hungry as long as she lived with us.

"I needed some orientation about my new duties so I went right away to Monsenhor Marcos [the parish priest]. I was still in doubt and I needed his counsel. The old monsenhor said that I should accept the child and that I should not fly in the face of what was undoubtedly God's plan for her. But, he warned, 'Raise her with caution and with distance. Keep her away from the true children of the family. Do not let her think that she is family. Never let her forget where she came from, and never be deceived into thinking that she can escape her blood and her history completely. Give her things very slowly, little by little, because people of her kind are opportunistic. They live only for the moment; they do not know the value of things. They are wanton and destructive.' The monsenhor told me to watch for signs of laziness in the child because *preguiça* is in the breed, the *gemo*, of these rural people. Padre Marcos gave me excellent orientation. Above all, he warned me not to let Erva completely 'penetrate' our family life. If the family was talking about a topic of importance, she should have respect and move apart from the discussion; she should not be allowed to think of herself as a true child of the family.

"My immediate responsibility, however, was to see that her physical, medical, and spiritual needs were cared for. Beyond that I wanted her to receive some education. The most immediate problem was her health and her physical being. When she arrived, she was quite repulsive. She was crawling with vermin; she had lice hopping off her head. Worst of all were the pinworms. She was tortured with itching and scratching every part of her body. When I took her outside with the maid to wash her off, we saw the pinworms exiting her rectum, taking flight up her buttocks and all the way up her back. They made it up this far [she points to just under the shoulder blades].

"I brought Erva to the home of my husband's *compadre*, who is a skin doctor. He told me to bring her over immediately if I didn't want my children infected with her diseases. He was shocked at the girl's condition, saying, 'Minha Nossa Senhora, I have never seen a child with so many worms and parasites!' He gave me a whole sack of medicines, saying, 'Let's just dose her one time with everything. Later we can do the feces exams and treat what's left over.'

"Within a month she was a different child. Let me show you the pictures of her before and after. Isn't that a radical transformation? She is a different child altogether. Well, not *altogether* because some things haven't changed. Until today she still carries the mark, the interior mark, of her history [her genetic and life histories]. Oh, how can I explain it? She's an odd child. She is very quiet, she hardly speaks at all, and she doesn't pay attention to things. She seems to live in a world all her own. I sometimes think that she is happiest of all when she is out in the garden taking care of the plants and flowers. One of her jobs is to help the boy who does our gardening. She takes twice the time her task should take because she's always talking to herself and humming; she even talks to the plants!

"I fear that Monsenhor Marcos was right and that she is lazy. No matter how patiently I instruct her in her duties, she rarely finishes a task. She will do half of what I or the maid or cook or the *babá* ask her to do. She's lacking in discipline. I have a little bell just for her; it's her own signal. I don't want to have to be yelling all over the house when I want her. But even after all this time she hasn't learned to respond to it.

"And there are other 'marks' as well. When she arrived, she was like an animal. At first I put her to sleep with the maid so she wouldn't feel lonely. But Dora yelled at me the next morning. She said that she couldn't sleep because of the stench coming from Erva's bed; she had urinated and defecated all over herself. We had to train her to use the toilet, and still some nights she forgets. And to this day Erva hides things all over the house. At first it was just little bits of food—bread, bananas, pieces of dried meat. I'd say to her, 'Erva, you don't have to hide food. This house is never lacking in fruits and sweets; you are allowed to eat as much as you want.' But that created another problem: Erva stuffs herself. Many times she eats so much that she cries from a stomachache afterward. Then there were other things that she would hide. Once all our medicines disappeared from the bathroom cabinet. Erva was responsible for cleaning the bathroom, but she refused to say where the medicines had gone. Later I found them myself, tucked behind the bidet!

"Sometimes I worry about her 'senses.' I wonder, Who *is* this strange creature that God brought to our door? Just the other night I told her, 'Erva, call all the people in to eat dinner.' We have *so many* mouths to feed—there's the maid, the old cook, the gardener, the washerwoman, the *babá,* and Erva [the household help eats apart from the family]. And do you know what she did? She opened the front gates and started to call in the people from the street! Before I could stop her, several street children were inside our garden! I reprimanded her: 'Senseless girl, what could you have been thinking? I meant all the people of the *casa,* not the people of the *rua!*'"

At this point in the narration I interrupted to ask if Erva was a foster child, really, or if she wasn't simply another sort of indentured servant. I realized that this was a rude question, breaking into the fantasy of mythical apparition and rescue that was being spun before my eyes, but Felipa accepted the challenge.

"For me, this child is a mission in life. I have not made her into a slave the way some of the wealthy treat their foster children or the way our grandmothers and great-grandmothers treated their adoptive children. In the days of the old *engenhos* almost every family had *filhos de criação* and not one or two but many of them. And they *were* slaves, really, until they had the sense to run away at thirteen or fourteen. My own mother kept a black girl as a kind of slave, and when my mother died, I inherited her as a middle-aged woman, a childlike adult who had never married and didn't know anything other than taking care of my mother! It was a burden, but I kept her until she died."

"What is the work that Erva is required to do?"

"When she gets up, she sets the table for breakfast. Then she eats with the other household workers. After that she goes out to clean the garden, her favorite job. When the *lavadeira* arrives around 10 A.M., Erva's job is to separate and sort all the clothes for washing. Later she helps to iron and fold them, and then she must put them away in their closets and bureaus. The organization of the closets and bureaus is her most important task. Then she has other duties: she helps the maid with the housecleaning and the dusting. After lunch she goes to school for a few hours, but she is not a very good scholar. When she comes home she has the evening coffee to prepare and her homework to do. Often she falls asleep over her books. I fear she has no head for studies."

"What is the mission of which you speak?"

"My mission with Erva is to secure her some kind of future. I want her to have a vocation in life. But so far her future remains a worry. I can't hand her her future the way that I can arrange the futures of my own children. I am not pretending that Erva is an adopted child. She is not. She does not carry the family name. Her name is simply Maria Erva da Santa. But when she leaves us, I want to feel that her life is made for her. I don't know if she has the aptitude to be a trusted person in domestic service. I don't know if I could recommend her to other families. But she may have a vocation for the kitchen; she's a marvel at baking cakes and making ices and ice creams. Perhaps she will marry and be a *dona da casa* herself! She has learned what a household is and what is required to keep it running. She knows about hygiene and cleanliness, and she knows that people must be fed three times a day, plus a midmorning and midafternoon snack.

"She doesn't have a lot, but she has two things in her favor. Erva is a *menina de sorte* [lucky child], and she has a strong patron saint. Since Erva arrived in October, the month of the rosary, I offered her to the protection of Our Lady of the Rosary, a powerful patron saint. This is the only inheritance I could give her, this and the fact that I fought to keep her out of the hands of her crazy old aunt, who came back to get her this year so that she could be 'sold' to a house of prostitution in the rural *zona!* I went to the judge, and we wrote up official 'donation papers' certifying that her aunt had freely given Erva to me with no strings attached. Erva may not be a true child of the family, but I will be responsible for her until she marries or leaves the home.

"Yes," Felipa concluded, "this child is my mission in life. I think there should be a campaign in Bom Jesus so that every wealthy family adopts one poor, unwanted, and neglected child. Every home, one foster child [*cada casa uma cria*]. I have already interested several women of good families in this neighborhood. Perhaps you could put us in touch with 'worthy cases' from the Alto do Cruzeiro."

The Addiction of Dependency

Casa, rua, and *mata* exist, then, as a dynamic tension that locks the social classes into a ruse, a travesty of interaction in which exploitation parades as benevolence and passive aggression masquerades as fawning dependency. The rural workers' discourse on their good and bad bosses offers a key to understanding the tenacity and resilience of *paternalismo* in Bom Jesus da Mata. The bad boss is no threat to the system, for he serves as a safe and contained internal critique. The *mau patrão* is individualized and cordoned off. He becomes the scapegoat of the system, subject to vicious ridicule and to occasional public shaming (as in the case of Dona Fátima). That the bad boss is said to have violated the trust between patron and client assumes that such a trust exists as the norm from which the bad boss has deviated. The bad boss can be treated as an aberration rather than as a manifestation, the true flowering of the logic and violence of *paternalismo*. The good boss, for her part, helps to smooth over, conceal, and sometimes resolve the contradictions inherent in the perverse relations of power and dominance.

The sharp lines that Lordes draws between her (mis)treatment at the hands of Dona Fátima (her bad boss) and her nurturance at the hands of Dona Júlia (her good boss) is reminiscent of Charles Dickens's juxtaposition of Scrooge and Fezziwig, a literary version of the bad boss/good boss scenario, in his allegory on late nineteenth-century capitalism in England, *A Christmas Carol*. Both Lordes and Dickens seem to imply that the relations between boss and client (under feudal or capitalist terms, as the case may be) can be rescued and reconstituted in a more humane fashion. But it is the Júlias and the Fezziwigs, not the Fátimas and Scrooges, who pose the greatest threat to the dependents' autonomy. The "good boss" in a "bad faith" economy rescues not only the exploited worker but also the exploitative and colonizing social system itself. And so the hungry and anxious worker can rest her weary head in the comforting space between the ample breasts of her *patroa*, fitting herself snugly like a revolver in its velvet-lined case. The smoking gun is silenced as the *moradores* rein in their own natural aggressivity toward those who have always compromised their humanity. The *moradores* have fallen into the great quagmire of gratitude toward their "benevolent" masters.

The lines drawn between dominator and dominated, master and servant, gradually become fuzzy as each comes to assume the attributes of the other. Domination is itself a form of dependency, and dependency is like nothing more than a drug or an addiction. The situation of the dependent worker locked into an intimate and personal relationship with a *patrão* is reminiscent of a parable told by Italian psychiatrist Franco Basaglia. It bears repeating here.

> An Asian fable tells of a serpent that crawled into the mouth of a sleeping man. It slid down into his stomach and settled there, imposing its will on him and depriving him of his freedom. The man now lived at the mercy of the serpent and he no longer belonged to himself. One day the serpent finally left; but the man no longer knew what to do with his freedom. During the long period of domination the man became so used to submitting his will to the serpent, all his wishes and impulses, that he lost the capacity to wish, to strive, or to act autonomously. Instead of freedom he found only the emptiness of the void, for the serpent had taken with it the man's new essence, which was acquired during the period of his captivity.

The man was left with the task of reclaiming, little by little, the former human content of his life. (Scheper-Hughes & Lovell 1987:85)

The people of the Alto have fallen prey to the serpent, hypnotized by its seductive dance of promised gratification. Albert Memmi, like Basaglia, refers to dependency as a form of possession, a "hypnosis" (1984:141) for which only an "exorcism" may be capable of liberating the dependent from the mesmerizing trance under which she has fallen.

4 Delírio de Fome
The Madness of Hunger

When I am hungry I want to eat one politician, hang another,
and burn a third.

Carolina Maria de Jesus

During the summer of the 1965 drought I was drawn one day by curiosity
to the jail cell of a young woman from an outlying rural area who had just
been apprehended for the murder of her infant son and her one-year-old
daughter. The infant had been smothered, and the little girl had been hacked
with a machete. Rosa, the mother, became for a brief period a central
attraction in Bom Jesus, as both rich and poor passed by her barred window,
which opened to a side street, to rain down invectives on her head: "Animal," she was called, "unnatural creature," "shameless woman." Face to face
with the withdrawn and timid slip of a girl (she seemed barely a teenager), I
made myself bold enough to ask the obvious: "Why did you do it?" She
replied as she must have for the hundredth time, "To stop them from crying
for milk." After a pause she added (in her own defense), "*Bichinhos não
sentem nada*"—"Little critters have no feelings."

When I related the story later that day to Nailza de Arruda, with whom I
was then sharing a tiny, mud-walled hut on the steep cliff path called the
Segunda Travessa de Bernardo Viera on the Alto do Cruzeiro, Nailza shook
her head and commented sadly, "It was the *delírio* [madness] of hunger." She
had seen many good people commit acts, for which they would later repent,
when driven to the brink by hunger madness. I remembered her words but
at the time considered them another example of the *Nordestino* imagination—vivid, dramatic, extravagant. Like the others who congregated to
taunt Rosa, I, too, felt that she was something of an "unnatural creature,"
rather than a creature of "nature." I soon had to reconsider.

Early one afternoon while Nailza, Zé Antônio, and I were still resting to
escape the inferno of midday, there was an impertinent knock on the door.
Thinking that it must be something quite serious, I pulled myself out of the
hammock and opened the upper half of the split door that opened into the

128

street. A small woman, whose expressionless face I did not immediately recognize, stood there with a small bundle in her arms that I knew at once to be a sick child. Before I could close the door with a stinging reprimand to come back at a more convenient hour, the woman had already unwrapped the clean sugar sacking to show a child of perhaps a year or so (it was often difficult to know) whose limbs were wasted, leaving what seemed a large head attached to sticks; a veritable, living stick figure. He was alive but very still, and he stared, I recall, intently and unblinkingly. He also had a full set of teeth, which was unexpected in one so malnourished.

Seeing that the child's condition was precarious, I rushed him to the local hospital of Bom Jesus, leaving his mother behind with Nailza for company. As a *visitadora*, I had the right to intern children such as these, but Dr. Tito frowned his disapproval. "It's too late for this one," he said, leaving me with an untrained practical nurse as together the two of us tried to find a usable vein in which to insert an intravenous tube. The once passive child threw its remaining energy into a fight against the tube, a reasonable enough response in a terrified and sick-to-death child. But the fight was just the beginning of an hour-long "delirium" during which the child went rigid, seemed to buckle, and then finally became wild, growling and snapping at our ministering hands until, thankfully, he died. I had not until then seen anything quite, as Brazilians would say, so "ugly" in my life. The cause of death penciled into the head nurse's copybook, the only record of hospitalized cases, read, "Malnutrition, third degree; acute dehydration." I was tempted to add *delírio de fome*—the madness of hunger.

I had occasion to witness other deaths like this over the years of my involvement with the people of the Alto do Cruzeiro, and they are not pretty. Sometimes, following death from hunger madness, the face becomes fixed in a terrible grimace, the *agonia da morte*. The people of Bom Jesus refer to deaths from malnutrition-dehydration (especially child deaths) with the very stigmatizing term, *doença de cão*, the "dog's disease."[1] They are referring to the similarities with death from rabies, which the people call *raiva*, rage, fury, madness. The madness—the *delírio*—of hunger is indeed very much like rabies, and death from hunger is indeed a dog's death.

The Taboo Against Hunger

The phenomenology of hunger in the Northeast must form the backdrop of any discussion of child death, mother love, the economy of sex, and the ecology of households. When Josué de Castro first published his classic book, *The Geography of Hunger*, he framed his discussion of worldwide patterns of starvation and undernutrition as the breaking of a long-standing and implicit scientific taboo. Hunger, he wrote, was a well-kept secret about modern human existence, so that of all the calamities "that have repeatedly devastated the world . . . it is hunger which is the least studied and discussed, least understood in its causes and effects" (1952:5). In short, hunger was a base and vulgar instinct from which science had averted its gaze. But even as the Brazilian nutritionist was writing these lines (and in the delay before its appearance in an English-language edition), they were already negated in the flood of biomedical and clinical studies that appeared in the wake of World War II. These were fueled by an almost obsessive need to document in minute detail, to quantify, every physical and psychological horror suffered by those interned in German concentration camps, abandoned in the Warsaw ghetto, and victimized by the famine that struck Holland in 1945.[2] Of these, perhaps the most detailed scientific examination of the effects of starvation on body and mind was the experimental study initiated in 1944 by Ancel Keys, Josef Brozek, and their colleagues (Brozek 1950; Keys et al. 1950) in the cavernous underworld of the University of Minnesota's Sports Stadium with thirty-two volunteers recruited from alternative-service conscientious objectors. (I refer to the biomedical and clinical findings of this detailed and definitive study on human starvation from time to time.)

What de Castro might have said, but what he failed to note, was that the attention of biomedical scientists to the subject of hunger had to wait until *white* Europeans began to suffer from the same conditions that had long afflicted black and brown peoples in many parts of the globe, including the southern part of the United States (Goldberger & Sydentricker 1944; National Research Council 1943; Hunt, Hunt, & Scheper 1970). The ravaged face of hunger was a shocking novelty to the Allied forces that liberated Bergen-Belsen on April 12, 1945, but it was a common reality during periods of drought and famine in the Brazilian Northeast, where there are, even today, many hunger victims, most of them very young, who die alone, unattended, and *desconhecido*, anonymously.

One might have expected anthropologists to turn their attention to some consideration of hunger in nonwhite and non-Western contexts, but up through the period of de Castro's work only three well-known monographs dealt in any great detail with hunger: two by Audrey Richards (1932, 1939) on the Bantu and Bemba peoples of Rhodesia and Alan Holmberg's (1950) study of hunger anxiety among the Siriono Indians of eastern Bolivia.[3] Yet even these pioneering works in the anthropology of hunger were disappointing. Ultimately, they were more concerned with documenting the social structure of the people studied than with documenting their hunger. During the brief preeminence of culture and personality studies (1940s–1960s), a few psychological anthropologists paid some attention to the experience of hunger, but they focused primarily on adult personality as shaped by the infant's early experiences, including the relative hunger of toddlers recently weaned from the mother's breast (see, for example, DuBois 1941, 1944). But these events had little reference to food scarcity and hunger in the society at large. Dorothy Shack (1969) and William Shack (1971) did, however, explore food scarcity, hunger anxiety, and ritual among the Gurage of Ethiopia.

Since the 1970s hunger and food practices have become a topic of interest to anthropologists, who could be described as falling into two interpretive camps: the bioecological and the symbolic. Among the ecologists, including the cultural materialists, malnutrition and chronic hunger tend to be viewed within a broad framework of biosocial adaptiveness (see Harris 1985; Cassidy 1980, 1982, 1987; Lepowsky 1985). These approaches range from the conventional nutritional anthropological studies of Gretel and Pertti Pelto (1983) and Lawrence Greene (1977), to the more controversial, neo-Malthusian approaches favored by some physical and biosocial anthropologists, including William Stini (1971, 1975). Among the neo-Malthusians, everything from small stature caused by childhood malnutrition (that is, stunted growth) to mortal forms of childhood malnutrition itself may be understood as contributing to a kind of biocultural homeostasis, a long-range evolutionary adaptiveness. William Stini, for example, argued, based on his study of human growth and development in an impoverished Colombian population, that small size, or "stunting," was adaptive there because it allowed a greater number of adults to survive on less food in a context of chronic scarcity of food resources. Claire Cassidy maintained that toddler malnutrition was a biosocially adaptive mechanism for population "pruning." In these studies hunger was recognized, but its brutal effects on particular human lives was subordinated to larger demographic or ecological concerns.

Among social and symbolic anthropologists, owing to the influence of French and British versions of structuralism (see Levi-Strauss 1964, 1965; M. Douglas 1970; Tambiah 1968, 1969), food, food taboos, and hunger tend to be understood as symbolic categories used in organizing social relations, ordering experience, or expressing or mediating contradictions. In this interpretive tradition food is less good to eat than it is "good to think"; it is a language rich in symbolic content. Food (as well as hunger) serves as a medium for complicated social transactions, as individuals and social groups use food to control others, establish and maintain sexual relations, avoid or initiate conflict, or express some aspect of cultural identity. In his elegant interpretation of hunger and social structure among the Trobriand Islanders, Stanley Tambiah (1968), for example, argued for the existence there of a symbolic equivalency between the yam house and the human belly, so that a central Trobriand rite, the *vilalia*, "is really a metaphorical analogy urging the human belly to restrain its hunger and greed for food" (1969:201). This theme was taken up later by Miriam Kahn (1986), who suggested that for the "always hungry" Wamirans of Melanesia, the perpetual famine to which the villagers referred was "metaphorical only," an expression of the universal conflict between individual desires and collective social needs. Among the Wamirans the statement "I am hungry" was to be understood as "I am feeling greedy; I don't want to share what I have." Here "famine" was a representation of the social, and the hunger of which Wamirans complained was metaphoric. In these symbolic studies hunger was sanitized and aestheticized. It was also denied.

The preference of cultural anthropologists for elegant homologies and their turning away, we might say, from the plain facts of hunger as a lived experience that consigns millions of third world people to an early grave are perhaps a manifestation of the "anxious taboo" against the study of hunger to which de Castro alluded. Perhaps hunger *as* hunger—a frightening human affliction—is simply "not good to think" for anthropologists who, if they think of hunger and famine at all, prefer to think of them as symbols and metaphors or as positive contributions to long-term adaption.

Among cultural anthropologists in recent times only Colin Turnbull (1972) gave a vivid and detailed ethnographic account of the collective experience of hunger, but this work has been largely ignored and discredited by his peers.[4] Turnbull studied a small population of hunters and foragers forced to resettle as agriculturalists on a barren wasteland in Uganda. Without the skills, inclination, or ability to cultivate subsistence crops during a drought, the Ik slowly starved to death, and so, too, did their society. Social bonds based on kinship and marriage, cooperation, sharing, and reciprocity went by the wayside as individuals fought for their long survival against all competitors, including their own parents and children. Turnbull concluded, "There is no goodness left for the Ik, only a full stomach, and that only for those whose stomachs are already full. But if there is no goodness, stop to think: there is no badness, and if there is no love, neither is there any hate" (1972:286). And neither is there any guilt or blame. At the end, what drove the Ik was not their culture but rather their human biology, which Turnbull referred to as the "survival machine": "They have not created it [i.e., the survival machine] willingly or consciously; it has created itself through their biological need for survival, out of the only materials available and in the only possible form" (285). Hunger destroyed the Ik as a people, and as a social group, although individual Ik survived. The lesson for Turnbull was the fragility of all social life and social institutions, even that most sacred of all sacred cows, the family. Everything, including notions of goodness and justice, gave way under the threat of starvation: "They had a simple choice of living or dying; they had already lost the rest—family, friendship, hope, love—and they made the same choice that most of us would make" (285).

Turnbull's description of the famished Ik was chilling; to some of his critics it was almost "too bad" to be believed. More than any other ethnographer, Turnbull broke the taboo of silence on hunger, and Turnbull and his book suffered the consequences. It was said that he had exaggerated the situation, that his account could not possibly be true because Africans were well known for their devotion to family and to children, even in the worst circumstances. The book was treated as an embarrassment. Soon it was forgotten, as were the Ik. And yet Turnbull's account of the destruction of Ik society has correlates in other descriptions of people and societies in calamity.

In their research on life in Warsaw and in the hungry Austrian village of Marienthal during the Great Depression, B. Zawadzki and Paul Lazarsfeld also described a people for whom "the consciousness of belonging together did not bind any longer" and among whom there "remained only scattered, loose, perplexed, and hopeless individuals" (1935:245). Reflecting on this instance, James Davies was moved to conclude that "without enough to eat there is not a society" (1963:17).

Nevertheless, in the extensive literature on the devastation wrought within the ultimate "culture of terror, space of death," the German concentration camps, where hunger remained the final arbiter of human values and social norms, the personal narratives of survivors are often ambiguous and contradictory.[5] There are those, like Bruno Bettelheim (1943, 1960), who stressed the desocialization process in the camps that was capable of transforming religious men and women and devoted family members into individual survival strategists reminiscent of the Ik. Keys et al. cited from the medical report made by a British physician, F. M. Lipscomb (1945), who was a member of the British Army team that liberated Bergen-Belsen in 1945:

> The most conspicuous abnormality was a degradation of moral standards characterized by increasing selfishness, more or less proportional to the degree of under-nutrition. In the first stage consideration for others was limited to personal friends, then the circle contracted to child or parent, and finally only the instinct to survive remained. Emotional response became progressively lowered and consciousness of sex was lost. Eventually all self-respect disappeared and the only interest left was to obtain something which could be eaten, even human flesh. . . . [There was as well] a blunting of sensitivity to scenes of cruelty and death. (1945:315)

More common, however, were the conflicts and radical alternations be-tween altruism and selfishness that Terrence Des Pres (1976), Elie Wiesel (1969), and others stressed in their writings on the behavior of the inmates of the death camps. Wiesel recalled, for example, the contradictory advice passed on to him as a new arrival at Auschwitz. In one instance he was told, "Listen to me, boy. Don't forget that you are in a concentration camp. Here every man has to fight for himself and not think of anyone else. Even of his father. Here there are no fathers, no brothers, no friends. Everyone lives and dies for himself alone" (1969:122). But another inmate warned, "We are all brothers, and we are all suffering the same fate. . . . Help one another. It is the only way to survive" (52). Similarly, a survivor of the camp at Treblinka explained, "In our group we shared everything; and the moment one of the group ate something without sharing it, we knew that it was the beginning of the end for him" (Des Pres 1976:96).

And so there is reason to question Turnbull's conclusion that acute hunger *necessarily* leads to the shedding of society, culture, and all social sanctions. The accumulated evidence indicates that responses to famine, chronic hunger, and scarcity vary among individuals and groups. Many societies have faced chronic food shortages and even acute starvation grace-fully. Among the small-scale societies traditionally studied by anthropolo-gists where seasonal hunger is often the norm, institutionalized patterns of food sharing rather than food hoarding are the most common response to food scarcity (see Y. Cohen 1961). It was just their acute consciousness of (and horror at) the eroding effects of famine that motivated the competitive food sharing and "fighting with food" that Michael Young (1971) described for a community of Papuan New Guineans.

The behavior of the rural Irish during the "great hunger" following the potato famine of 1845–1849 offers another contrast to Turnbull's study of the Ik in distress. During a brutal five years of famine, rural Irish peasants and squatters, living in hundreds of endangered, congested districts, faced acute starvation, disease, and a veritable die out of the population before they received massive and organized relief from England and the United States. The extent of the disaster in western Ireland approximated that of the Ik. Yet the Irish weathered the famine years with their culture and social institu-tions intact. Even in the most miserably affected region around Cork, fami-lies remained together. Nicholas Cummins, a Cork magistrate, paid a visit to Skibbereen and the surrounding countryside and later described what he saw in a letter to the Duke of Wellington that was published in *The Times* on December 24, 1846. On entering one wretched hovel he found "six famished and ghastly skeletons, to all appearances dead, huddled in a corner on some filthy straw. . . . I approached with horror and found by a low moaning they were alive—they were in fever [typhus], four children, a woman and what had once been a man" (cited in Woodham-Smith 1962:162). When forced to migrate, Irish famine victims did so in small domestic units—a father with his sons, a mother with her infants and small children. Cecil Woodham-Smith recorded instances of women and children trying to join road work teams sponsored by the Board of Works Relief Committees and other small families lying together by the roadside where death had cut short their exodus from the countryside (1962:145, 163).

Jonathan Swift might propose in his stinging, ironic prose that the Irish survived the famine by eating some of their "excess" progeny, but in fact Irish parents fed their children the only scraps of edible foods available while they themselves subsisted on stinging nettles and weeds. The great famine, rather than weakening traditional social institutions, had the paradoxical effect of strengthening them. The authority of the "old ones," the tendency toward patriarchal stem families, and patterns of celibacy and late marriage as population control measures became even more prominent in the decades following the famine throughout rural Ireland (see Connell 1955, 1968).

In other times and places—and the Alto do Cruzeiro is one example—where the threat of hunger, scarcity, and unmet needs is constant and chronic, traditional patterns of triage may determine the allocation of scarce resources within the household. In subsequent chapters I examine the logic and the cultural meanings underlying the practice of "selective neglect" that affects the life chances of those infants and babies thought of as "poor bets" for survival. Here I set the stage for that analysis by exploring hunger as it is experienced by adult cane cutters and their families on the Alto do Cruzeiro. Like Josué de Castro before me, I see the slow starvation of *Nordestinos* as a primary motivating force in social life.

Delírio de Fome: *The Lived Experience of Hunger*

To avoid the pitfalls of both materialist and symbolic reductionisms, I ground the following analysis of *Nordestino* hunger within a conceptual framework that allows for an understanding of the body as individually and collectively experienced, as socially represented in various symbolic and metaphorical idioms, and as subject to regulation, discipline, and control by larger political and economic processes, an insight fundamental to European critical theory. Margaret Lock and I (1987) referred to this as relations among the "three bodies." At the first and most self-evident level is the individual, or the "natural," body (the body personal) understood in the phenomenological sense of the immediately grasped and intuitively "true" experience of the body-self. The unquestionability of the body-self is, for Ludwig Wittgenstein, where all knowledge and certainty of the world begins. And yet it is difficult to imagine even the first, most "natural" intuition of the body-self as unmediated by cultural meanings and representation. And so even at this primary level of analysis, the biological, psychological, and symbolic meanings of hunger are merged in the experience of bodies that are mindful and minds that are *culturally* embodied. What does it mean then to speak of the primary, the existential, experience of hunger or to say that a population is "hungry"? The popular expression *delírio de fome* offers a starting point for our discussion.

In the context of this discussion the madness of hunger participates in various and sometimes ironical meanings, but its plainest one derives from the writings and folklore documenting the history of famine and drought in the Brazilian Northeast. The *delírio de fome* refers to the frightening end point reached in starvation. References to the madness of hunger can be found as early as the sixteenth century in the diaries and other records left by Portuguese, Dutch, and French navigators, who documented the raving madness caused by hunger aboard ship on the seemingly endless voyages to and from Brazil. Jean de Léry's *Histoire d'une Voyage Fait en la Terre du Brésil*, written in 1558 by a French Huguenot shoemaker who made the voyage to Brazil in the 1540s, recalled, "The food ran out completely at the beginning of May and two sailors died of hunger madness. . . . During such outright starvation the body becomes exhausted, nature swoons, and the senses are alienated, the spirit fades away, and this not only makes people ferocious but provokes a kind of madness, justifying the common saying that someone is 'going mad from hunger' " (cited by de Castro 1969:56–57). Hunger madness was also commonly observed among shipwrecked passengers. The ship physician who in 1896 accompanied the seven surviving passengers of the wrecked *Medusa* in an open boat on the high seas for a week until their rescue described their optical, later auditory, hallucinations. Some died in a state of delirium and all in the absence of feelings of hunger (Keys et al. 1950:807).

References to *delírio de fome* appear in the novels of Euclides da Cunha (1904) and José Américo Almeida (1928, 1937) and in the ethnographic writings of Roger Bastide (1958, 1964). Chico Bento, a character from the play *O Quinze* (The Drought in the Year 1915), describes his loss of moral scruples when "delirious with hunger" and "with trembling hands, his throat dry, and his eyes blackened, he clubbed down whatever stray animal crossed his path as he fled the land" (de Castro 1969:60). These writers captured a popular expression of the horror of hunger and hunger madness in what we might call the premodern era, when the phenomenon was widely recognized and feared and before it was "domesticated" by medicine in the clinics of Bom Jesus.

In its early context, *delírio de fome* may be taken to signify the unfettered, the primary experience of hunger. *Delírio de fome* is hunger before it was understood in the medical academy as "protein-calorie" or "protein-energy" malnutrition. It may be taken to represent, then, the subjective voice, the immediate experience, of hunger. It is the voice that emerges in the biting words of an angry *favelado*, Carolina Maria de Jesus, who wrote in her celebrated diary *Child of the Dark*, "When I am hungry I want to eat one politician, hang another, and burn a third" (1962:40). And it is the rage that provoked young Rosa to destroy her one-year-old daughter. *Delírio de fome* is also the panicked frenzy that can turn an enjoyable community *festa* on the Alto do Cruzeiro into a nightmare of chaos as adults vie with each other and with children to reach the banquet table first.

The hunger of the coastal sugarcane workers and their children is not the same as the starvation of the Ik or as the periodic famines that afflict the people of the Pernambucan *sertão*. The hunger of the *zona da mata* is constant and chronic, not much changed over the twenty-five-year period that I have known the region. It is the hunger of those who eat every day but of insufficient quantity, or of an inferior quality, or an impoverished variety, which leaves them dissatisfied and hungry. By contrast, the hunger of the drought-plagued *sertão*, the backlands and the badlands of Pernambuco, is cyclical, acute, and explosive. It descends ruthlessly on people who are generally energetic, self-sufficient, and well nourished. The popular culture of the Nordeste is replete with songs, narratives, prayers, and visual images of the flight of the "stricken ones," the famine and drought victims who are forced into marches across the barren lands of the *sertão* toward the coast and the *zona da mata*. The long, single file of *sertanejo retirantes* (expulsed ones) carrying their few possessions in their arms and on their heads is a generative image, like the flight of the Holy Family into Egypt, and is the most common theme represented in the famous ceramic folk art of Pernambuco. The flight through the backlands is often a death march. Descriptions of men, women, and children "with blackened skin glued to their bones" abound in the *Nordestino* literature. "More dead than alive," wrote Almeida, describing the fleeing victims of the drought of 1932. "Only their eyes alive, piercingly alive, their pupils reflecting the spasms and agonized concentrations of flashing vitality" (cited by de Castro 1969:57).

When pushed beyond endurance, hungry *Nordestinos*, normally a sober and law-abiding people, will sack marketplaces, warehouses, and trains during periods of drought, as they did in 1987–1988. In the past they have taken part in altogether futile armed "rebellions" against the state, led by half-crazed zealots such as the much celebrated Antônio Mendes Marciel, known as Antônio Conselheiro (see da Cunha 1904; Llosa 1985). And they have followed charismatic prophet-saints on penitential marches through the backlands, fasting, barefoot, and carrying the barbed whips of the *flagelantes* (penitents), as if their hunger were not penance enough for the angry, avenging God of the Nordeste. In the extremes of famine and drought, saints and messiahs as well as fierce *cangaceiros* (bandits) have arisen (see Bastide 1958, 1964). Some folk heroes of the Northeast, such as the beloved Padre Cícero of Ceará, have merged both traditions, as holy outlaws of sorts (see C. Slater 1986). The two traditions—messianisms and social banditry—capture the bimodal dimensions of *Nordestino* hunger: its spiritualized euphoria and its frenzied rage.

What the people of the Nordeste referred to as the *delírio* or *raiva* of hunger and dehydration, the scientists involved in the Minnesota starvation experiment (Keys et al. 1950) referred to as "hunger neurosis," the emotional lability that accompanied even gradual and controlled semistarvation in the laborary. But a nineteenth-century physician described similar symptoms among working classes in London during a period (1837–1838) of widespread unemployment and hunger: "The first [symptoms of starvation] are languor, exhaustion, and general debility with a distressing feeling of faintness and sinking in the chest, chilliness, vertigo, and a tendency to syncope, unsteadiness, the voice weak and tremulous. . . . The sufferer is often listless and depressed, and manifests apathy to his condition" (Howard 1839:27). In more advanced cases, "the feelings of prostration become overpowering . . . [so] that erect posture can only, with difficulty, be maintained. . . . Dizziness, transient dimness of vision, staggering are common. . . . Sometimes the patient manifests a highly nervous state; he is startled by any sudden voice and worried by the most trifling occurrences" (27).

The "stigmata" of slow starvation include both physiological and psychological changes. In addition to weight loss and wasting, edema, and changes in hair texture and skin pigmentation are the much-noted mood changes: initial depressions followed by faintness, lightheadedness, silliness, giddiness, brilliant flashes of insight, bravado, often accompanied by irritability. These are often followed by uncontrolled weeping; fierce, crazy anger; and the lashing out even at those who would be of assistance. Alternating with the rage are passivity and indifference, as if one were absorbed by some distant or interior reality.

In early-twentieth-century medical literature on the social personality of the Brazilian, references are made to the bipolar psychic rhythms of the *Nordestino*, who is said to possess a kind of "manic-depressive" personality, resulting in part from the cyclical drama of drought and famine (see Kretschmer 1927). Modernist Brazilian writers (see E. Freiro 1957; Prado 1931) referred more romantically to the "Brazilian melancholy," the celebrated *tristeza brasileira*, as the lasting signature of *Nordestino* hunger. Whereas Paulo Prado (1931) argued in his celebrated *Retrato do Brasil* that the Brazilian is inclined toward melancholy because of the unhappy "miscegenation" of the three races—the "listless" and "sentimental" Portuguese colonist, the enslaved African in permanent exile from his native land, and the mysterious and darkly savage Indian—Amadeu Amaral attributed the Brazilian sadness to another source. He wrote, "Our people possess the melancholy and sadness that belong to all poor, hungry, and weakened people throughout the world. . . . Much of the sadness can be blamed on health problems and on the insurmountable difficulties of life. . . . The proof is that in those regions possessing a healthy climate and decent wages, the *matuto* is no longer a diseased fungus, a miserable and unhappy parasite, but is a luxurious, flowering plant" (1948:83–84).

The psychological stigmata of hunger have been an important theme in modern literature, invoked as an expression of the marginality of the artist and as a metaphor of the madness of creation. Franz Kafka's (1971) short story "A Hunger Artist" and Knut Hamsun's (1967) autobiographical novel *Hunger* are cases in point. Hamsun described the erratic fluctuations experienced by the young protagonist, a starving writer, at once aimlessly detached and alienated, arrogant and dismissive, and also perversely alive, electric, visionary, and expectant. But nowhere in modern literature have I found a more evocative description of the deliriums of hunger than in Henry Miller's semiautobiographic *Tropic of Cancer*, where his protagonist, an American writer abroad in Paris, exalts in everything sensual, even his own starvation:

> My mind is curiously alert; it's as though my skull had a thousand mirrors inside it. My nerves are taut, vibrant! The notes are like glass balls dancing on a million jets of water. I've never been to a concert before on such an empty belly. Nothing escapes me, not even the tiniest pin falling. It's as though I had no clothes on and every pore of my body was a window, and all the windows open and the light flooding my gizzards. . . . How long this lasts I have no idea: I have lost all sense of time and place. After what seems like an eternity there follows an interval of semiconsciousness balanced by such a calm that I feel a great lake inside me, a lake of iridescent sheen, cool as jelly; and over this lake, rising in great swooping spi-

rals, there emerge flocks of birds of passage with long slim legs and brilliant plumage. . . . Suddenly the lights flare up. (1961:67–68)

The belief that hunger has marked the social character of the *Nordestino* remains a persistent theme in both Brazilian literature and popular culture. It is one of the stories that Northeast Brazilians tell themselves and others. In the Teatro Novo, the modernist film movement of the 1950s and 1960s, a specific kind of regional hero appeared. Set in the romantic backlands of the Northeast, the films often treat a young hero, a *matuto* or *sertanejo*, who, driven by hunger, thirst, or another consuming passion, crosses the desert wasteland in pursuit of some mad and lonely vision. In the film *Pagador de Promessas*, for example, a half-crazed and devout *matuto* insists on fulfilling his religious vow: to carry a huge wooden crucifix on his shoulders across the *sertão* and the *agreste* to a pilgrimage site in an interior town. He and his wife arrive, half-dead of exhaustion, hunger, and heat exposure, only to find the entrance to the church blocked by the parish priest, who fears the protagonist as a dangerous lunatic. The impassioned *matuto*, a Christ figure, dies on the church steps, stretched out on the cross of his own making.

During a severe drought in the mid-1960s that drove thousands of famished *Nordestinos* by truckloads to coastal cities looking for relief, a young *Nordestino* recording star cut a forty-five disk that hit the top of the charts for a brief period. Rendered in traditional singsong *repentista* fashion, "Pau de Arara" was a satire concerning a drought victim from the state of Ceará who escaped to the south of Brazil only to find himself dizzy with hunger and wandering the beaches of Copacabana in Rio. In desperation he learns that he can earn a few cruzeiros by entertaining small crowds of bikini-clad surfers with his "trick" of swallowing Gillette razor blades, later Coca-Cola bottle caps. The *pau de arara* (derogatory slang for *Nordestino* migrants) calls out to passersby, saying, "Kind sir, pay just five cruzeiros to watch me swallow a few Gillette blades! I'm so hungry. I haven't eaten a thing all day." As for the Gillette razors, the *pau de arara* says that they hurt a little going down but that once they hit the belly, "they're so hot and tasty!" Nevertheless, as soon as he gathers up a few more cruzeiros, *pau de arara* will be on his way again, returning to his beloved *sertão*. The song moved Brazilians of all social classes and walks in life, and it became a kind of theme song at grassroots political meetings until the Brazilian military recognized its "subversive" content and banned it from being played or sung in public.

The Face of Nordestino Hunger Today

The hunger of the Northeast is undoubtedly part of the popular folklore of the region, and it is a subject of modern Brazilian literature even as it appears in surrealist theater and film. But just how *real* is the hunger of the *Nordestino?* To what extent might the common and frequent references to a person *morrendo* or *caindo de fome* (dying or falling down from hunger) be a cultural convention, an expression of frustrated desires and longings that are more metaphorical than material? In accepting at face value Alto informants' descriptions of their *barrigas secas* (dry stomachs) and "trembling limbs," might not the naive anthropologist too willingly accept a collective myth similar to the symbolic "famine" of the Melanesian Wamirans? Is Galeano's reference to the Brazilian Northeast as a "concentration camp for more than thirty million people" a vulgar metaphor, a vile misappropriation of a space and an experience that have no equal and no parallel elsewhere?

In 1965 when I first joined Nailza and Zé Antônio in their tiny wattle-and-daub hut near the top of the Alto do Cruzeiro, I was still capable of shock at the conditions of Alto life, but over the years, and with the help of my Alto friends, I learned to *conformar* (adjust, accept) so as to be able to listen and observe in a relatively detached and dispassionate way. The scenes of sickness, hunger, and (especially) child death are now commonplace to me, and only rarely am I moved by a particularly poignant scene or image.

Perhaps it was the image of Terezinha carefully dividing four small rolls of bread into halves, one for each household member, regardless of age or size. What kind of blind justice was at work here, what radically egalitarian ethos? It was uncharacteristic behavior in hungry Alto households and therefore disturbing. Ordinarily, the heads of the household would take a disproportionate share so as to be able to work. But on this morning Seu Manoel, the father, took his tiny share without comment, shoving it into the pocket of his baggy pants. He would eat his later, after a few hours of work cleaning out the clogged drains and recently flooded main street of Bom Jesus.

"Won't you be hungry?"

"*Brasileiro ja se acostumou a fome.* [Brazilians have long since gotten used to hunger]," he said.

Or perhaps it was the words of Terezinha's seven-year-old son, Edilson, that reminded me that I could still feel something in the face of death. Edilson, who more than once had been given up for dead, continued to surprise everyone with his persistence in holding on to life. Edilson had survived, but he had not thrived, and he existed in a liminal social space midway between death and life. No one, especially not his mother, expected Edilson to survive his next crisis, his next uphill battle. He was very small and without strength. Terezinha showed me Edilson's latest affliction: a tumorlike growth on his neck that made it all but impossible for the child to swallow. "Now the little critter [*bichinho*] eats nothing at all," she said with pity.

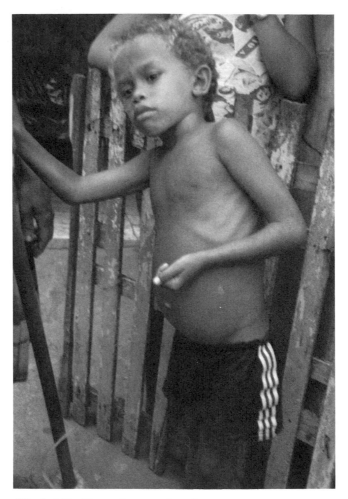

"Hush, Mãe, I'm ready to go there."

"He's not going to live long. Soon he will join the others (i.e., his dead siblings)."

"Don't talk like that in front of Edilson," I said to his mother, trying to protect the boy, forgetting that he had walked in a liminal space on the edge of death since his birth and that he was *bem conformado* (well adjusted) to his ghostlike social status. And so it was Edilson who silenced and corrected me so as to protect his mother. He tugged at her skirt anxiously to get her attention, and he said of his own death, "Hush, Mãe, hush. I'm not afraid; I'm ready to go there."

Or perhaps it was the memory of Seu Zacarias, the hungry and tuber-culous fruit vendor confined to a hammock in his one-room shanty with his young wife and two babies, begging me to intervene, to stop the public health officers from forcing him to go to Recife to die alone in a sanatorium there. "The nurses are bad women, I swear," Seu Zacarias pleaded. "They dance in the corridors at night; they play loud music. A sick man like me could never get any rest there at all."

And so I agreed to treat him at home, arriving every other day to give his injection until, finally, the flesh had melted away and there was only loose skin and the needle point hit bone. Or perhaps it just hit "home," for Zacarias said sadly, "*Sou osso mesmo* [I'm just bones]." And a skeleton he was, but a strangely animated skeleton who could set me off balance with his jarring, off-color humor, *himself* to the very end. For even skeletons in the Nordeste have the *animação*, the sexual vitality of the *brasileiro*. Then why did Zacarias's spirit in the face of death bring tears to my eyes and not the laughter he sought?

Or perhaps it was the lean-to of Maria José, the discredited widow, and her three children, dirty and the youngest one naked, dancing a *frevo* to a handmade drum and whistle.

"Where is your mother?"

"She's out looking for work," replied the oldest child, a girl with the shaved head of one who had been badly infected with head lice. With her shorn head, spindly legs, and torn shift the girl looked for all the world like a refugee from a prison camp. It was high noon and the children must have been hungry, but there was no sign of a fire. "Have you eaten today?"

"*Não*, nothing" was the predictable reply.

Her younger brother scowled and turned his back on me. "You are nosy; go away," his back announced. But I persisted.

"Let me see what you have in the house."

The girl pointed to two small reed baskets hanging from a rope thrown over a roof beam. In one there was half a coconut and a few shriveled peppers. In the other basket were several small dried fish, ugly and covered with tiny bugs. I was nauseated and quickly replaced the dirty cloth that had covered the basket.

"Tell me, is your *mãe* out begging?"

The girl looked down and nodded her head.

"Do you sometimes beg for your mother?"

"I used to, but not anymore."

"And why not?"

"I'm older now and I'm ashamed."

But now it was me suddenly struck with shame. I left the girl with fifty cruzados. She happily accepted the bill and said: "With fifteen cruzados I will buy a roll for each of us for lunch, and I will give thirty-five cruzados to my mother when she comes home." Like most Alto children, Francisca could

Looking in at the home of Maria José, the "bad widow."

not read, but she was quick with numbers, which she had not learned from school (she did not attend) but from "studying" precious *cruzado* notes. "Shall I dance for you?" she asked.

Or perhaps, finally, it was the *casa de nanicos* (house of the dwarfs) on the Rua da Cruz that jolted me from my state of conformity. Here were a grandmother, two adult daughters (one of them mother of a one-year-old baby), and six children, four of them *nanicos*. But these Brazilian "pygmies" (as the Brazilian nutritionist Nelson Chaves [1982] referred to such children) had been stunted by chronic hunger, not by genes. The boys, ranging in age

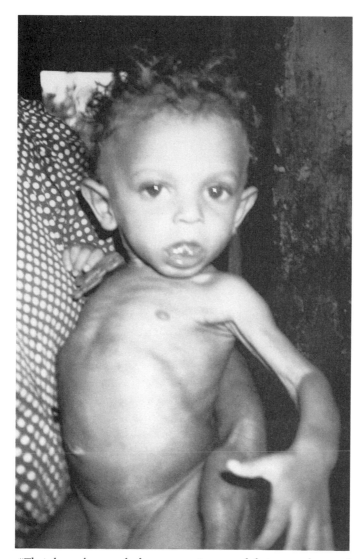

"Their breastbone and ribs are prominent, and their arms, legs, and buttocks are stripped of flesh."

from six to fifteen and in height from two and one-half to a little more than four feet, had been raised on *mingau* (manioc flour, water, salt), bean broth, and steamed cornmeal cakes. The two young girls had fared better, as was often the case in such households, possibly because they helped out in the food preparations. The youngest, eleven-month-old Paulo Ricardo, weighed barely five kilos and seemed likely, if he lived at all, to follow in the stunted footsteps of his little uncles. The adult women explained, "The boys in our house are all puny and weak; they don't like to eat much."

"The major cause of chronic undernutrition may be purely economic," wrote the authors of *The Biology of Human Starvation*, "but the primary cause of modern starvation is political strife, including war" (Keys et al. 1950:3). I do not want to quibble over words, but what I have been seeing on the Alto do Cruzeiro for two and a half decades is more than "malnutrition," and it is politically as well as economically caused, although in the absence of overt political strife or war. Adults, it is true, might be described as "chronically undernourished," in a weakened and debilitated state, prone to infections and opportunistic diseases. But it is overt hunger and starvation that one sees in babies and small children, the victims of a "famine" that is endemic, relentless, and political-economic in origin.

Since 1964, and with little letup over the decade (1975–1985) of the great economic miracle of Brazil, I have seen Alto children of one and two years who cannot sit up unaided, who do not or cannot speak, whose skin over the chest and upper part of the stomach is stretched so tightly that every curve of the breastbone and the ribs stands out. The arms, legs, and buttocks of these children are stripped of flesh so that the skin hangs in folds. The buttocks are discolored. The bones of the hungry child's face are fragile. The eyes are prominent, wide open, and often vacant; sometimes they have sunk back in the head. The hair is thin and wispy, often with patches of baldness, though the eyelashes can be exceptionally long. In some babies there is an extraordinary pallor, a severe anemia, that lends the child an unnatural, waxen appearance that mothers see as a harbinger of death. My daughter Jennifer, who often accompanied me in household visits, fell on an apt designation. She called them "snowball babies."

In addition to frequent stunting, older children and adults show other signs of chronic hunger. Vitamin deficiencies lead to changes in skin pigmentation, and one sees children who are speckled like Easter eggs with patches of white or gray on normally brown skin. There is a great deal of edema—swellings of the abdomen, limbs, and sometimes the face. The hair and skin of older children and adults can be dry and brittle. Skin infections are endemic in bodies that have virtually no resistance to scabies, impetigo, fungal infections, and all kinds of skin ulcers, invariably badly infected. Adults can live for years on end with the untreated and badly infected sores that squatters refer to as *pereba*. Seu Manoel and Terezinha, for example, both suffer from chronic skin infections on their feet and legs that have burrowed so deep that one avoids looking for fear of seeing bone. Alto

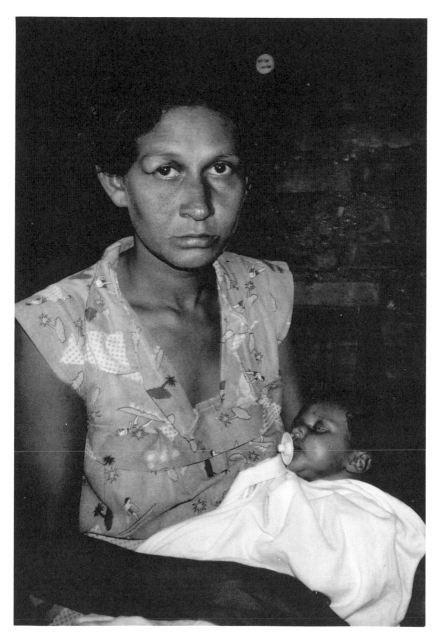

"Their heads are enormous, while their legs cannot sustain them."

residents not only learn to live with such painful and ugly afflictions; they learn to work with them as well, which for local washerwomen means soaking their infected legs or feet for many hours a day in the polluted waters of the local riverbed and for rural workers means walking many miles through the *mata* in open sandals.

Fazendo Feira: *Making Ends Meet*

The rural worker lost considerable buying power under the "new cruzado" scheme. In 1987–1988 the minimum wage purchased only half the groceries it did in 1982, and a family's *cesta básica* cost one and a half minimum wages. This situation had not changed significantly in 1989. Just the daily purchase of a kilo of bread alone cost a rural worker a large portion of his minimum wage. And, unfortunately, most residents of the Alto did not even have the security of a single minimum wage, as many were unemployed from February to September, when there was no cane to be cut.

Consequently, Saturday mornings were a time of nervous agitation on the Alto do Cruzeiro. It was the time when the market baskets had to be replenished. If there was a man in the household, marketing was generally his responsibility. He was expected to provide and purchase food for the family. The woman's responsibility was to economize and to make the food last, to make sure that the house was never *faltando comidas*, "without food," especially beans and a little bit of fresh meat. Within the hierarchy of consumption on the Alto do Cruzeiro, food *ideally* came before other wants and needs. One could postpone paying the rent, one could go without gas and cook with charcoal or twigs, one could always light the home with a kerosene lamp, and one could do without new clothing. Hunger was immediate, and *a comida não pode faltar* (you can't do without food) was the rule of thumb. But this rule was frequently bent as one emergency after another—an urgent need for medications, work clothes, transportation, school materials—"ate" away at the *feira* money. Meanwhile, *feira*, it was said, *come tudo*, "eats everything." And the specter of hunger was always in the foreground.

In 1988 Seu Manoel was paid about thirty-two dollars a month, about two-thirds a single minimum wage, as a municipal street cleaner. It was illegal, of course, for workers to be paid less than the minimum wage, but it was customary practice in the *município* all the same. His weekly paycheck could not provide for the basic necessities. Consequently, Terezinha sold *picolé* (popsicle) and penny candies from a small *barraca* (wooden stand) in front of their house. Their eldest son, Severino, age fifteen, was employed in various odd jobs and in scavenging. Pooling their collective labor and resources, this family of eight came up with one and a half minimum salaries, from which they purchased the following groceries on market day:[6]

1 kilo of *farinha*
4 kilos of sugar
2 kilos of brown or black beans
1 (or 2) kilos of rice
3 (200 gram) packages of cornmeal (*fubá*)
1 package of inexpensive coffee
(sometimes 1 or 2 packages of *macarrão*, a substitute for rice)
cooking oil, salt, garlic, parsley for flavoring, as needed
(a chicken or ½–1 kilo of chicken parts, if possible)
1 small plastic sack (200 grams) of the cheapest powdered
    milk for the nine-month-old baby
soap

In addition, almost every Sunday morning Manoel and one of his sons went to the river with his nets to supplement the family's diet with a few fish. Terezinha, for her part, tried to sell enough sweets from her *barraca* to provide for the morning bread, one small roll per person. Otherwise, the family breakfasted on *café simples*, "black coffee." The main meal, *almôço*, at midday was a serving of brown beans covered with *farinha* and usually one other starch, sometimes rice but more frequently *macarrão*, "spaghetti," which was prepared with oil and a bit of tomato or, more often than not, with *colorau*, a red food coloring. Dinner was *couscous simples*, steamed cornmeal cake made from *fubá*, salt, and water.

"The *caçula* [her youngest] yells at me," said Terezinha, "Mãe, you abuse me!"

"It's only because you annoy me so much!" Terezinha replied.

"But, Mãe, I am so hungry!"

"I can't help you. Only your papa can help us now."

"I want milk."

"*Posso, não.* I cannot help you, my daughter."

When there was not enough food to *mata fome* (kill, finish off, hunger), Manoel and the children asked for *garapa*, a glass of sugar water, and they went to sleep on that. And so the four kilos of sugar in the *feira* basket, which might seem excessive, was in fact a staple in this hungry family's diet.

There have been some changes in the diet of the people of the Alto since the 1960s, when brown beans slowly cooked for many hours with large, thick slices of native squash, pumpkin, and onions were the staple meal. Like the proverbial European peasants' "stone soup," beans were judged as much

Maria José cooking: camp rations.

by what could be added to the pot, especially, whenever possible, a bit of sun-dried beef (*carne de sol*) or beef jerky. On the Alto do Cruzeiro today beans are generally cooked *simples*, with only salt and cumin for flavor. The loss of garden plots has reduced the use of squash and other vegetables, while dried beef (as well as the much-loved salted codfish, *bacalhau*) has become prohibitively expensive and has largely disappeared from the market stalls and small *barracas* on the Alto. What have taken their place are bins of tiny, salted fish caught from the local river and dried in the street that runs through the *zona* (the red-light district), where the cars of the local bourgeoisie drive over them. Those who own cars never eat these fish, while the people of the Alto themselves often express their revulsion at having to eat them.

One Saturday afternoon in 1989 I passed by Dalina's house on the Rua dos Magos to find her in a state of great distress. The old woman had just returned from a local *barraca*, where she had been turned down when she asked to buy some bread and cheese for herself and her all-but-abandoned great-grandson, Gil, on credit. The shopkeeper relented, however, when he saw the pitiful state that Gil was in, and he offered her some of the local dried fish he had for sale. "That is kind of you, *compadre*," Dalina replied. "But as hungry as we are and even *de esmola* [as free charity], I wouldn't eat those nauseating little things."

In the 1960s many Alto women could be found on Saturday afternoons in their *quintals* (backyards) busily salting and preserving a kilo or more of fresh beef parts, which had not in most instances been purchased but rather had been earned by a family member who had spent part of the previous night working at the public abatoire, the *matadouro*, located at the base of the Alto. In exchange for slaughtering and butchering the cows that would be sold in *feira* the next day, many Alto residents were paid in kilos of nonchoice beef parts, often innards, which formed the basis of many traditional (but now increasingly rare) regional dishes, such as *feijoada* and *buchada* (a cow's stomach casing refilled with minced intestine). Today the *matadouro* has been moved farther outside of town and is no longer a primary part-time employer of Alto men and women because the process of slaughtering and butchering cows has been "modernized" and specialized; workers are no longer paid in beef parts. And so "meat hunger" has emerged as a dominant Alto complaint.

Increasingly, even beans have become prohibitive to the poorest Alto households, where *fubá* (dried cornmeal) has now replaced beans as the staple food. In the *casa de nanicos*, in the lean-to of Maria José, and in the home of Seu Chico, who has just arrived from the *mata* with his wife and seven children, beans have become something of a *festa* food, a party food. "In these days," Seu Chico says, "we learn to eat our *quarenta* [a probable mispronunciation of *polenta*, a cornmeal mush] and be content."

In the home of Antônio Campos everything is *parado* (dead). Unemployed for several months, Antônio is stretched out asleep on a plastic-covered sofa with more springs exposed than covered. His wife stands at the doorway with a crying toddler in her arms and two other small children at her side. Four other children are not at home. "Yes," she tells me, "the family is hungry a good deal of the time."

After he wakes up, Antônio explains how he manages to put together his family's weekly market basket: "I spend a lot of time in the house of my friends. They're out of work, too. We talk about one thing or another, asking ourselves, 'But what are we going to do? We can't be like this forever!' But when *feira* day comes I have to do something. *O jeito que tem* [the only thing to do] is to look for a friend and say, '*O meu amigo*, have you got there about two hundred cruzados you can give me so I can get the children some *farinha* and a little milk?' Well, if he can't help, then you go after another, and another. Or you try to find a shop that will sell you a little something on credit. If that doesn't work, my God, I don't even want to think about it."

But when it is a single woman alone with her children, the search can be even more frantic. If she is out of work, a woman will exhaust every resource, even stooping so low, Biu says, as to beg from an old lover or even from the *safado* (bum) who had deserted her and the children. "Who can stand by and listen to a child crying that its stomach is aching from hunger? You will do *anything*," she says. But children want more than just black beans, Biu continues. "They want meat, and here is the real struggle." Although Biu can resist her older children's "whines" for *comidas de luxo* (luxury foods), she breaks down, she says, when it is the baby, her *caçula*, little Mercea, who asks for meat. " 'Two pieces, Mãe,' she says, holding up her little fingers," and Biu takes away from an older child so that the stoical and melancholy little girl, who has never had the strength or "courage" to stand up or walk, can have her wish.

To see Biu, exhausted after a day's work in the cane fields, climb the treacherous backside of the Alto, balancing firewood on her shoulder and a basket on her head, while her two youngest children cheer from their perch outside their smoke-filled hut on the first sighting of their victorious *mãe*, reminds me of a passage from the diary of another strong shantytown woman. "I feel so sorry for my children," Carolina Maria de Jesus wrote in an entry dated May 13, 1958. "When they see the things to eat that I come home with they shout, '*Viva mamãe!*' Their outbursts please me. But I've lost the habit of smiling. Ten minutes later they want more food" (1962:34).

Camp Rations

The caloric intake of the rural worker in the *zona da mata* has been the subject of more than fifty years of research through the Instituto de Nu-trição at the Federal University of Pernambuco and the Fundação Joaquím Nabuco, both in Recife. The first scientific nutritional survey was conducted in the 1930s by the physician, nutritionist, human geographer, and human-ist without equal, Josué de Castro. He reported that the average daily intake of the rural worker in the area of the sugarcane monoculture was approx-imately 1,700 calories (1952:80). These initial studies were followed up by Nelson Chaves and his colleagues and students at the Fundação Joaquím Nabuco.[7] In the last book published before his death, Chaves (1982) reported that the conditions first noted by de Castro remained largely unchanged.

Amid the agroindustry of sugar cultivation, undernutrition is endemic and progressive, and workers' productive capacities are greatly reduced. Chaves attributed the low productivity of the Pernambucan cane cutter (half that of the cane cutters of São Paulo) to the chronic undernutrition of the *Nordestino* rural worker. "In Pernambuco the cane cutter's caloric intake is extremely low, averaging less than 1,500 calories per day" (1982:73).

Chaves referred to the so-called *preguiça tropical,* the "tropical laziness" of the rural workers as chronic fatigue, "nothing more than the natural defenses of an organism adapting to a hostile environment" (73). He argued that the slaves on the original sugar plantations of Pernambuco were better fed than today's rural wage laborers because the slave masters had a greater concern for the well-being of their tools of production. In contrast,

> the rural worker of today is primarily a carrier of worms, and his stature is diminishing considerably over time, so that it is actually approaching that of the African pygmy. The women of the region are also of low stature, their pelvic structures are reduced, and they suffer from mammary hydroplasia and sexual immaturity. They give birth to small, premature infants, and they are predisposed to both physical and mental fatigue. (81)

Chaves's radical conclusions concerning the gradual "pygmitization" of the rural poor *Nordestino* population (based on his group's statistical surveys and anthropometric measures) were both controversial and contested. Nevertheless, his measures have been verified in more recent nutritional, growth, and developmental studies that indicate gross differences in size and maturation of poor and privileged children in Pernambuco. In a recent study of 226 children, ages seven to seventeen, from poor and marginal rural migrant families living in new shantytowns of Recife, and a control of 674 wealthy children from the same city, the differences were striking. Whereas the mean values for weight and height of privileged children fell close to the fiftieth percentile by American and British standards, the mean for the poor children fell *below* the twenty-fifth percentile. The boys from poor homes were especially disadvantaged with respect to height measurements, which fell *below the fifth percentile* for all age groups (Linhares, Round, & Jones 1986).

Malaquias Batista Filho, a disciple of Nelson Chaves, published a recent book, *Nutrição, Alimentação, e Agricultura no Nordeste Brasileiro,* based on his statistical survey of the physical growth and development of rural children in the Northeast. His study indicated that two-thirds of all rural children showed signs of considerable undernutrition and stunting, and of these, 40 percent could be classified as nutritionally dwarfed, as *nanicos.*

These startling findings were published amid much heated public discussion and commentary in the newspapers of Recife. But they were unnoted by the public health personnel working in the state health post of Bom Jesus, where two mornings a week, rural mothers and their children fill that oxymoron called the "well-baby clinic" for immunizations. The babies and toddlers are routinely weighed and measured, and the obvious stunting and under-development of two- to four-year-old children is the rule rather than the exception. The functionary in charge reads out the height and weight statistics to the mother but never explains the implications of the child's often gross underdevelopment. The woman leaves the clinic without realizing just what she has been told. As for the health post workers, when asked why they do not do more for the malnourished children who appear each morning, they commonly reply, "What *can* we do? The health post can't prescribe food."

Current debates concerning world hunger, childhood malnutrition, and social policy continually redefine the parameters of the problem.[8] In the early 1980s the economist David Seckler (1982) initiated a heated contro-versy with his "small but healthy" hypothesis. Seckler suggested that per-haps as many as 80 percent to 90 percent of those people living in conditions of chronic food scarcity might fall under the designation "nutritionally stunted." But many of these, he argued, could be seen as small but otherwise healthy and "adapted" individuals requiring no special interventions. In place of a single, genetically determined human growth curve, Seckler proposed a multiplicity of potential growth curves that would respond to particular conditions, some favoring, and others inhibiting, growth. The analogy was that of people, like carp, transferred from a fishbowl to an outdoor pond, or vice versa. International food and aid programs, Seckler argued, should target only the very small proportion of malnourished and stunted individuals who were also chronically sick.

The response to Seckler's hypothesis has been strong and lively (see Messer 1986; Pelto & Pelto 1989). Most nutritional experts have rejected the notion of "small but healthy" as a spurious category unsupported by the worldwide evidence of the multiple medical, developmental, psychological, and social risks that accompany physical stunting resulting from malnutri-tion in early childhood. Not the least of these, with reference to Alto residents, is the high-risk spiral that turns malnourished children into small and undernourished women who give birth to premature, sickly and low-birth-weight infants who are at excessively high risk of mortality in the first weeks and months of life. On the Alto do Cruzeiro to be "small but healthy" is a contradiction in terms, especially to people who equate health with physical strength, size, and endurance. "Small but healthy?" Little Irene

Little Irene (far right): dwarfed by chronic malnutrition.

looked at me as if I were joking. "Look, Nancí, here it is a case of small but
lucky, lucky to be alive."

Stunting takes other, more gradual, and less obvious tolls on the people of
the Alto. They are the descendants of Mediterranean Europeans, West
Africans, and Amerindians, and when well fed and lucky, they can be tall,
muscular, and robust. This is the image they want to have of themselves.
But even though the range in size among individuals of the Alto is large, the
average female adult is five feet, one inch, and the average male is only a few
inches taller than she is. This leaves me—a rather "stunted" (five feet, four
inches) North American woman—often standing tall among the people of
the Alto at large community gatherings.

More striking, however, is the contrast between the stature of the children and adults of the Alto and of the middle- and upper-class residents of
Bom Jesus. The contrast begins at birth. In my reproductive history samples
(see chapter 7) the average Alto infant is born weighing about two and a half
kilos, whereas the average middle-class infant of Bom Jesus weighs three

and a half kilos at birth. Middle-class children reach puberty at an earlier age, and as teenagers and adults they conform to our norms for an average, although not particularly tall, population. These marked differences feed Alto people's profound sense of inferiority. They interpret their small stature and more delicate frames in racialist terms as evidence of the intrinsic "weakness" of their "breed" (*raça*). It is that which physically separates and marks them from the rich, the *gente fina*, of Bom Jesus. It is hardly, then, the biased projections of Texas-sized Americans foisting their hegemonic notions of "bigger is better" onto smaller and poorer populations that have Brazilian nutritionists so alarmed today about the pygmitization of poor rural *Nordestinos*. The problem is that stunting from malnutrition is almost invariably accompanied by delayed maturation, reproductive problems (including high risk of miscarriage and low-birth-weight infants), ill health, reduced energy, lowered self-esteem, and adverse effects during childhood on the ability to learn.

Childhood malnutrition has certainly contributed to the persistent and chronic illiteracy of the impoverished sectors of the Northeast, despite more than three generations of near universal primary school education. On the Alto do Cruzeiro, where illiteracy remains the norm and where only 30 percent of Alto women in my sample of seventy-four households could even sign their names, all attended primary school for at least a brief period of time before deciding that schooling was a waste of time. "I went to school for three years and never learned a thing," "Letters could never enter my head," and "School is not for *matutos*" were common explanations given for their illiteracy. But Alto children are not "slow" or "dumb" in any sense of the term, although, as in any population, there are ranges in intelligence. For the most part they are lively observers of human life and activity, full of sharp wit, and playful with words. Nonetheless, most Alto children are unable to concentrate in school, and it is the exceptional child who graduates from the final fifth grade class with any real knowledge of reading or writing.

The municipal primary school class held in the creche of the Alto do Cruzeiro, uninspirational to begin with and lacking in basic instructional materials, was filled with dozing and daydreaming children. During several visits to the classroom in 1988 and 1989, I encountered children who were grossly undersized for their ages; others, with obviously distended bellies, complained of stomachaches from parasites and worms, while still others were tormented by itching from lice, pinworms, scabies, and other common skin infections. Children of all ages and talents were exposed to the same repetitive lessons pitched always to the slowest learners. Antônio Marcos, age fourteen, and Valdecio, age nine, shared the same desk and assignments. Antônio was described by his teacher as "having a bit of a problem" (i.e., he had a profound mental disability), whereas Valdecio was exceptionally bright, although poorly educated. Later, I spent some time with each. Antônio thought that he was either five or seven years old, couldn't say exactly where he lived, and could not identify many of the animals and objects in a child's picture book. Valdecio, though small for his age, was bright-eyed, quick, and engaging. He liked to draw and had penned a Nazi insignia on his arm. No, he didn't know what it meant, but he had seen it on a movie poster, and he thought it was "handsome." He happily agreed to draw a picture of two things that were very important to him: a self-portrait next to the Cristo of the Alto do Cruzeiro and the Brazilian flag. Valdecio correctly identified the current president of Brazil, though he could not identify any of the candidates for the first democratic elections since the junta. Nevertheless, he knew the names of both the governor of Pernambuco and the newly elected mayor of Bom Jesus. Valdecio was also very clear on what were the primary responsibilities of a "good" president ("to build parks for the children") and of a "good" mayor ("to feed the people, especially milk and fruit").

Let me put the data on the average caloric intake in the *zona da mata* into a comparative context. The *Nordestino* rural worker, with his average caloric intake of between 1,500 and 1,700 calories, is considerably better nourished than were the Jews of the Warsaw ghetto of 1942. Tests and measurements of the survivors of the Warsaw ghetto indicated that most adults there had been subsisting on a diet of cabbage, bread, and potatoes that provided only 600 to 800 calories per day (Apfelbaum-Kowalski et al. 1946), similar to the diet of the internees at the Belsen concentration camp (Lipscomb 1945:313). At the Buchenwald concentration camp, however, an internee who later became a member of the French Academy of Medicine reported that the food allotment there in 1944 was usually about 1,750 calories per day, or some-what *more* than the average intake of the Nordestino sugarcane cutter today (Richet 1945).

The closest approximation of the dietary allowance of the rural worker in the *zona da mata,* however, is to that of the Minnesota starvation experiment (Keys et al. 1950), in which the thirty-two volunteers were submitted to twenty-four weeks of semistarvation; their daily intake was gradually reduced to a limit of 1,570 calories. Keys and his colleagues had designed an experimental study to observe the physiological and psychological effects not of malnutrition but of starvation. Insofar as their work still stands as the classic scientific study of human starvation, we might begin to consider the situation of the *Nordestino* rural worker and his or her family for what it really is: the slow starvation of a population trapped, as Galeano suggested, in a veritable concentration camp for more than thirty million people.

Empty Pockets and Full Bellies: Poverty and Food

Within the population of *os pobres* of the Alto do Cruzeiro the double stigma of hunger and sickness visibly stamps them as poor and marginal. Food and medicine are the idioms through which Alto people reflect on their social condition. Poverty is defined by food scarcity and by dependency on medications. The poor are those who are always sick, *só anda doente,* and always hungry, *passando fome.* Food separates the self-respecting poor, *os pobres,* from the miserable and the truly wretched, *os pobrezinhos* or *os pobretões.* The self-respecting poor organize their lives around the constant struggle to feed themselves and their children, but they "get by" and still have the strength to work. The truly wretched are those who must beg to eat and who are too sick or too weak to work.

The rich, by contrast, are those who *nem liga a comida,* who "don't pay any attention to food," because it is taken for granted. The rich are those to whom foods are offered (prepared and served up by those hungry poor who work in their kitchens) and whose appetites need to be coaxed and tempted. The rich can eat what they please, and they can choose to eat meat at every meal. They can select from among an enormous variety of plates according to well-developed preferences for particular tastes, textures, smells, and flavors. The poor are those who "grub" plain, heavy, basic foods that simply *enche a barriga,* "fill the belly."

Ramos, an *operário* in a local sugar factory, is a *pobre* who, although never lacking for food, shares the *pobrezinhos'* preoccupation with eating often and completely. He pities those unfortunates who cannot "stuff themselves" as much as he does. Ramos explains that he has a certain schedule to his meals: "I take my first meal early, around 6 A.M., about a half dozen fried bananas and five little rolls of bread. Then I go off to work, but by 11:30 A.M. I am already home and bugging my sister to see if lunch is ready. Then I eat a huge mound of beans, rice, *macarrão,* and as much meat as possible. My sister knows that I need the *fôrça de carne* [strength from meat] to work hard. Sometimes I'll have boiled manioc. Food, you know [and he smacks his lips], *real* food. Then I eat a good supper at night: yams, sweet manioc, couscous, bread, noodles, maybe a few sardines or an egg. *Filling* foods. If later on I feel like going out to the *praça* with some friends, I am again looking around the kitchen for a few loose bananas and some crackers to tide me over for the night."

Then Ramos adds thoughtfully, "Hunger is a terrible thing. On TV last week I saw that place . . . where is it that they are starving? Mozambique? . . . Where the children's ribs are showing and people are lying down because they are too weak to stand on their feet. I saw that and, girl, I just couldn't stand it. I started to cry and told my sister to turn the TV set off." The *pobrezinhos* are those who cannot afford to eat meat and who are always *sentindo falta,* "feeling something missing." The rich only *beliscam,* "nibble," like delicate little birds picking at tempting and novel tidbits. The poor shovel in piles of the same unappetizing, monotonous food so that even as they gobble it down, they are already half-disgusted and nauseated. *Me enjoei* or *Estou abusada*—"I'm revolted" or "I'm totally fed up" (with beans, rice, *farinha,* cornmeal, or *macarrão*) is commonly heard. The poor, then, are those who yearn for the *gosto,* the *sabor,* the strong "taste," of beef, *carne de sol,* or even chicken, beef innards, or eggs, all of which are delicacies in the diet of Alto people. Obviously, there is no "coddling" around meals, and it is important in poor households that everyone learns to accept the same diet. Although food preferences and food avoidances are sometimes expressed, they are not, indeed cannot possibly be, honored. A child or an adult who is totally fed up *(abusada)* with beans will simply have to do without. Consequently, there is a good deal of voluntary fasting among the poor because of strong food aversions, although chronic malnutrition surely contributes to these perplexing anorexias as well.

Biu's daughter, Xoxa, mentioned during our trek through the *mata* to find her mother's work crew that she had eaten no breakfast and would probably eat no lunch. She explained that she was completely *abusada* with plain food and that she yearned to eat *comidas de luxo.* "Such as?" She stopped for a moment, and then, wetting her lips and snapping her wrist in appreciation, she readily ticked them off: "Bread, hot dogs, pizza, cheese, cake, soda, ice cream." Some of these were foods she had not once tasted. On the return home we stopped at a small cafe where I ordered Xoxa a Brazilian-style hot dog, but she pushed away the plate because there were "greens"—onions, green peppers, and tomatoes—mixed in with the ground beef. "What I really wanted," she clarified, "was *carne pura* [plain meat]."

Among the poor of the Alto distinctions are drawn among *comidas* (real foods, basic foods, foods that satisfy), *comidas de luxo* (luxury foods, foods for the rich, foods that tempt the palate but tease the belly), *comidinhas* (little foods that only add variety and decoration), and finally *comidas para enganar a fome ou enganar a barriga* (foods to fool hunger or to fool the belly, worthless fillers and nutritionless distraction) (see Zaluar 1982). Beans remain the prototypical food, the food that satisfies and nourishes, so that to say that a house is *faltando feijão,* is to say that the house is *really* without food, that people are hungry. Rice alone or *macarrão* alone cannot fill the *buraco no estômago,* the "hole in the belly," but one can say that one ate and was satisfied if only beans were served. Ideally, however, a real meal consists of an ample combination of starches: beans, rice, *macarrão*, and, of course, *farinha* sprinkled liberally over the plate. The plate should be "built" in the same way that a Californian builds a salad. On the bottom are the beans, covered by rice, then *macarrão*, ending with a layer of *farinha*. In the poorest households where the silverware may consist of a few spoons, the mixture is rolled between the thumb and index finger into thick balls, which are then eaten by hand. In Alto households that are better off, fork and knife are used to cut the layers neatly into each other. The important thing is that the separate foods, flavors, and textures blend into one another.[9] For people with considerable anxiety about hunger and accustomed from early childhood to eating few but starchy and heavy meals, satisfaction (a word used in reference both to sex and eating) consists in a sensation of fullness, even heaviness, after a main meal.

Alto people often remark that the poor not only eat more than the rich but *must* do so, that their "inferior" constitutions require it. The rich appear only to nibble on teasing appetizers and frivolous luxury foods, yet they are never hungry, and their bodies mysteriously are fat, healthy, and beautiful. The poor seem to stuff themselves (they observe) on heavy foods just to stay alive, and they are still always hungry, and their bodies are thin, wasted, and worn out. And so the rich are sometimes described as people whose pockets are full but whose bellies are empty, and the poor are "people with empty pockets and full bellies."

Because of the pressure to eat quickly and amply at any one sitting—a trait that marks the eater with the stamp of *pobreza*—the people of the Alto do not like to eat in front of others. There is a great deal of shame associated with eating. Eating is almost as private an act as sex or defecation, probably because of its ability to reveal so much about the person. Eating in public gives one away; it shows the extent of one's desires, the seemingly bottomless pit of one's needs. The shame is double-barreled. In offering food to a visitor, one is risking embarrassment at the humble quality of the food or, even worse, at the humiliating possibility that there may not be enough. Conversely, to accept food in another's house can be an admission that one is hungry. One can eat too quickly, too sloppily, or too much. One's table manners may be wanting; one may be expected to use a fork rather than a spoon, or one may encounter a strange food on the table and not know how it is eaten. In all, one may show oneself to be a *matuto*. Better to pass it by, saying that one has just eaten, that one is not hungry. But then this may be taken as an insult to the household. A terrible dilemma, this eating with others. The more courageous sometimes accept an invitation to eat, if urged forcefully enough, but they refuse to make choices and eat only what is put on the plate. The polite answer to the impolite question "Would you like coffee or hot chocolate?" is the proverb *"Tudo que vem na rede é peixe*— Everything that comes up in the net is fish." In other words, whatever you want to give me is good; just don't ask me to make a choice.

This ambivalence is not a secret: all the inhabitants on the Alto are aware of these mixed emotions about food and eating, and they tease one another mercilessly, calling one another *matuto* if one refuses to eat. Ramos offered, "This shame of eating in front of others is terrible. I used to be like that myself, but I gave it up. I put it behind me because you only wind up hurting yourself." Poking fun at Zezinho, his *compadre* from the Alto do Cruzeiro, the radical agitator João Mariano commented, "This one here is something! In public he only picks at food, but in his own kitchen, my God, can he *eat!* The man piles food on his plate and into his mouth like a truck loading sugarcane." Zezinho just laughed and offered a rejoinder, "My friend is *rico mesmo* [really rich]. He doesn't have to eat anything at all. Tall as he is—a *negão* [a giant black]—but for breakfast he just eats *papa* [a typical baby food that is also eaten by the sick, frail, and elderly]. The rich don't know how to eat." This "good-natured" joking is quite barbed, for Zezinho is using food to question his bourgeois *compadre's* radical credentials. He is saying, "Can João Mariano really be trusted? Won't his 'background' win out in the end? Look, even the way he eats gives him away!" The joking also contains a racial slur and a put-down, for João Mariano is being reminded that although he may be rich, he is also a *negão.*

Although Biu often stopped by my house and gladly accepted a cup of coffee, she preferred not to eat with me; instead, she took whatever food I offered home with her. Her little *caçula* Mercea would eat, however, but only if I put her on the floor facing the wall, with a tin plate in her lap, and left the room so that she could eat with her fingers unobserved. Otherwise, she would sit quietly and soberly, adamantly refusing to touch anything that was offered. Her body posture communicated the sentiment "I may be a *pobre* and hungry, but I *do* have my pride."

Only old Dalina the water carrier had no "shame" and surprised me with her request that as a going away present I take her out to "an elegant restaurant in Recife." All her neighbors along the rocky ravine of the Rua dos Magos were shocked at Dalina's boldness. But at the old colonial Restaurante Leite, in the very heart of Recife, Dalina sat delightedly at a small table next to the blind piano player, who dedicated songs to her and kissed her wrinkled old hand. We winked at each other as Dalina ordered herself a very large, well-cooked steak.

In the food taxonomy of poor people of the Alto, foods that satisfy (i.e., *real* foods) are distinguished from foods that *não satisfazem,* that don't fill the belly. Foremost among these are fruits and vegetables, especially greens, always described as *verdurinhas* (little vegetables). Greens are valued insofar as they are colorful and pretty; they *enfeitar o prato*, "decorate the plate." But they are considered *fraquinha*. When Alto women suggest that vegetables are weak, they are not referring to the absence of nutritional value ("*Verduras têm muitas vitaminas, não é* [Vegetables have a lot of vitamins, right]?"); rather, the weakness of fruits and vegetables refers to their "lightness," their inability to satisfy. ("You would have to eat six plates to fill the belly.") Even relatively "heavy" fruits and vegetables such as bananas and corn are dismissed as not very filling. When in season, corn is eaten as a snack bought from street vendors and children who sell roasted ears to passersby. Boiled corn is used in various "party recipes" during the month of June when Saints João, Pedro, and Antônio have their feast days. Only *fubá* (cornmeal) is considered a *real staple* food.

Whereas beans, rice, *macarrão*, and other basic foods *mata fome*, "kill hunger," other foods only "fool hunger." *Garapa*, the sugar water given a hungry child at night, is the most common of these. But *farinha*, ordinarily a staple of the *Nordestino* diet, can also be viewed in this way. During lean times the main meal may consist of a "few beans" cooked in a great deal of water to produce a *caldo de feijão*, "bean broth," that is thickened with a great deal of *farinha*. Here, manioc meal serves as a food substitute more than as a food extender, its normal role. Sucking sugarcane is also an *engano*, a "trick" played on an empty stomach and one of the ways in which hungry workers are "fooled" by their bosses. Normally cane cutters may *chupar cana a vontade*, "suck cane whenever they wish," as long as they are not wasteful. They must cut and peel small "rounds" of cane during slack periods, not simply break open one new stalk after another, sucking juices and discarding the rest. But cane workers know that this "free cane" comes at a high price, and that it is used to extract energy and productivity from tired and hungry workers.

In addition to exploited workers, babies and toddlers are a common target of *engano* as mothers substitute *farinha de roça* (a crude, unrefined manioc flour) for expensive powdered milk to make a "weak" but filling *papa d'água* (watery cereal). "Babies fed on water soon have blood that turns to water," commented a disapproving older woman with reference to the listless, lifeless *papa d'água*–fed babies of the Alto do Cruzeiro. "Nonsense," replied another younger woman. "Weren't all five of my children raised on *papa d'água*?" "Not at all," corrected the old spinster. "You killed seven, and the other five managed to escape you!" Yet despite its deficiencies, *papa d'água* is filling, and many babies take it quite greedily (even newborns are finger fed with the thick gruel) and then are gratefully quiet for several hours. In this way even small babies learn early to conform to the adult pattern of heavy feedings and long delays between meals.

Between the ages of one and two years Alto children are finally weaned from *mingau* or *papa d'água* to adult food. There are no transitional, or "weaning," foods. A baby or toddler who rejects adult food (which may be offered quite early) is at a great disadvantage, for she will simply continue to be fed *mingau* alone, which is incapable of satisfying her nutritional needs. The resulting weak, stunted, or wasted toddler is said to be in that condition because of the child's own *má disposição para comer,* her "lack of interest in eating." Many a hungry toddler will cry and whine for whole milk, rejecting both *mingau* and beans. "What am I supposed to do?" asked Marlene with respect to her pale and severely malnourished two-year-old granddaughter. "I can't afford to give her fresh milk, and she won't eat with the rest of the family. The girl simply *não tem vontade de comer* [has no desire to eat or, it would seem, to live]." This unfortunate pattern helps to explain the oft-noted phenomenon in poor and shantytown households of relatively well-fed adults with emaciated toddlers. *Ao lado de adultos gordos viviam crianças muito magras,* commented Alba Zalur (1982:177) with respect to her study of *favela* families in Rio: "Side by side with fat adults are children who are extremely thin."

There is something to be said, however, for the basically egalitarian method of food distribution. Conforming to Alba Zalur's (1982:178, n. 7) observations in poor households in Rio de Janeiro, the principle that governs food allocation on the Alto do Cruzeiro is that of *o de encher mais o prato de quem come mais e encher menos de que come menos,* "filling the plates of those who eat more with more and filling the plates of those who eat less with less." Although this principle governs the formal distribution of food, as the mother serves family members as they arrive home from work or school according to her perceptions of each one's "inclination" (*disposição*) to eat, an informal distribution operates in the kitchen. Those who control the food preparations—women and their daughters—help themselves at will before and while the others are served. This practice helps to account for the frequency of mothers and daughters who are considerably better fed than adult men and boys in the female-centered life of the Alto. It is an unconscious, yet a fairly consistent, mechanism. Meanwhile, those who show the least *disposição* to eat are often the disadvantaged and malnourished toddlers, of whom mothers often say that the poor little creatures do not really have a "taste" for food—or for life.

Hunger and Sex

In popular Brazilian culture the idioms of food and sex, eating and making love, are interchangeable within a continual word play of mixed metaphors and meanings. Hunger (*fome*) is commonly used with reference to sexual desire, and intercourse is described as eating (*comendo*). The man's penis is a mouth that "eats" the "fruit" or the "apple" of the woman; the woman also "eats" with her *boca de baixo*, her mouth below. As mouths and genitals converge, "sexual pleasures are tied to the pleasures of the palate, and the definition of *sensualidade* (sensuality) is broadened and expanded" (Parker 1990:115). One thinks immediately of Jorge Amado's novel *Gabriela, Clove and Cinnamon* (1974) in which the dark, sultry heroine is a temptress of the table as well as of the bed or his *Dona Flor and Her Two Husbands* (1977), which contains elaborate recipes for heavy Afro-Brazilian dishes redolent with pungent flavors and aromas that can also be read as recipes for Brazilian eroticism and desire.

Brazilian erotic language is so linked to eating that following sex one can say appreciatively, "*Foi gostoso*" or "*Foi uma delícia!*" "It was tasty" or "It was really delicious!" The genitals represent a veritable Brazilian *feira*: a man's penis is a banana, a mango, a turnip, a cucumber, a squash, a sausage, or a stick of sugarcane, and his testicles are grapes, peanuts, or *pitomba* (a tropical fruit). Both breasts and penises flow with milk and honey, and a woman's breasts are ripe *mamãos* (papayas) waiting to be "sucked" and "licked." Richard Parker wrote that "building on the notion of desire as a kind of insatiable hunger, the erotic takes shape in a language of the *gostos* (tastes), *cheiros* (smells), and *sabores* (flavors)—a language of culinary metaphors in which *chupando* (sucking) the parts of the body is described, for example, as *chupando uma manga* (sucking a mango) or *chupando um picolé* (licking a popsicle, i.e., a penis)" (1990:115).

Consequently, there is a long tradition of *Nordestino* scholarship treating sex as compensatory gratification for hungry *Nordestinos*, beginning with de Castro (1952:66–67) and Chaves (1968) up through Fátima Quintas's (1986) more recent study of sex and poverty. De Castro concluded that although starvation depressed libido, chronic hunger might actually increase it. Later, Chaves (1968:149–153) hypothesized that chronic undernutrition contributed to the high fertility of poorly nourished *Nordestinos* by stimulating the sex hormones and initiating a premature menarche. (At least on the Alto do Cruzeiro, however, chronic malnutrition seems to have had the opposite effect; most young girls experience their first menstruation by the age of fourteen or fifteen, two years later than middle-class girls of Bom Jesus.)

Sexual vitality is, however, a variant of the "autoethnography" of *Nordestinos*, who do project themselves to each other and to outsiders as an erotic and intensely sensual, as well as sexual, people. To be devoid of sexuality is to be *morto*, "dead," and even the poorest residents of the Alto struggle to create a space for sensuality in their lives, especially during the period of *carnaval*, when thoughts and talk turn to the "carnal." Age and beauty, or lack thereof, are no barriers to the claim to sexual vitality. Once during a spontaneous house party on the Alto, an older woman, her body as thin as a rail, her skin as wrinkled and dry as parchment, her teeth missing, her foot badly infected but washed and painted with iodine, got up to dance a sexy *forro* with a handsome youth whose open shirt advertised his strength and virility. The two danced in a close embrace, their movements that of a single individual. Dona Maria's wrinkled face flushed with pleasure as the dancers were roundly cheered and as admiring comments were made on the sexual "fire" that still burned inside the skinny old woman.

Fátima Quintas spent five years probing sexual meanings and practices among poor women living in the urban shantytown in Recife. Although many of the women spoke of being oppressed by the men in their lives (their fathers, husbands, lovers, and even adolescent sons) as well as sexually repressed by conventional Catholic morals and scruples, others had quite a bit to say on the subject of hunger and sex. Rosália Antônia told Fátima, "Sure I'm hungry. Almost every day my house is without food. My compensation is screwing. You asked me if I take pleasure in sex? Of course I do! How else am I going to know that I'm alive if I don't screw? At least in sex I can feel my flesh moving around and I know that hunger hasn't killed me yet!" (1986:173). Although Rosália was not shy of sexual desire, nonetheless her pleasure was tied up with her hunger so that sex served as a kind of banner of protest against the meanness of her fate. Where hunger was equated with passivity, sex was associated with activity, so that Raquel offered, "I go hungry, but I have no control over it. Sex, to the contrary, is my decision, my right. Nobody can take it away from me. . . . I'm hungry because I don't have any money to buy food. But sex is free; and nobody can stop me from doing it" (175). Among the poor women of Recife hunger represented death, just as sex represented life. And if hunger was scarcity, sex was abundance. Hence, a middle-aged woman could still boast:

> I'm nothing but a bag of bones. But I'm still crazy about screwing. If you were to ask me why, I couldn't tell you. Every year I'm pregnant. I embroider one pregnancy onto the next. I have to get up at four in the morning. I hardly sleep at all. There's no time for me to take care of myself. I carry cans of water on my head, I prepare the meals, I feed the infant, but I still can always find time to screw. I'm all bones, alright, but I'm tough. (164)

On the Alto do Cruzeiro women spoke with more inhibition about their sex lives, although they could often reminisce about one or another lover who was "good in bed." There were, however, less positive ways in which hunger and sex were linked. On the main street of the Alto do Cruzeiro, for example, lived a number of prostitutes, often single mothers and many of them still in their early teens. For Madalena, the young mother of Paulo Ricardo in the house of dwarfs, there was no *gozo*, no "delight," in sex. Along with many others in her situation, it was sex that first brought trouble into her life, and now it was sex that brought food home to the hungry children. Rosa, an older prostitute, offered that sex was a "playground" for the rich but a "battleground" for the poor. And Madalena, using the same idiom used to express revulsion with food, said of sex, "Long ago *me enjoei*; I had my fill. Now I'm completely nauseated by 'screwing.' I only do it so I can buy Nestlé's [powdered milk] for Paulo Ricardo. My body is rotting with this terrible disease, and God is angry with me." Madalena, who had had her "fill" of sex and who was revolted by it, was only fifteen years old. Stricken with a strange fever that paralyzed her arms and later her legs, and lying on the floor of her hut wrapped in a torn and dirty blanket, Madalena refused medical assistance, convinced that her sickness was a *castigo* that she had coming to her because of her life as a "street woman" (*mulher da vida*).

One afternoon, on descending the backside of the Alto with Little Irene, we caught sight of a very young girl with a newborn in her arms. "Yours?" called out Irene. The girl nodded and Irene taunted her, "Another hungry baby for the Alto—*que beleza* [terrific]! Now here's somebody who loves to play the *brincadeira da gente* [poor people's game, i.e., sex]." The child-mother shook her head sadly and replied, "*O que brincadeira sem graça* [Oh what a game without any fun]!" Sex, like food, is another "commodity" that separates rich from poor in Bom Jesus da Mata. Medicine is still another dividing line, and in the next chapter we explore the process through which hunger is "appropriated" and "treated" within the clinics and pharmacies of Bom Jesus.

5   Nervoso

Medicine, Sickness, and Human Needs

There are few vigorous, well-built, healthy persons among the workers. . . . They are almost all weakly, of angular but not powerful build, lean [and] pale. . . . Nearly all suffer from indigestion, and consequently from a more or less hypochondriacal melancholy, irritable, nervous condition.
Friedrich Engels ([1845] 1958:118)

My sickness is both physical and moral.
Carolina Maria de Jesus (1962:83)

Nervous Hunger

In Bom Jesus one's ear is at first jarred by the frequent juxtapositions of the idioms *fome* and *nervos*, "hunger" and "nervousness," in the everyday conversation of the people of the Alto. Later, the expressions lose their special poignancy, and they come to seem natural, ordinary. A mother stops you on her way up the Alto to say that things aren't well, that her *meninos estão tão nervosos porque não têm nada para comer* (her children are nervous because they are hungry). Biu, on returning from *feira*, says, as she drops heavily into a chair and removes the food basket from her head, that she became dizzy and disoriented, made "nervous" by the high cost of meat. She was so *aperreada* (harassed), she says, that she almost lost her way coming home from the market.

I stop in to visit Auxiliadora, whose body is now wasted by the final stages of schistosomiasis, to find her shaking and crying. Her "nervous attack" (*ataque de nervos*) was prompted, she says, by uncovering the plate of food her favorite son, Biu, has sent her.[1] There in the midst of her beans was a fatty piece of salted *charque* (beef jerky). It will offend her "destroyed" liver. But to eat her beans *simples*, without any meat at all, makes her angry-nervous. And so she explains the "childish" tears of frustration that course freely down her cheeks.

Descending the hill I stop, as always, at the home of Terezinha. She says that Manoel came home from work *doente* (sick), his knees shaking, his legs caving in, so "weak and tired" that he could hardly swallow a few spoonfuls

167

of dinner. She says that her husband suffers from these "nervous crises" (*crises de nervos*) often, especially toward the end of the week when everyone is nervous because there is nothing left in the house to eat. But Manoel will recover, she adds, after he gets a glucose injection at Feliciano's pharmacy.

The theme of nervous hunger and nervous sickness is universal among the people of the Alto do Cruzeiro. It appears, for example, in the stories and vignettes told by youngsters in response to the Thematic Apperception Test (TAT), that I administered to a dozen Alto youths between the ages of nine and fifteen.[2] Their stories had a pressured, almost obsessive quality to them, overdetermined by a free-floating and intrusive hunger anxiety. There was little variety in the themes; the stories all seemed alike, and I soon gave up the exercise. Terezinha describes her fifteen-year-old son as "weak and useless" as well as "emotional and oversensitive," in short, *nervoso*. "He cries for no reason at all," she complains. The source of the boy's fatigue, emotional fragility, and chronic nervousness is made clear in his TAT stories:

Card 1 (boy sitting next to a violin): "This boy is thinking about his life. . . . He wants to be able to give things to his children when he grows up. He is going to see to it that they always have something to eat."

Card 3BM (kneeling figure next to a small object): "The boy is crying. . . . He is all alone in the world and he's hungry."

Card 3GF (a young woman with bowed head standing next to a door): "This woman is thinking about what she is going to put on the table when her husband comes home from work. The *feira* basket is empty, and she wishes she could run away. Her husband will be very angry with her."

Card 12M (a man leaning over a boy who is lying down): "This man found this boy on the street and brought him home, and he's trying to revive him. ["What was wrong with him?"] He collapsed from weakness."

Card 13BG (a barefoot boy in front of a log cabin): "This boy is very poor, and his mother and father leave the house every day to look for money and food for the family. Their situation is serious. He is the oldest son, and he stays at home to take care of the others, his brothers and sisters. Now he is crying about what might happen to them. ["What's that?"] Some of them could die."

There was hardly a card that did not elicit from Severino or the other Alto youths questioned a theme of deprivation, sickness, hunger, death, all of them laced with the characteristic symptoms of *nervoso*. This was the case even with pictures meant to evoke themes of sexuality, relaxation, or play. Pedro, an occasional street child whose mother's boyfriend often chased him out of the house, looked for a long time at the card with several men in overalls lying in the grass, supposedly "taking it easy" (card 9BM), before answering, "These men are 'drunk' from overwork. They are lying down in the sugarcane because the sun is so hot. This one here is too weak to get up again. ["Then what?" Pedro shook his head with a troubled expression on his twelve-year-old face.] He's not going to get hired next time. He's completely finished; he's washed up."

Hunger and deprivation have set the people of the Alto do Cruzeiro on edge, have made them lean, irritable, and nervous. Their lives are marked by a free-floating, ontological, existential insecurity. There is not enough, and it is almost inconceivable that there could ever be enough to satisfy basic needs. Perhaps this is what George Foster (1965) meant to imply in his model of "the limited good."[3] It is a worldview that conforms to the reproduction of scarcity in the conflict among *casa*, *rua*, and *mata*, plantation, town, and forest. Those who suffer chronic deprivations are, not surprisingly, nervous and insecure. Reflecting on their social condition, the foresters refer to themselves as "weak," "shaky," "irritable," "off balance," and paralyzed, as if without a leg to stand on. These metaphors used so often in the everyday conversations of Alto people mimic the physiological symptoms of hunger. There is an exchange of meanings, images, representations, between the body personal and the collective and symbolic body social.

If food and sex are idioms through which the people of the Alto reflect on their social condition as *os pobres*, nerves and nervousness provide an idiom through which they reflect on their hunger and hunger anxiety. The consequences are at once unintended and far-reaching. The prototypical limited good on the Alto do Cruzeiro is food, and nervous hunger is the prototypical form of *nervoso* or *doença de nervos* (nervous sickness), an expansive and polysemic folk syndrome. Here I explore the process through which a population, only recently incorporated into the biomedical health care system, becomes prey to the medicalization of their needs. *Nervos*, a rich folk conceptual scheme for describing relations among mind, body, and social body, is appropriated by medicine and transformed into something other: a biomedical disease that alienates mind from body and that conceals the social relations of sickness. The madness, the *delírio de fome*, once understood as a terrifying end point in the experience of angry and collective starvation, is transformed into a personal and "psychological" problem, one that requires medication. In this way hunger is isolated and denied, and an individualized discourse on sickness comes to replace a more radical and socialized discourse on hunger.

The medical appropriation of the folk syndrome *nervoso*, the failure of those in power to recognize in the diffuse symptoms of *nervos* the signs of nervous hunger, and their willingness to treat "it" with tranquilizers, vitamins, sleeping pills, and elixirs are glaring examples of bad faith and of the misuse of medical knowledge. They are also an oblique but powerful defense strategy of the state. The irritable hunger of the squatters exists as a standing critique of, and therefore a threat to, the social order, itself at this transformative juncture shaky, nervous, and irritable. Hence, the "nervous system," a notion I have borrowed from Taussig (1989a) but with a different interpretive slant so as to link the three bodies: the existential body self, the representational social body, and the body politic, all of them "nervous." The medicalization of hunger and childhood malnutrition in the clinics, pharmacies, and political chambers of Bom Jesus da Mata represents a macabre performance of distorted institutional and political relations. Gradually the hungry people of Bom Jesus da Mata have come to believe that they desperately need what is readily given to them, and they have forgotten that what they need most is what is cleverly denied. But there is more to the story than bad faith and false consciousness, for both obscure the symbolic uses of *nervoso*, its expression of the refusal of Alto men (in particular) to accept at face value the logic and terms of their abuse at the "foot" of the sugarcane. And so my analysis must be taken as incomplete and contradictory, like reality itself.

Critical Consciousness: The Method of Paulo Freire

The aspect of things that are most important for us are hidden
because of their simplicity and familiarity. (One is unable to
notice something because it is always right before one's eyes.)
      Ludwig Wittgenstein (cited in Sacks 1985:42)

Insofar as I am engaged here in an ongoing work of praxis—theory derived in the context of political practice—the themes I am addressing did not arise in a social vacuum. Rather, they emerged within open and often chaotic discussions of the weekly *assembléia geral* of UPAC, the squatters' association, since 1982 also the ecclesiastical base community of the Alto do Cruzeiro.[4]

The "method" of the Brazilian base community movement is derived from Paulo Freire's (1970, 1973) *conscientização,* meaning action based on critical reflection. The method begins at the "base," ground level, with the immediately perceived and the "practically" true, that is, the given, experiential world. This reality is then subjected to a relentless form of deconstruction and to critical, oppositional, and "negative" questioning. What is revealed and what is concealed in our commonsense perceptions of reality? Paradoxes are proposed. Whose interests are being served? Whose needs are being ignored? The Freire method is open and dialogic. Any member of the community can suggest "key words" or generative themes for critical reflection, discussion, and clarification, including such words as *fome, nervos, susto* (fright), *à míngua de* (for lack of, scarcity of), or *jeito* (a knack, way, means, solution). And so part of this analysis was derived in this public and contested manner at UPAC meetings with the residents of the Alto. Out of the dialogue, at least in theory, emerges a critical form of practice.

The essential insight, derived from European critical theory (see Geuss 1981:1–3) is that commonsense reality may be false, illusory, and oppressive. It is an insight shared with all contemporary critical epistemologies, including modern psychoanalysis, feminism, and Marxism. All variants of modern critical theory work at the essential task of stripping away the surface forms of reality to expose concealed and buried truths. Their aim then, is to "speak truth" to power and domination, in individuals and in submerged social groups or classes. These are reflexive, rather than objective, epistemologies. Theory is regarded as a tool for illumination and for praxis. Action without reflection is wrongheaded; reflection without action is self-indulgent.

At the heart of all critical theories and methods is a critique of ideology and power. Ideologies (whether political, economic, or religious) can mystify reality, obscure relations of power and domination, and prevent people from grasping their situation in the world. Specific forms of consciousness may be called "ideological" whenever they are invoked to sustain, legitimate, or stabilize particular institutions or social practices. When these institutional arrangements and practices reproduce inequality, domination, and human suffering, the aims of critical theory are emancipatory. The process of "liberation" is complicated, however, by the unreflexive complicity and psychological identification of people with the very ideologies and practices that are their own undoing. Here, Antonio Gramsci's notion of hegemony is useful. Gramsci (1971:chap. 1) recognized that the dominant classes exercised their power both directly through the state and indirectly through a merging with civil society and identification of their interests with broad cultural ideas and aims. It is through this blend of instrumental force and the expressive, contradictory (but also consensual) common sense of everyday culture that hegemony operates as a hybrid of coercion and consensus. The role of "traditional" intellectuals, the bourgeois agents of the social consensus, is pivotal in maintaining hegemonic ideas and practices.

Increasingly in modern bureaucratic states, technicians and professionals come to play the role of traditional intellectuals in sustaining commonsense definitions of reality through their highly specialized and validating forms of discourse. Gramsci anticipated Foucault, both in terms of understanding the capillary nature of diffuse power circuits in modern states and in terms of identifying the crucial role of "expert" forms of power/knowledge in sustaining the commonsense order of things. In the context of this discussion, doctors occupy the pivotal role of "traditional" intellectuals whose function, in part, is to misidentify, to fail to see the secret indignation of the sick poor expressed in the inchoate folk idiom *nervos*.

But anthropologists, too, can play the role of the "traditional" intellectual. The specific issues dealt with here, the concealment of hunger in the folk (ethnomedical), and later in the biomedical, discourse on *nervos*, concern the way that people can come not only to acquiesce but even to participate in their own undoing. For anthropologists to deny, because it implies a privileged position (i.e., the power of the outsider to name an ill or a wrong) and because it is not pretty, the extent to which dominated people come to play the role, finally, of their own executioners is to collaborate with the relations of power and silence that allow the destruction to continue.

Hence, my analysis is addressed to multiple audiences. First, it is offered to my *companheiros* in UPAC as a tool for discussion, reflection, and clarification and as a challenge to collective action. Second, it is addressed to my colleagues in anthropology. As social scientists (not social revolutionaries) critical practice implies for us not so much a practical as an epistemological struggle. Here the contested domain is anthropology itself. It concerns the way in which knowledge is generated, the interests it serves, and the challenge to make our discipline more relevant and nonoppressive to the people we study. And so the "bad faith" community to which I refer in this chapter has analogues in the applied anthropological community. What prevents *us* from developing a radical discourse on the suffering of those populations that, to use Taussig's (1978) apt turn of phrase, provide us with our livelihood? What prevents us from becoming "organic" intellectuals, willing to cast our lots with, and cleave to, the oppressed in the small, hopefully not totally meaningless ways that we can? Finally, this analysis is addressed to physician-practitioners as a challenge to participate in Brazil with the new Church in putting their resources and loyalties squarely on the side of suffering humanity . . . and letting the political chips and consequences fall where they may.

Nervos *and* Fraqueza: *Metaphors to Die By*

Excuse me doctor, but you left out something very important
in those questions. You never asked me anything about mental
problems. . . . The patient then proceeded to talk about
nervousness, *nervoso*, and he said that the biggest problem
that Brazilians had was hunger. He said that he himself was
extremely nervous and shaky and that he suffered from
palpitations in the head, that he'd gone to many doctors, had
many X-rays taken, but that he continued to be very nervous.
    Do Relatório Sobre o Nervoso (cited in Duarte 1986:143)

Nervos, nervoso, or *doença de nervos* is a large and expansive folk diagnostic category of distress. It is, along with such related conditions as *fraqueza*

(weakness) and *loucura* (madness), seething with meanings (sor
contradictory) that have to be unraveled and decoded for what th
veal as well as conceal. In fact, *nervos* is a common complaint amoi
marginalized people in many parts of the world, but especially ir
terranean and in Latin America. The phenomenon has been the subject of
extensive inquiries by anthropologists, who have tended (as with the analysis of hunger) toward symbolic and psychological interpretations. *Nervos* has
generally been understood as a flexible folk idiom of distress having its
probable origins in Greek humoral pathology. Often *nervos* is described as
the somatization of emotional stress originating in domestic or work relations. Gender conflicts (D. Davis 1983), status deprivation (Low 1981), and
marital tensions and suppressed rage (Lock & Dunk 1987) have been suspected in the etymology of *nervos* (or *nervios, nevra,* or "bad nerves,"
depending on locality). In all, *nervos* is a broad folk syndrome (hardly
culturally specific) under which can sometimes fall other common folk afflictions such as *pasmo* (nervous paralysis) or *susto* (magical fright), *mau
olhado* (evil eye), and "falling out" syndrome among poor black Americans.

What all of these ills have in common is a core set of symptoms. All are
"wasting" sicknesses, gravely debilitating, sometimes chronic, that leave the
victim weak, shaky, dizzy and disoriented, tired and confused, sad and
depressed, and alternately elated or enraged. It is curious that in the vast and
for the most part uninspiring literature on *nervos*, there is no mention of the
correspondence between the symptoms of *nervos* and the physiological
effects of hunger. I would not want to make the mistake of simply equating
the two (conceptually and symbolically, at least, *nervos* and *fome* are quite
distinct in the minds of the people of the Alto) or suggest that in stripping
away the cultural layers that surround a diagnosis of *nervos*, one will *always*
find the primary, existential, subjective experience of hunger, the *delírio de
fome*, at its base. Nonetheless, it does *not* seem likely that the situation I am
describing here is completely unique to Northeast Brazil.

On the Alto do Cruzeiro today *nervos* has become the primary idiom
through which both hunger and hunger anxiety (as well as many other ills
and afflictions) are expressed. People are more likely today to describe their
misery in terms of *nervos* than in terms of hunger. They will say, "I couldn't
sleep all night, and I woke up crying and shaking with *nervos*" before they
will say, "I went to bed hungry, and then I woke up shaking, nervous, and
angry," although the latter is often implied in the former. Sleeping disorders
are not surprising in a population raised from early childhood with the
mandate to go to bed early when they are hungry. People on the Alto sleep
off hunger the way we tend to sleep off a bad drunk.

Closely related to *nervos* is the idiom of *fraqueza;* a person who "suffers from nerves" is understood to be both sick and weak, lacking in strength, stamina, and resistance. And weakness has physical, social, and moral dimensions. Tired, overworked, and chronically malnourished squatters see themselves and their children as innately sick and weak, constitutionally nervous, and in need of medications and doctoring.

But this was not always so. There was a time, even at the start of the politically repressive years of the mid-1960s, when the people of the Alto spoke freely of fainting from hunger. Today one hears of people fainting from "weakness" or nerves, a presumed personal deficiency. There was a time not long ago when people of the Alto understood nervousness (and rage) as a primary symptom of hunger, as the *delírio de fome*. Today hunger (like racism) is a disallowed discourse in the shantytowns of Bom Jesus da Mata, and the rage and the dangerous madness of hunger have been metaphorized. "It doesn't help [*não adianta*] to complain of hunger," offers Manoel. Consequently, today the only "madness" of hunger is the delirium that allows hungry people to see in their wasted and tremulous limbs a chronic feebleness of body and mind.

The transition from a popular discourse on hunger to one on sickness is subtle but essential in the perception of the body and its needs. A hungry body needs food. A sick and "nervous" body needs medications. A hungry body exists as a potent critique of the society in which it exists. A sick body implicates no one. Such is the special privilege of sickness as a *neutral* social role, its exemptive status. In sickness there is (ideally) no blame, no guilt, no responsibility. Sickness falls into the moral category of bad things that "just happen" to people. Not only the sick person but society and its "sickening" social relations (see Illich 1976) are gotten off the hook. Although the abuses of the sickness exemption by "malingering" patients are well known to clinicians as well as to medical sociologists (see Parsons & Fox 1952), here I wish to explore a "malingering" social system.

Dialogues and Deconstructions: Decoding Popular Culture

I told [the director of a city school] that I was nervous and that there were times I actually thought of killing myself. She told me that I should try to be calmer. And I told her that there were days when I had nothing to feed my children.
> Carolina Maria de Jesus, (1962:92)

Here is the voice of Carolina Maria de Jesus, certainly one of the most passionate and literate voices to have come from the Brazilian *favela*—and one of the most critically self-reflexive as well. The clarity of Carolina's vision stands apart; she is one of Gramsci's "organic intellectuals" speaking out eloquently on behalf of her class.[5] Most individuals trapped by their poverty in a cycle of sickness, worry, and despair are less aware, less critically reflective about their lives, lives that are, as one woman of the Alto put it, "too painful to think about." It is not surprising, then, that attempts to elicit discussions about *nervos*, *fraqueza*, and *fome* so often resulted in popular interpretations that were fuzzy, inconsistent, and not infrequently contradictory. It is usual for the anthropologist to impose an order on her subject matter, to overlook the inconsistencies in the ways in which people make sense of the world in which they live. Here, an analysis of "epistemic murk" and contradiction is the task at hand.

We begin with the following conversation, which took place one afternoon on the doorstep of Black Irene's house, where several neighbors were gathered during the quiet part of the day after lunch. One can note the juxtaposition of folk and biomedical idioms and the considerable ambiguity and confusion that allow for the medicalization of hunger and hunger anxiety. Everything from anger, sadness, discontent, and hunger through parasitic infections is understood in terms of the folk ailment. *Nervos* functions as a "master illness" or a master explanatory model that is similar to the folk concept of "stress" as it is invoked by distressed middle-class North Americans.

Sebastiana initiated the discussion with a sigh: "As for me, I'm always sick; I have weak nerves."

"What are your symptoms?"

"Trembling, a chill in my bones. Sometimes I shake until I fall down."

Maria Teresa interjected, "There are many kinds of nerves: anger nerves, fear nerves, worrier's nerves, falling down nerves, overwork nerves, and sufferers' nerves."

"What are anger nerves about?"

Black Irene said, "That's like when your *patroa* says something that really ticks you off but because she's your boss you can't say anything, but inside you are so angry that you could kill her. The next day you are likely to wake up trembling with anger nerves."

"And fear nerves?"

Terezinha explained that her fifteen-year-old son, Severino, had suffered from *nervos de medo*, "fear nerves," ever since the night Black Irene's mother died: "Irene gave out such a blood-curdling yell in the middle of the night that we all woke with a great *susto*. Severino leapt from his hammock and ran to see what had happened. When he came back from Irene's house, he was so shook up that he collapsed on the floor clutching his heart in an *agonia* of *nervos*. Ever since that night he has suffered from *nervos*."

"But as for me," Beatrice broke in, "I suffer only from overwork nerves.

I've washed clothes all my life, for almost sixty years, and now my body is as beaten down and worn out as Dona Dora's bed sheets [a slur against her miserly *patroa*]. When I come home from the river with that heavy basin of wet laundry on my head, my knees begin to shake, and sometimes I lose my balance and fall right on my face. What humiliation!"

"Is there a cure for overwork nerves?"

"Sometimes I take tonics and vitamin A."

"Others take nerve pills and tranquilizers."

"Don't forget about sleeping pills."

"Why sleeping pills?"

"At night when everything is still," explained Sebastiana, "so dark, and so *esquisito* [strange], time passes by slowly. The night is long. I almost go mad with nerves at times like that. I think of so many things; so many sad and bitter thoughts cross my mind: memories of my childhood and how hard I was made to work at the foot of the cane and on an empty stomach. Then the tremors begin, and I have to get out of bed. It's no use, I won't sleep anymore that night. *A minha doença e minha vida mesmo*; my illness is really just my own life."

Terezinha added, "*E os aperreios da família*, and the worries and aggravations of family life."

"But you can get *nervos* from worms and parasites, too," broke in Black Irene, putting a new twist on the discussion. "I almost died from it. Twice they carried me in an ambulance to the hospital in Recife. The first time I was in crisis with pains and shaking. My mouth was full of blood. It was my liver; the worms had gotten to it. They were getting fat on me! The next time it was a crisis from amoebas. I had to take so many pills, every kind, but in the end it was useless. Amoebas never die. They leave eggs inside you and the pills can't kill them. So they just keep on growing and growing until they take up all the room inside you. Sometimes they're quiet, but when they wake up and start attacking you, that's when you have a *crise de nervos*."

Terezinha interjected, tapping on her own bloated belly, "*Tá vendo?* When I have an attack of amoebas I can feel them, tum, tum, tum, drumming on the inside of my belly. There's an army of the nasty things inside there. Sometimes I'll go for a whole week without defecating. What miserable things they are! Then, when I finally lie down at night, I can hear brr, brr, brr, *fervendo* [boiling] inside me. What are they doing now? I ask the doctor for pills to attack the amoebas, but he gives me nerve pills so that they won't keep me awake at night."

It is clear that *nervos* is a polysemic phenomenon, an explanation for tiredness, weakness, irritability, the shakes, headaches, angers and resentments, grief, parasitic infections . . . *and* hunger. What I wish to explore are the correspondences between *nervos* and hunger. I am not arguing, however, that *nervos* can be reduced to hunger alone or that *nervoso* is an exclusively poor or working-class phenomenon. *Nervos* is an elastic category, an all-purpose complaint, one that can be invoked by a frustrated middle class to express its dashed expectations in the wake of the decanonized economic miracle, by the urban working class to express its condition of relative powerlessness (see Duarte 1986; M. Cardoso 1987) *and* by an impoverished class of displaced sugarcane cutters and their families to express their hunger.

In this particular context, the relevant question to be asked is, How have these people come to see themselves primarily as nervous and only secondarily as hungry? How is it that the mortally tired cane cutters and washerwomen define themselves as weak rather than as exploited? Worse, when overwork and exploitation *are* recognized, how in the world do these get reinterpreted as an illness, *nervos de trabalhar muito*, for which the appropriate cure is a tonic, vitamin A, or a sugar injection? Finally, how does it happen that chronically hungry people "eat" medicines while going without food? As one woman commented on the choice between buying food or purchasing a tranquilizer for a nervous family member: "*Ou se come ou se faz outra coisa*—Either you can eat or you can do something else [with the money you have]." That something is, more often than not, a trip to the pharmacy, of which there are more than a dozen in the small town of Bom Jesus.

So I decided finally to challenge my friends on their *nervos* and *fraqueza*. During a small UPAC meeting with the leaders and several activist women of the Alto present, I launched the suggestion "Why don't we do some *conscientização* about *nervos*? People say they are nervous and weak, but a lot of what is called *nervos* looks like hunger to me. It's the *nervousness* of hunger."

The women laughed and shook their heads. "No, you're confused," they offered. "*Nervos* is one thing, and *fome* is another." Beatrice tried to explain: "*Fome* is like this: a person arrives at *feira* almost crazy, with a stomachache, shaking and nervous, and then she sees spots and bright lights in front of her eyes and hears a buzzing in her ears. The next thing she faints from hunger. *Nervos* is something else. It comes from weakness or from worries and perturbations in the head. You can't sleep, your heart pounds, your hands begin to shake and then your legs. You can have a headache. Finally, your legs get soft. They can't hold you up anymore, and so you fall over; you pass out."

"And the weakness, where does that come from?"

"That's because we are just like that, poor and weak."

"And hungry?"

"Yes, we are hungry, too . . . and sick."

"So weakness, hunger, and *nervos* are sometimes the same thing?"

"No, they are very different."

"You'll have to explain it better then."

Irene rushed in to rescue Beatrice: "*Fome* starts in your belly, and it rises up to your head and makes you dizzy and disoriented, without balance. If you eat something, you feel better right away. The trembling stops. *Nervos* begins in your head, and it can travel anywhere in the body—to your heart or to your liver or to your legs."

Biu interjected, "When I suffer a *crise de nervos*, it gives me an *agonia* in my heart. It can give a person a fit. It can paralyze you so you can't walk."

"Yes, *nervos* can even kill you," continued Beatrice.

"Do men suffer from *nervos?*"

Zefinha replied, "Here on the Alto a lot of men suffer from nerves. They have heart palpitations, headaches, no appetite, and tiredness. Poor things, some even have trouble walking up the Alto. Some get agitated and wild and try to beat their wife or children. Others have such pain that you can hear them screaming in the night."

"What's the difference between weakness and nerves?"

Biu answered, "*Fraqueza* comes from inside a person, from their own organism. Some people are born weak like that. They can't take much in life. Everything affects them strongly because their body isn't well organized. Every little thing that happens makes them sick. Then there is the weakness that comes from anemia in the blood or from parasites or from amoebas or from tired lungs."

"Is there a treatment for *fraqueza?*"

Zefinha replied, "You can drink a strong *vitamina caseira* [a homemade vitamin tonic] made from Nescau [a Nestlé's powdered-milk fortifier], pineapple, apples, beets, carrots, and oranges. If you drink that once a day, it will strengthen the blood."

"So then hunger *weakens* the blood?" I forged on.

"If you have weak blood," an elderly woman remarked, "you will suffer weakness in the head as well. The veins of the body are connected everywhere and so are the nerves. The nerves in our hands and feet are the same ones in our head. If you eat poorly, you can't be strong; it will affect the blood and the whole organism. Not enough food leads to *fraqueza*, naturally! Your head becomes weak because of a lack of food in the stomach and in the intestines. Weak food leads to weak blood, and weak blood will give you *nervos* because you will have no resistance to anything, and soon you are completely good for nothing."

"But *comadre* Conceição," broke in Teresa, "you can also get *nervos* because of worry. The thought begins in the head, and it starts to build up pressure and give you a headache; and then it spills over, and it can move from the head right to the heart of a person. Then the person can have an *ataque de nervos* with a terrible *agonia* in the chest. Isn't it the head that rules over the body? So bad thoughts can reach the heart and destroy a person because the heart sends bad blood [*sangue ruim*] everywhere in the body and to all the nerves."

Later, João Mariano, the political *orientador* of UPAC, who had been puzzling over the riddle of *nervos, fome,* and *fraqueza* since the foregoing meeting, suggested that I visit two men of the Alto, Seu Tomás and Severino Francisco, both of whom were cane cutters until they fell sick and weak from *nervos.* "I think maybe it is nervous hunger, as you say," my friend offered.

Severino Francisco, the proud owner of the tiny Barbearia Unisex (The Unisex Barber and Shave Shop, much to my amusement) on the Rua da Cruz of the Alto do Cruzeiro, looked considerably older than his thirty-five years. He invited me to step inside his shop, although there was barely room for the barber and his client seated on a sturdy kitchen chair in front of a fragment of what was once a much larger mirror. He had been expecting me, and he conducted the "interview" via the mirror so that he could observe his work and have eye contact with me simultaneously. He apologized for the "weak" condition of his business and mused about the expansion he could effect once he had purchased a "proper" barber's chair. He had been cutting hair for seven years, ever since he had been cut down by his illness. Yes, it was *nervos,* he assured me, although he added, "But the doctors here don't understand anything about this illness. All they know is how to write prescriptions."

Until the age of twenty Severino was a man "of health and of strength" on the Alto do Cruzeiro. He began cutting cane with his father when he was a boy of eight. His only schooling was a year of alphabetization in the local grade school. He worked in the cane without stop until his illness began with stomachaches, tiredness, and general malaise. He lost his appetite, and with his empty stomach, he suffered from the dry heaves. He lost his "taste" for food, and he now lived on coffee. Gradually his legs became weak and soft; they "collapsed" under him. He thought perhaps he might have burst a vein. Or maybe he had become sick from working in the cold rain while his body was heated up from the exertion of his labor. Or perhaps he had hurt himself by lifting too many stalks of cut cane. In any event, it had gotten so bad that he had had to quit working in the fields, and then he had begun his frustrating search for a true cure.

"What have the doctors told you?" I asked, knowing already from João

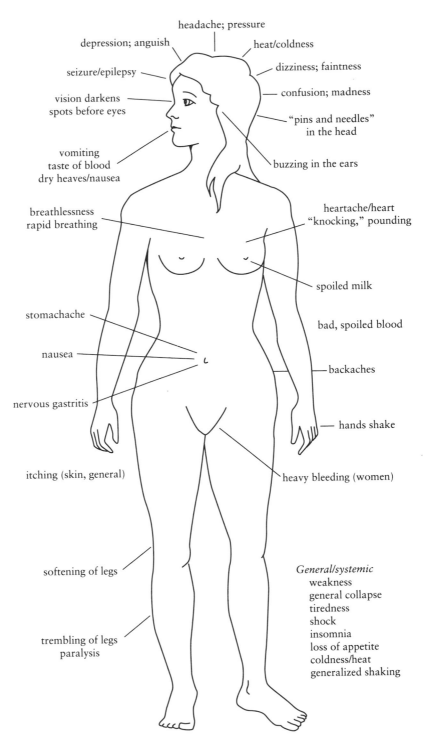

headache; pressure

depression; anguish

heat/coldness

seizure/epilepsy

dizziness; faintness

confusion; madness

vision darkens
spots before eyes

"pins and needles"
in the head

vomiting
taste of blood
dry heaves/nausea

buzzing in the ears

breathlessness
rapid breathing

heartache/heart
"knocking," pounding

spoiled milk

stomachache

bad, spoiled blood

nausea

backaches

nervous gastritis

hands shake

itching (skin, general)

heavy bleeding (women)

softening of legs

General/systemic
weakness
general collapse
tiredness
shock
insomnia
loss of appetite
coldness/heat
generalized shaking

trembling of legs
paralysis

Common sites and symptoms of *nervos*.

Mariano that Severino had been to every clinic in Bom Jesus as well as to hospitals in Recife.

"They don't know anything. They never told me what was wrong. They never operated on me. They just kept sending me home with *remédios* for my heart, for my blood, for my liver, for my nerves. Believe me, *só vivo de remédios* [I live on medications]."

Once, during a *crise de nervos*, he began to vomit blood, and he was carried by ambulance to a hospital in Recife, where he "really started going down hill." The nurses told his wife that there was no hope for him, and so she returned to Bom Jesus. The next day she sent for his body with a rented funeral car. But when the car arrived, the nurses exclaimed, "He got lucky; he escaped [death]!"

"But to tell you the truth, I don't know if I was lucky or not," Severino continued, "because I never did get better. Even today only a part of me is alive. I have no strength; my legs have no 'force' in them. All I have left are my hands [and he waved them gracefully in the air over the head of his young client]. My hands are as strong and as steady as a rock; the miserable *nervos* never got to them!

"At first I had no way of making a living. What does a cane cutter know besides his machete and his *foice* [sharp hoe]? I'm a donkey; I can't even read the sign outside my shop! And without my disability papers signed by the doctors, I can't get any benefits. Those bastards denied me what I had coming to me after all those years in the cane! So here I am today, a cane cutter cutting hair instead. Bah! As if this were any kind of work for a real man [*homem mesmo*]. This job is a *besteira* [a bit of nonsense]. Men today are worse than women [and he fairly glowered in his mirror at the nervous young man captive in his chair]. They want me to make them into little dolls with curls and waves and streaks in their hair. Tsk! The men today are all *viados* [queer]! And with all this, I barely make enough to feed my wife and children. The *caçula* [the last born] cries for milk all the time, but I have to deny her because out of the little *besteira* that I earn I have to put something aside every week for my medicines. The pharmacy won't let me buy them on credit. And like I told you, I live on medications. Would you call this a life?"

A group of men, unemployed and sitting in front of a little candy stand at the top of the Alto, directed me to the home of Seu Tomás. "Yes, his situation is truly *péssimo* [miserable]," they assured me and perhaps themselves as well. (It is always consoling to find one whose condition is even worse than one's own.) Seu Tomás and his wife were both thirty-two. Tomás apologized for not getting up from his hammock because he was "very weak." There was no place for me to sit down; even the earthen floor was muddy from the last rain. It was a miserable hut crowded with crying babies. "A poor house but rich in children," Seu Tomás joked, with a hint of sarcasm in his tremulous voice. He and his wife, Jane Antônia, had been married for nine years. They had seven children, of whom only one had died, thanks in part (he added) to the Franciscan nun, Sister Juliana, who had brought them a basket of food every week for the previous two years. Seu Tomás had been unemployed for those two years, unable to work in the sugarcane that had been his life since the age of nine.

"What is your problem?"

"A weakness in my lungs and tiredness," he replied, adding that the doctors could find no sign of tuberculosis.

"Anything else?"

"A coldness in my head, pains in my stomach, and a paralysis in my legs. There are days when my legs start to tremble and they can't hold up my body. I also have dizziness and fainting spells."

"Do you eat regular meals?"

"In this house it's a case of eat when you can, and when you can't, you try to sleep until the next day."

"What treatments have you received?"

At this Seu Tomás pulled himself with some difficulty out of his hammock and shuffled over to a small table in the corner. I noted that, like Severino Francisco, Tomás was able to walk but that his movements were stiff and awkward. Later, I asked to palpate his legs, which, although thin, were flexible and responsive to touch. I suspected that the "paralysis" of which Tomás and so many other Alto residents complained was part physical (hunger weakness) and part metaphorical or symbolic. Standing and walking concerned a good deal more than the "simple" acts of locomotion.

Men like Tomás are paralyzed within a stagnant semifeudal plantation economy that treats them as superfluous and dependent. The weakness of which these men complain is as much social structural as physical. They are trapped in a "weak" position. A healthy, vigorous person does not give a thought to the acts of breathing, seeing, walking. These come without thinking, and they go without saying. But these men (and women) have been made exquisitely aware and self-conscious of "automatic" bodily functions. They describe themselves as breathless, wobbly, disoriented, embarrassed, and unsure of their gait. How has this come about? We can begin by asking what it means—symbolically, existentially—to stand upright, to face the world squarely, standing on one's own two feet.

The psychiatrist Erwin Strauss provides us with a clue. Some years ago he wrote about patients in his practice who could "no longer master the seemingly banal arts of standing and walking. They [were] not paralyzed, but under certain conditions, they could not, or felt as if they could not, keep themselves upright. They tremble and quiver. Incomprehensible terror takes away their strength" (1966:137). Strauss analyzed his patients' existential dilemmas in terms of language. He noted that the expression *to be upright* carries two connotations. It means to be mobile, independent, free. It also means to be honest and just and to "stand by" one's deepest convictions. His patients had been morally compromised in some way. In the Brazilian instance I point to another connotation of "upright posture" in asking what the difference is between "standing up" to someone or something and "lying down," sinking, yielding, succumbing, giving up. In the cases of Severino Francisco and Seu Tomás, the language of the body is the language of defeat. It is as if they have had the wind knocked out of them or their chairs pulled out from under their legs. They have lost their balance. Yet one does not blame these men for their "succumbing" to the overwhelming forces of domination that have stolen their manhood. Their "failure of nerve" is understandable. The cards have been unfairly stacked against them. And yet one wishes, one hopes, one wants to hold out, for more than a chemical solution to their problems in living, indeed their very problem in "being" at all.

Among Tomás's collection of half-used medicines were the usual assortment of antibiotics, painkillers, worm medications, sleeping pills, and vitamins found in most Alto homes. Less common, however, was Tomás's antidepressant.

"Which of these are you taking now?"

Tomás picked up the antibiotic. "This was effective at first. The doctor gave it to me for my lungs. But then it began to offend me. Often I had to swallow the pills on a empty stomach, and they made my stomach pains worse."

"Why are you treating your nerves and not your hunger?"

He laughed. "Who ever heard, Dona Nancí, of a treatment for hunger? Food is the only cure for that."

"Which is worse—hunger or *nervos*?"

"Hunger is worse. When you are sick, like me, it takes a long time for you to die. When you are hungry, you can't be without food for more than a day. You *have* to get something to eat."

"Then why buy medicine rather than food?"

"With medicine you have to pay cash. Sometimes we can get food on credit."

"And yet you say that you and your children often go without food. Why is that?"

"It's easier to get help with *remédios*. You can show up at the *prefeitura*

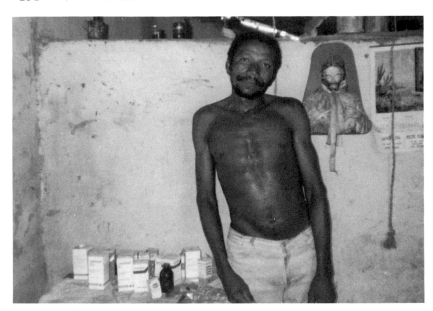

Seu Tomás, not quite upright and leaning against his medicine table.

with a prescription, and if it is in stock, Seu Félix will give it to you, or he will contribute something to the cost. But you can't go to the mayor and beg for food!"

"Why not?"

"Why not? Because it's not done. He will tell you to go out and work."

"But you are hungry because you are sick. Isn't that why he's giving you the *remédios?* If you are sick enough to be taking all these drugs, how can you possibly be well enough to work?"

"I'm a *matuto,* Dona Nancí; I have no head to answer a question like that." And so there the dialogue rested, but not before Seu Tomás struck up a pose, leaning and not quite "upright," in front of his table of not-so-magical medicines.

Embodied Lives, Somatic Culture

How are we to make sense of *nervos?* Are the *Nordestino* cane cutters suffering, in addition to everything else, from a kind of metaphorical delirium that clouds and obscures their vision? Is false consciousness sufficiently explanatory? Or can we best understand *nervos* as an alternative form of embodiment, or body praxis?

Embodiment concerns the ways that people come to "inhabit" their bodies so that these become in every sense of the term "habituated." This is a play on Marcel Mauss's (1950:97–119) original meaning of "habitus" (a term later appropriated by Pierre Bourdieu) by which Mauss mean' acquired habits and somatic tactics that represent the "cultural arts" of usi... and being in the body and in the world. From the phenomenological perspective, all the mundane activities of working, eating, grooming, resting and sleeping, having sex, and getting sick and getting well are forms of body praxis and expressive of dynamic social, cultural, and political relations.

It is easy to overlook the simple observation that people who live by and through their bodies in manual and wage labor—who live by their wits and by their guts—inhabit those bodies and experience them in ways very different from our own. I am suggesting that the structure of individual and collective sentiments down to the feel of one's body is a function of one's position and role in the technical and productive order. Nonetheless, the tendency in biomedicine, psychiatry, and conventional medical anthropology is to standardize our own socially constructed and culturally prescribed mind/body tactics and to understand and label the somatic tactics of others as deviant, pathological, irrational, or inadequate. Here I am referring to the exhaustive and generally unenlightening literature in medical anthropology on "somatization." Arthur and Joan Kleinman (1986), for example, understood "somatization" as a generally maladaptive and fairly primitive defense mechanism involving the deployment of the body in the production or exaggeration of symptoms as a way of expressing negative or hostile feelings. Here I am trying to recuperate and politicize the uses of the body and the secret language of the organs that play such a large part in the lives of many anthropological "subjects."

When I refer to the "somatic culture" of the displaced and marginalized sugarcane workers of the Alto do Cruzeiro, I mean to imply that theirs is a social class and culture that privilege the body and that instruct them in a close attention to the physical senses and symptoms. Here I am following the lead of the French phenomenologist Luc Boltanski (1984), who in his brilliant monograph translated into Portuguese as *As Classes Sociais e O Corpo* argued that somatic thinking and practice are commonly found among the working and popular classes that extract their basic subsistence from physical labor. He noted the tendency of the poor and working classes in France to communicate with and through the body so that, by contrast, the body praxis of the bourgeois and technical classes may appear alienated and impoverished. In the middle classes personal and social distress is expressed psychologically rather than physically, and the language of the body is silenced and denied. This, incidentally, is viewed as the norm in biomedicine and psychiatry and has consequently affected anthropological thinking as well.

Among the agricultural wage laborers living on the hillside shantytown of Alto do Cruzeiro, who sell their labor for as little as one dollar a day, socioeconomic and political contradictions often take shape in the "natural" contradictions of sick and afflicted bodies. In addition to the expectable epidemics of parasitic and other infectious diseases, there are the more unpredictable explosions of chaotic and unruly symptoms, whose causes do not readily materialize under the microscope. I am referring to symptoms like those associated with *nervos*, the trembling, fainting, seizures, and paralysis of limbs, symptoms that disrespect and breech mind and body, the individual and social bodies. In the exchange of meanings between the body personal and the social body, the nervous-hungry, nervous-weak body of the cane cutter offers itself both as metaphor and metonym for the socio-political system and for the weak position of the rural worker in the current economic order. In "lying down" on the job, in refusing to return to the work that has overdetermined most of their child and adult lives, the workers are employing a body language that can be seen as a form of surrender and as a language of defeat. But one can also see a drama of mockery and refusal. For if the folk ailment *nervos* attacks the legs, it leaves the arms and hands unparalyzed and free for less physically ruinous work, such as cutting hair. And so young men suffering from nervous paralysis can and do press their legitimate claims as "sick men" on their political bosses and patrons to find them alternative, "sitting down" work. In this context *nervos* may be seen as a version of the work slowdown or sickout, the so-called Italian strike.

But *nervos* is an expansive and polysemic folk concept. Women, too, suffer from *nervos*, both the *nervos de trabalhar muito* (the overwork nerves from which male cane cutters also suffer) and the *nervos de sofrer muito* (sufferers' nerves). Sufferers' nerves attack those who have endured a recent, especially a violent, shock or tragedy. Widows and the mothers of husbands and sons who have been murdered in violent altercations in the shantytown or abducted and "disappeared" by the active local death squads (see chapter 6) are especially prone to the mute, enraged, white-knuckled shaking of sufferers' nerves. In these instances Taussig's (1989a) notion of the "nervous system" as a generative metaphor linking the tensions of the anatomical nervous system with the chaos and irritability of an unstable social system is useful. And so one could read the current nervousness of the people of the Alto—expressed in an epidemic of *nervoso*—as a collective and embodied response to the nervous political system just now emerging after nearly a quarter century of repressive military rule but with many vestiges of the authoritarian police state still in place. On the Alto do Cruzeiro the military presence is most often felt in the late-night knock on the door, followed by the scuffle and abduction of a loved one—father, husband, or adolescent son.

The "epidemic" of sufferers' nerves, *sustos*, and *pasmos* signifies a general state of alarm, of panic. It is a way of expressing the state of things when one must move back and forth between an acceptance of the given situation as "normal," "expectable," and routine—as "normal" and predictable as one's hunger—and a partial awareness of the real "state of emergency" into which the community has been plunged (see Taussig 1989b:4). And so the rural workers and moradores of the Alto are thrown from time to time into a state of disequilibrium, nervous agitation, shock, crisis, *nervos*, especially following incidents of violence and police brutality in the shantytown. To raise one's voice in active political protest is impossible and wildly dangerous. To be totally silenced, however, is intolerable. One is a man or a woman, after all. Into "impossible" situations such as these, the nervous, shaking, agitated, angry body may be enlisted to keep alive the perception that a real "state of emergency" exists. In this instance nervous sickness "publicizes" the danger, the fright, the "abnormality of the normal." Black Elena, who has lost both her husband and eldest son to the local death squads, has been struck mute. She *cannot* speak. But she sits outside her hut near the top of the Cruzeiro, dressed in white, and she shakes and trembles and raises her clenched fists in a paroxysm of anger nerves. Who can reduce this complex, somatic, and political idiom to an insipid discourse on patient somatization?

The Body as Battleground: The Madness of Nervos

But there still remain the "negative" expressions of this somatic culture in the tendency of these same exploited and exhausted workers to blame their situation, their daily problems of basic survival, on bodies (their own) that have seemingly collapsed, given way on them. Insofar as they describe the body in terms of its immediate "use" value, they call it "good and strong" or "worthless." A man slaps at his wasted limbs (as though they were detachable appendages from the self) and says that they are now completely "useless." A woman pulls at her breasts or a man clutches his genitals and declares them "finished," "used up," "sucked dry." They describe organs that are "full of water" or "full of pus" and others that are *apodrecendo por dentro*, "rotting away from within." "Here," says Dona Irene, "put your ear to my belly. Can you hear that nasty army of critters, those amoebas, chomping away at my liver-loaf?"

In the folk system *nervos* may be understood as the zero point from which radiates a set of core conceptual oppositions: those between *força/fraqueza* (strength/weakness), *corpo/cabeça* (body/head, mind, morality), and *ricos/pobres* (rich/poor), as illustrated in Figure 5.1. Underlying and uniting these core oppositions is a single, unifying metaphor that gives shape and meaning

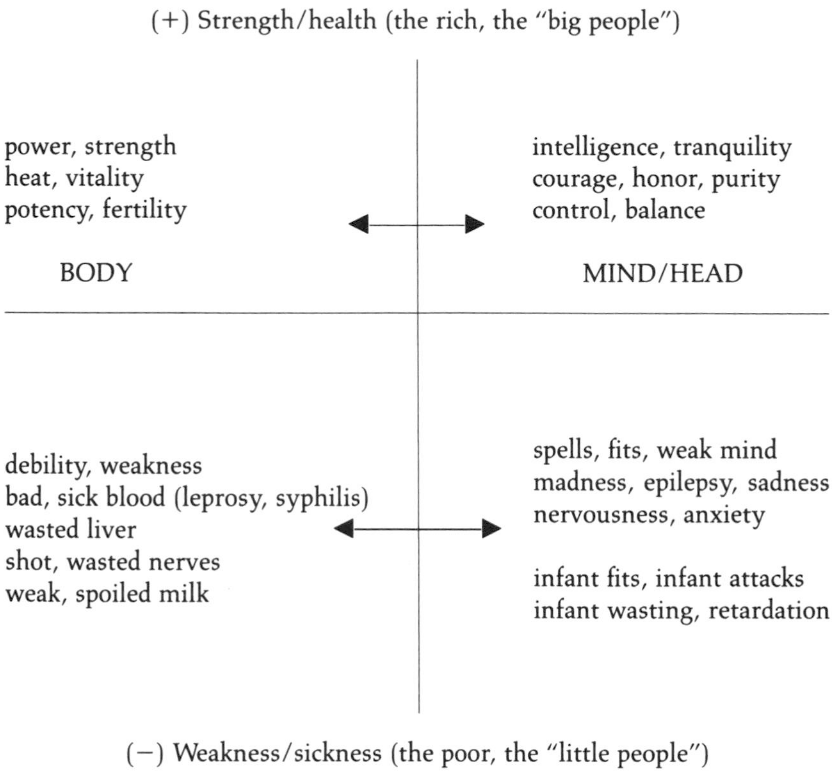

(+) Strength/health (the rich, the "big people")

power, strength heat, vitality potency, fertility BODY		intelligence, tranquility courage, honor, purity control, balance MIND/HEAD
debility, weakness bad, sick blood (leprosy, syphilis) wasted liver shot, wasted nerves weak, spoiled milk		spells, fits, weak mind madness, epilepsy, sadness nervousness, anxiety infant fits, infant attacks infant wasting, retardation

(−) Weakness/sickness (the poor, the "little people")

Fig. 5.1.   The phenomenology of *nervos*.

to people's day-to-day realities. It is the driving and compelling image of "life as a *luta*," as a series of uphill "struggles" along the *caminho*, the "path" of life. One cannot escape this generative metaphor; it crops up everywhere as an all-purpose explanation of the meaning of human existence. The *Nordestino* metaphor of the *luta* portrays life as a veritable battleground between strong and weak, powerful and powerless, young and old, male and female, and, above all, rich and poor. The *luta* requires strength, intelligence, cunning, courage, and know-how (*jeito*). But these physical, psychological, and moral qualities are seen as inequitably distributed, thereby putting the poor, the young, and the female in a relatively disadvantaged and "disgraced" position, making them particularly vulnerable to sickness, suffering, and death. Above all, it is *força*, an elusive, almost animistic constellation of strength, grace, beauty, and power, that triumphs. The folk concept of *força* is similar to what Max Weber (1944:358–386) meant by charisma. *Força* is the ultimate *jeito*, the real "knack" for survival. The rich and males have *força*; the poor and females have *fraqueza*.

These perceived class and gender differences emerge at birth. Alto women comment on the natural beauty of the infants of the rich, born fat, strong, fair, unblemished, pure, whereas their own infants are born weak, skinny, ugly, already blemished with marks and spots. Some poor infants are born weak and "wasted" before their lives have even begun, and they are labeled with the folk pediatric disorder *gasto* (spent), a quality of incurable *nervoso infantil*. Similarly, adolescent girls are prone to sickness at puberty, a time when the *força de mulher*—the female principle, sexual heat, and vitality—comes rushing from the girl's loins in her *regras*, her periodic menses, the "rules," the discipline of life. The softer among the girls sicken at this time, and some even die.

The rich fare better over all and at all stages of life, just as men fare better than women. The rich are "exempted" from the struggle that is life and appear to lead enchanted lives. Their days and nights are given to erotic pleasures (*sacanagem*) and to indulgence in rich and fatty foods; yet rarely do their bodies show the telltale signs of moral dissipation and wretched excess: bad blood and wasted livers. The poor, who can hardly afford to *brincar* (have fun, also used with reference to sex play) at all, are like "walking corpses" with their *sangue ruim, sangue fraco, sangue sujo* (bad, weak, dirty blood); their ruined and wasted livers (*fígado estragado*); and their dirty and pus-filled skin eruptions, leprosy, yaws, and syphilis. These illnesses come from "inside," and they are not sent from God but come from man, the wages of extravagance, sin, and wretched excess. The body reflects the interior moral life; it is a template for the soul and the spirit.

Within this ethno-anatomical system there are key sites that serve as conduits and filters for the body, trapping the many impurities that can attack the body from without and weaken it. The liver, the blood, and mother's milk are three such filters, and the very negative evaluation of this organ and these fluids by the people of the Alto reveals a profoundly damaged body image. The filter metaphor is particularly appropriate, however, to people accustomed to worrying about their contaminated water supply and who, in clearing the porous candle that traps filth and slime from their own water supply, often wonder aloud whether their own body "filters" may not be just as filthy.

One falls sick with tuberculosis, venereal disease, leprosy, liver disease, and heart disease because of the way one has lived: an agitated, nervous life given to excess. Bad blood or sick blood is the result of bad living, and people with these nervous diseases are said to be *estragado*, "wasted" by drugs, alcohol, or sex. If unchecked, these afflictions brought on by dissipation and excess lead to *loucura*, the most acute and dangerous form of *nervos*.

Dona Célia, once a powerful and feared old *mãe de santos* (a priestess in

Célia, the Sorceress.

the Afro-Brazilian possession religion, Xangô), fell sick after Easter in 1987. Within a few months her already lean body became even more wasted, an *esqueleto* (skeleton), she commented sadly, and she lacked the strength to pull herself out of her hammock. A stay at the local hospital resolved nothing, and she was discharged without a diagnosis or any treatment beyond intravenous *soro* (sugar, salt, potassium, water). "So many ways of being sick," mused Célia, "and yet only one treatment for all the *pobres.*" Her illness, she said, was *nervos*. Her nerves were frayed and jumpy and brought on wild flutterings in her chest, so that her heart seemed like a wild, caged bird beating its wings to escape. There were other symptoms as well, but it was an infernal itching that was driving her mad.

When I visited her, Célia was straddling her tattered old hammock, busily casting a spell to bring about the return from São Paulo of an errant husband who had abandoned his young wife, leaving her both very lonely and very pregnant. I waited respectfully until the long incantation was completed and the candle at her feet was almost extinguished.

"That will 'burn' his ears all right," Célia reassured the tearful young client with a roguish smile on her face. The Franciscan sister, Juliana, passing by the open door, shook her head and said disapprovingly, "Can a reunion brought about by magic be worth anything?"

"Oh, it's worth something, Sister," replied Célia. "I work with the spirit messengers of the saints, not with the devil!"

"How are you doing, *comadre* Célia?" I inquired.

"Poorly, *comadre,*" she replied. "I no longer sleep, and the vexation [*vexame*] in my chest never leaves me. I can't eat and every day I grow weaker. I have a terrible *frieza* [coldness] in my head, and it's difficult for me to concentrate. I can't even remember my spells, I'm becoming so forgetful. But it's the strange itch, the *coceira esquisita*, that I can't stand. It gives me such agony, I fear that I am going to lose my mind."

Célia's neighbors were divided on the diagnosis. Most accepted that Célia's illness was *nervos*, but they disagreed on its origins, whether it came *por dentro* or *por fora* (from inside Célia or from outside) and whether it was a "natural" disease that came from God or an evil disease that came from man (through witchcraft). Those who were friendly to the old woman said that Célia was simply "wasted" from years of hard fieldwork. In other words, hers was simply a case of *nervos de trabalhar muito*. But those who were fearful of the old woman, resented her, or accused her of witchcraft dismissed *nervos* as secondary to her "true" illness: *lepra* (leprosy) resulting from her "sick" and "dirty" blood, the wages of the old sorceress' extravagance. They pointed to Célia's many moral infractions: her ritualized use of marijuana and other drugs in the practice of Xangô, her casting of spells both for good and evil, her many lovers over the years—in short, her generally independent and irreverent attitude toward the dominant Catholic mores of the community.

I stood helplessly by as Célia gradually began to slip away, daily growing more thin and haggard from her ordeal. It was painful to see a once strong and powerfully built woman so physically reduced and humbled. Although I was able to reassure Célia that she was suffering from a bad case of scabies, not from the dreaded *lepra*, I could do nothing to alleviate her nervous symptoms: her weakness, her melancholy, the *agonia* in her heart, and her adamant refusal to eat the small bits of food offered to her by her loyal friends and her few compassionate neighbors. Everything filled her with "nausea," she said. It was no use; she would never eat again.

As a going away present I brought Célia a hand-carved black *figa* (a wooden fetish, in the shape of a clenched fist with a thumb clasped between the fore and middle fingers, used to ward off evil) that I had purchased in Bahia, where Afro-Brazilian religion is practiced with greater acceptance and with more openness than in rural Pernambuco. Célia was so weak that she could barely speak, but she grabbed onto the holy object with a passion that startled me. After implanting a forceful kiss on the *figa*, with it she made a sweeping sign of the cross over her own withered body, and then she blessed me with it as well. I have been blessed many times in my life as a Catholic, but never did I feel as protected and enclosed as in that moment, or as humble.

Less than a week later (but after I had already left Bom Jesus), a few friends gathered to carry Célia in a municipal coffin to her pauper's grave in the local cemetery. There would be no marker and no inscription to honor the remains of the devout sorceress, so I could not visit the grave on my return. Célia's sullen and blasphemous daughter, Ninha, cursed her dead mother and tossed her magical apparatus in the place where pigs forage and garbage is burned on the Alto do Cruzeiro. "She'll pay for that," said Nita Maravilhosa, Nita the Marvelous, who was the old sorceress's apprentice on the Alto do Cruzeiro.

What prevented Célia from eating was, in part, her fear of an impending descent into total madness, *loucura*, the final stage and end point of *nervoso*. "Do you think I am losing my mind?" she would ask me fearfully, and I would try to reassure her, but without success. During this same period, at the time of Célia's rapid decline and anorexia, there were several cases of *loucura*, and the Alto was astir with the scandalous behavior of Vera-Lúcia, the *doida*, the "wild woman" of the Rua dos Índios. Here, the madness of hunger and the hunger of madness merged once and for all in a case of *nervoso* that would not soon be forgotten.

"Vera-Lúcia would never do that," her fifty-two-year-old mother said without looking up from the floor, where she sat busily weaving a large basket of rushes. "She would never kill her own child." I had come to the slippery cliff called the second crossway of the Rua dos Índios in search of a woman named Vera-Lúcia who had registered the deaths of three small children during a period of eighteen months. The last to die, a two-year-old named Maria das Graças, was treated in the local hospital, and her death certificate listed the cause of death as *pancada na cabeça*, "a blow to the head."

"The baby was pushed down the ravine by the crazy deaf-mute daughter of Maria Santos," offered Vera's mother. "The other two died of *gasto*." As we spoke, Vera-Lúcia, her belly huge with another child, sat rocking in a corner with a slightly bemused, absorbed, and distant expression. When I walked over and gently ran my hand over her abdomen, Vera lashed out, "Take care of your own belly; mine is full of shit." Her mother then dropped all pretense to explain how impossible it was for a poor widow to care for a daughter who was both crazy and violent.

"When Vera-Lúcia is having a fit, an *ataque de nervos*," she began, "there is no one who can control her. She is totally fierce. You have to tie her down, or else she will break everything in the house. It's a *quebradeira mesmo*: glass breaking, plates flying, chairs overturned, name calling, bad words, even cursing Jesus and the saints. Sometimes she is so raving that she foams like a wild dog. But without the right connections, I can't even have her taken away to the asylum in Recife. I wonder whether living with a *doida* can make you crazy as well.

"Even as a baby Vera was always sick. She had weak nerves, and she suffered from *pereba* [infected sores] in her mouth and on her head. She couldn't eat anything except *papa d'água*, and she was as skinny as a stick. Once she came so close to dying that I carried her to church with the candle in her hand. It was a pity that God didn't take her then. But she survived, and now look what I have! A weak family can't support a person so *nervoso* and *fraca de juízo* as this. Once she woke up in a fit. It was during the full moon, and she began to bang her head against the wall, shaking and trembling all over with foam coming from her mouth. I washed a piece of raw meat around her mouth and threw it to a stray dog hoping that the *raiva* [madness] might pass into the animal and leave my daughter alone, but it was not to be. The wretched dog lived! I'll tell you something: with these nervous attacks there are no cures. If doctors knew how to cure this disease, the hospitals for the *doidos* in Recife wouldn't be so crowded. One has to accept what God wants. I only wish that God had wanted to take her when she was a baby."

"How long has she been ill this time?"

"Since Holy Week; since the night of Holy Thursday up until this day I have had no peace. On Good Friday I got on my knees and started praying, 'Blood of Christ, you have the power. Remove this nervous attack from my daughter; make her well.' But Vera heard me praying, and she yelled from the next room, 'I'd like to see this wretched blood of Christ spilled on the floor!' I shuddered at her blasphemies. I can only think that she has been bewitched by a sorcerer. Only Jesus can heal her, but I am afraid to bring her to church.

"Once I gave her a little statue of Cristo Redentor [a replica of the famous Christ Redeemer, the patron saint of Rio, who stands with arms outstretched at the top of Corcovado], and she became agitated. She smashed it to bits, saying, 'Once you were Cristo Redentor [Christ the Redeemer], but now you are Cristo Rebentado [Christ the Destroyed]!' And she laughed so that it froze my blood. On the night of Good Friday I walked her to the top of the Alto, and when we reached the crucifix, she became wild again. She flung herself at the cross, saying, 'Jesus, come down from there; I want to kill you myself!' But she didn't mean it because the next night she ran out of the house, and I found her at the foot of the cross where she was hitting herself with a *foice*. 'Just let me die here,' she was saying. I embraced her and she was shivering; there had been a terrible downpour. She began to cry, and finally she was able to pray, 'If you are Jesus, come down from your cross.' They say that even the devil can quote the Bible, but what she said didn't come from the devil, Nancí. Vera said to the Cristo, 'Feed your lambs; feed your sheep.' "

Such is the madness of *nervos* and the hunger of madness on the Alto do Cruzeiro. But despite her prayers, Vera-Lúcia didn't get better, and her new baby daughter survived only a few weeks. "It was a blessing," her mother told me when I returned in 1988 during the celebrations of *carnaval*. Vera-Lúcia was putting on her makeup and costume to join a local *bloco* of "Gypsies" who would be dancing in the streets below the Alto. A diagonal smear of very red lipstick traversed her lips to her chin. She flashed me a wild-eyed grin.

Nervos is a social illness. It speaks to the ruptures, fault lines, and glaring social contradictions in *Nordestino* society. It is a commentary on the precarious conditions of Alto life. *Doença de nervos* announces a general crisis or general collapse of the body as well as a disorganization of social relations. What, after all, does it mean to say, as did Sebastiana, "My sickness is really just my life," my nervous, agitated, threatened life? *Fraqueza* is as much a statement of social as of individual "weakness," for the people of the Alto are accustomed to referring to their home, work, food, or marketplace (as well as their own bodies) as *fraco*. The metaphor of the *luta* and its accompanying moral economy of the body, expressed through the idioms of nervousness and weakness, are a microcosm of the moral economy of the plantation society in which strength, force, and power always win. *Nervos* and *fraqueza* are poignant reminders of the miserable conditions of Alto life, where individuals must often compete for precious little.

Rather than a torrent of indiscriminate sensations and symptoms, *nervos* is a somewhat inchoate, oblique, but nonetheless critical reflection by the poor on their bodies and on the work that has sapped their force and their vitality, leaving them dizzy, unbalanced, and, as it were, without "a leg to stand on" (cf. Sacks 1984). But *nervos* is also the "double," the second and "social" illness that has gathered around the primary experience of chronic hunger, a hunger that has made them irritable, depressed, angry, and tired and has paralyzed them so that they sense their legs giving way beneath the weight of their affliction.

On the one hand, *nervos* speaks to a profound sort of mind/body alienation, a collective delusion such that the sick-poor of the Alto can, like Seu Manoel, fall into a mood of self-blaming that is painful to witness, angrily calling himself a worthless *rato de mato* (forest rat) who is *inutilizado*, "useless," a zero. On the other hand, the discourse on *nervos* speaks obliquely to the structural "weaknesses" of the social, economic, and moral order. The idiom of *nervos* also allows hungry, irritable, and angry *Nordestinos* a "safe" way to express and register their anger and discontent. The recent history of the persecution of the Peasant Leagues and the rural labor movement in Pernambuco has impressed on rural workers the political reality in which they live. If it is dangerous to engage in political protest, and if it is, as Biu suggests, pointless to *reclamar com Deus*, to "complain to, or argue with, God" (and it would seem so), hungry and frustrated people are left with the possibility of transforming angry and nervous hunger into an illness, covertly expressing their disallowed feelings and sensations through the idiom of *nervos*, now cast as a "mental" problem. When they do so, the health care system, the pharmaceutical industry, commerce, and the political machinery of the community are fully prepared to back them up in their unhappy and anything but free "choice" of symptoms.

Medicine and the Bad Faith Community— The "Nervous System"

The old is dying and the new cannot be born; in this inter-
regnum there arises a great diversity of morbid symptoms.
Antonio Gramsci (1971:110)

The modern state of Brazil is faced at this conjuncture, this transition from brutal military politics to more democratic forms of civil society, with a serious dilemma: what to do with the explosive problems of poverty, hunger, and indigency among its marginals, such as the former squatters inhabiting the Alto do Cruzeiro today. The modern bureaucratic state becomes more concerned with "organizing" than with "punishing" peoples' collective needs. In this way civil society "defends" itself against its "natural enemy": the poor, the indigent, the marginal. At this juncture the role that medicine and medical professionals can play as "traditional intellectuals" in reinterpreting and reorganizing peoples' needs is crucial.

Modern medicine has transformative qualities as doctors, nurses, pharmacists, and other health professionals contribute to the process whereby more and more forms of human discontent are filtered through ever-expanding categories of sickness, which are then treated, if not "cured," pharmaceutically. Although the medicalization of life (and its social and political consequences) has long been understood as a feature of advanced industrial societies, medical anthropologists have been slow to explore the process and the effects of "medicalization" in those parts of the world where it is happening for the first time. Here I want to show how medicine first begins to capture the imagination of people who, until quite recently, interpreted their lives and their afflictions and experienced their bodies in radically different ways. My attention to this topic was first stimulated by a wonderful aside (a footnote, in fact) in which Pierre Bourdieu recorded the words of an old Algerian peasant woman who explained what it meant to be sick before doctors became a permanent feature of village life: "In the old days, folk didn't know what illness was. They went to bed and they died. It's only nowadays that we're learning words like liver, lung . . . intestines, stomach . . . and I don't know what! . . . And now everyone is sick, everyone's complaining of something. Who's sick nowadays? Who's well? Everyone complains, they all run to the doctor. Everyone knows what's wrong with him now" (1977:166). Or do they? Here I am exploring the "usefulness" to the state of the medicalization of distress in a sick-hungry and restless population.

The expansion of clinical medicine into rural Pernambuco and into the consciousness of the rural population over the past three decades has been phenomenal and exponential. When I first arrived to take up a position at the state health post in 1964, there were few available health "resources." There was the privately owned Barbosa family hospital but without its current medical clinics and huge maternity wing. Wealthy women delivered their babies in Recife. Alto women gave birth at home assisted by a traditional *parteira* or *curiosa*, as the midwives were called. There were a half dozen doctors in private practice in Bom Jesus, but there were no medical clinics for the poor, with the exception of the state health post, located a few kilometers outside of town, where feces samples were examined, immunizations given, and teeth extracted. It was not a much-frequented place, and I soon left the health post to take the state's immunization program into the primary schools and homes of people on the Alto. In the role of *visitadora,* I was expected to try overcoming the "resistance" of the poor to medical care. In one sense (but not the one intended) that was an accurate term.

When people on the Alto got sick, then, which they did with great frequency—given almost endemic schistosomiasis and many active cases of tuberculosis and malaria—they drew on their rich store of herbal medicines, on the practical expertise of older women in the household, or on more specialized women healers who lived on almost every hillside path. When they were mortally sick, they were sometimes taken to the Barbosa hospital, which was understood by the Alto people as a place one went, often never to return. Home birth was universal and doctors were generally mistrusted, by women in particular. My efforts to coax a few Alto women suffering through difficult or problematic pregnancies into one of the private clinics in town were almost always met with firm refusals. I was told that the doctors were "men," after all, and that the women would not allow themselves to be "taken advantage of" in intimate medical examinations. Even when I stayed with them during the most minimal and modest prenatal exams, the women of the Alto would tremble from head to foot and sometimes cry when asked to lift their skirts to a stranger.

When Dona Amor was still a young woman in the 1950s and was working for a wealthy family in town, she suffered a serious accident to her eye at the hands of the youngest child in the household. Her *patroa* insisted that Amor be taken to the local hospital, but Amor at first refused, even though it might have cost her her eye. She had never done this before. But her *patroa* won.

"They took me there, and I spent a night of anxiety in the hospital, I can tell you! The next morning they brought in three doctors to operate on my eye. By then I was prepared for anything, for whatever pain they would inflict on me. But when the doctor brought me into the operating room and told me to lie down, I fell apart, *acabou a môça!* Even my own father never saw me lying down! And when I realized that I was going to have to take off my clothes in front of three men, I was finished. This would *never* do. *Sou môça intata* [I am an intact virgin] to this day! [Amor was eighty-five at the telling of her story.] 'Lie down, my daughter,' the head doctor said gently, but I was shaking so hard I could hear my teeth rattling in my head. Finally, I managed to go behind a screen and take some of my clothes off. They put me on a table and covered me with a big sheet. And there I was, dying of shame the whole time. I could never have gotten through it except for the head doctor, who told me a story while he was cutting away at my eye. It was about the old woman who couldn't get into heaven because Saint Peter said that she needed to take a bath and wash her hair and change her clothes first. It was a long story, and it made me want to laugh; but the other doctors didn't think it was funny at all, and they told the head doctor to stop fooling around and do his job right, *direitinho.*"

By far the most direct contact people then had with biomedicine came through the two family pharmacies in downtown Bom Jesus, both of which functioned like clinics and apothecary shops, where a small and limited assortment of modern, biomedical drugs were measured, rolled into little paper cones, and sold alongside herbal and homeopathic remedies. Many an afternoon I spent in the large back room of Rute and Washington's shop, taking powders out of huge jars with wooden lids, mixing them as directed, and rolling them into the paper cone-shaped packets for sale and distribution. The large, slow fan creaked and groaned overhead. Occasionally, a barefoot man from the countryside would break into our lazy concentration with a petition to administer an injection. Rute and I would take turns giving the injection, listening to the client's story, and offering practical medical advice. The only thing he paid for was the content of the injection—the medical service and the "consultation" were always free.

By 1982, when I returned, all this had changed. The hospital was greatly expanded and included an all-day walk-in clinic and a large maternity ward where almost all poor women now gave birth. There were a dozen modern pharmacies in Bom Jesus, and Rute's pharmacy was under renovation. No longer an apothecary, Rute's had a long sanitary counter surrounded by shelves of both domestic and imported drugs, including the controversial drugs Depo-Provera, the day-after contraceptive, and Prolixin, the long-acting antipsychotic injection. Meanwhile, the number of private doctors and clinics had increased tenfold. In 1980 the *prefeito* inaugurated the first municipal clinic, operating in an abandoned state-owned building in front of the *prefeitura.* It functioned all day in two shifts and was always crowded with women and children from the Alto and other poor *bairros* of urban and rural Bom Jesus. Many people, however, still preferred to get their consultation directly from the mayor, and the opening of the municipal clinic did not stem the tide of sick people waiting to talk with the *doutor,* Félix himself.

In 1989 there was another quantum leap as the *município* installed its first "secretary of health," who now supervised a whole system of municipal free clinics. The original municipal "post" had gone through a process of fission, now radiating out into a circuit of more than a dozen little "miniposts," as they were called, one for each poor Alto and *bairro* of Bom Jesus and for the most populated rural villas within the radius of the *município.* These were opened in tiny storefronts, in Protestant and Catholic chapels, in the backs of little shops, wherever a space could be found. Most clinics had only a table and chair, a small supply of basic first aid and injection materials, and a prescription pad. From "centralized" to "capillary," the diffusion of medicine, or at least some semblance or "ruse" of it, was accomplished.

Accompanying this process (which had some beneficial aspects as well) was a transformation in the popular idioms of distress as these were increasingly "medicalized." The traditional folk idiom, *nervoso*, was one instance of the larger transformative process. *Nervos* created a crevice, a space, for the insertion of medical thinking and practice into the everyday experience of people's lives. It became a vehicle for the medicalization and domestication of people's needs.

Misery wears many faces: that of indigency, hunger, madness, and despair. When misery is forced, as I am arguing here, to express itself in the form and language of sickness, there is always a consequent danger. In the clinic misery is confronted with an array of techniques and interventions that isolate it and guarantee that from it no other "voice" will be heard. Medicine is, among other things, a technical practice for "rationalizing" human misery and for containing it to safe quarters, keeping it "in its place," and so cutting off its potential for generating an active critique.

Where once *delírio de fome* was a popular representation of the tragic experience of the body with frenzied hunger, *nervoso* now represents the tragic experience of tormented and worried bodies with a nervous social and political system. *Nervoso*, once lifted out of the context of popular culture and welcomed into the hospitals, clinics, and pharmacies of Bom Jesus da Mata, becomes the "rational" discourse by power about disallowed and "irrational" hunger. Hunger and other unmet and basic human needs are isolated by a process that excludes them by redefining them as something other than what they are.

The Charisma of Medicine

I do not wish to leave you with the impression of a conspiratorial plot by doctors and pharmacists to lure poor and nervous-hungry people into a dysfunctional dependency on injections and drugs and into a form of self-delusion and alienation. Here is where Gramsci's notion of hegemony is useful. In general, medicine does not act on people coercively but rather through the subtle transformation of everyday knowledge and practice concerning the body—body praxis. By the time people start lining up in clinics and waiting long hours for three-minute consultations and a prescription, it is not because they have been "forced" to do so; and once inside those clinics they do not have the doctor's social and medical views thrust on them. They go because to a great extent they have already come to share those views (see Frankenberg 1988). This is how hegemony operates and why one encounters such resistance in attempting to challenge notions and relationships that are now part of the shared commonsense world.

Because the people of the Alto do Cruzeiro suffer, truly suffer, from headaches, tremors, weakness, tiredness, irritability, angry weeping, and other symptoms of nervous hunger, they look to healers, doctors, pharmacists, and political bosses and patrons in Bom Jesus for a "cure" to their afflictions. Sickness is recognized as a "crisis" manifesting itself dramatically and brutally, visiting itself on the body with a vengeance. Likewise, medical therapy is understood as a rapid, violent, and immediate assault on the ailing body, symbolized in the injection, intravenous *soro*, extraction of teeth, and surgical removal of organs. The people of the Alto look for strong, powerfully acting medications, drugs that will reinvigorate the body, "animate" the senses, and "fortify the bones." And so they line up in clinics, in drugstores, in the mayor's office, in the municipal dispensary, and they ask for *remédios:* "strong," powerful drugs to transform them into healthy, lively, and healthy bodies, to reclaim the strength and vitality they describe as having "lost." And they do not leave until they get these magical, potent drugs: antibiotics, painkillers, vitamins, tonics, "nerve pills," tranquilizers, and sleeping pills. And they get them, if they are "lucky," even without paying for them.

One cannot underestimate the lethal attractiveness of drugs to an illiterate population (unable to read warning labels) and emerging from a popular culture with a long tradition of "magical medicines." The indigenous Brazilian *pajé* was, among other things, a *curandeiro* whose power derived largely from his knowledge of a vast repertoire of herbal medicines (G. Freyre 1986a:266; Araujo 1979). The contemporary herbalist, such as Dr. Raiz who operates several large stalls in the weekly *feira* of Bom Jesus, has command, or so he says, of "several hundred" healing plants, roots, and barks, which he prescribes in great quantities and in combinations called "cocktails" that mix herbs and modern pharmaceuticals, including antibiotics. In visiting door to door to inquire about medications currently in use, I came to think of my Alto friends as "eating" and "drinking" their drugs as daily requirements rather like fuel and food (see Helman 1981).

An altogether horrifying illustration of the magnetism of drugs to relatively isolated populations in Brazil comes from the small town of Goiana in central Brazil, where in September 1987 several individuals were exposed to radioactive contamination. A hapless junkyard dealer came across a lead cylinder containing a capsule of radioactive cesium 137 (used in the treatment of cancer) that had been carelessly discarded when a local medical clinic was abandoned. By the time Brazilian doctors and public officials were aware of

"Can you give me some help so I can have these two refilled?"

what had happened and were able to control the contamination, more than two hundred townspeople had been exposed to the deadly but mysteriously beautiful bluish dust found inside the capsule. Several individuals, captivated by the glowing substance, rubbed it on their faces and bodies or powdered their hair with it, and one person even swallowed some, thinking it to have magically therapeutic or beautifying properties. As in this rather extreme case, so, too, in more ordinary circumstances, poor people expect "strong" medicines to have the power to restore them to health and strength.

Medicine and politics are closely intertwined in small, interior towns like Bom Jesus, where the aristocratic, dynastic families produce the community's landowners, politicians, and doctors. Often these roles are combined in a single dominant personality. In Bom Jesus da Mata the large, powerful, and sugar-rich Barbosa family has controlled municipal politics, the municipal health clinics, the hospital, the *maternidade*, and the town's only newspaper for a half century. The director of the hospital, named after his father, is a powerful state senator and older brother of the mayor. Dr. Urbano returns to Bom Jesus every weekend to meet his "constituency" in the wards of his family's hospital. The *prefeito* himself, and without the benefit of medical training, runs his inner chambers like a walk-in clinic and a "people's pharmacy." From his desk drawers and file cabinets he distributes various *remédios*, eyeglasses, false teeth, tonics, and vitamins to the long lines of hungry sick-poor who come begging his intercession in their miseries. He keeps a monogrammed notepad handy on which he scribbles "prescriptions" to be gotten from a local pharmacist who maintains close connections to "the family."

The old sugar plantation's moral and political economy is still felt in "modernizing" Bom Jesus, where political leaders are expected to be patrons rather like "godfathers," who bestow gifts and favors in exchange for loyalty. Increasingly today the gifts and favors sought and bestowed are medicines, some highly toxic. They are, at their worst, when given to nervous-hungry people, gifts of poison. The ancient Greeks did not distinguish between the word for drug and the word for poison—a single word, *pharmakon,* implied both the power to cure and the power to kill, an apt designation for this context. There is an irony to the old custom of the interior whereby the poor refer to all their social superiors with the courtesy title *doutor.* In the past this was meant to acknowledge the university education and learning of the rural elite. Today, when a rural worker calls a superior *doutor,* he is meaning to invest his *patrão* with the mystique and power of medicine.

But why medicine? If it is power that the leading political families want, why don't they simply distribute food to hungry people? Health is today, and throughout the Third World, the political symbol that is most subject to manipulation. Political slogans such as "health for all by the year 2000," "community health," and "the therapeutic community" filter down to small, interior communities, where they are often used as a "cover" for acts of violence and malicious neglect practiced against the poor in the economic and political spheres. There are power and domination to be had from defining a population as "sick" or "nervous" and in need of the "doctoring" hands of a political administration that swathes itself in medical symbols. To acknowledge hunger, which is not a disease but a social illness, would be tantamount to political suicide for leaders whose power has come from the same plantation economy that has produced the hunger in the first place. And because the poor have come to invest drugs with such magical efficacy, it is all too easy for their faith to be subverted and used against them. If hunger cannot be satisfied, it can at least be tranquilized, so that medicine, even more than religion, comes to actualize the Marxist platitude on the drugging of the masses.

The physicians working in the public hospital and clinics of Bom Jesus da Mata cannot be held solely responsible for the drug fetishes of the local populace. Doctors do not control the flood of harmful pharmaceuticals coming from the United States, Germany, and Switzerland (see Silverman 1976), nor are they responsible for the relatively free circulation of restricted drugs through pharmacies that occupy so strategic a position in both the small towns and large cities of Brazil today. For many Alto residents the pharmacies remain their only dependable source of primary health care. Local druggists and their young assistants diagnose symptoms and recommend specific drugs. Most apply injections in the shop. Even though each pharmacy is periodically sent a government list of "restricted" and "controlled" substances, the only drugs I ever saw withheld from local residents without a prescription were abortifacients and antipsychotic medications.

Nonetheless, local physicians do participate in the irrational "drugging" of a sick-hungry population either because they have themselves fallen under the spell of the latest drug propaganda or because they are, as one clinic doctor describes himself, "totally demoralized" by the functions they perform and the political interests they serve in the small community. At the main municipal clinic functioning out of a new wing of the private Barbosa Family Hospital, several doctors take turns staffing the morning and afternoon shifts. Two dental students staff the dental clinic, where teeth are extracted on request. Approximately thirty patients are attended at each clinic shift on a first come, first served basis. No individual records and no record of the drugs prescribed to each client are kept. A daily summary of patients seen and drugs prescribed is submitted on a monthly basis to the mayor's office. There is no fee for consultation, but the quality of the medical care received is so poor that it fools no one, least of all the sick-poor themselves, who say that the clinic only represents more "bureaucracy." A woman, waiting in the crowded hallway that served the municipal clinic, has this to say: "The medicine for the poor is worthless. It's 'street medicine,' medicine 'on the run.' There's no diagnosis, no examination. They don't want to handle us. Maybe they're afraid that poverty, like disease, is contagious. So without exams, without referrals, with whatever drugs are handy, we die of grippe, of fevers, of diarrheas, or of many things we don't even know what they are. We are like walking corpses."

Another woman adds, "So many children walk around this clinic with their knees shaking from hunger. The doctors send us away. They don't touch us. They don't even look inside our mouths. Aren't they supposed to do that? How can they know what is wrong with us? If I had my life to live over again, I would be a pharmacist. They take more care in treating us than the doctors. The doctors only know one question: 'Well, tell me what you are feeling?' And already they are writing out a prescription. We die off and we die off, and we never even know from what."

Later that same day I speak to a young dentist working at the clinic who agrees with the clients: "This health post is a scandal, a danger really. People are worse off coming here than treating themselves. There are no conditions here, no way to run a proper clinic: no instruments, no proper medicines, no sterile conditions. Look at this room and what do you see? A chair! Nothing else. All I do is pull teeth. People come in with a healthy set of teeth but with a pain they can't bear. All they need is a filling. If I tell them that is the solution they reply that they can't afford a private dentist. So against my conscience, I pull the tooth. If I were to send them home, the way I'd like, I'd be out of my job. It is a total demoralization, but we do it. Mine is a political appointment. I'm here to please; maybe appease is a better word. It's all politics in any case. My job is not only to extract teeth but to extract votes as well."

Appeasement does seem an appropriate word for the care given to the sick-poor who daily attend a municipal clinic. By the time I arrived at the municipal health post on the morning of July 12, 1987 (for one of several dozen such clinic observations made between 1982 and 1989), the attending clinic physician, Dr. Luíz, had already seen more than a dozen patients. It was just barely 8 A.M. There were still forty or more people crowded into the waiting room hoping to be seen that morning. The young physician, a hospital surgeon, welcomed me into the consulting room as he had on previous mornings. Interested in his work, and critical of the organization of health care and of the patients who came for treatment, Dr. Luíz was a talkative and open informant. As a surgeon and a specialist, he considered his weekly shift in the clinic an annoyance, and he obliged the *prefeito* only to secure his regular position at the Barbosa Hospital. Although he considered the clinic a bit of a sham, he also blamed the patients who presented him with a host of nonspecific ailments.

"They come in with headaches, no appetite, tiredness, and they hurt all over. They present a whole body in pain or in crisis, with an ailment that attacks them everywhere! That's impossible. How am I supposed to treat that? I'm a surgeon, not a magician! They say they are weak, that they are nervous. They say their head pounds, their heart is racing in their chest, their legs are shaking. It's a litany of complaints from head to toe. Yes, they all have worms, they all have amoebas, they all have parasites. But parasites can't explain everything. How am I supposed to make a diagnosis?"

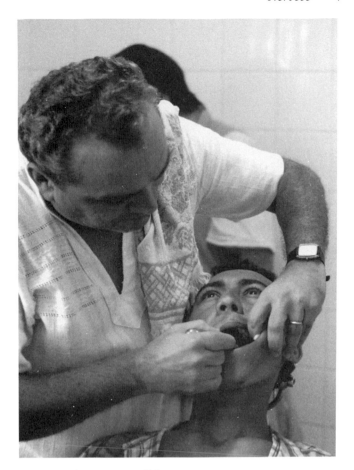

Dr. "Tiradentes": "It will be out in a minute!"

But he didn't even try. It was too "demoralizing," he said. On this particular day, as on the others I observed, most of the clinic patients were women, many of them accompanied by small children. In keeping with the political agenda of the clinic, the consulting room was bare, consisting only of a table and two chairs. The old examining table, pushed against a back wall, was covered with a plastic sheet and never used. In this clinic, at least, Foucault's (1975:93) hostile "medical gaze" would never graze or penetrate the "sanctity" of the sick individual. Here no bodies would be touched, or heart and lungs listened to, no organs palpated. Here diagnosis was the privilege of the patient: "Oh, doctor, mine is a problem with the kidneys." At most the doctor translated the nonspecific torrent of symptoms, or the folk syndrome, into a functional or psychosomatic category hardly more specific than the *nervos* or *sustos* referred to by the patients. Although doctor and patient sometimes used the same words in communicating with each other, each was almost completely ignorant of the other's often very specific meanings. And neither particularly respected the other. "Doctors don't know anything about my illness," the patients complained with great frequency. "Those people 'enjoy' being sick," retaliated Dr. Luíz. "Being sick makes the 'little people' feel important, valuable, long suffering. They are terrific actors."

Given the basic ground rules of clinic interactions (no physical exam, no diagnosis), the average consultation took less than three minutes, allowing Dr. Luíz to see more than the required number of patients and still leave the clinic for an early lunch at 11:30 A.M. Because the wait was so long and the attention received so minimal, most clinic patients came prepared, and once admitted to the consulting room, they attempted to take charge of the situation by initiating the interaction with a direct request. Several approached the doctor carrying old prescription bottles either to get a refill or to complain that they were useless. Generally what ensued was a negotiation over access to costly antibiotics, controlled or restricted drugs, and surgery (especially sterilizations) at the expense of the município.

The futility of the clinic interaction was captured in a genre of Pernambucan folk art: miniature ceramic figures found in the marketplace. Doctors were a popular subject and (along with the military police) were often portrayed in compromising poses as inept, brutal, disgusting, or corrupt. In one popular representation, a doctor and a patient (fully clothed) sit across from each other so that they gazed in opposite directions. There was no contact and no communication. It was a scathing, and all too accurate, commentary.

On the morning in question, twelve of the twenty-three clinic patients presented symptoms of nervos, often in conjunction with other ailments. By contrast, on a general clinic morning in August 1982, only five of twenty-nine patients presented nervous symptoms. I cannot hazard a guess about the general prevalence of this complaint among the poor of Bom Jesus. Clinic doctors always complained of an "excess" of these "neurotic" symptoms, whereas in a felt needs survey that I conducted among residents of the Alto, desanimação (dispiritedness), weakness, and nervos were among the five most frequently cited health problems.

Of the twelve patients who reported nervous symptoms to Dr. Luíz, nine received a prescription for a tranquilizer or a sleeping pill; five received (separately or in addition) a tonic (fortificante). In two instances women received tranquilizers in the absence of any nervous complaints. A young woman with a gynecological problem resulting from a botched delivery in which the infant died was prescribed a major tranquilizer in the absence of any psychological symptoms.[6] In another instance a single woman, age thirty-eight, was denied a request for a hysterectomy and sent home with a scolding, sanctimonious lecture on the womanly "duty" of childbearing.

An obvious subtext ran through these women's nervous complaints: the free-floating anxiety of women saddled with too many, too sick, and too needy-hungry children and with too little support in rearing them. The symptoms of irritability, sadness, fatigue, headaches, and nervousness were often the prelude to a request for a sterilization, a request that was rarely granted. For these "nervous" women and their fussy, malnourished children, tranquilizers and sleeping pills were easier to come by than either food or tubal ligations.

The link between *nervos* and hunger was perhaps nowhere more poignantly illustrated than in the case of a young single mother who presented her nine-month-old baby as suffering from a *nervoso infantil*. The mother complained that her small, listless, and extremely anemic little girl was "irritable" and "fussy" and that she cried all through the night, thus annoying other family members, especially the child's grandmother. The old woman was the economic mainstay of a large household with many dependent children and several unemployed adults. The old woman had to rise each morning before dawn and walk a great distance to the ceramic factory where she worked. The perpetually fussy and crying toddler kept her awake, and she had threatened to put her daughter and child out if she couldn't get the child to be quiet at night. The mother requested something that would calm the nervous child and make her sleep. The herbal teas recommended by a local *curandeira* had not worked. Throughout the brief interview the little girl hid her head in her mother's shoulder and whined in a pitiful manner. She was an unattractive child: pale and thin, unhappy, insecure, and both physically and socially underdeveloped. Dr. Luíz gave the mother a broadly disapproving look and shook his head, saying that he was a principled doctor and would not prescribe sleeping pills to a child younger than four years. Instead, he wrote the distraught young woman a prescription for vitamins that she was told to pick up at the *prefeitura*.

As on many other occasions the doctor failed to acknowledge the mother's very real distress and the child's gross state of undernutrition, for which the vitamins were merely an insult. That the child was "nervous-hungry" goes without saying, just as the causes of death on the burial certificates for the two hundred to three hundred children registered each year at the *cartório civil* of Bom Jesus da Mata go "without saying." In this way the reality of hunger can remain a fiercely guarded community secret. And so there is a consequent failure to see what should be right before one's eyes and an evasion of responsibility and accountability. In all, there is a dissociation from reality, a kind of collective psychosis.

"She cries all night long; no one in the house can get any sleep."

The Brazilian novelist Clarice Lispector captured a similar moment in a poignant scene from her novel *A Hora da Estrela* (The Hour of the Star). Macabea, a naive and pathetic young *matuta* from the Northeast who has migrated to the south of Brazil, where she is both underpaid and underfed as a typist, consults a doctor for the first time because she is feeling so badly. After a cursory medical examination the following dialogue takes place:

"Are you on a diet, child?"

Macabea didn't know how to respond.

"What are you eating?"

"Hot dogs."

"Just that?"

"Sometimes I eat a ham sandwich."

"And what do you drink? Milk?"

"Only coffee and soft drinks."

"Do you ever vomit?"

"Never!" she exclaimed with shock. She wasn't crazy to waste food like that! The doctor knew, of course, that Macabea wasn't skinny because of dieting. But it was easier to say this. It was just something to do while he was filling out a prescription for a tonic. . . .

"This question of a hot dog diet is purely neurotic. You ought to see a psychiatrist."

The doctor had no values. Medicine was, to him, just a way of making money. It had nothing to do with the love of a profession or of the sick. In fact, he was inattentive and he thought that poverty was something ugly and distasteful. (1977:76–77, my translation)

Jean-Paul Sartre's (1956) *Being and Nothingness* contains a brilliant existential analysis of "bad faith," referring to the ways that people pretend to themselves and to others that they are not really involved in or responsible for what they are doing or for the consequences of their actions. In the existential view of things, bad faith is the refusal to "make oneself," to strike out freely and responsibly, to take hold of one's situation. Bad faith allows for "history" to be made by others; it entails a passive acceptance of the definition of one's reality as proposed by others. In this instance, the "bad faith" is collective, and it exists on many levels: among the doctors and pharmacists who allow their knowledge and their skills to be abused; among the politicians and power brokers who want to represent themselves as community servants and benefactors, while on another level they know full well what they are doing; and among the sick-poor themselves, who, even while they are critical of the medical mistreatment they receive, continue to hold out for a medical solution to their social dilemmas and their political and economic troubles. In effect, we have a situation, similar to the one described by Pierre Bourdieu, where no one wants to betray "the best-kept and the worst-kept secret (one that everyone must keep) [so as not to break] the law of silence which guarantees the complicity of collective bad faith" (1977:173).

The best-kept and worst-kept secret in Bom Jesus da Mata is that adults are nervous-hungry and that hungry infants are dumped in common graves after they have been turned away from clinics with nothing more than vitamin drops or a packet of *soro*, as if these were miracle solutions to the problems of hunger and need. And so the refusal to recognize, the failure to *see*, the signs of hunger or to see them as something other than what they really are represents the worst instance of collective bad faith in Bom Jesus.

Gil-Anderson: The Violence of Hunger

One of the most injurious of these [new] patent medicines is a
drink prepared with opiates, chiefly laudanum, under the name
of Godfrey's Cordial. Women who work at home and have
their own and other people's children to take care of, give
them this drink to keep them quiet and, as many believe, to
strengthen them. They often begin to give this medicine to
newly born children and continue, without knowing the effects
of this 'heart's ease,' until they die. . . . The [general] effects
upon children so treated may be readily imagined: they are
pale, feeble, wilted, and usually die before completing the
second year.
                    Friedrich Engels ([1845] 1958:161)

In visiting the miserable hovel of an old friend, Dalina of the Rua dos Magos, I was taken aback to see in the same room a skeleton of a toddler in the arms of an older child. The boy was Gil-Anderson, Dalina's unfortunate great-grandson. "What is wrong with him?" I asked. He was "sick," Dalina replied. He didn't "like" to eat; food "disgusted" him. Unconvinced by the possibility of so pronounced a death instinct in a tiny child, I asked to see Gil's mother, a stocky, seventeen-year-old girl named Maria dos Prazeres (Mary of the Pleasures, her real name). Prazeres explained that Gil, although eleven months old, ate only a tablespoon of powdered milk in a baby bottle of water each day. She showed me his food: a dirty and almost empty can of Nestlé's milk. The child weighed no more than three or four kilos and looked startlingly like E.T. Because the boy showed no signs of fever, pain, or even diarrhea, I challenged the mother: "Your baby is not sick; he's hungry. Babies that are starved lose their appetite."

Prazeres replied that he was most certainly "sick" because she had taken

Gil to the clinic, to the hospital, and to various pharmacies in town, and each had given her *remédios* to cure him. I asked to see the medicines and was taken to a tiny lean-to behind Dalina's hovel where, over the child's hammock, was a shelf with more than a dozen bottles and tubes of prescription drugs, all opened and partly used and displayed like saints on a home altar. There were in the collection antibiotics, painkillers, tranquilizers, sleeping pills, and, most painful of all, an appetite stimulant. The child was being "fed" medicines (including a medicine to make him hungry) and then "denied" food. I was much taken with Gil-Anderson, whose startled little expression seemed to convey so much premature wisdom and sadness (but hunger has a way of expressing itself in this way), and I decided to intervene. The same day Sister Juliana and I returned with a vegetable soup, mashed fruits, and fresh milk, which Gil-Anderson at first spit out (thinking, I am sure, that here was more bitter-tasting medicine for him) and then gingerly, later greedily, ate, but in small quantities. His mother said she was surprised that he could eat such things. Each day, however, the foods that I brought (meant to last the little fellow for two or three days) would vanish, as the adults and older children in Dalina's household confessed to eating foods that Gil "didn't like" to prevent them from "going to waste."

This, too, is the madness of hunger, for hunger can turn adults into competitors with their own children. The failure of Dalina to recognize her great-grandson's hunger (so preoccupied was she with her own) is understandable. The "turning away" of the doctors and those pharmacists who gave or sold Maria painkillers and sleeping pills for her starving son is less easily swallowed. Death is, after all, the ultimate soporific, and they need not have bothered.

In the final analysis, the medicalization of hunger is symptomatic of a nervous system, individual and social. Hunger has made the people of the Alto lean, nervous, and desperate. Sometimes it has made them violent. Such nervousness has in the past, under the idiom *delírio de fome*, exploded into a rage that contributed to the many "primitive" rebellions in the backlands of Pernambuco, Ceará, and Paraíba: the fierce struggles at Canudos led by Antônio Conselheiro, the social banditry of Lampião and his Maria Bonita, and the mystical reign of Padre Cícero in Juàzeiro do Norte. The nervous-hungry *Nordestino* continues to be feared today as a potential foot soldier in a revolutionary reserve army.

Into this potentially explosive situation, doctors, nurses, pharmacists, and the first few timid psychologists to appear on the landscape are recruited in an effort to domesticate and pacify an angry-hungry population. It is an uneasy alliance, however, and I do not mean to suggest that Bom Jesus does

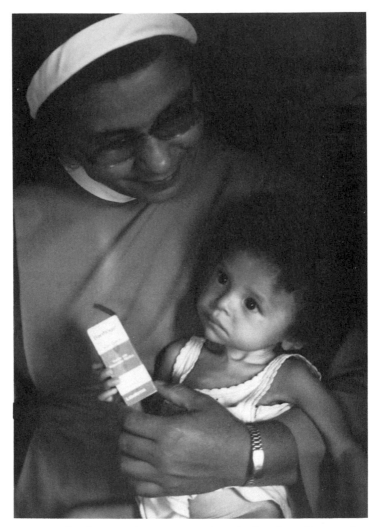

Pensive Gil and Sister Juliana: "Poor Gil: no food; only medications for him."

not have its share of social critics among the ranks of both doctors and patients. As I suggested earlier, this analysis developed over time and within the process of political engagement with the members of a base community movement. To date, however, their analysis is rudimentary and inchoate with respect to differentiating hunger from sickness and the need for food from the need for medication. And so they speak of being *enganados* (fooled) by doctors and by politicians, but they are not quite sure in just what ways they are being deceived.

Toward a Liberation Medicine: A Pedagogy for Patients (and Practitioners)

Despite their intuitive understandings that something is amiss, people of the Alto remain perplexed about the social and political nature of *nervos*. They have not grasped how their own folk idiom has been appropriated by clinic physicians and used against them. Meanwhile, the doctors of Bom Jesus da Mata do not appreciate that when the poor people of the Alto complain of nervousness, they are not expressing quite the same neurotic symptoms as one of Dr. Freud's Viennese patients. These doctors might be best advised to return to the basics of their medicine, attend to the primary symptoms of their patients' wasted bodies, and thereby treat as well their tormented minds and frayed emotions.

For people of the Alto one answer lies in subjecting *nervos* to oppositional and critical thinking within the context of their base community meetings so as to denaturalize the concept, to render it somewhat "strange," "exotic," and anything other than commonsensical. In this way "common sense" can be replaced by "good" sense (see Gramsci 1957:90–93), thereby allowing a new discourse (or an older one)—a discourse on nervous *hunger*—to take the place of *nervoso*.

The irony has not been lost on me that it is the "odd fellow" anthropologist who argues against medicine working with and through a popular folk idiom, in this case *nervos*. There is also an irony in calling on already normally reductionist physicians to return to the "basics" of their practice, to treat the "hungry body" so the "nervous mind" will follow, a blatant example of Cartesian thinking. All this would seem to situate me on the side of Susan Sontag (1979), arguing that bodies and diseases be demetaphorized and treated for what they (presumably) really are: plain and "natural" things. Strip away the ragged metaphor of *nervos*, and you will find the bare skeleton of "hunger" shivering under its mantle. But my argument is not, as is Sontag's, against the "poetics" of illness, for hunger and thirst are no more "objects" and "things" than is any other aspect of human relations. Hunger and thirst are mindful as well as embodied states, and they come trailing their own metaphorical meanings and symbolic associations. Happy are those, or blessed are those, after all, who *hunger* and *thirst* after justice. . . . So perhaps I am arguing for the substitution of one set of metaphors for another. If so, that would not make me unhappy.

But we cannot forget that whatever else illness is (an unfortunate brush with nature, a fall from grace, a rupture, a disequilibrium, and so on), it is also an act of refusal, an oblique form of protest, and therefore it, too, can contain the elements necessary for critique and liberation. This is the case with hunger and its double, *nervos*. *Nervos* (like other illnesses) can express itself negatively in various ways: as a refusal to work or to struggle under oppressive and self-defeating conditions, a refusal to endure what is not endurable, a refusal to "cope." The person assuming the sick "role" says, "I will not, I simply *cannot*, any longer." It is the strategy of Bartleby the Scrivener, who "prefers not to." This certainly seems to be the case with Severino Francisco and Seu Tomás, the nervous-paralyzed cane cutters who simply had had enough and had reached the ends of their ropes.

As Talcott Parsons (1972) recognized, sickness poses a real threat to the social and moral order of things. It is a form of passive resistance that can be a most effective political strategy. Nevertheless, it does require that inchoate and largely unconscious, personal, and symbolic expressions of negation and refusal be transformed into more instrumental, collective, and conscious action. We began by considering *nervos* as the double, as the second reality that coalesces around the cultural images, meanings, and metaphors that attach to particularly dreaded diseases and conditions—in this case, hunger. The original ailment comes to assume a "second nature," a superimposed "other" reality. These doubles can be seen as creative attempts by people to grapple with and explain the meaning of suffering. They are attempts to answer the existential question of the sufferer: "Why me, oh God, why me?" The idiom of *nervos* at the very least provides an agitated, nervous, and hungry population with a less dangerous way of addressing their pain and registering their discontent and defiance. Through the idiom of *nervos*, the terror and violence of hunger are socialized and domesticated, their social origins concealed. But this idiom also contains within it the possibilities for critical reflection. "My illness is really just my own life," said Sebastiana. And Carolina de Jesus reached a similar conclusion: "My sickness is both physical and moral."

The sufferer of *nervos* has two possibilities: he can be open and responsive to the covert language of the organs, recognizing in his trembling hands and "paralyzed" legs the language of suffering, protest, defiance, and resistance. Or he can silence it, cut it off by surrendering more and more of his consciousness and pain to the technical domain of medicine, where they will be transformed into a "disease" to be treated with an injection, a nerve pill, a soporific. Once safely medicated, however, the scream of protest is silenced, and the desperate message in the bottle is lost.

Both Karl Marx and Talcott Parsons were aware of the eroding effects of the organization of personal life and work in industrializing, capitalist societies on the human body and spirit, although their specific sympathies and loyalties in this process diverged radically. Marx understood religion as "the sigh of the oppressed," an expression of workers' frustration. Parsons similarly viewed medicine as providing frustrated workers with an escape into the lure and haven of chronic sickness, an allowable and sanctioned form of deviancy. But where Marx aligned himself squarely on the side of suffering humanity, Parsons' sympathies were with an insufferable social and economic order. Parsons recognized that the sick role was risky, that it had to be closely monitored lest a "sickness strike" spread like wildfire among disaffected and dis-eased people in society at large. He identified one of the covert functions of medicine in industrialized societies as the control of discontent expressed through the medium of illness and the diffusion of its revolutionary potential. And so the physician had to be "trained" not to see the secret indignation of the sick and wherever possible to transform active protest into passive forms of breakdown. If organized religion was an opiate of the poor, medicine was an opiate of the sick (and the hungry), where the metaphor was actualized, as we have seen, in the "drugging" of hungry bodies and tormented minds.

But medicine, like religion, wears two faces. It can provide the antidote against experiencing the pain of one's existence, or it can be transformed into a "critical practice of freedom." By means of an odd alchemy combining the insights of Marx and Parsons we can see, especially in the context of Northeast Brazil, that both popular religion and folk idioms of sickness can function as febrile expressions of protest against the demand to suffer, hunger, and die unnecessarily or absurdly. In recent decades the religiously devout but impoverished and excluded masses of Central and South America have discovered the revolutionary potential of a "liberation theology" (see Lancaster 1988) by forming ecclesiastical base communities where the Scriptures are read and reflected on in terms of practical realities and are interpreted in a Marxist key. Medicine, too, can serve as a point of critical reflection and practice. It is not by coincidence that so many revolutionary workers in Central and South America have been priests and nuns as well as doctors and nurses, those who have exercised a "preferential option," for the sick-poor by virtue of their privileged access and proximity to the suffering and the afflicted.

Medicine, the hospital, and the clinic (in Foucault's enlarged sense of the term) can be isolated, closed off, from the external world and from the experiential world of patients. Or they can provide a space where new ways of addressing and responding to human misery are worked out. From out of the indistinct panorama of human needs, some voices are raised in anguish and in anger, protesting their own sense of impotence. One of these is the voice of *nervos*. We might conclude by asking what medicine might become if, beyond the humanitarian goals that it expouses, it could see in the suffering that enters the clinic an expression of the tragic experience of the world. We might have the basis for a liberation medicine, a new medicine, like a new theology, fashioned out of hope.

6 Everyday Violence
Bodies, Death, and Silence

> What's true? What's false? Who knows how to evaluate
> anymore?
>
> Seu João Gallo, *morador*, Alto do Cruzeiro

This chapter takes my various reflections on nervous hunger, delirium, and the mindful bodies of *Nordestino* sugarcane cutters to their final and logical conclusion. I ground my discussion in the problem of the "disappeared," for the specter of missing, lost, disappeared, or otherwise out-of-place bodies and body parts haunts these pages even as it haunts the imaginations of the displaced people of the Alto do Cruzeiro, who understand that their bodies, their lives, and their deaths are generally thought of as dispensable, as hardly worth counting at all. In this context even the most interpretive and qualitative of ethnographers becomes an obsessive counter, a folk demographer, her function that of the village clerk, the keeper of the records recording and numbering the anonymous dead and disappeared.

And yet short of a theological meditation on the passions of the soul, what meaning have these empty spaces, these missing and disappeared bodies? I hope to show the difference they make when the everyday, lived experience of a large number of threatened people is introduced into current debates on the state, the politics of fear, and the problem of the disappeared.

The Breakdown of Consensus

The multiple and contradictory social realities of Bom Jesus and its surrounds contribute to fleeting perceptions of the community as a ruthless, unstable, amoral place. There is a sense of almost desperate vitality and of chaos threatening to unleash itself, so that Bom Jesus sometimes feels like a place where almost anything can happen. If there are rules to discipline and govern public interactions, they appear to exist only in the negative, to be violated, scoffed at. Only fools would obey a stop sign; never mind that the slow and fussy *solteirona* (old maid) of the Chaves family was knocked down by a speeding Fiat as she tried to cross the main *praça* of Bom Jesus on her way home from Mass. The obvious contradictions do at times rise to the surface and threaten a social consensus that is, at best, tentative and fragile. The guise of civility is rent by sudden explosions of violence, some apparently calculated, others merely reactive.

In 1986 the children of one of the wealthiest landowners in Bom Jesus were kidnapped in front of their home in broad daylight by masked *desperados*—angry "social bandits" from the interior of the state—who later demanded, and received, a huge ransom. The band of unemployed field hands then declared "war on the greedy *latifundiários*."

During the 1987 drought hungry rural workers throughout the *zona da mata* began looting stores, warehouses, and train depots, thereby forcing the governor of Pernambuco to send emergency rations to divert the looters. In an interview with the press the governor blamed the looting on the expulsion of rural workers from their *roçados*, which led to a "savage, violent, and disorderly urbanization" (Riding 1988:1-A4), an "occupation and siege" mentality evidenced in the social geography of shantytown "invasions" and squatter camps throughout the state.

Several young men of the Alto do Cruzeiro, each of them black, young, and in trouble with the law for petty theft, drunkenness, vagrancy, glue sniffing, and other infractions, were seized from their homes just after Christmas in 1987 by unidentified men "in uniform" and were "disappeared." A few weeks later two of the bodies were found slashed, mutilated, and dumped between rows of sugarcane. The police arrived with graphic photos for family members. "How do you expect me to recognize *meu homem* [my man] in this picture?" Dona Elena screamed hysterically. Similar events were repeated in 1988 and 1989. Finally they came late one night for the teenage son of Black Irene, the boy everyone on the Alto knew affectionately as Nego De. The existence of paramilitary "death squads" with close ties to the local police force is suspected, but on this topic people are generally silent; if and when they do speak, it is in a rapid and complicated form of sign language. No one else wants to be marked.

In February 1987 Evandro Cavalcanti Filho, a young lawyer for the Pernambucan rural workers syndicate, representing 120 peasant families in dispute with local landowners in the area of Surubim, was shot dead in front of his wife and children on the patio of their home. One of the gunmen (a suspected informant) was shot and killed by military police.

One year later, in February 1988, a small group of *posseiros*, traditional squatters using the abandoned and marginal fields of a local plantation called the Engenho Patrimônio, a few miles outside of Bom Jesus, were ambushed by *capangas*, hired gunmen in the employ of the *senhor latifundiário*. The peasants were quietly tending their *roçados* when the gunmen opened fire without warning. One peasant was maimed; another, a twenty-three-year-old father of a small family, was killed.

In 1989 rumors surfaced concerning the disappearance of street children, *meninos da rua* and *moleques*, several of whom lived in the open-air marketplace, took shelter at night in between the stalls and under canvas awnings, and helped themselves to bits of produce from crates and baskets. Even though many of the vendors were tolerant of the hungry street urchins, others enlisted the help of the local police in a local "pest control" campaign.

Throughout all, Bom Jesus da Mata continued to perceive itself as a quiet, peaceable interior town in the *zona da mata*, far from the violence and chaos of the large cities on the coast. As the initial excitement of each incident blew over, life resumed its normal course. The kidnappers were apprehended and the frightened children returned to their parents, but only a fraction of the ransom money was recovered. The sacking and looting of markets continued throughout the *zona da mata*, and a state of emergency was declared just before Holy Week in 1988, when suddenly the skies opened and torrential rains swept many Alto residents from their homes, which disappeared down rushing ravines of the shantytown. The *castigo* of drought was replaced by the *castigo* of floods. "Life is harsh. Man makes, but God destroys," said the *moradores* of the Alto do Cruzeiro philosophically.

The hired gunmen from the Engenho Patrimônio were arrested and then freed immediately on bail. The owner of the *engenho* was never cited or brought to trial. As of 1989 three ex-military police officers were in prison awaiting trial for the murder of Evandro Cavalcanti, but the special investigator appointed to the inquiry had resigned from the case, and another one had not been appointed. The disappearance of young black men continues on the Alto do Cruzeiro and in other poor *bairros* of Bom Jesus and is treated as a nonissue, not even thought worthy of a column in the mimeographed opposition newspaper of Bom Jesus. "Why should we criticize the 'execution' of *malandros* [good-for-nothings], rogues, and scoundrels?" asked a progressive lawyer of Bom Jesus and a frequent contributor to the alternative liberal newspaper. "The police have to be free to go about their business," said Mariazinha, the old woman who lived in a small room behind the church and who took care of the altar flowers. "The police know what they're doing. It's best to keep your mouth shut," she advised, zipping her lips to show me exactly what she meant.

Padre Agostino Leal shook his head sadly. "Is it possible that they murdered Nego De? What a shame! He was in reform. I trusted him. He even attended my Wednesday night Criminals' Circle." Then, after a pause, the good padre added ruefully, "I guess it was just too late for Nego De."

Violence and the Taken-for-Granted World

The tradition of the oppressed teaches us that the "state of emergency" in which we live is not the exception but the rule. We must attain to a conception of history that is in keeping with this insight. . . . One reason why Fascism has a chance is that in the name of progress its opponents treat it as a historical norm.

Walter Benjamin (cited in Taussig 1989b:64)

Writing about El Salvador in 1982, Joan Didion noted in her characteristically spartan prose that "the dead and pieces of the dead turn up everywhere, everyday, as taken-for-granted as in a nightmare or in a horror movie" (1982:9). In *Salvador* there are walls of bodies; they are strewn across the landscape, and they pile up in open graves, in ditches, in public restrooms, in bus stations, along the sides of the road. "Vultures, of course, suggest the presence of a body. A knot of children on the street suggest the presence of a body" (9). Some bodies even turn up in a place called Puerto del Diablo, a well-known tourist site described in Didion's inflight magazine as a location "offering excellent subjects for color photography."

It is the anonymity and the routinization of it all that strikes the naive reader as so terrifying. Who are all these *desaparecidos*—the unknown and the "disappeared"—both the poor souls with plucked eyes and exposed, mutilated genitals lying in a ditch and those unidentifiable men in uniform standing over the ditches with guns in their hands? It is the contradiction of wartime crimes against ordinary peacetime citizens that is so appalling. Later we can expect the unraveling, the recriminations, the not-so-guilty confessions, the church-run commissions, the government-sponsored investigations, the arrests of tense and unyielding men in uniform, and finally the optimistic reports—Brazil, Argentina (later, perhaps even El Salvador) *nunca mais*. Quoth the raven, "*Nunca mais.*" After the fall, after the aberration, we expect a return to the normative, to peacetime sobriety, to notions of civil society, human rights, the sanctity of the person (Mauss's *personne morale*), *habeas corpus*, and the unalienable rights to the ownership of one's body.

But here I intrude with a shadowy question. What if the disappearances, the piling up of civilians in common graves, the anonymity, and the routinization of violence and indifference were not, in fact, an aberration? What if the social spaces before and after such seemingly chaotic and inexplicable acts were filled with rumors and whisperings, with hints and allegations of what could happen, especially to those thought of by agents of the social consensus as neither persons nor individuals? What if a climate of anxious, ontological insecurity about the rights to ownership of one's body was fostered by a studied, bureaucratic indifference to the lives and deaths of "marginals," criminals and other no-account people? What if the public routinization of daily mortifications and little abominations, piling up like so many corpses on the social landscape, provided the text and blueprint for what only appeared later to be aberrant, inexplicable, and extraordinary outbreaks of state violence against citizens?

In fact, the "extraordinary" outbreaks of state violence against citizens, as in Didion's *Salvador*, during the Argentine "Dirty War" (Suarez-Orozco 1987, 1990), in Guatemala up through the present day (Paul 1988; Green 1989), or in the harshest period following the Brazilian military coup of 1964 (Dassin 1986) entail the generalizing to recalcitrant members of the middle classes what is, in fact, normatively practiced in threats or open violence against the poor, marginal, and "disorderly" popular classes. For the popular classes every day is, as Taussig (1989b) succinctly put it, "terror as usual." A state of emergency occurs when the violence that is normally contained to that social space suddenly explodes into open violence against the "less dangerous" social classes. What makes the outbreaks "extraordinary," then, is only that the violent tactics are turned against "respectable" citizens, those usually shielded from state, especially police, terrorism.

If, in the following ethnographic fragments, I seem to be taking an unduly harsh and critical view of the "state" of things in Brazil, let me hasten to say at the outset that I view this interpretation as generalizable to other bureaucratic states at a comparable level of political-economic "development" and in a different form to those characterized by a more "developed" stage of industrial capitalism such as our own. Violence is also "taken for granted" and routinized in parts of our police underworld operating through SWAT team attacks on suspected crack houses and crack dealers in inner-city neighborhoods. And state terrorism takes other forms as well. It is found in the cool jargon of nuclear weapons researchers, our own silent, yet deadly, technicians of practical knowledge. Carol Cohn (1987) penetrated this clean, closed world and returned with a chilling description of the way our nuclear scientists have created a soothing and normalizing discourse with which to discuss our government's capacity for blowing populations of bodies to smithereens. "Bio-power," indeed.

I share with Michel Foucault his suspiciousness of the state as a social formation that spawns what Franco Basaglia (1987a) called the official and legalized "institutions of violence." Yet Foucault (1979) believed that public spectacles of torture and execution had gone the way of the ancien régime. The use of torture by the state, associated with criminal proceedings, was abolished throughout the Western world in the eighteenth and nineteenth centuries, so that Victor Hugo could confidently announce in 1874 that "torture has ceased to exist" (Peters 1985:6). In Foucault's analysis, the mutilated body as the icon of state repression and control gave way to the more aestheticized and spiritualized character of public discipline, regulation, and punishment. The retreat from the body allowed for new assaults on the mind and the moral character of citizens. The new objects of discipline and surveillance were the passions, will, thought, and desire.

In advanced industrialized societies and in modern, bureaucratic, and welfare states, the institutions of violence generally operate more covertly. A whole array of educational, social welfare, medical, psychiatric, and legal experts collaborate in the management and control of sentiments and practices that threaten the stability of the state and the fragile consensus on which it claims to base its legitimacy. We can call these institutions, agents, and practices the "softer" forms of social control, the gloved hand of the state. But even the most "advanced" state can resort to threats of violence or to open violence against "disorderly" citizens whenever the normal institutions for generating social consensus are weakening or changing. I think that this is the situation we are rapidly approaching today in the United States with respect to the general tolerance of violent police actions in our urban inner cities on behalf of combating the "drug war."

The Brazilian state has been thrown into considerable turmoil in recent years by the democratic "awakenings" of previously excluded and alienated populations to new forms of political praxis and mobilization in the proliferation of highly politicized shantytown associations, mothers clubs, squatters unions, rural workers defense leagues, and so on, many of these supported by the clergy and hierarchy of the "new" Catholic church. The changing allegiance of the Catholic church, which, following the Latin American Bishops' Conference at Medellín withdrew much of its traditional support from the traditional landowning and industrial political-economic elite of Brazil, produced a crisis. Bishops and clergy throughout the country have in the last decade increasingly taken the side of peasants, squatters, Indians, and small landholders in disputes with *latifundários* and multinational companies, and they have publicly denounced the use of violence in extracting forced labor from plantation workers and in evicting peasants from their traditional holdings. In 1980 the Brazilian National Bishops' Conference released a statement that implicated not only landowners and hired *pistoleiros* in perpetrating the violence but also the state itself: "There is ample proof that such violence involves not only hired thugs and professional gunmen, but also the police, judges, and officers of the judiciary" (cited in Amnesty International 1988:3). The result was a stepped-up campaign of police-initiated harassment culminating in the murder of priests and religious sisters associated with rural trade unions, land rights claims, and shantytown associations throughout Brazil.

Northeast Brazil is still at a transitional stage of state formation that contains many traditional and semifeudal structures, including its legacy of local political bosses (*coroneis*) spawned by an agrarian *latifundista* class of powerful plantation estate masters and their many dependents (see Lewin 1987). To this day most sugar plantation estates are protected by privately owned police forces or at least by hired *pistoleiros*. The web of political loyalties among the intermarried big houses and leading families of the interior leads directly to the governor and to the state legislature, which is still controlled by a traditional agrarian oligarchy. Consequently, civil police, appointed by local politicians, often collaborate with hired gunmen in the employ of the plantation estates owners and sometimes participate themselves in the operations of the "death squads," a widespread and pernicious form of police "moonlighting" in Brazil.

One could compare the semifeudal organization of contemporary Northeast Brazil with Anton Blok's (1974) description of the state and state terrorism in Sicily in the early decades of the twentieth century. In both cases state power is mediated through a class of landholding intermediaries and their hired guns: the *coroneis* and their *capangas* in the Brazilian case and the *gabelotti*, the wealthy leaseholders and landlords who supported the rural mafia, in the Sicilian case. The Sicilian mafia evolved in the late nineteenth and early twentieth centuries when the modern state superimposed itself on a marginal peasant society that was still feudal in its basic features. The mafia served as a kind of modus vivendi mediating the claims of the new state apparatus with traditional landowners and big men. Acts of graphic public violence underscored the authority of the traditional power elite and of the newly emergent state as well.

Similarly, Northeast Brazil has not yet produced the range of modern social institutions, scientific ideologies, or specialized "technicians of practical knowledge" (a term first used by Sartre) to manage and individualize (and so contain) public expressions of dissent and discontent. The health and social welfare agencies, psychiatric clinics, occupational therapies, or varieties of counseling that help to bolster a wavering consent to the prevailing order of things are not yet completely in place. Clinical medicine in the interior of Brazil is, as we have seen, fairly brutal and unsophisticated in its goals and techniques. In the interior of Northeast Brazil there are only the police, a judiciary that has generally failed to prosecute cases of police brutality, the prison, the FEBEM federal reform schools for criminalized or simply marginalized youth, and the local death squads, all of them violent institutions.

There are three public security and law enforcement institutions in Brazil: the federal, civil, and military police. The federal police, under the jurisdiction of the Ministry of Justice, supervises immigration, protects the national frontiers, and investigates the black market and drug contraband in the country. Civil police are generally under the jurisdiction of the *município*, and the chief of police (*delegado de polícia*) is usually appointed by the mayor and is financially dependent on him and the town councilmen. In addition to the officially appointed civil police, a large number of ex-officio *vigias* (night watchmen) are nominated or tacitly approved by the chief of police. *Vigias* patrol virtually every *bairro* of Bom Jesus and are supported by weekly "dues" collected (or extracted) from each household on their beat. All *vigias* and most civil police have no formal training, and most are recruited from the poorer social classes. Often civil police and *vigias* are difficult to distinguish from thugs and vigilantes. In addition to these is the military police, which, under the jurisdiction of both the army and the state, is responsible for maintaining public order and security. It is the military police that is usually called on to enforce, often with violence, the evictions of traditional squatters. Throughout the years of the dictatorship (1964–1985), military police officers were heavily implicated in the disappearances, tortures, and deaths of suspected subversives in Bom Jesus as elsewhere in Brazil. The process of democratization has been painfully slow and has yet to challenge the local presence and the fearful psychological hold of the military police over the poorer populations (Amnesty International 1988, 1990). Consequently, poor *Nordestinos* have been living for many years with state violence and threats of violence. The alternative to "softer" forms of persuasion and control is direct attack on citizens: arrest and interrogation, imprisonment, disappearance, and, finally, torture, mutilation, and killing.

At certain levels of political-economic development—and the sugar plantation zone is one of these—violence and threats or fear of violence are sufficient to guarantee the "public order." In any case, violence is the only technique of public discipline available to a military government such as the one that ruled Brazil for twenty-one years and that still plays an important role in the state today. The military is not an educational, charitable, or social welfare institution; violence is intrinsic to its nature and logic. Violence is usually the only tactic the military has at its disposal to control citizens even during peacetime (see also Basaglia 1987b:143–168).

One of the ways that modern military dictatorships have legitimized the use of violent acts against citizens is through the legal loophole of the *crimen exceptum*—that is, the "extraordinary crime" that warrants extraordinary and often cruel punishment. The concept may be extended to extraordinary situations warranting extraordinary measures to protect the state. And so, paradoxically, during an era of expansion and centralization in which the Brazilian state commands great strength and power to mobilize vast resources, state policy is nonetheless based on a concept of extreme vulnerability. The fear of subversive or simply of criminal activity can become obsessional (see Suarez-Orozco 1987), and torture may be used in an attempt to assert, as Elaine Scarry put it, the "incontestable reality" of a particular state's control over the population. "It is, of course," she continued, "precisely because the reality of power is so highly contestable, the regime so unstable, that torture is being used" (1985:27). And so I have borrowed Franco Basaglia's notion of "peacetime crimes" as a way of addressing the routinization of violence in everyday aspects of contemporary *Nordestino* society.

What, then, is the rationale for turning a military, wartime arsenal against private citizens. What crimes have they committed (or do they threaten to commit)? What makes some citizens assume the character of "threats" or "dangers" to the state so as to make violence an acceptable form of social control, the legitimate "business" of the police? (Remember the words of Mariazinha, the religious spinster: "The police have to be free to go about their business.") The "dangerousness" of the poor and marginal classes derives directly from their condition of desperate want. Hunger and need always pose a threat to the artificial stability of the state. Following Basaglia (1987a:122), we can say that the marginals of the Alto do Cruzeiro are guilty of "criminal needs."

In the specific instance of the *posseiros* (peasants who, by Brazilian law, acquire *legal* tenure in unused, though privately owned, plantation lands) who were ambushed by hired gunmen working for the owner of Engenho Patrimônio, the squatters were "executed" by criminals who were never brought to trial. The "crimes" of the poor, of the desperate—of the *posseiro* whose very way of life stands as a negation of "modern," bourgeois notions of property rights or of Nego De, whose petty thievery helped maintain his mother and siblings after the murder of his father—are understood as "race" crimes and as "naturally," rather than socially, produced. Nego De and other poor, young black men like him steal because it is thought to be in their "nature," "blood," or "race" to steal. They are *malandros*, and they are described in racist terms as *bichos da Africa*. Their crimes can be punished with impunity and without due process. *Posseiros*, with their precapitalist notions of "the commons," are viewed as dangerous retrogrades, and the gunmen contracted to kill them do so with the full, often explicit, understanding and tacit approval of the local police. Those few gunmen who are apprehended usually escape from jail with the help of local prison guards.

Meanwhile, the violent crimes of the wealthy classes are understood and forgiven as socially produced. Landowners must "protect" their patrimonies; politicians are "put into" totally corrupting situations. Lies and bribes are endemic to politics; they are part of the "game" of power. People are surprised to find an honest political leader or a fair and just employer. There is no such cultural and political immunity for the peasant squatters who occupy lands because they have no other way to survive or for Nego De, who was better able to sustain a large and desperate household by stealing than by "honest" work for one dollar a day in the cane fields. Although these are crimes of need, they are neither excused nor understood in social terms. Instead, they are seen as base, instinctual crimes that are natural to an "inferior" and "mulatto" population.

Increasingly today race and racial hatred have emerged as subliminal subtexts in the popular discourses that justify violent and illegal police actions in shantytown communities. Remnants of the older racial "harmony ideology" of *Nordestino* plantation society still render it "impolite" for the powerful and educated classes to comment in public on racial differences (while in private and behind closed doors racist discourse is rampant and particularly grotesque and virulent). But this same "polite" society can thereby fail to see, fail to recognize, that police persecution is now aimed at a specific segment and shade of the shantytown population. Even my radical black friend, João Mariano, was profoundly embarrassed when I raised the question of the racial nature of Alto disappearances at a study group formed by the small, literate, leftist intelligentsia of Bom Jesus, and the discussion was tabled.

Here we can begin to see the workings of a hegemonic discourse on criminality/deviance/marginality and on the "appropriateness" of police and state violence in which all segments of the population participate and to which they acquiesce, often contrary to their own class or race interests. How is this extraordinary consensus forged, and how is it maintained in the face of living (and dying) contradictions? Why is there so little expressed (or even submerged and seething) outrage against police and death squad terrorism in the shantytown? Why is there no strongly articulated human rights position among even the most progressive forces and parties of Bom Jesus? What has made the people of the Alto so fearful of democratic and liberal reforms?

In an attempt to answer these questions my analysis proceeds in two directions: ideology and practice. The first, relying heavily on the writings of contemporary Brazilian social scientists, concerns the political ideology of democracy, the state, and citizenship in Brazil. The second, based on my observations of everyday life in Brazil, explores the mundane rituals and routines of humiliation and violence that assault the bodies and minds of the *moradores* as they go about the complicated business of trying to survive. Both tend to reinforce an acceptance of "terror as usual."

Citizenship and Justice in Brazil

We tend to think of the Western political traditions and concepts of democracy, citizenship, and the modern state—as well as the necessary preconditions for their existence—as universally shared among modern nations. But as the recent events in Eastern Europe indicate—especially the difficulty with which newly liberated citizens are attempting to "reclaim the public" and recreate civil society following the "fall" of repressive and totalitarian communist regimes—the concepts of democracy, equality, and civil society may have very specific and different cultural and historical referents. In Eastern Europe the relationship between civil society and the state was perceived not in terms of collaboration and consensus but rather in terms of mutual hostility and antagonism (see Kligman 1990:394).

In Brazil the political traditions of republican democracy and equality, influenced by both the French and American revolutions, have always been mediated by traditional notions of hierarchy, privilege, and distinction. The Brazilian constitution, like the American constitution, was adopted before slavery was abolished, and by the end of the nineteenth century the public sphere had been constituted exclusively for a very small, elite group (Schwartz 1977; Caldeira 1990). Liberty and democracy became the exclusive preserves of the dominant minority, those educated and landed men (and, later, women) of breeding, culture, and distinction. Civil liberties and human rights were cast as "privileges" and "favors" bestowed by superiors on subordinates within relations structured by notions of personal honor and loyalty. "Favors" included everything from personal protection, material goods, jobs, and status to the right to vote. Consequently, up through the first half of the twentieth century in the Northeast, votes and elections were controlled by a few local big men and their clients.

Roberto da Matta pointed out that although Brazilian law is based on liberal and democratic principles of universalism and equality, its practice often diverges from theory and it "tends to be applied in a rigorous way only to the masses who have neither powerful relatives nor important family names." He went on to state that "in a society like Brazil's universal laws may be used for the exploitation of labor rather than for the liberation of society." Those who are wealthy or who have political connections can always manage to "slip under or over legal barriers" (1984:233).

Brazil's system of criminal justice is a "mixed system" containing elements of both the American and the European civil law tradition (Kant 1990). Contrary to the American system, there is no common-law tradition whereby precedents and jury verdicts can actually participate, in conjunction with the legislature, in making the law. And in addition to many egalitarian, and individual rights protected by the Brazilian crimin system (such as the right to counsel and to *ampla defesa*—that is to produce any possible evidence on equal footing with the prosecution), there are other, more traditional, and less liberal traditions. First among these is the tradition of progressing from a position of "systematic suspicion," rather than from an assumption of innocence, and, relatedly, the judge's "interrogation" of the accused relying on information produced by prior police investigations that are "inquisitorial" in nature. In the words of one police chief interviewed by Roberto de Lima Kant, police interrogations entail "a proceeding *against everything* and *everyone* to find out the *truth* of the facts" (1990:6). Within this inquisitorial system, "torture becomes a legitimate—if unofficial—means of police investigation for obtaining information or a confession" (7). In all, "Brazilian criminal proceedings are organized to show a gradual, step by step, ritual of progressive incrimination and humiliation, the outcome of which must be either the confession or the acquittal. The legal proceedings are represented as a punishment in themselves" (22).

Within this political and legal context, one can understand the *moradores'* awesome fear of the judicial system and their reluctance to use the courts to redress even the most horrendous violations of their basic human rights. And, as Teresa Caldeira (1990) noted, the first stirrings of a new political discourse on "human rights," initiated by the progressive wing of the Catholic church and by leftist political parties in Brazil in the late 1970s and early 1980s and fueled in part by the international work of Amnesty International, was readily subverted by the Right. Powerful conservative forces in Brazil translated "human rights" into a profane discourse on special favors, dispensations, and privileges for criminals. Worse, the Brazilian Right played unfairly on the general population's fears of an escalating urban violence. These fears are particularly pronounced in poor, marginalized, and shantytown communities. And so, for example, following a 1989 presidential address broadcast on the radio and over loudspeakers in town announcing much-needed proposed prison reforms in Brazil, the immediate response of many residents of the Alto seemed paradoxical. Black Zulaide, for example, began to wail and wring her hands: "Now we are finished for sure," she kept repeating. "Even our president has turned against us. He wants to set all the criminals free so that they can kill and steal and rape us at will." It seemed to have escaped Black Zulaide that her own sons had at various times suffered at the hands of police at the local jail and that the prison reform act was meant to protect *her* class in particular. Nevertheless, Zulaide's fears had been fueled by the negative commentary of the police, following the broadcast, on the effects these criminal reforms would have on the people of Bom

Jesus but especially on those living in "dangerous" *bairros* such as the Alto do Cruzeiro and needing the firm hand of the law to make life minimally "safe."

Similarly, Teresa Caldeira offered two illustrations of right-wing ideological warfare that equated the defense of human rights with the defense of special privileges for criminals. The first is from the "Manifesto of the Association of Police Chiefs" of the state of São Paulo, which was addressed to the general population of the city on October 4, 1985. The manifesto takes to task the reformist policies of the then-ruling central-leftist political coalition, the PMDB:

> The situation today is one of total anxiety for you and total tranquility for those who kill, rob, and rape. Your family is destroyed and your patrimony acquired with much sacrifice is being reduced. . . . How many crimes have occurred in your neighborhood, and how many criminals were found responsible for them? . . . The bandits are protected by so called human rights, something that the government considers that you, an honest and hard working citizen, do not deserve. (1990:6)

Her second example is taken from an article published on September 11, 1983, in the largest daily newspaper of São Paulo, *A Folha de São Paulo*, written by an army colonel and the state secretary of public security:

> The population's dissatisfaction with the police, including the demand for tougher practices . . . originates from the trumped up philosophy of "human rights" applied in favor of bandits and criminals. This philosophy gives preference to the marginal, protecting his "right" to go around armed, robbing, killing, and raping at will. (6)

Under the political ideology of favors and privileges, extended only to those who behave well, human rights cannot logically be extended to criminals and marginals, those who have broken, or who simply live outside, the law. When this negative conception of human rights is superimposed on a very narrow definition of "crime" that does not recognize the criminal and violent acts of the powerful and the elite, it is easy to see how everyday violence against the poor is routinized and defended, even by some of the poor themselves.

Mundane Surrealism

In Mario Vargas Llosa's novel *The Real Life of Alejandro Mayta*, the Peruvian narrator comments on the relations of imagination to politics and of literary fiction to history:

Information in this country has ceased to be objective and has become pure fantasy—in newspapers, radio, television, and in ordinary conversation. To report among us now means either to interpret reality according to our desires or fears, or to say simply what is convenient. It is an attempt to make up for our ignorance of what is going on—which in our heart of hearts we understand as irremediable and definitive. Since it is impossible to know what is really happening, we Peruvians lie, invent, dream, and take refuge in illusion. Because of these strange circumstances, Peruvian life, a life in which so few actually do read, has become literary. (1986:246)

The magical realism of Latin American fiction has its counterparts in the mundane surrealism of ethnographic description, where it is also difficult to separate fact from fiction, rumor and fantasy from historical event, and the events of the imagination from the events of the everyday political drama. The blurring of fiction and reality creates a kind of mass hysteria and paranoia that can be seen as a new technique of social control in which everyone suspects and fears every other: a collective hostile gaze, a human panopticon (see Foucault 1979), is created. But when this expresses itself positively and a state of alarm or a state of emergency is produced—as in the epidemic of *susto* discussed in chapter 5—the shocks reveal the disorder in the order and call into question the "normality of the abnormal," which is finally shown for what it really is.

Peacetime Crimes

The peoples' death was as it had always been:
as if nobody had died, nothing,
as if those stones were falling
on the earth, or water on water. . . .
Nobody hid this crime.
This crime was committed
in the middle of the Plaza.
    Pablo Neruda (1991:186–187)

What makes the political tactic of disappearance so nauseating—a tactic used strategically throughout Brazil during the military years (1964–1985) against suspected subversives and "agitators" and now applied to a different and perhaps an even more terrifying context (i.e., against the shantytown poor and the economic marginals now thought of as a species of public enemy)—is that it does not occur in a vacuum. Rather, the disappearances occur as part of a larger context of wholly expectable, indeed even anticipated, behavior. Among the people of the Alto, disappearances form part of the backdrop of everyday life and confirm their worst fears and anxieties—that of losing themselves and their loved ones to the random forces and institutionalized violence of the state.

The practices of "everyday violence" constitute another sort of state "terror," one that operates in the ordinary, mundane world of the *moradores* both in the form of rumors and wild imaginings and in the daily enactments of various public rituals that bring the people of the Alto into contact with the state: in public clinics and hospitals, in the civil registry office, in the public morgue, and in the municipal cemetery. These scenes provide the larger context that makes the more exceptional and strategic, politically motivated disappearances not only allowable but also predictable and expected.

"You gringos," a Salvadorian peasant told an American visitor, "are always worried about violence done with machine guns and machetes. But there is another kind of violence that you should be aware of, too. I used to work on a hacienda. My job was to take care of the dueño's dogs. I gave them meat and bowls of milk, food that I couldn't give my own family. When the dogs were sick, I took them to the veterinarian. When my children were sick, the dueño gave me his sympathy, but no medicine as they died" (cited in Chomsky 1985:6; also in Clements 1987:ix).

Similarly, the *moradores* of the Alto speak of bodies that are routinely violated and abused, mutilated and lost, disappeared into anonymous public spaces—hospitals and prisons but also morgues and the public cemetery. And they speak of themselves as the "anonymous," the "nobodies" of Bom Jesus da Mata. For if one is a "somebody," a *fildalgo* (a son of a person of influence), and a "person" in the aristocratic world of the plantation *casa grande*, and if one is an "individual" in the more open, competitive, and bourgeois world of the new market economy (the *rua*), then one is surely a nobody, a mere *fulano-de-tal* (a so-and-so) and João Pequeno (little guy) in the anonymous world of the sugarcane cutter (the *mata*).

Moradores refer, for example, to their collective invisibility, to the ways they are lost to the public census and to other state and municipal statistics. The otherwise carefully drafted municipal street map of Bom Jesus includes the Alto do Cruzeiro, but more than two-thirds of its tangle of congested, unpaved roads and paths are not included, leaving it a semiotic zero of more than five thousand people in the midst of the bustling market town. CELPE, the state-owned power and light company, keeps track, of course, of those streets and houses that have access to electricity, but the names the company has assigned to identify the many intersecting *bicos*, *travessas*, and *ruas* of the Alto do not conform to the names used among the *moradores* themselves. The usual right of the "colonizer" to name the space he has claimed is not extended to the marginal settlers of the Alto do Cruzeiro.

The people of the Alto are invisible and discounted in many other ways. Of no account in life, the people of the Alto are equally of no account in death. On average, more than half of all deaths in the *município* are of shantytown children under the age of five, the majority of them the victims of acute and chronic malnutrition. But one would have to read between the lines because the death of Alto children is so routine and so inconsequential that for more than three-fourths of recorded deaths, the cause of death is left blank on the death certificates and in the ledger books of the municipal civil registry office. In a highly bureaucratic society in which triplicates of every form are required for the most banal of events (registering a car, for example), the registration of child death is informal, and anyone may serve as a witness. Their deaths, like their lives, are quite invisible, and we may as well speak of their bodies, too, as having been disappeared.

The various mundane and everyday tactics of disappearance are practiced perversely and strategically against people who view their world and express their own political goals in terms of bodily idioms and metaphors. The people of the Alto inhabit a world with a comfortable human shape, a world that is intimately embodied. I have already suggested that the *moradores* of the Alto "think" the world with their bodies within a somatic culture. At their base community meetings the people of the Alto say to each other with conviction and with feeling, "Every man should be the *dono* [owner] of his own body." Not only their politics but their spirituality can be described as "embodied" in a popular Catholicism, with its many expressions of the carnal and of physical union with Jesus, with His mother Mary, and with the multitude of saints, more than enough for every day of the year and to guide every human purpose. There is a saint for every locale, for every activity, and for every part of the body. And the body parts of the saints, splintered into the tiniest relics, are guarded and venerated as sacred objects.

Embodiment does not end with death for the people of the Alto. Death is itself no stranger to people who handle a corpse with confidence, if not with ease. ("When you die, Dona Nancí," little Zefinha used to say affectionately, "I'm going to be the first to eat your big legs," the highest compliment she could think of to pay me.) On the death of a loved one, a local photographer will often be called to take a photo of the adult or child in her or his coffin. That same photo will be retouched to erase the most apparent signs of death, and it will become the formal portrait that is hung proudly on the wall. The deceased continue to appear in visions, dreams, and apparitions through which they make their demands for simple pleasures and creature comforts explicit. As wretched *almas penadas*, "restless souls" from purgatory, the dead may request food and drink or a pair of shoes or stockings to cover feet that are cold and blistered from endless wandering. Because the people of the

Alto imagine their own souls to have a human shape, they will bury an amputated foot in a tiny coffin in the local cemetery so that later it can be reunited with its owner, who can then face his Master whole and standing "on his own two feet."

Against these compelling images of bodily autonomy and certitude is the reality of bodies that are simultaneously discounted and preyed on and sometimes mutilated and dismembered. And so the people of the Alto come to imagine that there is nothing so bad, so terrible that it cannot happen to them, to their bodies, because of sickness (*por culpa de doença*), because of doctors (*por culpa dos médicos*), because of politics and power (*por culpa de política*), or because of the state and its unwieldy, hostile bureaucracy (*por culpa da burocracia*).

I am not going so far as to suggest that the fears of mutilation and of misplacement of the body are not shared with other social classes of Brazil, which also "privilege" the body in a culture that prides itself on its heightened expressions and pleasures of the sensual. What is, however, specific to the marginal classes of the Alto do Cruzeiro is a self-conscious sort of thinking with and through the body, a "remembering" of the body and of one's "rights" in it and to it. The affluent social classes take for granted these rights to bodily integrity and autonomy to the extent that they "go without saying." The police oppressors know their victims all too well, well enough to mutilate, castrate, make disappear, misplace, or otherwise lose the bodies of the poor, to actualize their very worst fears. It is the sharing of symbols between the torturer and the tortured that makes the terror so effective (see Scarry 1985:38–45; Suarez-Orozco 1987).

The unquestionability of the body was, for Wittgenstein, where all knowledge and certainty began. "If you do know that here is one hand," he began his last book, *On Certainty*, "we'll grant you all the rest" (1969:2e). And yet Wittgenstein himself, writing this book while he was working with patients hospitalized during the war, was forced to reflect on the circumstances that might take away the certainty of the body. Here, in the context of *Nordestino* life, I am exploring another set of circumstances that have given a great many people grounds to lose their sense of bodily certitude to terrible bouts of existential doubt—"My God, my God, what ever will become of us?"—the fear of being made to vanish, to disappear without a trace.

It is reminiscent of the situation described by Taussig with reference to a similar political situation in Colombia: "I am referring to a state of doubleness of social being in which one moves in bursts between somehow accepting the situation as normal, only to be thrown into a panic or shocked into disorientation by an event, a rumor, a sight, something said, or not said—

something even while it requires the normal in order to make its impact, destroys it" (1989b:8). The intolerableness of the situation is increased by its ambiguity. Consciousness moves in and out of an acceptance of the state of things as normal and expectable—violence as taken for granted and sudden ruptures whereby one is suddenly thrown into a state of shock (*susto, pasmo, nervios*)—that is endemic, a graphic body metaphor secretly expressing and publicizing the reality of the untenable situation. There are nervous, anxious whisperings, suggestions, hints. Strange rumors surface.

The Disappeared: Traffic in Organs

And so the *moradores'* feelings of vulnerability, of a profound sort of on-tological insecurity, are manifested in a free-floating anxiety and in rumors (that are never publicly squelched or denied) about the disposability, ano-nymity, and interchangeability of their bodies and body parts. They imagine that even their own chronically sick and wasted bodies may be viewed by those more powerful than themselves (by *os que mandam*, those who give the orders) as a reservoir of "spare parts." I am referring to a rumor that first surfaced on the Alto do Cruzeiro (and throughout the interior of the state) in the mid-1980s and that has been circulating there ever since. It concerns the abduction and mutilation of young and healthy shantytown residents (espe-cially children), who are eyed greedily for their body parts, especially eyes, heart, lungs, and liver. It was said that the teaching hospitals of Recife and the large medical centers throughout Brazil were engaged in an active traffic in body parts, a traffic with international dimensions.

Shantytown residents reported multiple sightings of large blue or yellow vans, driven by foreign agents (usually North American or Japanese), who were said to patrol poor neighborhoods looking for small stray children whom the drivers mistakenly believed no one in the overpopulated slums and shantytowns would ever miss. The children would be nabbed and shoved into the trunks of the vans. Some were murdered and mutilated for their organs, and their discarded bodies were found by the side of the road or were tossed outside the walls of municipal cemeteries. Others were taken and sold indirectly to hospitals and major medical centers, and the remains of their eviscerated bodies were said to turn up in hospital dumpsters.

"They are looking for 'donor organs,'" my clever research assistant, Little Irene, said. "You may think that this is nonsense, but we have seen things with our own eyes in the hospitals and in the public morgues, and we know better."

"Bah, these are stories invented by the poor and illiterate," countered my friend Casorte, the new socialist manager of the municipal cemetery of Bom Jesus, in August 1989. "I have been working here for over a year," he said. "I arrive at six in the morning, and I leave at seven at night. Never have I seen anything. Where are the bodies or even the traces of blood left behind?"

When overnight the life-sized body of Christ disappeared from the huge cross that gives the shantytown of Alto do Cruzeiro its name, the skeptical and the irreverent wondered aloud whether the same kidnappers were responsible. They suggested that community leaders search the dumpsters of the local hospital to find out if the Christ had had His organs removed. But among the devout and the more simple, the "missing Cristo" of the Alto increased people's sense of threat and physical vulnerability. Dona Amor wiped a stray tear from her wrinkled cheek and confided in a hoarse whisper, "They've taken Him, and we don't know where they have hid Him." "But who?" "Os grandes," she replied. "But why?" I persisted, and she answered in a word: "Política." Dona Amor was referring to the politics of power, to all the inchoate forces summoned by the poor to explain and account for the misery of their lives. Whereas for us politics is something remote that happens elsewhere and in a separate discourse with its own vocabulary and etiquette, for the Nordestino peasant-workers política is imminent and omnipresent. It accounts for and explains everything, even the size of one's coffin and the depth of one's grave.

The body-snatching rumors were so widespread in the favelas and poor neighborhoods of Pernambuco that local journalists soon picked up the story and went to great lengths to expose the credulity of the population, sometimes cruelly satirizing people's fears as bogeyman stories. But to the illiterate, or partly literate, the newspaper and radio coverage only added further validity to the rumors. "Yes, it's true," insisted Dona Aparecida, pacing anxiously in front of her house on the Rua do Cruzeiro. "I heard it on the radio yesterday. They are reporting it in Recife. Now what will become of us and our poor children?" And she started to cry.

The stories had reached such proportions that my attempts one morning to rescue little Mercea, Biu's perpetually sick and fussy three-year-old, backfired when I attempted to get her into the back seat of a taxi, even as she was carried in the arms of Xoxa, her older sister. As soon as I gave the order "To the hospital and quick!" the already terrified little toddler, in the midst of a severe respiratory crisis, began to choke, scream, and go rigid. "Does she think I'm Papa-Figo [the Brazilian bogeyman]?" the annoyed cab driver asked.[1] No amount of coaxing could convince Mercea that her tormented little body was not going to be sold to the ghoulish doctors. Biu had instructed her little girl well: "Don't let anyone take you outside the house."

Even more children than usual were kept out of school during this period, and others were sent away to live with distant kin in the mata. Meanwhile, small children, like Mercea, who were left at home while their mothers were

at work in the cane fields or in the houses of the wealthy found th
virtual prisoners, locked into small, dark huts with even the wooder
securely fastened. On several occasions I had to comfort a sobbing child ...
through a crack in a door or shutter, would beg me to liberate her from her
dark and lonely cell.

As a result of these organ theft rumors, there are a fascination and horror
with autopsy, plastic surgery, and organ transplant operations, which are
sometimes understood quite fantastically. "So many of the rich are having
plastic surgery and organ transplants," offered an older Alto woman, "that
we really don't know whose body we are talking to anymore." As the people
of the Alto see it, the ring of organ exchange proceeds from the bodies of the
young, the poor, and the beautiful to the bodies of the old, the rich, and the
ugly and from Brazilians in the Southern Hemisphere to North Americans,
Germans, and Japanese. The people of the Alto can all too easily imagine
that their bodies may be eyed longingly as a reservoir of spare parts by those
with money.

It was just this perceived injustice of unfair and unequal exchange of
organs and body parts that kept Dona Carminha in search of extraordinary
medical help for her only living son, Tomás, who was blinded when he was
eight years old because of a poorly treated eye infection. Secondary scar
tissue had grown over the cornea of both eyes, and the boy, entering
adolescence, lived in a world of impenetrable blackness to which his mother
refused to let him make the slightest adjustment or accommodation. She
was convinced that the boy's blindness was temporary and would someday
be reversed through an eye transplant. The obstacle, as she understood it,
was that the "eye banks" were reserved, like everything else in Brazil, for *os
ricos*, those, she said, who could afford to pay "interest." She had taken the
boy to Recife and then by bus, to Rio, where she lived in a *favela* with distant
relations while she relentlessly pursued one impossible option after another.
Although she could not read and was terrified of the city, she learned to make
her way, she said, and went from hospital to hospital and clinic to clinic until
she finally exhausted all possible options there. Yet she persisted in her belief
that there was still hope for her son, that somewhere she would find a doctor
of conscience, *um doutor santo*, who would be willing to put his hands into
the till and come up with a new pair of eyes for her son. (Her story put me in
mind of the images I knew as a child of Santa Lucia, with her plucked eyes
resting on a dish held in her hands.) Didn't they give new eyes to the rich?
Carminha asked me. And wasn't her own son *gente* (a good person) just like
them and equal before the "eyes" of God? How could the doctors not "see"
what they were doing, she continued. Were they so "blind"? Her husband,
patient and long-suffering Seu Evanildo, sighed, shaking his head at me.

"Maybe," I said gently, "maybe, Carminha, it *is*, as the doctors have told you, too late for your son's eyes. Maybe he will have to learn how to walk in the shadows." "Never," she said, "I will never give up as long as I have the strength to walk the streets and I have a mouth to speak. I will take him to Texas if that is the only solution."

The rumor that the "rich are eating us" or "eating our children" is not exclusive to these impoverished *Nordestinos*. One can find similar stories in other places and historical periods—for example, in the "blood libel" stories that European Catholic peasants spread against Jewish merchants, who were accused of using the blood of Christian babies for Passover rituals, and in the contemporary Pishtaco myths found among Andean Indians. The Andean version, held widely from the colonial period to this day (see Oliver-Smith 1969; Taussig 1987b:211–241), maintained that sugar mills could not be started up at the beginning of the milling season without being greased with human fat, normally Indian fat and preferably Indian children's fat. The mills ran by feeding on human bodies, an apt enough metaphor. The Indians mistrusted all aspects of the milling industry—the factory with its heavy machinery, electric power plants, and engineers who managed them. The Indians had reason enough to be suspicious because mill and factory owners had both exploited the labor and mistreated the bodies of the Indian population since the beginning of the conquest.

There are modern versions of the Pishtaco tale. In the 1950s Peruvian villagers told Eugene Hammel (personal communication) that airplane jet engines could not be started up without human fat and that Indian children were stolen to provide it. It was also rumored during a famine in the southern highlands of the Andes in the 1960s that U.S. grains and other surplus foods that were being sent to Peru through the Food for Peace program were designed to fatten up Andean babies for the U.S. Air Force. When USAID programs began to provide Andean children with a nourishing school lunch, the Indians stopped sending their children to school altogether. Finally, in the 1980s Bruce Winterhalder, a biological anthropologist from the University of North Carolina, found his attempts to study the physiological effects of high altitude on Andean Indians stymied by the rumor that the anthropologist and his team of assistants were modern-day Pishtacos. They believed that the researchers were measuring the fat folds of adults and children with calipers to select the fattest for their nefarious, cannibalistic purposes.

The *Nordestino* rumors about kidnapped children and organ theft for medical procedures are more complicated than the blood libel or Pishtaco myths. Even though beliefs about greasing the engines of sugar mills and jet planes with human fat vividly express people's fears of exploitation by the rich and powerful, they remain metaphorical, speaking only to symbolic, not to actual, truths. *Nordestino* fears and rumors of body and organ snatching by medical institutions are grounded in a historical reality going back as far as Renaissance anatomists and surgeons (see Lindburgh 1975) and in a new biomedical technology that is real and in some respects monstrous enough. The "Baby Parts Story Just Won't Die" (see *San Francisco Sunday Examiner and Chronicle,* September 30, 1990, B-7) because the "misinformed" shantytown residents are onto something. They are on the right track and are refusing to give up on their intuitive sense that something is seriously amiss.

Certainly the scarcity of organ donors for transplant surgery and the development of new techniques for the medical use of fetal tissues have created a gruesome market for human "organ harvesting," one with international dimensions. There are several sources of human organs and body tissues for transplant surgery and for basic medical research. The primary source of "spare parts" comes from "neomorts"—that is, brain-dead hospital patients whose vital organs may be kept "alive" and "available" for days, even weeks, via machines that can push and pull oxygen out of lungs, electrically shock the heart into beating, and keep the blood warm and circulating through body tissues. This process of maintaining life-in-death is fairly routinized today in American hospitals. Another source is from still living, yet doomed, anencephalic infants, and a third comes, relatedly, from the brain tissue taken from aborted fetuses. In Berkeley, California, the Hana Biologics Company is currently developing techniques to produce insulin-producing cells from aborted fetuses to transplant into patients with diabetes. The company hopes to accomplish the same for Parkinson's disease. Craig McMullen, the president of the company, deals with the ethics of this procedure rather cursorily: "We take a waste product of society and use it to find a cure for diseases affecting millions of people" (*San Francisco Chronicle,* October 6, 1987, 6).

Information and disinformation about these and other seemingly magical medical innovations are rapidly picked up by the media and disseminated worldwide. Consequently, the organ theft rumor has spread rapidly throughout the Third World, even in the absence of literacy, newspapers, and television sets. Perhaps the medical practice that most reflects the anxieties underlying the organ theft rumors is the use of living, healthy, unrelated donors who are paid to "donate" a spare organ, most commonly a kidney. The business of organ transplants is conducted today in a multi- and transnational space. For example, between 1984 and 1988, 131 patients from three renal units in the United Arab Emirates and Oman traveled of their own accord to Bombay, India, where they purchased, through local brokers, kidneys from living donors, most of them from impoverished shantytowns outside Bombay. The donor's "extra" kidney was surgically removed for transplant, and the "donor" was compensated between $2,600 and $3,300 for the missing body part.

This subject was treated in a recent issue of *The Lancet*, perhaps the premier medical journal in the world. A. K. Salahudeen et al. (1990) analyzed the high mortality among the Arab recipients of the purchased kidneys. There was no parallel follow-up or discussion, however, of the possible adverse effects on the health and mortality of the organ donors. The authors did, however, comment on the ethics of organ sale. While they condemned the practice of "rampant commercialism" in Bombay (without mentioning the rampant commercialism of the Arab participants), they considered ethically "acceptable" the practice of "rewarded gifting" or "compensated gifting" whereby living, unrelated donors are "rewarded" for the inconvenience of the procedure and for the loss of earnings during the period of recovery. Citing studies by C. T. Patel (1988) and K. C. Reddy et al. (1990), *The Lancet* authors concluded that financial incentives for living organ donors may be considered "moral and justified" on the grounds that "kidney donation is a good act. It is a gift of life" (1990:727).

The language of *The Lancet* article evoked an early and formative essay by Talcott Parsons, Renée Fox, and Victor Lidz in which the authors drew on religious imagery and the biblical idea of self-sacrifice as the ethical basis underlying the then still very experimental medical technology that made heart transplants possible. The donation of an organ, they wrote, was the most literal gift of life that a person could offer or receive:

> The donor contributes a vital part of his (her) body to a terminally ill, dying recipient, in order to save and maintain that other person's life. Because of the magnitude of this gift exchange . . . participating in a transplantation can be a transcendent experience for those involved. . . . It may epitomize for them man's highest capacity to make the sacrificial gift of life-in-death, that is supreme love, commitment, and communion. In this sense . . . deep religious elements, some of them explicitly Christian, are at least latently present in the transplant situation. (1972:412)

Obviously, there are many ethical and political dilemmas involved in the question of organ transplants that are being creatively addressed by shantytown residents. While Western Europeans and North Americans persist in thinking of organ transplants as "gifts" donated freely by loving and altruistic people, to the people of the Alto, whose bodies are so routinely preyed on by the wealthy and the powerful (in economic and symbolic exchanges that have international dimensions), the organ transplant implies less a gift than a commodity. In place of the gift of life, there is a suspicion of a theft of life in which they will serve as the unwilling and unknowing sacrificial lambs.

The body parts rumor is so persistent and widespread today among poor and vulnerable people living in urban shantytowns on the fringes of modern social life that in November 1988 the European Parliament passed a resolution condemning the "traffic" in Central and South American children for international adoption, an undersupervised commercial as well as a charitable activity that sometimes involves such children in prostitution and pornography and possibly even, as the rumor suggests, in a covert traffic in baby parts (see R. Smith 1989; Raymond 1989).

At the very least the organ theft rumor should give pause to those medical technicians and political leaders in the United States who have sometimes made indecent proposals for the acquisition of scarce donor organs.[2] The Brazilian rumors express poor people's perceptions, grounded in an economic and biotechnomedical reality, that their bodies and the bodies of their children may be worth more dead than alive to the rich and the powerful.[3]

And so the rumors of the "medically" disappeared and mutilated bodies continue unabated, coexisting, of course, with actual cases of politically motivated abductions and mutilations of Alto men and young boys, about which people are too afraid to speak, so that when touching on *this* subject *moradores* are suddenly struck mute. The rumors of "what can happen next" express, albeit obliquely and surrealistically, the *moradores'* implicit and intuitive understanding that something is amiss.

The Disappeared: Traffic in Children

Por este pão pra comer	For this good bread to eat
Por este chão pra dormir	For this hard ground on which to sleep
Por me deixar respirar	For letting me breathe
Por me deixar existir	For letting me exist
Deus lhe pague!	God reward you!

Chico Buarque, popular song (cited in Pires 1986:39)

The anxious stories of shantytown children snatched up for their organs may also be a reflection of the active roundup of small street urchins, thousands of whom disappear each year into Brazilian prisons and federal correctional and education reform facilities that are viewed with suspicion and horror by shantytown residents (see Fonseca 1987). But the stories of physical and sexual abuse of children detained in Brazil's correctional institutions are matched by equally horrible stories of abuse, battering, mutilation, and death on the streets (see Allsebrook & Swift 1989). Benedicto

Rodrigues dos Santos, the head of the Brazilian National Street Children's Movement, reported the violent deaths of 1,397 street children between 1984 and 1989 alone. Many of these were the victims of one version of "urban renewal," and similar to the death squad assassinations of adult marginals, the bodies of some of these "lost" street children were also mutilated.

It is curious to note how the official public discourse about street children has changed in Brazil (and more widely in Latin America as well) over the past two decades. In the 1960s street urchins were accepted as a fairly permanent feature of the urban landscape, and they were referred to affectionately as *moleques*, that is, "ragamuffins," "scamps," or "rascals," or any small black child. *Moleques* were "streetwise" kids, cute, and cunning, sometimes sexually precocious, and invariably economically enterprising. They tried to make themselves useful in myriad small ways, some of these bordering on the deviant. Think of Fagin's "boys" from *Oliver Twist*, especially the Artful Dodger, and you have it. Many *moleques* survived by "adopting" a particular affluent household, where they often ate and slept in a courtyard or patio. Hardly a Peace Corps volunteer in Brazil in the 1960s didn't have a special *moleque*, who attached himself or herself to the volunteer for the duration of the stay. A few of these "loose" and "excess" children were adopted and brought back to the United States.

Today, street children in Brazil tend to be viewed as both a public scandal and public nuisance. They are now referred to either as "abandoned" children or as marginals. The first connotes pity for the child (and blame for the neglectful mother), whereas the second connotes fear. But both labels justify radical interventions and the removal of these all too public "pests" from the landscape of modern, congested cities in Brazil. Yet today's abandoned and criminalized street children seem no more neglected and no more (or less) dangerous than yesterday's playful *moleques.* Most of the children are today, as they were in the 1960s, "supernumerary" children of impoverished single mothers. And although they may be quite on their own economically, most are still emotionally and socially attached to a larger family unit. In fact, street children, most of them boys, are quite sentimental on the topic of mothers, their own mothers in particular. When asked why they begged, stole, or lived in the streets, the children often replied that they were doing it to help their mothers. Most shared a percentage of their earnings with their mothers, whom they visited each evening. "Fifty-fifty," said Giomar proudly with his raspy, boy-man voice. "Oh, *chê!*" his nine-year-old friend Aldimar corrected him. "Since when did you ever give your mother more than a third?" (I was more impressed, however, with the math skills of two street children who had never been to school.)

Self-portrait of Luiz: "Begging." Happy to be alive!

A band of street children who had attached themselves to us in 1987 liked nothing better than to be invited indoors to use our indoor toilet, to wash up with soap and water, and, afterward, to flop on the floor and draw with magic marker pens. Their sketches were curious. Given free hand to draw what- ever came into their heads, most drew self-portraits or conventional nuclear family portraits, even when there was no "papa" living in the house or when the child himself had long since left home. The street children also liked religious themes, the crucifixion in particular, colored in with lots of bloody red. But their self-portraits tended to be smiling and upbeat, like the one that eleven-year-old Luiz sketched of himself, posing with his beggar's sack.

The main shadow that is cast over the lives of street children today is their fear of the police and of the FEBEM children's asylums in Bom Jesus and in nearby Recife. "You won't ever turn me in to FEBEM, will you, Nancí?" I was made to answer many times over. "They kill children there," Luiz insisted. The more I denied that this could be so, the more the children ticked off the names of friends who had been "roughed up" or hurt at one of the Federal Schools for the Well-Being of Minors, as the FEBEM institutes are misnamed. "Why do you think that they built the FEBEM school so close to the cemetery of Bom Jesus?" asked José Roberto, aged 12, with a quiver of fear in his voice. No one can tell these experienced street children that their fears for their physical safety are groundless.

By the same token, one cannot suggest to Alto women that their fears of child snatching are fantastic and groundless in light of the active domestic and international black market in Brazilian children (see Scheper-Hughes 1990). The thriving trade in babies has affected the lives of a dozen or more Alto women with results that are complex and ambiguous. In the absence of any formal child protective service, with the exception of the punitive FEBEM asylums, child arrest, child stealing, and child saving are hopelessly muddled. When coercion, bribery, and trickery are involved in Brazilian child adoption, the humanitarian gesture is easily unmasked as little more than institutionalized reproductive theft that puts the bodies of poor women in the Third World at the disposal of affluent men and women in Brazil and elsewhere. But regardless of the form it takes, the trade in babies has contributed to the chronic state of panic that I am describing and to Alto residents' perceptions of bodily destinies that are out of their control.

When Maria Lordes, the mother of five sickly and malnourished children living in a miserable hovel on the hillside path called the Vulture's Beak on the Alto do Cruzeiro, was approached by her wealthy *patroa*, the woman for whom she washed clothes for less than one dollar a week, who asked to "borrow" her pretty little four-year-old *galega* (fair-haired, fair-skinned child), Maria readily agreed. The woman said she would keep the child overnight just for amusement and would return her in the morning. Maria sent her little girl off just as she was: untidy, barefoot, and without even a change of clothes or her little pink comb with its missing teeth.

That night passed and then another. Maria was worried, but she assumed that her child was happy and having a good time, and Maria did not want to anger her boss by appearing anxious or mistrustful. After almost a week had gone by, Maria's husband, Manoel Francisco, came home from the plantation several hours to the north where he had been working as a sugarcane cutter. When he returned to find that his favorite daughter was missing, he pushed Maria against the wall of their hut and called her a "stupid woman." He went frantically in search of the little girl, but on arriving at the house of his wife's *patroa*, he learned it was already too late: the little girl had been sent by bus to Recife to an "orphanage" that specialized in overseas adoption.

"I did your wife a favor," the *patroa* said to Manoel. "Leave your daughter alone and soon she will be on her way to America to become the daughter of a rich man. That pretty *galega* of yours had no future in your household. Don't be selfish. Give her a chance." The woman would give no further information, and when Manoel became insistent, she called on one of her houseboys to have him forcibly removed from her patio.

Had they lodged a complaint with the police? I asked. "And do you think that the police would take a complaint from us, Dona Nancí?" I was told. No, said Maria, adding that although she was still very angry at having been tricked, she had come to accept what had happened, to *se conformar* (adjust) to her and her daughter's fate. Marcela was most certainly better off where she was now. Later Maria withdrew into the little back room where the members of the family slept crisscrossed in hammocks of various sizes and colors, and she emerged with a small plastic basket that contained all her daughter's earthly possessions: a couple of tattered cotton shifts, her chewed-up pacifier on its string, a pair of plastic flip-flops, the comb, and a tiny mirror. "Marcela was so vain, so proud of her blond hair and fair skin," her mother said wistfully, "and look what happened to us because of it." Maria's oldest daughter picked up the objects and turned them over. There were tears glistening in the corners of her eyes. "Does she miss her little sister often?" I asked. "Don't mind her," Dona Maria replied, pushing the girl away roughly. "She's only crying for herself, that it was her bad fortune *not* to have been stolen!"

"But do you still miss your little girl?"

"I don't think of her too often now. But when I go into her things, it makes me sad. I feel so bad to see the little bit that she left behind, and I think to myself, 'Why don't you just throw the things out? Even if by some miracle she would walk through that door, she could never use them anymore.' When Manoel catches me looking at her things, he starts up again, arguing about my stupidity. But now I yell back at him: 'What are you saying? Do you want Marcela back here amid all this want, all this abuse and maltreatment? Let her escape! What can we do with another child when we already have too many? Don't cry for her. We are the ones to be pitied, the ones who were left behind.'" Later Maria added that sometimes when she was alone, she could get really wound up and she would curse the American who changed her life, saying, "Damn that rich woman! Why doesn't she come back and get the rest of us as well!"

Each year close to fifteen hundred children leave Brazil legally to live with adoptive parents in Europe (especially Italy, Scandinavia, and Germany), the United States, and Israel. But if one counts the more clandestine traffic that relies on the falsification of documents and political and bureaucratic corruption at the local, state, national, and international levels, the number of children leaving Brazil has been estimated at three thousand per year, or about fifty children per week. The clandestine and black markets work through murky channels by relying especially on employers and *patroas* to put pressure on female workers and to exploit the ignorance of poor, rural women, like Maria, whose children are living in a state of real poverty and neglect. On what grounds could Maria defend herself? She was afraid of the police and received no sympathy from her *patroa*, who dismissed her complaint by saying, "You already killed two of your children by neglect; did you want to finish off your pretty little blonde as well?"

Child protection, such as there is on the Alto do Cruzeiro, often takes the form of child theft. And even where a radical intervention may be justified to save a child's life, the unpredictable form it takes attacks women at the core of their fragile existence and increases their feelings of hopelessness and powerlessness. The bad widow Maria José came within a hair's breadth of losing her youngest child, a fair-haired and rosy-cheeked little cherub. Although the little tyke was generally filthy and often left to play with stray goats and in the rubbish pile behind the unfinished mud lean-to where the family lived, he was healthy enough and better fed than many Alto toddlers. He was also better cared for than his lice-infested older sister and scarecrow-skinny brother. The brunt of scarcity falls in disequal proportions on children in any given Alto household, and this one was no exception.

The Franciscan sister, Irmã Juliana, made a visit to the young widow only to find her smoke-filled hovel empty, save for a couple of pigs rooting about in a pile of dirty rags near the twig fire. Fearing a possible fire hazard, Juliana kicked the pile of rags away from the flames only to have them respond with a howl. When she realized that inside the bundle was a little boy covered with dirt and feces, the nun scooped him up and was about to leave with him when his older sister arrived home and begged Juliana not to take her baby brother away, for her mother would surely "kill" her for having left him unattended. Juliana relented when the girl promised to wash the baby and take better care of him. When the nun returned the next day, she argued with Maria José to give her child to a Franciscan home for abandoned children in a nearby town. The widow adamantly refused; threats followed. Sister Juliana vowed she would do nothing more for the widow, not help her with weekly food baskets or with bricks and cement to construct a proper home. The widow replied angrily, "I may be a poor and miserable cur, but I am not so depraved as to trade my beautiful baby for a basket of food and a roof over my head."

Stories like these circulate wildly among the *moradores* of the Alto, who take from them the lesson that they are powerless before the big people of Bom Jesus, who can dispose of them and their children as they wish. True, the women of the Alto agreed, Maria José was not a particularly doting mother, but it was "wrong" of the nun to force the widow to choose between food and a house *or* her child.

Nonetheless, each year many thousands of children change parents in Brazil. Some of this "circulation of children" is traditional and voluntary, as in the pattern of the informal fosterage of *filhos de criação* discussed in chapter 3. Some of it is formal and bureaucratized, but much of the exchange, as we have seen, remains coerced, illegal, and covert.

One of the reasons that *moradores* so fear the asylums of FEBEM is that these institutions also serve as intermediaries in the domestic adoption process, transferring poor and "abandoned" children from their neglectful birth mothers to adoptive mothers elsewhere in the country (see Fonseca 1987:22). Meanwhile, temporary and informal fosterage is problematic because of the ease with which any middle-class woman can go to a civil registry office and *limpar a certidão*—that is, be issued a new birth certificate with her own name listed as the child's natural parent.

One young Alto mother told of the unfortunate day when, on her way to the post office, she stopped at the front gates of a big house in town to ask for a cup of water for herself and her one-year-old daughter. The *dona da casa* requested that the child be brought inside for a few moments. The cup of water was brought out to the thirsty woman, but her baby was not. The mother cried out in protest, but the wooden door and the gates were slammed in her face. The woman was told to leave or the police would be called. Before the week was out the mistress of the big house had registered the child in her own name. The wealthy woman had taken advantage of a Brazilian law that allows for the transfer of legal rights in a child from its birth mother to another woman at the *latter's* request (see Código Civil 1916; Lei 4655, 1965; Código de Menores 1979). Local courts in Brazil favor the rights of the middle class to adopt, almost at will, the needy and often neglected children of the poor.

And so these incidents feed bizarre rumors, such as the organ theft stories, and the rumors feed a culture of fear and suspicion in which ambiguity contributes to the experience of uncertainty and powerlessness, which then present themselves as a kind of "fatalism" and despair. The privileging of rumor over reality, of the fear of what can happen over the reality of what has already come to pass, may be seen as a kind of collective delirium. Or by way of another analogy, it is not difficult to drive people crazy by telling them that their fears or beliefs are groundless or that they are "paranoid" when, in fact, everyone is actually talking about them behind their backs. The elements of reproductive trafficking in poor women and children that I describe here contain, as Janice Raymond recently put it, "all the worst elements of human rights violations" (1989:245). This trafficking involves the barter and sale of human beings, coercion, and the uprooting of children from their homes and sometimes from their cultures and countries of origin. Finally, we cannot eliminate the suspicion, kept alive in the form of a strange and outrageous rumor that refuses to die, that within the clandestine international black market in babies, there are some violations resulting, more often than we may know, in the medical abuse or death of such children.

Everyday Violence: Hospital Clinics

The body and organ theft rumors also have their basis in poor people's mundane encounters with a clinical and medical reality that does view and treat their bodies and body parts and those of their children as "dispensable." When Seu Antônio, a rural cane cutter from the Alto do Cruzeiro, appeared in a local clinic following a series of small strokes that left his eye damaged and his vision impaired, the clinic doctor said, without even bothering to examine the afflicted eye, "Well, it's not worth anything; let's just have it removed." While the wealthy indulge themselves in the very latest medical technologies—plastic surgery and body sculpting are now almost routine among the middle-aged and middle class in this region—the frequent accident victims among the cane cutters and mill workers on the plantations return home from the hospital with grotesque scars and badly set bones that leave them permanently disfigured or disabled.

Seu João Gallo was one of the young leaders of the shantytown association in the 1960s. He was spirited and lively, known as a particularly good dancer of the *Nordestino forró,* a sexy version of the two-step. Often in those days João would try to teach me to dance after UPAC meetings, and I would stumble along to everyone's amusement except my own. My feet and hips simply would not move to the complicated and smooth steps he so effortlessly made. "Is that you, João, truly?" I asked the defeated-looking man with deep furrows cut into his brow. He was seated uncomfortably on a chair outside his hut set into a niche of the Alto that looked out over the *mata.* He greeted me with the taunt that perhaps I was now altogether "too grand" a person to recognize an old beau who today was a "cripple." His story was a not uncommon one. While away working in São Paulo on a road construction gang, he'd been knocked down by a car that came speeding out of nowhere. He never knew what hit him. As a temporary worker without proper documents, he had been treated as a "charity" patient in the general hospital, which explained the ugly and botched repair work on his leg that left it both useless and ugly. Not even minimal cosmetic surgery had been attempted to hide the brutal effects of the trauma, although Brazilian plastic surgeons practicing in Rio de Janeiro and São Paulo are considered among the finest in the world.

The frequency of sudden and violent death in this vulnerable population leads to a confusion between killing and dying so that the people of the Alto speak routinely of relatives "killed" by pharmacists who prescribed, knowingly or not, the wrong medication or by surgeons in Recife whose steady hands slipped fatally during the course of otherwise routine operations. It is hardly surprising, then, that one encounters among the poor a nagging and persistent anxiety about what can happen to their bodies, anonymous enough in Bom Jesus, once they leave the *município*. No one from the Alto travels beyond Bom Jesus, especially not to the capital city of Recife, without his proper identification papers. There are too many stories of *companheiros* and family members who were transported to Recife for medical treatments and then were "lost" in the web of exchanges of charity patients among public, private, and teaching hospitals. On several occasions I was recruited in the search for a "missing person," a hospitalized patient who had gotten lost, as people say, "in the bureaucracy" and discovered that it was next to impossible to trace "anonymous" bodies attached to "generic" interior names such as José or Maria da Silva.

I think of Nilda Gomes, who in 1982 suddenly found herself mother to four grandchildren after their mother "disappeared" into a hospital in Recife. "And now these poor children are orphans," sighed Nilda as the two youngest ones put their heads in their grandmother's lap and cried pitifully. In her desperation Nilda had "arranged" some money from the *prefeito* to cover her bus fare into Recife, where she went to find her missing daughter or at least, she said, to find out what had been done with her body. ("I am afraid they gave her up to the medical students. She was burned all over her body from the house fire, and she would certainly be a great curiosity to them," Nilda commented sadly.) But when she arrived at the Hospital das Clínicas in Recife, the old woman was made to wait many hours. Finally Nilda was told that there was no record of her daughter ever having been registered at the hospital. "Liars!" Nilda accused the nurses. "Murderers!" And for her troubles she was physically pushed out into the street.

"It's always like that with the poor," said Nilda somewhat philosophically. "Our lives and our deaths are very cheap. The nurses and doctors look at us and they say, 'Well, what does it matter, one more or one less?' And when we arrive in the city in our ugly clothes without knowing how to speak properly or how to behave, they make us wait and tell us nothing. It's for this reason that we are so afraid of hospitals and why we fight with the *prefeito* to let us travel in the ambulance with our family members."

Maria Luiza, the "good widow," would most certainly have agreed. Maria's husband, Cosmos, was a popular handyman on the Alto. When a badly infected sore on his leg failed to heal ("It was so deep," Maria said, "that you could see to his bones"), Cosmos went to the local hospital, where Dr. Francisco gave him a half dozen ill-advised injections, one each week. "But he didn't get any better," the patient little woman said without a trace of rancor. "Cosmos would scream at night with the pain so it would freeze your blood." Finally, they took Cosmos by ambulance to the Hospital das Clínicas in Recife, but he was rejected by admitting staff that did not want to take responsibility for a man who was so close to death. Later, Cosmos was taken to the Hospital de Restauração, where his leg was amputated. Nonetheless, a few days later Maria received an order from the hospital to get her husband's body if she did not want him sent to the Medical-Legal Institute, the ML, as people called the public morgue in Recife. The *prefeito* refused to send the municipal ambulance. "You are entitled to only *one* trip," Seu Félix scolded the widow, "and the municipal ambulance is not a hearse"—a phrase I was to hear on several occasions.

"Cosmos died screaming and banging his head," Maria Luiza continued. At least, that is what a nurse offered her for consolation when she arrived at the hospital in a battered, rural taxi cab with a recalcitrant taxi driver who did not want to carry a "stiff" back into the interior. "But I was firm," the widow concluded. "I told him that a deal was a deal and that he had already agreed to the fare in Bom Jesus." "But you didn't tell me about *him*," the driver muttered. "And if I had," replied the stoic little woman, "would you ever have agreed to take me?"

Because the poor believe that those who arrive deathly ill to public hospitals, without medical insurance, official documents, or without family members to identify and protect them, often become fodder for medical experimentation and organ theft, it is hardly surprising that so many *moradores* resist hospitalization altogether. Above all, the poor fear dying in the charity wards of urban public hospitals where their remains may be "donated" to medical students as a way of canceling their unpaid medical debts. "Little people like ourselves," Little Irene cautioned, "can have *anything* done to them." Stories like the following one, told by a washerwoman from Recife, confirm some of those suspicions.

"When I was working in Recife," she began, "I became the lover of a man who had a huge, ugly ulcer on his leg. I felt sorry for him, and so I would go to his house and wash his clothes for him, and he would visit my house from time to time. We were going along like this as lovers for several years when all of a sudden and without warning, he died. The city sent for his body. I decided to follow him to make sure that his body wouldn't be lost. He didn't have a single document, so I was going to serve as his witness and as his identification papers. But by the time I got to the public morgue, they had already sent his body to the medical school for the students to practice on. So I followed him there, and what I saw happening at the school I could not allow. They had his body hung up, and they were already cutting off little pieces of him. I demanded the body back, and after a lot of arguing they let me take it home with me. It's true, he was only a beggar, a *tirador de esmolas*, who sometimes did magic tricks on the bridge in Recife to amuse people. But I was the one who washed his clothes and took care of his wound, and so you could say that I was the owner of his body."

And when Biu's little girl, Mercea, who had been sick for a very long time, finally died in late February 1988 just as they arrived at the emergency room of the hospital, Biu and her half-sister Antonieta wisked the child's body away despite the protest of the clinic staff. They buried Mercea hurriedly that same day, as is customary. I accompanied Biu to the *cartório civil*, where she and Antonieta registered the child as having died at home unattended that morning. I was asked to sign as a "witness." I did so but later asked for an explanation. "We were afraid of the state," Antonieta said simply. "We didn't want an autopsy or Mercea's body tampered with. She is *our* child, and we are the *donas* of her body."

But Mercea, like most of the more than three hundred children who die in Bom Jesus each year, was buried in an unmarked grave, although in her own little coffin purchased on credit. In less than six months her grave was cleared to make room for another "little angel," and her remains were tossed in the deep well that is called the "bone depository" (*depósito de ossos*). And so Mercea's older sister, Xoxa (who was away working on a plantation at the time of her baby sister's death), could not on her return home locate the little grave. This made it difficult for Xoxa to offer her sister the pretty white stockings that Mercea told Xoxa in a dream that she wanted. "Your vision was a true one," Biu told her eldest daughter. "In our rush to bury Mercea we had to put her into the ground barefoot."

Everyday Violence:
The Social World of the Cemetery

Alas, poor Yorick!
William Shakespeare, *Hamlet*, Act V, Scene I

Nenhum dos mortos daqui	None of the dead from here
vem vestido de caixão.	are carried in a coffin. They
Portanto eles não se enterram	are not so much buried as
são derramados no chão.	dumped into the ground.

Cemitérios Pernambucanos (cited in de Castro 1966:vi)

While going throughout the death registry books in the *cartório civil* in Bom Jesus, I came across the following handwritten entry. There were many others just like it. It encapsulated something about the violence of hunger, exclusion, and marginality in this community:

Died: September 18, 1985, Luíza Alvez da Conceição, female, brown, aged thirty-three, unmarried

Cause of Death: Dehydration, acute malnutrition
Observations: The deceased left behind no living children and no possessions. She was illiterate. She did not vote.

I was later able to determine that she died in the municipal hospital, that
she was carried to the graveyard in a borrowed coffin, and that she was put in
her shallow grave wrapped only in a worn hospital sheet. Within the year
her remains, too, would be exhumed, and she, too, would be permanently
disappeared.

Nowhere, perhaps, is the anonymity and disposability of their bodies and
their lives made more explicitly clear to the peasant-workers of Bom Jesus
than in the symbolic violence directed to their remains in the municipal
cemetery, a social space that in microcosm reproduces the social and political
structure of the community. The bodies of their loved ones accumulate in
unmarked graves and in the municipal graveyard's bone depository, while
the wealthy and middle classes build family vaults and elaborate marble
tombstones that are privately owned, permanent, and inviolate, even when
fallen out of use for many generations.

"It's bad enough for the poor who die in the hospital," said Seu Jaime, a
hospital orderly and servant. "Their families have to come and pick them up
and wake them at home. But those who are hurt on the highways or on the
plantations and are brought here without any documents, *coitados,* they are
just thrown outside on the stones in the back of the hospital. After a few
days the *prefeito's* men come with the *bandeja* [a tin-lined coffin that is
returned to the *prefeitura*] and take the body to the cemetery. They won't
even have a grave. Those who are too poor to buy their own plot, and all the
'unknowns' are put together in the same place. Their bones are all mixed
together." Lordes interrupted Jaime to ask anxiously, "Do you think that
Jesus will be able to sort all of them out on the day of the Last Judgment?"

Although the bodies of the poor have, as Thomas Laqueur (1983:109)
noted, always been treated with less care and buried with less splendor than
the bodies of the rich, it is only in fairly recent times—if Laqueur is correct,
between 1750 and 1850—that the idea of a proper and well-appointed burial
came to signify the sum total of a person's social worth (see also Aries 1974;
Urbain 1978; Rodrigues 1983). With the advent of bourgeois society and
values, death—rather than the great "equalizer" of men and women—
became the ultimate discriminator. Eventually, the social distinctions that
separated the living were brought to bear on the architecture and geography
concerning the disposal of the dead.

The social history of the Brazilian funeral begins in the colonial plantation *casas grandes* of the Northeast with the extravagant displays of splendor

with which the feudal patriarchs and their family members were put to rest. The masters and mistresses of the great estates were buried in "silks, religious robes, decorations, medals, jewels; the babies all painted with rouge, clusters of blond hair, angel's wings; the virgins dressed in white, a garland of orange flowers and sky-blue ribbons" (Freyre 1986a:440). Their remains were placed in family vaults in private chapels, with their portraits kept in glass cases in the sanctuary among the images of Christ and the saints. Votive lamps and fresh-cut flowers were offered to both. A dead woman's braids or an infant's curls might be preserved in the chapel as if they were holy relics. Freyre interpreted these practices as a cult of the dead that put him in mind of the ancient Greeks and Romans. Of course, for the plantation slaves there were no elaborate funerals, and *their* bodies were simply wrapped in palm leaf mats and buried in the space reserved for slaves in the small graveyard outside the chapel.

By the mid-nineteenth century the competing domains of *casa* and *rua,* the world of the traditional rural aristocracy and of the modern town, came into direct conflict over the treatment and disposal of the dead. The traditional elite of the feudal *casa grande* began to lose out to the new, liberal, progressive bourgeoisie of the town, which sought to "modernize" and "rationalize" all aspects of social life, including burial customs. This new class drew for support on the rhetoric of medicine and public hygiene. The traditional customs of burying the elite in partly opened vaults and catacombs in family chapels or churchyards and the disposal of the urban poor in pauper trenches were both condemned as unsanitary. "How long can the dead continue to enjoy the unhappy perogative of poisoning the lives of living persons?" asked Jose Martins da Cruz Joabim rhetorically on the occasion of the installation of the Medical Society of Rio in 1830 (cited in Freyre 1986a:439). At about this time the first cemeteries for slaves, paupers, and heretics were founded by the Misericórdia, but a public health report prepared by the Medical Society of Rio de Janeiro (1832) considered these charitable ventures to constitute a veritable public health hazard. The corpses "were thrown in heaps in a huge trench . . . barely covered over with earth, the layers of earth being poorly pressed down . . . so that the bones would come out with the ligaments and membranes still clinging to them" (cited in Freyre 1986a:441, n. 92).

Eventually, even the remains of the elite that were once preserved as precious family relics came to be viewed as dangerous sources of contamination through the emissions of foul airs and gasses called "miasmas" that were believed to cause sickness when inhaled. And so new municipal codes were passed that regulated the disposal of the dead, introducing death certificates, mandating the construction of walled public cemeteries, and in general transferring power and control from religious to secular authorities. Every *município* was ordered to construct a public cemetery enclosed by high, white walls at the outskirts of town (see Rodrigues 1983).

These new cemeteries were truly "public," and *all* citizens—including heretics, paupers, and unbaptized babies—were to be buried there under law. Forced to rub shoulders with the public, the wealthy and middle classes sought to distinguish their resting places from those of the common lot. Those who could afford to do so purchased private spaces within the public cemetery for the construction of elaborate family catacombs reminiscent of the plantation mausoleums. Those who could not afford either a catacomb or a modest individual grave were buried at the expense and at the mercy of the *município*. In this way the cemetery became the final arbiter of one's individual, family, and social identity.

The Good Death: "Six Feet Under and a Coffin"

Essa cova em que estás	This grave you lie in,
com palmos medida	measured by hand,
é a conta menor	represents the small
que tiraste em vida	space you occupied in life
É de bom tamanho	But it's a good-sized grave,
nem large, nem fundo,	neither wide nor deep.
é a parte que te cabe	It's all you'll ever get
deste latifúndio.	from this plantation
É uma cova grande	It's a large enough grave
para tua carne pouca	for your small bit of flesh.
mas a terra dada	When it's a pauper's grave,
não se abre a boca.	you can't complain.

João Cabral de Melo Neto, "Morte e Vida da Severina" (as recited by Dona Amor, Bom Jesus da Mata)

And so the cemetery became a mirror world, a symbolic representation of the social world that the dead had presumably left behind. And the image of the handsome burial (*o bom enterro*) came to play on the popular consciousness against the abhorrent image of the "ugly" or mean burial, the *enterro dos pobres*, the "poor people's funeral." "It is to die," said Dona Amor, her voice quivering with emotion, "*no pior desprezo do mundo*, in the greatest contempt in the world."

The good burial was equated in the popular mind with the idea of the "happy death," one that liberated the soul from its wretched sufferings on earth. No matter how mean or miserable the conditions of one's earthly existence, the "good" Catholic who lived and died in the state of grace was guaranteed a "good death" and an eventual reunion with Jesus, Mary, and the saints. But even the best Catholics might die with some debts to be squared with the Almighty, requiring a period of "detention" in purgatory. All the more important, then, to be served a "decent" burial in a well-marked grave where loved ones could light a candle and offer a prayer to help liberate the soul from purgatory. But the proper burial also had its social referents as well, and to "go into the hole without a coffin" represented the worst kind of social stigma: "Abandoned in life, abandoned in death," again noted Dona Amor.

But before the people of the Alto had come to live in the *rua*, they lived and died in the *mata* and were usually buried there as well. Dona Xiquinha, a local "praying woman" (i.e., an older woman who cures minor ailments by prayer) who also prepares the dead for burial, explained how it was when she was a little girl living on an *engenho*.

"In the old days, the dead were put back into their *redes* [hammocks] when they died. In those days it took only two people to carry a man to his grave: one took hold of the cords in front, and one took the cords at the other end. For an adult the *rede* was closed, the sides were thrown together, but if it was a *moça* or a *moço* [i.e., virgin, male or female, young *or* old, as in the case of some elderly women], the *rede* would be open because they had no sins to hide.[4] Babies always had open *redes*, of course, and their eyes were left open because soon they would be able to see God. Those who could would put their loved ones *no chão* [into the ground] wrapped up in their *redes*. But if the need was great, the body would have to go into the ground wrapped only in a sheet, and the *rede* would go back to the family, poor things."

The rural people of the *zona da mata* always struggled to assure for themselves and their loved ones a decent burial, and eventually this came to mean, in the words of Zé de Souza, a founding member of the Peasant Leagues, "six feet under and a coffin of one's own" (de Castro 1969:7). This slogan became the rallying cry of the Peasant Leagues, which adopted as one of their first projects a rural mobilization around the burial needs of the dead: land rights for the dead, rather than for the living. "Before the leagues," Zé de Souza explained, "when one of us died the coffin was lent by the *município*, and after the body had been carried to the common grave, the coffin went back to the municipal warehouse." He continued, "Today the [Peasant] League pays for the funeral, and the coffin is buried with the dead. That's what the League did for us, *meu filho*" (cited in de Castro 1969:12).

In fact, funeral societies have been common in Northeast Brazil throughout this century. They were formed in rural communities so that people might avoid the humiliation of a poor people's burial. The horror of the pauper's funeral in which the coffin stopped at the mouth of the grave remained strong among the people of the Alto. The travesty of the poor people's burial was the supreme humiliation, a mortification that seemed to the peasants to carry over into eternity.

One of the reasons for the relative popularity of Seu Félix, an otherwise much criticized mayor, was his inauguration of the municipal coffin factory and coffin distribution program in the 1960s, which local radicals had satirized as "a baby for every hovel and a coffin for every baby." Until that time, however, there was only the despised *bate-queixo*, the unadorned and unlined (hence, "chin-knocker" or "jaw-breaker") borrowed municipal coffin, or a more elaborate charity coffin donated by some local benefactor. Dona Clarice recalled the latter custom well: "When I was a girl there were always a few rich patrons in Bom Jesus who would request in their wills that they be buried like paupers in the ground and that their own coffins be left at the cemetery and loaned out to those poor souls who had no one to bury them. It was a blessing for the poor to be carried to the cemetery in grand style, but it was still shameful to have to dump the body in the ground without its coffin. Today, thanks to our 'godfather,' Seu Félix, we all go into the ground, each with his own, proper box. Only babies are sometimes buried without a coffin because their parents think that a coffin is wasteful for a little angel."

Anxiety about a "good burial" was keen enough to appear as a common theme in Alto children's drawings as well as in their TAT stories. When ten-year-old Giomar was asked to draw a panoramic scene of Bom Jesus, he sketched the three shantytown hills that encircle the town, but he neglected to draw the "downtown" of Bom Jesus. Instead, he drew the municipal graveyard located on the outskirts of town. Similarly, in his response to card 13MF (the picture of a man turning away from a partly nude woman in bed), Giomar told this story: "This man in crying because 'his woman' just died. He's worried about a lot of things. He is wondering if he can find enough money to bury her good."

I wondered how so young a boy had come to be so preoccupied with death and burial. It did not take very much probing to learn that Giomar's father had been shot by nameless people as they were breaking into his mother's house one night. The *município* had sent for the body, and it was buried in a "charity" coffin. "But in a pretty spot under a mango tree," Giomar assured me, fiercely wiping the tears from his dirt-stained face. Later that day Giomar and I went to visit his father's grave, but when we got there we could not locate the place where he had been buried. "They even took the *mangueira* away," said Giomar angrily. On our way home Giomar "slipped" me to scale the wall of a private, enclosed garden. He refused to respond to my calls. He was "picking mangoes," he told me. I made the Brazilian gesture

Dona Amor: "If our sweet Savior could come into this world resting in hay, my sweet mother can leave this world in a pauper coffin lined with paper."

for washing my hands of the matter and went home thinking about the boy's anger in the cemetery.

Laqueur wrote that in nineteenth-century England "the pauper funeral had become perhaps the dominant representation of vulnerability, of the possibility of falling irrevocably from the grace of society. . . . It was an image which worked on the poor . . . who would sell their beds out from under them sooner than have parish funerals" (1983:125). Indeed, much the same could be said of the *moradores* of the Alto. Black Irene, for example, admitted that the only thing capable of forcing her back into domestic service for her bad boss, Dona Carminha, was her even greater fear of dying a pauper. "Even a bad and abusive boss," said Irene, "must still, in the end, act like a mother and bury her miserable child. Yes, I would go back to my *patroa* and die with her if there was no other solution in the end."

But it was Dona Amor, herself nearing ninety years, who perhaps had the most to say on the subject of the good burial, and she took up the better part of a long rainy afternoon in 1988 to record for me, in her grand oratorical style, the story of the death and burial of her mother. What follows is a much reduced and edited transcription of that narrative.

"My mother, may Jesus and His angels embrace her, lost a bunch of children. Only a few of us survived. We suffered a lot in growing up, until everyone left and there was only me working to keep my mother housed and fed in her old age. We went on and on like this until finally one day, I walked out of the house and I prayed, 'My Heavenly Father, excuse the weakness of my flesh for saying this to You—if I sin it is only because of the misery I am living in—but if I have to live only to see my old mother slowly die of hunger, I would prefer her to die now. The future is in Your hands. You have the power. Do with me whatever it is I deserve, for I am a miserable sinner.' I cried some more, and I said, 'Take her or take me; take her or me. It's in Your hands. But as a matter of fact, if You take her, it would actually be a little bit better for me because I am still strong and I can work for a living. She, poor thing, can no longer live without me.'

"Well, it turned out that it was only a week before my mother suffered the terrible fall that was to claim her life. . . . She called me to her side and said, 'My love, I am not going to escape death this time, so don't forget about the little brass box where I have hidden away the money for my funeral.' She wanted me to go and order her coffin and her *mortalha* [burial clothes and coffin decorations]. 'My God,' I thought, 'what will I do now?' You see, my little saint, I had to spend a long time nursing Mama after the fall, and during that time I could not work. So from time to time I had to take out a few notes and coins from the brass box. I took out only what was needed, not a penny more. I could recognize the value of the bills from their colors. After all, was I going to let her and me die of hunger, *querida*, knowing all along that there was money set aside?

"I was always a long-suffering woman, and all the suffering I accepted with goodwill as sent by God. It often fell to me to take care of sick people on the Alto, not only my mother but anyone who needed a prayer recited or a sponge bath. All these things I did with pleasure and satisfaction. But I have to confess, I *did* take that money without telling my mother.

"When mother's end grew near, my brothers and sisters came home from the *mata* to be with her. While I was out she told them, 'It gives me some satisfaction to know that the money for my burial is carefully put away. Before I die I would like to see my coffin.' When I came home my sisters asked me, 'Where is mama's money for her funeral?' 'Well, let's get it down and see,' I said. When we opened the box there were only three or four mil reis [worth about $2]. My sisters accused me of hiding the money to keep for myself after mother died. Then I explained what had happened, but they refused to believe me.

"I felt very bad after this, and I walked the streets all that afternoon. When I came home my mother was very, very weak. I said to her, 'Mama, I am not going to be seeing you very much any more.' And we both cried.

And all I could think of was that my mother would die without anything put aside for her burial. But I lied to her: 'Don't worry, Mãe. I will go down into the street and order your funeral things.' 'That's a good girl,' she said. My mother was a simple person. It never would have entered her head that I could have spent the money from her special brass box.

"I went to my old boss's house. 'What is it?' he said. 'Has your mother died?' "

" 'Not yet,' I said, 'but she is at the portals of death, and I'm here to borrow the money I need so I can arrange her funeral.'

" 'I don't have any money here,' he said. Imagine that! And he was the manager of a big bank! But he said, 'Just take this check, and with it you can buy what you need.' Well, *minha santa*, ignorant race that I am, did I understand anything about bank checks? I thought my patron was tricking me, and so I took the check from him, but outside I tore it up and threw it away. Before I left the house of my patron, his wife said to me, 'Now run off quickly to the coffin shop, and pick out everything that you need.' But I thought to myself, 'How could I ever do that with my mother still alive in her bed? God deliver me!'

"On the way home I was full of agony. What was going to happen to me after my mother died? Who would be left to worry about how *I* went into the ground? I thought of my unmarried cousin who died a pauper *no pior desprezo no mundo*, in the worst kind of neglect and disregard. How much worse off was myself, who had nothing and no one left in the world!

"Finally the night arrived when my mother died in my arms, just like a little baby. She didn't weigh very much anymore. When the end finally came, I was calm. God finally brought some peace into my heart, and I decided that I would make the best of it. So I made up a good fire of twigs, and I sent a neighbor's child to borrow a plastic pan. Imagine! I had to wash my mother with a borrowed basin. Excuse me for telling you, but I washed every part of her body. I washed her good and with nice hot water. I straightened her up and warmed up her feet, and I combed her hair. I even put a little cologne on her head. I took out her own best clothes, which I had washed, mended, and ironed, and I dressed her up. Then I wrapped her up nice and tight in her covers. I did everything without the help of a single person.

"I left her in the bed, and I went to look for someone to help me move her out into the front room. As my luck would have it, there was a gravedigger's apprentice who was passing along the street. 'Hey, hey,' a neighbor called to him. 'Go inside that house because Amor's mother has died and she needs help bringing her bed into the front room.'

"The boy thought that my neighbor was making fun of him because he worked at the cemetery, and so he came into the house full of jokes. Well, he was plenty surprised to see my mother lying there all right! But he was a good boy, and he helped me move her, and he sat up with me until very late that night.

"I was waiting for the coffin to arrive. I had sent for one from the old folks home run by the *Vicentinos*. It was very late by the time the assistant came carrying the coffin on his head up the hill. And the shameless boy greeted me saying, 'Come and look at the piece of crap the *Vicentinos* have sent you!'

"*Porcaria*, nothing!" I replied. He was talking about *my mother's* coffin, and I told him that anything the *Vicentinos* sent us was good. But he insisted that it was a piece of rubbish because it was a charity coffin, decorated with paper and not with fabric and ribbons.

" 'Mother's coffin has nothing wrong with it,' I said. 'It is just the way she wanted it to be. Didn't she tell me before she died that she wanted to be buried the same as my own father had? And his coffin was just like this one. So I am content. If our sweet Savior could come into this world in a manger lined with hay, then my mother can surely leave this world in a coffin lined with paper!'

"The boy said, 'Well, is she going to be buried in her old tattered clothes, then?' At this I began to *me endoidar* [go mad]. 'No,' I thought to myself, 'I *can't* put her into the ground with her old, patched clothes.' So I told him to wait, that the *mortalha* was coming. I ran to my sister-in-law and I said, 'Hey, there, do you have five mil reis to loan me until tomorrow?' 'I have,' she said. 'Well, give it to me then so that I can bury my mother properly.' With the money in my hand I ran to a woman who cut out the cloth to put in the coffin, and she quickly sewed some new clothes for my mother. She even came and helped me dress her in the coffin.

"Finally, everything was just right. But my brothers and sisters said that I had fooled everyone and that I still had my mother's funeral money hidden away. Poor things! Poor things! God above forgive them! God Almighty save them! For I am the victor! I am still walking around on this earth, and long ago they have left it!"

I did not ask Amor how she would be buried or whether she had a nest egg with her funeral money squirreled away. But I do know that Amor, like the other *moradores* of the Alto do Cruzeiro, does not remember the dead—not even her own mother—by visiting the local cemetery. There is no point in doing so, not even on November 2, All Souls' Day, the universal Day of the Dead in Latin America. The local cemetery, like Potter's Field in New York City, is a place to be avoided. It stands as a forceful reminder of the fragile *inexistência* of the poor, their socially constituted being and nothingness.

Pauper Funerals, Misplaced Bodies, and the State

Today in the small, compact, walled enclosure of the municipal cemetery of Bom Jesus, the conflicting social realities of *casa, rua*, and *mata*—the colliding worlds of the feudal *casa grande*, of the "streets" of the modern town, and of the peasant countryside—and their accompanying definitions of person, individual, and anonymous nonentity are graphically reproduced. In the municipal cemetery of Bom Jesus one is immediately struck by its density. At the entrance is the *vila nobre*, as Casorte refers to the aristocratic section of the graveyard with its huge, white stone mausoleums, family homes that are miniature reproductions of the plantation society's *casas grandes*. Here the coffins rest on cement benches *above* ground, the preferred form of burial in Bom Jesus, as throughout Brazil.

People in Bom Jesus have a marked fear, as they say, of "going into dirt" or "going into a hole" and being eaten by bugs, and so they prefer aboveground entombment. They also fear being buried alive. These fears are shared with the people of the Alto. Dona Xiquinha, the elderly praying woman of the Alto who prepared bodies for burial, offers, "Those who can afford to, have their own catacombs. Nobody wants to go into the hole, into the dirt, to be eaten by insects. But the poor, *coitados*, they have no choice." On the fear of being buried alive Xiquinha had this to say: "We became afraid after the time of the cholera, the sickness that took so many people there were hardly any living left. They buried so many and so quickly that they even buried some people who were still alive. So for this reason we like to leave the coffin unnailed, and we want to have a *velório* [wake] for one night. It is prohibited to bury a person on the same day he dies, but infants can go into the ground right away."

Some of the mausoleums are constructed to look like family chapels complete with altar and votive lamp. With the passage of time the disintegrated remains are swept into an urn or pottery container and placed to the side, making room for a new occupant. The family remains are treated collectively but are never removed from the family vault. They are the property of the family. With the transformation of rural society and the consolidation of family plantations into large industrial sugar mills and refining factories, many of the original big families of the sugar estates have left the *município*, and their family vaults have fallen into a state of disuse and disrepair, thereby projecting the image of aristocratic families now fallen on hard times.

Leaving the *vila nobre*, one comes on the graveyard's *rua burguesa*, a representation of the modern town with a paved street alongside of which are individual graves with personalized tombstones. At once the traditional

"Look, corn decorates the graves of *matutos*."

The Bone Depository: "They have counted my hands and feet; they have numbered all my bones."

notion of the "person" gives way to the modern notion of the "individual" freed from familistic constraints. These new marble niches are also built above ground, and some carry air vents.

Beyond the *vila nobre* and the *rua burguesa* of the cemetery lies the *mata*, the field where small mounds of earth cover the new graves of the anonymous poor, which are marked, if at all, by small white wooden crosses and decorated with stalks of corn rather than with fresh or plastic flowers. No individual or family names grace these graves. Anonymous in life, they carry their *inexistência* (as Casorte puts it) with them into the grave. Into the looking glass that is the funeral space, the poor and humble classes are destined to be unreflected.

For the poor of Bom Jesus and of the Alto do Cruzeiro, who are buried at the public's expense, their graves are not their own. Because of overcrowding, they can expect to keep their spaces only for a year for an adult, six months or less for a child. Pauper graves are shallow—two feet is common for a child—and when the site is needed again, the order is given to exhume the remains. The partly disintegrated coffin, made of plywood and cardboard, is tossed over the west walls of the cemetery, where it is burned. What remains ("hair and all"), says Casorte, making an evil face, is tossed into the deep well that is called the *depósito dos ossos*.

The rapidity of the transfer from shallow, individual grave to collective bone depository is understood by all as a necessary (i.e., a hygienic) evil, one

Angel graves: two feet under and a cardboard coffin.

that entails a certain violation of the bodies of the deceased. "It's not ugly," Casorte says, trying to persuade me to come closer to the bone well, to overcome my reluctance to "examine" its contents as he pulls off the stone cover to expose the multitude of the anonymous dead of Bom Jesus. "They have counted my hands and my feet"—the words of the Easter psalm returns to me—"they have numbered all my bones." My eye catches sight of cloth, and I turn away. "Socks," Casorte says, "socks last forever. It's because they're synthetic." And I think back to little Mercea and her bare feet. "Shall I jump in?" Casorte offers teasingly. And then he pulls out a small fibula that must have belonged to a very young person. "Enough, Casorte," I say, and we return to his "office" at the back of the cemetery to go over his books to see if his burial figures matched the deaths recorded that year at the *cartório civil*. I ask Casorte how many of the 162 children buried in the cemetery in the first six months of 1989 (it was July of that year) were "bourgeois" children, falling into his preferred usage. Only two babies, he replies, were *not* buried as paupers that year. The others would all soon join the multitude of skeletal angels in the bone depository. "Is that any way to treat angels?" I ask, for we have both descended into a devilish sort of gallows humor, united by our politics and by our anger.

As we speak a middle-aged, working-class woman raps on the open door of the office. She enters apologetically, explaining that this is her fifth attempt to talk to Casorte about a "personal matter" of great importance. She asks to purchase the space where her father and husband are both buried so that no one could "mess" with their remains. She adds, "I don't want anyone to *arrancar eles* [drag them up, as though by the roots]." Casorte is gentle with the woman and asks her to fill out a form, reassuring her that her wishes can be arranged. She leaves, with relief evident on her careworn face.

As Casorte accompanies me out to the front gate of the cemetery, he offers to show me the antique *bate-queixo* or *quebra-queixo* (jawbreaker), as the old borrowed pauper coffin is called because of the way the bones rattled on its hard surface without so much as a piece of felt or cloth under the body. But just then Seu Cristavão, a local coffin maker, appears. Sweating profusely and mopping his face, he stops to lean on a tombstone. Next to him he places a tiny child's coffin that he has been carrying in the crook of his arm. The shoe-box-size coffin is decorated in a dark blue fabric, with silver paper stars glued across the top. "It looks like the American flag," quips Casorte, and then he adds, "Here's another little angel going into the pit." "But where," I asked, "was the procession of the angels?" Sometimes, Casorte explains, the mother or father will pay Seu Cristavão or another owner of a *casa funerária* to deliver the coffin for them. And once in a while a cab driver will "deliver" a baby in his or her coffin as a favor to the mother, who was, perhaps, too ill to arrange a proper funeral. "But the saddest thing of all," he says, "is to see a *matuto*, dressed in his one good suit, arrive from the country in the back of a hired cab, with the baby coffin resting on his knees." Seu Cristavão and I have crossed paths on many other occasions. "Why the *pesquisas* [research]?" the coffin maker taunts. "Just put down that they all died of hunger." I promise to quote him.

I return the following morning to complete the count of child burials for 1989. Casorte is late, and while I am waiting for him at the front gates, a municipal truck pulls up quickly, and two stocky young men jump out of the cab, slamming its doors. They immediately engage the disabled gravedigger in a mock fist fight and then ask him to run and get the *bandeja* (serving plate), a euphemism for the tin coffin that is used to pick up and deliver unidentified bodies. "This one," says the older of the two men, "is a real mess, a *morte desastrada*," the victim of a "violent assassination." His remains had been found in the fields of an *engenho* outside of the town. He had been shot and mutilated. The body had lain unclaimed for two days in the "morgue" of the local hospital. The mayor now requested that the body, which was "already beginning to offend the hospital workers," be brought to the cemetery and kept there for another few days. If by the weekend no one showed up to claim it, the judge would give the orders for it to be buried as a *desconhecido*, an "unknown person."

"Is it possible," I ask, "that *no one* really knows who the man was?" The municipal workers look away, offering no reply. Later, Casorte explains that with assassinations like these, in which no one knows exactly what is involved, the relatives and friends are afraid to show their faces or to have anything to do with the body. "They are afraid"—and here Casorte brings the conversation to a hurried conclusion—"that they could be the next ones marked."

The Public Morgue / Bureau of Missing and Disappeared Persons

But what the *moradores* of the Alto fear most of all is the police summons to appear in Recife at the ML to identify the body of a loved one who met a violent or precipitous end. Here the bodies of the unknown, the unregistered, and the pauperized rub shoulders with the bodies of the assassinated, the murdered, and the disappeared. Of the two—the unknown and the violently killed—the latter are more stigmatized because theirs were "sudden deaths," *mortes de repente*, and by definition "bad deaths" as well. People say of them that they died alone, *sem dizer aí Jesus*, "without calling on Jesus."

As Casorte says, it takes a considerable amount of courage to appear in the morgue of the local hospital, the holding space in the back of the municipal cemetery, or the dreaded cavernous underworld of the ML in Recife to identify and claim a lost, unknown, or disappeared body. It is not a job for the faint of heart or the weak of stomach. Among the *moradores* of the Alto do Cruzeiro it is a job for women, for wives and mothers in particular.

Elena Morena did not want to go to the ML for a second time when notified by her sister in August 1989. Elena rocked back and forth on her little stool with her arms crossed and beat her fists against her hard, small breasts. The tears rolled down her cheeks, but not a word escaped from lips pressed together so tightly they seemed to lose all their color. Two years before Elena's husband had been murdered by local policemen. "In uniform," she said. They came to Elena's door in the dead of night, dragged her husband, Sérgio, from the house, and murdered him, dumping his mutilated remains on a country road. A few days later more police officers appeared with photos, asking Elena to identify the body as it was when it was found, and they carried the collapsing, grieving woman to the morgue, where she was forced to make the identification in person. She was given no explanation for the assassination by the police, but it was widely rumored on the Alto do Cruzeiro that Sérgio was a thief.

Sérgio was, in fact, a local guard, a *vigia* chosen by the *delegacia* of Bom Jesus to police his immediate vicinity near the top of the Alto. He was murdered within a few days of having given up guard duty to work for himself. Sérgio was not the first *vigia* to die on the Rua da Cruz of the Alto in 1989. He had come into his position following the murder of the previous *vigia* during an argument with some off-duty policemen on the street at the base of the hill where pineapples were sold at Saturday *feira*. The shots could be heard halfway up the Alto.

After Elena reported the murder to the judge of Bom Jesus, demanding not justice but merely the widow's pension that had been denied her, police harassment of the family continued. Elena began to fear for the safety of Jorge, her eldest son. She urged Jorge to take up residence with her sister, who lived in a poor neighborhood in Recife. On a quiet Wednesday night, just a few days after Jorge had moved to Recife, he went to a corner stand to buy a Coke and talk with some of the local boys. Two men rushed up to him, hit him across the head, and shot him twice in the back. They left him lying in the street. Within minutes children and stray dogs formed an agitated circle around him. Jorge was dead before the ambulance arrived.

As soon as her sister sent word, Elena rushed to the city to identify and claim her son's body, which meant another descent into the hades of the ML. Elena shuddered in the telling: "It is a place, Nancí, that no human wants to enter, not even once in her life. But *two* times. . . ." Her one consolation was that her friends had taken up a collection so that Elena could get the body from the morgue and back to Bom Jesus for a proper burial, one fitting a handsome youth, the joy, she said, of her "old" age. Elena was forty-two at the time.

"And what would have happened if you hadn't the money?"

"Those who can pay for the burial get to take the body home with them. Those who can't, lose it."

"Where does it go?"

"The doctors get it, and they can take from it what they want."

"And the rest?"

"Who knows what they do with the bones? Maybe the *urubus* [vultures] get them. This is the fate of the poor, Nancí. *Nem donos do corpo deles, eles são* [They don't even own their own bodies]."

It is no coincidence that the Brazilian filmmaker Marcel Camus retold the Orpheus legend around the magical disappearance of Orpheus's beautiful lover, Euridice, during *carnaval* celebrations on a hillside shantytown, a *favela*, of Rio de Janeiro. In the 1959 masterpiece *Black Orpheus* (*Orfeu Negro*), Orfeu searches frantically for his "disappeared" lover amid the frenzied crush of Rio's streets during the four days of the festival. He is directed to the Department of Missing Persons on the thirteenth floor of a modern high-rise building. But, of course, during *carnaval* the corridors are deserted, except for a minor clerk—poor, black, and illiterate—who is sweeping up pieces of shredded and discarded paper. Confetti? Reports of missing persons?

"Is this the Missing Persons Department?" Orfeu asks anxiously.

"It is," replies the old man, "but I have never seen a missing person here." And he opens the door to an office that is stacked with papers.

"Here are your missing persons. You see? Nothing but paper. Fifteen floors of it, and all for nothing. Can you read? I can't, but you may look through them if you like. But if you ask me, you'll never find a lost person in papers. That's where they get lost forever. . . . Do you think that papers are ever sorry for a man?"

From the Missing Persons Bureau, Orfeu goes to a Xangô meeting to contact his dead lover through spirit mediums. He fails, and from there he must go to the public morgue, where, like Elena Morena, Black Irene, and many other women of the Alto do Cruzeiro who have had to face the same, he is met by a cold, unfeeling functionary who tries to dissuade Orfeu from carrying the body of his loved one away.

"You know a body is always useful for science. And if you just left it here, it would save you a lot of money."

Orfeu roughly pushes the functionary aside and kisses the cold lips of his beloved Euridice, who is lying on a stone slab among the anonymous dead still in their *carnaval* costumes, here in the underworld of Rio.

These brief, potent scenes evoke, even thirty years later, some key themes of shantytown life: the anxious, ontological insecurity of the *favelados* and their worst fears—separation, loss, disappearance, and violent, inexplicable physical assault on the body. Camus also captured the images of an indifferent bureaucracy that turns a deaf ear to the cries of the people, transforming their misery into mountains of paper that are discarded and swept away by the illiterate custodian to whom the words are meaningless.

Postscript

On the last day of the liberation theology missions in mid-August 1989, on the evening of the ritual bonfire into which effigies and images of the "social sins" of the community were thrown and burned, the Alto women whose husbands or adult sons had disappeared were called forward. Tentatively, a half dozen women made their way to the front of the makeshift altar under the still empty gaze of the crucifix of O Cruzeiro. One of the women was Black Irene, whose scream on the night that the men came to take away her eldest and favorite son, Nego De, was heard up and down the length of the Alto and all along the Rua da Cruz. It is said to reverberate there still.

But on this night Irene was silent, stunned by her own daring in coming forward to make her dangerous loss public. The simple prayers recited, an Ave Maria, a Pai Nosso, the deeds silently recorded, the people of the Alto returned to their homes, mulling these events over in their hearts.

Later that same night a little street urchin, a *moleque* known to everyone on the Alto as Pitomba (after a fruit he frequently stole and then resold in the marketplace) disappeared from the steps of the church where he normally slept. The next morning it was said that someone reported seeing his body, eviscerated and tossed outside the west wall of the cemetery, in the place where the partly disintegrated coffins of recently exhumed infants were burned. The Franciscan nuns of the chapel of Santa Lúcia, who occasionally ministered to the street children of Bom Jesus, fervently prayed that the boy's itinerant soul might be received, indeed welcomed, by his heavenly Father.

But the boy's body, like that of the missing Cristo, was never recovered, and the story remains unverified.

7 Two Feet Under and a Cardboard Coffin

The Social Production of Indifference to Child Death

A child died today in the favela. He was two months old. If he
had lived he would have gone hungry anyway.

Carolina Maria de Jesus (1962:108)

The opposite of love is not hate, but indifference.

Elie Wiesel (1990:174)

Forebodings

"Why do the church bells ring so often?" I asked Nailza de Arruda soon after
I had moved into a corner of her tiny mud-walled hut near the top of the Alto
do Cruzeiro. It was the dry and blazingly hot summer of 1964, the months
following the military coup, and save for the rusty, clanging bells of Nossa
Senhora das Dores Church, an eerie quiet had settled over the town. Beneath
the quiet, however, were chaos and panic.

"It's nothing," replied Nailza, "just another little angel gone to heaven."
Nailza had sent more than her share of little angels to heaven, and sometimes at night I could hear her engaged in a muffled, yet passionate, discourse with one of them: two-year-old Joana. Joana's photograph, taken as
she lay eyes opened and propped up in her tiny cardboard coffin, hung on a
wall next to the photo of Nailza and Zé Antônio taken on the day the couple
had eloped a few years before. Zé Antônio, uncomfortable in his one good,
starched, white shirt, looked into the camera every bit as startled as the
uncanny wide-eyed toddler in her white dress.

Nailza could barely remember the names of the other infants and babies
who came and went in close succession. Some had died unnamed and had
been hastily baptized in their coffins. Few lived more than a month or two.
Only Joana, properly baptized in church at the close of her first year and
placed under the protection of a powerful saint, Joan of Arc, had been
expected to live. And Nailza had dangerously allowed herself to love the
little girl. In addressing the dead child, Nailza's voice would range from
tearful imploring to angry recrimination: "Why did you leave me? Was

268

your patron saint so greedy that she could not allow me one child on this earth?" Zé Antônio advised me to ignore Nailza's odd behavior, which he understood as a kind of madness that, like the birth and death of children, came and went.

It was not long after that Nailza was again noticeably pregnant, and the nightly prayers to Joana ceased, momentarily replaced by the furtive noises of stolen marital intimacies. By day, Nailza's appetite and her normally high spirits returned, much to my relief. The peacefulness was, however, soon rent by the premature birth of a stillborn son. I helped Nailza dig a shallow grave in our *quintal*, the trash-littered excuse for a backyard where pigs and stray goats foraged and where we hoped to dig a pit latrine before the start of the winter rains. No bells would ring for this tiny fellow, nor would there be any procession of the angels accompanying his body to the grave-yard. Stillbirths remained (in those days prior to hospital delivery for Alto women) outside the net of public and medical surveillance. And when curious neighbors commented the next day on Nailza's flat stomach, she tossed off their questions with a flippant "Yes, free and unburdened, thanks be to God!" Or with a sharp laugh, she would deny having been pregnant at all. Even living with Nailza in our close quarters, I had a hard time knowing what she was experiencing in the weeks and months that followed, except that Joana's photo disappeared from the wall, and her name was never again mentioned as long as I lived in that house. The stillborn son returned Nailza to her senses and to an acceptance of the reality in which she lived. Neigh-bors would say approvingly that Nailza had learned to *se conformar* to the unalterable conditions of her existence. But at what price I wondered, at what physical, psychic, and social cost to Nailza and other women like her and at what risk to their seemingly unbroken succession of "replacement" babies and subsequent angel-children?

At the time I first posed them, these questions held only immediate and pragmatic value for me. As a community health worker specializing in ma-ternal and child health, I wanted to know just what was necessary to propose and introduce "appropriate" kinds of intervention. Should sick-to-death infants be treated at home or in the clinic? Could one teach young mothers how to administer intramuscular injections of water-salt-sugar solution under the infant's clavicle as a dangerous but desperate "last ditch effort" at saving severely dehydrated babies? Would collectivizing child care through a cooperatively run day care center allow for the simultaneous rescue of Alto children and their mothers? It was the 1960s, and I struggled to maintain a positive view of shantytown life, which (prior to my training in cultural anthropology) meant the attribution of all forms of human misery and suffering to purely exogenous causes—poverty, racism, class exploitation, political and economic imperialism, and so on. And like so many of my North American compatriots, with our terrible fear of human difference, I projected onto my Alto friends and neighbors a comforting illusion of familiarity and sameness. We were all very much alike, very much the same (I liked to think) beneath the superficial veneer of cultural differences.

Both views eventually proved themselves inadequate, and I clung to them in the face of a good deal of cognitive incongruity. But I managed to bury the conflict in a mad whirl of activities, in attending to the multitude of small, day-to-day crises surrounding the work of the shantytown association and the building (later the running) of the cooperative day nursery, the creche. There was no time for abstract, philosophical reflection and musings on the human condition, on the nature of human nature, or on the varieties of response to the stresses of chronic hunger, deprivation, sickness, and premature death. Then, too, there was always the specter of depression and despair hovering anxiously at my shoulders, spurring me on to further activity, often at the expense of understanding.

Buried, perhaps, but never completely banished, for when I returned to Brazil for the first time in 1982, I came back to understand events that had puzzled me then and that continue even today, following four more field trips, to elude easy or definitive interpretation. My primary research questions were overdetermined at the outset. They were the ones that first crystallized during a veritable die out of Alto babies during a severe drought in 1965. The food and water shortages and the political and economic chaos occasioned by the military coup of the spring of 1964 were reflected in the spidery, difficult to read, handwritten entries on births and deaths in the yellowed pages of the huge ledger books kept at the *cartório civil*. Almost five hundred babies died in the *município* that year, and three hundred of these came from the shantytown population of less than five thousand individuals. But it wasn't the deaths that surprised me. It would take no Rudolf Virchow to crack some mysterious epidemiological puzzle. There were reasons enough for the deaths in the miserable conditions of shantytown life. Rather, what puzzled me was the seeming "indifference" of Alto women to the deaths of their babies and their willingness to attribute to their own offspring an "aversion" to life that made their deaths seem wholly natural, indeed all but expected. I shall try to explain what I mean.

Within the first month of my arrival in Bom Jesus, a young mother came to me with a very sick and wasted baby. Seeing that the child's condition was precarious, I rushed with him to the local hospital, where he died soon after, the desperate efforts of myself and two clinic attendants notwithstanding. I was devastated and frightened. I had come from a society in which (at least to my limited knowledge and experience) babies didn't die, or if they did, where it was a great human tragedy for all concerned. How could I break the news to the child's mother? Would she hold me responsible for the death? Would I be forced to leave my post of duty so soon after my arrival? Selfish concerns, mind you. Meanwhile, I had to trek all the way through town and climb the Alto with the tiny, yet strangely heavy, dead weight in my arms. It was almost more than I could bear, and I wept bitter and angry tears all along the way. To my great wonder and perplexity, however, the young woman took the news and the bundle from my arms placidly, almost casually and indifferently. Noting my red eyes and tear-stained face, the woman turned to comment to a neighbor woman standing by, "*Hein, hein, coitada! Engraçada, não é;* Tsk! Tsk! Poor thing! Funny, isn't she?" What was funny or amusing seemed to be my inappropriate display of grief and my concern over a matter of so little consequence. No one, least of all the mother, had expected the little tyke to live in any case.

Later that afternoon I returned to the home to attend the brief and understated wake. The small group of women and children who had gathered was mainly concerned with hearing me speak my then-fractured Portuguese, and gales of laughter followed my awkward attempts at expressing myself. Many had never heard a foreigner speak their language before, and they judged my accent completely unintelligible. The baby in its sky blue cardboard coffin was balanced precariously on a simple, straight-backed kitchen chair. No one had bothered to clear off the table, which was cluttered with dishes and knicknacks. A small knot of barefoot children played dominoes on the floor, and when a fight broke out among the players, the coffin was very nearly knocked over during the fray. No one corrected the children as they bumped into the chair, rocking its silent cradle. After an hour or so had passed, an older woman (she may have been the child's grandmother) called on some of the children to form a procession of angels to carry the baby to the cemetery. A couple of older girls were chosen as pallbearers. One refused, saying that she was "too old." Another complained that she was "always" the one chosen, and she pointed to another little girl, who ran off to hide, giggling. As the procession was about to leave, I asked whether a prayer would be recited. "It's only a baby," one of the women scolded, while the children bounded off down the hill, with the unfastened lid of the coffin flapping madly up and down. "Slow down!" a neighbor called to the children from her open door. "It's not a circus, you know."

Like the women who were listening to me and not understanding a word, I stood there dumbly, hearing and seeing but failing to grasp the meaning of the social drama being played out before me for the first of many times that year. We were strangers to each other and mutually unintelligible. I was faced, although I did not have the words for it then, with the opacity of culture. My only point of reference was the casual indifference and aliena-tion implied in Mersault's opening lines in Albert Camus's *L'étranger*, which I had read for a French class earlier that year. The words returned to me with a new force and power: *Aujourd'hui, maman est morte. Ou peut-être c'est hier, je ne sais pas.* "Mother died today, or possibly yesterday. I don't know [or care, it seemed]" (1955:21).

What had made death so small, of such little account on the Alto do Cruzeiro? Had the exposure to altogether too much sickness, hunger, and loss turned these women's hearts to stone? Because the indifference ap-peared in women who were ordinarily vibrant, emotionally charged, and sometimes quite sentimental when it came to remembrances of things and relationships past, it required some explanation.

In this first of three chapters on child death and mother love, I begin with a discussion of the "routinization" of child death in the creation of an "average expectable environment" of child death, meaning a set of condi-tions that places the infant at great jeopardy of sickness and death, accom-panied by the normalization of this state of affairs in both public and private life.[1] In the otherwise highly bureaucratic world of Bom Jesus, child death has yet to seize the imagination of political leaders, administrative and civil servants, physicians, and priests or religious officials as an urgent and pressing social problem about which "something must be done." Rather, there is a failure to see or to recognize as problematic what is considered to be the norm (as well as normal, expectable) for poor and marginal families. Michel Foucault (1975, 1980) has written of the hostile gaze, the punitive net of surveillance cast by the state and its disciplinary and biomedical technicians over the sick and deviant majority. Here, I am writing about an averted gaze, the turning away of the state and its agents in their failure to see, to acknowledge what should be right before their eyes.

In subsequent chapters I move from the public to the private realm, from *rua* to *casa*, to explore the conditions that normalize infant deaths within the family and that place all infants at high risk. The apparent indifference of Alto mothers toward the deaths of some of their infants is but a pale reflection of the "official" indifference of church and state to the plight of poor mothers and children. Although the routinization of child death in the miserable context of shantytown life is easy to understand, its routinization in the formal institutions of public life in Bom Jesus is difficult to accept uncritically. Here, the "social production of indifference" (see Herzfeld 1991) takes on a more malevolent, even sinister, cast.

I begin by sketching some historical and demographic features of child mortality worldwide and for Brazil as a whole, and I relate these broader patterns to the specific ethnographic instance: Bom Jesus da Mata during the twenty-five-year period 1964–1989. Drawing on municipal statistics and hospital records and on the reproductive histories of a large sample of Alto women, I show the interlocking threats of micro- and macroparasitism in maintaining a high level of what demographers refer to as "reproductive wastage" in poor women.

The Discovery of Child Mortality

Throughout much of human history, as in a good deal of the developing world today, women have had to give birth and nurture infants under environmental and social conditions inimical to child survival as well as hostile to their own well-being. Consequently, a high rate of infant and child mortality has been a fairly standard feature of human reproduction (see M. Cohen 1989:130–131). The dialectic between birth and death, survival and loss, remains a powerful one in the lives of most people living on the peripheries of the modern industrialized world, either as marginalized rural workers or as urban shantytown dwellers. In these contexts disease epidemics, food shortages, contaminated water, and inadequate medical care interact with patterns of high fertility and sometimes prejudicial forms of infant care to consign millions of children to an early grave.

In the world in which most of us live, the dialectic between fertility and mortality has lost its edge and is buried in the back of our consciousness. For most Europeans and North Americans each birth signifies new life, not the threat of premature death. But it was not so long ago in our own "Western" world that reproduction was as unpredictable and death as "random" and chaotic as they are in Northeast Brazil today. In many rural areas and in the squalid tenements of the urban slums of nineteenth-century England and America, there was hardly a family that had not experienced firsthand the death of an infant or a small child. Public health and sanitation, child and adult labor laws, and social welfare legislation had yet to vanquish the great uncertainties of human existence. A walking tour through any New England churchyard, with its symmetrical rows of infant tombstones, gives silent testimony to the fickleness of life to those who lived and died on the threshold of the great epidemiologic and demographic transitions.[2]

The mundaneness and ubiquitousness of child death—a fairly permanent feature of the history of childhood until quite recently—contributed to an array of private and public responses and to individual and collective defenses. One of the most common of these was the failure to recognize childhood mortality as a significant personal or social problem and to "naturalize" and normalize an infant death rate that, in various times and places, had sometimes reached 40 percent of all live births. Consequently, childhood mortality rates were difficult to discern up through the mid- to late-nineteenth century for Europe and North America. Often they were not tabulated apart from adult deaths. Child mortality remained hidden insofar as it had yet to achieve the status of a social or a medical problem in which the state had a clear vested interest.

One obstacle to the "discovery" of child mortality was the tendency of medical professionals and public officials alike to treat infant death as normal and routine, part of the "natural order" of things. This was reflected in the way the British Registrar General classified the causes of deaths in infants and small children. Many of these deaths were tabulated under the heading "diseases of growth, nutrition, and decay," which included deaths from "old age," "debility," and "natural causes" along with deaths from "wasting" (usually childhood malnutrition) and "prematurity" (Armstrong 1986:221; Wright 1988:306). It was only in 1907 that birth registration became compulsory in England (Armstrong 1983:15); about the same time the country launched its first national campaign against infant and childhood mortality. With the passage of the Registration Act of 1834, every death had to be publicly recorded as to its cause in the form of a medical disease so as to replace the so-called natural deaths of the old and of babies. An infant mortality rate was created in 1875, thus suggesting for the first time a social awareness of these premature deaths and a recognition of the infant as a discrete entity (Armstrong 1986:212).

Pediatrics, meanwhile, was a relative latecomer to medical specialization: the British Pediatric Association was founded in 1928, and in the United States pediatric medicine developed only when women began entering the medical profession and the medical academy at the turn of the century. Relatedly, childhood malnutrition and diarrhea, two of the greatest killers of young children, were not identified as pediatric diseases until the twentieth century. In the first instance, "misrecognition"—the failure to understand the social relations of infant wasting as hunger (rather than as a congenital or constitutional defect in the child)—was responsible for the omission. In the second instance, professional self-interest led British doctors to suppress diarrhea as a diagnostic category; because diarrhea was deemed a "trivial" illness by the general population, physicians feared that parents might attribute incompetence to those doctors involved in the treatment of fatal pediatric cases.

It is ironic that the discovery of childhood malnutrition (first identified as a pediatric disease in 1933) and the more specific diagnoses of marasmus, kwashiorkor, and PEM (protein-energy malnutrition) had to await Western medical doctors encountering these disorders in the tropics and adopting a traditional Ghanaian term as their clinical diagnostic category. Kwashiorkor is an Ewe term for an infantile wasting disease that is caused by an insufficient intake of protein, producing apathy, edema, and partial loss of pigmentation. It is generally associated with stunted growth, delayed development, and chronic diarrhea, and it is recognized as a serious, potentially fatal, childhood disorder. In the native etiological system kwashiorkor is recognized as a socially produced disease of childhood: it is said to be the disease of the "deposed" child, who, following the birth of a younger sibling, is weaned from the breast to a low-protein maize diet. Protein-calorie malnutrition in children (of which there was an epidemic in nineteenth-century England [see, for example, Engels (1845) 1958:160–190]) only entered medical nosology when British doctors working in the colonies discovered it as a "tropical" disease.[3]

In short, the social construction, or (as Armstrong preferred) the social "invention," of child mortality and, later, child survival as important social and medical problems about which something must be done is of fairly recent vintage. In many parts of Europe and in North America up through the mid-nineteenth century, high infant mortality was not regarded as intolerable or unacceptable but rather as a fairly predictable and expected occurrence. For one thing, child mortality had always had a clear class reference that allowed it to remain hidden: the children of the rural and urban poor and working classes were mostly afflicted. As Foucault wrote: "It was of little importance whether *these* people lived or died, since their reproduction was [thought of] as something that took care of itself in any case" (1980:126). It would take class and political conflict and economic emergencies (such as the new labor requirements of a more advanced stage of urban industrialization) to provoke state interest in the regulation of fertility and the control of population, including a concern with child mortality and child survival, which, in recent years, have achieved the status of a "master" social and political problem in the developing world.[4] And so gradually the "naturalness" of infant death was called into question, and the infant was no longer regarded as "one of death's natural habitats, but rather as a terrain in which death was an obscene intrusion" (Wright 1988:306).

But in many Third World countries mired in a relatively crude form of dependent capitalism and still characterized by a high mortality and a high, "untamed" fertility, the naturalness of infant and child mortality has yet to be questioned, and parents may understand a baby's life as a provisional and undependable thing—a candle whose flame is as likely to flicker and go out as to burn brightly and continuously. There, child death may be viewed less as a tragedy than as a predictable and relatively minor misfortune, one to be accepted with equanimity and resignation as an unalterable fact of human existence.

Following from a high expectancy of loss, reproductive and child-tending habits may be based on a thinking in sets, on a presumption of the inter-changeability and replaceability of offspring (see Imhof 1985). Reckonings of the social, moral, and economic value of the individual child may be measured against those of older children, adults, or the family unit as a whole. These moral evaluations are in turn influenced by such "external" contingencies as population pressures, subsistence strategies, household composition, cultural ideas concerning the nature of infancy and childhood and definitions of personhood, and religious beliefs about the soul and its immortality, all of which are explored in the following pages.

I wish to make it clear from the outset that the apparent indifference of Alto women toward the lives and deaths of some of their infants is contin-uous with, and a pale reflection of, the official bureaucratic indifference of local agents of church and state to the problem of child mortality in North-east Brazil today. The social production of official indifference is similar to what Bourdieu (1977:172–183) meant by *meconnaissance*, or "misrecogni-tion," the largely unconscious rejection of the "unthinkable" and "unname-able," especially those social relations that must be concealed and misread so as to guarantee complicity in the collective bad faith alluded to earlier. What cannot be recognized in this instance are the social determinants of the overproduction of *Nordestino* angel-babies.

Child Death in the Northeast: The Colonial Context

In his *Guia Médico das Maẽs de Família,* published in Rio de Janeiro in 1843, J. B. M. Imbert cautioned the mistresses of the large estates of the Northeast to exercise caution in selecting *babás* and wet-nurses for their newborns from among their female slaves living in the traditional *senzalas*. While suggesting that black slave women were more physically suited to the task of lactation than were white and free women (1843:89), Imbert also noted the unhygienic infant care practices of slave women that contributed to a high infant mortality in the slave quarters:

> The Negro women ordinarily cut the cord very far from the navel and are more and more inclined to follow the pernicious custom of putting pepper on it and covering it with castor oil or some other ir-ritant. Having done this the perverse creatures squeeze the child's belly to the point of suffocating it. This cuts the life-thread of many, many young ones and contributes to the development in the navel of that inflammation which goes by the name of the seven day sick-ness. (Cited in Freyre 1986a:381)

In addition, Imbert noted that slave women tended to ignore the "weak digestive organs of the newborn" and to feed infants a gruel made up of the same kinds of "coarse food such as the mothers themselves are accustomed to eating." He warned the plantation mistresses to be on their guard against black nursemaids bringing their dangerous practices inside the big houses. But he also advocated that the mistresses try to educate their slaves so as to curb these practices in the slave quarters as well, for "the Negro women that give birth are augmenting their master's capital" (cited in Freyre 1986a:382).

The concern with the slave master's primary means of production promoted some interest in the question of black infant mortality in the colonial period and may have contributed to the negligible differences in the birthrates and infant death rates of the slave and free populations as recorded for a number of *Nordestino* plantations and *fazendas* in Brazil for the late eighteenth and early nineteenth centuries. Freyre cited, for example, a census taken in the sugar plantation community of São Antônio, Pernambuco, in 1827 that showed comparable adult and child death rates for free whites, free mulattoes, and enslaved blacks. Nevertheless, even if the differences between the free and slave child mortality were negligible (and Freyre's selective use of questionable historical sources must certainly be questioned), child mortality was still extremely high in both *casa grande* and *senzala*. The premature death of infants and their mothers for many successive generations in the colonial and postcolonial periods "reduced by something approaching fifty percent the production of human beings in the Big House and in the slave hut" (Freyre 1986a:385). This was reflected, for example, in the writings of Maria Graham, the British diarist who traveled through Brazil in the early nineteenth century. She recorded in her published *Journal of a Voyage to Brazil* that, according to the mistress of an *engenho* in Mata-Paciência, less than half the Negroes born on that estate lived to be ten years old.

The high infant death rate of the slaves was affected by the "economic circumstances of their domestic life and labor" (Freyre 1986a:377). Many slave women who worked in the fields were forced to carry their infants and small babies strapped to their backs in cloth slings. One chronicler cited by Freyre, F. A. Brandão, Jr., told of an estate master in Maranhão who obliged his female slaves to deposit their infants in the field shack on plantation lands for the duration of their mothers' workday. The infants were suspended in hammocks or left alone on floor mats, while more mobile toddlers were sometimes buried up to their chest in holes dug in the ground so as to curtail their movements over long stretches of time.

By contrast, the high mortality in the big house was due largely to the failure of the Portuguese colonists to adapt their traditional childrearing practices to a new environment. The European planters brought with them to the New World the practices of swaddling and head bundling that contributed to the death of infants exposed to the often sweltering heat of the tropics. In his *Memórias Históricas de Pernambuco*, published in 1844, Fernandes Gama noted that although the original Portuguese planter class suffered an extremely high infant mortality ("two-thirds of them died shortly after birth"), successive generations of plantation mistresses eventually learned to adopt more practical approaches to infant care, and they did not suffer as much "reproductive waste" as their mothers and grandmothers had.

But even though Brazilian infant and child mortality decreased in Brazil beginning in the second half of the sixteenth century, it remained high. Child death was first elevated to a national concern in Brazil during the late nineteenth century, when it became one of the problems addressed by the hygienists of the Second Empire. At a meeting of the Brazilian Academy of Medicine held in Rio de Janeiro in 1846, the subject of child mortality was raised for general discussion and debate. The physicians in session directed their attention to two main issues: child mortality and pediatric illnesses. Their explanations of child mortality ranged from climatic considerations (dampness, humidity, tropical airs, radical changes in temperature), to inappropriate pediatric feeding practices, to the exposure of vulnerable infants to tropical diseases. Virtually all the conference participants implicated the institution of Negro slave wet-nursing in the high infant mortality. The black nurse was accused of transmitting syphilis and other venereal and skin diseases to the suckling infant via contact with her skin and contaminated milk. These physicians also attacked as unhygienic the common slave practice of hand-feeding infants with premasticated adult foods, and they criticized the *babás'* customs concerning the care of the umbilical cord, infant head shaping, underdressing of babies, and the use of traditional herbal remedies for common childhood sicknesses.

The first Brazilian medical text to deal exclusively with the problem of child mortality was José Maria Teixeira, *Causas da Mortalidade das Crianças no Rio de Janeiro*, published in 1887. It remains a unique statement of late-nineteenth-century social medicine. In contrast to the prevailing medical opinions of his day, Teixeira laid the blame for high childhood mortality on the political economy of slavery itself and all the perversions that it reproduced in both the big house and *senzala*. Teixeira cited the great disparity in the ages of married couples that was customary among the plantation elite, the poor education and poor maternal preparation of both white and slave mothers, and the frequency of unwanted, illicit births produced in master-slave sexual relations. As an aside he noted that child death was not treated as a great misfortune in the big house because plantation women married young and there would always be another newborn to replace a dead sibling.

Child Death Today:
The Modernization of Child Mortality

Finally, we come to the question of what advantage can be
taken [on behalf of child survival] of the prevailing winds of
free enterprise now blowing across both developing and
industrialized worlds. . . . The decade of the 1980s will
perhaps . . . be remembered as the decade in which economic
theories began to change with remarkable suddenness.
Enterprise systems and market mechanisms are now being
more fervently embraced by almost every nation, including
many with long marriages to other ideologies.

James P. Grant (1990:65)

Approximately one million children younger than five die each year in
Brazil, or about forty children every hour. An estimated 25 percent of all
infant deaths in Latin America occur in Brazil, and of these more than 50
percent take place in the Nordeste, which has an estimated infant mortality
rate of 116/1,000 live births, one of the highest in the hemisphere and
comparable to the poorest parts of Africa (IBGE 1986:38). Official statistics
are, however, at best an approximation of an underreported phenomenon.[5]
The inefficiency of basic public health and medical services in the Northeast
is such that an estimated two-thirds of those infants who die do so without a
medical diagnosis.

Hence, counting dead infants in Northeast Brazil is every bit as daunting
as U.S. census workers' attempts to count the homeless in American cities.
Much of the problem is tucked away from public scrutiny. Nonetheless, this
is a startling reality coming from the world's eighth largest economy, the
largest in the Southern Hemisphere. Insofar as infant and child mortality
rates may be taken as a particularly sensitive barometer of how well or how
badly a nation (region, community, or household) is faring at a given time,
what accounts for the persistent and perversely high child mortality in
Brazil as a whole and for the Northeast in particular?

One tendency has been to explain the high rates of child death and disease in the Third World as the almost inevitable consequences of impersonal ecological, climatic, or demographic conditions, such as the perennial
droughts of the Brazilian Nordeste or the "tropical" climate of the coastal
regions, with its plagues of microparasites and "exotic" infectious diseases.
Alternatively, explanation is sought in the "rampant," uncontrolled fertility
of the poor, which leads to food shortages and gross pediatric malnutrition.
The followers of classic demographic transition theory identify economic
and social "underdevelopment" as the key culprit, and they predict—based

on analogy with the recent history of Europe—that with advances in industrialization and with the penetration of modern, capitalist modes and relations of production into the "backward" hinterlands of Brazil, both the high infant mortality and the high "replacement" fertility will decline. That such has not been the case for Brazil, which over the past four decades of phenomenal economic growth and despite a marked decline in fertility has maintained a high infant mortality (indeed, in some cases, the economy and infant mortality have expanded in tandem), requires some explanation. What each of the ecological, population studies, and demographic transition theory approaches has obscured is the role of pernicious class relations in the social production of child morbidity and mortality. In other words, the foregoing equations have failed to note the macroparasitism of uncontained "market forces" that has fed and preyed on the bodies of the young, the vulnerable, and the powerless. Economic expansion and "development" have been waged in Brazil largely at the expense of the general social welfare and sometimes at the price of child survival. Hence, I refer to the "modernization" of child death with the same irony with which feminists describe the "feminization" of poverty in the United States in the late twentieth century.

And so despite the modernization of the Brazilian economy and its transformation in the second half of the twentieth century into a world-class superpower, glossed in the late 1970s as the Brazilian economic miracle (see Singer 1972), the rates of infant and child mortality did not show everywhere the expected decline. In fact, the mortality and fertility rates increased in some years for the most populous centers of the country. It is true that one observes for Brazil *as a whole* an initial and precipitous decline of 50 percent in child mortality between 1940 and 1970 and a decline in the average number of births from 5.8 in 1970 to about 3.3 in 1985 (see Berguó 1986). But when one begins to break down these aggregate data, certain patterns emerge that tell a different story, one that I refer to as the modernization of child mortality. By this, I mean, on the one hand, the "taming," "standardizing," and containing of child death to one level of society— the very poorest, especially those millions of rural exiles now living in the teeming shantytowns and *mocambos* that encircle São Paulo, Brasília, Belo Horizonte, Rio de Janeiro, Recife, and Forteleza. On the other hand, I mean the replacement of the "old" childhood killers, especially tetanus and other infectious childhood diseases now controlled by immunization, by the "new" killers, especially infant malnutrition and diarrhea-caused dehydration, both related to bottle-feeding. Under the new childhood mortality pattern, death comes to children at an even earlier age.

The "old" pattern of child mortality that characterized Brazil from the

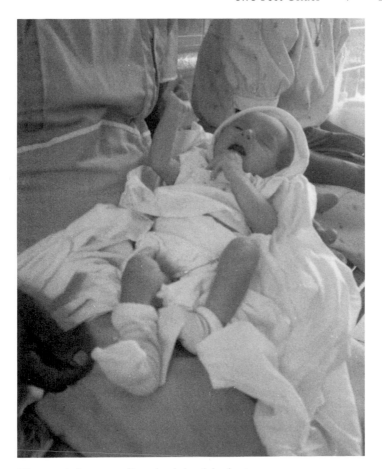

The new infant mortality: death by dehydration.

colonial period up through the mid-twentieth century was one of exceedingly high mortality affecting all social classes and races in Brazilian society. Epidemics of infectious diseases—measles, smallpox, malaria, pneumonia, and various tropical fevers—carried away the infants and small children of rich, poor, black, white, and mulatto alike. In addition, the poorer populations suffered the double jeopardy of malnutrition and gastrointestinal problems related to their impoverished and unsanitary living conditions. The rapid industrialization, urbanization, and modernization of Brazilian society and social and public institutions during the twentieth century have brought about the expected demographic and epidemiological transitions for the middle and upper classes and initially for the urban working classes as well. In addition to greatly improved standards of living, these social classes benefited during the decade of the 1970s from expanded and improved medical care, immunization, birth control and day care facilities, and possibly the world's largest national breast-feeding promotion campaign, initiated in March 1981.

These same social and biomedical forces had little or no impact on the morbidity and mortality of Brazil's poorest popular classes, while the economic "revolution" affected them adversely. This explains certain discrepancies and contradictions in the nation's changing epidemiological profile. Never again would black and white, rich and poor, master and worker, patron and client, bureaucrat, civil servant, and peasant alike share the same risk of child morbidity and mortality that Freyre described for the colonial and postcolonial period in Brazil. Child death had been vanquished in the *casas grandes, praças,* and main *ruas* of town and country. But it has not disappeared; child death has retreated to the back streets, muddy roads, and squalid hillsides of Brazil, where it has become the "privilege" of the *favela* and the shantytown alone. And there it will remain, requiring more than UNICEF's program of universal immunization, breast-feeding promotion, and oral rehydration (ORT) to dislodge it. Here, the social and economic roots of child death run very deep and very wide, indeed. They drink from the polluted groundwater produced by the unleashing of the same market forces cautiously welcomed in the 1990 UNICEF report *The State of the World's Children* (Grant 1990).

Consequently, one finds in Brazil today two contradictory epidemiological profiles, one for the rich and middle classes and the other for the poor. It is as if history had bifurcated, producing the expected demographic transition for part of the country, leaving the rest to die the way they always had: of sickness, hunger, and gross neglect.

And so beginning in 1966, two years after the Brazilian military coup, infant and child mortality began to rise in some regions. W. Leser (1972), for example, examined the evolution of child mortality in São Paulo between 1909 and 1970, noting the general tendency toward decline until 1961. After that date, but especially in the early 1970s, the rates rose again. Later, Roberto Macedo (1988) examined the effects of specific indices of the growing economic crisis in Brazil on the health, welfare, and mortality of children in the state of São Paulo throughout the 1980s. Rising rates of urban unemployment, worsening income distribution, and decline or stagnation in the production of basic food staples over the period 1975–1985 were highly correlated with the rise in infant mortality, a marked increase in the percentage of low-birth-weight infants in São Paulo's two major public hospitals, and a sharp rise in the number of abandoned street children, especially during 1982–1984.

In 1970 the Pan American Health Organization (PAHO) directed a large, comparative study of child mortality patterns (see Puffer & Serrano 1973) in fifteen rural and urban sites in the Americas (Argentina, Brazil, Colombia, Bolivia, Canada, Chile, El Salvador, Jamaica, Mexico, and the United States). The researchers identified Recife, the capital of Pernambuco and a mere ninety kilometers from Bom Jesus da Mata, as having the highest rates of infant mortality, of child deaths from malnutrition, and of infant deaths related to low birth weight of all urban centers sampled. Recife also had the poorest and most crowded living conditions. Even so, the PAHO investigators did not include the many congested shantytowns and peripheral neighborhoods that encircle the capital. We can well imagine that the *actual* infant mortality rate of Recife was considerably higher than the reported 91.2/ 1,000 live births. The woman identified by the PAHO investigators as the most likely to have lost an infant during the study years—an illiterate rural migrant who was marginally employed—could be any Alto woman older than thirty-five.

A team of physicians and epidemiologists at the University of Salvador, Bahia (see Paim, Netto Dias, & Duarte de Araújo 1980), closely monitored child mortality in that city (the fifth most populous in Brazil) and found that following a reduction by 53 percent in infant mortality between 1940 and 1966, the rate of decline was reduced dramatically until 1968, when mortality began to rise, reaching its highest point in 1971. Using multiple regression analysis, the team was able to identify the factors that most influenced child morbidity and mortality in Salvador for the period 1962– 1973. Health care and access to pediatric assistance were less significant than real wages, water supply, and educational level.

Similarly, Charles Wood (1977), an American researcher working for the Ford Foundation in Brazil, where he was also affiliated with a large planning and development agency in the city of Belo Horizonte, investigated the relationship between the conservative economic policies of the military government and the increase in infant mortality in two of Brazil's most important and populous urban centers, São Paulo and Belo Horizonte. He argued that in the years following the coup of 1964, the military junta supervised a transfer of the national income from the poorest 40 percent to the richest 10 percent of the population, thereby precipitating a decline in the standard of living for the largest number of people; the epidemiological consequences were disastrous. During the 1960s infant mortality in São Paulo rose more than 40 percent; in Belo Horizonte the rate of child death increased almost 70 percent between 1960 and 1973. There was, Wood discovered, a direct and negative correlation between real wages and infant mortality: as family income and purchasing power of workers declined in São Paulo and Belo Horizonte during the 1970s, the rates of infant mortality correspondingly increased (Wood 1977:58–59). Meanwhile, of course, development and business were "booming" in Brazil.

Because the rise in infant mortality occurred in Brazil's capital cities, such as Recife and Salvador in the Nordeste, and in regional metropolises, such as São Paulo and Belo Horizonte, in the industrialized south, the richest part of the country, economic development is not of itself predictive of a child survival revolution. In fact, it is the young who have suffered the brunt of the cost of economic expansion. Part of the cost of servicing Brazil's massive foreign debt has been severe cuts in public spending, including child health, welfare, and education programs.

Here, then, is the net result of Latin American nations' headlong rush at midcentury into the World Bank version of economic development: in the 1980s the economies of Latin America suffered their most severe setback in fifty years, which erased the economic boom of the 1970s (Albanez, Bastelo, Cornia, & Jespersen 1989:1). Of the ten Latin American countries for which there were reliable data, only one nation, Cuba, showed an unambiguous and steady decline in rates of infant mortality throughout the 1980s. Cuba, which already had the lowest mortality rates for the Southern Hemisphere, continued to advance its own child survival campaign successfully, so that from 1980 to 1986 the rates decreased from 16.6/1,000 to 13.6/1,000, just when the rates for infant mortality were rising or were stagnant for other Latin American nations because of inflation, foreign debt, and declining real wages for the working classes (Albanez et al. 1989:36). In this instance, Cuba's isolation from Western market forces and from the World Bank's economic development policies for Latin America served it well with respect to insulation from the long-term side effects of those policies on the health and well-being of the population.

The case of Brazil is particularly illustrative. The share of the government's total expenditures in interest payments in servicing the foreign debt rose from 7.2 percent in 1980 to 29.4 percent in 1985, while total expenditures in health decreased from 7.8 percent to 6.4 percent in 1985, just when infant mortality rates were beginning to show a significant rise (see Chahard & Cevini 1988). Real minimum wages fell 33 percent between 1981 and 1988, while food prices rose, so that the number of hours of labor at the minimum wage necessary to feed a family increased by more than a half in some years. On the Alto do Cruzeiro, where as much as 75 percent of family income is spent on basic food purchases, the net result was hunger. This was most marked during 1982–1984 when cornmeal began to replace beans and rice as a staple food, much to the detriment of child health and nutrition in particular.

The irregular and incomplete epidemiological transition that I am describing for Brazil as the modernization of child mortality is perhaps not so very different from what occurred in Europe at the beginning of the nineteenth century after the introduction of smallpox vaccination. There, the causes of death from smallpox among infants and small children were "taken over" by increased deaths caused by gastrointestinal illnesses (Imhof 1985:4). As René Dubos (1960) warned against the conceits of biomedical science, the advance against disease is never won, as one new pattern of morbidity and mortality comes to supplant the old, and the utopia of health or survival for all remains as elusive as a mirage in the desert.

In the interior of Northeast Brazil today, many poor infants and babies still manage (despite vigorous immunization campaigns) to escape vaccination until they reach school age, but they are generally protected against the old scourges of childhood—measles, smallpox, diphtheria, whooping cough, and so on—by the immunization of the majority, which reduces the risk for all. But there is no immunization against malnutrition and chronic diarrhea. Oral rehydration therapy can "save" a poor infant on the brink of death a half dozen times or more until, finally, the little one simply refuses and dies of hunger several weeks or months later. Jairnilson Paim, an epidemiologist at the Federal University of Salvador, and his colleagues estimated that only 2 percent of the Northeast Brazilian infant mortality rate can be reduced through immunization (see Paim, Dias, and De Araújo 1980:332).

The question to be asked is whether it is really an advantage to be rescued from one sickness only to be killed later of another more prolonged and painful one? We can ask ourselves a related question in light of the epidemiological transition that has occurred in our own society over the past hundred years as death from infectious disease—from polio and tuberculosis and from pneumonia-influenza-bronchitis—has been largely displaced by death at a later age from heart disease and cancer. Death from infectious disease is often premature but quick. Pneumonia was long and affectionately called the "old man's friend" in the United States because it brought a relatively quick death to the sufferer. Death from the "new" chronic diseases of old age are prolonged, painful, and both socially and psychologically troublesome, as one must observe the slow, yet irreversible, loss of the body's capacities and functions as well as the diminution of one's social roles, social network, and economic resources. These are large moral and ethical concerns, questions that are being debated by bioethicists (see Callahan 1990) and discussed in medical schools throughout the country. Adults can express their wishes through living wills, in malpractice law suits, and in the columns of the nation's newspapers. They can, at least hypothetically, have some say about how they *wish* to die.

The infants and babies of Northeast Brazil have no say. They cannot protest the international child survival programs and campaigns that can cruelly (although unintentionally) prolong their suffering and death. I try in the following pages to articulate the suffering of those—both women and children—who are too young to speak or whose words and opinions have been ignored or discredited and yet whose bodies are on the line. But how can one initiate a dialogue (especially in the case of infants) with the speechless? Only, perhaps, in the wordless space and primitive solidarity of "being there" and "bearing witness" to the suffering of the silent or silenced others—in this instance, mothers and babies. With all its pretensions and all of its difficulties, I know of no other way to proceed.

The Overproduction of Angels:
Keeping Track, Losing Count

The child shall be registered immediately after birth and shall have the right from birth to a name.

Article 7, United Nations Convention
on the Rights of the Child (1989)

Throughout Northeast Brazil, whenever one asks a poor woman how many children she has in her family, she invariably replies with the formula, "X children, y living." Sometimes she may say, "Y living, z angels." Women themselves, unlike the local and state bureaucracies, keep close track of their reproductive issue, counting the living along with the dead, stillborn, and miscarried. Each little angel is proudly tabulated, a flower in the mother's crown of thorns, each the sign of special graces and indulgences accumulating in the afterlife. There are a great many angels to keep track of. It is just as well that so many women are doing the counting.

When I first began in 1982 to try documenting the extent of infant and child mortality in the _município_, I was stymied by the difficulty in finding reliable local statistics. I was referred by various public officials of Bom Jesus to the office of the local IBGE, the national central statistics bureau. This was a small rented room across the hall from a local dentist's office in "downtown" Bom Jesus and was closed each time I went there. Finally, one afternoon I encountered a civil servant sleeping in a chair in the otherwise empty office. There was not so much as a typewriter or a file cabinet. "No," I was told, "there are no statistics kept here—no numbers at all." Everything, I was told, was tabulated and sent off to the central office in Recife.

The application of some local political pressure, however, yielded summaries of vital statistics for the community for selected years in the 1970s. In 1977, 761 live births (599 in hospital, 162 at home) and 311 deaths of infants were recorded, yielding an IMR (infant mortality rate) of 409/1,000. In 1978, 896 live births (719 in hospital, 177 at home) and 320 infant deaths yielded an infant mortality rate of 357/1,000. If these statistics were reliable, they indicated that between 36 percent and 41 percent of all infants in the *município* were dying in the first twelve months of their lives, a state of affairs that was immediately and roundly denied by the mayor as an absurdity. "My *município* is growing, not declining," he insisted, and Seu Félix sent me to the local hospital to corroborate the IBGE statistics with the records on births and deaths kept there.

The Barbosa Hospital and Maternity Center is one of three hospitals serving the entire region of the *zona da mata—norte* of Pernambuco and Paraíba. Although privately owned by the Barbosa family, the hospital primarily serves the needs of the rural popular classes, many of whom receive medical services without charge. Hence, the hospital attracts a large clientele that extends far beyond the limits of the municipality, and its statistics reflected a regional, not a municipal, pattern. Nonetheless, the head nurse gave me access to her records. For 1981 a total of 3,213 deliveries were recorded, of which 807 were of indigent, or nonpaying, patients. The remaining deliveries were covered by the national health care security system or by the rural workers health fund. There were 98 (3.1 percent) stillbirths and 38 (1.2 percent) perinatal deaths in the maternity wing for that year. When I returned in 1987 the figures for the previous year were 2,730 deliveries, of which 68 (2.5 percent) were stillborn and 27 (1 percent) died within forty-eight hours postpartum. Official death certificates were issued in the name of attending physicians, but these were generally filled out by a nurse or hospital functionary. And the causes of death, when given at all, were perfunctory: "prematurity" and "heart and respiratory failure" were the most common diagnoses. One hospital physician had a disproportionately high number of stillbirths and perinatal deaths in his practice at the maternity wing. But no one seemed to be keeping track too closely or carefully.

After I had begun, through various and sometimes creative means, to assess the extent of child mortality in Bom Jesus, I made a visit to the first and newly appointed secretary of health for Bom Jesus. Responding to inquiries about the greatest health risks to the population of the *município*, the debonair and energetic Dr. Ricardo offered without a moment's hesitation, "Stress." And he began to outline his proposals for a stress-reduction education program that would target the substantial business and professional class of the community. Heart problems and cancer were, the secretary of health continued, the two greatest causes of death in the bustling little metropolis. When confronted with the data painstakingly culled from the civil registry office in Bom Jesus indicating that almost a half of all deaths in the *município* each year were of children under the age of five and that diarrhea, not heart disease, and hunger, not stress, were the main pathogens, Dr. Ricardo sighed and raised his eyes to the heavens: "Oh, child mortality! If we were to talk child mortality . . . an absurdity, surely. And unknowable as well."

"What do you mean?"

"When I took over this office last August, the municipal administration had no figures on child mortality, none whatsoever. I had to send for them from the state, and they were unusable: an infant mortality of 120 percent!"

"How can that be?"

"And why not? It's quite straightforward. The official figures said that of every 100 infants born in Bom Jesus, 120 of them died before they reached the age of one year! What a disaster! No wonder we are so underdeveloped in Brazil—more of us die than are even born!"

"Surely there are other ways of counting the dead," I suggested. "For example, how many charity baby coffins does the mayor's office distribute each month?"

"Oh, there's no limit there, no limit at all. We give the people as many as they want. In fact, the more they want, the better! It's one of the things we take care of very efficiently and well."

The doctor was pulling my leg, of course, but his remarks captured both the social embarrassment and the bureaucratic indifference toward child mortality as a premodern plague in a self-consciously modernizing interior town.

Later that day I stopped in again to visit Seu Moacir, the municipal "carpenter," although what he "carpenters" for the city are poor people's coffins, mostly baby coffins. Nonetheless, Moacir strongly objected to being called the municipal coffin maker or having his crowded annex to the back of the municipal chambers referred to as a coffin workshop or a *casa funerária*. And so the discreet sign over his door read, "Municipal Woodworks." But even here there was some deception at play, for the media in which Moacir worked were as much cardboard and papier-mâché as plywood and pine. His "product," he told me, cost the city between two and eight dollars apiece, depending on size.

Yes, he was quite busy, Moacir said, but he could answer a few questions. He has been the municipal carpenter since 1965, when Seu Félix decided that every citizen had the right to a decent burial. There were more than twice as many baby coffins requested as adult ones. February and March were the "busiest" months for his work. Why? Perhaps it was, he hazarded a guess, because people liked to marry in June after the *festas juninas* were over and boys and girls on the Alto had begun to "pair up." Moacir was a man of few words, and his own curiosity in the matters I was raising was limited. But

Seu Moacir, municipal "carpenter."

the craftsman in him readily agreed to pose for pictures, and he held up both an adult coffin and a baby one, pointing out that the style was similar for both—a cardboard top and a plywood bottom.

All adult coffins, regardless of sex, were painted a muddy brown ("Earth tone," said Moacir), and all children's coffins, males and females, to the age of seven were painted "sky blue, the favorite color of the Virgin." Moacir noted a detail: there were no fasteners on the children's coffins because parents preferred to put their angels into the ground as unencumbered as

Children's coffins: all in a row.

possible so that the children's spirits were free to escape their premature graves. Moacir found it difficult to estimate how many coffins "left" the workshop each week: "Some days as many as five or six will leave the shop. And then there are days when there are no requests at all." But, he added, "this doesn't affect my productivity. I just keep on working steadily so that coffins are never lacking in the *município*. I don't like to fall behind in my work; even on a holiday a comrade can find me, and I will have a coffin in stock that will serve his needs."

I asked Moacir if he would be willing to go over his requisitions for the previous few weeks, and, somewhat reluctantly, he agreed. We moved over to a cluttered desk with slips of paper in small, untidy piles. "Here," he said picking up one pile, "I'll read them out to you. But I warn you, things are a little chaotic. Here's one: baby, female, three months, June 22, 1987." And he continued, "Newborn, male, June 17, 1987. Female, about six months, June 11, 1987. Male, four months, June 17, 1987."

Then something had him stumped, and he had a hard time reading the slip of paper. As I approached him to look at it myself, he put it down abruptly: "This has nothing to do with anything. It's an order for seventeen sacks of cement! I warned you that everything was all mixed up here."

When I learned that all the requisition orders were referred back to Seu João in the town hall, I approached João himself for access to the records on all materials furnished by the *prefeitura*. Grumbling, Seu João got down the ledger books, but he warned me not to trust any of them: "If you want numbers," he suggested, "just double everything that's put down here— our inventory is incomplete." In the books that documented in neat columns the "movement" of all supplies in and out of the *prefeitura*, the data on baby coffins were there, interspersed with data on Brillo pads, light bulbs, chlorine bleach, kerosene, toilet paper, cement, alcohol, and soap. In a six-month period in 1988 the *prefeitura* had distributed 131 free infant and child coffins.

When I asked Seu João, who was delighted to get his books back so quickly, why the data on baby coffins were not kept separately, he replied, "Because it wouldn't be of interest to anyone." The deaths of these children, like their brief lives, are invisible and of little or no account.

Finally, I was referred to the *cartório civil* of Bom Jesus, a small, airless, and windowless office privately owned and run by the formidable Dona Leona and her humorless twenty-year-old son. Here, for a small fee, the vital statistics of the community—births, deaths, marriages, and (since 1986) divorces were registered by hand in one of several large ledger books. I was invited to borrow one of the two chairs and a small space at a desk to count the entries for selected years, an occupation that took the greater part of many mornings in Bom Jesus da Mata in 1987 and later again in 1988 and 1989.

Dona Leona has maintained the *cartório* for thirty years, and she worked in "cooperation" with the mayor's office. The town hall furnishes a space in the municipal cemetery and a charity coffin only to those who have registered a death at the *cartório civil*. Consequently, the data on child deaths since 1966 are fairly complete, with the exception of stillbirths and perinatal deaths, many of which are neither registered nor buried in the municipal graveyard. Late abortions and stillbirths, many of them occurring at home on the Alto do Cruzeiro, are buried privately in the *mato* or in the backyard, and there is no question of a medical record or a death certificate. Moreover, until relatively recently, the deaths of unbaptized babies of any age went unregistered. As "pagan" infants they were stigmatized creatures and were buried covertly by their parents at a crossroads in the country, the place where Exu, the Afro-Brazilian deity, and his host of unbaptized spirit infants congregate to serve as messengers for good and ill in the world.

In addition to these, about one-fifth of all Alto births today still take place at home, keeping the half dozen elderly midwives (called *parteiras* or *curiosas*) fairly regularly employed. The *parteiras* who work today in virtual isolation from the medical institutions of Bom Jesus (following years of unsuccessful attempts to regulate them and to incorporate them into the extension work of the state health post) especially fear running afoul of the "bureaucracy" and the medical profession in Bom Jesus. Consequently, the *parteiras* do not encourage registration of infant births or deaths in which they were involved. Moreover, stillbirths and perinatal deaths are roundly denied by the midwives, who actively compete with each other for an ever-constricting market.

Although, with these exceptions, the data on infant mortality at the *cartório civil* can be taken as fairly complete and reliable, there is no possibility of ascertaining a reliable infant mortality *rate*. Although universal birth registration is mandatory today, there is no way to enforce it at the local level. In practice, most poor families delay registration until the child has to confront the "state" for the first time—usually on registering for primary school. Otherwise, an individual may not be registered until he or she wants to enter the work force, marry, join the military, or receive some medical or social benefit from the state. Moreover, although all registrations of infant deaths (to age one) also require birth certificates, registrations of child deaths older than one year do not require that the births of the children also be registered. Somewhat more reliable, then, is a calculation of the proportion of child to adult deaths for the community as a whole for the years selected for study. I selected the three years advisedly: 1965, the year following the Brazilian military coup and, as I recalled it, the year of the great die out of Alto babies; 1985, twenty years later and following the crash of the great economic miracle; and 1987, the period of democratization and preparation for the transfer of authority from military to civilian rule, also the year of the cruzado novo and significant fiscal reforms aimed at restructuring the economy with respect to inflation and the debt crisis.

Public records, whether official censuses, birth or baptismal certificates, marriage or divorce records, or death or burial certificates, are obviously not "neutral" documents. They are not in any sense "pure" sources of data. Censuses and other public records count only certain things, not others. They count some things better than others, as in this instance they count infant and child deaths better than births. They reveal a society's particular system of classification. So they are not so much mirrors of reality as they are filters, or "collective representations," as Émile Durkheim might put it. It is just those images and collective representations—in this case, of the child and of child death—that I am after. How are the records kept? What events are kept track of? What is thought hardly worth noting or counting at all? And what can this tell us about the collective invisibility of women and children in particular?

Those relatives who arrive at the *cartório civil* to register the death of a child in Bom Jesus are briefly interviewed by Dona Leona according to the following formula. They are asked to testify, "on their honor," to the time and date of the death, the place of death (usually the home address), the sex of the child, the child's "color," the name of the child's mother and father, the father's (but not the mother's) birthplace, the father's (but not the mother's) profession, and the name of the cemetery. The reporting relative is then asked to sign the form or to affix his or her mark (an X), and two other individuals are asked to testify as "witnesses" to the accuracy of the account.

What we can learn from this particular record is the following: the sex, age, name, and "race" of the child; the marital status of the parents; the neighborhood or street in which they live; the father's occupation; and the place of death. In those few instances where the child died in the hospital and was also issued a death certificate, Dona Leona noted the name of the attending physician and his or her diagnosis.

While copying the birth and child death data at the registry office, I was able to observe many interactions between Dona Leona and the people of Bom Jesus, especially the poor of the Alto, who appeared each day to register the death of a child. Most often it was the father of the child who appeared, but occasionally it was a grandmother, a grandfather, an aunt, a godparent, or even an older sibling. Mothers, however, never appeared in the *cartório* to register the death of one of their own children. The registration and burial of the child usually took place within twelve to twenty-four hours of the child's death.

Dona Leona was generally distant and officious; if provoked, she could be gruff and dismissive, especially if the relative was uncertain of basic "details," such as the name of the child, the complete names of the child's parents, the marital status of the parents, or the exact time and location of the death. Many of these seemingly obvious and necessarily bureaucratic details were anathema to the people of the Alto and had little relevance to their everyday lives. "Name of the deceased?" Dona Leona snapped. And I saw a father turn anxiously to his sister-in-law to ask her, "Whatever *is* the name of our little Fiapo [a common nickname meaning little bit of nothing]?" Explaining where one lived in response to the bureaucratic question "Street and house number?" could be taxing. There were no official house numbers and only descriptive and informal nicknames for many of the dirt paths and hillside ledges on which *moradores* had built their homes on the Alto do Cruzeiro. Living arrangements were often informal, and couples frequently did not know each other's surnames. On one occasion, when a father could not produce the full name of his common-law wife, his *compadre* whispered to him, "Well, just let it be Araújo da Silva, then" and so "married" the couple on the spot. Dona Leona was not amused by these "lapses" of memory in her clients, and she was not above giving them an occasional dressing down.

As the end of the day approached, Dona Leona could be testy; her work kept her busy, and she liked to have her books in order by 4 P.M. so that she could go home early. Those who rushed in at the last minute, as did Dona Aparecida of the Rua dos Magos, could face an impassive and bureaucratic wall of resistance. Aparecida had just run from the Barbosa Hospital at one end of Bom Jesus to the *cartório civil* at the other end to register the death of a premature grandson who had been born and who had died earlier that day. Her daughter, the infant's mother, was doing poorly in the hospital and had begun to hemorrhage. The baby's father was away working on a distant plantation and knew nothing of the events that had transpired. It fell to Aparecida to bury her grandson, but in her anxiety over her deathly ill daughter, she had forgotten to register the death earlier in the day, and now Seu Moacir refused to give her the little coffin until she had done so.

"But where is the marriage certificate?" Dona Leona inquired, as the older woman attempted to register her grandson as the "legitimate" son of her daughter and son-in-law. "And how would I know where my daughter keeps such things?" replied the grandmother, who was sent away in search of the document and told to return with it the following day. And so Dona Leona got to go home early, as usual. The infant, meanwhile, wrapped in its *mortália* (winding sheet), lay overnight in a hospital storage room that served on occasion as a morgue for indigent patients.

Dona Leona tried hard to run a tight ship, but she was often frustrated. "Color of the deceased?" she asked. And here the relatives were often puzzled. Some fathers pointed to their own skin, saying, "Well, she was my child." In other words, "Judge for yourself, if you wish." Another young father, when asked the color of his deceased four-month-old infant, replied, "It was just a baby—it didn't have any color yet." Usually Dona Leona simply designated the color of the infant based on a local cultural category: poor equaled "brown." She never asked the parents to supply the missing "cause of death," however. In the absence of an official death certificate and a medical diagnosis, there was, she said, no way to know, and she was content to leave that space blank on most of the forms.

The state, then—represented in the personages of minor civil servants such as Moacir and Dona Leona—contributes to the routinization and normalization of child death by its implacable opacity, its refusal to comprehend, and its consequent inability to act responsively to the human suffering that presents itself. Bureaucrats and civil servants respond to pain and difference with a studied indifference—*la belle indifférence*. Normally, this is expressed in the bureaucracy's "deaf ear," its interminable off-putting delays and postponements, its failure to note the dire consequences of its indecisiveness. But there is another side to bureaucratic indifference that is more

Table 7.1. Births and deaths in Bom Jesus da Mata.

	1965	[1977]ᵃ	[1978]ᵃ	1985	1987	1989 (Jan.–July)
All deaths (adults and children)	1,117	N/A	N/A	507	444	327
All births	760	[761]	[896]	951	722	N/A
Infant/child deaths (< 5 years)	497	N/A	N/A	214	170	162
Infant deaths (< 1 year)	375	[311]	[320]	165	152	155
Child deaths (1–5 years)	122	N/A	N/A	49	18	7
IMR	.493	[.409]	[.357]	.174	.211	N/A

Source: *Cartório civil*, Bom Jesus, based on computations from individual records of each death.
ᵃSummary data, supplied by local IBGE office.

characteristic in this instance: the rapid dispatch. It conveys that nothing of any consequence, nothing worth noting, has really taken place. Two or three minutes to "process" each dead infant or child should suffice.

"But look at this," I spoke (out of turn) from my perusal of the death registry books in the *cartório* on one occasion. "Here is the name of a woman on the Rua dos Índios of the Alto do Cruzeiro who has lost three small children within the space of a few months. What do you think could be going on? Shouldn't someone look into it?"

"I wouldn't know," Dona Leona replied coolly. "My job is only to record the dead, not to hold an inquest once they're gone."

I was sufficiently abashed to go quietly back to my "clerking" of the records, scratching away in my copybooks, a modern-day Bartleby the Scrivener, refusing to leave where I was decidedly unwanted and just barely tolerated. Table 7.1 shows what my clerking revealed.

In 1965 a total of 497 child deaths (of those born live through age five) were recorded. Three hundred seventy-five, or 78 percent, of the deaths were of infants in the first twelve months of life. These infant deaths came from a total of 760 recorded births for 1965, a figure that included all children born in that year and registered in that year or born in 1965 but registered in subsequent years. Even if we assume that some born in that year escaped registration altogether, 1965 (with an infant mortality rate of 493/1,000 live births) was a year the bells of Nossa Senhora das Dores tolled incessantly. And when they tolled, it was for the "holy innocents" of Bom

Jesus and its rural surrounds, the most immediate victims of Brazil's "quiet and bloodless" military coup. Quiet, indeed, but perhaps not quite so bloodless after all. Of all deaths in Bom Jesus in 1965, 44.5 percent were of children younger than five years. The high proportion of child to adult deaths did not change radically over the next two decades.

With the establishment of mandatory birth registration in the mid-1970s, birth statistics are now more reliable than previously, although they are still incomplete. Twenty years later, in 1985, 214 child deaths were registered, of which 165, or 77 percent, were of infants younger than one from a total of 951 registered births. The infant mortality rate had decreased significantly to 174/1,000 live births. Of all registered deaths in Bom Jesus in 1985, 42.2 percent were of children younger than five years.

In 1987, the final complete year studied, 170 infant and child deaths were registered. Of these, 152, or 89.4 percent, were infants, with 722 recorded live births for the *município* that year. Of all deaths that year, 38.2 percent were of children younger than five years. When I returned again in 1989 I was able to review births and deaths during the first seven months of that year (January–July). The data indicated a significant upward turn in child, and especially infant, deaths. There were already 162 infant and child deaths recorded, of which 96 percent were infants. Meanwhile, the proportion of child to adult deaths had increased to 49.5 percent—that is, in 1989 half of all deaths in the *município* were of babies in their first year of life.

In all, the data indicate a decisive decline in infant and child mortality in the twenty-year period 1965–1985, beginning from an apparent 49 percent infant mortality in 1965. It must be recalled, however, that 1965 was by all accounts an extraordinary year for child deaths, the year of the great die out of Alto babies, resulting from a severe drought combined with the economic and social chaos occasioned by the military coup d'état of March 1964. Many social programs that were put into place by the state government led by the progressive, socialist governor, Miguel Arraes, were dismantled in 1965, with immediate and disastrous effects on the poorest populations. The high infant mortality was the most immediate indicator of the disruptions caused by the political and economic upheavals.

In these data we can begin to detect the modernization of child mortality pattern that I suggested for the nation as a whole—that is, the standardizing of child death within the first twelve months of life and its containment to the poorest and marginalized social classes. Although in the aggregate data for the three years that I personally surveyed 82.9 percent of all child deaths occurred in the first year of life and 57.7 percent in the first six months, in breaking down the figures, we can see that in the past few years *infant* death has come to replace *child* death almost completely. Between 1965 and 1989 the percentage of child deaths after the first year of life through five years declined from 25 percent to 4 percent. By 1989, 96 percent of all child deaths were of infants in the first twelve months of life. Today, older babies and toddlers of Bom Jesus are reasonably safe from chaotic and premature death. At the close of the decade of the 1980s, it was safe to say (as the popular culture indeed dictated) that if a child survived her or his first year, the family could bring out the baptismal clothes and celebrate a formal, rather than a hurried, last-minute, christening: the child would live. Figure 7.1 demonstrates the changing pattern of child mortality in Bom Jesus.

If we take together all 881 cases of infant and child death culled from the records of the *cartório civil* for the years 1965, 1985, and 1987, some significant features of child mortality in the *município* emerge. Male infants and babies are at a slightly greater risk of mortality (54.1 percent male, 45.9 percent female overall) immediately postpartum (a predictable and fairly universal phenomenon [see Waldron 1983]), but even more so in the first five months of life, when there is some evidence of maternal influence and selectiveness in the relative survivability of babies. Figures 7.2, 7.3, and 7.4 show the relative disadvantage of male children at various ages.

Seasonality is a factor in child mortality in Bom Jesus. "There is a time to be born and a time to die," wrote the authors of Ecclesiastes, and in Bom Jesus da Mata children die "in season," particularly in February and June, the months of *festa* as well as the beginning and end, respectively, of the season of unemployment among the sugarcane cutters. By mid-February the harvest season is completed and the vast majority of Alto men are out of work. February is also the end of summer and a time of drought and thirst when the water supply is low and tempers are short. But February is also the time of Brazilian *carnaval*, when thoughts turn to the sensual, the festive, the imaginary, and the fantastic. It is, wrote Roberto da Matta (1983), "a time of forgetting." Indeed, among those mundane and bothersome things that are "forgotten" during this time of laughter and license are the needs of sick and vulnerable infants and small babies, some of whom are "lost" in the festive shuffle. And so the municipal coffin maker's folk theory is substantiated in the data.

June is the month of winter holidays—the *festas juninas* of Saints Antônio, João, Pedro, and Paulo. Schools are closed, and the main streets are decorated for block parties, street dancing, and enactments of folk pageants such as the *casamento matuto* (the country yokel's shotgun wedding). As in February, during this festive cycle, too, the mayor's office, Justice Department, hospital, health posts, and clinics operate at low gear. It is not a good time to be sick or needy, child or adult alike. If the months of December through February assault small bodies with the relentless heat of summer

Fig. 7.1. Registered deaths by sex and by age group in Bom Jesus da Mata, 1965, 1985, 1987.

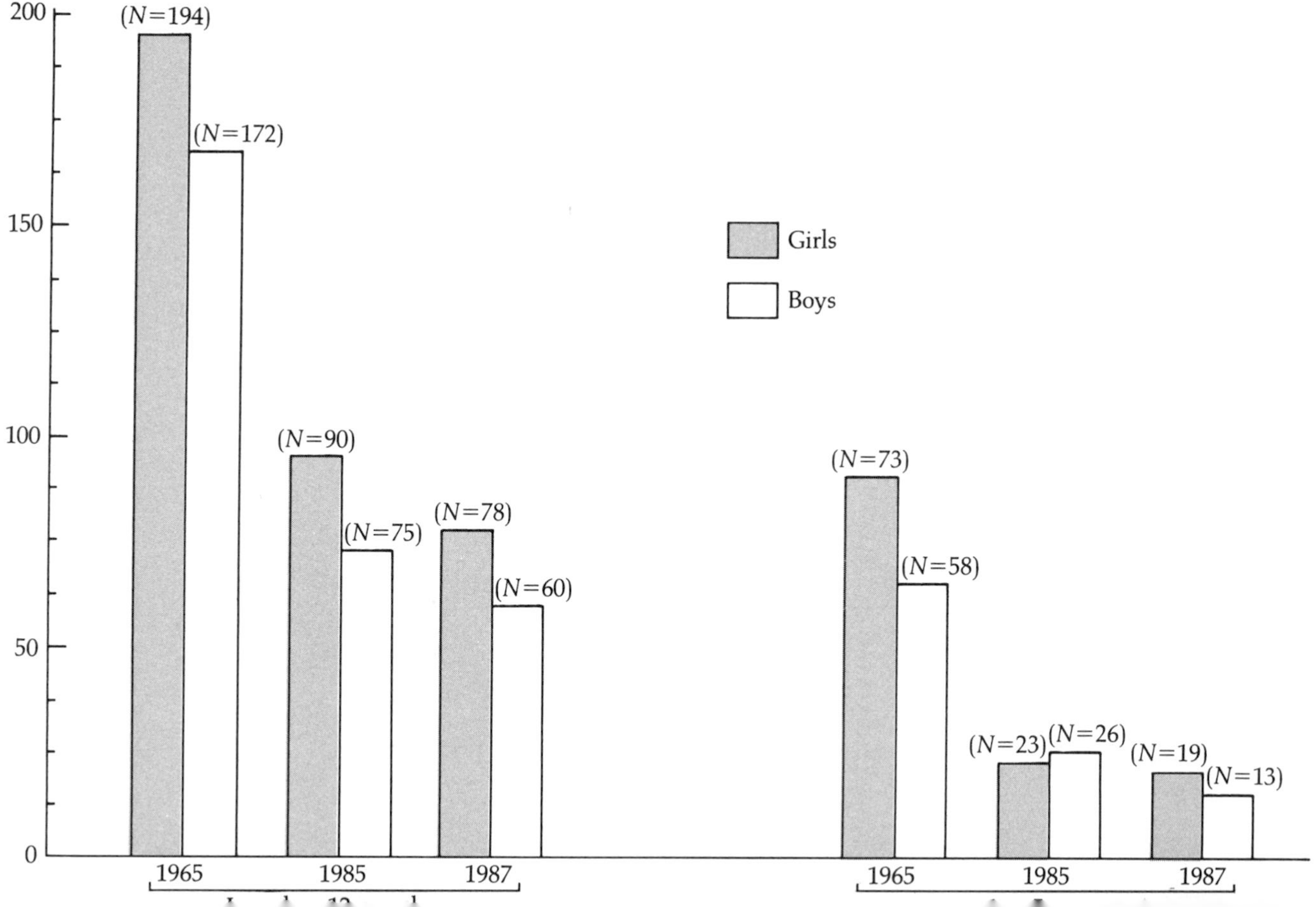

Fig. 7.2. Registered deaths in the first year for boys and girls, 1965.

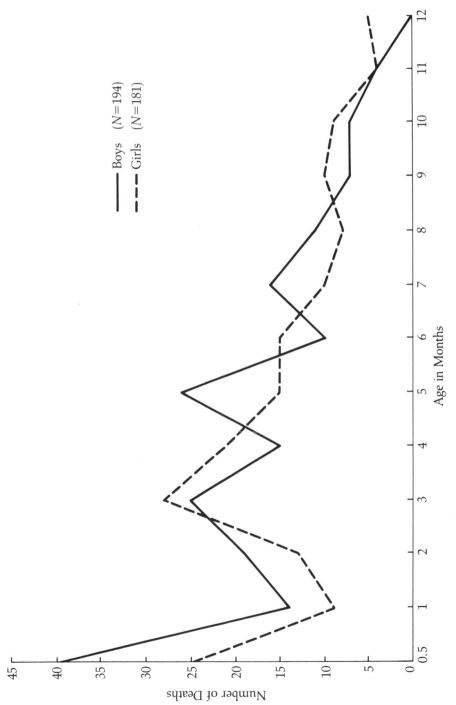

Boys   (N=194)
Girls   (N=181)

Number of Deaths

Age in Months

Source: *Cartório civil,* Bom Jesus da Mata.

Fig. 7.3. Registered deaths in the first year for boys and girls, 1985.

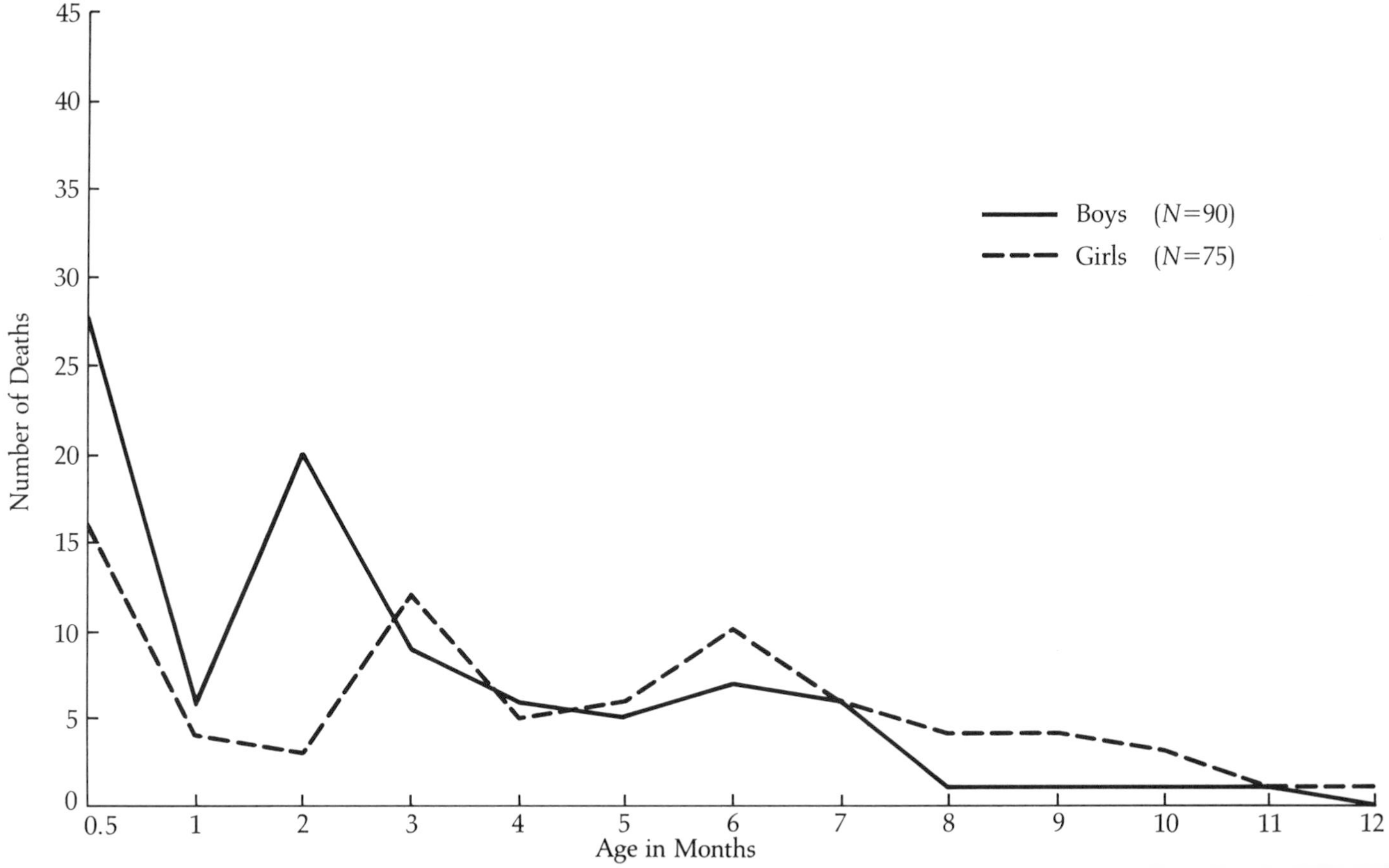

Boys (N=90)
Girls (N=75)

Number of Deaths

Age in Months

Fig. 7.4. Registered deaths in the first year for boys and girls, 1987.

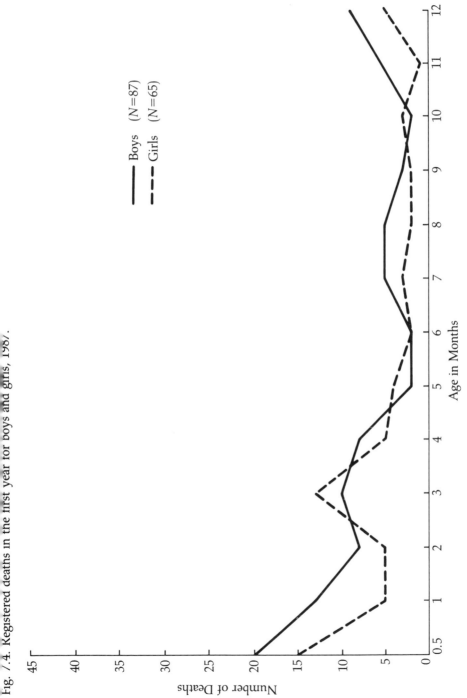

Source: *Cartório civil*, Bom Jesus da Mata.

and the drought, June marks the start of the winter downpours that turn the Alto into a running cesspool of backed-up latrines and wet garbage that carry in their wake new cases of infant and adult diarrheas. In addition, winter brings the flus and respiratory ailments to which so many Alto infants succumb.

From the birth and death records kept at the *cartório civil* we can also learn something about the families and households most prone to losing one or more children. Of the parents who lost children in the years sampled, 32.3 percent were from the rural districts of the *município*, living on large plantation estates and *fazendas*, while 67.6 percent were from the town of Bom Jesus itself. Of these, close to 87 percent of the child deaths occurred in the poor and marginal *bairros* of Bom Jesus, especially in the Alto do Cruzeiro, the largest and poorest of the peripheral neighborhoods of Bom Jesus.

Overall, 38 percent of the babies were registered as "white" and 62 percent as "brown," "mulatto," or "black." The proportion of white to brown infant and child deaths decreased precipitously between 1965 and the 1980s. This is a feature of the modernization of child mortality—its containment to the poor *favelas*, shantytowns, and rural districts where to be poor means, culturally speaking, to be brown or black. Of the 881 cases of child death, 38.3 percent of the parents were legally married, while 30.4 percent of the parents appeared to be living together in what *moradores* referred to as conjugal *amizade*, "friendship." In 30.9 percent of the child deaths, the mother was listed as single, and no father was identified. In those 496 instances in which the father's profession was listed, the majority, 328 (66 percent), listed agriculture as their profession. The remainder were scattered among the various trades and crafts of Bom Jesus: construction, carpentry, pottery, hammock making, and shoemaking. Fifty-nine fathers were listed as menial laborers and "servants."

Perhaps the most persistent feature of child mortality in Bom Jesus is its privacy and anonymity: 79.2 percent of all infant and child deaths occur at home without medical intervention or observation. Consequently, the causes of death for the vast majority of children younger than five in Bom Jesus da Mata remain unknown. But even among the 175 babies who died in the local hospital in 1965, 1985, 1987, 16 of these left the hospital for the cemetery without a cause of death listed on their official *óbitos*. A child could even die in the local hospital "unobserved." Of the 159 children with a medical diagnosis on their *atestados de óbitos*, the most frequent "cause of death" given (34.8 percent) was simply "cessation of heart beat and respiration." They died, one might suppose, of having lived. Dehydration was the next most common diagnosis (22.2 percent), followed by prematurity (14.8 percent). A dozen children died of falls, bruises, or blows to the body; *pancada na cabeça*, a "strike or blow to the head," was the commonest of these. Several carried the extraordinary medical opinion that the cause of death was acute infantile suffering. Only 3.4 percent of the deaths of infants and children in the hospital were attributed to acute or severe malnutrition, while only 1.7 percent of the infant and child deaths in the hospital were attributed to infant diarrhea. One wonders, amid the sea of froth and brine that carried away the infants and babies of the Alto do Cruzeiro, what kind of professional prudery it was that "failed to see" what every mother of the Alto do Cruzeiro knew without ever being told. "They die," said one woman going straight to the heart of the matter, "because their bodies turn to water."

On my return in 1989 I checked to see if the proportion of hospital to home, public to private, deaths had changed. In the first half of 1989 fully 71 percent of all child deaths still occurred at home; 29 percent occurred in the hospital, which represented only a slight increase in medically treated and observed child deaths. But the indifference to medical diagnosis had not changed: "Respiration stopped, heart stopped" remained the preferred medical diagnosis in cases of child death.

Reproductive Histories: Alto Women's Voices

My search to understand the extent and meaning of child mortality was not, however, contained to the public records, such as they were. If anyone in Bom Jesus understood the phenomenon, it was most certainly the women of the Alto do Cruzeiro themselves. To track their reproductive life histories, I began in 1982 with a sample of seventy-two Alto women; the sample eventually encompassed more than one hundred Alto women, and in 1989 I added a small sample of Alto men. Insofar as I have previously published the findings of my initial survey (1984, 1985), I reproduce here only the most significant features of Alto fertility and mortality, as gleaned from the personal reproductive histories, and I correct some of my initial findings in light of subsequent research.

My initial sample of Alto women was an opportunistic one, comprising the first women to volunteer following an open meeting in the abandoned creche of the shantytown. Many more women volunteered for the long interview than I could possibly have completed during a field trip that was also concerned with time-consuming general ethnographic work in the community. At the original meeting with Alto women I explained in general terms the purpose of the reproductive interviews. Because my work on the Alto during the 1960s had focused on maternal and child health, the current research agenda was both familiar to, and compatible with, the interests of the women themselves. My only criterion for inclusion in the study was that the woman had been pregnant at least once. Consequently, the women spanned three generations of mothers, ranging in age from nineteen to seventy-six. This gave me the opportunity to compare reproductive patterns over time.

Throughout the process of eliciting women's life and reproductive stories, I was aided by a talented assistant, Irene Lopes da Silva, a resident of the Alto do Cruzeiro and one of the original founders of the shantytown association and the creche. She was among the first women I sought out on my return in 1982. Although both ill from a recent miscarriage and dispirited on the morning I found her "camping out" as a squatter amid the dilapidated and abandoned public washstands of the creche that she had helped to build in the 1960s, Irene was up from her hammock on the following day and ready to work as my primary research assistant. By 1988 Irene was able to conduct ethnographic interviews and take elliptical and somewhat idiosyncratic field-notes on her own. I wager that Irene, with less than three years of formal schooling, is as good a descriptive ethnographer as many graduate schools of anthropology have produced. She has the gift of the sociological imagination as she intuitively links the individual "worries" and "troubles" of Alto women to larger social, economic ills and to the political issues confronting contemporary Brazil. Her curiosity about human life, will, and action is enormous, and I am much in her debt with respect to understanding Alto women's moral choices and dilemmas.

The questions I put to Alto women were not only concerned with patterns of fertility and mortality but also with issues of value, choice, and meaning. I wanted to understand what infant and child death meant to Alto women and how they explained and interpreted their lives and their actions as women, wives and lovers, and mothers. What were the effects of scarcity and deprivation on women's abilities to nurture, "hold," love, and hope. What kinds of resilience did they have, and how were their "survivor" values and practices passed on to their children? For it was as survivors that many Alto women saw themselves. "*Vingaremos!*" they said, meaning that they did *and* will continue to survive despite the odds and that they would "take vengeance" on a life that had often treated them so unfairly.

A profile of the "average" woman in my Alto sample could read as follows: she was born on an *engenho*, where she grew up at the foot of the sugarcane; she attended primary school briefly, and although she could do sums with great facility, she could not read or write. Only a third of the women could, and with some difficulty, sign their names, a skill that until very recently determined one's legal and civil status as a voting citizen (an *eleitor*) or a nonvoting citizen. It was a biographical note that was carefully recorded on each person's death certificate.

After establishing a household with a man—often by "running off" with him (*fugindo*) and less often by having a civil or religious ceremony—she moved with her companion and children several times before finally coming to settle in town. Her husband or current companion was often described as "good" but *meio-fraco*, weak-poor, unskilled, unemployed, or, worse, sickly and dependent or as a *cachaceiro*, a "rum drinker." They might have broken up and come back together several times. Although most of the seventy-two women first interviewed in 1982 valued monogamy and marriage, less than half of them, thirty-two (or 44 percent), had a stable, long-term union that was recognized by church, state, or both. The remaining forty women (56 percent) described themselves as *solteiras*, as "single women," although eighteen of these were at the time of the interview living in a relatively stable relationship with one man, while fifteen had lived off and on in a series of relatively unstable relationships with different men. The remaining seven women described themselves as recently "abandoned." Nonetheless, Alto women were philosophical: "Terrible without them, but even worse with them," they often said of the "weaker" sex.

"Two men already left me," said Little Irene. "Do you think I need another? Nothing doing! Men are so jealous; I don't need any of these bandits around here. When my old man came around to 'visit' me the other night, I laughed in his face. I take whatever money he wants to give me for the children, but I won't let him pass the night with me as long as he has another little 'piece' around. What some of the younger women haven't learned yet is that marriage is a kind of slavery."

Edilene, aged forty-seven, agreed: "I prefer my children to my husbands. The husbands were all drunkards, and when they drank they would abuse me. But I would just up and leave them. It's much better to be alone than to take abuse. Some of it is my own fault; the men I arranged for myself were pretty but worthless. I have no 'knack' for men, so it's better that I remain single after all."

Nonetheless, there were many men and women on the Alto who shared a deep and lasting affection for each other, as did Black Irene and her second "husband," who came to live with her after Irene had already given birth to a child by another man. They lived happily together (*amigados*) for thirteen years. She had seven children by him, and then just before he died, they married. "Ours was a good marriage," Black Irene explained, soon after her husband was murdered. "I always wanted to be the one to die first. We weren't like those brutal couples that fight all the time, so that when one finally dies the other one brushes his hands and says, 'Good riddance.' No, we lived together in harmony. Whatever Seu Manoel [Irene always referred to her late husband formally and by title] wanted I wanted, and vice versa.

Whatever time of day Seu Manoel would come home, I would have his dinner ready. I never complained if he was late. And if I was late with his dinner, he never complained either. He would just sit patiently and wait until I called him to the table. A milder man than Seu Manoel would be hard to find here on the Alto do Cruzeiro. With love in your heart you can face almost anything."

The "average" Alto woman worked, at least part-time, taking in laundry or doing other domestic work for the wealthy families of Bom Jesus, clearing the fields of the smaller estates and sugar plantations, doing piecework for the local hammock industry, or selling produce at the weekly *feira*. If there was a man in the household, he was most likely a worker in the cane who was seasonally employed and unemployed in turn. Or he might have worked as a municipal laborer or street cleaner, earning only a fraction of a single minimum wage. If he was extremely lucky, he landed a job in a shoe or a textile factory. If he was unlucky, like Seu Biu de Papião, he collected paper and cardboard from the streets and garbage dumps for resale. A wife and husband's combined weekly income in 1982 averaged twenty-four dollars, or one and a half minimum salaries. This had dropped to only sixteen dollars a week in 1987, plunging the vast majority of Alto households from just ordinary to absolute misery. Women counted the members of the nuclear family from above and below: the dead angel-babies and wandering souls above along with the *desgraçados*, the unlucky and the accursed ones, still struggling below.

The seventy-two women in the sample reported a staggering 688 pregnancies among them, staggering in that half the women had yet to complete their reproductive lives. The "average" woman in the sample (see Table 7.2) had experienced 9.5 pregnancies and had 4.2 living children. She had 1.6 miscarriages, abortions, or stillbirths, and she had lost 3.6 small children (2.9 of those infants) among those born live to her.

I am often asked how "dependable" these women were with respect to their accuracy and truthfulness in reporting on their reproductive lives. Most but not all of the interviews were conducted in the creche and in a public context. The details of fertility were not, in any event, a private matter on the Alto do Cruzeiro, with the exception of a certain delicacy around young, especially male, children. Pregnancy, abortion, stillbirths, and child deaths were common topics of gossip and conversation among Alto women, and at any given interview session a woman might have been accompanied to the creche by her mother, adult daughters, siblings, or female neighbors. Together they corroborated the particular woman's history, serving as one another's memory checks and guides. The events of pregnancy, birth, and child death were a vital part of women's culture,

Table 7.2. Reproductive histories of Alto women.

	Total Number	Number per Woman
Pregnancies	688	9.5
Children surviving to age 5	308[a]	4.2
Miscarriages/abortions	93	1.3
Stillbirths	16	.3
Infant deaths (birth – 1 year)	208	2.9
Child deaths (1+ – 5 years)	47	.7

Source: Anthropological interviews of three generations of Alto women who gave birth between the 1930s and the 1980s.
Note: $N = 72$ women, ages 19–76, with a median age of 39 years.
[a]Minus 16 deaths of older children, 6–17 years.

transmitted from mother to daughter, so that adult daughters could recite their own mother's full reproductive history, including abortions, miscarriages, and deaths.

Although every woman could recall, without prompting, the exact number of pregnancies she had had (as a point of female honor and pride), a few of the older women could not recall the names of all their babies who died in infancy or the circumstances surrounding each death. There was a tendency for all the women to "round off" the ages of their children at death. If a child died as an infant, she or he tended to die at "two weeks," "one month," or "three months." A somewhat disproportionate number of Alto babies were said to have died at "three months," which was, I suspect, a convention invoked by mothers whenever an infant died quite young without any signs of teeth but not a newborn. There were certain mnemonic devices that women used to aid them in reconstructing what were sometimes awesome reproductive histories with as many as twenty pregnancies to account for. The women always began from the firstborn to the last born, and they used the formula encostado de, as when Zulaide explained that Zé Antônio came "leaning up against" Maria das Graças, and "pressing up against" Zé came Marivalva, and so on. I was impressed that even though Alto infants might not have been given names during their brief lives, they were always given Christian names at death, so that no Alto infant meets his or her Maker unnamed or anonymously. Insofar as newborns were frequently named after a preceding sibling who had died, mothers would sometimes recall their pregnancies in this fashion: "After Zulaide there was a long 'line' of Claudios—four in a row—but only the last one lived long enough to know his own name."

Interviewing Alto women: "My story is a long one; do you mind if I smoke?"

Perhaps a dozen women came to the interview carrying a small box or a tin can in which they had carefully stored a paper recording the birth or baptismal dates and names of each of their children. As most of the women were illiterate, they often had a *patroa* write these down as a favor. These folk "documents" were highly valued, so much so that when Dona Maria's wattle-and-daub house collapsed during the winter rains of 1987, she went back into the ruins the next day searching the broken clay pot fragments to find the handwritten record of her children's births and her widowed husband's hospital admission and funeral papers. In general the women were excellent reproductive historians, with one exception: I suspect that abortions, miscarriages, and stillbirths were underreported.

The reproductive histories of these women indicate certain patterns, some of which corroborate the statistics collected at the *cartório civil*. The period of

Table 7.3. Sex and age at death of Alto children.

	Male	Female	Sex?	Total		
Postpartum (1–15 days)	25	13	1	39		
15+ days – 3 months	51	37		88	173	
4 – 6 months	21	25		46	(67.8%)	208
6+ months – 1 year	14	21		35		(81.5%)
1+ – 2 years	11	10		21		
2+ – 5 years	10	16		26		
Total	132	122		255		

Source: Anthropological interviews of Alto women, aged 19 to 76, covering births between the 1930s and the 1980s.
Note: $N = 255$ deaths.

greatest risk for Alto babies is during the first twelve months of life, by which time 81.5 percent of all child deaths take place (see Table 7.3). But if one begins to break these aggregate data down by generation of Alto women (as I do in Table 7.4), we can see the same pattern I discussed earlier: infant death increasingly comes to predominate over child death in the younger generation of Alto mothers, those from nineteen to thirty-nine years of age. Bottle- and hand-feeding, in addition to patterns of mortal "selective neglect" directed at certain sickly and disadvantaged neonates and infants, both of which are products of disorderly and chaotic economic development, contribute disproportionately to the death of infants.

The reproductive histories of these impoverished women do not, however, suggest a particularly strong sex bias in child survival, although male infants are again shown to be more vulnerable immediately postpartum and up through the first three months of life. Perhaps reflecting this mortality pattern, Alto mothers were certainly more inclined to attribute a constitutional "weakness" (fraqueza) to their infant sons than to their infant daughters who did not survive. The absence of a "sex bias" in mortality is supported by the women, each of whom was questioned about ideal family size, sex preferences, and perceived differences in offspring.

Despite a strong and pervasive ideology of male dominance in Brazilian culture at large (although it was somewhat muted in the female-centered life of the shantytown), Alto women expressed no consistent pattern of sex preference, and all agreed that a woman would want to have a balance of sons and daughters. Boys were said to be "easy" to care for (once they survived infancy), relatively "independent" from a young age, and "useful" to the household: small boys could be sent out "foraging" in the marketplace. They could earn small bits of cash carrying large baskets of produce on their heads for those able to pay, and little boys were not ashamed to beg (or even to steal) if necessity brought them to that. Besides, mothers added, boys were "entertaining"—what mother didn't take pride in her growing son's skill and dexterity with a soccer ball or, later, luck with young girls?

But daughters, too, were loved and highly valued—what mother didn't enjoy dressing up a little daughter or seeing her go off proudly to school with at least an initial determination to master her numbers and letters? Daughters were not only a mother's helpmate at home; when they grew up they often became a mother's closest, lifelong companion. And although distance, dissension, and alienation between mothers and adult daughters occurred on the Alto (as anywhere else in the world), it was considered both a tragedy and an aberration. In general, Alto women tended to stay in close proximity to their daughters so that small clusters of intergenerational, female-centered households built around the *matriz* (mother church but also the source or foundation of anything, in this instance, the first mother) were common on the Alto. Yes, a woman would be short-changed indeed not to have at least one *casal* (boy-girl couple) to rear in life.

With respect to birth order and survival, a clear pattern emerged. Among the generation of women older than forty with completed reproductive histories, the safest and most protected children were those who occupied the "middle ranks," neither the first nor the last child born. The deaths of Alto babies tended to come "in runs," often at the beginning or at the close of a woman's fertile years. In the earlier years the mother's youth and relative inexperience sometimes played a part in her children's deaths, as did the fact that many Alto women were single and unsupported during the earlier pregnancies and births. One older woman summed up a situation that was not altogether unique: "It looks like I had to lose the first half dozen so I could learn enough from my mistakes to save the second half dozen." A woman's advancing age, her mental and physical fatigue, and the drain on already limited resources made by several other older siblings contributed to the higher mortality risk of children born later. Some older women were explicit about their feelings toward the birth of their late-born and supernumerary children: they had had enough, the children were an unwanted burden, and the mothers were grateful when some of the children died in infancy. Nevertheless, the *caçula,* the last-born child to survive infancy, was generally loved and indulged by all: she had "adjourned" (*encerrou*) her mother's seemingly inevitable appointment with procreation, and that fact alone increased her value.

Before turning to a consideration of Alto mothers' perceptions of the

Table 7.4. Fertility, mortality, and ideal family size, by generation of Alto women.

	For Each Younger Woman[a]	For Each Older Woman[b]
Total pregnancies to date	6.6	12.4
Total living children	3.1	3.4
Total infant/child mortality	2.4	4.7
Abortion, miscarriage	1.1	4.3
Ideal family size	2.6	3.5

Source: Anthropological interviews of Alto women.
[a]$N = 36$. These women ranged in age from 19 to 39, with a median age of 30.
[b]$N = 36$. These women ranged in age from 40 to 76, with a median age of 50.

primary causes of infant and child death, I want to elaborate a bit more, by way of comparison across time (generational) and social space (class), on the social epidemiology of child mortality in Bom Jesus da Mata. As grim as the situation first appears, it is actually worse than I have described. The record of pregnancies, births, and infant deaths, as summarized in Tables 7.2 and 7.3, is incomplete. Many of the children reported as living at the time of the initial interview (1982) were deathly sick babies, and some of these have died in the interim. I did not try to follow up every woman in my original sample, but I maintained reasonably close contact with twenty-eight of the households, and on subsequent field trips between 1987 and 1989 I recorded an additional nine deaths from these households alone. A few of these additional child deaths were of new infants, whose births were not, of course, even recorded in the 1982 interviews.

Recall that only *half* of the original seventy-two women interviewed had completed their reproductive years. If we separate out the older cohort of women (median age = fifty years) from the younger women still in their childbearing years (median age = thirty years), we can see that the "average" Alto woman had experienced 12.4, not 9.5, pregnancies and 4.7, not 3.6, infant and child deaths (see Table 7.4). These figures are not, however, necessarily predictive of the younger generation of Alto women, whose reproductive thinking and practices differ somewhat from those of the older generation.

Generally in demography one cannot depend entirely on completed life courses across historical time; one must look closely at incomplete data as well. One way to do this is to compare the experience of first and second births between older women of completed fertility and younger women of

Table 7.5. Child mortality by generation of Alto mothers, first two pregnancies only.

	Younger Women[a]	Older Women[b]
Pregnancies	69[c]	72[d]
Miscarriages/stillbirths	5	4
Infant deaths (birth – 1 year)	27	14
	(13 male, 14 female)	(10 male, 4 female)
Child deaths (1+ – 5 years)	0	7
		(3 male, 4 female)
Older child deaths (5+ – 12 years)	1	2
	(male)	(1 male, 1 female)
Living children	36	46
	(24 male, 12 female)	(24 male, 22 female)

Source: Anthropological interviews of Alto women.
[a]$N = 36$. These women ranged in age from 19 to 39 .
[b]$N = 36$. These women ranged in age from 40 to 76.
[c]Three younger women had had only one pregnancy to date.
[d]One older woman gave birth to twins at her second delivery.

incomplete fertility. Table 7.5 demonstrates the extent to which things are getting worse for the younger generation of Alto women and their babies. The younger women already show an "excess" of ten deaths, or an additional 1.4 per woman, over the preceding generation of Alto mothers, this without us even knowing (or wanting to predict) how many others from among the younger generation's still-young infants and babies are yet to die in the months to come. Looking at these figures with their built-in question marks puts one in mind of Ebenezer Scrooge's last eerie visitation: the ghost of Christmas yet to come. And we wonder, along with Scrooge, whether the premonitions of deaths foretold in these incomplete figures represent what *must* happen or only what *may* come to pass.

Mortal Ills, Fated Deaths

Whereas doctors in the clinics and hospitals of Bom Jesus were unconcerned about properly diagnosing and recording the causes of infant and child deaths for the poor of Bom Jesus, Alto women readily shared with me their notions of the causes of childhood mortality. I posed the question in two ways. I asked a general question: "Why do so many babies die on the Alto do Cruzeiro?" Then in the course of recording personal reproductive histories, I asked each woman to tell me at length about the circumstances surrounding each child's death, including her perception of the baby's key symptoms, the various steps she took to remedy the illness, and her understanding of the cause of the death. The two questions elicited very different answers.

In response to the general question on the incidence and causes of high child mortality in the community, Alto women were quick to reply with blanket condemnations of the hostile environment in which they and their children were forced to live and die. They responded:

"Our children die because we are poor and hungry."

"They die because the water we drink is filthy with germs."

"They die because we cannot afford to keep shoes on their feet."

"They die because we get worthless medical care."

"They die of neglect. Often we have to leave them alone in the house when we go to work. So you wash them, feed them, give them a pacifier, close the door, and say a prayer to the Virgin hoping that they will still be alive when you get home. Yes, they die of neglect [à míngua] but it's not due to a lack of goodwill toward our children. The problem isn't one of *vontade* [willingness] but one of *poder* [power or ability]."

When asked what it is that infants need most to survive the first and most precarious year of life, Alto women invariably answered that it was *food*, pure and simple: "Can it be that mothers of ten, twelve, even sixteen children don't know what a child needs to survive? Of course we know! Rich people's children have proper food. Our children are fed catch as catch can. Some days we have one ingredient for the baby's *mingau*, but we don't have the other. We may have the *farinha* but not the sugar. Or we have the sugar but not the powdered milk. And so we improvise. What else can we do?"

Another shook her head in perplexity: "I don't know why so many die. Some babies are born strong and healthy enough. Their stomachs when they are round and full give one such pleasure! But something is wrong with the food we give them. No matter how much we feed them, they lose their fat and turn into toothpicks. It makes one discouraged."

Still another could identify the exact problem and its remedy: "They die from the miserable *engano* [ruse] of *papa d'água*. Babies need food to live. Most older babies require at least two cans [four hundred grams each] of powdered milk a week. But people here can afford only one can, and so the babies are fed mostly on water. Soon their blood turns to water as well. Money would solve all our problems."

Many others agreed with her: "Here on the Alto there are a multitude of children who live in neglect, eating garbage that other people leave behind, sucking on banana skins and on orange peels. It's because their parents don't earn enough to feed them, and the only solution is to set the children out on the streets."

In short, Alto mothers gave highly politicized answers to the question of child mortality in general, ones that stressed the external constraints on the ability to care for their offspring. But when these same women were asked to explain why any of *their own* children died, their answers were more clinical, and the causes of death were seen as more proximate, sometimes as *internal to the child*. Often the dead infant was judged as lacking a vital life force, his or her own "will" to live. And not a single Alto mother stated that hunger was the cause of death for any of her own children, although many of the dead babies were described as having "wasted" or "withered" away, "shriveled up," or "shrunk to nothing." In response to what may have caused a particular infant to "waste away," Alto women often replied that the baby was born with a "fragile," "nervous," or "weak" constitution. Hunger, it seemed, only killed Alto children in the abstract. It may kill *your* children (perhaps) but not any of mine. It may be that Alto mothers had to exercise a certain amount of denial because the alternative—the recognition that one's own child is slowly starving to death—is too painful or, given the role that mothers sometimes play in reducing food and liquid (see chapter 8), too rife with psychological conflict.

Alto women distinguished between child deaths viewed as "natural" (coming from God or from nature) and those suspected to be caused by sorcery, evil eye, and magical possession. They attributed most of their own children's deaths to natural causes, especially to communicable diseases. But the women also explained child deaths in terms of failures in proper nurturing, including disregard for the normal "lying-in" precautions for mother and newborn, mortal forms of neglect, and strong and passionate emotions. Table 7.6 gives a very condensed rendering of Alto mother's perceptions of the major pathogens affecting the lives of their offspring.

Alto mothers considered simple diarrhea the greatest single killer of their babies, carrying away 71 of the 255 children who died. But more "complex" and complicated forms of diarrhea were also implicated in the folk category *doença de criança*, "child sickness," and in some cases of *dentição* (teething illness), *gasto* (wasting illness), *susto* (fright sickness), and *fraqueza* (general weakness and debility). Were we to include all the folk pediatric diagnoses in which diarrhea was at least a secondary symptom, then as many as 189 of the 255 deaths, 74 percent of all infant and child deaths on the Alto, could be attributed to diarrhea. Mothers distinguished among many different subtypes (*qualidades*) of infant diarrhea (e.g., *intestino, quentura, barriga desmantelada*), based on color, consistency, smell, and force of the stools. Mothers saved the dirty nappies of their ailing babies to discuss the differential diagnoses with neighbors and elderly healing women of the Alto. In all, mothers recognized the severity of this disease in particular as a primary child-killer on the Alto. Among the other communicable diseases

Table 7.6.   Causes of infant/child deaths (Alto mothers' explanations).

Cause	Number
Diarrhea/vomiting	71
Measles, smallpox, pneumonia, and other infectious childhood diseases	41
Doença de criança (doomed child syndrome, various subtypes)	39
Fraqueza (weakness, wasting)	37
Pasmo, susto (fright, shock, and other malignant emotions)	14
Dentição (malignant teething)	13
Diseases of skin, liver, blood	13
De repente (sudden death)	9
Mal trato (conscious, if unintentional, neglect)	6
Resguardo quebrado (lying-in precautions broken, violated)	5
Castigo (punishment, divine retribution)	4
Cause unknown to mother	3

Source: Anthropological interviews of Alto women.
Note: $N = 255$ deaths.

commonly cited by mothers were (in order of importance) measles, pneumonia and other respiratory ailments, infant jaundice, tetanus, fevers, whooping cough, smallpox, and other skin diseases and infections.

Underlying and uniting these diverse etiological notions were the same structural principles that informed Alto people's beliefs about the "nervous" body. Here, once again, life was conceptualized as a *luta*, a power "struggle" between large and small, strong and weak. Infants were born both "weak" and "hot"; their tiny systems were easily overwhelmed. Poor infants were already compromised in the womb. Born (as the women said) of prematurely aged fathers whose blood was "sick and wasted" and whose semen was "tired" and of mothers whose breasts offered blood and infection instead of rich milk, it is little wonder that Alto babies were described as born "already thirsty and starving in the womb," as "bruised and discolored," their "tongues swollen in their mouths."

The babies of the rich were described as coming into the world fat and fair and "greedy" for life. They emerged from the womb with a lusty cry. The babies of the Alto, "poor things," came out of the womb "like wet little birds, barely chirping" and with a "nausea" for food. "Our babies," I was often told, were "born already *wanting* to die." Although few Alto mothers could give me the accurate birth weights of their offspring, their descriptions of "skinny," "wasted," "pale," "quiet" newborns, infants who came into the world with no *gosto* (taste) for life and no will to suckle, seemed very much the descriptions of preterm and low-birth-weight infants, babies all too aptly described by Alto women as born already "disadvantaged."[6]

What mothers expectantly looked for in their newborn infants were qualities that showed a readiness for the uphill struggle that was life. And so Alto mothers expressed a preference for those babies who evidenced early on the physical, psychological, and social characteristics of fighters and survivors. Active, quick, responsive, and playful infants were much preferred to quiet, docile, inactive infants, infants described as "dull," "listless," and spiritless. Although differences in infant temperament were believed to be innate, in a precarious environment such as the Alto parasitic infection, malnutrition, and dehydration reproduced these same traits in a great many infants. A particularly lethal form of negative feedback sometimes resulted when Alto mothers gradually withdrew from listless infants whose "passivity" was the result of hunger itself.

Conversely, for an Alto mother to say proudly of a child that she or he suffered many "crises" during the first year of life but "conquered" or "endured" the struggle was a mother's fondest testimony to some hidden inner strength or drive within the child. And so fat, resilient babies were described as having *força*, an innate charismatic power and strength. Many frail infants easily succumbed to death from teething because the innate *força* of the teeth straining against the soft gums holding the teeth captive overwhelmed the little body, making the infant vulnerable to any of several lethal and incurable child diseases. Perhaps the ethnopediatric illness *gasto* best captured the image of the beleaguered little body unable to resist powerful forces. In *gasto*, a fatal form of infant gastroenteritis, the infant's body offered no "resistance" and was quickly reduced to a hollow tube or sieve. Whatever went into the infant's mouth emerged directly in virulent bouts of vomiting and diarrhea. The infant was quickly "spent," "wasted," used up; her fight and her vital energy were gone.

Breasts, Bottles, and the Somatization of Scarcity

A fairly direct and positive correlation exists between infant survival and breast-feeding. A government-sponsored study in São Paulo found that among bottle-fed infants 32 percent were malnourished, compared with 9 percent of breast-fed infants. More recently, a team of researchers from the Department of Social Medicine at the Federal University of Pelotas studying the effects of mixed and bottle feeding on infant survival in a large case control study of two urban areas in the south of Brazil found that breast-fed infants who received even *supplemental* bottles of infant formula were at four times greater risk of dying than were breast-fed–only infants. The mortality risk jumped to fourteen times greater for infants who received no breast milk at all (Victora et al. 1989).

Bottle-fed infants are exposed to contaminated water; overly diluted powdered-milk formulas; unsterilized bottles, nipples, dishes, and spoons; and shortages in the supply and distribution of commercial milk. The evidence is so incontrovertible that a number of governments have taken unprecedented steps to end the practices of hand- and bottle-feeding infants. Legislation passed in Papua New Guinea in 1977 made baby bottles and plastic nipples available only by prescription. In 1980 the Nicaraguan Sandinista government implemented labor regulations that allowed mothers to breast-feed on the job, restricted the sale of infant milk formulas, and issued strong warnings on the labels of all infant food products.

Despite measures such as these, each generation of mothers in the Third World is less likely than the previous one to breast-feed offspring. This is especially true of rural migrants to urban areas, where wage labor and the work available to women are incompatible with breast-feeding. Consequently, powdered milk is one of the most readily available food commodities on the shelves of local *supermercados*, where it is sold in large, economical plastic sacks as well as in the more expensive, vitamin-enriched infant formula cans distributed by the Nestlé company. In Brazil the decline in breast-feeding has been precipitous; between 1940 and 1975 the percentage of babies breast-fed *for any length of time* fell from 96 percent to less than 40 percent (cited in Grant 1983:4). Since that time it has decreased even further.

Alto mothers of the present generation used the breast as an initial, and not very dependable, supplement to the staple infant food, *mingau*, that is offered to the newborn as early as the second day of life, following the cleansing herbal tea given to all infants immediately postpartum. Maternal colostrum is rejected as a "dirty" substance. It is manually extracted and thrown away. Most Alto mothers do offer the breast to their newborn by the third or fourth day postpartum but *always* in combination with, and usually following, *mingau*. Because hungry babies are quieted first with *mingau*, which is made of such a thick consistency that it is often finger-fed the newborn, it is not surprising that so many infants are "uninterested" in the breast when it is offered. Before long—usually in just a few days—mother's milk "fails." Alto infants are not put to the breast often enough, or hungrily enough, to suck vigorously and build up the mother's milk supply. And Alto mothers, like so many women elsewhere in the world (see Gussler & Briesemeister 1980), explain their failure to breast-feed in terms of "insufficient milk."

There is no doubt that the infant mortality rate of the Alto do Cruzeiro could be reduced by half if *mingau* and powdered milk were replaced by breast-feeding. Nevertheless, nothing short of draconian measures could dislodge the practice of artificial infant feeding on the Alto do Cruzeiro. A national breast-feeding promotion campaign launched in Brazil in 1981 had little effect on the poor and illiterate women of the Alto, as elsewhere in Brazil. Meanwhile, the efforts of a local education campaign on the part of a number of concerned doctors, pharmacists, priests, and nuns have been poorly received by poor women, for whom breast-feeding is no longer really an option. Seu Wellington, a local pharmacist and social reformer, tried his best to turn the poor women of Bom Jesus away from their powdered-milk dependency. He sometimes used his pharmacy as a schoolroom or a pulpit. He explained, "I try to teach through analogy. I say to young mothers, 'Did you ever see a cat making *mingau* for its kittens, and yet most stray kittens on the Alto are better fed than your babies.' "

"*Mentira* [lie]!" interrupted a mother who was within earshot of our conversation. "Didn't I rear all mine with *mingau?*"

"And how many were there, Dona Maria?"

"Seven," she replied.

"And living today?"

"Three."

"Well, then, don't talk about rearing your children with *mingau.* You killed four of them with it, and the other three just managed to escape."

On another occasion an anxious young father arrived at the pharmacy with a sick and malnourished baby in search of medicines only to be scolded by Seu Wellington: "Who is the boss in your household? If *you* are, go home and break that blasted baby bottle and force that woman of yours to breast-feed!" When the man protested that his wife was ill and quite weak, that she had no strength to breast-feed, Seu Wellington countered, "That is just laziness in your woman. Go home immediately and show her who is the boss. Otherwise you will soon have a little angel to bury." The man left the pharmacy in a great state of perplexity and agitation, not knowing which way to turn.

The weekly purchase of the requisite four-hundred-gram tin of powdered milk for the household infant or baby is a chronic anxiety on the Alto do Cruzeiro today. Powdered milk (costing between two and three dollars per box, small plastic sack, or can) is the single most expensive food purchase made by most young Alto families, and it consumes about a fifth of their weekly income. It is little wonder that the quantity of milk purchased does not radically increase with the age and size of the current baby. The standard purchase remains one can or box per "baby," whether the baby is an infant or an eight-month-old. What differs is the "quality" of the milk purchased and the extent to which it is diluted and starch filler is added. In general, the older the baby is, the lower is the quality of powdered milk purchased and the greater is the amount of manioc flour and sugar and water added to the *mingau*. It is believed necessary to give the newborn infant a "good start" in life by using the most expensive and "specialized" Nestlé milk formula, Nestogeno, first semester, recognized by its bright purple label with its picture of a sweetly sleeping, fat infant. After the first couple of months mothers may substitute Nestogeno for an "inferior," domestic brand of powdered whole or skimmed milk, at roughly half the cost of the Nestlé formula.

Even unschooled and illiterate mothers of the Alto make it their business to be well informed on the many different varieties of powdered milk sold locally—those designed for the neonate, those for babies in their first six months of life, those for babies in the second "semester" of their first year, and so on. There are many different tins and boxes of powdered milk, some fortified with iron and other vitamins and minerals, some without. I counted eleven different varieties of infant milk products available on the shelves of the central *supermercado* of Bom Jesus one morning in 1988: Nestogeno (recommended for the newborn), Nanon (for the baby aged six months to one year), Pelagron (fortified with iron), *Semilko* (a milk-substitute product with iron), *Ninho* (whole-milk powdered milk for the baby older than one), Nidex (a sugary, vitamin-enriched milk "supplement"). In addition to these (all Nestlé products), there were the following alternative brands of "baby milk": *Glória* (an inexpensive, skimmed, powdered-milk product manufactured by Fleischmann and Royal Industries); Molico, CIPE, Leite Componesa, and *Itambé* (Brazilian domestic brands of inexpensive, partly skimmed powdered milk). Some of these were produced at local sugar mills.

The array of "choices" was quite daunting, and the display of infant-formula powdered-milk tins and boxes took up a full aisle of the local supermarket, more than for any other food product. The "consumer consciousness" concerning the variety of commercial infant formulas in Bom Jesus was unlike anything I had ever seen. It was in a class by itself. The elderly midwife Norinha offered that she had simply "given up" because she no longer felt confident enough to instruct new mothers on the feeding of their infants: "Infant feeding is like a science today, and as for me, unfortunately, I am just a poor, illiterate woman."

It is too bad that the illiterate women of Bom Jesus cannot at least read the tiny, mandatory warnings printed on the brightly colored labels of all the canned Nestlé milk formulas (a concession by the industry to end the international boycott of its products that began in 1978). On the labels are such dire warnings as:

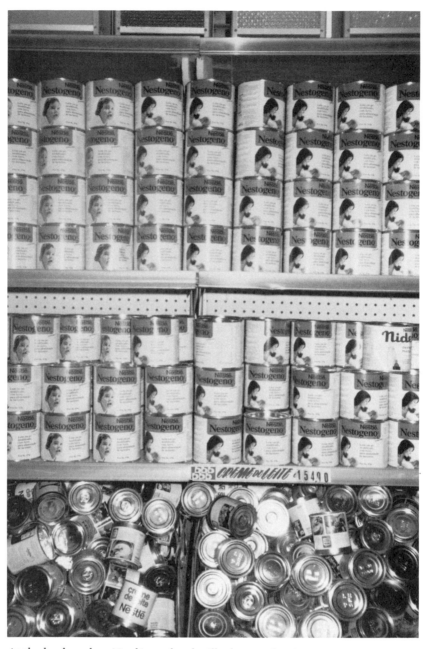

At the local market: Nestlé powdered milk, dozens of varieties.

"Before you use this milk, make sure you consult a physician."
"Powdered-milk formulas should be used only for healthy infants."
"Mother's milk is the best milk for infants."
"Remember to hold your infant when you feed him. An infant who feeds himself can easily strangle."
"By the age of six months you should supplement the milk formula with vitamin-rich cereals, eggs, fruits, and vegetables."
"If you mix this formula without boiling the water first, your baby can get very sick."
"Only make up one bottle of milk at a time if you do not have refrigeration."

Most of the warnings are inappropriate in any case. What Alto home has refrigeration? What Alto mother can consult a physician for advice on making up a *mingau*? Who can afford to boil water for every *mingau*? How can a mother hold her baby for each feeding when she must leave the baby in a hammock while she is away at work?

Alto mothers do recognize, however, that not all infants can tolerate powdered-milk *mingau*, and when a first crisis of diarrhea and vomiting occurs—often as early as the second week of life—women do experiment with different types of powdered milk, and they frequently vary the *mingau* recipe, substituting rice or corn starch for the offending manioc flour, adding more or less sugar, carefully filtering (if not boiling) the water, and so on. In very severe cases of pediatric diarrhea the infant is taken off *mingau* entirely and given only *soro* or an herbal tea to "calm" the intestines. But *no* mother tries to wean her sick infant from the bottle and *mingau* to the breast as an alternative.

The contemporary pattern of bottle- and hand-feeding differs markedly from the infant feeding practices of the older generation of Alto women, most of whom raised their infants and babies on rural plantations and *fazendas* where breast-feeding and woman's work were not so incompatible and where fresh cow's milk was plentiful and sometimes free to plantation workers and their families as part of the traditional terms of labor. Virtually all the older generation of Alto women breast-fed their firstborn children for a year or longer, though many then failed to breast-feed their latter-born children, allowing the older siblings to take over much of the rearing of their baby brothers and sisters. *Mingaus* and *papas* made from fresh, whole cow's milk were even in the previous generation an integral part of the infant's diet, but they were introduced later and after the nursing mother's milk supply was well established. But breast-feeding was not enough even then to curtail a high mortality, although the children of these older women died largely of communicable diseases, not of marasmic wasting and chronic diarrhea/dehydration, the commerciogenic plague of the current generation of Alto babies.

The almost complete erosion of breast-feeding occurred during a very brief historical period. Twenty-five years ago, when I first lived on the Alto, women supplemented their breast milk with goat's milk *mingau*. The milk goats ran freely along the rocky ledges of the Alto, and they were raised by every other household. Today, with the erosion of the hillside, the milk goats have virtually disappeared. Only a half dozen women raise them, and tied up and contained to small sheds, they are pathetic and sickly looking for the most part. Their owners say that their young goats now die as "easily" as their babies. No creatures seem to be faring very well on the Alto today. And commercial powdered milk is the only substitute for the breast.

In the mid-1960s the only available powdered milk was supplied freely to Alto residents under the U.S. Food for Peace program. The women of the Alto were happy to receive the milk (which I myself distributed), but they used it only for cooking and for café au lait for themselves and hot milk drinks for their older children. They were "suspicious" of the "American milk" and fearful of giving it to their fragile infants and small babies. They did not believe that it was "real" milk at all; they thought it was made from "plants" (perhaps they meant soybeans), although others said it was manufactured from whitewash, while local "communists" spread the rumor that it was made from ground-up baby bones. I recall being offended by these rumors and "doing my best" to correct them. I assured Alto women that the powdered milk, mixed carefully with filtered or boiled water, could be given safely to small babies. Just as firmly the women informed me that the American milk gave their infants diarrhea, vomiting, and blindness. Much later I learned about the "night blindness" caused by vitamin A deficiency in babies fed exclusively on formulas made from powdered skimmed milk, such as the sacks of milk the U.S. government was pouring into Brazil and other underdeveloped nations at that time. Perhaps the communists were not so wrong after all. The Food for Peace program distributed powdered milk throughout the Northeast region during the 1960s and eventually fostered a powdered-milk dependency in the populace, which Nestlé and other companies took advantage of when the free distribution ended in the 1970s.

But why did the women of the Alto give up their original resistance to powdered milk? How were they turned into avid consumers of a product that they do not need, that they cannot afford to buy, and that contributes to the death of their children? If we assume that people behave according to the ground rules of a "minimal rationality" (see Mohanty 1989), we ought to look for the internal logic that informs the "choices" that people make.[7] But perhaps it is disingenuous to ask poor women who are often heads of households with four or more dependent children, in addition to the current baby, what their infant feeding "choices" and "preferences" are. If they "prefer" to live at all, they must often work as temporary wage laborers and rear their infants as best they can and with whatever is at hand. In the desperate situation in which many Alto women find themselves, bottle-feeding is really the only possible "choice."

Black Irene breast-fed each of her children for a few months until she had to return to work. Her *patroas* would never allow her to enter their homes if they even suspected that she were lactating. "*Dá nojo* [It's disgusting]!" Irene exclaimed, gesticulating to indicate heavy, pendulous breasts dripping milk. One could not run the risk of suddenly having a wet blouse, she explained, in the middle of serving the family a meal: "It would make everyone lose their appetites."

In the transition from semisubsistence peasants to wage laborers, whereby food becomes a commody that is purchased, rather than grown on one's rented *roçado*, it does not take much of an imaginative leap to begin thinking of infant food as a prepackaged commodity as well. There are radical changes, too, in the relations between the sexes that further promote bottle-feeding. As marriages become less formal, more consensual, and more transitory in the shantytown (as opposed to the rural *vila*), the responsibilities of mothers and fathers to their offspring are altered, and the ways of symbolically establishing a child's legitimacy take on new forms, some of them harmful.

Shantytown households and families are "made up" through a creative form of bricolage in which we can think of a mother and her children as the stable core and husbands and fathers as detachable and circulating units. Consequently, the definition of a "husband" on the Alto do Cruzeiro is a functional one. A husband is the man who provides food for his woman and her children, regardless of whether he is living with them. Insofar as many men on the Alto provide (or try to provide) food to more than one household of women and children simultaneously, it is difficult to conceptualize the community as fundamentally monogamous, although monogamy remains the idealized norm. All Alto women—especially those who are not living with the father of their newborns—both hope and expect the putative father to recognize and "claim" his offspring by means of a highly symbolic transaction. That is, within a few days of the birth of the baby, the father is expected to provide the infant her or his first weeks' supply of expensive Nestogeno. The definition of father on the Alto do Cruzeiro is the man who arrives at least once a week bearing the prestigious purple-labeled can of Nestlé or, when relations are strained, who has the can of milk sent to the household through a friend or intermediary. In fact, this is how a woman's

Papa: baby's "milk."

current lover and father of her child is often greeted. As he sheepishly enters the door of the hut, a woman will say to her newborn, without looking up at her man, "Clap your hands, little one; your milk has arrived!"

I learned of the significance of this transaction when, in the course of instructing a young single mother of the Alto in the gentle art of breast-feeding and after many weeks of orienting her, the young girl could not contain her joy in showing me the "gift" she had just received that afternoon from a "special" person. My face fell when I saw it to be not one, but several, large cans of Nestlé's Nestogeno. The girl's shy and embarrassed excitement and palpable pleasure alerted me to smile with her, rather than spoil what was clearly a special moment. The child's father had appeared. The pretty cans of milk, displayed on the table in the front room, symbolized her newborn son's birth certificate and her own proof that she, too, was "claimed." Unfortunately, a mother who breast-feeds her infant is thought of either as an abandoned woman or as a woman whose husband does not "provide" for her or for his offspring. It can also mean that the husband is no longer sexually "jealous" (i.e., desirous) of his woman's body, letting her breasts be "ruined" by a sucking infant. In this context, breast-feeding is a kind of social stigma.

But one can probe even further into some of the unconscious sources of Alto's women's rejection of breast-feeding. It is supported by women's mistrust of their own bodies and their abilities to nurture an infant. Most Alto women believed that they could not produce sufficient milk, that they were too poor, too weak, or too "wasted" to do so. One woman tugged at her breast, saying, "It's easy *for you* to say we ought to be feeding our own babies, but look here, our infants can suck and suck, and all they will ever get is blood or pus."

"Why is that?"

"Because we are totally weak, used up, finished, no good. We have nothing to give to our own children, not even our own milk."

Another woman broke in to say, "If we were to nurse our babies directly, we would all die of tuberculosis. Weak people can't give much milk."

When I suggested that even poorly nourished women could generally produce an abundant supply of breast milk, an older woman pulled me up short by saying, "Don't some of us raise goats, and don't we know that some goats give milk and others are dry? It is the same with us."

Nevertheless, the more that I observed infant feeding practices in Alto homes, the more I learned about the social production of scarcity. Because women were anxious about the survivability of their often small, puny infants, they hastened to offer them a heavy, thickened "pap" to fill their tiny bellies and (as we might say) to "stick to their ribs." In contrast to thickened powdered milk or even to fresh goat's milk, human milk appeared blue, thin, watery. It could not possibly be "good," Alto women reasoned. It was not rich enough or "strong" enough. It was thin and watery because they themselves were thin and had watery blood. I could not convince the women that all breast milk looked much the same as their own. In offering infants *mingau* from the very start and offering the breast only as an afterthought, Alto women could not build up an adequate supply of milk, which required active stimulation and fairly continuous sucking in the early days and weeks of breast-feeding. Within days of relative disuse, Alto women did notice a gradual decline in their breast milk and could say with reason, "I have very little milk."

What has been lost on the Alto do Cruzeiro through the commercialization of infant feeding is the whole "culture" of breast-feeding: the seemingly (but not really) "intuitive" knowledge of how breast-feeding is done, what breast milk "should" look like, how a mother knows when a small baby has had enough, and so forth. My point is that breast-feeding is no more "natural" or any less "cultural" than cooking. Breast-feeding is a form of body praxis. Like swimming, dancing, or making love, breast-feeding must be learned, and the knowledge of "how" to do it comfortably and well (though with many cultural variations) can be lost.

Finally, many women accused their babies of "refusing" the breast when it was offered. And they could hardly blame the infant, they said, for their milk was simply "no good." I was told by dozens of women that their breast milk was "bad." They described it as salty, watery, bitter, sour, infected, dirty, and diseased. In all, the women perceived their milk as "unfit" for the infant and as little more than a vehicle of contamination, no better than the polluted waters of the Capibaribe River. Not only a woman's weakness and her sickness but even her sins could be transmitted through nursing. When a newborn died suddenly on the Alto, mothers sometimes took comfort in the belief that an unbaptized baby, if it had never been breast-fed, could go directly to heaven free of the stain of original sin passed into the infant through the mother's breast.

In all, we can see the representational uses of the body as a medium of exchange between personal and social metaphors, symbols, and meanings. When their milk supply begins to falter, Alto women are quick to see in this an indication of their own weakness. Similarly, when they refer to their own milk as scanty, curdled, bitter, or sour, breast milk is a powerful metaphor speaking to the scarcity and bitterness of their lives as women. The rejection of the "goodness" of their breast milk derives from a political economy of the emotions expressed in the somatization of scarcity and deprivation. Through the medium of the body, the contradictions of the social order are reproduced in the disquieting image of needy, hungry, dependent women who must withhold their milk from their babies to keep from being devoured by them first: "If we would feed them, they would make us sick and skinny and old." The perceived inability to breast-feed reinforces these young women's already deeply eroded sense of inner goodness, self-worth, and self-sufficiency, which is embodied in the autonomous act of nursing one's newborn. What has been taken from these women is their belief in their ability to give: "We have *nothing* to give our children." And so the cycle of economic dependency is complete. From autonomous *roçado* to commercial *supermercado*, and from autonomous breast to canned Nestogeno, the ruse is total. And its consequences are nothing less than deadly.

Social Class and Reproduction

I am suggesting that poverty interacts in many different ways to produce child mortality and to shape reproductive thinking and practice. But which is cause? Which is effect? Do so many babies die because there are too many of them to begin with, or are there so many babies because so many of them die? Do women have more babies because they are poor? Or are they poor because they have so many babies?

In 1988 I took my study of reproductive histories into the most comfortable and bourgeois neighborhood of Bom Jesus, a half dozen suburban streets of modern, ranch-style homes with tiled patios, fringed hammocks, large swimming pools, and pet dogs. My sample of twenty-three middle- and upper-class women was, like the Alto sample, an opportunistic one. I began with a trusted friend, the wife of a middle-aged bank officer, and she introduced me to her circle of friends at a local and exclusive private social club. All members of the social club had been screened for their bourgeois credentials before being admitted. These women in turn introduced me to friends of their own.

The profile of the "average" woman in this small "control" group stands in obvious and marked contrast to that of the Alto women. The sample was drawn, after all, from the class of local *patroas*. This average affluent woman of Bom Jesus was born in the *município* of Bom Jesus on her father's *fazenda* or plantation estate, where she was reared as a favored *menina de engenho*, a true *filha da terra*, a child of the sugar mill, a daughter of the land. She was educated by German nuns at the Colégio of Santa Lúcia in Bom Jesus and then later sent off to Recife to study literature and language, history, the arts, or pedagogy. But she did not leave normal school or the university with a diploma, and she never had time to put her skills to practical use, for she returned home to marry young. Most had their first child by the age of twenty-one or twenty-two. But first she was a local debutante and had her formal "coming out" party at the age of fifteen. She dated carefully, choosing her suitors from among the "better" and "older" families of the *município*. She married "close to home," often a cousin or distant relation. Although her husband may have come from the landed "aristocracy," he is in all likelihood not an "agriculturalist" himself but a professional or a man of commerce and banking. She was not a virgin at marriage, but she was married in white in both religious and civil ceremonies and with much festivity. After marriage she settled into the comfortable, matronly role of *dona da casa*, managing a large household of family members, live-in domestics, and hired help.

The twenty-three middle- and upper-class women, ranging in age from twenty-four to forty-eight (median age, thirty-eight), reported a total of 76 pregnancies among them, or 3.3 per woman. (Compare Table 7.7 with Table 7.2.) Among them they experienced only *one* infant death (of a preterm, premature infant), one stillbirth, and seven miscarriages and abortions.

Table 7.7. Reproductive histories of middle-class women, Bom Jesus da Mata, 1988 (control group).

	Total Number	Number per Woman	
Pregnancies	76	3.30	
Living children	67	2.90	
Miscarriages/abortions	7	0.30	} 0.34
Stillbirths	1	.04	
Infant deaths (birth – 1 year)	1	.04	} .04
Child deaths (13 months – 5 years)	0	0.00	

Source: Anthropological interviews of women of Bom Jesus da Mata.
Note: $N = 23$. These women ranged in age from 24 to 48, with a median age of 38.

They had 67 living children, or 2.9 per woman. Clearly, mortality and fertility patterns are thoroughly modernized in this middle-class population, for whom child death is as shocking and aberrant as for affluent women anywhere else in the world. These women do not speak of "angels" populating the heavens, nor do they take comfort in homely Catholic pieties about the afterlife and "God's will" with respect to infant and child death.

Although in this sample of women there were no infants deaths (apart from the one premature infant who died on the day of birth) to grieve, over the years I have encountered a few other cases of child death in Bom Jesus among the middle classes. Terezinha Cavalcanti, the thirty-four-year-old daughter of one of the oldest landed families in the *município*, lost her fourth child in 1981, a baby son at the age of ten months. I visited her at home a year later, and Terezinha was still in mourning for the lost child: "He was the strongest and the healthiest one of all," she told me. "As an infant he never had to see a doctor. The sickness struck without warning. He took sick overnight. He died in my arms on the way to the hospital in Recife." The child was never diagnosed, but the cause of death was a high fever with convulsions, "probably encephalitis," she said.

The family decided against an autopsy and took the baby home for an elaborate wake. His grave is well marked by a large marble headstone flanked on either side by a stone guardian angel and a replica of the family watchdog. I had occasion to visit the grave with Terezinha, who always carried photos of the baby on her person; she would take them out and show them to anyone willing to hear her short, painful story. What tormented

Terezinha was the knowledge that she could never "replace" the lost child, for at the time of his delivery she had had a tubal ligation to prevent further pregnancies. By all appearances, Terezinha was deeply depressed, and her mother often consulted me for practical advice on how she might best respond to her daughter's suffering.

Similarly, a local doctor in Bom Jesus who had lost a five-year-old son to leukemia was "inconsolable" for months following the death. The child was his firstborn son and his namesake. No one in Bom Jesus seemed able to help the man overcome his grief. Finally, the doctor went to the famous archbishop of Recife-Olinda, Dom Helder Câmara, for spiritual advice and comfort. There he asked the elderly "saint" if the death of this favorite child was "God's will" to which he must somehow learn to adjust. Dom Helder shocked the grieving man by saying, "God is not a cannibal—he doesn't wish any child to die. The death of your son was a terrible *human* tragedy, not the workings of a willful or capricious Deity. But let us pray for the strength to pass through this terrible hour." Both men knelt together and wept, Dom Helder as much as the doctor, for his grief recalled to the elderly prelate the death of six of his own thirteen siblings during an epidemic of "croup" when Dom Helder was still himself a child.

Middle-class infants and small babies are not completely protected from the scourge of life-threatening diarrheas, fevers, respiratory infections, and other pediatric diseases. Although there was only one death, two other women interviewed came very close to losing a child, one to croup and another to diarrhea/dehydration. Both infants were rescued, however, by prompt and appropriate medical attention in Bom Jesus. And several of the middle-class mothers boasted that none of their children was ever put on a course of antibiotics, this in contrast to the babies of the Alto, who were fed a steady diet of medications, including many different varieties of strong antibiotics.

Among the affluent women of Bom Jesus, reproduction was described as a controlled and rationalized, rather than a chaotic and fearful, process. All births took place in urban hospitals and maternity centers, and a large number of these were cesarean sections. While interviewing a middle-class woman on her patio, I noticed her six-year-old daughter and friends playing "hospital." We interrupted the interview so that I could watch the play-birth just as the "nurse" called for the "doctor" to deliver the baby. The mother was anesthetized, her belly was cut open, and the "birth" was pronounced a success by the little girls, although the infant was immediately put on intravenous feedings! Because surgical births have become so normalized among the middle and upper classes of Northeast Brazil (see Janowitz 1982)—and newspapers in Recife reported C-section rates approaching 70 percent for private maternity patients—poor women frequently complained of medical "maltreatment" at the local maternity ward: they were forced to give birth "naturally," although sedated.

If Women Could Choose:
Fertility, Mortality, and Ideal Family Size

Had those women on the Alto [do Cruzeiro] refrained from
the momentary, fleeting pleasures of irresponsible orgasms,
there would be no dead babies to bury. Furthermore, by
solidifying commitment, one man to one woman, until death
do they part, by practicing abstinence and responsible sex, a
way out of poverty and oppression might more easily be
found.

Unpublished letter in response
to Nancy Scheper-Hughes (1989)

During a lull in the conversation at a diocesan dinner for the bishop of Oakland attended by invited Catholic faculty of the University of California at Berkeley in the fall of 1989, I was asked about my research interests by the Dominican philosopher seated at my right. I summarized some of the foregoing figures on fertility and mortality. The Dominican philosopher's response was learned but coolly indifferent. He said, "Interesting, but throughout history poor women have probably always lost more children than they were able to raise. No doubt they are more accustomed to death than we are." Indeed, they are, I replied, but at great cost to their bodies and their spirits. Our conversation was cut short, however, for just then the bishop of Oakland got up to address the gathering, managing skillfully to sidestep the critical questions from the floor on the church's continuing condemnation of artificial birth control, abortion, and education for "safe sex" in response to the current AIDS crisis. It was not a terribly friendly audience.

We know that educated Catholics in North America, long exposed to a religiously pluralistic environment, exercise a good deal of independence from official church teachings on sexual and reproductive ethics. But to what extent do these same teachings influence reproductive thinking and practice in Bom Jesus, where 85 percent of the population describes itself as Catholic? Do the words of Pope John Paul II fall on receptive and fertile ground here, and do they contribute to the seemingly self-defeating tendencies of poor Alto women who plunge themselves into a lockstep dance of repeated pregnancy and repeated child death?

In short, why *do* these poor Brazilian women have so many babies? Are they ignorant of birth control methods, or are they spiritually battered by

Table 7.8. "If women could choose": ideal family size.

	Total Pregnancies	Living Children	Ideal Family Size
Middle-class women	3.3	2.9	4.5
Alto women	9.5	4.2	3.0

Source: Anthropological interviews of Alto and Bom Jesus women.

the sterile and uncompassionate teachings of the Catholic church with respect to sexuality? Are they also passive objects of the reproductive whims of selfish husbands and lovers? Alternatively, do these women simply value fertility, pregnancy, childbearing, and childrearing to the extent that they "overproduce" for the "love" of it? Or, like Alice in *Through the Looking Glass* racing just to stay in place, do these women give birth again and again only to hold on to the precious few who manage to escape death?

A frequent response worldwide to infant death is pregnancy, an attempt to quickly replace what was lost. The evidence of high infant mortality "driving" up rates of fertility is generally accepted today by most demographers and epidemiologists (see Imhof 1985; Ware 1977; Choudhury, Khan, & Chen 1976). The reproductive histories of Alto women represent, in plain terms, gross reproductive waste, draining the physical, economic, social, and psychological resources of women who bear again and again such vulnerable offspring. But how many children do Alto women actually want? And how much are they willing to go through to achieve that goal? Do the women of the shantytown differ significantly in their reproductive goals, practices, and outcomes from middle-class women in the town of Bom Jesus da Mata? Here, comparison across class in the same small community can show the effects of scarcity on reproductive thinking and practice and help us to tease apart what is culturally shared from what is class driven.

In all, while it takes the "average" Alto woman almost 10 pregnancies to rear 4 living children, middle-class women of Bom Jesus have 3.3 pregnancies to rear 2.9 living children (see Table 7.8). In other words, the average Alto woman labors through 6 more pregnancies than the average middle-class woman to have 1 child in excess of her more affluent "sisters." The women of the Alto, then, are not prodigious reproducers; they must simply work much harder than affluent women to produce a medium-sized family.

When asked what each considered an ideal-sized family, the poor women of the Alto expressed a preference for many fewer children than the number of pregnancies they had experienced. Poor women also wanted fewer children (3.0) than did middle-class women (4.5). Whereas the small sample of affluent women clustered closely around the mean age of thirty-eight, the Alto women represented two generations of women, an older, postreproductive group and a younger, still fertile group. So, referring back to Table 7.4, we can see that the younger generation of Alto women actually considered 2.6 an ideal family size, while for those older Alto women who agreed to answer this "irrelevant" question, 3.5 was the ideal-sized family. Here is what a few younger Alto women had to say about family size:

"A pair; that's plenty for a poor family" (aged thirty-two).

"Two is good; if I could, I would have only one boy and one girl" (aged nineteen).

"Three or four—that's enough!" (aged twenty-four).

"Two are more than enough these days" (aged twenty-five).

"More than three is an agony. I've had seven . . . too many, too many" (aged thirty-three).

"Two of each sex. When you have too many children, you are in the middle of a great confusion. You don't know where to turn. If one wants something and you give it to him you end up taking something away from another" (aged twenty-nine).

"Whatever God decides, that is good. But for myself, what I would have liked was two of each sex, and all of them living" (aged thirty-one, lost seven of ten children).

And here is what a few of the older women of the Alto (forty and older) had to say:

"Three would be good. If there had been only three in my family, we could have lived better. But God didn't want this—He gave me all of these" (aged forty-four, mother of nine children, six living).

"Two are plenty for us. Everything for the poor is a struggle. We want to put them into school, and it is a sacrifice. We want to feed them and dress them, and we can't" (aged seventy).

"Ten, at least ten children. I would have preferred to have raised all of mine, to have lost none of them. I gave birth nine times, and I raised five of them, in addition to two others that belonged to my husband from another woman. They were good children; I loved all of them" (aged fifty-six).

"Six. Three boys for their father in the *roçado* and three girls for me at home" (aged fifty-two).

"Four or less—more than that and they start to die on you" (aged forty-seven).

Those older women who "refused" the question replied indirectly:

"Ideal family size? That's hard to say. I myself had so many that I am tired, worth nothing anymore. My desire was always to conform to God's will because all that God does is good. I love to hear the words of the holy Mass wishing goodwill to all. It is a small sacrifice, then, to conform to His wishes" (aged seventy-six).

"Whatever God sends us is good" (aged seventy-four).

"It's not for us to say. But sometimes I think it would have been better if God had decided to take them all, though He was right to leave me with just these two. They served me well" (aged sixty-six).

In general, Alto women were more conservative than middle-class women on the subject of birth control. "Who doesn't want children shouldn't marry," older Alto women often said. But poor women were also pragmatists who understood that unlimited fertility was not an unlimited good: "I hope to God that I won't have any more children," a forty-two-year-old Alto woman offered. "But I won't do anything to prevent it either. If God is willing, then I will have to be willing, too."

Nonetheless, *most* poor women younger than forty had had some experience with birth control, usually the pill.[8] Many had used the pill for brief periods of birth spacing but rarely for more than six to eight months at a time. The pill was described as an effective but "dangerous" form of birth control. It was uniformly disliked by Alto women, an attitude widely shared among all women of Bom Jesus across class. The pill was said to cause nausea, headaches, swelling, extreme nervousness . . . and cancer. While readily available in most pharmacies of Bom Jesus and sold without prescription for a modest fee that would *not* be entirely prohibitive to the poor, the pill was considered an "unnatural" form of birth control that adversely affected, as one Alto woman put it, "the whole organization of the nervous system." Contraceptive creams, jellies, and pastes were known and sometimes used by the younger women of the Alto. Diaphragms were unknown and unavailable in local drugstores, while condoms were generally used only by local men when visiting prostitutes in the *zona* of Bom Jesus.

The older generation of Alto women had had recourse to a vast array of herbal teas, washes, baths, and infusions said to affect fertility in a variety of ways but most commonly to "bring on" a late period. These traditional remedies were never referred to as having "abortive" properties but rather as "regulating the normal menstrual cycle. Sister Christiana, another Franciscan nun who ministers to the sick and especially to women and small children of the poor *bairros* of the parish, is well versed in the medicinal and fertility-regulating qualities of various indigenous plants, a knowledge she readily shares with the young women of the Alto. Sister Christiana describes the *mata* (the wilds) as "God's own pharmacy," and she teaches poor women at religious base community meetings that whatever can be effected through "natural" herbs and plants is "good," an expression of God the Creator's intent.

Little Irene and I went to each of the half dozen medicinal herbal stalls in the *feira*, where we collected samples of menstrual-inducing herbs, leaves, roots, and bark. There we encountered Dr. Raiz (Dr. Roots), who, reluctantly at first, told us about the properties of various abortifacient plants, among them *cabacinha* (also called *cabacinha-riscada* and *aboboraovos*), *senna* (any one of several species of cassia); *quinaquina* (*cinchona offinalis*, also known as *guamixinga* and *murta-do-mato*). Dr. Raiz believed that his vast knowledge of healing herbs, roots, and barks (several hundred of them) was a gift from God and that his was an *obra da natureza*, a "work of nature." Therefore, he said, he would not "cooperate" with those who asked him to use his gift for ill. He would only "treat" women for menstrual periods up to fifteen days late. After that date the women would have to look "elsewhere" for help, perhaps (he said) with a local midwife or a curing woman willing to use her knowledge in that way. Or the women could go to Feliciano's pharmacy for an abortion injection or an abortion "cocktail."

Later, I visited several local healing women (*rezadeiras, parteiras,* and *curandeiras*) of the Alto, and we walked the *mata* looking for samples of green herbs, berries, nuts, roots, and leaves used to stimulate delayed menstrual periods. Four more abortifacients were added to the list in this way: *aroeira* (*Schinus molle*), which is used either as a tea or a douche; *caju roxo* (a variety of the common cashew); *arruda* (common rue used as a douche); and *cravo do reino* (a species of clove). To what extent these natural remedies were efficacious, I could not say. Nonetheless, the knowledge and practice of menstrual induction were fairly widespread among the women of the Alto and known even to some of the religious sisters of Bom Jesus, who, like Christiana, participated in the popular church's new alternative medicine ministry to the sick-poor. In so doing the women (including the nuns) acted with considerable independence from some central tenets of Catholic orthodoxy regarding the nature of the embryo and the beginnings of human life. They did so by taking advantage of the considerable ambiguity surrounding menstruation. A late period might be seen as the first sign of pregnancy *or* as the symptom of a sluggish system requiring an herbal purgative.

It seems, then, that menstrual-inducing pharmaceuticals, like Depo-Provera, might be compatible with this orientation. And, indeed, several younger women of the Alto said that they had used the "injection method" of birth control. Despite the controversy surrounding Depo-Provera in the United States because of its links to uterine cancer (see Petchesky 1984:8), the drug was not listed as a "controlled" or "regulated" substance on the Brazilian government's published inventory. The drug was sold at local pharmacies in three different injectable dosages, and I purchased a small sample injection without prescription at Rute's pharmacy. Rute, who was strongly opposed to abortion, did not associate the drug with its abortifacient effects. She believed that the drug was recommended to "promote fertility" by normalizing irregular menstrual cycles. Indeed, the accompanying directions indicated its use for the control of endometriosis and the treatment of amenorrhea, the latter an indirect reference to the drug's abortive properties.

There was another way that Alto women manipulated ambiguity with respect to induced abortion. Most women knew that it was dangerous to take any medications in the early stages of pregnancy. Because, however, so many poor women *so anda doente*, were constantly sick and "eating" so many different and often "contradictory" drugs, abortion sometimes resulted as the "unintended" consequence, a side effect, of their tendency to overmedicate. Such was the case with Little Irene, who, as you recall, was quite ill when I found her on that morning in 1982 and asked her to be my field assistant. Irene had many different somatic complaints; a suspected pregnancy and an induced "miscarriage" were only two of her troubles. As we plunged into the first few days of interviewing, Irene frequently alluded in an offhand and lighthearted way to the unwanted pregnancy she had just been relieved of. During an interview in the creche, Marlene asked Irene about her pregnancy. Irene replied, "I'm free! It was because of all the drugs I was taking. I'm like a walking drugstore! I'm sick with so many different problems I finally just took everything at once. I made myself a drug cocktail and *pronto!* The next morning when I went to relieve myself—plop! There it was, a little sack of white stuff this long. [She indicated that it was half as long as her index finger.] For sure it was all those medicines I took."

Marlene exclaimed, "For shame, Irene. What a *big* sin!"

Irene replied without skipping a beat, "There was no sin at all! I'm no more responsible for this abortion than a woman who lost hers because of a great *susto!* I was sick, doubled over with pain. I thought I was going to die. And now I'm totally cured! How could that be wrong? I have three other children still at home to look after."

Nonetheless, virtually all Alto women (Irene included) vigorously condemned medically induced abortion, whether by surgical procedures in the hospital or by the manipulations of local midwives at home. Fully intentional abortions like these constituted a grave sin, an offense against God and the Virgin. "Once it's *really* in there," Alto women cautioned, "it's too late." Because medical abortions in Bom Jesus required several weeks of gestation, the ambiguous period immediately following a "late period" had passed by the time of such an abortion. Nothing is less ambiguous than a clinical abortion, and those half dozen Alto women in my sample who admitted to having an abortion considered themselves guilty of a mortal sin. Abortion, they maintained, was morally wrong (as well as illegal in Brazil), even if dire necessity had led them to it. The soul of an unbaptized, aborted fetus was an anomaly, the soul of a child unborn, and older praying women warned that such restless souls hovered near crossroads and sometimes got into mischief: "They hold it against their mothers—they never forget who brought them to their end." Consequently, induced abortions were often held responsible for all quality of misfortune in the world: drought, floods, evil landlords, the deaths of older children, and disease epidemics. On this point the women of the Alto stood strongly by orthodox church teachings, and they often said quite straightforwardly, "The pope forbids it."

The small, mainly evangelical Protestant churches of Bom Jesus also forbade abortion among their members, although these churches had not yet gained a foothold on the Alto do Cruzeiro. There, Catholicism competed only with Xangô and Umbanda, the Afro-Brazilian possession religions, and these, too, both strongly condemned abortion.[9] Nita the Marvelous explained that Exu, the trickster (devil and messenger) of Umbanda, was legion and was always accompanied by his "women" and their host of pagan child spirits. These *almas inválidas* (disabled souls) belonged to the multitude of aborted and unbaptized fetuses. "Beware these evil spirits," warned Nita, "for they are the most dangerous of all." The baptized spirits that did Exu's bidding were civilized, endowed with reason and with a knowledge of good and evil, and they could discriminate between the two. But the mischief of the crippled pagan souls of the unbaptized and unborn knew no bounds. They were primitive spirits, poorly evolved, and totally unsocialized, said Nita, and they were to blame for much evil in the world. "And yet," she sighed, "they are not the guilty ones. They are not responsible for what they do. They have no conscience. Who are to blame are their mothers, those base and low-life women who destroy their progeny in the womb. And in the end, *they* are the ones who will suffer because they will go into the next world *devendo o espíritu a Deus* [owing a soul to God]."

In contrast to the moral sensibilities regarding abortion, sterilization emerged as the preferred form of birth control among women of all social classes in Bom Jesus even though sterilization was viewed, equal to abortion, as a serious mortal sin by the Catholic church. For middle-class women who were able to afford it, sterilization was also the most commonly practiced form of family planning. Similarly, while local doctors expressed considerable moral conflict over medicalized abortions, they expressed no qualms about sterilization once a woman had demonstrated her "good gender citizenship" by producing an "adequate" number of children. Often I was asked to serve as a *despachante* in arranging, through various political and medical "connections," for the free sterilization of an Alto woman who could not afford to pay for her own. Political leaders in Bom Jesus complained that expensive sterilizations (at about one hundred fifty dollars each) were among the most popular political "favors" distributed to poor women voters. Nevertheless, Seu Félix denied that local women ever received the operations at municipal expense . . . except during municipal elections when he was forced to keep pace with his political opponents.

The women of Bom Jesus, both rich and poor, did not see any contradiction in their moral condemnation of medical abortion and their widespread acceptance of sterilization. The latter, they said, did not involve "killing" a fetus. And tubal ligations were second only to delivery as the most common medical practice for women inpatients as the local hospital. Overall, however, the morality that guided reproductive thinking and practice for both rich and poor women in Bom Jesus was contained within a very Catholic discourse on the "natural" (as though with oblique reference to a kind of Thomistic natural law). Women, they agreed, had a duty to "cooperate" with God and with nature. This was equivalent to a "duty to procreate" (see Noonan 1966:193), although not indefinitely. At a certain point a womanly pragmatics took over. Once a woman had had four or five or twelve children, she might decide to put an end to her reproductive years. A twenty-seven-year-old Alto woman, an active member of the women's altar society of the local church and pregnant herself for the second time, could say; "I want only these two children. I hope to have my tubes tied while I am in the hospital for the birth. My husband has agreed. The only problem is with the hospital. The doctors don't like to do these operations for those of us who can only pay the minimum allowed through the rural workers medical fund. They make the poor suffer through seven or eight pregnancies before they finally take pity on us."

The young woman was correct. Unless one was very well connected politically, it was almost impossible to get a tubal ligation after only two pregnancies. Consequently, only 13 percent of the seventy-two Alto women were able to arrange for their sterilization, although many more had tried to do so. By contrast, fourteen of the twenty-three middle-class women interviewed had already had tubal ligations, which they viewed as the expected and normative practice of family planning among their peers. Among the middle and upper classes of Bom Jesus, once a woman and her husband had agreed that they had had enough children, a tubal ligation was scheduled, along with a "uterus-lifting" and "vaginal-tightening" operation that had become fashionable among middle-class women wanting to maintain their husbands' sexual interest. "No man likes a flabby old woman," I was told more than once with a wink. Male sterilization, however, had made no inroads into Bom Jesus at all. Only one local man, a lawyer, was known to have had a vasectomy, and he was ridiculed as a man who had been too willing to sacrifice himself to a form of symbolic castration.

While middle-class women of Bom Jesus were strong believers in "family planning" for themselves, they were even stronger supporters of "population control" for the poorer classes of the town. And while Alto women emphasized pregnancy and childbearing as a womanly "duty," the middle-class and wealthy women of Bom Jesus tended to view procreation as a "right" to be exercised only when there were sufficient resources to assure each child a decent upbringing. In response to my question "How many children are good for a poor family?" one middle-class woman snapped, "*None*, not one!" Claudinette was more gentle but firm: "If it is a sin to say this, forgive me, but I think that for a poor woman to raise a child only so that it will suffer and go hungry, I think it would be better if that child had never been born."

Many middle-class women interviewed shared the belief that the negative teachings of the Catholic church had a greater effect on the poor, who were more "vulnerable" and at the same time more "devout" and "obedient." Dona Elizabete pulled from her purse a small pamphlet that had been distributed at Mass on the previous Sunday. It had formed the basis of the weekly sermon, which had treated the subject of "chastity," sexual purity, within and outside of marriage. The pamphlet descried a decline in the spirit of self-mortification in the modern world and the proliferation of sinful practices: promiscuity, fornication, adultery, homosexuality, bestiality, masturbation, and so on. It condemned even within marriage any sexual practices that deviated from "natural" law, such as anal intercourse, the use of sexual stimulants (whether dildos or erotic videotapes), and artificial birth control. Elizabete was incensed at a message that equated bestiality and masturbation, on the one hand, and "pornography" and birth control, on the other. She believed that the church's misguided efforts would be ridiculed by sophisticated Catholics and uncritically accepted by the illiterate popular classes. Either way, she said, it was a disservice to the church in Brazil. Herself the mother of four grown children, Elizabete had her own tubes tied when she was only thirty-four years old. "I know that the pope is against this," she said, "but this is a sin that I will have to carry with me." Had she confessed it to the local priest? "No," she replied. "You only confess sins that you repent." Did she still receive Holy Communion? "Yes," she answered. "This matter concerns me and God alone."

In all, the independent reproductive practices of the middle classes of Bom Jesus are not too dissimilar from those of North American Catholics. Those of the poor are another matter. If official church teachings affect their reproductive patterns, contributing to the high fertility/high mortality cycle that I have described for the women of the Alto do Cruzeiro, the church has the devil to pay in terms of accountability. But Catholic teachings are deflected and creatively refashioned on the Alto within the context of a lively popular culture of spirituality and an alternative, folk bioethics concerning the definitions, meanings, and value of early human life (to which I now turn).

8   (M)Other Love
Culture, Scarcity,
and Maternal Thinking

Maternal practices begin in love, a love which for most women
is as intense, confusing, ambivalent, poignantly sweet as any
they will experience.

Sara Ruddick (1980:344)

The following chapters are about culture, scarcity, and maternal thinking.
They explore maternal beliefs, sentiments, and practices as these bear on
child survival on the Alto do Cruzeiro. The argument builds on an earlier
and controversial article I wrote on this topic (1985), which I have since
restudied, rethought, and mulled over with the women of the Alto on three
return field trips since 1987.[1] I trust I can do better justice to it than when I
began. If, however, I cannot establish here some basis for empathy, for a
shared understanding of sentiments and practices that seem so very different
from our own and therefore so profoundly disturbing, I shall have failed.
One difficulty is that over the years I have come to participate in the
worldview expressed by these women, and their sentiments and practices
now seem to me all too commonsensical and expected. I must struggle to
recapture a sense of its initial "strangeness" so as to identify, at least initially,
with the reader and his or her reluctance to accept a set of practices driven by
an alternative womanly morality, one that will be experience-distant to a
great many. It is a dilemma common to all ethnographic writing: how do we
represent the other to the other? But here the stakes are very high indeed.

The subject of my study is love and death on the Alto do Cruzeiro,
specifically *mother* love and *child* death. It is about the meanings and effects
of deprivation, loss, and abandonment on the ability to love, nurture, trust,
and have and keep faith in the broadest senses of these terms. It treats the
individual and the personal as well as the collective and cultural dimensions
of maternal practices in an environment hostile to the survival and well-
being of mothers and infants. I argue that a high expectancy of child death is
a powerful shaper of maternal thinking and practice as evidenced, in particular, in delayed attachment to infants sometimes thought of as temporary
household "visitors." This detachment can be mortal at times, contributing

340

to the severe neglect of certain infants and to a "failure" to mourn the death
of very young babies. I am *not* arguing that mother love, as we understand
it, is deficient or absent in this threatened little human community but
rather that its life history, its course, is different, shaped by overwhelming
economic and cultural constraints. And so I trace the gradual unfolding of
maternal love and attentive, "holding" care once the risk of loss (through
chaotic and unpredictable early death) seems to have passed. This discussion
is embedded in an examination of the cultural construction of emotions, and
it attempts to overcome the distinctions between "natural" and "socialized"
affects, between "deep" private feelings and "superficial" public sentiments,
between conscious and unconscious emotional expressions. In its attempts
to show how emotion is shaped by political and economic context as well as
by culture, this discussion can be understood as a "political economy" of the
emotions.[2]

A second goal of this discussion is rather more abstract and theoretical. It
represents an attempt to forge a dialogue between competing views of
maternal thinking and practice. My analysis and findings challenge the
psychological infant attachment and maternal "bonding" theorists *and* those
cultural feminists who argue for a singular conception of women's goals,
interests, and moral visions. I am referring to those who emphasize an
essentially "womanly" ethic and ethos of maternal responsiveness, atten-
tiveness, and caring labor. In its most reductionist form this appears in the
developmental and clinical literature on maternal "bonding" understood as a
universal maternal script. In its more complex and "socialized" form it
surfaces in the writings of those feminists who argue for a "poetics" of
motherhood and for a specifically female moral voice and sensibility expressed in an "ethic of care." The latter, in attempting to recover the muted
and marginalized voices of women, can paradoxically do violence to the
different experiences and sensibilities of poor and Third World women
whose moral visions may not conform to the feminist paradigm. In arguing
for a common female ethic, the cultural feminist analysis can doubly mar-
ginalize poor women. Sara Ruddick, for example, has posited certain universal "interests that appear to govern maternal practice throughout the
species" so as to make "mother love appear altogether natural" (1980: 347–
348). Her persuasive writings on "maternal thinking" and "maternal practice" (Ruddick 1989) provide the touchstone for the following set of critical
reflections.

Mother love is anything *other* than natural and instead represents a
matrix of images, meanings, sentiments, and practices that are everywhere
socially and culturally produced. In place of a poetics of motherhood, I refer
to the pragmatics of motherhood, for, to paraphrase Marx, these shantytown

women create their own culture, but they do not create it just as they please or under circumstances chosen by themselves. Consequently, mother love is best bracketed and understood as (m)other loves. The following discussion obviously makes no claims to universality. Nor is it an argument for a "culture of poverty" addressed specifically to the situation of shantytown mothers and children. Although it does not surprise me to discover some resonances and resemblances with mothering practices at other times and places, it is to the particularities of the Brazilian situation that the following is addressed.[3] The women and children whose painful lives I dare to expose here are the end in and of themselves of my analysis.

What I discovered while working as a medic in the Alto do Cruzeiro during the 1960s was that while it was possible, and hardly difficult, to rescue infants and toddlers from premature death from diarrhea and dehydration by using a simple sugar, salt, and water solution (even bottled Coca-Cola worked fine in a pinch), it was more difficult to enlist mothers themselves in the rescue of a child they perceived as ill-fated for life or as better off dead. More difficult still was to coax some desperate young mothers to take back into the bosom of the family a baby they had already come to think of as a little winged angel, a fragile bird, or a household guest or visitor more than as a permanent family member. And so Alto babies "successfully" rescued and treated in the hospital rehydration clinic or in the creche and returned home were sometimes dead before I had the chance to make a follow-up house call. Eventually I learned to inquire warily before intervening: "Dona Maria, do you think we should try to save this child?" or, even more boldly, "Dona Auxiliadora, is this a child worth keeping?" And if the answer was no, as it sometimes was, I learned to keep my distance.

Later, I learned that the high expectancy of death and the ability to face death with stoicism and equanimity produced patterns of nurturing that differentiated those infants thought of as "thrivers" and as "keepers" from those thought of as born "already wanting to die." The survivors and keepers were nurtured, while the stigmatized or "doomed" infants were allowed to die à míngua, "of neglect." Mothers sometimes stepped back and allowed nature to take its course. This pattern I first (and rather unfortunately) labeled "ethnoeugenic selective neglect" (Scheper-Hughes 1984:540). Today I simply call it "mortal neglect." Both are unhappy terms, and it is little wonder that some critics have been offended by what they saw as a lapse in cultural relativism or as a failure of solidarity with my female "subjects." Claire Cassidy's (1980) earlier notion of "benign neglect" perhaps comes closer to the women's own perceptions of their actions. Nevertheless, translated to the North American context, "benign neglect" conjures up images of unkempt and unsupervised, yet otherwise happy and carefree, older street urchins riding subway trains on hot summer nights in New York City. The mortally neglected infants and babies I am referring to here are often (although not always) prettily kept: washed, such hair as they have combed, and their emaciated little bodies dusted with sweet-smelling talcum powders. When they die, they usually do so with candles propped up in tiny waxen hands to light their way to the afterlife. At least some of these little "angels" have been freely "offered up" to Jesus and His Mother, although "returned" to whence they came is closer to the popular idiom.

Because of the difficult subject of this research, I am forced to create a pact with the reader. These are not "ordinary" lives that I am describing. Rather, they are often short, violent, and hungry lives. I am offering here a glimpse into *Nordestino* life through a glass darkly. Hence, the reading entails a descent into a Brazilian heart of darkness, and as it begins to touch on and evoke, as Peter Homans noted (1987), some of our worst fears and unconscious dreads about "human nature" and about mothers and babies in particular, the reader may feel righteous indignation. Why am I being served this? Conversely, what is an appropriate and respectful distance to take with the subjects of my inquiry, one that is neither so close as to violate their own sense of decorum or too distanced so as to render them the mere objects of anthropology's discriminating, sometimes incriminating, "gaze"? I begin, then as always, with stories (some of them stories within stories) because storytelling, intrinsic to the art of ethnography, offers the possibility of a personal, yet respectfully distanced, rendering of events from the "once upon a time" or "long ago and far away."

Lordes and Zezinho:
The Ambiguities of Mother Love

In 1966 I was called on for a second time to help Lordes, my young neighbor, deliver a child, this one a fair and robust little tyke with a lusty cry. But while Lordes showed great interest in the newborn, she ignored Zé, who spent his days miserably curled up in a fetal position and lying on a piece of urine-soaked cardboard beneath his mother's hammock. The days passed and with Lordes's limited energy and attention given over to the newborn, Zezinho's days seemed numbered. I finally decided to intervene. In taking Zé away from Lordes and bringing him to the relative safety of the creche, I repeated the words that Alto women often used when deciding to rescue a *criança condenada* (condemned child) from a relative or neighbor. "Give me that child," I said, "for he'll never escape death in your house!" Lordes did not protest, but the creche mothers laughed at my efforts on behalf of such a hopeless case. Zezinho himself resisted the rescue with a perversity matching my own. He refused to eat, and he wailed pitifully whenever anyone approached him. The creche mothers advised to leave Zezinho alone. They said that they had seen many babies like this one, and "if a baby *wants* to die, it *will* die." There was no sense in frustrating him so, for here was a child who was completely "lifeless," without any "fight" at all. His eyes were already sinking to the back of his head, a sign that he had already begun his journey into the next life. It was very wrong, the creche mothers warned, to fight with death.

Their philosophy was alien to me, and I continued to do battle with the boy, who finally succumbed: he began to eat, although he never did more than pick at his food with lack of interest. Indeed, it did seem that Zé had no *gosto*, no "taste" for life. As he gained a few kilos, Zé's huge head finally had something to balance on. His wispy, light hair began to grow in, and his funny, wizened, old man face grew younger once his first two teeth (long imprisoned in shrunken gums) erupted. Gradually, too, Zezinho developed an odd and ambivalent attachment to his surrogate mother, who, when frustrated, was known to angrily force-feed him. Then the power struggle was on in earnest; once when Zé spit his *mingau* in my face, I turned him over and swatted him soundly on his skinny, leathery backside. He wouldn't even give the satisfaction of crying. Throughout all, Zé's legs remained weak and bowed, and long before he could stand upright, he would drag them behind him in a funny sort of hand crawl. Once he became accustomed to it, Zé liked being held, and he would wrap his spindly arms tightly around my neck and his legs around my waist. He reminded one of a frightened Brazilian spider monkey. His anger at being loosed from that uncomfortable, stranglehold position was formidable. Zé even learned to smile, although it more resembled a pained grimace. Withal, I was proud of my "success" and of proving the creche mothers wrong. Zé *would* live after all!

There were many other little ones in the creche like Zezinho, but none had arrived quite so wasted as he, and none ever engaged me in quite the same way. But as the time approached to return Zé to his mother, my first doubts began to surface. Could it be true, as the creche mothers hinted, that Zé would never be "quite right," that he would always live in the shadows "looking" for death, a death I had tricked once but would be unable to forestall forever? Such "fatalistic" sentiments were not limited to the creche mothers by any means. A visiting pediatrician from the American Midwest took a dim view of the creche. At first I could not understand his negative reactions. What could be wrong? Each of the thirty-some creche babies wore hand-laundered cotton diapers with the monogram UPAC stitched onto each. There were handmade canvas cot-cribs and even a playpen donated by the German sisters of the local convent. In the midst of the tour of the facilities, the doctor turned away and wearily rested his head on his elbow against the wall. "What do you think you are doing?" he asked.

I had to shake myself out of my own accommodation to see what the American pediatrician was noting: that the diapers, so white from having been beaten against stones and bleached by the sun to sterilize them, were covering fleshless little bottoms. The high point of the day was the weighing-in ritual, and we would cheer when a ten-month-old would weigh in at a fraction over his "normal" six or seven kilos: "*Gordinho* [fatty]!" or "*Guloso* [greedy]," we would say in mocking jest but also in encouragement. The "toddlers" in their playpens sat on their mats passively, without crying but also without playing. They moved themselves away from the brightly colored plastic toys, unfamiliar objects altogether. The creche had something of the grotesque about it, for it was a child care center, a place where healthy, active babies should have been howling and laughing and fighting among themselves. From the visiting doctor's clinical perspective, virtually all the creche babies were seriously physically and "developmentally delayed" and likely to remain so, carrying their early damage into what could only become highly compromised adult lives.

What *was* I doing, indeed? Could Zé ever be "right" again? Could he develop normally after the traumas he had been through? Worse, perhaps, were the traumas yet to come, as I would soon be returning him to Lordes in her miserable lean-to on the trash-littered Vultures' Path. Would he have been better off dead after all that I had put him through? And what of Lordes? Was this fair to her? She barely had enough to sustain herself and her newborn. But Lordes did agree to take Zezinho back, and she seemed more interested in him now that he looked a bit more human than spider monkey. Meanwhile, my own interest in the child began to wane. I was beginning to "let go." By this time I was becoming better socialized to Alto life. Never again would I put so much effort where the odds were so poor.

When I returned to Bom Jesus and the Alto in 1982 among the women who formed my original research sample was Lordes, no longer living in her lean-to but still in desperate straits and still fighting to put together some semblance of a life for her five living children, the oldest of whom was Zé, now a young man of seventeen. Zé struck me as a slight, quiet, reserved young man with an ironic, inward-turning smile and a droll sense of humor. He had long, thin, yet obviously strong, arms; I could see that they had always served him well, compensating for legs still somewhat bowed. Much was made of my reunion with Lordes and Zé, and the story was told again and again of how I had whisked Zé away from Lordes when he was all but given up for dead and had force-fed him like a fiesta turkey. Zé laughed the hardest of all at these "survivor tales" and at his own near-miss with death at the hands of an "indifferent" mother who often forgot to feed and bathe him. Zé and his mother obviously enjoyed a close and affectionate relation-

Lordes and Zezinho (with cigarette): "This boy is my arms and legs."

ship, and while we spoke, Zé draped his arm protectively around his little mother's shoulders. There was no bitterness or resentment, and when I asked Zé alone and in private who had been his best friend in life, the one person he could always count on for support, he took a long drag on his cigarette and replied without a trace of irony, "Mãezinha [my little mother], of course!" For her part, Lordes gave "homage" to her son as her *filho eleito*, her "elect," or favorite, son, her "arms and legs," she called him, more important to her than the shadowy, older man with whom she was then living and more beloved than any other of her living children.

To understand Lordes (and Zezinho) better, I asked my old friend if she would be willing to tell me her life story. Lordes readily agreed, although she blushed modestly as she asked, "Do you think people 'there' would find anything of interest in my life?" I assured her that "they" would. When I arrived the following Saturday to the dirt road along the banks of the Capibaribe River in the Campo de Sete where Lordes was living with elderly widower Seu Jaime, her door was bolted shut and her five-year-old cried pitifully from within, begging me to spring him from his dark cage. Some neighbors sitting in a circle at the end of the street assured me that Lordes was expecting me and that she would be home from the river soon.

We managed to liberate the child, who, happily seated on the lap of a neighbor, was the first to spy his beloved mama coming up the river trail, her head bouncing under the weight of a heavy basin of wet laundry. Although Lordes had been out in the sun all morning and was fairly splattered with brown freckles, she was still very much the *galega*, "fair one," of her childhood nickname. Lordes bore little resemblance to her oldest half-sister, Antonieta, with Antonieta's coppery skin and her high, Amerindian cheekbones, and even less did she resemble her half-sister, Biu, the darkest of the three with her warm brown skin, dark brown hair, and black, black eyes. It was as if the three "races" of the Northeast had united under the banner of their mother's notorious "promiscuity." "*Mãe era fogo* [Mom was dynamite]," the half-sisters liked to say in referring to their mother's casual indifference to monogamy and in explaining why each of them had a different father.

After awkwardly embracing, Lordes and I quickly entered her cramped but neat little cinder block house. Time has been kind to Lordes, who was sliding toward rock-bottom *pobridão* (grinding poverty) when I first encountered her in her lean-to of cardboard, sticks, and discarded Food for Peace bean sacks. Her present surroundings, though simple in the extreme, were pleasant, the few furnishings and wall hangings arranged with evident care. All the more must she have suffered the indignity of her Alto campsite.

"So you want my life story? Well, my history is really something, almost like a television soap opera. I was born in 1948 on the Engenho Bela Vista, but my mother soon gave me away to her sister, my aunt, Tia, because Mãe had to be gone from the house working. My father was good to Mãe until she got pregnant. That's when he started to abuse her, and after I was born he wouldn't have anything more to do with either of us. When the second baby was born, Pai walked out on us for good. We have not heard from him since; I don't even know his name. The baby boy wasn't any good anyway. He only lived a few weeks. But Mãe made her way in spite of these problems. She wasn't one to sit and cry about spilled milk.

"Mãe washed clothes seven days a week, and one of my first jobs was to find her at the river and bring her lunch. She never washed clothes in the same place, so I had to learn how to walk the *mata* from an early age. I had other jobs, too. It fell to me to gather the *capim* [grasses] for the animals and to search for kindling wood, all the outdoor jobs. I wasn't much good at housework. Antonieta was better at that.

"I never learned to read or write, although Mama and Auntie tried to make me go to school. It was no use. I learned to sign my name, but not very well, because it is a complicated name and it has a lot of parts to it. When I was about five years old Mãe took me away from Tia and gave me to another woman, a woman who lived next to us on the plantation. It was during this time that my aunt found a job as a maid in Recife, and she could take only one child with her. So we got divided up. Mama took Biu, Tia took Antonieta, and I stayed at Bela Vista with my godmother, Dona Graças.

"My *madrinha* was a real mother to me. Dona Graças raised me with care and great sacrifice. In those days food was scarce, and some days all we had to eat was the coarsest manioc flour, *farinha de roça*. I found it hard to swallow because of a sickness that injured my throat when I was a small baby. It made my godmother sad to see me getting skinny, so she begged a few spoonfuls of the finest whitest *farinha* every day from her *patroa* so that she could make me a smooth custard. When there was no other food, Madrinha would take an ear of hard Indian corn, and she would roast it and coax me into eating the dried kernels one by one. I was close to dying more than once, but my godmother fought with me to stay alive. And she won!

"When I was fifteen I married for the first time. I became the legitimate wife of Severino José da Silva. But it was a marriage that wasn't worth much, and it soon fell apart. We lived in a tiny room built onto the side of Tia's house on the Alto do Cruzeiro, so small you could only lie down in it. Severino was miserable the whole time we were together. He never wanted to marry me; it was Mama and Auntie who forced him into it. In those days when a boy ruined a virgin, he was made to marry the girl, and if he refused, the judge could put him behind bars. So when it happened like that to me, Mãe and Tia went to the judge and made a formal complaint against Severino. When he heard what my family was up to, he ran away. But a boy of fifteen doesn't have too many places to hide, and within a week he was back on the Alto staying with friends. José Leiteiro, the old *pai dos santos* (Xangô master), spotted Severino, and he ran down the path, grabbed him, and tied him up good. Then José called Mãe and Tia, and the three of them carried Severino to the judge. Severino refused to have me, and so the judge locked him up. Severino stayed in jail for two weeks until he gave in. When they let him out, I was standing right there in my best dress, and they married us on the spot with two police for witnesses. It was a real *casamento matuto*, a shotgun wedding!

"Even though we didn't have a good start to our marriage, I was determined to make it turn out all right. I worked myself sick. I did everything I could to put food on the table, but all Severino did was lie around and mope. He was lovesick, but not for his bride! You see, all along Severino had promised himself to another woman, and during the time that he was living with me, he was always thinking about *her*. That's why he had put up such a fight not to marry me. Finally, he left me to live with his other woman. By then I was almost glad to be rid of him.

"Well, once Severino was gone, I had to figure out what to do. First I lived with Mãe, then Auntie, and then with our neighbor Beatrice. Bea found me a live-in job as an assistant to a shoemaker and his wife in town. I lived with them for two years, and then I outgrew it. So I left to work outside of town in a ceramic factory, and that's where I met my second husband, Nelson. Nelson's job was firing roof tiles, and he was very skilled at this. I can't really say that Nelson was my 'husband,' though, because I was still legally married to Severino. And I can't even say that we 'lived together' because Nelson was very attached to his old grandmother, and he never stopped living with her the whole time we were together.

"At first Nelson was good to me. Every Saturday he would climb the Alto to visit, and he always brought a basket of groceries for the week. He never once came empty-handed. And so everyone really thought of him as my husband. But after I got pregnant, everything changed. Nelson began to abuse me. It looked like I was going to follow in my mother's footsteps. I was actually glad that my firstborn died right away. Things got better for a little bit, and then I was pregnant again. After Zezinho was born, things went from bad to worse. I was living in a hovel without even a roof over my head. It was worse than living in an outhouse. Virgin Mary, goats on the Alto lived better than me! But I clung to Nelson thinking that he would change. I had it in my head that he mistreated me only because he was so young and still very attached to his grandmother. But finally I began to see that Nelson was abusing me for the fun of it. It was a kind of sport. He wanted to keep making me pregnant just so he could threaten to leave me again and again. I was young and emotional and so I cried a lot, but once I saw what he was up to, I got stronger, and I put him out for good.

"That was all well and good, but there I was still living in my stick house with my stick baby, Zezinho. What a mess, and I was only eighteen years old! I was my mother's daughter for sure. That's when I decided to go to Ferreiras to find work picking vegetables. I spent three months working in the tomato fields, and that's where I met Milton, my third husband, the one you liked so well and whose tongue was so tied up in his mouth that no one could understand him. They put us working together on the same *quadro*, and he looked over at me, and I looked over at him, and before long nature had its way. I was too afraid to say anything when I got pregnant again because Mama and Tia were losing patience with me. So I tried to hide it, and I never told anyone at all about Milton.

"I was low and dispirited during this time. It was the only time in my life that I didn't have energy for anything. I didn't have any interest in Zezinho, and I never did anything to prepare for the birth of Wagner. That's how it happened that I had to call on you at the last minute to cut the cord. I didn't care about anything. I *wanted* that baby to die and Zezinho, too. But it turned out to be a pretty baby. Still, they were the cause of my misery! I was so unhappy that I didn't pay any attention when you took Zé away to raise him in the creche. You could have taken him and never brought him back, for all it mattered to me then. *Oxente*, and today that boy is my arms and legs, more than a husband, better than any husband could ever be!

"After Wagner was born there was no reason to hide what was going on. So finally Milton came to visit, carrying a big sack of fresh corn on his head to give as a present to Mãe. He told both Mãe and Tia that he was responsible for the baby. And that's how he became my third husband. Well, with Milton I finally had some luck. It worked out, and I wound up living with him for fourteen years. I was pregnant ten more times with him. I had three miscarriages and seven live births, and of those I managed to raise four. So we didn't do badly. The three of his that died all died quickly. The first one died in his hammock while I was away working. One of the older children killed him. He got too close and yelled in his ear. He just frightened that baby to death. He died of *susto* in less than a day, and I didn't suffer very much. The other two were weak and sickly from birth. They had no 'knack' for life. The other four came into the world ready to confront [*enfrentar*] hardship and suffering, and so naturally they lived.

"Although things were going along well enough with Milton, I took a fancy to leave him and take up with Seu Jaime, the old widower I live with now. What can I say? First you love one, and then another one comes along, and your heart goes out to him. Isn't it Jesus that made us this way? Didn't he put these feelings into our hearts? If it is wrong, then we will be punished. That I know. Milton accepted it without much of a fuss. He went back to live in the *mata*, and people say that he has found himself another wife on the Engenho Votas and that he has a new family already. I'll say one thing about Milton: he has never forgotten his own children, and he always sends us produce from his *roçado*.

"I have been living with my old man for almost four years now, and it hasn't been easy. Because of our sin, violence entered our lives. The first real trouble came from Jaime's side. A group of his first wife's relatives stoned him one night as he was coming home from work. They left him bleeding and unconscious on the sidewalk. 'My poor old man,' I said, 'what have they done to you all because of me?' How was it their business anyway? Jaime's first wife was dead, and he was free to do what he wanted with the rest of his life, even throw it away on a woman such as me! Jaime's old in-laws were Protestants, and they didn't want to see their family tainted by association with the likes of me. By bringing Seu Jaime down, I was bringing shame on them as well.

"Seu Jaime was so injured that he couldn't go back to work for a long time. I thought that we might have to move back to a shanty on the Alto. But then as luck would have it, my first husband, Severino, died suddenly, and as I was still his legal wife and not the other woman he'd lived with all these years, I was entitled to the widow's pension. So in the end it paid off, and Severino's pension brought a little bit of comfort into our lives. Now I hope that we are entering a period of calm and tranquility and that God has finally forgiven us."

Our Lady of Sorrows

Mother, behold your Son; Son, behold your Mother.

John 19:25

Lordes and Jaime's period of tranquility was short-lived, however. Perhaps God had not forgiven them after all. Or perhaps it was that death once again came stalking Zezinho as if to square an old and bad debt. On my next return to Bom Jesus in 1987 I was told the news immediately: "Go find Lordes—she has suffered a terrible tragedy. She is mad with grief." I found Lordes at home disconsolate, plunged into a profound mourning. With tears coursing freely down her suddenly, prematurely aged cheeks, Lordes explained that her favorite son, "her arms and legs," had been brutally murdered on the night of the feast of São Pedro by his lover's ex-husband. Zé had been fooled; he never knew that his girlfriend had a husband. Lordes struck her breast in grief.

"If only my Zé were alive today, my life would not be one of suffering and misery. Not one of my other children turned out like him. On the day he died he left my house filled with enough groceries for a month. It was as if he knew he would be leaving me. I couldn't eat for weeks after the murder, and it pained me to look at all the food he had left me: yams, manioc, pimientos, beans. . . . These other wretched children of mine, they only know how to drive me crazy by asking for things. As soon as Zé was old enough to work, he said to me, 'Little Mama, now you are free. You will never have to worry again. You won't have to depend on some worthless bum to feed and protect you. I will see that you always have enough to eat and a bed to sleep on. I will be your protector. And he was! He was like a mother to me! He never forgot me, even after he found a woman of his own. How many mothers can say that about their son?"

With Seu Jaime sitting next to her, passively holding his distraught wife's hand, Lordes told what happened on the night that her son's life was taken: "I had a premonition that something bad was about to happen. All during the days of the *festas juninas* I warned Zé to be careful. I told him that it was during fiesta time that people take advantage of the chaos to do evil things, to get into fights, to take drugs, to steal, even to kill. Zé became impatient with my fears. On the eve of São João, Zé came home very late, and I was up waiting for him, biting on my knuckles. Zezinho was so angry that he spoke to me like he never had before, for he was always very respectful. But this time he said, 'Old woman, get off my case. Can't you understand that I am a man now and that I need to be about my own business? When I am out late, you know where you can find me: I am at the home of Rosita, my sweetheart.'

"It was on the next market day, the eve of São Pedro, that Zé brought me home those groceries. He called it my 'holiday basket,' trying to make up for the mean words he had thrown at me. But I still wasn't consoled. He left to work the afternoon shift at the factory, and when he came home it was already late. He put the radio on very loud, playing *forró* music. I begged him, 'Zezinho, for the love of God, it's late. Put that music down low. My head is pounding.' He refused. So I yelled at him again. Finally, he slammed the radio off, and he rushed out in a bad mood. It was the vesper of Saint Peter's, the night of the festivities, and before he left I grabbed him by the shoulders, begging him to be careful. I told him that a mother cannot stop herself from worrying and that I had a 'bad feeling' that night. Zé laughed and kissed me good-bye. To make amends he asked me for my blessing. *Ai, meu filho,* it is my one comfort!

"I tried to lie down next to Jaime, but I couldn't get my mind off Zezinho. Finally, I drifted off to a restless sleep, half awake, my ears cocked to hear the latch and to know finally that he was home safe. But I was awakened instead by the sound of grunting, 'Ugr! Ugr!' the ugly noise that a huge pig makes when it is angry or frightened. I thought it must really be a hog that had gotten into the food that I had stored away in the back of the house, but when I went out to look with my flashlight, everything was black and silent and tranquil. You see, that was the moment of his death. Zé was letting me know of his final *agonia*, his death throes. Just as I turned around to go back to bed, a bat swooped down on me. It swirled around my head and around my shoulders, then around my belly. It wouldn't leave me! I swung my arms around to defend myself saying, 'Holy Virgin Mary, protect me from this mad creature! Leave me; leave me at once!' And just as suddenly as it came, it swooped back up into the black sky and out of sight. That was his soul telling me good-bye.

"I went back to bed and slept fitfully until finally there was a clamoring at the door. I sat straight up in bed. Oh, I knew, I knew! A sharp pain pierced me in my chest, and then I had no doubt. Jaime jumped up out of bed, and I followed him to the front door. When we opened it, there was a crowd of people outside. As soon as they saw me, someone cried out, 'Protect the mother! Don't tell her! Bring her inside for the love of God!'

" 'No,' I screamed, 'for the love of God, tell me! Tell me what has happened to my son? What have they done to my child? Is he in jail?'

" 'No, Little Mother Lordes, he is dead,' a young boy was brave enough to say. 'His body is in the hospital. You can go and get it now.'

"That was the end. I fell down into a heap on the ground, completely demolished. Jaime rushed out into the crowd and to the hospital. He left me there on the ground. I don't remember what happened to me after that. On his way to the hospital Jaime met a man with a long woolen cape who said, 'I know who murdered your son, and I know where he is hiding.' But Jaime was too distraught to grab the man and take him with him. Instead, he ran on all the way to the end of town to get the body, to bring Zezinho home to me, what was left of my son."

Lordes could go on no more, and after she went inside to lie down, Jaime put his finger to his lips to silence me while he reached up for a box hidden away among his things. In it was a photograph of Zezinho, taken as he was found, bleeding and already dead, sprawled awkwardly across the steps leading down the backside of the Alto do Cruzeiro. His eyes were open, and the blood was seeping through his shirt. I turned away quickly, stifling a scream. My head began to spin.

"The mother must *never* see this," said Seu Jaime. "She must never know that I have the photo hidden away. It would *kill* her altogether." I wished that Jaime had remembered that one time, long ago, the dead man had been my "son" as well.

Mother Love and Child Death

Love is always ambivalent and dangerous. Why should we think that it is any less so between a mother and her children? And yet it has been the fate of mothers throughout history to appear in strange and distorted forms. Mothers are sometimes portrayed as larger than life, as all-powerful, and sometimes as all-destructive. Or mothers are represented as powerless, helplessly dependent, and angelic. Historians, anthropologists, philosophers, and the "public" at large are influenced by old cultural myths and stereotypes about childhood innocence and maternal affection as well as their opposites. The "terrible" power attributed to mothers is based on the perception that the infant cannot survive for very long without considerable nurturing love and care, and normally that has been the responsibility of mothers. The infant's life is a vulnerable thing and depends to a great extent on the mother's good will. Sara Ruddick (1989:34–38) has captured the contradictions well in noting that mothers, while so totally in control of the lives and well-being of their infants and small babies, are themselves under the dominion and control of others, usually of men. Simultaneously powerful and powerless, it is no wonder that artists, scholars, and psychoanalysts can never seem to agree whether "mother" was the primary *agent* or the primary *victim* of various domestic tragedies. And so myths of a savagely protective "maternal instinct" compete at various times and places with the myth of the equally powerful, devouring, "infanticidal" mother.

Whenever we try to pierce the meanings of lives very different from our own, we face two interpretive risks. On the one hand, we may be tempted to attribute our own ways of thinking and feeling to "other" mothers. Any suggestion of radically different existential premises (such as those, for example, that guide selective neglect in Northeast Brazil) is rejected out of hand as impossible, unthinkable. To describe some poor women as aiding and abetting the deaths of certain of their infants can only be seen as "victim blaming." But the alternative is to cast women as passive "victims" of their fate, as powerless, without will, agency, or subjectivity. Part of the difficulty lies in the confusion between *causality* and *blame*. There must be a way to look dispassionately at the problem of child survival and conclude that a child died from mortal neglect, even at her or his mother's own hands, without also blaming the mother—that is, without holding her personally and morally accountable.

Related to this is the persistent idea that mothers, *all* mothers, *must* feel grief, a "depth of sorrow," in reaction to infant death. Women who do not show an "appropriate" grief are judged by psychoanalytic fiat to be "repressing" their "natural" maternal sentiments, to be covering them over with a culturally prescribed but *superficial* stoicism, or they may be seen as emotionally ravaged, "numbed" by grief, and traumatized by shock. But it was indifference, not numbing or shock, that I often observed. The traumatized individual does not shrug her shoulders and say cheerily, "It's better the baby should die than either you or me" and quickly become pregnant because little babies are interchangeable and easily replaced.

One may experience discomfort in the face of profound human differences, some of which challenge our cultural notions of the "normal" and the "ethical." But to attribute "sameness" across vast social, economic, and cultural divides is a serious error for the anthropologist, who must begin, although cautiously, from a respectful assumption of difference. Here we want to direct our gaze to the ways of seeing, thinking, and feeling that represent these women's experience of being-in-the-world and, as faithful Catholics, their being-beyond-this-world. This means avoiding the temptation of all "essentializing" and "universalizing" discourses, whether they originate in the biomedical and psychological sciences or in philosophical or cultural feminism.

On the other hand, there is the danger of overdistancing ourselves from those we are trying to understand so as to suggest that there is no common ground at all. This is found in some deconstructionist and postmodernist theories of gender politics where the categories of "woman" and "mother" are rigorously problematized and deconstructed out of existence.[4] Less radically, one can see the "overproduction of difference" in the writings of those modern social historians who have suggested that mother love is an invention of the "modern" world and that until very recently in human history women scarcely knew how to love their children (see Aries 1962; Badinter 1981; de Mause 1974; Shorter 1975). The language of these historians can be extreme and off-putting.

"The history of childhood," wrote de Mause, "is a nightmare from which we have only recently begun to awaken. The further back in history one goes . . . the more likely children are to be killed, abandoned, beaten, terrorized, and sexually abused" (1974:1). Edward Shorter concurred. With respect to early modern England he wrote that "mothers viewed the development and happiness of infants younger than two with indifference," which was why their "children vanished in the ghastly slaughter of the innocents that was traditional child-rearing" (1975:168, 204). Writers in this genre have often pointed to such "child-hostile" and covertly "infanticidal" cultural institutions as "wet-nursing," "foundling homes" (Trexler 1973), the early introduction of baby "pap" and other unnutritious weaning foods (Phillips 1978; Fildes 1986), and the common use of laudanum syrup and other narcotic "pacifiers" (Engels [1845] 1958:161) throughout the early modern period of Europe, which contributed to high rates of infant and child mortality.

William Langer (1974:360–361), for example, referred to the wet nurses of early modern Europe as those "angel makers" and "baby killers" who kept the infant coffin makers busily employed in Italy and France from the fourteenth through the nineteenth centuries. Wet nurses, recruited from the poorest social classes and paid but a pittance for the servitude of their bodies in nurturing the infants of more affluent classes, were poorly motivated and rarely punished for the frequent deaths of the infants charged to their indifferent care. Maria Piers (1978) referred to the institution of wet-nursing as little more than a public license to kill unwanted and excess babies in societies in which active infanticide was sanctimoniously condemned by church and state. Thomas McKeown (1976) argued that such culturally established but harmful infant- and child-tending practices as these served to check population growth in Europe for many centuries.

Nevertheless, social historians continue to debate whether the observed indifference of mothers to the fate of their infants in the early modern period was merely a reaction or an actual contributor to the death of young children. Most historians have tended to reject the mortal neglect hypothesis for an interpretation of maternal indifference as less the cause than the effect of high infant and childhood mortality. In this view the distanced emotions are but an "unconscious source of emotional armour against the risk of seeing the object of their affection die" (Badinter 1980:58). But where early human life is precarious in inhospitable urban slums and shantytowns, maternal indifference (whether intentionally or not) exaggerates the risks and exposes vulnerable infants to premature death. Nonetheless, in identifying the role of neglect in the etiology of infant mortality, one must be careful not to isolate it from its origins in pernicious social and economic relations. The attention to mothering and mother love can obscure the fact that the greatest threats to child survival from the early modern period to this day (and through all stages of industrialization) have been extreme poverty and exploitative female wage labor.

So perhaps there is a middle ground between the two rather extreme approaches to mother love—the sentimentalized maternal "poetics" and the mindlessly automatic "maternal bonding" theorists, on the one hand, and the "absence of love" theorists, on the other. Between these is the reality of maternal thinking and practice grounded in specific historical and cultural realities and bounded by different economic and demographic constraints. Maternal practices always begin as a response to "the historical reality of a biological child in a particular social world" (Ruddick 1980:348).

Seen in the context of a particular social world and historical reality, the story of Lordes and Zé conveys the ambiguities of mothering on the Alto do Cruzeiro where mortal selective neglect *and* intense maternal attachment coexist. Alto mothers, like Lordes, do sometimes turn away from certain ill-fated babies and abandon them to an early death in which their own neglect sometimes plays a final and definitive part. But maternal indifference does not always lead to death, and should an infant or a toddler show, like Zé, that he has a hidden "talent" for life, his mother may greet the "doomed" child's surprising turnabout with grateful joy and deep and lasting affection. And these same "neglectful" mothers can exclaim, like Lordes, that they live only for their grown children, some of whom only survived in spite of them. In so doing, these women are neither hypocritical nor self-delusional.

One of the benefits of returning to the Alto do Cruzeiro after a sixteen-year hiatus was the chance to observe the happy outcomes of several memorable cases of severe, selective neglect, children who survived and were later able to win their way inside the domestic circle of protective custody and parental love. Whatever else it is, the customary practice of selective neglect on the Alto do Cruzeiro is not what we in the United States mean by child abuse. It is not motivated by anger, hate, or aggression toward the small baby, for that would be seen as grotesque and unnatural by the people of the Alto. The impoverished, neglected, and often abandoned women of the Alto are more likely to express "pity" than anger toward a frighteningly sick, needy, and overly demanding baby. Moreover, Alto mothers are entirely disinclined to strike what is seen as an innocent and irrational little creature, and (unless they are mad or psychotic) they never project images of evil or badness onto an infant.

Mother love is a richly elaborated theme on the Alto do Cruzeiro, as in Brazilian *Nordestino* culture and society at large (see Aragão 1983), and it is celebrated in folklore and folk art, in popular music, and in an intense devotion to the Virgin Mother and to São Antônio, the patron saint of mothers and children. But it is especially the mature Mary, the widow standing tearfully at the foot of the cross or sitting in its shadow while cradling the dead adult Jesus in her arms, her own heart (like Lordes's) pierced with a sword, that is the popular image of long-suffering motherhood and of tormented but sanctified mother love in this community. Our Lady of Sorrows, Nossa Senhora das Dores, reigns over Bom Jesus as the *município*'s patron saint. Her statue is taken down from its grotto over the main altar of the church, and bedecked with many floral wreaths she is paraded through town on various holy days during the year (see Figure 8.1). But images of the young mother Mary at the creche, holding her fat infant in her arms or suckling Him at her white breast, that are so common to Catholic imagery and iconography in northern Europe and North America (see Fernandez 1979:70–71; Kristeva 1980:237–270) are curiously absent in Bom Jesus da Mata even during the Christmas season. On the Alto do

Our Lady of Sorrows.

Cruzeiro the birth of a child is hardly a time of rejoicing, and mother love follows a tortured path, often beginning with a rocky start and fraught with many risks, dangers, separations, and deaths.

On the inhospitable, rocky outcrop of the Alto do Cruzeiro mother love grows slowly, tentatively, and fearfully. The cheerful and resilient "maternal optimism," of which Ruddick (1989:74) wrote, that allows the mother to greet each new life born to her hopefully gives way in the shantytown to dark clouds of maternal pessimism, doubt, and despair rooted in the un- happy experience of repeated infant death. "Can it be," asked Margarita, "that Jesus wants me to leave this world without having raised a single, living child?" And so the doubt allows a mother to reject an infant born weak and sickly as a child not worth keeping, a child without a knack for life. Or maternal optimism can degenerate into its opposite, a "cheery denial" (Rud- dick 1989:75), so that a plump Maria das Prazeres can breezily dismiss her skeletal son's anorexia, born of the child's frustrated hunger, by saying of him, "Gil doesn't 'like' to eat so we don't 'waste' any food on him."

Holding on and Letting Go— The Pragmatics of Mothering

What mother among us living in a secure and protected household has not once in her life had to suppress the wild impulse to throttle a child—even a helpless infant—within an inch of her or his crying, complaining, demand- ing life?[5] And what middle-class mother has not on more than one occasion "forgotten" about a child, left a terrified toddler to wander through racks of women's dresses on the crowded floor of a midtown department store while herself absorbed in a shopping frenzy? What mother has not put a fussy, "hyperactive" child down to nap once too often in the day or in winter sent older children out to play in the "fresh air," even as their red fingers were near frozen, so as to enjoy uninterruptedly a cup of coffee and a long and much anticipated visit with a dear friend? Yes, we have all done these or similar things with (at least we like to think) little harm done.

Most mothers, despite such "lapses," fall into that broad and forgiving category that D. W. Winnicott called "ordinary, devoted mothers" or, al- ternatively, "good enough" mothers (1987:16). For Winnicott, "holding" is the root or generative metaphor of nurturing, the "prototype of all infant care" (37). Indulging the infant in her or his basic need for enfolding, protective "holding" allows the newborn to feel both "*secure* enough" and "*real* enough" to begin developing an autonomous ego. In Eriksonian terms, "good enough holding" anchors the infant's "basic trust" in the world (Erikson 1950:247–251). Ordinary, devoted mothering has, for Winnicott, an overdetermined and existential quality about it. It is where humans start from: a mother and an infant, each "naturally" adapted to nourish the other. In most instances the mother knows by "intuition," or she readily finds out by experience, how to hold and handle a baby so that both she and the infant are comfortable.

As a child psychoanalyst, Winnicott was concerned with the psychological and developmental risks to the young baby resulting from the odd "failures" in what he called "the ordinary, devoted mother principle." Gross disturbances in early nurturing, which Winnicott described in both actual and metaphorical terms as "letting baby down" rather than "holding baby up," can produce "unthinkable anxieties" in the infant. He referred to the infant's fears of falling apart, of "going to pieces," of "falling forever," and to feelings of utter and total isolation. "I've watched and talked to thousands of mothers," wrote Winnicott, "and you see how they pick up the baby, supporting the head and body. If you have got a child's body and head in your hands and do not think of that as a unity, and reach for a handkerchief or something, then the head has gone back and the child is in two pieces— head and body; the child screams and never forgets it. *The awful thing is that nothing is ever forgotten*" (1986:55).

The continuity of life has been broken for the infant, and the child emerges from this painful drama of "having been let go of" with a residue of anxiety and a lack of confidence in things, including a solid belief in his or her own reality. Such instances of gross failure in protective and nurturant "holding" are, however, extremely rare, and Winnicott, who more than any other child psychoanalyst tended to side with mothers, suggested that normal child development requires only ordinary and "good enough," not perfect or excellent, mothering. His clinical experiences as a pediatrician and later as a child psychoanalyst working with thousands of English mothers and children led Winnicott to the conclusion that the ordinary, good enough home is common, even usual. But even though Winnicott's benevolent theory of nurturing and his innate trust of mothers are refreshing, they are based on an overly optimistic view of the *infant's* adaptiveness.

Within the physically threatening context of shantytown life, where so much greater vigilance is required to keep an infant alive, even the smallest lapse in maternal attention and care can sometimes be fatal. Not all creche babies were saved as little Zé was; some failed to escape death despite the organized efforts of a mothering cooperative bent on child survival. And Alto women's perception of infants as somewhat strange, transient, and undependable creatures seemed warranted. Marcelinho, the abandoned infant adopted and reared by Nailza and me in 1965, suffered a series of intestinal crises that brought him to the brink of death several times in his first year of life. We viewed the infant with caution and always with a hint of "suspicion." He lived, but my strong North American belief (based on the calm reassurances of Benjamin Spock) in the natural resilience and hardiness of babies was forever shaken.

And Winnicott was strangely silent on the topic of the "good enough" baby, although sickly and handicapped babies "let mothers down" often enough. In the context of the Brazilian shantytown the meaning of good enough mothering changes. It puts a terrible burden on women who, having been "let go of" and "let down" so often themselves as well as left "holding the baby," are sometimes unable to summon up the extraordinary courage needed to "hold on" or "hold fast" to each fragile infant. Here, good enough mothering can require almost superhuman effort. As one poor Brazilian woman told another ethnographer who asked why so many infants and babies died in her community: "Look, mister, I think that here it's easy for *anyone* to die" (Nations & Rebhun 1988:175). And indeed it is.

On the Alto do Cruzeiro the threats to infants and small children in the environment seem to come from everywhere: the polluted and overly "treated" public faucet water, the gritty dirt under little bare feet, the insects in the air, the sluggish and insidious snails along the muddy banks of the river, the ticks on domestic animals, the "kissing bugs" (i.e., Chagas' disease) burrowed into the mud walls of huts, the worms in the pit latrine, the mad dogs roaming the garbage pits of the Alto, the spoiled milk left out overnight, the salted and sun-dried meat covered with maggots in a dish under the roof beam, the tuberculin fruit vendor in the public market, the wheezing, pneumatic child next door. There are reasons enough for child death in the material conditions of shantytown life. One need go no further. The various WHO and UNICEF child survival campaigns have been built around combating these environmental risks to young children in impoverished Third World communities. But my inquiry does not rest there, driven as it is by the more existential dimensions of the problem: the shaping of consciousness, reflexivity, and action in those women who are forced to make decisions and moral choices that no woman should have to make. What does mothering mean for those women who are forced to participate in the shantytown's culture and space of death? If maternal thinking is, as some suggest, a universal and natural script, what does it mean to women for whom scarcity, sickness, and child death have made that love frantic?

Sara Ruddick has suggested that although some economic and social conditions, such as extreme poverty or social isolation, can erode maternal affection, they do not kill that love. Her understanding of mother love carried resonances of Winnicott as she referred to the metaphysical attitude of "holding"—holding *on*, holding *up*, holding *close*, holding *dear*. Maternal thinking, she suggested, begins with a stance of protectiveness, "an attitude governed, above all, by the priority of keeping over acquiring, of conserving the fragile, of maintaining whatever is at hand and necessary to the child's life" (1980:350). It is, she continued, citing Adrienne Rich (1977) "an attitude elicited by the work of 'world-*protection*, world-*preservation*, world-*repair* . . . the invisible weaving of a frayed and threadbare family life'" (1980:350). Holding is an attempt on the part of the mother to "minimize risk"; it is a "way of seeing with an eye toward maintaining the minimal harmony, material resources, and skills necessary for maintaining a child in safety" (1989:79). Ruddick recognized the attendant "risks" and "dangers" of the metaphysical stance of "holding"—its degeneration into maternal overprotectiveness, holding too close, too tight, too fast, stifling the creativity and need for adventure in small children, especially in comfortable surroundings where the actual risks to child safety may be few.

But what of mothering in an environment like the Alto where the risks to child health and safety are legion, so many, in fact, that mothers must necessarily concede to a certain "humility," even "passivity," toward a world that is in so many respects beyond their control? Among the mothers of the Alto maternal thinking and practice are often guided by another, quite opposite metaphysical stance, one that can be called, in light of the women's own choice of metaphors, "letting go." If holding has the double connotations of loving, maternal care (to have and to hold), on the one hand, and of retentive, restraining holding on or holding back, on the other, letting go also has a double valence. In its most negative sense, letting go can be thought of as letting loose destructive maternal power, as in child-battering and other forms of physical abuse. But malicious child abuse is extremely rare on the Alto do Cruzeiro, where babies and young children are often idealized as "innocents" who should not be physically disciplined or restrained. But letting go in the form of abandonment is not uncommon on the Alto, and the occasional neonate is found from time to time where he or she was let go in a backyard rubbish heap. And the abandonment of newborns by their overwrought mothers is so common in the maternity wing of the local hospital that a copybook is kept hanging on a cord just outside the nursery in which the data on abandonments and informal adoptions are recorded. There is no stigma in leaving an infant behind, although the birth mother is required by the nursing staff to remain in the hospital until a prospective adoptive parent can be found. The mother rarely has to wait more than a few days. Once an adoptive parent or couple appears—and there is no regulation of the process save for the few instances in which the nurse on duty takes a personal dislike to a potential adoptive parent—the birth mother need only sign her name (or affix her mark) after a statement declaring that she has freely given up her infant son or daughter born on such a date and time at the hospital. The adoptive parent is free to register the infant as her own birth child at the *cartório civil*, and most do so. In 1986 twelve newborns, eight males and four females, were left behind in the nursery by their mothers. In 1987 ten newborns, seven girls and three boys, were abandoned. Although all the birth mothers were poor, some of them wretchedly so, and only six could sign their own names, as many of them were older (thirty and older) as younger mothers (sixteen to twenty-nine), and almost an equal number were living with a spouse or lover as those who reported themselves to be "single," "separated," or "abandoned."

But here I want to reflect on another meaning of letting go. Among the women of the Alto to let go also implies a metaphysical stance of calm and reasonable resignation to events that cannot easily be changed or overcome. This is expressed in the women's frequent exhorting of each other, especially in times of great difficulty, to "let it go," "let it pass," "let it be": *Deixe, menina—deixe isso, deixe as coisas como são para ver como ficam.* In other words, "Leave it be, girl; leave things alone, and see how they turn out for themselves." This attitude demands a leap of faith and of trust, one not easy for most Alto women to achieve. Nonetheless, the pursuit of a blessed calm—what the early Christian monks and Church Fathers called "holy indifference"—in the face of turmoil and worldly adversity remains a cherished religious value among *Nordestino* peasant Catholics. It is a value that is often misunderstood and diminished by secular anthropologists who refer to it as "peasant fatalism." Some ethnographers who insist on seeing poor *Nordestino* women as very much like themselves deny that this particular existential stance exists at all (see, for example, Nations & Rebhun 1988). But the ethos of "holy resignation" in the face of chronic "troubles" exists, and it informs maternal thinking and practice. It is present each time Alto mothers say that their infants are "like birds," nervous and flighty creatures that are here today and gone tomorrow. A perfectly good mother can in good faith and with a clear conscience let go of an infant who "wants" to escape life, just as one may set free into the heavens a miserable wild bird that was beating its wings against its cage.

"What does it mean, *really*," I asked Doralice, an older woman of the Alto who often intervenes in poor households to rescue young and vulnerable mothers and their threatened infants, "to say that infants are like birds?"

"It means that . . . well, there is another expression you should know first. It is that all of us, our lives, are like burning candles. At any moment we can suddenly 'go out without warning [*a qualquer momento apaga*].' But for the infant this is even more so. The grownup, the adult, is very attached to life. One doesn't want to leave it with ease or without a struggle. But infants are not so connected, and their light can be extinguished very easily. As far as they are concerned, *tanto faz*, alive or dead, it makes no real difference to them. There is not that strong *vontade* to live that marks the big person. And so we say that 'infants are like little birds,' here one moment, flying off the next. That is how we like to think about their deaths, too. We like to imagine our dead infants as little winged angels flying off to heaven to gather noisily around the thrones of Jesus and Mary, bringing pleasure to them and hope for us on earth."

And so a good part of learning how to mother on the Alto includes knowing when to let go of a child who shows that he wants to die. The other part is knowing just when it is safe to let oneself go enough to love a child, to trust him or her to be willing to enter the *luta* that is this life on earth.

We can think of these women as existentialists in their view of the world, a view that casts life and death not as polar opposites but as points along a continuum called the *caminho*, the "path" of being. Their words and actions suggest a faith in death as a valid part of existence, so that death, too, must be *lived.* Over some of their very young children falls a shadow, an "inevitable death-certainty" (as Ludwig Binswanger [1958:294] called it), that troubles and continually disrupts their short-lived existence. Here, the pragmatics— in more deft hands than my own we might even speak of an alternative "poetics"—of mothering is one that requires calling on all the resources and strengths necessary to help one's own sickly, disabled, or weak infant or young baby to let go, that is, to die quickly and well. Although in dying the infant ceases to exist in normal space and time, she passes into eternity where she exists entombed in an eternal moment of transcendent love, as imagined by Doralice and other women of the Alto. Or perhaps we should say "hoped for" by Doralice because she added this disclaimer: "Well, this is what we say, this is what we tell each other. But to tell you the truth, I don't know if these stories of the afterlife are true or not. We *want* to believe the best for our children. How else could we stand all the suffering?"

A Criança Condenada

What does it mean to let go of a baby? What is the logic that informs this traditional practice? Alto mothers spoke, at first covertly (often lowering their voices and looking about nervously to see who might be in earshot), of a folk syndrome, a cluster of signs and symptoms in the newborn and young baby that are greatly feared and from which mothers (and fathers) recoil. One way or the other, premature death is in the cards for these babies, and parents hope that it will be a rapid, not particularly "ugly" death. They certainly do not want to see their little ones suffer. These hopeless cases are referred to by the very general and euphemistic terms *child sickness (doença* de criança) and child attack (ataque de menino). Sometimes the syndrome is simply referred to as that illness or the ugly disease. Mothers avoid repeating the specific and highly stigmatizing names or descriptions of the conditions subsumed under "child sickness, child attack." These include gasto (wasted, spent, passive), batendo (convulsed), olhos fundos (sunken eyes), doença de cão (frothing, raving madness), pasmo (witless), roxo (red), pálido (white), susto (soul shocked), corpo mole (body soft, uncoordinated), and corpo duro (body rigid, convulsed).

The infant afflicted with one or more of these "dangerous" and "ugly" symptoms is generally understood as doomed, "as good as dead," or even as "better off dead." Consequently, little is done to keep him or her alive. The sequela that follows a folk diagnosis of child sickness may be understood as a not uncommon practice of passive euthanasia traditional to the people of the Alto. The practice of letting go an infant and young baby is recognized by old and young across at least four generations of moradores of the Alto do Cruzeiro and by men as well as by women. It exists within the context of a "popular," or folk, Catholicism that is independent of the formal teachings of the Catholic church in this regard.[6]

Because these ugly sicknesses are not easily or readily talked about, even among women, for fear of "calling them up," and because there are so many different forms and varieties of child sickness and child attack, it is difficult to estimate just how many Alto babies die with their mothers suspecting the worst and sometimes hastening their end. Of the 255 infant and child deaths reported by the Alto women in my sample (see Table 7.6), 39 of the deaths were directly attributed to "child sickness." But one can also suspect an additional 37 babies said to have died of weakness, the 14 deaths from fright sickness, at least some of the deaths from teething sickness, and many of those said to have died "suddenly," de repente. In all, these folk diagnoses would account for 110, or 43 percent, of the child deaths reported by Alto mothers. Whatever else it is, child sickness is not a rare phenomenon in the shantytown; Alto mothers view it as one of the most common causes of the premature deaths of their children. Although child sickness and child attack can afflict children from birth to age five and even seven, on the Alto do Cruzeiro, where the vast majority of all child deaths occur in the first twelve months of life, the condemned child syndrome is in reality the condemned infant syndrome.

The symptoms and signs of child sickness refer to a host of serious pediatric conditions that, although not necessarily fatal, are deemed likely to leave the mother with a permanently damaged or severely disabled child: excessively weak or frail, retarded or mad, mute, epileptic, paralytic, crippled—in short, "unprepared for life." The key symptoms that both alert and alarm mothers to a possible case of child sickness or child attack include rapid emaciation; virulent and uncontrolled pediatric diarrhea; deathly pale skin or flushed and red spotted skin; fits and convulsions with bubbles, saliva, or froth from the mouth; glazed or sunken eyes; weakness and lethargy; a loose, uncoordinated body; an inability to focus the eyes or steady the head. Within the folk etiological system almost any "ordinary" illness can "turn into" a case of doomed child sickness; therefore mothers must learn to differentiate between a "light and ordinary" case of *susto* and one that has "turned" into a "heavy" and presumably terminal case of child attack.

Women say that there are seven, sometimes fourteen or twenty-one, different types of child sickness, each of these subsumed under the two main poles, chronic (*doença de criança*) and acute (*ataque de menino*). There is little agreement among women on the identified "varieties" and subtypes. Midwives, praying women, and other traditional healers of the Alto recognize many more varieties than do ordinary Alto women. Dona Maria the midwife insisted that there were as many as twenty-one recognizable types of child sickness, but even when applying great concentration, she could come up with only twelve.

"First there is *gasto*, the most common form of child sickness. Many infants come into the world that way, sickly and wasted. Then there is the kind where the child's body is bruised, battered, or crushed and the type where the infant cries and cries without stop. Another kind comes from a great fright that startles the baby, who never gets over it. Then there is the kind where the baby has purple lips and purple fingernails. How many is that?"

"I think that's about five, Dona Maria; you have a lot to go yet."

"I still have more in my head. There's the one that gives nonstop vomiting and green, foul-smelling diarrhea. There's the kind that expresses itself in yelling and making ugly faces. [She demonstrated.] There's another that makes the baby sleep too much, with a laziness so great that he doesn't even wake up to suck or to eat. This one is related to the one that makes the infant stupid so that it drools all the time. There's the ugly kind that gives fits in the child, with eyes that roll to the back of the head or eyes that 'flicker-flicker' fast like this. [She demonstrated.] There's the kind that makes the child bang its head and throw its body against the ground. Finally, there is the kind that makes the child defective, paralyzed, and crippled. That's it."

Despite the lack of agreement on the specifics, all the women noted the two main varieties: (1) wasting and passivity and (2) convulsions and wild fits. Table 8.1 summarizes the most commonly identified subtypes of child sickness.

Each master symptom alerts the mother to the precarious ontological

Table 8.1. Qualities and symptoms of the doomed child syndrome.

Chronic Child Sickness (Doença de Criança)	Acute Child Attack (Ataque de Menino)
Gradual wasting; premature aging (gasto)	Suddenness of onset (de repente)
Weakness, frailty (fraqueza)	Screaming (gritando); colicky crying (chorando)
Paralysis (aleijado); lethargy, inactivity, passivity (preguiça)	Fits, seizures, head banging (batendo, bate-bate)
Retardation (boba); shocked, witless (pasmo)	Foaming, spittle, drooling from mouth (espumando)
Body, limbs soft (corpo mole)	Body rigid (corpo duro); neck stiff, body extended
Pale, white, ghostly (pálido)	Discoloration, purple or red blotches on stomach, buttocks (roxo); purple fingernails
Teething (denticão); trapped teeth (dentes recolhidos)	
Eyes sunken, fallen to back of head (olhos fundos)	Shallow, rapid breathing (falta de ar)
Fallen fontanelle (moleira funda)	Acute startle reflex (susto)
	Explosive, loose, green stools, vomiting (dobrando e vomitando direto)

status of her child. "There are various qualities of child sickness," said Jurema. "Some die with rose-colored marks all over their body. Others die purple, almost black, colored. It's very ugly. With these diseases it can take a long time for the baby to die. It takes a lot out of the mother. It makes you sad. But still, these sicknesses we do not treat. If you treat them, the child will never be good [bonzinho], never worth anything. Some become crazy. Others are weak and sickly their whole life. They can never work or take care of themselves."

Dona Norinha, the elderly midwife, added the following: "Who doesn't know what this disease is? It's what an infant gets from a susto in the womb because of an angry mother. Her anger poisons the infant's blood, and so it is born small, defective, soft, stupid, its body all slack. Sometimes the tongue hangs out of the mouth, and the eyes never focus anywhere. Months pass but the infant never learns to hold its head up." In response to how many different types of child sickness there were, the old midwife turned into a tease, and pointing to the crowd of children gathered outside her open door, she said, "Why, there's one type for each and every child. One like him, one like her, one like that little one over there." And the children screamed and scattered to their respective homes.

The chronic sufferers are those infants born small and "wasted." They are often deathly pale babies, mothers say, as well as passive and unresponsive. Such infants demonstrate no vital force or liveliness. They do not suck vigorously. They hardly cry. They are "uninterested" in food and, seemingly, in life itself. Here is what some women said:

"They are very pale. They frighten easily."

"Some are very lazy infants. You put the bottle to their mouths, and their lips are soft, not tense. They just let the *mingau* dribble to the sides of their mouths. They don't pull or tug."

"They come into the world with an aversion to life. They are overly sensitive and are soon fed up [*abusado*] with milk, with *mingau*—food doesn't interest them; it doesn't hold their attention. You see, they are neither here nor there."

Women label such "transitional" or liminal infants—infants existing somewhere between this world and the next—as *difícil de criar*, "difficult to raise." They are difficult not because they are overly demanding but because they are so underdemanding, too willing and too likely to die. Others are difficult because they will cause much grief and suffering to the mother if they do live. Although many present themselves like this at birth, others are infants who, though born sound, soon show little "resistance" and no "fight" against the early childhood killers, especially diarrheas, respiratory infections, skin diseases, and tropical fevers. These are babies who "fold" too easily; they are too *mole*. Weakness is the most common symptom of "chronic" child sickness. I was told that rich people are able to raise such "weak" and "difficult" babies, but poor people need babies who are strong from the start. "They die with this disease," said one mother, "because they *have* to die. If they were meant to live, it would happen that way as well. I think that if they were always weak, they wouldn't be able to defend themselves in life. So it is really better to let the weak ones die."

These babies die, mothers say, *à míngua*, of slow and gradual neglect. The term, a colloquialism, specifically indicates a death from wasting. Its literal meaning is to "shrink" or "shrivel up." The same expression is used by women who have been recently abandoned by a husband or a lover. They say that their "worst fear" is that they will be left to die *à míngua*, abandoned and hungry, wandering the streets like a miserable cur. Most infants presented as suffering from chronic and wasting child sickness are simply tiny famine victims whose hunger is often complicated by severe diarrhea and dehydration. The deaths from hunger can be painfully slow as babies sometimes summon an incredible energy to put up a final resistance, and the parents can suffer a great deal in the process. "It hurts the mother to see her baby delay so in dying," says Seu Manoel with reference to the death of a one-year-old daughter the year before from chronic child sickness. "The mother didn't cry, but *I* cried for her, seeing our little bit of nothing slowly disappear. But God is God. If we didn't have a mighty faith in Him, we would put a rope around our neck and kill ourselves."

There is no expressed guilt or blame for those who aid such deaths, for babies allowed to die *à míngua* are seen as wanting to die. Those wanting to live will survive no matter what. One young woman speaks of the recent death of her fifth child, a little girl of four months, in this way: "I was sick all through the pregnancy and her infancy. I didn't pay any attention to her [*nem ligou, não*]. With all that I have to attend to, I didn't fuss. I couldn't do everything just right. I didn't boil her water. I didn't take a lot of care with her *mingau*. I wasn't vigilant against the flies and mosquitoes. And I don't fight with the older children to make them wear shoes all the time. It's rare to find a child who doesn't love playing in the mud. I can't stop all manner of sickness from coming to my children. If they have the strength, the courage for life, they will live despite everything. And if they don't, it doesn't matter what you do to prevent it; they will die anyway. That's what I can see. Julieta died because she never grabbed the nipple. She *herself* never took hold [of life itself]. If she died it was because she herself, on seeing what was ahead, what was in store for her, *she* decided to die."

Sometimes an older woman or a midwife intervenes and helps a mother to decide at birth whether to keep a baby (in the popular idiom, to wash a newborn) or to put the infant "aside." The elderly midwife Dona Maria explains, "When a baby is born *saudável* [healthy and robust], I instruct the mother to give the infant a cleansing herbal tea, a *chá de erva santa*. This will clean out its system and strengthen the baby. But if the infant is born puny and wasted or *incômodo* [ill-fated], I instruct her to withhold the tea."

"Why?"

"Because the tea may cure the baby."

"What's wrong with that?"

"Because in some cases it is better if it dies. If she cures it, the baby will be damaged. It will never be worth anything. So I tell her to dust the infant with Johnson's baby powder and to wait for Jesus to come and take it."

"Does she feed the baby anything?"

"No one is going to let a newborn die of hunger. We let *Jesus* decide the appropriate hour, according to His plan, not ours."

"What is the infant fed then?"

"The mother may give just a little bit of weak milk, nothing to strengthen or to fortify the infant, no strong, whole milk, no vitamins. She is to give only that little *mingau de água* [watery gruel]. Just a small taste a couple of times a day will do. And then she can wait for Jesus to decide the rest."

The mother, then, has merely allowed "nature" to take its course. She sees herself as cooperating with God's plan and not (as in the case of induced abortion) as thwarting God. The true, real cause of death is seen as a deficiency in the child, not in his or her poor, distracted mother. Zulaide, pregnant for the fifth time at the age of thirty-two, speaks of her puny one-year-old son sitting in her lap, "He's still living, but he won't be for long! He can't stand up; he can't speak a word. He spends most of his day on the floor because I can't hold him in my arms all day. He has fevers and diarrheas, diarrheas and fevers. The doctors say that he will be like this unless I take him to the Children's Hospital in Recife. But I can't afford to treat him special. I couldn't breast-feed him because I am not in good health. It wouldn't help him or me, would it? I can't make him special foods. He's no better than the others! So he gets the same inferior quality of milk in bulk that they do. I know it is too weak for him, and that's why he is so witless. But if he dies, so be it. He is *not* the only one I have."

At the other, and more frightening and extreme, pole are those "doomed" infants who die suddenly and violently. They are often recognized by a red flush or by purple blotches or other marks or discolorations of the skin or fingernails. These babies are given to fits, their little bodies may go into contortions, their backs and necks may become rigid or extended. They sometimes shake their heads violently, "wanting" to bang themselves against a wall or floor. They screech, make terrible faces, and sometimes foam at the mouth. They can look like wild, rabid animals, their mothers say. *Moradores* suspect that the cycles of the moon may play a part in the illness. They are described as "red" babies in contrast to the pale, chronic, "white" babies. Child attack babies can die quickly, sometimes overnight. The infant can be dead before the mother is even aware that anything is wrong. Célia's fated twin infants, for example, gave her "no trouble" in dying: they simply "shook, rolled their eyes to the back of their heads, and were still." Other infants can suffer repeated "attacks," and this is particularly "heavy" for the mother because she may have to act decisively. She may have to "remove" the infant; there are others in the family to think about and to protect. "When the infant begins the *bate-bate*, banging its head around, we put it on the floor to the back of the house, and we leave it alone," offers Zefinha, the mother of two infants who died of child attack. Alto women speak plainly of "putting an infant aside to die" (*a gente bota o menino fora para morrer*). Seu Zé de Mello, a seventy-year-old cane cutter, referred obliquely to child attack during a life history interview in 1989. He referred to child attack as the "sickness of wild, fierce, crazy babies who are reared on the floor [that is, not in the arms, not nurtured]." High fevers often accompany the fearful convulsions, and mothers pray that death comes quickly.

Although any number of common childhood conditions can reproduce the symptoms of child attack—encephalitis, meningitis, umbilical tetanus—most infants presented as victims of this dreaded and acute disease are babies whose bodies are thrown into shock because of the electrolyte imbalance accompanying severe diarrhea/dehydration.[7] It is the *delírio de sede*, the "madness of thirst." All of these life-threatening diseases—but especially the madness of thirst—are virulent but medically treatable conditions.[8] And Alto mothers are themselves aware that child-saving interventions exist for such afflicted infants: "*Treated, yes*, the baby can live," agreed Rosália, "but we *do not* treat it." "Why not?" "*Não adianta*," was her reply; "there's no use" (i.e., even when treated, the baby will emerge too damaged).

I decided to investigate further. At the Fundação Joaquim Nabuco in Recife I researched the archives for references to child sickness and child attack, but nowhere did I find an entry for *doença de criança* or *ataque de menino*. Finally, in a handbook on popular remedies, *Remédios Populares do Nordeste* (Maior 1986:37), I found a reference to "infantile convulsions," which the author noted were sometimes referred to popularly as *ataque de menino*. Although the women of the Alto disowned any cure, Mário Santo Maior listed several, among them immersing the child in a very cold or a scalding bath, vigorously rubbing the child's body with alcohol, feeding the child an herbal tea made of eucalyptus leaves and watermelon seeds, and giving the infant a shock by a few, sharp slaps to the face to return him to his senses.

Among popular healers in Bom Jesus, however, from the herbalists working in the public market, to the Xangô masters, to the elderly praying women of the Alto, the answer to my question was always the same: "This disease we do not treat." Dona Marcela, a praying woman, referred to the various types of child sickness as *doenção*, a "great big sickness." And her comment echoed that of Dona Rosália. "Yes," she said, "it is possible that somewhere there is a cure for these things, but it is better in these cases to do nothing at all." Dona Maria do Carmel listed all the pediatric ills that God allowed her to cure—choking, splinters, evil eye (*olhado*), and the light *sustos*. Among the illnesses that she did *not* treat were child attack, madness, and the *doença de menino*. "Why not?" "Because God hasn't given it to me to cure them."

"Yes, I know how to 'pray' all the *usual* childhood sicknesses," said the midwife Norinha. "I 'pray' to cure fevers, fallen womb, fallen fontanelle, and light *susto*, but to tell you the truth, I don't put too much faith in these prayers. And I don't want to take responsibility for the lives of all the children I help bring into the world! If I did I'd be godmother to the whole Alto, and my little house would be crowded with the world's children. I recite my prayers only for babies to be born safely, not to cure them once they're here." As for child sickness, Norinha replied abruptly, "I have *nothing* to do with that. Go talk with Nita the Marvelous; maybe she knows some cure." But Nita the Marvelous, a Xangô practitioner specializing in pediatric disease and working under the spiritual protection of the child saints Cosmos and Damião, was no help either. Nita agreed with her mentor, the great sorceress Dona Célia, that "the only cure for *doença de menino* is death itself."

Dr. Raiz, the herbalist who sold many dozens of curing herbs in the outdoor market, was outspoken. Yes, there was a cure for child attack, if one caught it at the very start of the disease. "The mothers you are talking about rarely pay attention. This class of women is too poor to take care of themselves, let alone a damaged child."

"What is this early cure?"

"The first time a child convulses, the mother should put salt in its mouth and cut the child anywhere on the body. She should take a virgin calabash, one that has never been used before, cut it in half, and put it on top of the child's stomach. The calabash will draw out the evil if it was caused by some mischief that was 'placed' on the child [i.e., by sorcery]. It is a simple cure. But among the women we are talking about, they don't want to know about a cure; they are *afraid* of a cure."

"Why is that?"

"There is a cure but never a *complete* cure. At best the baby can be 40 percent cured. Child sickness is similar to stroke in an old comrade. When an old person is felled by a stroke, aren't there things one can do? He may never be completely well, but he can recover some of his speech and movement. But if you say, the way these women do with their children, 'Ah, *não tem jeito*' [There's no solution], well, naturally, he will just lie there. The old man will remain totally useless, paralyzed and mute. It is the same way with child attack."

Meanwhile, most clinic doctors in Bom Jesus knew nothing of child sickness and child attack, although a few had heard poor mothers use the terms. "Child sickness?" Dr. Antônio, the medical director of the municipal health clinic, replied. "Isn't that measles and whooping cough, that sort of thing?" Dr. Fernando, another clinic doctor, shook his head. "No, I don't think I have ever come across it," he said. But during a *cafezinho* break at the hospital clinic with Dr. Gloria and several nurses, my question elicited a positive response. "Yes, we know," the nurses said. But they deferred to Dr. Gloria, whose words were both clinical and chilling: "Child sickness is used with reference to the *criança condenada*, a species of rejected child. The mother has given up, and she is no longer attending to its needs. She will come into the clinic with a baby showing signs of third-degree malnutrition and dehydration. I take one look and say that the child can be saved only if we hospitalize it. But the mother wants no part of it. She says that the infant has *aquele* [that] disease—she won't even name it—and that there is no solution. No solution, that is, but death. In her mind the baby is already as good as dead. She is no longer interested in keeping this particular child's life going. She wants the flame to go out. The maternal sentiment is absent. It just isn't there. The afflicted child is like some object that is broken and useless [*inútil*]."

"But they *do* come to the clinic all the same. Isn't that contradictory?"

"Sometimes the women come to the clinic because they want a pretext. They want to avoid the *fofoca*, the gossip of the neighbors who might say that after all the mother let her baby die of neglect. The mother comes to the clinic looking for medicines so that later she can say, 'I went to *this* clinic and to *that* clinic, but the medicines the doctors gave me were 'weak'; they weren't worth anything. Or she will say, 'I spent so much money on expensive drugs, but in the end nothing helped.' She won't listen when I tell her that medicines aren't the real solution for her baby."

A nurse interrupted to say on behalf of the mothers, "But it is only because they are so afraid of this disease. Sometimes there is a 'crisis' of fever and the baby has a convulsion, and the mother thinks immediately that here are the signs of epilepsy. The poor people are truly revolted by that disease; they have a kind of horror of it, as if it were the devil's own sickness. They are so frightened of convulsions and fits in the baby that they will burn its clothing and hammer nails into the mud floor to prevent it from returning. Some mothers hide the fact that the baby has been sick in this way; they pretend that the sickness was a light one. The blemish, the taint, is very heavy."

Difference and Danger: Stigma, Rejection, and Death

I approach the topic of stigma as it is related to child attack and child death with some trepidation, for I do not wish to add to the burden of lives already pushed close to the margins of endurance. But the turning away in fear and rejection from certain "condemned" babies is, as Dr. Gloria suggested, implicated in infant and child death on the Alto do Cruzeiro.

Stigma is undesired difference. It is everything that makes us turn away from another human being in fear, disgust, anger, pity, or loathing. To stigmatize another human is the most antisocial of human acts, for it consigns the victim to a living death on the margins of human interaction. In the case of infants, it allows one to say, with considerable risk to the baby, that this one is not yet (or perhaps ever will be) a person at all: "*Hein, hein, coitado, mas o bichinho não sente nada, não é* [Tsk! Tsk! Poor thing, but the little critter doesn't have any feelings, right]?"

Stigma is discourse, a language of human relationships that relates self to other, normal to abnormal, healthy to sick, strong to weak. It involves all those exclusionary, dichotomous contradictions that allow us to draw safe boundaries around the acceptable, the permissible, the desirable, so as to contain our own fears and phobias about sickness, death and decay, madness and violence, sexuality and chaos. The tactics of separation allow us to say that *this* person is *gente*, one of us, and that person is *other*. Erving Goffman (1963) referred to the first encounter between "normal" and stigmatized "other" as a sociological primal scene, a special moment when the moral economy that governs social relations is unmasked and the society reveals itself in the very phenomena that it disowns, excludes, and rejects.

I shall never forget one such "primal scene." It was in February 1966, and I was in a crowded bus crossing the desert *sertão* of Pernambuco on my way with a busload of rural pilgrims to the city of Juàzeiro do Norte, birthplace of the great local saint and miracle worker Padre Cícero (Cícero Romão Batista). Since the death of the so-called *padrinho da gente* (everybody's godfather), Juàzeiro do Norte had become a celebrated site of pilgrimage (see Slater 1986). We were all in high spirits after several hours of travel inland from Recife, and we had begun to entertain one another with songs and travel stories. Jugs of cheap, sweet red wine were passed back and forth. Each of us carried our secret petitions that we would lay at the feet of the huge ceramic statue of Padre Cícero, requests for miraculous cures, for the recovery of lost objects or missing or disappeared persons, for success in love, marriage, business, child bearing, and so on. It was a special moment, a time out of time.

Along the way, deep into the *sertão,* the bus was flagged down by a couple standing along the edge of the open and barren highway with no shelter from the brutal sun save a battered black umbrella. One was a young woman, a *matuta*, in a long-sleeved, modest cotton dress. She removed a pair of sturdy shoes from a paper bag and slipped them on her feet just as the bus came to a halt. Alongside her was an elderly *campesino* in plastic sandals and straw hat. He was very frail and extremely thin. His daughter (or so I assumed) was solicitous toward him and gently helped to lift him onto the bus. It was a desperate stretch of empty road, and they must have walked some distance to get to the highway and then waited some time for a bus to pass. Once settled in the back of the bus they could not make themselves invisible, for it soon became apparent that the old man was sick, very sick indeed. His hacking paroxysms of coughing were punctuated by his spitting into a tin can carried for that purpose. The singing and jovial spirit of camaraderie were broken by the man's incessant, choking, tubercular cough.

Not too much time passed before the bus driver again pulled to an abrupt halt. He motioned for the couple to come forward, and the girl bent down to whisper a few words to the driver, who did not respond. He simply opened the front door of the bus and officiously waved the couple out. Not one of us protested as the pair slowly and gingerly descended from the bus onto another parched, empty piece of highway. It would be hours before another bus came their way. We continued on in silence for quite some time until one passenger let free a nervous, yet loud and cracking, fart. The tension broke and we laughed, each pointing to the other accusingly. Some brought out bottles of cheap cologne to sprinkle around the seats, "purifying" the air. The singing and the jocular mood resumed as before "the incident." We were safe, a "community" once again.

We have all observed, or even ourselves participated in, such primal scenes of inclusion/exclusion. With the possible exception of AIDS babies, however, we are not accustomed to thinking about stigma with reference to *very* little people. But I am going to suggest that the rejection of "failed" babies is the prototype of *all* stigmatization. Whereas stigma may consign the spurned adult to a life of exclusion and marginality, the stigmatization of a hopelessly dependent neonate or infant is inevitably a death sentence. The sickly, wasted, or congenitally deformed infant challenges the tentative and fragile symbolic boundaries between human and nonhuman, natural and supernatural, normal and abominable. Such infants may fall out of category, and they can be viewed with caution or with revulsion as a source of pollution, disorder, and danger. The African Nuer studied by E. E. Evans-Pritchard (1956) referred to the physically deformed infant as a "crocodile" child and to twins (another kind of birth anomaly) as birds. Few Nuer twins or crocodile infants survived, and when they died Nuer said of them that they "swam" or "flew" away. Birds return (or are returned) to air, and amphibious infants return (or are returned) to water, the medium in which each really belongs.

Elsewhere, physically different and stigmatized infants may be rejected as "witch babies" or as "fairy children." Among the rural Irish of West Kerry, old people still speak of "changelings," sickly or wasted little creatures that the fairies would leave in a cot or a cradle in the place where the healthy human infant should have been (Scheper-Hughes 1979; Eberly 1988). Irish changelings, like Nuer bird-twins, were often "helped" to return to the spirit world from whence they came, in some cases by burning them in the family hearth. Carolyn Sargent (1987) studied birth practices among the West African Bariba of the People's Republic of Benin, where a traditional form of infanticide was practiced until very recently to rid the community of dangerous witches held responsible for all manner of human misfortune. Witches were believed to present themselves at birth in the form of various physical anomalies, among them breech presentation, congenital deformity, and facial or dental abnormalities. Such infants were traditionally exposed, poisoned, or starved. When the Bariba came to live in ethnically diverse urban communities and to give birth in modern hospitals, the killing of stigmatized witch infants was, of course, prohibited. Instead, such marked infants now live, carrying their stigmas with them and suffering an inordinate amount of consequent physical abuse and neglect. Witch babies grow up into witch children and later into community scapegoats, blamed for all manner of unfortunate events.

In the Brazilian Amazon infanticide was normatively practiced by many Amerindian peoples in the interests of social hygiene. Today, church and state intervene, as they do in most parts of the world. Nevertheless, Thomas Gregor reported that infanticide is still practiced today, although covertly, by the Mehinaku Indians in the case of twins, illegitimate births, and birth defects. The birth of a deformed infant is referred to as a *kanupa*, a forbidden or a tabooed thing, and it is a source of great shame to the parents. At birth each infant is carefully examined: "We look at its face, at its eyes, its nose, and at its genitals, its rectum, its ears, its toes and fingers. If there is anything wrong, then the baby is forbidden. It is disgusting to us. And so it is buried" (1988:4).

Moreover, the Mehinaku contrast their own native wisdom with the irrational behavior of those urban Brazilians who allow their deformed babies to live: "The Brazilians have many worthless, disgusting individuals among them. There are people we have seen without eyes, without noses, without ears, without legs. In São Paulo there was even a man with two rectums. If such a child were born here it would be buried in the ground immediately. Not nearby, no, but over there, far away! That is why we are beautiful!" (4). While stigmatized shantytown infants would not be buried in a hole or poisoned, such children are sometimes viewed and treated as a "taboo" thing, and some of these are, as we have seen, gradually, yet mortally, neglected.

I do not wish to suggest, however, that Brazilians are more prone to stigmatizing the sick or the different than we are. Social life in rural Northeast Brazil tends, if anything, to be more, rather than less, tolerant of human difference than elsewhere. The sickly and the disabled who survive childhood are, with few exceptions, well integrated into public and community life. Meanwhile, madness circulates freely in the marketplace and in the downtown plazas of Bom Jesus in the form of known and tolerated village fools, clowns, and madmen and women. The blind, the deaf, the lame, and the leprous are common sights in Bom Jesus, particularly on market day, when professional beggars come into town. Tropical, infectious, and communicable diseases are not uncommon, even among the middle and upper classes, and there is little attempt to exclude many of the sick from active participation in town life.

Nonetheless, certain forms of sickness are particularly loathed and feared, so much so that few will repeat even the name of the disease. In the 1960s, when it was still rampant in the Northeast, tuberculosis was one of these highly stigmatized diseases. It connoted squalor, filth, promiscuity. Generally it was hidden, and always it was denied. Today, epilepsy, acute psychotic episodes, and rabies fall into the category of dreaded and profoundly stigmatizing diseases, and, largely by analogy, so do the acute symptoms of child sickness and child attack, which appear to mimic epilepsy and madness.

I have no data on the prevalence of epilepsy in Bom Jesus, but rabies remains a real threat. In 1986, seven residents of Bom Jesus were bitten by rabid animals, and all received the painful course of injections at the local health post. Five of the seven animals were identified and destroyed. Hardly a field trip to Bom Jesus passes without at least one incident of a chaotic mad-dog pursuit, often culminating in a collective killing of the suspected animal in the streets and *praças* of Bom Jesus. The killing can take on a festive quality, and sometimes merely scroungy, hungry, stray curs without signs of the disease are attacked and killed by roving gangs of animated street children armed with sticks and stones. It is unfortunate that infant child attack is often equated with rabies and is sometimes referred to with revulsion as the *doença de cão*, "dog's disease" (rabies). Maria Pãozinho spoke from sad experience: "People are afraid of child attack. It is a foul disease, the same as rabies in a dog. It is a *moléstia mental* [mental perturbation]. My baby son suffered from attacks, and he would spit his food right out on the floor. My other children were hungry, and they would run to pick up the tainted morsels that he had spit out and put it into their own mouths. I would scream at them to stay away. But thanks be to God, none of them caught it from him."

"And what happened to your afflicted son?"

"He was sick for a long time, ever since he was two years old. After a *susto* he began knocking himself against the wall, *se batendo, se batendo*, without stop. I prayed to God to take him and not to leave me with such a child. I made many vows to Jesus, the Virgin, and São Severino de Ramos that they might take him. But he waited to die until he was ten years old, when a fever finally claimed him."

"Who can possibly raise such a defective child?" I was asked rhetorically on many different occasions (with respect to child attack), and the answer was invariably: "Only saints," living saints such as Dona Marta or Dona

Amor (see chapter 3), those exemplary, dedicated women who had devoted their lives to raising a demented (*doido*), sickly (*fraco*), crippled (*aleijado*), paralyzed, or wild (*brabo*) child on the Alto do Cruzeiro. The efforts of such women, in light of the social and economic realities of Alto life, were nothing short of heroic.

João-Fabiano, for example, is a gangly, healthy twelve-year-old, all sprawling adolescent arms and legs. His movements, however, are jerky and uncoordinated, and he is both mute and autistic. The neighbors say that he is crazy (*doido*), wild (*brabo*), and altogether defective (*defeituoso*). They are afraid of him. But to the children living nearby his hut on the far side of the Alto, João-Fabiano is a great source of sport and entertainment. They throw stones at him whenever he approaches. They imitate his grunts, and they run squealing if he pays them any mind. Dona Marta tries to keep her son safely inside their tiny two room hut as much as possible during the day, but this is complicated by the presence of her husband, four other children, and a grown daughter living there as well with two other small children. There is hardly room for a "wild child" like Fabiano, who rocks, knocks his head, and shrieks from his favorite place on the floor under the table when he is not tangled up in his patient mother's arms intently scanning her face as if it were a treasure map. "He cannot get enough of my face," his tired mother offers. "But when I ask him to give me a real embrace, he scampers away screaming. When I ask him if he understands me, he seems to be following me. And, look, when I ask him, 'Do you love me, Fabiano?' he gets so agitated trying to speak. He is trying to say, 'I do.' But I fear that he will kill me in the end."

Dona Marta attributes her son's condition to a *susto* experienced as a toddler when she took him visiting at the house of a crazy person on the Alto. The *doido* frightened Fabiano so much that he ran outside and fell into a mud hole. He came home soaked, dirty, and babbling nonsense and has been sick since that time. He was even worse, Dona Marta adds, before he was hospitalized at an asylum in Recife for three years. Today he is taking ninety drops of liquid chlorpromazine three times a day. The antipsychotic medicine "calms" Fabiano down enough so that he can sleep. Before he had the medication, Fabiano cried and thrashed himself around and banged his head on the floor. He was *bobo* (stupid) and *bêbedo* (drunk, dizzy, and uncoordinated). It was pure misery, she says. "What unhappiness in this house with one child who can walk but can't talk and another [a reference to one of her grandchildren] who can talk but can't walk." Although her neighbors refer to Fabiano as afflicted with the terrible disease, Dona Marta herself long resisted the diagnosis of hopeless child attack, and she tried "everything" to cure her son, all in vain. I did not, of course, ask this poor

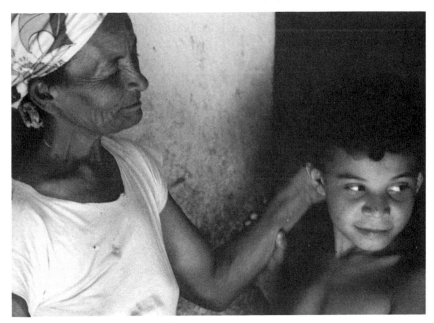

Mother love: Dona Marta with her autistic son.

distracted woman whether she would agree with those neighbors who say of Fabiano, without batting an eye, "It would have been better if that boy had been allowed to die as a baby, rather than grow up afflicted with that ugly disease."

Indeed, this is the very same advice that Dona Maria the midwife gives to Alto mothers in cases of suspected child sickness or child attack in a newborn. Dona Maria bases it on her own sad experience. "It is harsh to say this, but sometimes I warn the new mother right away, 'This one we won't need to wash, no.' "

"But are you always sure about this?"

"Yes, it happened to me, so I know. No one is immunized against that disease. It can strike anyone. My own daughter was born *d'aquele jeito* [that way], little and weak, and I decided right away to let her go. But it didn't happen the way I wanted, no. My *comadre* came visiting that same day, and she took pity on the little creature. She gave her a good, cleansing tea, and then she gave her a little *mingau*. And so the girl lived until she was fourteen, stupid and senseless the whole time. My child only grunted. She never learned to walk or to talk. She survived pretty long, but in the end finally she died. She was 'born dying,' and because of my *comadre*, I had to suffer a long time until she finally did die."

What people of the Alto fear most of all is a public spectacle in which one of their own children could be involved. Anything, even early death, is better than to confront a scene such as the one that occurred in August 1989 in the manioc market on *feira* day, when the "defective" son of Seu Daniel "fell down" with the terrible, shaking, falling disease (i.e., epilepsy/madness) in view of hundreds of local people.

As the vendors were preparing to pack up their sacks of produce and head for home, there was a ruckus near the door of the enclosed market, and a crowd formed rapidly around a young boy of about fifteen who was either in a deep trance state or at the start of a grand mal seizure. He was violently twitching and drooling at the mouth, and his eyes were unfocused. "Virgin Mary, Our Lady, protect us," said an older woman standing at the outer rim of the circle, "I think it is *that* disease, the falling down sickness!" The boy in a semisomnambulant state, shaking and growling, lunged with bared teeth for the throat of a woman. The crowd screamed and scattered in all directions, creating a stampede for the door. Marcelo, the agile young manager of the municipal market, jumped the boy from behind and pinned him to the ground. He needed help. The boy's strength, in the midst of a severe fit, appeared superhuman, prodigious. He thrashed arms and legs, foaming freely at the mouth, his eyes lost in the back of his head. The crowd alternated between screams of fear and wonder at the boy and cries of encouragement to Marcelo and two other men attempting to carry the boy out of the market. I followed the parade. The boy was brought first to Feliciano's pharmacy for a tranquilizer injection, but no attendant there dared to approach the wild child. Nor would any taxi driver agree to take them to the local hospital. Finally, the afflicted boy's older brothers arrived in a pickup truck. After expertly roping their brother like a young steer, they tossed him in the back of the truck. Later I learned that he was taken to the home of Dona Maria Umbandista on the Rua da Matadoro, where he was pacified, at least temporarily.

A visit with Dona Maria Umbandista in the company of Marcelo on the following day proved instructive. After receiving permission from her spirit familiar, Ogum (Saint George), Dona Maria and her apprenticed daughter emerged from their small *salão de trabalho*, their sacred "workroom," and agreed to talk to us about the boy's affliction. It helped that Dona Maria's elderly father, although very nearly blind, recognized me as "the *moça* of the Alto."

The boy was indeed, Dona Maria began, "touched" with the falling disease (i.e., epilepsy) because of spirit possession. When he was carried over her doorstep, the possessed boy was screaming, "I am Zé Pilenta [a troublesome mulatto spirit with a taste for cigarettes, women, and rum], and I want to drink your blood. I want to see your blood spilled on the floor." The boy's older brothers were beside themselves. Two other *curandeiras* had refused to treat the boy, saying that his sickness was too "heavy" for them to deal with. They suggested Dona Maria as a last resort. The tiny woman agreed to accept the boy as a patient and asked that he be brought inside while she prepared herself in her workroom. In a few minutes she emerged dressed in her ritual clothes, including the scabbard and sword of her protector, Ogum/Saint George. Thus armed as a warrior and in a protective trance with Ogum at her shoulders, Dona Maria did battle with the boy's spirit, laying her hands and Ogum's sword on his head and shoulders, demanding the spirit to depart, which it did almost at once. The boy fell back onto the bed exhausted and sweating profusely. He blinked his eyes, which came into focus, and then begged for a glass of water. After gulping down three cups of sugar water, he asked Dona Maria what had transpired. He recalled nothing. She told the brothers to take the boy home to rest for twenty-four hours, after which they might return for a complete diagnosis and therapy. Dona Maria's hunch was that the boy was possessed not by Zé Pilenta, a mere mischief maker, but by a much more powerful and dangerous spirit, Exu of the Seven Crossroads himself.

Dona Maria's elderly father, who was sitting with us in the front room, bent down to trace in the dirt floor with the tip of his walking stick the four quadrants of the crossroads, "the place," he explained, "where everything bad collects." It was the place where women "trashed" their aborted fetuses and where the pagan souls of the unbaptized gathered to do the bidding of the Evil One. In the dead center of "all this evil," the old man continued, Exu lived. The unfortunate man or woman possessed by Exu was in serious trouble. There were only three possible outcomes: he (or she) killed someone, committed suicide, or was killed by others first. The one possessed by Exu was doomed.

With such frightening examples, it is little wonder that Alto women sometimes see the premature death of certain marked children as the only solution. Child sickness, especially acute child attack, has something of the uncanny about it. The infant appears "touched" by some unnamed power or force. The illness is heavy, of the kind more appropriate to adults. Acute child attack presents and looks very much like the symptoms of epilepsy, rabies, stroke, malevolent spirit possession, schizophrenia, all of them highly stigmatized conditions on the Alto do Cruzeiro. There is often a suspicion of magical foul play, for these "evil," shaking sicknesses mimic the deep trance states of the Xangô adepts and their spirit familiars. Could the infant have been "sorcerized"? Has something heavy, a curse, been "put" on the child? Such babies are fierce. They foam at the mouth. They bite like animals. But chronic child sickness also appears as premature aging, as if

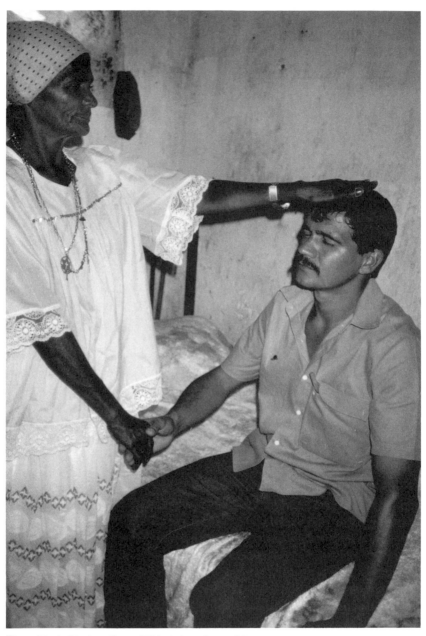

Dona Maria Umbandista: "This is how I cured him: 'Be gone, Exu!' "

one's beautiful little infant had been replaced by a wizened and toothless old man, one with a soft body and limbs without strength or definition. Their wrinkled, pale, pinched-in little faces can make these babies appear much wiser and sadder than their months or years allow. All this adds to the perception of their "untimeliness" and the strangeness of the disease.

In all, child sickness, especially child attack, is an "infectious" and polluting condition, and a careful mother protects her other children from contact with the contaminating sibling. An older child will be slapped for eating the tainted baby's leftovers. But it is also believed that the sickness in its earliest stages can be magically transferred to stray animals. While her baby is in the throes of an acute attack, a mother may take a small piece of raw meat and wash it around in her wild child's mouth. If after throwing the "infected" meat to a stray dog, the animal begins to show signs of rabies, her own afflicted baby will be spared. The dreaded disease has now passed into the body of the animal "familiar."

Otherwise, the afflicted infant or small baby is isolated. No one tries to pick up or rock such a child. She or he will often remain hidden away in the folds of a too large hammock. No one blames a mother for turning away from such ill-fated infants and babies. Neither does the mother hold herself responsible for deaths that are hastened by a reduction in food and liquid. Because the principle underlying maternal care and nurturance on the Alto is based on "demand," hungry and dehydrated babies are allowed to refuse their meals. Such babies eventually withdraw and shy away from human contact. They become fussy and profoundly unhappy creatures, difficult to engage and impossible to satisfy. Although slowly starving to death, such babies rarely demand to be fed or held. Because they are so passive, they can be left alone for long periods of time. Consequently, their feeble whimpers signaling a final crisis may be heard by no one while their mothers are away working in the *roçado* or in the big house, and many such babies die alone and unattended, their faces set into a final, startled grimace—an ultimate *susto*—that they will take with them into their tiny graves.

A mother's single responsibility is to thrust a candle into the dying infant's hands to help light the path on the journey to the afterlife. After the hurried burial of such a baby, the older children, who formed the funeral procession, come home and change their clothes to remove all traces of the stigmatized illness. Meanwhile, the dead infant's clothes and diapers are burned or buried, and holy water or the favorite cologne of Xangô is sprinkled around the corners and roof beams to purify the house. If one is not careful, the dead child may return to "pull away" another child into the grave after it. Dona Xiquinha explained, "Once a little boy on the Rua Fun da Mala died suddenly of the accursed disease. Less than a month later his

Child attack: the madness of hunger.

baby brother died as well. The father wanted to bury the two in the same place, and when he uncovered the grave of the first, he found the dead infant completely intact and smiling, waiting for his brother. Imagine! Normally in the heat of these tropics it takes only seven days for a baby to begin to disintegrate [*estoura*] in the grave."

"But what *really* is this *doença de criança* so I can explain it better to people back there?" I demanded of a small group of Alto women, two of them local healers. "And why is it *so* feared?" "Pronto!" Dona Maria slapped her hands together and replied, "Isn't this child sickness another term for death itself? And isn't child attack the very same death throes [*agonia da morte*] that we all must suffer at the moment of our deaths? Who can stand in death's way? When death comes to claim its due, *you* will die, and *I* will die. No one will escape. It's the same with our babies." It would appear from this that child attack is, above all, the personification of death in its final struggle. It is death marked, engraved, on the child, and it is death in its cruelest form: premature death, death suffered before its time. And it is an agonized death, "undeserved" by an innocent baby. Child sickness or child attack is all liminality; it is not just death but death out of its proper time and place.

Whatever the trajectory that leads up to a diagnosis of fatal child sickness, once the label has been affixed, a mantle of social death begins to envelop the small child, and the parents begin to prepare for the child's untimely end. The process is not too dissimilar to the social death and death by suggestion involved in Australian "bone pointing" and "voodoo death" in otherwise healthy individuals who have been sorcerized. W. Lloyd Warner described the following sequence of events in Arnhem Land, which has some resemblance to the social reactions to child sickness in Bom Jesus today: "The attitude taken is that the [sorcerized] man is 'half-dead' and will shortly die. The effect . . . is sufficient to set up certain psychophysiological reactions which tend to destroy him. Pressure is then applied through mortuary rites which perform the function of attempting to remove him from the society of the living to that of the dead, further destroying his desire to live" (1959:9). In recent years the classical psychogenic argument (see Cannon 1942) has been challenged in favor of a more material explanation suggesting that the actual mechanism of death in sorcerized individuals may be dehydration through the confiscation of liquids (Eastwell 1982).

In the case of the condemned child syndrome, the suggestibility of the infant is irrelevant, although severely malnourished babies do eventually lose their will to live, as their mothers so readily note. The analogies are stronger with respect to the resignation of the infant's mother and father to the inevitability of their child's death, their moving away from the child, and her or his ultimate isolation. Nor can one discount the confiscation of food and liquid, especially in small bodies already dehydrated by acute attacks of diarrhea, as when Dona Norinha cautions newly delivered mothers to give "only the smallest taste" of *mingau* to the sick infant a couple of times a day. The designated baby is just as surely trapped in the "given up–giving up complex" (see Engel 1968) as are the sorcerized aborigine of Arnhem Land. Harry Eastwell (1982) referred to the Australian social death practices as desirable euthanasia, especially among the very sick and very old when a "natural" death might be prolonged and painful. The same could be said of some cases of the doomed child syndrome in Northeast Brazil.

But ultimately I remained frustrated. The folk category of child sickness was impossibly loose, fluid, elastic, and nonspecific. It was ambiguous. How could a mother be *certain* that before her was a case of nontreatable *gasto* as opposed to an ordinary case of pediatric diarrhea? How could a mother discriminate between ordinary teething and the more dreaded and potentially fatal symptoms of trapped teeth? When was a *susto* just a bad fright, a mere startle reflex in an infant, and when was it likely to knock the soul right out of the baby? Nations and Rebhun (1988) are probably correct in suggesting that most cases of child sickness, or doomed child syndrome, are diagnosed after the fact of a child's death. Then, for certain, one can say, *"Não teve jeito"* (There was no solution, no hope, no cure). The evidence is right before one's eyes in a little blue coffin. This is compatible with the way that poor Brazilians generally diagnose their ills—that is, through a process (see Loyola 1984) of "successive elimination," a method of trial and error that reduces all the possible diagnoses down to the last one to be eliminated, a kind of differential diagnosis.

During the taping of a *carnaval* video in February 1988 (de Mello & Scheper-Hughes 1988), Neninha, who was prettily posing for an interview in front of her house, was annoyed by a sad-faced little child who kept getting in the way of the camera. Neninha finally chased her away, and the little one withdrew into a dilapidated annex at the back of Neninha's small house. The little girl belonged to a "desperate" family of rural migrants who had recently arrived from the *mata*. Inside the little annex sat a grim-looking woman in her early forties holding an infant who seemed very close to dying. The child was very white and quite still, with deep, vacant eyes. The husband, a much younger man in his late twenties, was seated on the straw mattress next to his wife. They were expecting the baby to die soon, he said. She was their third daughter. A week earlier the infant's two-year-old sister had died. Soon there would be only the firstborn left. I asked if they knew about *soro*, and they said they did, and they repeated the rehydration formula known to almost everyone today. Was the infant being fed?

"No, she is very sick with diarrhea."

"Not even rice water?"

"No, *nada* [nothing]."

"Is she baptized?"

"We will baptize her on Sunday."

"She may not live until Sunday."

"*Como Deus quise* [As God wishes], then."

Not wanting to pry any further, I left the shack, but uneasily. Outside a small knot of older creche women motioned for me to join them. In lowered voices they commented on the miserable situation of the afflicted drought victims. "*Péssimo* [abysmal]," said Teresa, whose own family had suffered hunger so many times. Plans were made to get emergency rations to the household. "What about the baby?" I asked. There was silence until Marlene spoke out: "They are letting the baby go. The father says it has that disease; there is no cure. He has forbidden his wife to give *soro* to the baby." It was better, he said, to let the baby die. The women, knowing my suspiciousness of the doomed child syndrome, awaited my reaction. But I was at a loss, and not for the first time. If not the infant, certainly the whole situation seemed doomed, the doomed family syndrome. I was tempted to say, "I think they are suffering from *doença de família*," but even black humor did not seem appropriate.

On the following day I returned to the hovel to find the situation unchanged. I questioned the father while the video camera rolled: "What is wrong with your baby?"

"It's *aquele mesmo*."

"How do you know?"

"It has the red marks on its body."

"Show me."

Gingerly the mother lifted the infant's tiny little shirt and cloth diaper to reveal a very wasted and pale but unblemished body.

"But I don't see them."

"The marks have gone away; they have retreated *inside* the baby," the father explained.

So I challenged him: "Nonsense. Men don't know anything about the ugly disease. It's something that concerns only women."

"You are wrong. Many men know about this sickness. I myself was only a boy this high when I buried my baby brother in the *mata*."

How could I have forgotten that boys, too, form part of the procession of the angels to the graveyard? Abashed, I took my leave, tucking a hundred cruzados under a chipped coffee cup. But I never saw the couple again. The baby died later that same day, unbaptized, and by dawn the remaining three had packed their few belongings and returned to the drought-plagued countryside.

I began to pay more attention to the role of men, and to fathers in particular, when in 1987 I returned to the household of Terezinha to find that Edilson, her "doomed" toddler, decided to surprise everyone and escape

Terezinha and Edilson: "He's content to sit on the floor and play with the roaches."

death after all. The last time I had seen Terezinha in 1982, she spoke continually of the little boy's "hopelessness," his refusal to swallow more than a few tablespoons of *mingau* each day, his need for "expensive" treatments that could be gotten only at the expense of her other children. Edilson was dying of *gasto*, Terezinha was quite certain, and though she often said that she took "pity" on the little fellow, she rarely held him, saying, "He's contented enough, poor thing, to sit on the floor and play with the *baratas* [large cockroaches]." I brought the boy some antibiotics, and Terezinha posed for a few photos to have as a keepsake once Edilson was gone.

But when I returned in 1987 there was the impish and undersized little boy playing soccer with a rag-ball just outside his house. Although he was nearly seven, Edilson appeared more like a four-year-old, though a terribly bright and precocious one. Terezinha invited me inside to explain what had happened. Manoel, who was laid up with a badly infected foot, was seated beside her.

"At about the time you left," Terezinha began, "I had given up. You saw the shape Edilson was in. Then he had one last terrible crisis. He was vomiting green and had a belly so swollen and tender he wouldn't let anyone touch him. He just lay curled up and miserable. I took pity on him and decided to take him one last time to the hospital clinic. The nurses said to leave him there, but I said, 'No, let me just take him home to die.' I thought for sure he would be gone in the next day or two. I just left him quietly in his hammock. I didn't want to bother him anymore.

"That night when Manoel came home from work he asked about Edilson, and I told him that it was no use, that there was no cure for the boy. But Manoel wouldn't listen. He is much smarter than I am. 'What is hopeless,' he said, 'is the local hospital. We have to carry the boy to a real clinic. So Manoel wrapped up our little bag of bones and carried him to the private clinic of Dr. Francisco Melo. This is a clinic for rich people who can afford to pay a lot. I would never have had the courage to show up there. But Manoel works for the mayor [as a construction worker's assistant], and he figured that he had as good a right as anyone to get a consultation for his son, even if he didn't have a cruzado to pay for it. When Manoel was finally called inside the consulting room, he fell apart altogether. He became very emotional and could hardly speak. He said, 'Oh doctor, I'm mad with grief. Look, I'm losing my child. I beg you to have a look at him. My wife has already given up. She refuses to do any more for him. I don't have a nickel to pay you, so I am asking you, in the name of your patron saint and for the love that he had for the poor, to attend to my dying son.' Dr. Francisco replied, 'Keep your money. I don't want any of it.' And he examined Edilson very carefully. He said, 'Your wife is right. Your son is almost dead. He will have to go to the Children's Hospital in Recife if you want to save him now.'

"But when Manoel arrived with Edilson at the town square, the municipal ambulance was already overloaded, and he was sent away. He rushed back to Dr. Francisco's clinic, and the doctor said, 'The only chance now is for me to treat the child here.' He gave Manoel a prescription for an antibiotic, and he gave the boy injections of *soro*. Manoel returned every morning for ten days, and the treatment worked. Edilson fooled death, and he got better, well almost. I hate to think what would have happened if Manoel hadn't forced himself on the sainted doctor."

Manoel was quiet throughout his wife's narration, so I asked him why it was that he could see some life in his child where his wife saw only death. Manoel replied, "Many women don't understand a lot about babies. They don't know, for example, when a baby is lying or not. Sometimes when the child cries and cries, the way Edilson did, they think he is crying for no reason, and so they hit him on the head to make him stop. But Edilson was only crying because he was hungry. His only sickness was hunger and lack of care." Terezinha fidgeted nervously throughout her husband's narration, but she did not contradict him.

Obviously, these selective neglect practices are not fully conscious or intentional maneuvers. Consciousness constantly shifts back and forth between allowed and disallowed levels of awareness. People are continually "checking" themselves and each other. On the morning that two neighbor girls called me to attend the burial of a one-month-old infant whose mother I had been urging unsuccessfully to breast-feed, the girls begged me not to "scold" the young mother but to tell her that I was sorry her baby was so sick and that Jesus had to take him. The girls looked down at their dusty sandals as they informed me of the proper Alto etiquette for infant wakes. "Yes," I agreed, of course. "But what do *you* think?" I asked. Xoxa, the younger of the two girls, blurted out, "Dona Nancí, that baby never did get enough to eat. But you must *never* say that!" The shifting levels of consciousness were also apparent at base community meetings when I took the liberty of suggesting child sickness as a topic for critical reflection through *conscientização*.

But even as some women like Terezinha (or the couple in the foregoing vignette) were all too willing "to see only death" in a child, other Alto women and men were equally likely to deny the apparent hopelessness of another infant's highly compromised condition. On one depressing afternoon awash in torrential rains, I took a shortcut past Teresa Gomes's house. Several men were resting on her windowsill and taking advantage of Teresa's new television, which was tuned to a soccer game. The men were quite drunk, and one of them commented offhandedly, "The only time Brazilians are happy is when their country is winning a soccer game. The rest is misery and decline." Teresa rescued me from the men and greeted me warmly, insisting that I come in until the rains subsided. Inside the neat little hut with Teresa were her two teenaged daughters, each with a newborn, and a small circle of neighbor women. Teresa sat with her two infant grandchildren in her ample lap, one in the crook of each arm. She was loving toward both, but whereas one infant was round, pretty, and pink, the other was puny and jaundiced.

While changing the diaper of the obviously wasted and sickly infant, Teresa initiated a discussion of the child's illness. Everyone had an opinion, even some of the men. All agreed that the baby's condition was precarious, but they disagreed as to the cause and the cure. The men tended to suspect that the baby's decline was brought about by a change in the brand of her powdered milk. In response to a nationwide price freeze to fight the country's inflation, local shopkeepers had hidden away the stock of many popular and expensive commodities, including Nestogeno Integral, the whole-milk infant "formula" that discriminating Alto parents preferred to give their very young babies. Mothers now had to rely on inferior, domestic brands of powdered milk, and many Alto babies had sickened, and some had died in the interim. A man leaning on Teresa's window ledge boasted that he managed to find one large can of Nestogeno for his two-month-old infant, but for his one-year-old he had purchased only the bulk skimmed, powdered milk sold in plastic sacks.

The women turned their attention to the sick infant. Teresa thought that the problem had begun with the eruption of a boil on the infant's chest near her heart that had adversely affected her whole system. Following the infection came diarrhea, and the infant was being sustained on *soro* purchased from the pharmacy in premeasured packets. Teresa explained how she had rubbed chicken fat over the boil to express the pus until there was only blood. But still the infant continued to weaken. Twice she carried the baby to the health post, but she was never able to see a doctor, and each time she went home unattended. The baby's mother broke in to say that perhaps she was responsible for the infant's problem, as she had taken so many medicines during her pregnancy. "The only solution now," she said, "is to pool our money and get the baby diagnosed and treated properly at Feliciano's pharmacy."

At this point the women began to gather around the baby's diaper, examining the feces closely: their consistency, smell, and color. Teresa saved all the dirty diapers in a pile to compare them and note small changes from day to day. Everyone was talking at once, each offering her advice. One woman recommended a different powdered-milk formula; another suggested giving the infant a mashed banana; another disagreed, saying that fresh fruit might kill a baby as fragile as this one. The women complained that the local doctors disagreed among themselves. Some said to withhold food during an acute crisis of diarrhea, and others said to give food to the infant. No one was sure; everyone was confused.

The infant herself seemed all leather and bones; her breastbone was particularly prominent. Although six months old, the baby's motions were like a newborn's, and her tongue hung from her mouth. The baby's eyes were unfocused and didn't follow a finger that was passed in front of her. Her disproportionately large head lolled back and forth like a rag doll's. Infants like these were usually referred to as *bobo* and *mole*, sure diagnostic signs of chronic and hopeless child sickness. But not one of these women mentioned that possibility at all. Rather, they were clearly intent on helping Teresa and her daughter to find a cure for the baby.

Just then Biu stuck her head in the doorway. She had just returned from Recife and wanted to talk with me "urgently." Usually that meant she needed money, so I tried to divert her attention to the sick baby. Biu was not one to mince words, and when it came to advice on babies, she spoke with the authority of one who had lost many children. "This is a case for the hospital in Recife," she said. "You must go immediately to Seu Félix and request a space in the ambulance. My daughter Sonia died looking just like this one." Biu turned to the young mother and asked, "Are you feeding this baby anything?" Teresa's daughter took offense. The baby's emaciation was not from *mau trato* (poor care), she said, but from the sickness itself. The chest boil may have poisoned her blood. Had the mother taken a bad fright during her pregnancy? "No," she replied, just the ordinary, everyday little disturbances one always had, nothing that would have caused such a problem in a baby.

"The baby is so wasted," I broke in to say, using the key word *gasto* for effect to see if anyone would take me up on it. The mother turned the baby over to show that it had no flesh at all on its legs and buttocks. "Ay," she said sadly, "just bones." The women once again took out the pile of dirty diapers and began to compare notes and observations. As more women crowded into the little room, the event took on the aspect of an ethnomedical "grand rounds." Biu rubbed the feces between the ends of the diaper to judge their texture, and she declared them to be "green and cheesy, just like my Sonia's before she died." Another woman found traces of blood and mucus in the diaper, indicating that the infant's diarrhea had taken a serious turn indeed. But the mother herself noted, somewhat reluctantly, that it was neither the wasted body nor the quality of the feces that really worried her but rather the infant's bobbing head. "Something is not right," she said. "Her head just bounces around, and her mouth is always open. You think she would get tired keeping it open like that."

"Well, if you want my opinion," said Biu, "it's *that* paralysis." But the other women reacted strongly, defending the baby. "Look," said Teresa, "if the baby weren't so skinny, she would have great force in her legs," and as she spoke she stood the poor creature on her lap to demonstrate the power of her wasted legs, but not very convincingly. Another middle-aged woman added with an odd twist of logic, "If this baby weren't so skinny, she would be a *meninão* [giant baby]!" But Biu again exhorted the mother to take the baby to the large teaching hospital in Recife. The mother resisted Biu's advice, saying that she did not know her way around the city and that she would be terrified in the giant hospital. But Biu told how well attended she had been in the emergency room when she brought her daughter Sonia there. Nevertheless, it was not a very convincing argument because Sonia arrived home dead anyway.

As I was about to leave, one of the men at the window approached me. His eyes were very red, and his breath smelled of cheap rum. "Excuse me, Dona Nancí," he said, "but I have a word to say. I did everything, everything in the world together with you to save my baby many years ago when you were still living in that little hut over there. But if God wants to take a child, there is nothing that anyone can do to prevent it. After God took my little Graças, I made a vow to the Holy Virgin. I swore that I would never sleep with another man again as long as I lived. And I have kept that vow, haven't I?" The men nodded in agreement. My confusion turned to embarrassment when I realized that "he" was a cross-dressed, transvestite woman. The death of her little girl so hardened the woman (who I then recognized as my old neighbor Irma) against her gender and sex that she crossed the divide and joined the men of the Alto, certainly one of the more extreme anger-grief reactions I encountered.

Sacrifice and the Generative Scapegoat

And so after all is said and done, I still do not know exactly what prompts a mother or a father to conclude that a baby is a victim of child sickness or child attack and is therefore under a death sentence. Nevertheless, the flexibility of the diagnosis allows parents and healing women the greatest amount of autonomy in judging the relative survivability of infants and small babies. The key symptoms of child sickness are extremely general and open-ended, covering most of the ordinary signs and symptoms of childhood distress, from explosive vomiting and diarrhea to skin rashes and birthmarks, from teething problems and irritability to frailty, passivity, and the obviously frightening problem of infantile convulsions. But external contingencies in the household at the time of an infant's sickness are at least as important as the "quality" of the infant.

We need only think back to Lordes at the time she was so strapped, living "in her stick house with her little stick baby, Zezinho." Her current boyfriend had abandoned her when she was close to the delivery of yet another unwanted child. She was barely able to sustain herself. Where would she find the energy to fight for so seemingly "hopeless" and unattractive a child as Zezinho? Conditions like these are "ideal" for the doomed child syndrome to come into play. The condemned child syndrome shifts the responsibility for the child's future to the hands of God. It might be thought of as a divine social security program.

Sometimes I think of the "given-up-on" or the condemned babies of the Alto do Cruzeiro in terms of ritual scapegoating and sacrifice as discussed by René Girard (1987a, 1987b). Girard built his theory of religion around the idea of sacrificial violence and the surrogate victim, or the "generative scapegoat," the one (like Jesus) who is assigned to assume the blame for the sins of others (1987a:73–105). What happens in ritual sacrifice is killing, and so violence and death, argued Girard, are the cornerstones of religion and social life. In popular culture the generative scapegoat is the agreed-on victim whose suffering or death helps to resolve unbearable social "tensions, conflicts, and difficulties of all kinds" (74). It is important that the scapegoating remain unconscious and that it be directed toward outsiders, "imperfectly assimilated" people of some kind, be they foreigners, the disabled, the sick, or, as I argue here, infants.

In a way, we can consider the given-up, offered-up angel-babies of Bom Jesus as prototypic generative scapegoats, sacrificed in the face of terrible domestic conflicts about scarcity and survival. And that is just how their mothers sometimes spoke of them. The Christian notion of the sacrificial lamb provided a means of deriving meaning from the otherwise "senseless" assertions women made to the effect that their babies "had" to die. I used this particular theme to guide critical reflection at a UPAC base community meeting among the women of the Alto. The presence of Sister Juliana, the barefoot Franciscan nun, perhaps allowed the discussion to take a more "theological" turn than it might have otherwise. After an opening prayer led by the sister, I raised the first question: "What does it mean," I asked, "to say that a baby *has* to die or that she dies because she *wants* to die?"

Terezinha was the first to speak. "It means that God takes them to save us from suffering."

"What she means," broke in Zefinha, "is that God knows the future better than you or me. It could be that if the baby were to live, he would cause much suffering in the mother. He could turn out a thief, or a murderer, or a *cabo safado*, a good-for-nothing. And so they die as babies to *save* us from pain and suffering, not to give us pain."

Luiza added, "I kept giving birth and mine kept on dying. But I never gave up hope. Perhaps the first nine had to die so that the last five could live."

"I, myself," said Fátima, "don't have too much hope for this one [the sickly, listless one-year-old in her lap]. She has no blood. If God wants her, then I would be happy for her and for me! I would be happy to have a *coração santa* [a little sacred heart] in heaven. My grandmother says that a child who dies without ever having touched its mother's nipple [i.e., without ever having been breast-fed] is without original sin, and she goes right to heaven. She is very pleasing to the Virgin. And this one of mine is *pure, pure.*"

"Yes, I'm sure that your little one is pure and pleasing to God and the Virgin, but why would God want babies to suffer so much in dying as they do?" I asked.

"Don't ask me," answered Edite Cosmos. "I did *everything* to keep mine healthy and alive, but God didn't want me to have them. I think that these ugly diseases are sent by God to punish us for the sins of the world. And yet the babies don't deserve this. We ourselves are the sinners, but the punishment falls heavily on them."

"Be quiet, Edite," said another. "They die, just like Jesus died, to save us from pain and suffering. Isn't that right, Sister Juliana?"

But Juliana, a native of the dry *sertão* where babies did not die, she said, like flies as they did in the sugar zone, was not so sure that the women were right in their thinking. "I don't think Jesus wants all your babies," she said. "I think He wants them to live." But Sister Juliana was a nun, and the Alto women didn't pay her too much attention. What could she possibly know about babies?

The sacrificial baby theme appeared in many other guises—in the belief, for example, that infants named after powerful patron saints often became "the first fruits" offered to them. The saints could claim the newborns as their rightful "due," a "payment" in exchange for protection of the household. So when a mother affixed the same saint's name on a series of children, each of whom died after the other, it was a "protective" strategy. Eventually the saint would be satisfied and would leave the household in peace. An anxious mother explained, "I told Saint Sebastião not to be greedy. I reminded him that he had *already* taken enough of my babies, to look elsewhere and to leave this little, last-born Sebastião for me."

But not all Alto women were so easily resigned to greedy saints or a hungry Deity. Angry blasphemies sometimes slipped from the lips of grieving women. A grief-ravaged woman cried out to Dona Amor, the saintly old praying woman, "What good did it do me, *meu* Amor, to give birth to a child, with so much pain and sacrifice, only to have God come to look for him and eat him?"

"God, *eat* him?" I had never heard anyone use such an expression before.

"Yes, *senhora!* Wasn't it horrible for her to curse God in that way? Only a crazy person would use such words. She should have recalled the words of

São Antônio, 'Don't grieve. God has the power; He knows what He is doing.' "

Amor then launched into a long folk narrative, which she performed in the nasal country-western style of the Pernambucan *repentista* singer. She called it the "Prayer to São Antônio." It opened with the story of a prosperous and happy young man, devoted to São Antônio, who put his home, wife, young children, and all his possessions under the saint's protection: "I love São Antônio; he is a powerful saint." But things began to turn out badly for the protagonist. Like Job, he suffered a series of domestic tragedies. First his favorite horse died, strangled in his barn. Angered, the man cursed his patron saint: "What kind of patron are you? You haven't any power!" His wife, frightened by her husband's blasphemy, praised the saint: "São Antôn is a good saint, and he is to be praised. Better that the horse should die than either one of us!"

But the next year the couple lost a baby son, and again the man cursed his patron saint: "I trusted you. I put all of my possessions under your care, my favorite horse and my own son, and look what you have done!" But his wife reassured him again, saying, "Don't mind what has happened. Children can be replaced. Better that a child should die than either you or me [*Melhor morrer menino do que um de nos morrer*]." This time the husband was not so easily consoled: "Say what you like, woman, but I am losing my faith." With the passage of another year, his wife, too, died. The husband returned from the fields to find her body already cold. He angrily knocked over the home altar, and the statue of Saint Anthony crashed to the floor. The man left in great distress to arrange for his wife's burial.

Along the way he met a priest passing by on a small donkey. The priest asked the young man why he was so downcast, and the man told all that had come to pass: "I lost everything in the world that was dear to me." The priest got off his donkey and began to walk side by side with the man and to explain why these things had happened. He pulled out a photo and showed the man what would have been in store for him: his own neck broken in a fall from the horse. "The horse would have stumbled, and you would not have escaped death. São Antônio, like the good saint he is, saved you from this end. And as for what happened to the horse, the same goes for your child." The priest produced another photo, this one of his now fully grown son tied up as a prisoner and surrounded by angry and jeering military guards. The priest urged the man: "Have a good look. Here is what would have happened. Your son by the age of fifteen would have become a thief, stealing everything in sight, bringing down dishonor on your name. He would have faced execution in the barracks. But São Antônio, like the good saint he is, decided to free you from this agony." And, of course, as for what happened to the infant son, likewise his mother, and from inside his black cassock the priest produced the third and most agonizing photo, this one of his wife entangled in the arms of a naked man, her beautiful long hair in passionate disarray. The man asked the priest fearfully, "Is that man me?" And the priest replied sadly, "No, my son, it is not. Your wife would have run off with another man and fallen into disgrace. But São Antônio, like the good saint he is, killed her first to save you from such sorrow to come." The man was stunned and speechless, and the priest, revealing himself to the man as São Antônio himself, put his arm about the man's shoulder and concluded, "Now that you have finally heard all, be resigned and be content. Make no pacts with the devil. Run home and light a candle to your good patron, who loves and cares for you well."

In this folk motif not only the small child but the man's horse and his wife are transformed into sacrificial victims to preserve the safety, sanity, and faith of the protagonist. Few *moradores* of the Alto lose a cherished animal, and only some experience the loss of a young spouse, but virtually all have lost a baby, and many have lost several. And the words of consolation from Amor's folk ballad are often repeated on the Alto. "Better the child should die," women say to each other, "than either you or me."

It was finally, however, while arguing about the "hopelessness" of child sickness with Dona Maria do Carmel, a devoutly religious praying woman of the Alto, that the theme of child death as religious sacrifice came unexpectedly to the fore. "How can you, Dona Maria, a *beata*, a religious woman of the church, tell me that you will do nothing to rescue a doomed child, to save him from parents who have decided to give him up?" I asked. "You have told me that you don't believe in abortion, that it is the greatest of sins, and yet you, a healing woman, would just stand by and watch a sick child die à *míngua?*"

It was getting close to the last few days of my stay in Bom Jesus, and I was risking a lot, pushing about as far as I could go, standing on our "common ground" as Catholics who met each Sunday at the altar rail. She stood there quietly, eyeing me fixedly, which was quite disconcerting because Dona Maria had one eye that refused to hold its ground and darted about independently of the other. She was quite ready to turn the tables on me.

"I know what you think," she said. "You think that all these hungry, sickly babies of the Alto would be better off if they had never been born at all. But we, who are a people of faith, believe that *all* children were born into this world for a purpose, even if that purpose was so that they could die. Where is your faith in an afterlife?"

When I didn't reply and seemed somewhat repentant, she decided to

Cure by crucifixion: the only hope for a doomed sickness.

initiate me finally into one of the secrets of child sickness. "No, there is no cure for child sickness," she said, "but there is something a praying woman like me can do if the disease has not yet taken full hold of the baby but is only beginning to show its face. The mother can come to me early, and I can do something. But there is no guarantee."

"What can you do?"

"I cannot discuss it, especially not one woman to another woman, or the power will be broken."

"Can you show it to me then?"

"Come back tomorrow, very early, before anyone else is up, even before the water carriers have gone to the public spigot. Bring me a little child, and I will show you how to prevent the dreaded sickness from taking hold of him. But you must promise not to ask me any questions before or after."

The next morning I arrived with a one-year-old boy "borrowed" from Nininha on the way up to Dona Maria's hut. The little one still had sleep in his eyes. It was just before sunrise. Dona Maria was waiting for us. She smiled at the little boy and went to the back room. She came out with a white sheet that she laid on the dirt floor, and she gestured that the boy be stretched out on the sheet, his legs together and his arms extended outward. Next she took out a rather large hammer and four large rusted nails. She put the nails in her mouth, and as she bent down over the boy and tried to position one of the nails near his right hand, the boy stiffened and began to cry hysterically. Dona Maria shook her head back and forth, indicating to him not to be afraid, to be quiet, but it was no use. The little one refused to stay in place. I went across a ravine and found a house with an older child, too old really, but at least he could be quieted. The boy smiled nervously, but he followed Dona Maria's instructions, and he barely flinched as she "nailed" his hands, feet, and head to a symbolic and invisible cross while reciting the Pai Nosso and the Ave Maria.

After the crucifixion, Dona Maria asked the boy to rise up quickly to his feet. She motioned to him to remove his shorts and shirt. These were rolled up tightly, and Dona Maria indicated that they would be burned far out in the *mata*. "And now," she said to the boy, "from now on your name will be João. You must not tell anyone what you have seen." I left, as promised, without asking any questions, but I pondered the possible meanings of this symbolic enactment of crucifixion and resurrection. The doomed child, like the doomed Christ, "needs" to die so that others may live. I wondered, too, whether the simple ritual evoked in women of the Alto a painful, if only partly conscious, awareness that mothers must at times sacrifice their own children. I recall reading not so long ago that Jesus of Nazareth died not of the wounds afflicted by the Roman soldiers who scourged and crucified him but rather, like so many of the little angels of the Alto do Cruzeiro, of dehydration and thirst.

9 Our Lady of Sorrows
A Political Economy
of the Emotions

They do not grieve the way we do.
General William Westmoreland, Vietnam, 1968

1) Sir, their light hearts turned to stone.
It is not remembered whether in gardens
stone lanterns illumined peasant ways.
2) Perhaps they gathered once to delight in blossom,
but after the children were killed
there were no more buds.
3) Sir, laughter is bitter to the burned mouth.
Denise Levertov (1987:123)

What finally can be said of these Alto women? How do they make sense of their lives and of their babies' foreshortened lives? What, after all, does mother love look like in this inhospitable context? Are grief, remorse, and anger present, although deeply repressed? If so, where shall we look for them? Or if we take Alto women at their word, are these feelings absent? And if so, what does this tell us about the nature of emotions and affects? Moreover, how are the mothers able to do what they feel they must do? What is the human cost to those who are forced into moral dilemmas and into choices that no woman should have to make? What are the moral visions that guide their actions? How do they protect themselves from being overwhelmed at times (as we might) by ambivalence and doubt?

I have been chastised for presenting an "unflattering" portrait of poor women, women who are themselves the victims of severe social and institutional neglect. True, I have described these women as allowing, even helping, some of their children to die. But I do not see these practices as unnatural, inhuman, or unwomanly but rather as reasonable responses to unreasonable constraints and contingencies. In the earlier chapters of this book I tried to establish the larger context, with all its social and economic ills, within which these Alto women move and reason, act and make choices, limited those these may be. Here, I want to unravel the personal and existential dimensions of love and death on the Alto do Cruzeiro and especially the shaping of women's consciousness and subjectivity.

Whenever social scientists involve themselves in the study of women's lives—especially in practices surrounding sexuality, reproduction, and nurturing—they frequently come up against theories of human (and maternal) nature that have been uncritically derived from assumptions and values implicit in the structure of the "modern," Western, bourgeois family. I refer to theories proposing essential, or universal, womanly scripts, such as Marshall Klaus and John Kennell's (1976) "maternal bonding," Sara Ruddick's (1989) "maternal thinking," Nancy Chodorow's (1978) "feminine personality," and Carol Gilligan's (1982) "womanly ethos," all of which on closer examination can be found to be both culture and history bound. I find these theories inadequate insofar as they posit a very specific cultural "norm" as general or universal and thereby alienate the experiences of many poor, working-class, and Third World women, who become a feminist version of the non-Western other.

Contemporary theories of maternal sentiment—of mother love as we know and understand it—are the product of a very specific historical context. The invention of mother love corresponds not only with the rise of the modern, bourgeois, nuclear family (as Elizabeth Badinter [1980] pointed out) but also with the demographic transition: the precipitous decline in infant mortality and female fertility. My argument is a materialist one: mother love as defined in the psychological, social-historical, and sociological literatures is far from universal or innate and represents instead an ideological, symbolic representation grounded in the basic material conditions that define women's reproductive lives. The journalist who reviewed my research for the science page of the Brazilian daily *Folha de São Paulo* (see Bonalume Neto 1989), in a feature article entitled "Anthropologist Calls Mother Love a Bourgeois Myth," may have overstated my case. But in effect I suppose it is close enough to what I am saying.

The radical transition from an "old" to a "new" mortality pattern that has occurred in Europe in the past hundred years, and that is now occurring in the more prosperous parts of Brazil, has been accompanied by a "new," lowered fertility pattern (see World Bank 1991:ix; Faria 1989). These demographic changes, wherever they occur, affect perceptions of human life, personhood, life stages (including the "invention" of modern childhood and adolescence), and family roles and social sentiments (including mother love). They also alter perceptions concerning the relative value of the individual as measured against the collectivity (whether nuclear or extended family, lineage, or community).

Modern notions of mother love derive, in the first instance, from a "new" reproductive "strategy": to give birth to few infants and to "invest" heavily (emotionally as well as materially) in each one from birth onward. This reproductive strategy was alien to most of European history through the early modern period, and it does not reflect the maternal thinking and practice of a great many women living in poverty and in many parts of the Third World today.[1] Under conditions of high mortality and high fertility, as still obtain on the Alto do Cruzeiro, a different, or a pre–demographic transition, reproductive strategy obtains: to give birth to many children and, on the expectation that only a few will survive infancy, to invest selectively in those considered the "best bets" for survival in terms of preferred sex, birth order, appearance, health, or perceived viability. Of course, to introduce the language of "investment" and "strategy" is already a deep cultural distortion. This is *our* cultural idiom, the language of the free market, in which infants are perceived as valuable biological and social commodities. I do not wish to suggest that reproductive thinking conforms everywhere to capitalist equations of "cost-benefit" analysis. Brazilian women do not keep a balance sheet on their offspring. Many Alto women are willing, as we have seen, to try raising "as many as God sees fit to send" them. But the limited material conditions of their lives make this ideal impossible, a contradiction of the reality in which they live and reproduce.

And so what I am calling an "old" reproductive strategy comes into play. It demands a very different sort of maternal thinking, and it just as surely calls forth different maternal attachments, feelings, and sentiments, such as those implicated in the mortal neglect of "high-risk" infants and babies on the Alto do Cruzeiro or the absence of deep grieving or a profound sense of loss accompanying the death of each and every fragile child. These very different patterns of maternal thinking and feeling are not merely "superficial" cultural conventions covering a more deeply constituted universal "truth" about female psychology and gender. Rather, these same cultural conventions are in and of themselves constitutive of a multiplicity of truths conforming to radically different experiences of reproduction and motherhood.

In seeking to create a woman-centered interpretive paradigm, many contemporary scholars have reconceptualized psychological and philosophical concepts of self and other, object relations, and moral reasoning by incorporating the "wild crescent" of women's experience. For example, feminist revisions of human psychological development have suggested that women develop a less autonomous, more socially embedded sense of self. Nancy Chodorow's (1978) classic revision of Freudian psychology posits a female adult identity defined more in terms of relationship than independence and characterized by fluid and flexible ego boundaries that tend to merge, rather than differentiate, self from other. She suggested that women are more comfortable with intimacy and proximity, with a sense of close, even collapsed, distances with others. Unlike males, who above all fear engulfment by encroaching others, women fear isolation. The feminist revision of human psychology is widely accepted today, and the feminist debate concerns only whether female empathy, social embeddedness, responsiveness to others, and fluid ego boundaries are positive or negative characteristics for modern women. Sara Ruddick (1989), Evelyn Fox-Keller (1983, 1985), and Carol Gilligan (1982) have celebrated, even idealized, the intuitive, empathic womanly ethos. Others, including Jane Flax (1980), have argued that autonomy and a strong, individuated sense of "self" remain prerequisites of healthy psychological growth and development. Here I question the paradigm of an essentialist "female" psychology itself. The "object relations" that take shape in the womanly experiences of pregnancy, birthing, and early mothering may just as "naturally" reproduce maternal sentiments of distance and estrangement as of attachment and empathy.

The Muted Moral Voices of Women

Don't pity the infants who died here on the Alto do Cruzeiro.
Don't waste your tears on them. Pity us instead. Weep for
their mothers who are condemned to live.
Black Irene, Moradora, Alto do Cruzeiro

On the Alto do Cruzeiro the survival of any one child is generally subordinated to the well-being of the entire domestic group, especially to that household core made up of adult women and their older, and therefore more dependable, children. In a world of great uncertainty about life and death it makes no sense at all to put any *one* person—not a parent, not a husband or lover, and certainly not a sickly toddler or fragile infant—at the center of anything.

As we have seen, in the desperate context of shantytown life mothers do sometimes favor the survival of older and healthier children, and sometimes of their own selves, over that of younger and weaker family members. One does encounter often enough the unsettling image of relatively well-fed adults and older children side by side with famished toddlers and marasmic infants. Such were the cases in the household of Terezinha, Manoel, and Edilson and in the household of Dalina, Prazeres, and Gil-Anderson. Gil was the one-year-old skeletal toddler I encountered on the Rua dos Magos whose stocky seventeen-year-old mother, Prazeres, had been feeding him various patent medicines (including sedatives) while simultaneously, and largely unconsciously, denying him food.

When Prazeres refused to have Gil hospitalized in Recife, where I was sure he could be saved, I resorted to bringing fresh milk, mashed vegetables, and a hearty meat broth for the famished little boy every other day. But I discovered that the food that I brought for the little boy was being distributed among the bigger and healthier household members, including Gil's great-grandmother, Dalina, my oldest *comadre* on the Alto do Cruzeiro. Meanwhile, the antibiotic skin cream that my field assistant, Cecilia de Mello, brought to heal the badly infected diaper rash of Gil's newborn infant cousin, the youngest member of the household, was being passed around among the teenage women of the household to use for their skin "blemishes." But Cecilia's and my immediate and self-righteous indignation passed as we had to confront the inappropriateness of our "humanitarian" gestures. Our too frequent visits and, if I may be excused, our "half-assed" interventions on behalf of this altogether miserable and threatened household only provoked jealousy and conflict.

"Why were you *wasting* so much money on Gil?" old Dalina asked, when there were older children and working adults who were also sick and "hungry." Gil's mother, Prazeres, had a painful toothache, and the side of her face was dangerously swollen. Her aunt had a stomachache resulting from some spoiled fish she had eaten the night before. She was doubled over with pain and could not therefore get the laundry back to her *patroa* on time, which might cost her the coming week's market money. A twelve-year-old nephew lay on the tattered straw mattress in the front room, his face turned to the wall hiding his unmanly tears; his stubbed toe was badly infected, and the pain (when I thought to inquire) was, the boy admitted, "unbearable." Dalina's youngest son, a twenty-four-year-old alcoholic, had begun to show signs of madness. Was he now sniffing glue as well? He was sleeping on the floor in the back room. "Be careful you don't trip over him," warned Dalina, as I went out back to use the latrine. "He's *brabo.*" Old Dalina's legs were edemic, but she still went out twice a day to the public *chafariz* to collect a dozen large cans of water, which she would resell at a few cents a can to the neighbors along her hillside path. Dalina must have been ancient; she was already an "old woman" in the 1960s when she carried water to my little Alto house. Dalina complained of a nervous attack that had left her shaky and unable to balance the heavy cans of water on her head. She said she had fallen down on the descent from the *chafariz* earlier that day, and now her bones were sore. When I walked shamefacedly across the tiny room to comfort her, she began to cry, "You used to be a mother to me. When I was hungry, you brought me good things to eat. When I was sick you took me to the hospital. Don't you care about me anymore?"

The fact is that life on the Alto do Cruzeiro resembles nothing so much as a battlefield or an emergency room in a crowded inner-city hospital. Consequently, moral thinking is not guided by the blind justice and commitment to abstract universal principles that Lawrence Kohlberg (1981) equated with

Dalina: "Don't you care about me anymore?"

highly developed ethical reasoning and that Carol Gilligan (1982) later attacked for its unconscious male bias. The moral thinking of women of the Alto conforms in a very general sort of way to Gilligan's notion of a womanly nurturance that is fundamentally relativist, concrete, and context specific. But the premises on which the womanly ethic of "care" and "responsibility" are based on the rocky hillside of the Alto do Cruzeiro are quite different from those described by Gilligan.

In the shantytown, day-to-day moral thinking is guided by a "lifeboat ethics" (Hardin 1974). The central ethical dilemma of the lifeboat concerns the decisions as to who among the shipwrecked is to be saved when it would spell certain disaster to try saving all. Infants and toddlers first? Women and children? The young and the strong? The hardworking? The brave and the beautiful? The wise old men? The sick and the vulnerable? In emergency situations the morality of triage—the rudimentary pragmatics of saving the salvageable—often supersedes other, more aesthetic or more egalitarian ethical principles. In the specific instance just cited, Gil-Anderson was not viewed as salvageable. He could not walk, he did not speak, and he was, as everyone in the family agreed, an unattractive child. His aunt noted with pity that he looked like the movie character E. T. (the extraterrestrial), which she had seen on a poster displayed in downtown Bom Jesus. And he did, poor little hungry fellow.

It is unfair to ask these women to defend their moral thinking under what can only be described as cruel and unusual circumstances. Do we ask the survivors of prison and refugee camps or released prisoners of war to describe the moral visions and moral reasoning that obtain in those inhuman contexts? It would be unseemly to do so. Moreover, what of the "moral voices" and visions of Alto men, who are decidedly absent here? The burden of child survival and the responsibility for governing the moral economy and distributive justice within the Alto household fall unfairly on the shoulders of Alto women, those who are single and those who are not. Perhaps the most exploitative relationship of all is that which demands of poor women not only that they give birth again and again and again, as these women do, but that they must display "appropriate" maternal sentiments.

After reading my first article on maternal thinking in the shantytown, David Daube, a distinguished professor of Roman and religious law at the University of California, Berkeley, told me the following anecdote (see also Daube 1987:75–80). Some time previously Daube had shared with his wife, Helen, then a Jungian therapist, a curious event that had taken place in Strasbourg a few years after the end of World War II. Daube and some scholarly friends were lunching at an elegant restaurant, and a lively, animated hum of conversation filled the dining room. Suddenly, however, a reverential hush fell across all the tables as an elderly, distinguished-looking gentleman, accompanied by some friends, entered the restaurant. It lasted until the man took his seat. Daube was told that the man had been a public official in the city during the time of the German occupation and that two of his sons had been captured by the Nazis in a sweep of the downtown area. All the young men taken in the *razzia* were to be killed. The official, who had his connections, gained access to the commandant who was just about to give the order to have the dozen or so random victims shot in the courtyard. The official begged that his own sons be spared. The commandant listened and then nodded nonchalantly toward the window overlooking the enclosed courtyard. "All right," he said, "you may take one of them." The official stopped dead in his tracks. He could not bring himself to make the inhuman and evil selection. Both sons were executed together.

On hearing the story, Helen was unmoved by the moral scruples of the Strasbourg official. She said that he was to be pitied, rather than admired. Actually, he was something of a coward, she continued, because he did not want to make a choice that would haunt him the rest of his life. His guilt would have been unbearable. Daube argued with Helen in terms of the "higher" ethical principles involved. Had the official accepted the offer, he would have been made into a collaborator with evil, participating in the Nazis' arbitrary toying with human life. Helen listened and then calmly replied, "You may be right. But a woman would have gone home with one of her sons."

The disagreement between himself and his wife, Daube noted, might have some reference to the controversy surrounding my research. It concerned, in part, the difference between the moral visions of those guided by abstract, universalist principles of justice, fairness, and equality and the moral visions of those guided by relativist principles in which concrete, proximate, personal considerations and relationships of responsibility and care mediate disembodied moral abstractions. Gilligan identified this tension as an "essential" difference between the moral visions of men and women. The uncompromising, universalist reasoning of the Strasbourg official (and of men, are we to suppose?) represents the "moral majority," the dominant moral voice of society. The voice of Helen ("But a woman would have gone home with one of her sons") represents the muted, submerged "moral voice" of women, of mothers in particular.

This discourse, however, recreates an essentializing gender-based dichotomy between "male" and "female" moral thinking. It is more useful, I think, to see the difference in terms of social position with respect to the dominant moral ideology. Social class is at least as important as gender in the instance I am describing. Nevertheless, Helen's corrective that a "woman would have gone home with one of her sons" is certainly reminiscent of the Alto mother who prayed that God spare her favorite child and content Himself by taking another of her children instead. And it resonates with the Alto mother who said of her dying toddler, "Let him die, then. He's not the only one I have." This kind of motherly pragmatics is also found in the several entries in the "adoption" book at the local hospital nursery in which the smaller and weaker of newborn twins was left behind by their impoverished mother.

The everyday violence of shantytown life daily recreates the dilemma of the Strasbourg official for Alto women, who are forced to participate in the community's "space of death" by making innumerable, little "selections" that have life-and-death consequences. Mothers must decide on the quality and strength of the powdered milk and *mingau* given to younger and older, stronger and weaker children; on the claims to the small amount of carefully filtered or boiled water that is kept in a special clay pot; who shall receive emergency medical care; and who will get a new pair of sandals. Yes, an Alto mother "would have gone home with one of her sons," and she would have picked the one more able to confront the *luta*, even if it meant leaving behind the younger, the gentler, or the more beloved of the two. When an Alto mother says, "It is better to let the weak ones die," her thinking is similar to that of Medea, who would sooner slaughter her defenseless children than leave them abandoned and helpless in a hostile world.

These reflections may cause us to cast doubt on the renowned "wisdom" of Solomon, the son of David and his successor as king of Israel. Born the illegitimate son of Bathsheba, David's partner in adultery, Solomon had rather strong faith in the power of the maternal bond. When two harlots came before Solomon for the mediation of a dispute involving their claim to the same newborn infant (1 Kings 3), Solomon heard out their accusations and counteraccusations and ordered that a sword be brought to him. The king "cleverly" demanded that the contested infant be cut in half and divided equally between the two women. The one agreed to the mediation, saying, "Let neither of us have it; cut it in two." The other protested, saying, "Oh, sir, let her have the baby! Whatever you do, do not kill it." On hearing their responses, the king ordered that the living baby be given to the woman who refused to have the infant killed, for "she is its mother." Solomon's subjects marveled at the wisdom of their king. Although Solomon's decision was a just one, invoking the contemporary principle of "the best interests" of the child, I am not so convinced that the infant was necessarily sent home with the natural mother. Maternal thinking should not be sentimentalized. The morality that guides mothers, especially poor mothers, may not follow "conventional" wisdom or dominant moral discourses concerning justice and equality.

Alto women allow, even help, some of their children to die, but they themselves are forced to live. To many Alto women, like Black Irene, this is the ultimate irony, their version of the existential "black hole" (see Daube 1983). Here, in full is what Black Irene told me from the depths of her despair following the murder of her husband and, the following year, the death squad assassination of her eldest and beloved son, Nego De.

"I am three times cursed. My husband was murdered before my own eyes. And I could not protect my son. The police made me pick over the mutilated bodies in the morgue to find my De. And now I am forced to go on living. I only wish I had the luxury to hang myself. My husband could die. My son could die. But I *cannot die.* I am the *matriz.* My children and grandchildren still suck from my roots. Don't pity the young men and the infants who have died here on the Alto do Cruzeiro. Don't waste any tears on them. Pity us, Nancí. Weep for the mothers who are condemned to live."

Basic Strangeness: Mothers and Their Others

The arrival of a child is, I believe, the first and often the only opportunity a woman has to experience the Other in its radical separation from herself.

Julia Kristeva (1977:99)

Underlying the feminist theory of female object relations is the experience of pregnancy, birth, and motherhood in which self and other are merged during a long period of forced nurturance/dependency. Chodorow's (1978:65–87) theory of the reproduction of mothering, for example, draws heavily on John Bowlby's ethologically based ideas on mother-infant attachment. Modeled after research on "imprinting" in birds, Bowlby (1969) posited a parallel sequence of innate infant attachment scripts, later expanded to include notions of maternal bonding. Such innate infant behaviors as clinging, rooting, and shaping the nipple and such "automatic" maternal behaviors as smiling, cooing, gazing, nuzzling, sniffing, stroking, and enfolding the infant were carefully observed, documented, and quantified in an effort to show the "naturalness" of mother-infant relations. Maternal "bonding" (see Klaus & Kennell 1976) was said to be "activated" in the mother in response to the infant's crying, smiling, and sucking. It was suggested that human mothering has a strong, unlearned component (see Rossi 1977) and that women are both physiologically and psychologically prepared to nurture their young. The automatic "milk letdown" reflex in nursing mothers' response to signs of infant distress is a case in point.

In his three-volume study of human attachment, separation, and loss, John Bowlby (1969, 1973, 1980) argued that attachment is a primary, rather than a secondary, instinct, as Freud had posited. Infant attachment, Bowlby wrote, is "a class of social behavior of an importance equivalent to that of mating behavior," with a "biological function specific to itself" (1969:179). In other words, mother-infant attachment is cast as a biologically "protected" sequence of behaviors. Bowlby's empirical research on the tiny, institutionalized war orphans in England following World War II led him to conclude that the "attachment" instinct in infants is awakened by six months of age and remains intense through the end of the third year of life, after which the child becomes gradually more self-sufficient. Curiously, however, maternal attachment to the infant is said to follow a more immediate trajectory. Klaus and Kennell identified a "critical" or a "sensitive" period for maternal bonding immediately postpartum, "in the first minutes and hours of life" (1976:14).

Bonding theory, backed up by a large body of often questionable clinical research, has had a profound effect on obstetrical practices in Europe and the United States, where it has wide currency among medical and social work professionals.[2] And it has shaped the way social theorists and even feminist philosophers and writers think about maternity and mother love, which has acquired the status of an empirically demonstrated scientific "truth." Although some cross-cultural research has shown the cultural and environmental parameters of mother-infant attachments (see deVries 1987; LeVine 1990), by and large these studies have done little to alter the accepted model of mothering (and maternal bonding) that predominates in the scientific community and in popular culture.

Yet it should hardly be surprising to find that poor women, with a cumulative experience of multiple child deaths and repeated pregnancy, respond differently to their newborns and babies than do middle-class women with both a greater control over their fertility and a higher expectancy of child survival. In a context of high infant mortality a woman must be fairly well convinced that infants are, at the very least, replaceable, or she would be disinclined to attempt pregnancy at all.

On the Alto do Cruzeiro infants, like husbands and boyfriends, are best thought of as temporary attachments. Both tend to disappoint women. And disappointment, Freudians suggest (see Homans 1988), is closely related to an inability to mourn. One of the ways that Alto women arm themselves against disappointment and loss is through a much more gradual and "delayed" process of maternal attachment to their newborns. I have called this a process of guarded, watchful waiting. Rather than allow themselves the sort of unrestrained, even passionate, *jouissance* and fierce, exclusive, almost sexual jealousy with which materially secure mothers can sometimes greet their newborns, poor women of the Alto are more restrained and emotionally distant from their infants. But this distance does not preclude a great deal of physical contact or the expression of a pitying affection for the "poor little critter." Born themselves into an environment of scarcity, loss, and disappointment and raised as children who buried some of their own siblings, Alto women approach each pregnancy ambivalently and each birth warily. And they may greet the frail or sickly newborn, as we have seen, with a seeming "lack" of empathy.

In contrast to the male maternal bonding theorists, Maria Piers offered a more womanly view of mothering that recognizes the deep ambivalence and estrangement that many women experience in their first encounters with their newborns. Piers referred to a not uncommon psychological state of maternal disconnectedness that she called "basic strangeness" (1978:37). The new mother may not immediately postpartum recognize in her newborn another human being. The neonate may strike her as a disturbingly animate "object." Existentially speaking, "basic strangeness" is prior to the "stage" of recognition, protective nurturing, and reciprocal attachment that Erik Erikson (1950:247–251) called "basic trust." Piers wrote that "basic strangeness precedes basic trust. It marks the beginning of life and its end. In the intervening years, however, many situations occur that drive us back partially or wholly into that state. Basic strangeness denotes primarily the opposite of empathy. It is a state in which we 'turn off' toward others and are unable to experience them as fellow human beings" (1978:38).

The development of the infant's basic trust in the world (represented in the good enough and trustworthy mother) has a little-noted correlate: the mother's basic trust in the infant, specifically in her or his "willingness" to survive. Basic strangeness may reveal deep insecurities in the mother, her lack of trust in the world, her fears of abandonment and loss, which cause her to hold the infant and her attachment to the baby at bay. Alto infants must, like mothers, prove themselves worthy of trust and attachment. In this sense, we might speak of *all* infants as requiring "adoption."

Although maternal estrangement may be more characteristic of women who give birth in conditions of great personal insecurity and "abject poverty" (Piers 1978:39), psychologists have begun to recognize that a great many altogether "average" and secure women react with feelings of estrangement and even dislike toward their newborns. In a study of the maternal reactions of a large sample of healthy, middle-class English mothers, K. M. Robson and R. Kumar (1980) found that 40 percent of first-time mothers and 25 percent of more experienced mothers reported feelings of "indifference" or "dislike" on holding their newborn infants for the first time. Moreover, these feelings of estrangement often lasted during the first few weeks home from the hospital. Maternal sentiments of basic strangeness may indeed precede maternal attachment for a great many women. If the experience of birth can predispose a great many women to a primary, existential experience of separation and distance, rather than one of relationship and empathy, as the cultural feminists suppose, another, more pluralistic model of female "psychologies" is needed.

Moreover, although classical bonding theory predicts long-term negative consequences of a woman's "failure" to bond to her neonate in the early hours and days following birth, the majority of initially "estranged" mothers in Robson and Kumar's sample became (like Lordes and her Zé) more loving and accepting of their infants as their babies matured and became more "human" and interesting.[3] A failure to bond at birth should not be taken to mean a permanent rejection of the child by any means. Human attachments are infinitely more complex and variable than are implied in the "maternal scripts" that begin in the stable and barnyard and that ethologically oriented bonding theorists use as prototypical models of human behavior. As Sara Ruddick pointed out, *all* human mothers are "adoptive" mothers. The biological act of birthing a child does not commit the *human* mother—as it does some nonhuman animal mothers—to the nurturance and protection of her offspring. When a woman commits herself to the preservation and care of her infant, she is consciously "adopting" the child as her own. This is a voluntary social act, independent of the more "coerced" act of giving birth. "To adopt," wrote Ruddick, "is to make a space, a 'peace' where the promise of birth can survive. . . . All mothers-in-the-world are adoptive" (1989:218).

The hegemonic biomedical model of maternal bonding makes the experience of alternative maternal emotions seem unnatural, indeed almost criminal, in the United States today. North American women are literally bombarded in doctors' offices, clinics, and hospitals with literature and classes on proper maternal behavior and feelings. They are exposed to so much emotional "prompting" by LaMaze counselors, doctors, and pediatric nurses that most American women probably do manage to produce the "appropriate" sentiments of euphoria, love, and passionate, jealous attachment to the infant while still in the hospital. Those who do not, especially if they are poor, single, "welfare" mothers, run the risk of early social intervention. The "failure to bond" carries a heavy clinical judgment. It implies that the neonate may be at serious risk. No doubt a great many women work very hard to conform to the emotional expectations defined by the bonding script.

Maternal sentiments, whether in the context of Northeast Brazil or the United States, are shaped by larger "political" agendas and goals. The conventionally isolated, patriarchal nuclear family of the American suburbs "requires" intense maternal involvement in the newborn. The "epoxy glue" theory of mother-infant bonding is a caricature of a social situation in which mother and infant are indeed "stuck" with each other. The bonding script "naturalizes" this social artifice. Conversely, the social and political indifference to the survival and well-being of shantytown mothers and infants in Brazil is reproduced in maternal emotions of "indifference" and "stoicism" to child death there. Emotion work, to borrow a felicitous phrase from Arlie Hochshild (1979), puts the mindful body at the service of the body politic. North American women are no different from the Brazilian women of the Alto in "producing" sentiments that respond to hidden political agendas and that are useful to the "state" of things. Emotions are both personal, deeply private events and public, ideological constructs, as the rhetoric of mother love, and its absence, illustrates.

The Cultural Construction of the Infant

What Piers called maternal basic strangeness can be less pejoratively described, following the lead of O. W. James (1980), as a slowness to anthropomorphize the infant. This refers to the long process—call it socialization, if you will—whereby parents gradually and in stages attribute to their babies such human characteristics as consciousness, will, intentionality, self-awareness, capacity for suffering, and memory. The timing of this process is arbitrary and conforms to social categories of the person and to cultural constructions of infancy and childhood. Some people are eager to begin this process immediately at birth; others are slower to do so, as are the women and men of the Alto do Cruzeiro.

And so the mother who said of her severely malnourished baby with evident pity, "Poor little tyke! But after all, little critters have no feelings," can be understood in terms of delayed anthropomorphization rather than in terms of a "failure" of appropriate maternal empathy. The baby is seen, in this instance, as incapable of real human suffering. Some North American pediatricians are equally casual about infant sensibilities. Until very recently it was common for newborn males to be circumcised without anesthesia on the grounds that infants have little or no consciousness of pain. In marked contrast is the "new generation" of pediatricians, altogether maternal men such as Benjamin Spock and T. Barry Brazelton. Brazelton delights in staging "conversations" with one- and two-day-old infants. Or so Brazelton thinks and would like others to think, too.

The anthropomorphization of the fetus, neonate, infant, and baby is everywhere subject to cultural "nomination," and it is always a "courtesy" anthropomorphization. For it will be many months before the infant can display an undoubtedly "human" smile, and years will pass before she can turn a "twitch" into a meaningful "wink," as Clifford Geertz (1974) once described the essence of cultural transformation. Parents (mothers in particular) begin to enculturate infants, turning "raw" and "savage" neonates into "cooked" and "civilized" babies, by granting the infant a courtesy human status and then (like T. Barry Brazelton) acting toward the baby "as if" she could understand and respond intelligently. In this way human socialization proceeds and eventually succeeds in producing a bona fide human person. Whereas North American parents are generally eager to anthropomorphize their newborns, Brazilian shantytown mothers are relatively slow to do so. Conversely, whereas many North American women are reluctant to attribute any human status to the fetus, shantytown women do grant their fetuses a protective human soul. The cultural logic that informs courtesy anthropomorphization is not airtight; contradictions abound.

The women of the Alto are slow to "personalize" infants by attributing specific meanings to their whimpers, cries, facial expressions, flailing of arms and legs, kicks and screams, except in the negative instance, when these are seen as signs of child attack. Alto women do not scan the infant's face to note resemblances to other family members. At most what is commented on is whether the infant is light or dark skinned and whether he or she is big and strong or puny and weak. Naming practices follow a similar logic: many Alto infants can remain unnamed and unbaptized until they reach the first birthday or until a serious illness provokes an emergency baptism and/or burial. Until that time they will simply be referred to as *nene* (baby), little one, skinny one, or some other affectionate, yet impersonal, pet name. Infants who die unbaptized are named and baptized in their coffins. Anyone may be called on to give a name to a baby, and if that name doesn't stick, another will be given at a later date. Small children circulate among relatives and are often reared by more than one mother; on moving into a new household, the child may be given a different name or nickname.

These child naming practices can be understood within the larger social context of Alto life, where "individualism" has made fewer inroads than it has in Brazilian cosmopolitan society and culture. Roberto da Matta (1983:180–185), drawing on a long debate in social anthropology beginning with Mauss (1938) and followed by Dumont (1970), J. S. LaFontaine (1985), and others, argued that the Anglo-Saxon notion of the "individual" as a bounded, unique, integrated, motivational, and cognitive universe, a dynamic epicenter of awareness, emotion, judgment, and action, is a rather unique notion in the West. This concept of the individual remains somewhat exotic to traditional *Nordestino* society, which is still hierarchical, patriarchal, and personalistic in the sense that family, kinship, and other social roles define one's place and social identity.

For the traditional landed classes of the *zona da mata*, this means that one's identity is inherited through family bloodlines, as in any other oligarchy. One is a Cavalcanti, a Sá Barreto, or a Ferreira-Lima, and that preempts other, more individual, or unique characteristics of the person. But for the landless squatters of O Cruzeiro, where family names mean very little, it is not unusual for men and women not to know the full family names of their spouses. Here, individuals acquire their names and their social personas in a variety of social contexts. Consequently, personal names are often nicknames, some of them funny and affectionate (Fofa for puffy and soft), others merely descriptive (Irene Preta, Black Irene). Others are social relational, as when a woman is described as Maria *de* Lal or Maria *de* Sofia, that is, Maria the mother of Lal or Maria the employee of Dona Sofia. Men are similarly named in terms of various social and occupational roles (i.e., Oscar de Prestação, Oscar who sells on credit) and in terms of relationships to kin and to employers. As work roles and other social relationships change, so can the personal names. In this social context the notion of the person "as a complex of social relationships" (Radcliffe-Brown 1940:193) predominates over the notion of the individual as a unique and indivisible unit.

Infant naming patterns reveal this same kind of "thinking in roles," and no one infant is viewed as totally unique. Infants can substitute for or replace one another. A newborn can inherit the name of an older, deceased sibling, and several children in the same family may be given a variant of the same personal name. Our firm belief that every child has a constitutional right, as it were, to his or her own individual name reflects our markedly individualistic way of thinking. It is unfortunate that this conception of the individual has recently been codified in the United Nations Convention on the Rights of the Child, which states (article 7) that "the child shall be registered immediately after birth and shall have the right from birth to a name." Certainly, few of us would tolerate having been given the same name as a sibling (dead or alive), which would be viewed as an assault on the unalienable right to an individualized "self." Yet our own highly individualized naming practice has a recent social history that corresponds to the decline in family firms, especially the family farm. Until the late nineteenth century naming practices in the United States and western Europe were very similar to the ones I am referring to here. And in parts of rural America they persist to this day.[4]

The Alto infant gradually and slowly comes to earn his personal claim to full human status and with it his claim to a personal name and his right to the affections and passionate attachment of his mother. Until that time the affection shown the infant and young baby is general and nonspecific. "Who doesn't enjoy a baby?" people ask. But when asked what it is in particular that brings them enjoyment, they are puzzled and reply, "I don't know. Because she is no trouble?" or "Because he eats his *mingau*?" The attention given the infant does not focus on any distinguishing traits that identify the infant as a separate little person.

Similarly, Alto infants are not held a great deal today. The newly delivered mother is cautioned not to *pegar* (pick up) the infant until the forty-day *resguarda*, or lying-in period, has passed. There is no custom of backpacks or side slings among the *moradores*, although older babies are carried, somewhat gingerly, sidesaddle and across their mother's arm. The newborn sleeps in mother's bed or hammock for the first several weeks, after which she is moved into her own hammock or crib. The hammock provides the most stimulation the young baby receives; she is rocked. Therefore, Alto infants can most often be found lying on their backs. I have seen altogether doting grandmothers get on their knees on a bed to engage the newborn in a playful *en face* dialogue rather than lift the infant up and hold her in their arms. And young Alto mothers often hold their infants on their laps, with the head to their knees at a very awkward position from which to offer the baby a bottle.

In all, what is created is a social environment that minimizes the "individual" nature of the infant. The infant is viewed as human, to be sure, but as decidedly less human than the older child and certainly than the adult. Hence, it is entirely plausible that Alto women who have lost one or more young babies do not feel the depth of sorrow and grief that our theories of attachment, separation, and loss suggest must or *should* be there. In earlier chapters I referred to the political and public processes that routinize child death as the average, expectable outcome for poor families and to the indifference of the Catholic clergy to infant death amid obsessive Catholic cant on the social evils of birth control and abortion. Here; I refer to the various cultural practices and scripts that allow for death without weeping. Foremost among these is the traditional *velório de anjinho,* the "angel wake."

Angel-Babies: The Velório de Anjinhos

If he died at this angelic age, the small child became an object
of adoration. The mother rejoiced over the death of the
angel . . . weeping with delight because the Lord had carried
away her fifth child.

Gilberto Freyre (1986a:58)

From colonial Brazil to the present the death of an infant or a very young child was treated as a blessing among the popular classes, an event "to be accepted almost joyfully, at any rate without horror" (Freyre 1986b:144). The dead baby was an *anjinho,* a "little cherub," or an *inocente,* a "blameless creature" who died unregretted because his or her future happiness was assured. The bodies of the little angels were washed, their curls were prettily arranged, and they were dressed in sky blue or white shirts, with the cord of the Virgin tied around their waists. Their little hands folded in prayerful repose, their eyes left open and expectantly awaiting the Beatific Vision, angel-babies were covered with wild flowers, including floral wreaths on their heads. Little petition prayers and messages to the saints were tucked into their hands to be delivered to the Virgin on arrival. Even the poorest were arranged on wooden planks laden with flowers or in large, decorated cardboard boxes "of the kind used for men's shirts" (Freyre 1986b:388). The *velório de anjinho* was immortalized in Euclides da Cunha's classic, *Rebellion in the Backlands:* "The death of a child is a holiday. In the hut the poor parents' guitars twang joyfully amid the tears; the noisy, passionate samba is danced again and the quatrains of the poetic challengers loudly resound; while at one side, between two tallow candles, wreathed in flowers, the dead infant is laid out, reflecting in its last smile, fixed in death, the supreme contentment of one who is going back to heaven and eternal bliss" (1944:113).

The festive celebration of angel wakes, derived from the Iberian Peninsula, has been noted throughout Latin America from the Andes of Peru to the pampas of Argentina to the tropical coastal regions of Brazil and Colombia (see Foster 1960:143–166; Schechter 1983, 1988; Belote & Belote 1984; Dominguez 1960; Lenz 1953). It is found among Amerindians, blacks, whites, and *criollos* and among the wealthy as well as the poor. Roger Bastide

(1941) attributed the angel wake customs to the introduction of the "baroque" in Brazil, whereas Freyre (1986b:388) suggested that the Jesuits introduced *anjinho* beliefs to console native women for the alarming death rate of Indian children resulting from colonization.

All-night drinking, feasting, party games, courting rituals, special musical performances, and dances cross many culture areas in South America, where the infant wake may last for three or four consecutive days (Schechter 1983). Weeping is proscribed at the infant wake because a mother's tears make the angel-baby's path slippery and dampen its delicate wings (Nations & Rebhun 1988). Rather, the mother is expected to express her joy, as did the plantation mistress from Rio de Janeiro who exclaimed, "Oh, how happy I am! Oh, how happy I am! When I die and go to the gates of Heaven I shall not fail of admittance, for there will be five little children pressing toward me, pulling at my skirts, and saying, 'Oh, mother, do come in, do come in'" (Freyre 1986b:388). In rural Venezuela, the mother of the dead baby generally opens the dancing at her child's wake so that her angel may rise happily to the kingdom of heaven (Dominguez 1960:31).

The body of the dead infant was fetishized during traditional angel wakes in rural Latin America. The little corpse was sometimes taken out of the tiny coffin and handled like a doll or live baby. The corpse could be displayed like a saint, propped up on a home altar in between candlesticks and vases of sweet-smelling flowers. Or the dead child might be seated in a little chair, elevated on a small platform, set up inside an open box, tied to a ladder placed on top of the casket (to suggest the angel's ascent into heaven), or even tied to a swing suspended on ropes from the house beam. The infant's flight on the swing was said to symbolize the baby's transformation into an angel. The custom of leasing out angel-corpses to enliven local fiestas was described for the late nineteenth through the twentieth centuries in the Argentine pampas as well as in Venezuela, Chile, and Ecuador (see Ebelot 1943; Lillo 1942). In all, the traditional infant wake was a grand pretext for "unbridled merrymaking," perhaps (some suggested) as a culturally institutionalized "defense" against grief and mourning in a context in which infant death was all too common.

But what of a situation where neither festive joy nor deep grief is present? My own startlingly different ethnographic observations of angel-babies and the *velório de anjinho* in Bom Jesus today lead me to another set of conclusions, which I must touch on as a prelude to my final discussion of mother love, attachment, grief, and moral thinking. In Bom Jesus today, where an angel-baby is sent to heaven on the average of one every other day, infant wakes are brief, rarely lasting more than a couple hours, and dispensed with a minimum of ceremony. The *velório* of an infant younger than one is at best perfunctory. There are no musical accompaniments, no songs, no prayers, no ritual performances of any kind. Neither food nor drink is offered the casual visitor, most of them curious neighborhood children. Household life simply goes on as usual around the infant in her or his little casket, which may be placed on the kitchen table or across one or two straight-backed kitchen chairs. The infant's grandmother or godmother is in charge, in addition to the older woman who specializes in preparing the body for burial. There is neither great joy nor grief expressed, and the infant is rarely the focus of conversation.

I recall one particularly poignant infant wake that took place in an Alto household in 1987 on the day following the celebration of the one-year-old birthday party and formal christening of another child of the household. Mariana, the middle-aged mother of the one-year-old *caçula*, had purchased christening clothes, a large decorative birthday cake with candles, soft drinks, a wine punch for the adults, balloons, and party favors. The frosted cake was the centerpiece, and Mariana was quite protective of it, frequently brushing away flies that gathered near it and more than once dusting away a persistent procession of little ants. A borrowed record player was turned up loud; samba and lambada music blasted into the main street of the Alto, and the dancing spilled outside of the tiny house. The fiesta lasted for the better part of that Sunday afternoon and early evening. The little birthday girl in her ruffled dress was the center of a great deal of praise and attention. Meanwhile, Mariana's oldest, sixteen-year-old daughter, herself the single mother of a four-month-old infant, sat out the festivities very much on the margins. Her boyfriend was nowhere in evidence. To engage and entertain the girl a bit, I asked if I might take a peek at her baby. She brought me into the back room where her infant, in an advanced stage of marasmic malnutrition, had been left to sleep through the party. She slept very deeply, indeed, for the next morning I was called back for her brief, understated wake and burial.

The young mother sat in the front room repairing a fishing net. The grandmother's only comment was the usual *moradora* words of consolation: "Man makes; God takes." The "snowball baby" in her white tunic, decoratively strewn with sweet forget-me-nots, took the place of the birthday cake as the centerpiece on the table in the front room. A few crumbs of cake and frosting left over from the day before were still on the table, and a couple of deflated pink balloons lolled about on the mud floor. The crepe paper decorations were still in place. The previous day's little birthday girl seemed confused by the muted and ambivalent sentiments so soon after her own animated party, and she was fussy and demanding, insisting to be lifted up to see her infant niece. Finally, Mariana carried the child over to the table and let her peek inside the little casket. "Baby, baby," said the toddler. "Yes," repeated her tired mother, "baby is sleeping," and as Mariana leaned over to adjust the infant in her little cardboard pauper's coffin, I saw her hand once again, almost instinctively, brush away a line of ants, but this time from the infant's frosted, white face.

Men are rarely present at a *velório de anjinho*. Female relatives, neighbor women, and children often mill about. Meanwhile, however, the women and young girls of the household often go about their regular housework. They wash clothes at the back of the house, sort beans in preparation for the main meal, and do piecework for the local hammock industry, while the children do homework, play checkers, cut out paper dolls, or read comic books on the floor.

The procession of the angels to the cemetery is formed on the spur of the moment from the children who happen to be present. No special clothes are worn. There may or may not be a small floral wreath carried in front of the ragtag little parade. Some adults, but never the infant's own mother, may follow the procession to the graveyard. On one occasion the father, god-father, and paternal grandfather attended the funeral of a firstborn child, and all were deeply and visibly affected. On another occasion the godfather (and uncle to the dead child) followed the children's procession at some distance while walking his bicycle. Although he came as far as the graveyard, before the baby was put into the grave, the godfather left to attend a previously scheduled soccer game.

The procession of the angels takes the main, and only paved, street of the Alto, but once at the foot of the hill it veers away from the main *praça* of town and bypasses the church of Nossa Senhora das Dores. The procession does not stop (as it once did) for the priest's blessing; consequently, the bells of Our Lady of Sorrows no longer toll for the death of each child of Bom Jesus da Mata. That way of counting the dead has gone the way of many other folk Catholic pieties, swept away by the reformist spirit of the Vatican Council and by the socialist philosophy of the new regime of liberation theology. And no priest accompanies the procession to the cemetery, where the body is disposed of casually and unceremonially. Children bury children in Bom Jesus da Mata today. Where once clergymen and religious sisters taught patience and resignation to child death and other domestic tragedies, which were said to reveal the imponderable workings of God's will, the new church participates in the public indifference and social embarrassment toward infant death, which exists only as a bloody breech, a rupture with, and a glaring contradiction to the hierarchy's prolife and pronatalist teach-ings. So instead of the church *praça* in the dead center of Bom Jesus, the procession of the angels discreetly passes through the back streets of town,

Angel procession to the municipal graveyard.

under the trestles of the railroad or across the tracks, through the open-air yam market, past the rural sugar workers syndicate building, just under the barred windows of the municipal jail, close to the edge of the new reform school for abandoned street children run by the FEBEM, and up the muddy trail to the municipal cemetery at the farthest edge of town. The children know the route by heart; most have been part of other processions to bury dead siblings or playmates' siblings. The procession shares the street with cars, trucks, donkeys, wagons, and carts. Most cars and trucks hurriedly whiz by, and the children have to run to the side of the road with their little charge.

At the cemetery Seu Valdimar, the disabled and often ill-tempered municipal gravedigger and an assistant lead the children to the common space where pauper children are buried. The temporary space is normally already waiting, and in a few minutes the coffin is placed in the grave and covered over, thereby leaving a small, fresh mound to mark the space. No prayers are recited, and no sign of the cross is made as the coffin goes into its shallow grave. Valdimar often chides the children for one reason or another. It may be that the coffin is larger than expected, and he will have to enlarge the grave. Or he may scold the children for not tacking closed the top of the coffin, although he surely knows well the customs of the region. "Didn't you have any nails, any tacks?" he asked the brother of one deceased child.

"Soon the bugs will get to your little sister," he said unnecessarily. Other times Valdimar can be gentle with the children, in his own gruff way. "Have you any flowers?" Valdimar once asked the older sister of a little toddler who had just been buried. "No," she shook her head sadly. "Well, hurry up and get some, then. . . . I haven't all day." Permission granted, the children scampered off in opposite directions to pull up flowers from other fresh graves. "Not *that* many; be careful," yelled Valdimar. And the children returned to scatter the picked flowers on top of the little one's grave. That is normally the extent of the ceremony, except the washing off of muddy hands and feet in the public spigot on the way out.

If an adult is present, the children in the procession have the right to expect a treat on the way home. "*Picolé* [ices] *Picolé*!" the cry may go up, and the responsible adult will be pulled toward a little storefront shack. I have seen a grandfather gather the children into a small shop and carefully count out his few, wrinkled cruzados and negotiate quietly with the shopkeeper so that every child in the procession could have two pieces of hard candy. He himself carefully distributed the sweets, two by two to each child, a sad, gentle smile on his face.

I have tried to imagine, working slowly, intuitively, and unobtrusively with the people of the Alto and with women and children in particular, what meaning the angel-baby and the *velório de anjinho* has for them. At times it seems as if the dead infant were a "transitional object" for the women of the Alto, not only in the ritual, anthropological sense of a liminal being in between social statuses ("Neither here nor there," as one mother said of her dying infant) but in the psychoanalytic sense of a liminal, transitional "attachment" (as to a teddy bear or a "rubby" blanket), which, created out of the imagination, has a self-soothing quality (see Winnicott 1964:167–172). *Anjinhos* allow Alto mothers to "let go" of so many of their young children by allowing them to "hold on" to an idealized image of spirit-children populating the heavens, as close, really, as the stars can seem on a still night. All transitional objects ultimately foster autonomy and independence through the breaking or the breaking out of "impossible" attachments (as in infancy the "rubby blanket" or teddy bear substitutes for the "impossible" desire to have mother's breast available at will). Just so, for Alto women, *anjinhos* in heaven substitute for the impossible attachment to half-live babies in the hammock.

The shaping of the emotions and responses at child death is formed in early childhood as Alto children, mere babies themselves, are schooled in the normalization of child death as they are sooner or later delegated the role of their dead siblings' and playmates' pallbearers and undertakers. The average Alto girl between the ages of five and thirteen participates in two or more angel processions each year. The average boy participates in at least one a year. One notes, in the reactions and fantasy play of Alto children, the awesome power of these early "primal scenes" in shaping, routinizing, and muting later adult responses to child death.

Many little girls on the Alto do Cruzeiro have no baby dolls to play with. Nor do they tend to fashion them out of available scrap materials, such as torn socks or the corn husks discarded on the main streets after *feira* in the harvest months of June and July. Nor do they fashion dolls and play furniture from the red clay that is commonly found not far from the banks of the local river. Alto girls prefer active games, circle dances, and pretend "talent shows" in which they can imitate the beautiful and seductive children's television star, Xuxa. Girls covet the cheap, plastic soccer balls that any of their older brothers are lucky enough to own. Playing with dolls and playing house are of little interest to Alto girls. I soon learned to bring costume jewelry, hair ribbons, play cosmetics, and small, battery-run video games as gifts for Alto girls and to leave at home the pretty little baby dolls, which elicited so little interest or curiosity. In a half dozen of the more prosperous Alto homes where the children have an abundance of toys, girls are given dolls as presents, but these are treated as display, rather than play, objects and are often kept in the original cellophane-covered boxes standing up on a shelf and are taken down for visitors to admire and are then carefully replaced.

I am tempted to suggest why Alto children are so uninterested in a form of play that is so common among little girls the world over. This lack of interest is born, perhaps, of an early and negative association between lifeless dolls in pretty cardboard boxes and lifeless siblings in decorated cardboard coffins. This possibility was brought home to me during a conversation with Xiquinha, the elderly praying woman of the Alto, who had been washing and dressing dead children for their angel wakes since she was seven and a half. In the following conversation, Xiquinha explained how she became a specialist in angel wakes at so tender an age.

"Whenever a baby died on the Rua dos Sapos, where I had been raised since I was a tiny child, a neighbor would call for me because I always enjoyed dressing the baby for its wake. The other little girls would run away; some didn't even like being in the procession of the angels. But not me; I adored it all. I would take the baby on my lap across my knees, and it was *just like a little doll for me to play with*. Little angel-bodies are different from [dead] big bodies. Angel-bodies stay soft and flexible, so you can handle them easily. I would wash it and put on its blue or white clothes and a veil for the little girls and, if their mother had one, a blue ribbon around their waist. All little angel-girls are dressed like little brides. White is the color of virgins, which all of them are. When an infant is stillborn, people call it an angel-*carobim* [i.e., possibly derived from cherubim] because it is untouched by this world. Blue is the color that the Virgin Mary loves best. So you want to have the little angels dressed that way when they arrive to greet the Virgin at the gates of heaven."

When my Brazilian informants tell me that they do not weep, that they are pleased to have a little *coração santa* in heaven looking after them, I am inclined to believe them and to take them at face value. In most cases the socialization experience has been adequate. Angel-baby beliefs not only "console" *moradores*, they shape and determine the way that death is experienced.

Once as my then-fifteen-year-old daughter, Jennifer, and I were on our way up the Alto to an angel wake near the very top of the hill, Jennifer burst into angry tears. She was to have been the "official" photographer at the wake because the mother of the baby was unable to pay for a professional photographer from the town. I had quite insensitively offered Jennifer's services without asking her permission. "I don't want to photograph a dead baby," she yelled at me, quite reasonably. I apologized and brought her inside Terezinha's house along the way to compose herself. Terezinha and her teenage daughter Rosália were quite concerned. Why was Jennifer so upset? Did she have "boyfriend troubles"? Rosália wanted to know. When I explained that she was upset about having to attend an infant wake, they stared at her unbelievingly. "Why?" they asked. "It's only a baby!"

On only one occasion out of the dozens of angel wakes and burials that I have witnessed over the years did a child express a subdued, yet nonetheless ravaged, grief. It was just as little Mercea's body was going into the dirt that her seven-year-old cousin, Leonardo, turned to me to say in an anxious aside: "Nancí, I don't want any more of mine to die." Ashamed, I put aside my camera and my dog-eared, rain-soaked notebook and allowed myself, too, to sit down on a low marble stone and rediscover and feel pain and grief for a moment: "I don't either, Leonardo. I don't either."

Grief Work: A Political Economy of the Emotions

Sorrow concealed, like an oven stopp'd,
Doth burn the heart to cinders where it is.
                    William Shakespeare, *Titus Andronicus*

And so when an infant dies on the Alto do Cruzeiro, few tears are shed, and women are likely to say that the death came as a blessing or a great relief. "I feel free" or "I feel unburdened" is what many say. This is not to suggest, however, that the women are "cold" and unfeeling, for very often the

Leonardo at his little cousin's grave: "I don't want any more of ours to die."

mother expresses pity (*pena*) for the dead child, saying, "*Faz pena* [what a shame], *menina*, to see them suffer and die." But pity is distinctly different from the sentiments of grief (*desgosto, nojo, luto*), sadness (*tristeza*), depression (*depressão, deprimida*), or bittersweet longing or yearning for a lost or dead loved one (*saudade*). And just as there is no immediate display of grief or mourning in many Alto mothers, I have found no evidence of "delayed" or "displaced" grief in the days, weeks, and months following the death of an infant, unless, perhaps, a new pregnancy can be seen as a symptom of displaced grief.

I made a point of visiting the homes of women who had recently lost an infant, both to offer support and observe their responses to death. What I found did not conform to the conventional biomedical wisdom concerning "normal" grieving following child death, a model of "human" behavior that is, in part, the creation of a few influential psychologists, among them John Bowlby (1961a, 1961b, 1980), Elisabeth Kübler-Ross (1969), and Robert Jay Lifton (1967, 1975, 1979).

Several days following the death and burial of her first baby, a three-month-old daughter named Daniella, I visited the young mother, Anita, to see how she was getting along. She had been calm, composed, and dry-eyed during the wake and had gone back to work on the next day.

"Are you *triste* [sad]?" I asked.

"No, ma'am, not much; Mario says I'll soon have another."

"Did you cry?"

"Oh, no! It's not good to cry, for it will keep the baby from rising up to heaven."

"Did you sleep all right?"

"Oh, yes, I was very tired yesterday."

"Did you eat well?"

"No, I didn't," she said sadly. But then the resilient girl added, "There was nothing in the house to eat but *fubá* [cornmeal], and I *hate* fubá!" Then Anita went outside, humming along with a popular tune on the radio, to wash clothes. I stayed behind to chat with a few of her neighbors, who confirmed that one does not really miss a very young baby.

Sometimes, it is more obvious why grief at the death of an innocent "angel" is not forthcoming. When Dona Amor received word that her first and only grandson was born puny and weak to her adopted and mentally disabled teenage daughter, who had been seduced and raped by a pimp, the old woman hurriedly lit a candle to São Antônio, her patron saint. She begged the saint to carry off the day-old infant, born, she said, of a "race of beasts." Amor's prayers were answered later that same day. Laughing and clapping her hands, Amor told how she went to the local *casa funerária* to pick out the little coffin. She carried it to the hospital, where she washed and dressed the infant in his baptismal/burial clothes. Then jauntily, as if "it were a basket of fruit," Amor put the little casket on her head and started off across town to the municipal cemetery. When street children laughed to see Dona Amor balancing the little coffin on her head in a solitary procession, the old woman shooed them off, saying, "There is no shame in burying the dead." There was certainly no sorrow either.

Against these altogether normative responses to infant death on the Alto do Cruzeiro are the modern psychiatric theories of "healthy" versus "disordered" mourning, which constitute a hegemonic theory of the emotions. The psychologists and psychiatrists of mourning (see Freud 1957:244–245; Bowlby 1980; Lifton 1967) consider child death, and infant death in particular, to be among the most wrenching of all experiences of loss, especially for the mother who may not yet feel herself to be separate from the newborn. "Infant death is," Marshall Klaus remarked, "a kind of death to the self not dissimilar to the loss of a limb" (personal communication). Bowlby (1980:113–124) described the phases of *normal* mourning after the death of a young child as follows: numbing and shock, disbelief, anger, depression, disorganization, and reorganization.

Every major hospital today has clinical social workers and nurses who specialize in helping women (and men) to grieve the premature death of an infant. They distribute helpful booklets, such as "Newborn Death" (Johnson, Cunningham, Ewing, Hatcher, & Dannen 1982) to the bereaved parents. The advice offered is succinct and *very* direct. It counsels the parents to "see, hold, touch, and name your [dead] newborn" and stresses the importance of the mother's presence at a graveside service and burial (1). Weeping over the death is cast as a human right and a necessity: "We have finally come to realize that crying is a strength. . . . Remember, you have a right to cry when your baby dies. Allowing your tears to come, while talking to others, can help you move through your grief" (4). But the booklet cautions against taking to heart the "insensitive" comments of relatives and friends who may not know the "right" things to say. Those around may offer just the kind of advice and comfort that "you *don't* need": "Every parent will hear some well-meaning person say that you can have another baby. You'll get the 'don't cry' messages, and 'just forget about it' statements. Some people will act as if your baby never existed. Others will act as if you can be a *little* sad, but not as much as if your baby were older. It's as if they think the amount of sadness is somehow connected to the size of the dead person" (8).

If the inherent psychological conflicts produced by the loss of an infant or a very young child are not resolved, various pathologies are believed likely to occur, of which chronic mourning (similar to Freud's notion of melancholia) or its opposite, a "prolonged absence of conscious grieving" (Bowlby 1980:139), is common. The absence of grief or the "inability to mourn" was first identified by Helene Deutsch (1937) in her clinical practice with women, some of whom were evidently rather "merry" widows. The "denial" of an "appropriate" grief may last, Bowlby wrote, for years, decades, and even in some cases "for the rest of a person's life" (1980:139). The "disordered mourner" may feel relief and may be quite cheerful and seem well adjusted. Some may even report feelings of relief and euphoria following the death of a loved one. But such feelings are disallowed and pathologized. Lifton was direct: "To be unable to mourn is to be unable to enter into the great human cycle of death and rebirth; it is to be unable to 'live again' " (1975:vii). Those who cannot grieve are scarcely human. This is a weighty moralism, indeed.

It strikes me as no coincidence that so much of the psychological literature on disordered mourning concerns *female* patients who appear to be at a "high risk" of producing, according to the canons of psychotherapy, the wrong emotions in response to death, either too much or too little sadness. In the grief and mourning literature, as in the attachment and bonding literature, we are faced with a biomedical prescription concerning the womanly duty not only to marry and procreate but to *love* offspring and mourn the family's dead. Emotion work is frequently gendered work. And we may want to consider whether the psychological theories on maternal love, attachment, grief, and mourning are not a "rhetoric of control" (M. Rosaldo 1984) and a discourse on power "by other means."

Catherine Lutz (1988) recently pointed out in this regard that conventional biomedical theories of emotion represent an American "ethnopsychology" based on Western notions of mind and body, feeling and reason, nature and culture, self and other, male and female, and individual and society. Psychotherapy is concerned with fostering emotional expression; with "speaking truth" to the deeply repressed, hidden spaces of individual emotional life; and with overcoming the "cultural" constraints that produce distortions and defenses against knowing what one is *really* thinking and feeling.[5] There is a presumed binary split between public sentiments and private feelings, between what is cultural and what is "natural." Culture emerges as an artificial facade concealing the dangerous intensity of hidden or unconscious human passions and desires. What is "real" and "authentic" is just what is most concealed from view.

Along this same binary divide, women and the female are associated with nature, body, and feeling, just as men and the male are associated with culture, mind, and reason. It is expected that women will be more emotionally responsive than men; consequently, society relegates more emotion work, including love work and grief work, to them. In the extensive psychological literature on grief and bereavement (see, for example, Glick, Weiss, & Parkes 1974:263–265; Scheff 1979), it is assumed that the sexes differ in emotionality. Men are said to cry less than women following the death of a family member and are less often depressed. Often they do not appear to be deeply moved or touched by death. But this is treated as appropriate gender behavior. There is no respected body of psychological research on the "inability of men to cry" comparable to the research on the "inability of mothers to love." And the clinical portraits of "failure to grieve" are almost exclusively concerned with the absence of "appropriate" emotionality in women following the death of a spouse or a child.

Bereavement customs worldwide (see Kligman 1988; Rosenblatt, Walsh, & Jackson 1976:26–27) commonly assign women to prolonged and ritualized grieving, both during the funeral services and long after they are over. It is widows who commonly cut their hair, cover themselves with ashes, mutilate their bodies, or shroud themselves in black for the remainder of their lives, while widowers walk freely, indistinguishable from "ordinary" men. This cross-cultural "specialization" of women in the division of emotional labor may be related to the generally lower status of women in the societies observed. Just as women may be coerced into feeding males before they themselves eat or into carrying the heaviest loads, they may be coerced into assuming the emotional burden for grief work. Just as plebeians were expected to weep openly on the death of their king, women are expected to show proper "deference" by weeping publicly for the death of kin.

Alternatively, the expectation that women will grieve for the dead may be an extension of the division of labor found in many traditional rural and peasant societies that delegates to older women specialists the task of washing and dressing the bodies of the dead, as they do, for example, in the two ethnographic instances that I know best: western Ireland and rural Northeast Brazil. In "Ballybran," Ireland, the old women who dress the dead are also expected to recite long and sorrowful ritualized laments; on the Alto do Cruzeiro the old women who dress the dead are expected to recite special mortuary prayers, but they do so only for dead adults. "Why pray for angel-babies who have no need of our prayers?" asked Xiquinha. "It's *their* job to pray for us!" Given the often "coerced" nature of pregnancy on the Alto do Cruzeiro—recall, for example, the sexual and reproductive life of Lordes, whose second husband sadistically "enjoyed" seeing her pregnant again and again—it is also possible that the refusal to grieve for the death of their infants is at times a gesture of defiance. It could be a way of saying, "You can make me pregnant, but you cannot make me love all of them . . . or *keep* all of them either."

Death Without Weeping

And so I maintain that Alto women generally face child death stoically, even with a kind of *belle indifférence* that is a culturally appropriate response. No one on the Alto do Cruzeiro criticizes a mother for not grieving for the death of a baby. No psychiatrist, pediatrician, or social worker visits the mother at home or tells her in the clinic what she is "supposed" to be feeling at a particular "phase" in her mourning. She is not told that crying is a healthy (and womanly) response to child death or that it is "natural" to feel bitter and resentful (which reduces anger to a manageable medical "symptom") or that she must "confront" her loss and get over her unhealthy emotional "numbness."

Poor Brazilians "work" on the self and emotions in a very different fashion. Instead of the mandate to mourn, the Alto mother is coached by those around her, men as well as women, in the art of resignation (*conformação*) and "holy indifference" to the vagaries of one's fate on earth and a hopefulness of a better life beyond. In this cultural milieu a deficit of emotion is not viewed as unhealthy or problematic (as in the overly repressed Anglo-Saxon culture of the United States); rather, an excess is. To experience strong emotions and passions—of love and lust, envy and anger, ecstasy and joy, grief and longing—is for most Brazilians, rich as well as poor, urban as well as rural, the most "natural" and expected occurrence. It is what being human is all about. But if allowed to run riot, these emotions are understood as the harbingers of much misery and suffering. Excessive emotions can bring down large and powerful households as well as small and humble ones. They can ruin lives and livelihoods. They can destroy relationships. They can cause physical as well as mental sickness. The Brazilian folk ethnopsychology of emotion is based on a very different construction of the body, self, personhood, and society. One can, for example, contrast the once popular belief in American society that cancers were caused by the repressions of the inner self, by passion turned inward and feeding on itself (see Sontag 1979), with the popular belief in Brazilian culture that emotional outbursts can dissipate the individual, poison the blood, and cause tuberculosis or cancer.

The strong mandate *not* to express grief at the death of a baby, and most especially not to shed tears at the wake, is strongly reinforced by a *Nordestino* folk piety, a belief that for the brief hours that the infant is in the coffin, she is neither human child nor blessed little angel. She is something other: a spirit-child struggling to leave this world and find its way into the next. It must climb. The path is dark. A mother's tears can impede the way, make the road slippery so that the spirit-child will lose her footing, or the tears will fall on her wings and dampen them so that she cannot fly. Dona Amor told of a "silly" neighbor who was weeping freely for the death of her toddler when she was interrupted by the voice of her child calling to her from his coffin: "Mama, don't cry for me because my *mortália* is very heavy and wet with your tears." "You see," Amor said, "the child had to struggle even after death, and his mother was making it worse for him. The little one wasn't an angel yet because angels never speak. They are mute. But he was no longer a human child either. He was an *alma penanda* [wretched, wandering soul]."

"What is the fate of such a child?"

"Sometimes they are trapped in their graves. Sometimes when you pass by the cemetery, you can see little bubbles and foam pushing up from the ground where such infants are buried. And late at night you can even hear the sound of the lost souls of the child-spirits wailing."

In all, what is being created is an environment that teaches women to contain their affections and hold back their grief during the precarious first year of the child's life. The question remains, however, whether these cultural "conventions" actually succeed in producing the desired effects or whether the dry-eyed stoicism and nonchalant air of Alto mothers are merely "superficial" and skin-deep, covering up a "depth of sorrow," loss, and longing. Nations and Rebhun, for example, maintained that the lack of grief is mere facade: "The inner experience of grief may be hidden by the flat affect of impoverished Brazilians. This behavior is part of a culturally mandated norm of mourning behavior; rather than signify the *absence* of strong emotion at child and infant death, it reveals the *presence* of grief" (1988:158).

What they wish to suggest, drawing inspiration from the writings of Robert J. Lifton and other psychologists of mourning, is that the "blankness" and "flat affect" that they observed in certain poor women of the Northeast "is the blankness of the shell-shocked" (160). They continued, "The loss is too great to bear, too great to speak of, too great to experience fully. . . . Their seeming indifference is a mask, a wall against the unbearable. . . . While flamboyantly open about such emotions as happiness and sexual jealousy, they adopt a generally flat affect when discussing painful topics" (158).

Although I have no doubt (and have gone to great lengths to show) that the local culture is organized to defend women against the psychological ravagings of grief, I assume that the culture is quite successful in doing so and that we may take the women at their word when they say, "No, I felt no grief. The baby's death was a blessing." One need not speak of "masks" or "disguises" or engage in second-guessing on the basis of alien and imported psychological concepts of the self. Nations and Rebhun assumed a "divided self" that conforms to our Western ethnopsychiatry: a split between a public and a private self and between a "true" and a "false" self-expression. Moreover, when they suggested that the "mothers' flat affect in response to infant deaths is due more to folk Catholic beliefs than to a lack of emotional attachment to infants" (141), they projected a very secular view of religious belief as a superficial feature of the interior life, rather than as a powerful force that penetrates and constitutes the person.

Until recently, most cultural and symbolic anthropologists tended to restrict their interest in emotions to occasions when they were contained within formal, public, collective, highly stylized, and "distanced" rites and rituals, such as in healing, spirit possession, initiation, and other life cycle events. They left the discussion of the more private, idiosyncratic feelings of individual, suffering subjects to psychoanalytic and biomedical anthropologists, who generally reduced them to a discourse on universal drives and instincts.[6] This division of labor, based on a false dichotomy between collective, "cultural" sentiments and individual, "natural" passions, leads to a stratigraphic model of human nature in which biology emerges as the base and culture as the mere veneer or patina, as the series of carnival masks and disguises alluded to previously.

But the view taken here is that emotions do not precede or stand outside of culture; they are part of culture and of strategic importance to our understanding of the ways in which people shape and are shaped by their world. Emotions are not reified things in and of themselves, subject to an internal, hydraulic mechanism regulating their buildup, control, and release. Catherine Lutz (1988) and Lila Abu-Lughod (1986), among others, understand emotions as "historical inventions" and as "rhetorical strategies" used by individuals to express themselves, to make claims on others, to promote or elicit certain kinds of behaviors, and so on. In other words, emotions are discourse; they are constructed and produced in language and in human interaction. They cannot be understood outside of the cultures that produce them. The most radical statement of this position is that without our cultures, we *simply would not know how to feel*.

In fieldwork, as in daily life, we often encounter radical difference, and we come up against things we do not like or with which we cannot immediately identify or empathize. These "discoveries" can make us supremely uncomfortable. As anthropologists with a commitment to cross-cultural understanding, we worry—as well we should—how our written materials will be read and received by those who have not experienced the pleasures (as well as the pains) of living with the complex people whose lives we are trying to describe. Consciously or unconsciously we may "screen out" or simply refuse to accept at face value what we see or what we are being told, as, for example, when Renato Rosaldo (1980) at first refused to believe that his Ilongot friends were capable of headhunting, as they insisted, for the simple, expressive "joy" of it as well as to "kill" the sadness and anger they felt. Rosaldo preferred to believe that there was a more "rational" and "instrumental" purpose behind Ilongot headhunting, such as avenging the death of a loved one. But his informants, after listening attentively to Rosaldo's explanation of the anthropologists' model of exchange theory, replied that "Ilongots simply did not think any such thing" at all (1983:180).

The temptation to second-guess our informants is particularly keen when their own explanations of their lives are "experience-distant" or counter-intuitive to our own sociological or psychological understandings of human behavior. Sometimes, as in Rosaldo's case, it is because people's explanations may appear, as they did to him, "too simple, thin, opaque, implausible, stereotypic, or otherwise unsatisfying" (179). Similarly, Thomas Gregor, who investigated the "psychological impact" of infanticide among the Brazilian Amazonian Mehinaku Indians, found that he could not accept the villagers' claims that infanticide was easily accomplished and left no residue of guilt or blame: "We profoundly reject interring healthy children and therefore we assume that deep down the Mehinaku must feel the same way. Yet they claim otherwise. They institutionalize infanticide and assume that it is nearly painless: "The white man really feels for his infant. We do not. Infants are not precious to us" (1988:6).

These statements produced cognitive dissonance for Gregor, who began from the premise of a "universal human imperative requiring that children be protected and nurtured" (3). While aware of the danger of projecting his own moral repugnance toward infanticide on the Amerindian villagers, Gregor found himself ultimately unable to "take Mehinaku opinion at face value" (6). The oft-repeated phrase "Infants are not precious to us," while emblematic of the "official" culture of Mehinaku infanticide, was covering a large reservoir of personal ambivalence and doubt. The Mehinaku mother, Gregor wrote, who brought an infant to term simply could not "be emotionally neutral about infanticide" (6) because she was subject to the same psychobiological feelings as the Western mother. And so Mehinaku cultural practices were interpreted as psychological "defenses" and "distancing devices": the rejected neonate was not referred to as a "baby" but rather as a *kanupa*, a "tabooed" or "forbidden" thing; the infanticidal act was accomplished very rapidly; and so forth. These led Gregor to conclude that, despite what the Indians told him, "Mehinaku infants are, in fact, precious to the villagers and infanticide is edged with moral and emotional ambivalence" (19). The burden of proof was, however, very thin, overinterpreted, and extremely circumstantial. It would not hold up in court. And it strikes me as indefensible to argue in a post hoc fashion that Mehinaku villagers *must* consider all their newborns precious because Western psychobiological theories tell us that all humans *are* this way.

Gregor's detailed descriptions of Mehinaku beliefs and practices toward their *kanupa* lead me to think that these women view and treat some of their neonates as prehumans, just as many women in the United States view and treat their fetuses. If we want to draw comparisons and analogies, it may be more appropriate to consider Mehinaku neonaticide as a form of "postpartum abortion." It seems to be practiced with similar intent and with a similar range of sentiments, explanations, and emotions. And just as Gregor would second-guess his informants' *real* feelings on the matter, some psychologists similarly dismiss the apparent psychological relief and the "indifference" of middle-class women who have had to abort a fetus as "denial" of their loss, grief, and deep moral ambivalence. With theories such as these, what is being "denied" are the disparate voices and moral sensibilities of women.

Renato Rosaldo, while later recovering from a profound personal loss in his own life, was moved to reflect (1983) on his initial refusal to "hear" what his Ilongot informants told him about "grief and the headhunter's rage." In rethinking Ilongot emotions in light of his own recent experience, Rosaldo came to accept that one could indeed feel a passionate, murderous, yet almost joyously self-affirming, rage in response to the death of a loved one. Or perhaps his own experience of grief was shaped by his Ilongot teachers, for fieldwork *is* transformative of the self. And so Rosaldo returned from his own mourning to challenge his anthropological colleagues to pay more attention to what their informants were telling them and to make room in their highly abstract theorizing for the often unanticipated "force" and intensity of emotions in human life.

Tristeza e Saudades

Saudade! Saudade!	*Saudade! Saudade!*
Palavra tão triste	Such a sad word
e ouvi-la faz bem.	I hear it and I feel good.

   Antônio Nobre (cited in Figueiredo 1988:4)

The *moradores* of the Alto are passionate people who express their emotions with freedom and with a range of nuances in sentiment and sensibility that defy translation. "Take *saudades*," my friends often say. "Do you even have a word for it?" Based on their knowledge of American film, television, and rock music, Brazilians throughout the country tend to view North Americans as a cold, unfeeling, and emotionally wooden people, a people without a heart. Often I am taunted: "Americans are rich and smart, but they are sexless, passionless," or they lack a depth or experience of emotional abandon and joy [*alegria, animação*] or delicious sexual jealousy or bittersweet longing and sorrow [*saudades*]. Brazilians, they say of themselves, are sensual, vibrant, alive, also deeply sentimental, heavy, melancholy, sad. They describe themselves, above all, as a people of feeling. Consequently, I almost always feel more "at home" on the Alto do Cruzeiro, where my own occasional "excesses" of joy, sadness, fear, anger, revulsion, or attachment are not censored (as they so often are in the United States) but rather are understood and excused as "only human."

In referring to themselves as a passionate, emotional, melancholy, and tragic "race" (a term they sometimes use), my friends are expressing the dominant and "official" cultural self-identity, which has been a favorite subject of Brazilian poets, writers, filmmakers, historians, and social anthropologists from Euclides da Cunha (1904) and Paulo Prado (1931), up through Gilberto Freyre (1986a, 1986b). (Also see Amaral 1948; Leite 1976; de Andrade 1941.) With the possible exception of Roberto da Matta and his emphasis on the joyous, playful, Bakhtinian spirit of the *carnavalesco*—the *alegria brasileira*—much of the literature written by Brazilians about themselves eventually returns to the subject of "Brazilian sadness" and melancholy, the *tristeza brasileira*. And so Paulo Prado (1928) opened his classic work on the Brazilian soul with the poignant words, "*Numa terra radiosa vive um povo triste*; in a radiant land lives a sad people."

This mantle of sadness was assumed, Prado suggested, in the history of the colonial encounter and in the violence, destruction, and rape of the lands and people who eventually gave birth to the Brazilian nation. Eduardo Freiro repeated the famous lines of Olavo Bilac: "The Brazilian is naturally sad because of the melancholy of the three races that contributes to his being. The Portuguese is as nostalgic as the listless sound of his *fados* [a plaintive song about fate and human destiny]; the African is oppressed, beaten down, and his revolts are the painful cries against his permanent state of exile; the Indian is long-suffering, his lamentations echoing the resigned complaints of the rivers and the patient murmurings of the mysterious forests" (1957:13, my translation).

The celebrated *tristeza brasileira* that so dominated the modernist movement in Brazil in the early decades of the twentieth century and whose spirit was reflected in Levi-Strauss' *Tristes Tropiques*, is a highly self-conscious form of national self-construction. It affects the way Brazilians understand themselves in everyday life. The reckless surrender to *carnaval*, for example, is understood even by the impoverished residents of the Alto do Cruzeiro as a necessary corrective to the sadness and melancholy of the everyday. But this "nationalized" sadness is not only banished—as when *carnaval* revelers and dancers sing out, "*Tristeza vai se embora*; Sadness, be gone!"—it is also coddled, institutionalized, and even savored in the generative theme of Brazilian *saudades*.

It is not true that Northeast Brazilians generally "express painful topics" in a "blank" or an emotionless way. Quite the opposite is the case. No, the absence of grief, the emotional indifference to infant death, is something else and is perhaps in a class by itself. When I began to examine this topic, one of the things that first struck me as rather "odd" was the choice of words women used to express their feelings following the death of a small baby. They did not say that they were *triste, deprimida, desgostosa* (disappointed, sorrowed), or *acabada* (beaten down or laid low) by the event, words they commonly used in other, related contexts, as when, for example, an older child died, a lover abandoned a woman, or an adult child moved far away. Nor did they ever speak of *saudades* for the dead infant.

In the days, weeks, and months (or even years) following all these other sad events, Alto women spoke at great length of their poignant "longing" for the missing object of their affections. And they wept freely in the telling. Eventually they began, through the process of recollection in often exquisite detail, to *matar* their *saudades* (kill their longing or lovesickness). They did so by reliving and reexperiencing, in a very sensual way, various moments shared with the loved one. It could happen by evoking the memory of the brilliant colors of the sky on a particular night of lovemaking or the musky smell of a favorite son's fresh sweat as he rushed in happily and victoriously from a neighborhood soccer game, or it could be the cool, sweet taste of coconut water that one's mother or one's spouse went through the trouble of getting when one was feverish and thirsty. The memory, returned to consciousness through these vivid, little physical details, so evoked the feelings one had for the missing loved one that it was physically painful and forced one to cry out, "*Ai, que saudade!*" and sometimes to strike one's chest or the table or the wall. The memory of the loved one was painful, but it was also impossibly sweet, and *no one* preferred emotional or mental amnesia to these ambivalent, bittersweet recollections. And so one could even say, "*Ai, que saudades de saudades que eu não tenho!* Oh, what sad longings for the longings that I don't have."

Saudades, as my Brazilian friends suggested, though a key term, is not an easily translated one, and herein lies the problem of cultural interpretation. As Lutz noted, the translation process "involves much more than a simple one-to-one linking of concepts in one language with concepts in another" (1988:78). The anthropologist must also supply the larger cultural context within which the words are used and accumulate their various meanings, some of them subliminal. *Saudade* reflects a great deal about the ways in which Northeast Brazilians view themselves and their ways of thinking, being, feeling, and acting in the world. So to suggest that *saudade* can be simply translated as "sad longing," "poignant memory," "yearning," "nostalgia," or "homesickness" (see the various entries in Taylor 1970:571) is misleading. Nostalgia, while sharing with *saudade* the complex interactions of joy and sorrow, is a greatly debased sentiment in American usage today. We think of nostalgia as a superficial, often false emotion. Brazilians think of their *saudade* as the purest expression of the Brazilian soul, of their heightened sensibility and awareness of the natural and social environment in which they live, of their acute sensitivity to the human condition and to its tragedies, and of loss, longing, and, in particular, memory itself.

Eurico Figueiredo, a Portuguese psychiatrist, noted in an unpublished essay, "Saudade e Depressão," the difficulty of locating the "exact sense" of the concept of *saudade*, which requires, among other things, a mastery of Portuguese and Brazilian poetry that I cannot claim for myself. Figueiredo stressed the complex associations between pleasure and regret, desire and pain, attachment and loss. It is not to be confused, he said, with the biomedical concept of depression, which has medicalized and reduced the associations among painful longing, burning desire, and unbearable loss to a psychiatric symptom.

Think for a moment how infrequently today we refer to ourselves as desperately sad or sick with longing and desire. So transformed are we by medicine and psychiatry that we can speak to each other today only of our "depressions." Although I am sure that many readers also know what lovesickness is, we tend to denigrate it as an adolescent experience of first passion. Similarly, our understandings of mourning the dead have been reduced to a medicalized discourse that makes it difficult for us to grasp the Brazilian uses of *saudades* in this context as well. Some Protestant Americans might be inclined to view as morbid, maudlin, or baroque, for example, the penitential rituals in Roman Catholic celebrations of Holy Week, with their sensual recalling to "memory" of the physical suffering and death of Jesus. Yet this is a spiritualized expression of Brazilian *saudade*. And to Brazilian Catholics these graphic Lenten rites of embodied memory are central to their faith (see Bastide 1964:62). Perhaps only "homesickness" (by analogy and containment to one instance of loss) is the one sentiment left in our lexicon that captures something of what Brazilians mean by *saudade*.

I am belaboring this discussion because the notion of *saudades* offers a key to understanding "death without weeping" on the Alto do Cruzeiro. Infant death is the one context of loss in which people, mothers in particular, never refer to their *saudades*. When I realized this, late into my research, I began to ask *moradores* to talk to me in general about their *saudades*. I learned that there were *saudades* for a loved one who was gone or (more abstractly) for a love that had turned sour or bitter. But one could also have *saudades* for particular smells, foods, colors, or sensations from the past that were associated with poignant events and loved ones. One could have *saudades* for the good times one had had at a *festa* or at *carnaval*. "But these are 'light' or merely 'entertaining' *saudades*," I was told. It was the loss of a loved one through death that provided the most potent source of *saudades*. An Alto mother spoke of her young daughter's *saudades* in the days and weeks following the "sudden" death of the girl's father in a work-related accident: "Edilene could not eat or sleep, and she cried without stopping. Throughout the day she would lie on our bed wrapped up in her father's clothes, his stained work shirt and pants, his sandals, holding onto his half-used bottle of cologne and his photo. She refused to give them up, not even so I could wash the soiled clothes. Finally, I had to hide her father's things; they were so full of *saudades* for her. As long as they were in sight, she couldn't go on with her life. I had to force her to return to school. Even today she sometimes begs me, 'Mama, where have you put my papa's things so that I can keep him nearby me?' It breaks my heart, but I cannot let her even see those objects; I fear they will make her sick."

But whereas mothers (like Lordes and Black Irene) who lost older children and adult sons grieve for those children for months and years on end through the idiom of their *saudades*, Alto women did not refer to *saudades* or *tristeza* when talking about the death of their infants and young angel-babies. In these contexts, it was not sadness, sorrow, or wrenching, tortured, yet sweet, longing that they felt; it was pity.

After leaving the home of Anita, who had just buried her three-month-old daughter and who assured me that she was not feeling sad, I stopped to chat with a few of the young girl's neighbors, one of whom, a middle-aged woman called Mazie, had taken a nurturing interest in the girl and her sickly baby. Mazie assured me that Anita would be fine: "There is little sorrow for the death of an infant up until the age of eight or nine months. Really, it is only after the baby is a year old that we begin to grieve, to have *saudades* for the child."

"Why is that?"

"There is little grief [*desgosto*] because the infant is without a history [*não tem história mesmo*]. The infant's story is not yet made up; it has no shape to it. And so the loss is not a big one; it is not heavy. The death passes over one lightly, and it is soon and easily forgotten."

Another woman agreed with Mazie and interjected, "It is only the older child who *faz mais falta* [whose absence is felt]. At the death of an older child a mother has more compassion, more feeling."

Mazie continued, "Yes, because once the child is *formada* [once the child's life and person have some shape], we are beginning to know something about him, what he is like, the things that make him happy, the things in this world that he takes pleasure in, the foods he likes to eat, the way he likes to sleep curled up or stretched out, sucking his *chupeta* [plastic pacifier] or sucking on his fingers, all the little things that make him the person that he is. Well, then, at that age, even as early as eight months of age, you can't stand to see them go. *Then* there is sadness; then there are *saudades*."

Another neighbor added, "It happens when the child is beginning to walk and to grab onto things [*pegar as coisas*], to recognize people. Then one notices his absence, and one *sente mais* [suffers more]."

Just then Anita came out to join us. She had finished washing her clothes. No one tried to change the subject, so I continued, "Does it make a difference when you baptize the babies and give them their names?"

Mazie, who was very active in the church, replied, "Some baptize their infants right away, sick or well. Others wait for a heavy sickness to scare them into baptism. But the baby will always have a name, whether they are baptized or not. But it is only their official name—say, Maria da Conceição or João. To have a *real* name, a baby has to live long enough to have a little, endearing nickname. For that is how we actually come to love our babies, when they begin to show us who they are and what kind of being we now have here. We can begin to see the kind of child he will be, wild or gentle, fast or slow, *sabido* [smart] or *jeitoso* [cunning]. As his history begins to gather around him, that's when, oh, my God, we don't want him to leave us!"

To engage Anita in the conversation, I said, "Your infant was given a very pretty name."

"Oh, yes, thank you."

A curious onlooker asked, "And what was your little one's name?"

Anita looked over to her older neighbor for help. She seemed to have quite forgotten it. Mazie shook her head at the girl and chided her, "And wasn't it Daniella that we put onto her, girl?"

"Oh, yes," and Anita smiled in relief, "that was her name."

"There was no time for the name to take," Mazie explained.

"Why do women say that they have *tanta pena* [so much pity] at the death of their newborns, but not sadness or sorrow?"

Mazie again said, "It is because they feel sorry for the infants because they died without knowing anything in this world, not even who their mother is. They die innocent but also dumb, like little animals, and so we say, '*Hein, hein, que pena!*'"

I left the scene mulling it over, and I brought the topic up again later that week while I was relaxing at the home of Antonieta. Lucienne, Antonieta's eldest daughter, a generation removed but now a world apart from the shantytown, was a kindergarten teacher, and she usually enjoyed explaining things to me slowly and patiently. She never seemed to mind when I returned to ask the same question again, with a slightly different twist, a few days later. I suppose she considered me a slow learner. We began going over the various shades of meaning of *saudade*, most of which conformed to what I had already learned. So I asked her to tell me about the nuances of meaning implied when people said they "had pity" (*tenham pena*) for someone. Lucienne perked up immediately.

"Yes, this is something you should know. In polite company one should try to avoid this expression. It lacks a certain delicacy. It should not be used in reply to someone who has been ill or lost a loved one, no, no. If you must, you could say that you feel 'compassion' for them. But it is better simply to offer your prayers."

"I don't understand."

"*Pena* is the worst word there is, and only simple people without any education would use it. *Pena* is a word that messes with people's feelings, that gets under the scab and opens up their wound. It is too invasive, and often it is false. It could mean that you are actually glad that the misfortune occurred. Envy or jealousy could be involved. *Pena* is a crude word; it is more appropriate to use when referring to suffering animals than to suffering humans."

"What's that you say? Tell me more about pity for animals."

"We sometimes say that we feel pity for an ignorant beast that is about to suffer. We say, 'Poor thing, I feel sorry for it.' Don't you know how it is that in every household there are women who can kill chickens and turkeys or even goats and pigs without feeling anything? That's like Mama and my grandmother. They can just lop the head off a squealing chicken without batting an eye. And then there are soft people, like me, who can't do it. I begin to feel for the dumb beast, and as the knife is about to fall I say, '*Hein, hein, coitada, tenho tanta pena do bichinho* [Tsk! Tsk! Poor thing, I have such pity for the little creature].' Mama gets angry when I say that, and she tells me to get out of the courtyard."

"Why does she get *angry* with you?"

"Mãe says that when you express pity in front of the animal as it is about to die, it will suffer more in dying. The animal senses your emotion, and that gives it more consciousness of its pain and death. So it is better to kill them quickly and without any show of feeling. That way the creature will die without knowing anything about its death."

"It dies more unconsciously?"

"Yes, that is what Mama means. So, all in all, we like to avoid the term *pena*—it is a difficult word to use properly because it has double meanings."

We can juxtapose *saudade* and *pena* and see that they are contradictory emotions: where *saudade* unites and attaches, *pena* distances and separates. To evoke *saudades* protects and conserves; indeed, it enshrines memory. *Saudade* has been described as the ultimate nourishment of love (*o alimento principal do amor*). *Pena* is evoked for creatures who are assumed to be preconscious and presentient: infants and dumb animals. *Saudade* is a positive emotion; it is linked with pleasurable and satisfying past experiences. *Pena* is linked with painful and conflicted memories; it carries only negative meanings. There is no pleasure mixed with the pain. As the poet Camões wrote:

"Do mal ficam as mágoas da lembrança
e do bem, se alguém houve, as saudades."

Only the bruises remain from painful memories;
from the good ones, if there were any, are *saudades*.
(Cited in Figueiredo 1988:3)

Saudade is an immediate and proximate emotion; it strikes and is felt inside, in the heart and chest of the person. *Pena* is outside the self; it is not the pain *of* the sufferer but regret *for* the pain of the one who must suffer (and die). It is a condescending pity for the creature in its own lack of conscious understanding of its fate. The infant dies and leaves behind no trail of bittersweet memories. Love and loss grow with memory. Mourning arises when the lost object was loved for his own sake. It can occur only when one individual is capable of empathy with another, when one recognizes that this "other" person has enriched one through his otherness. And so "naturally," Alto women say, their older and more grown children are more dear to them than ever a small baby could be, and their deaths are, of course, deeply grieved.

I do not wish to leave you with the impression that these women, so preoccupied with their own survival and needs, never suffer or experience grief at the death of their babies. In talking with Alto women about their lives and those of their many children, amid the generally resigned and impassive numbering of the death of so many infants, the memory of a *particular* death, a poignant loss, would sometimes flood the consciousness of the woman and shatter the stoicism that was the norm. These were deaths of older babies, toddlers, and nearly grown children, those who had been expected to live and in whom the woman had dared to trust . . . and to love. Dona Norinha had given birth to eleven children, six of whom she "gave to Jesus." But it was only in the telling of the death of her four-year-old and favorite child that her composure disappeared.

"She was so beautiful; you would have to see her yourself to know what I mean. And *sabida* before her years. She understood everything. The neighbors said, 'Never mind. You'll never raise that one.' And they were right. She was so beautiful and smart that Jesus wanted her all to Himself. What could I do? When she became ill, I almost went crazy. I couldn't sleep. I couldn't eat. I could only think, 'God doesn't want me to have this child. He doesn't want me to have any comfort in this world.' But I had such friendship with this one child. I begged Jesus to 'forget' her, to take another one of mine in her place. But my daughter didn't like it when I prayed like that. Finally, she said, 'Mama, Mama, let me go.' I yelled at her, 'Then die—go away; leave me alone then.' I was so *angry* at her. Why was she so willing to go? Well, the poor little thing died like that, telling me that she would be all right, asking me to forgive her, telling me not to cry."

Even in this touching love story we can see the desperation and terrible neediness in the mother that let her see her dying child as a deserter. But, of course, whenever a woman of the Alto broke down in the telling of the death of a child, other women present scolded the woman, and soon I, too, fell into the ritualized words of consolation: "You are strong, Dona Maria. Be grateful that you are still alive. Resign yourself. It is useless to grieve. You have your own life to think about. You must endure." And, inevitably, the woman "came to her senses" and wiped away her unwomanly tears. As she did so, I wondered for how many generations women the world over have been telling each other similar words, shaping their experience of loss, controlling unruly reactions to what might otherwise be unbearable. If there is, as some feminists want to suggest, a universal sisterhood of women, and I doubt it, but if there is, it would have its origins in this collective comforting of those weeping women, like the biblical Rachel, whose children are no more.

One of the benefits of working in the same community over a quarter century is that one does get to see, if not the final chapter, at least the working out of various problems and dilemmas over time. One category of children who are particularly loved by their mothers and other family members are the survivors of what had been presumed to be fatal afflictions. Those resilient children who beat the odds and proved themselves willing to "fight" death, even after they had been "given up" for dead—Lordes's Zé, Auxiliadora's firstborn, Biu-Biu, Mercea's older brother, João—are celebrated for their hardheadedness. They are the "elect" of the family and of a community that boasts its toughness of spirit, and this is how they are referred to: my *filho* or *filha eleito*, "chosen" one. And even years after the events had transpired, *moradores* can be choked with emotion in recalling how their own child or sibling "escaped" death.

At a base community meeting one evening I presented a slide show of portraits taken of my Alto friends over the various field trips to Brazil. The creche hall was packed and animated as scenes of the Alto and its residents going back to the mid-1960s were flashed against a torn sheet tacked to the wall. When the enlarged portraits of individual residents appeared, the roars of laughter and appreciation were deafening. Midway into the presentation the slide of a mother with her toddler presenting a bloated belly came onto the screen, again to squeals of delighted laughter. João Mariano, the political *orientador* of UPAC, led the discussion and tried to calm everyone down. "What does this baby have?" he asked. "Worms!" the adults and children yelled back. "And who here has not suffered with worms?" (Silence.) "How did this child get sick?"

"Crawling barefoot on the ground."

"Putting mud and dirt into its mouth."

"Sucking on a dirty baby bottle."

"The house has no pit latrine."

And how might this problem be solved?"

"Medical exams."

"Worm pills."

"No!" Terezinha suddenly jumped to her feet. "No, for the child will *still* be without shoes, and the house *still* won't have a latrine, and the children will *still* be drinking 'amoeba juice' from the public water spigot."

"So what is the answer then?" asked João Mariano.

"Building latrines."

"*União!*—working together!"

A few moments and several slides later and up came the enlarged image of Terezinha herself taken with her marasmic baby, Edilson, in 1982. (See p. 388.) Again there was laughter. Terezinha, sitting in one of the front rows and embarrassed by her harried and frazzled image on the screen, in- stinctively attempted to smooth her wild hair into place. "My baby, my baby . . ." she began to say, but emotion prevented her from going on.

João Mariano helped her out: "*Comadre* Terezinha's baby was very sick when this slide was taken. Many of you have had children just as sick as Edilson. What can be done for such children?"

"*Nada*, they just die," several voices volunteered.

But suddenly Terezinha was once again on her feet, and she spun around agitatedly to face the audience. She was a shy woman who did not normally speak her mind at community meetings, although she faithfully attended them all. But now her face was flushed with emotion, and her voice broke as she said, "No, you are wrong! Some of them survive. My own survived. Mine lived! Ai, my little son! Ai, my little *homem* [man-child]!" Collapsed and weeping, Terezinha was comforted by several neighbors and helped back to her seat.

"And what do we say, *minha gente*, to our *companheira* Terezinha?" asked João Mariano.

The response was a spontaneous burst of applause. To grieve for the one who almost got away and didn't was both allowed and very common. As with *saudades*, the tears for the one who might have died, who came within an inch of dying, were ambivalent and bittersweet. They were tears of regret and anxiety, but they were also tears of relief. The poignant memory was relived from a safe position, for as Terezinha cast about anxiously, there he was, her little *macaco* (as she now called him), her "little monkey," and she grabbed him and pressed him to herself.

Alto women are religious specialists during one brief period of the annual liturgical cycle: Holy Week. *Semana Santa* belongs to them, to the *beatas* of the *morro*, crucifix hill, the *alto do amor*, the "hillside of love" dedicated to the crucified Christ. On Holy Thursday the *beatas* gather in the convent of the Franciscan sisters, where they retrieve the life-sized plaster cast image of Nossa Senhora da Piedade (Our Lady of Mercy, Our Lady of Pity) that they will carry in silent procession to the church plaza. Just as they arrive at the door of the church, they are met by the older men, who are just leaving the sacristy carrying their image raised on a pedestal, that of Nosso Senhor dos Passos, Jesus of Calvary, with his purple robes and long doll's hair matted with blood from his crown of thorns, dragging the heavy cross behind him. As the two images meet, Our Lady of Pity shows her face. Stripped of her veil, Mary's agonized and tear-stained face is made plainly visible to all. There are gasps of astonished recognition and then applause from the crowd of "humble" people who have gathered for the events that mark the center of their spiritual life.

"Why do the people clap their hands at this holy encounter?" I was asked by the good *padre* of Bom Jesus, an urban man from Recife who still found some of the local, "country" customs perplexing.

"You are their priest," I replied. "Why don't *you* ask them?"

"But *you* are their anthropologist," the priest teased in return.

On Good Friday, the holy women of the Alto again gather at the church. They are dressed in white with the red sash of their sodality, the laywomen's

Our Lady of Pity.

society dedicated to the bleeding and Sacred Heart of Jesus. Now it is their charge to lead the procession honoring the passion and death of Jesus, the Processão do Nosso Senhor Morto. The corpus of the dead Cristo, temporarily removed from his tomb under the altar, will be carried through Bom Jesus on a catafalque in a death procession. His body is covered by a red cloth. But first the padre begins with a reading of the passion followed by the *via sacra*, the Stations of the Cross. And so the story is told: Jesus with his disciples, Jesus sweating blood at the garden of Gethsemane, Jesus kissed by Judas, Jesus carried away to the high priests and then to Pilate, Jesus scourged and the crown of thorns crushed into his head, and Jesus made to carry his cross.

The tension in the church mounts as the priest now walks station to

Our Lord of Calvary.

station around the church and as he pauses to recall the meeting between Jesus and the holy women of Jerusalem. Then, following the crucifixion, the tension reaches a crescendo with the padre's recitation of the words, "Aba, Aba [Father, Father, my God], why have you forsaken me?" A spontaneous cry rings out in the crowded church. It comes from the knot of holy women of the Alto. Are they saying what I think I hear? *"Ai, meu filho! Ai, meu filho!* My son, my son!"

Our Lady of Sorrows looks down benevolently from her pedestal behind the tabernacle. She points, as always, to the opening in the loose folds of her white shift, where her heart is exposed and pierced with six daggers. She could be any one of the holy women of the Alto do Cruzeiro. I wait for the sound of applause.

10 A Knack for Life
The Everyday Tactics of Survival

> It wasn't ruthlessness that enabled an individual to survive—
> it was an intangible quality, not particular to educated or
> sophisticated individuals. Anyone might have it. It is perhaps
> best described as an overriding thirst—perhaps, too, a talent
> for life.
>
> Death camp survivor (cited in Des Pres 1976:192)

But where, you may ask, in these dark lives is there space for the Brazilian joie de vivre, the celebrated vitality and *animação* that are captured in Brazilian song and dance, in film and literature, and, most of all, in the Brazilian *carnaval*, with its great, joyful, bounding leaps of the *frevo* and its erotic and life-affirming samba? Have hunger, sickness, and scarcity all but extinguished these expressions of Brazilianity in my Alto friends? What makes life worth living for these people? What gives women the strength to go on with their reproductive lives in the face of such adversity? What accounts for the differential effects of chronic deprivation, loss, and trauma on Alto residents? And what distinguishes those women and children who escape with minimal scarring and with a vitality of mind and body that is as indisputable as it is seemingly inexplicable from those who survive but remain in a chronic state of vulnerability, dependency, and siege, as ontologically insecure as any of R. D. Laing's patients, yet without even the odd defenses that descent into madness sometimes affords?

These and other questions surfaced at a bar near the University of Chicago to which a few distinguished colleagues and I had repaired following a symposium on comparative human development in the fall of 1987 (see Stigler, Shweder, & Herdt 1990). I had presented a paper on hunger, sickness, and child death in Bom Jesus that closed with the hopeful, but to some listeners puzzling, description of Alto women who, despite all, emerged with a strong, intact belief in their right to be alive, to take up space, and to *gozar*—to "take pleasure" in food, dance, or sex, and even (like Biu) in hard, physical, plantation fieldwork. And so the conversation that evening turned to the women of the Alto do Cruzeiro and specifically to their personal and collective resilience in the face of adversity—their "spirit of survival"—and beyond that to their spirit of pleasure and joyful affirmation of life. In short,

446

what did it mean to say of a favorite adult child, "*Ele vingou! Escapou a morte!* He beat the odds. He escaped death!" and to follow with the affirmation "My God, does he have a lust for life!"?

The topic of resilience in the face of adversity has received considerable attention in recent years. B. F. Steele (1986), for example, wrote of famous world figures who were successful despite, or even because of, miserable childhoods or terrible early life experiences. And George Valliant (1977) noted that personal strength and resilience seem to depend on life skills acquired largely through having had to overcome the odds (see also Garmezy & Neuchterlain 1972; Rutter 1985; Sheehy 1986). Strength becomes most apparent, Vaillant wrote, "when the going gets tough" (1977:13). There was plenty of "tough going" on the Alto do Cruzeiro. But where was I to begin to look for the sources of strength, resilience, and relative invulnerability in the shantytown?

You Tell Me

These particular questions would not have too much currency to the people of the Alto, whose understandings of such things conform, on the one hand, to a belief that God has predetermined what life has in store ("Who can write one line against the script already written down in the Great Book?") and, on the other, to a belief in the power of luck, chance, and good fortune. And so people will often preface talking about a positive accomplishment with the statement "It was my good luck that . . ." when in fact there were considerable skill and effort on their part. And all *moradores* of the Alto consider themselves to be survivors of sorts. In response to the visiting American pediatrician who suggested that all the severely malnourished and neglected creche babies would probably grow up into warped, damaged adults, Dona Biu, the women's leader, countered, "Oh, *xente* [shucks], if that were the case, we would *all* be crazy here. Who on this rock [the rocky hillside of the Alto] was raised without hunger, without suffering, without having at least once just barely escaped death?"

Although psychodynamic self-analysis is obviously not a native practice among the people of the Alto, as a result, in part, of the style of questioning and the close and intense scrutiny that I have introduced into their lives, some *moradores* have begun to think in personally self-reflexive ways, for better or worse. Xoxa, the young teenage daughter of Biu, started working with me in 1987, beginning from a state of original and blissful naïveté. Three years later she was an introspective young woman who enjoyed thinking aloud with me about "why" things were the way they were in her own life and family, among her neighbors, and in the community at large. But when we began in 1987 Xoxa was at particularly loose ends. She was not in school, and she could not find work that suited her. She refused to work as a domestic, but unlike her mother, Biu, she was equally opposed to working in the sugarcane. Instead, she stayed at home and kept house for her younger siblings, often feeling like a prisoner there. She resented having to mother her younger siblings, especially the sickly and dependent "baby," Mercea. I proposed to Xoxa that she reconsider attending some afternoon classes at a local school to give literacy one last try. Xoxa seemed mildly interested in my suggestion but complained that she had no proper clothing or shoes. A deal was made: I would provide the clothes and a few necessary school supplies, and she would agree to attend school regularly. Xoxa was delighted with the stylish short skirt, pert white blouse, and handsome sandals I brought her the next day. The teacher at a local school was expecting Xoxa that same afternoon. But when I climbed the hill later that day Xoxa was outside her hut spinning around and around in her new skirt and sandals, admiring herself in a large puddle in front of the public water spigot. I lost my temper at Xoxa, and I angrily compared her life to that of her first cousins, Antonieta's eldest daughters, Lucienne, Lucia, and Lucy.

"Why do you think that *their* lives have turned out so much better than yours?" I asked Xoxa. "How do you think it happened that Lucienne now wears fine clothes and teaches kindergarten in town? Why do you think that Lucia is engaged to a 'rich' man who works in a gas station in Bom Jesus?" I taunted the child out of some anxious and antediluvian, although caring, peasant past of my own. "Why," I asked Xoxa finally, "do your cousins have embroidered sheets and pillowcases piling up in their bedrooms, all ready for their marriages? Why are your and your sister's lives so different, so much more wretched than theirs?"

Xoxa began to cry, more out of humiliation because I was *dando uma caroa em ela*, picking on her in public and making such an awful row, than because my stupid questions had wounded her or penetrated her consciousness in any way.

"I don't know why," she replied angrily.

"Have you never thought to compare your life and your mother's life to Tia Antonieta and her family?"

"No, never, I swear," she replied, as if I were asking her to commit a crime, to fly in the face of destiny. Then she raised her tear-stained face to me with a defiant challenge: "*You* tell me, Nanci. You tell me why our lives are so wretched."

It was not the first, or the last, time that I would be chastened by the sharp little girl. I was abashed and could not, of course, answer my own question, save with reference to sociological and psychological platitudes in which I no longer believed. So I decided to pursue the life histories of the three sisters—

Antonieta, Lordes, and Biu—to see if in their own narratives I might find some clues. I cannot say that any of my Alto friends are truly "invulnerable"—all are at risk and perceive themselves that way; recall the shantytown woman who said, "Look mister, I think that here it is easy enough for anyone to die." Nonetheless, the life stories of these sisters do show different degrees of resilience and rather different "survival strategies," some more successful than others.

The three half-sisters were born within six years of each other, the only children of the rather small and quiet, yet irrepressibly independent, rural woman who to this day I still know only as Mãe. Each daughter was fathered by a different man, and each was partly reared by their mother's only sister, Tia Josefa, during their early childhood years on a small sugarcane plantation just outside Bom Jesus da Mata. There was little to distinguish among them in their earliest life experiences, but by the time the tough little family had moved to the Alto do Cruzeiro during the girls' early adolescence, the paths of the sisters had already begun to diverge, moving their lives in quite different directions. Nonetheless, all three were graced with good looks, native intelligence, and a formidable work ethic.

By Alto reckonings, Antonieta has led the most charmed life, though to us it may seem the most ordinary and conventional, if charmingly told, one, filled with many difficulties and perturbations but eventually achieving some semblance of tranquility and minimal security. But to her old neighbors on the Alto do Cruzeiro, Antonieta's life *is* charmed, and she is seen as extraordinary in her success and in her good luck, which seemed to swoop down at just the right moment to deliver her and her husband, Severino, from the far more predictable and painful outcomes of her younger and more vulnerable sisters. Tonieta, after all, managed to escape the Alto, and she and her children move comfortably along the margins of Bom Jesus "society." She and her family are known and respected.

It seems as if, as she tells her life story, Antonieta had always fixed her sights on a "better" life. She refused to be knocked down or overwhelmed by adverse life experiences; rather, she had a facility for turning bad situations into advantageous ones. She tended to "reframe" bad events in her past as if they were actually fortunate ones. And so Antonieta tossed off her mother's cavalier sexual behavior, which robbed her of a father when she was still an infant, as if it were an altogether admirable personality trait, a proud boast: "Mama was like that, a real firebrand!" Similarly, when jilted by her first lover, Antonieta did not brood over it but used a jealous suitor to her advantage, quickly arranging a new engagement for herself using the same engagement ring that her faithless first suitor had given her. Confronted by obstacles to her marriage, Antonieta fought her future in-laws and her husband's jealous and powerful *patroa* to make their marriage "doubly" secure by marrying Severino in both church and civil ceremonies.

Antonieta formed many different relations for survival. She was never above using her beauty, her wit, or plain trickery to get others to help her through difficult situations. She made the best of patron-client relations, using political favors without selling herself short. But her only real and lasting loyalties were to her large family and to a few carefully chosen best friends, some of them of "humble" origins like herself but others middle-class teachers in the school where Antonieta works as a kitchen aid. Were Antonieta not so winsome and so direct about her various *jeitos* for getting by, one might see these in a less positive light as crafty and self-serving manipulations. But Antonieta has also been unstintingly generous, opening her already large and crowded household to three foster children, two of these rescued from less fortunate relations.

Antonieta did not beat the odds by means of conventional middle-class strategies, such as careful "family planning." Her fifteen pregnancies match those of her younger and more desperate sister, Biu, and surpass the thirteen pregnancies of Lordes. If anything, Antonieta's crowd of bright and handsome children—all of them relatively well educated locally—have helped Antonieta and Severino bootstrap themselves out of grinding poverty. All the children have been contributing to the family larder since they were able to find paid chores in the neighborhood. And they are a decided social advantage as well, for her children are in no way tainted by association with the stigmatized shantytown of Antonieta and Severino's origins.

Of the three sisters, Lordes, the youngest, told a personal history (see chapter 8) that is the most normative for women her age from the Alto do Cruzeiro. She suffered her predictable share of bad lovers, abandonments, "premature" pregnancies, infant deaths, destitution, and sickness. But Lordes also found some later relief in the form of two long-term and relatively secure relationships with men who "adored" her. Similar to her older sister and her mother, Lordes sometimes "used" people to foster her own ends. After forcing her first boyfriend to marry her against his will, Lordes happily helped herself to a widow's pension in his name that in all fairness belonged to the woman and children with whom her long estranged "husband" had really made his life soon after he and Lordes parted ways. Likewise, Lordes walked out on her third common-law husband, a poor, rustic man who had fathered many of her children and who was uniquely devoted to her, to take up with an elderly widower, Seu Jaime, who had a better pension and who could promise Lordes a small house of their own in town. Seu Jaime is, for his own part, a rare sort of man, kindly, unassuming, unselfish, and protective of his much younger "wife" and her many children by other men. Part of Lordes's "good fortune" is her simplicity and sweetness of nature. She projects an aura of vulnerability, and she tends to bring out the nurturing side of older men. To this day, Lordes's third husband, Milton, admits to being in love with his former common-law wife, who treated him so unfairly, and he never forgets to send her produce from his own little *sítio*, even though he now has a new family of his own. "Yes," he admitted ruefully one afternoon, "I am still 'soft' on that little *galega* of mine."

By everyone's standards on the Alto do Cruzeiro, Biu's life has been hard and brutish, an example of what can go wrong, of how low one can fall, of how bad and mean life can be for some women. And yet Biu is the hardest working of the sisters and the most independent and uncompromising. Despite her adamant refusal to marry, Biu's conjugal life has been conservative. She took one common-law husband at the age of fifteen and remained with him, off and on, for almost as many years. Although she left him several times, it was never to take up with another man. And it was only after Valdimar's death that Biu formed a second and, again a long-term, relationship with another common-law husband. Although Oscar ultimately proved unfaithful, Biu remains loyal to him, and she still wants to be buried next to him "in the end."

Biu is full of initiative, and she is proud of the "survivor spirit" that allows her to pick herself up and try again and again. Yet she remains soft and vulnerable where she should be hardest, at the very core of her being. Of the three half-sisters, it is Biu, "unbossed and unbought," whom I love the most. But it may be just these same endearing traits that have contributed to Biu's permanent state of risk and misery. If so, this is "bad news" for women, indeed.

Lordes was the first to tell her life history in 1987, following the death of Zezinho, her favorite son; Biu and Antonieta told their narratives against the background of *carnaval* drums and whistles in 1988. We were interrupted more than once so that Biu and I could go out in pursuit of the revelers. But meanwhile, not even *carnaval* could keep the wheels of destiny from spinning, indeed from grinding, relentlessly on.

Antonieta the Invincible

When I first came to live next door to her on the Alto do Cruzeiro in 1964, Antonieta was a young married mother pregnant for the second time. She was a strikingly beautiful woman, with even features and a small, shapely body. Her skin was a coppery brown, her cheekbones high and Amerindian, and her eyes almond shaped and very, very dark. We did not become intimates until the day that Nailza and Zé Antônio, the young couple I was living with, left suddenly for Mato Grosso, taking my adoptive son, Marcelinho, with them. I sought Antonieta out for consolation, and soon we became close friends. I began taking most of my meals in her neat little brick home, escaping the dark and dingy confines of my now empty and lonely mud hut. As the months and years passed, one pregnancy followed fast on the other, but rather than fall more deeply into poverty and debt, Tonieta's little family seemed to prosper in ways that other Alto households did not.

As old friends our relationship is something else, and when I stop by Antonieta's home, it is usually "after hours" when I am "off duty" as an anthropologist. It is a time for the two of us to kick off our sandals, open a few bottles of very cold beer, and gossip, complain, or rest, saying nothing at all. But as a research "subject," Tonieta had put me off several times. Yet the "interview" had been promised, and if it was to happen at all, *carnaval* was an ideal time, with the men and older boys off in the streets for the duration of the festival. The normally busy and boisterous house seemed dead and deserted, left to Antonieta and her two eldest daughters, each one temporarily abandoned by her young husband. The women had been left at home to watch Rio's *carnaval* parades on the small black and white television set, its screen covered with a sheet of multicolored plastic to give an illusion of color to the picture on the screen. "Leave *carnaval* to the men," Antonieta consoled her daughters. "It's a *besteira* [nonsense], anyway. And lighting up a pungent "Hollywood" brand cigarette, Antonieta began her life story.

"I was born in Itabaiana [in the nearby state of Paraíba] in July of 1942, but when I was only a week old Mãe and Pai moved to the outskirts of Bom Jesus to work on the Engenho Bela Vista. It was a big plantation, and it was where everyone found work when they first moved into town from the countryside. There was work for everyone in the *roçados* and in the *casa de farinha*, where manioc flour was milled for sale, and there was always work in the cane fields.

"I don't remember anything about my papa because Mama left him before I reached my senses. You see Mama never married men; she just took them, and when she met another that she liked better, she would go off with him. That's what happened to my father. Soon after we moved to Bela Vista, Mama found herself a rich older man who owned a large *sítio* on the plantation. After a short while she left Papa to live with him. As soon as Papa found out that Mama had 'put the horns on him,' he took off. He left town, and we never heard from him again. When Mama went off to live with her new lover, I was sent to live with my mother's sister, Tia Josefa. It was really Auntie who raised Mama's children: me, Biu, and, later, Lordes. Mama was a ball of fire, and when she was young, she was too busy to take care of us. I won't apologize for Mama. That was her way, and she never saw any harm in it. So why should I? Mãe had so many lovers that I couldn't count them, and I bet she couldn't either. That's how it happened that Biu and Lordes and I each had different fathers.

"Well, Mama stayed with her rich old man for five years, and during this whole time she gradually gave away his belongings—food, clothing, money, even his silverware—to her friends and neighbors. She robbed the old man blind! Mama was like that. She told the neighbors to go into his fields and to take whatever they wanted because the old man was so rich he hardly paid attention to what he owned. This is what Mama herself has told us. She's not the least bit ashamed of it. You might call it 'stealing,' but that's not how Mãe looked at it at all. To her way of thinking it was just that the old man had so much of everything and her neighbors had so little that it was right and just to share some of it around. The old man never suspected that Mãe was the thief in his house, and when Mama left his household, it was because she herself chose to leave it. She left him to take up with the father of Lordes. This man planted vegetables that he sold every week in *feira,* so people called him Severino das Verduras. They lived together for a while, happily enough, and they had two children, but only Lordes lived.

"During this time I was living with Tia Josefa, and I was in charge of the household. Tia's work was washing people's clothes, and she had to be away from the house a good deal of the time. So it was left to me, from the age of six or seven, to do all the housework, the shopping, and the cooking. It seems like I am still always cooking! By the time I was eight years old, I had started to help with the laundry. I would go to the *patroa's* house and collect the dirty clothes into a big bundle balanced on my head. When I was about eleven years old Tia and Mama moved away from Bela Vista and to the Alto do Cruzeiro. I was sent to school for the first time in a building they called the Escola de Tiros [Gunshot School] because it had once had something to do with the military. But I left it after a year without learning anything. I went to school totally unprepared, and there was no one at home to help me with my alphabet. I didn't even know how to hold a pencil in my hand!

"The person who really taught me how to read was Severino's father, my father-in-law. Of course, he wasn't my father-in-law then; he was a neighbor, a man who worked hard all day in the cane fields. At night he would come home, and after dinner people would gather together in his tiny hut to recite the rosary. After prayers his 'students' would come, and he would teach us the alphabet so that we really learned it. He was a very religious man, and he taught the children of the Alto for the love of it. He had been successful in teaching his own children to read, and so he thought that he could teach other people's children as well. And he did.

"In those days Alto people didn't trust the public schools at all, but there were always a few older people who took in students at night, and for a few *mil reis* they would teach children to read and write and do their sums. These were old-fashioned country people, and the only way they knew how to teach was to drum these things into your head. But you never felt ashamed in these homes the way you did when you went to school in town. On the Alto we were all pretty much the same. Nobody was any better off than anyone else. So if you didn't understand something, you could ask a question, and no one would laugh at you.

"At fifteen and a half I became engaged for the first time to a boy from Recife whom I hardly knew at all. He stayed in Bom Jesus for about a year while he worked at the hospital making X-rays for the patients. I met him at a dance, and we began to see each other. He gave me a beautiful gold ring as an engagement present before he left. He said he would send for me as soon as he had found a place for us to live in Recife.

"When I began to wear the engagement ring, I noticed that Severino started to act differently toward me. He was very jealous of my fiancé, Geraldo. But he never said anything outright. He was such a *matuto* he could hardly speak up at all! But I could see that he was jealous, and I took advantage of it. I used to eat at his house quite a lot. I did this because we didn't have much food in Tia's house, and I was shameless. I would drop by at dinnertime, and I'd sit at the edges of the table and talk while the others would eat. They always invited me to eat, but I always refused politely. But they enjoyed my company, and as we would talk I would nibble around the edges of the dinner. I would sample little bits of dried beef, of *farofa* [a manioc dish], of *couscous* [cornmeal cake]. They always seemed to have enough to share, and the food was very simple, very rustic. So there I was stealing food right out of their mouths! I knew I was taking advantage of Severino because he was so lovesick for me.

"About this time I began to wonder about my fiancé because I hadn't heard from him since he left for Recife; several weeks had passed. I sent a message to him through the bus driver, but the driver came back saying that he could not find word of him anywhere, that it seemed he had left Recife altogether. So my fiancé had disappeared! Geraldo left me without so much as a good-bye! Well, I didn't waste any time on tears. I began a romance with Severino right away. After a year we wanted to get married. But we had our difficulties. Severino was still working in the cane fields outside of town, and he earned next to nothing; every penny that he did earn, he handed over to his parents. I wondered how we would ever be able to marry at this rate.

"I insisted that we get engaged so that everyone would know our intentions. But Severino didn't even have enough money to buy me the simplest engagement ring. So I said, 'Look, Severino, Geraldo left me with this perfectly good engagement ring, solid gold. Let's just use his ring as our ring. Who will know the difference?' After some coaxing Severino finally agreed. And look what a good ring it was that Geraldo had left me with. It still shines after all these years! So I must have meant something to him after all.

"Once Severino and I became engaged, he found work in town as a bricklayer's assistant. But soon he was out of work. There just weren't too many jobs to be had outside of the sugarcane. Things got so bad in Bom Jesus that Severino's parents decided to return to the countryside to live. They left their little house on the Alto with their two eldest sons, Severino and Antônio. This was all the better for me. Now I could come over and visit and cook and eat with them whenever I wanted. But finally the time came when Severino could not stay back any longer. He *had* to find work, and so he announced one night that he was going to return to the *mata* to work with his parents on their little *sítio*. I began to cry because this would certainly spell the end of our marriage plans.

"On his way home that afternoon Severino stopped off at church to say a prayer. He prayed hard to São Antônio to find him some work in Bom Jesus so that he would not have to leave me. Then he came home slowly and sadly. I helped him pack up his small bundle of patched work clothes, and he set off by foot for his parents' *roçado.* It was a good four- or five-hour walk through the countryside. Along the way he met an old man, who asked Severino where he was headed. After Severino explained his situation, the man said, 'How old are you, son?' 'Nineteen,' lied Severino, for he was barely sixteen at the time. 'Well,' said the old man, 'I have just come back from talking to the principal of a large elementary school in Bom Jesus, and the woman, Dona Dora, asked me to find a good, dependable boy to work for her as a custodian. You seem like a good fellow.' Severino turned on his heels, and the two men started back for Bom Jesus together. But when they got to the home of Dona Dora, the principal was in a terrible mood. She was abusive, throwing things around, and she even yelled at the poor old man. But she called Severino into her office, and after talking with him for a few minutes, she offered him the job.

"Severino was so excited that he came running up the Alto to find me and to tell me the good news. We danced around the table in Tia's house! But our problems didn't end there. We still didn't have a place to live. We needed to have our own house. There was a small piece of land in front of Tia's house, just big enough for a little home. It was nothing but a little ledge in a cliff, but it would be our own. Severino went for help from the bricklayer he had once worked for. The bricklayer liked Severino and agreed to help him build our house, but on one condition: Severino had to promise that he would become a Protestant once the house was completed. Well, Severino wanted the house badly, and so he agreed and the deal was made.

"When Severino got his first paycheck, it came late and in a large sum, and with it he was able to buy enough bricks and cement to call on the bricklayer and his assistants. The house was little and solid, and it went up in no time at all. Just as the job was nearing completion, Severino had to confess to his old boss, who had been so good to him, that he really did not want to become a Protestant after all. He said that he had searched his soul, and the truth was that he didn't have the heart to go through with it. It wasn't in him to leave the saints and the Blessed Virgin behind. Well, the man really respected Severino as an honest person and a diligent worker, and so he agreed to finish working on our house anyway, even though Severino had broken his half of the bargain. And so we finally had our little home! Everyone admired our brick home. No one else had anything like it. In those days the very poorest houses on the Alto were made of straw, and most of the houses were made of sticks and dried mud. There was hardly any such thing as a tile roof until we set the fashion.

"Once the house was ready, we ran into another set of difficulties with Severino's parents. They were upright, old-fashioned country people, and they didn't want a marriage at all because I wasn't a *filha de família*. That is, my mother lived outside the laws of the church, and I was an illegitimate child. My parents weren't ever married to each other. But Severino's parents were married in the church, and they were very religious people. They didn't want their oldest son to marry someone from a family like mine. So, finally, Severino owned up to me that his parents would never give their approval to our marriage. In fact, they were totally opposed to it. I was shaken, although it didn't surprise me. What surprised me, really, was Severino's persistence because he was such a shy and respectful son who always lived in harmony with his parents. He asked me, 'Do you have the courage to fight for this marriage?' I said that I did. After all, I had nothing to lose by it and everything to gain. As for Severino, he stood to lose a lot because of me.

"As it happened, Dona Dora favored Severino of all her workers at the school, and she always tried to help him out. When she learned that Severino was building a home on the Alto (although she never suspected that he was planning to move me into it!), she gave him a cartload of used furniture, almost everything that we needed: tables, chairs, trunks, a *guarda-roupa* [wardrobe]. There was everything except the bed, which Severino bought brand new with a covered straw mattress. We paid for it in two installments. Meanwhile, I was carefully laying away a proper trousseau of embroidered sheets and towels, cups and dishes, and new clothes for the day we would be married.

"When Severino's father came to visit his son, he began to suspect that we might be going ahead with our plans without the old man's permission or his blessing. He looked around him, and he said with amazement, 'Severino, my son, you are going to marry like a rich man!' He was really impressed with our new bed, and he said, 'When your mother and I married, we married in the church, but all we had to sleep on was a *cama de varra* [a low bed made from twigs] and a mattress that your mother made out of sugar sacks from the mill that she sewed together and stuffed with banana leaves.' Severino's father really thought that his son had become a wealthy man.

"Tia Josefa helped the marriage along by buying me some pretty white fabric so that I could sew my wedding dress. It was going to have a short skirt and long sleeves, a very simple design, so that we could hide the fact that we were getting married. I had learned how to sew, and I was very handy with an old, battered sewing machine that I had acquired, so that I was even sewing clothes for other people. It was one of the ways I was making money to support us. But I worked on the wedding dress in secret.

"I was the one who made all the arrangements. I went to the civil registry office to get the marriage license. They wanted my birth certificate, and I was stumped. Nobody in our house ever looked after things like that, and I was pretty sure that there wasn't any birth certificate. But I knew that I was baptized, and they said that I could use that certificate instead. It meant that I had to go by train all the way back to Itabaiana where I was born and baptized to get the document. I spent a night in the train station because I couldn't afford a hotel, and I didn't know anyone there. But I managed to come back with the papers I needed. Then, I put away all my wedding things into a large trunk. We had two of everything: two sheets, two towels, two plates, two cups, two glasses, two spoons.

"Severino announced the banns of marriage in church, and we started the paperwork in the *cartório civil*. In those days you married in the church, in the civil registry office, or in both. We decided on both. This was a hard marriage to bring off, and we really wanted it to stick. But as it turned out, when we arrived at the registry office to sign the official papers, we were told that Severino's boss, Dona Dora, had gotten there first, and she had put a stop to the civil proceedings. Dona Dora was a tough woman. In the years that she was the director of Elizabete Lira School everyone said that she was the real boss of Bom Jesus, even more than the mayor. Whatever Dona Dora said, it was law. And she did not want her pet, Severino, to marry a woman like me. She had hoped that he could do better and marry a teacher at least. She was afraid that I would pull him down, a poor and unschooled person like me.

"There was nothing we could do. We had to turn around and leave the

registry office. The next day we went to the church, where we were married
with just our two witnesses. This is how we got married, finally, on April 8,
1962. We crept out of our houses in secret that morning, but after the wedding service there was nothing to hide, and we walked back up the Alto together holding hands and smiling. We were properly married in the church,
and now we had the right to live together in peace. Severino carried me over
the doorstep into our new house in his arms so that everyone could see what
we had done. And then we went across the street to Tia's house, and then we
walked all the way to Severino's parents' house to announce our wedding.
Severino's father was angry, and he said to us, 'Why did you two even
bother to marry? Why didn't you just live together? People like you,' he said
to me, 'don't need to marry. You only need to shack up.' He was referring to
my background and to my mother's past. But I didn't answer him back. I
stood there quietly and took the abuse in silence. After all, I had won. He
was going to be my father-in-law whether he liked it or not. And he had a
right to be angry because Severino had disobeyed him and deceived him.

"We went home for our first meal together in our new house. There was
hardly anything in the house to eat. There were some black beans, salted,
dried fish, a coarse *farinha*, rice, and cornmeal, hardly enough to get us
through our first week together. I was thinking that I would make us corn
bread and dried codfish for our wedding meal. But when we got home there
was a surprise waiting for us. Seu Fermino, our wedding sponsor, had sent
us a large turkey. And so we spent our first week together stuffing ourselves
with turkey—it was a real party!

"I got pregnant less than a month after we married. When I was huge
with a big belly, we went back to the civil registry office to be married legally
in the eyes of the state. We wanted to make sure that our baby would carry
Severino's name, and a church wedding wasn't enough to do that. We chose
the feast day of Severino's favorite saint, Francis of Assisi, the saint of the
poor, for our civil wedding. And so on October 4 we arrived at the *cartório*
and talked the functionary into letting us marry for our baby's sake. We
promised to keep it a secret from Dona Dora. The woman relented and we
were married. And that's how it happened that each time we married, we had
to do it in secret, like thieves in the night. But here we are together more
than twenty-five years later and with ten children. So, we were *teimosa*
[hardheaded], but we proved them wrong.

"Soon after we married there was a political crisis, and all public employees were without their salaries. So we passed the first six months of our
marriage without any money. But if we didn't have any money, we didn't
spend any either. How can you spend what you don't have? We made do by
eating at the home of an old *patroa* of mine, Dona Maria de Jesus, and she

was as good as her name. Finally, the state paid Severino everything that it owed him. When he got his money, we went right out and we bought a little gas stove with a canister of gas. It was the first gas cook stove to appear on the Alto do Cruzeiro. Until that time we cooked our meals, like everyone else, on a little clay stand with charcoal. I always hated it. Charcoal made the walls black, and it filled the house with smoke.

"Even after we bought the cook stove there was still some money left over, and with it we bought a beautiful layette for the new baby—all the diapers and shirts and cloths and towels a newborn would need. So we were all prepared when Célia was born in February. I gave birth at home and without any trouble. She was a pretty baby and healthy. But I fed her *mingau*, and she soon got sick with diarrhea and vomiting, and she died after only a few months. I listened to my mama after that, and I vowed that I would nurse the next babies the old-fashioned way with my own milk.

"I got pregnant again right away with Luciano, and then our luck began to change. I made a promise to Saint Lúcia, and she has been good to us. From then on almost all our babies lived. Severino got a second job as a construction worker for the *município*, and when he brought home his first paycheck from the new job, he asked me, 'How shall we spend this? Shall we buy a new layette for the next baby?' I thought about this for a while, and then I said, 'No, let's use the money for a radio, and later on when I'm closer to delivery, we can kill the pig that I am raising out back to pay for the layette.' But Luciano was born a month early, and there wasn't time to sell the pig or to buy him a new layette, so we just used the one that we had bought for Célia.

"Luciano was born on July 24, 1964, and once he came along, everything started to look up for us. The babies came one after the other. After Luciano came Lucienne. But we can skip over this part of my life because this is when you, and then later Dona Bets [a second Peace Corps worker], came to live next door to us. We called this the 'time of the Americans.' Before you left Lúcia was born, and I was pregnant again with Lucy. And just at the time you were leaving the Alto, so were we because Dona Dora got it into her head that we should move down from the shantytown and into a brand-new custodian's house that she had built on the grounds of the school. Soon after we moved I had a pair of twins, both girls, but they didn't make it. Twins are the hardest things to raise in this world. I began to think I wasn't going to have any more sons, but then came Lauriano, followed by Luzivan. The babies came one after the other, there were fifteen in all, and of these ten survived, so our house was never lacking in children. And as if we didn't have enough of our own, we started to take in the children of others.

"First, we took in Edilene from my sister Biu after Valdimar hung himself. We raised Edilene like a daughter for eight years, but she deceived us. She got pregnant at sixteen and ran off to live with a boyfriend even younger than herself. Leonardo came to live with us when he was barely one year old. He was the son of Severino's younger brother, Antônio. Antônio's wife had given birth to twins in their home in the country, and one of them was doing well, while the other one, Leonardo, was in such a state of misery that I took pity on him. When I first saw him Leonardo was nine months old and weighed less than two kilos. No one was taking care of him, and he was left out in the sun all day so that his skin was burned and peeling. He was yellow with hepatitis, and his little belly was bloated with worms. He lay on the ground like a newborn all curled up. He didn't know how to use his arms and legs. They just dangled in front of him like this. His bones were soft; there was no calcium in them. And he was toothless and as bald as Dr. Urbano Neto!

"I took Leonardo home with me and carried him to the private office of Dr. Antônio, and he asked me, 'Can a poor woman like you with so many children of your own afford to take care of this miserable creature?' 'No, I cannot,' I replied, 'but nor can I leave him to die in the home of my brother-in-law.' 'In that case,' said Dr. Antônio, 'I will help you save the child.' And he was true to his word; he never charged me anything for all the consultations I had over Leonardo. Dr. Antônio said that the boy carried no heavy or untreatable diseases and that what ailed him were hunger and thirst. After only nine days with me his weight increased to two kilos and three hundred grams. After fifteen days with me he weighed two kilos and seven hundred grams. After a month he weighed three kilos. And he is still growing fast to this day.

"Our third foster child is our *caçula*, Luciana, who came to us left in a basket on our doorstep. By this time we had come to live in our own large new home on the Alto de Independência, and we were known far and wide as a strong family that loved children. The little baby girl was tiny but well cared for, plump and rosy with her ears already pierced with tiny gold earrings. What suffering and anguish must have brought this treasure to our door! She had a note pinned to her dress: 'God bless you, *madrinha da gente* [godmother to all the poor people]. Please take care of my precious baby.' And we have, even though by this time I had had my tubes tied and had given up the idea that I would ever raise another child. But we have never regretted it. God has been good to us, and the only shadow that has ever crossed our path since those early years was the time of the inquest, the one that almost destroyed us.

"Until we left the Alto I was still washing clothes for a living, and that, as you know, is hard, mean work. But Dona Dora finally forgave me for marrying Severino, and she invited me to work in the kitchen at the primary school. Now both Severino and I were working at the school, and things went very well for us there, as they did for all the workers and teachers. Dona Dora had a knack for getting things for the school, and whatever was available in Recife, Dora went out and got it. She would go into Recife by bus, and she would come back by truck, bringing all kinds of supplies, especially food. She brought back sacks of food—beans, fine white flour, bulgur wheat, and powdered milk, along with huge cans of margarine and oil. She would give the food away to anyone who needed it, not just to the schoolchildren. She gave big sacks of food to me and Severino and to all the school workers and their families. Later, she would send for the poor people from the Alto, and they would line up in the schoolyard, and she would give food away to them, too. It was like a big party, and no one was ever sent away empty-handed. Dona Dora explained that the food was there to feed people, wasn't it? And it was free. It came from the United States. What harm as long as it was eaten?

"Dona Dora was getting to be so powerful that many people were afraid of her. But whatever she did, it was because she wanted what was best for everyone. Remember what I told you about my mama? Dona Dora was the same way. She wanted to make people happy. She felt a responsibility toward the whole *município*. The way Dona Dora handled the free foods was the way she handled everything else. She would get grants and new teaching positions for the school, and she would hand these around as though she were dealing a deck of cards. She would get a position for one person, and she would divide it into two jobs. Or she would find work for one person, and if it turned out that he didn't need it after all, she would have him sign the money over to someone else who did. But Dora never took anything for herself. She was no thief; she was just breaking the law.

"This is where we came into it because Dora had a special fondness for Severino. She trusted him more than anyone in the city. She always said that Severino was a man of total confidence. You could trust him 100 percent. She would send Severino into Recife to pick up supplies, to deposit money in various accounts, to deliver confidential messages, everything, everything. She also asked Severino to sign some of the payroll checks that went to the wrong people. Severino was a *matuto*, but he wasn't a donkey. He knew that what he was doing for Dona Dora was wrong in the eyes of the law, but he also knew that Dora was doing these things to help out people who were as poor as we were. So in the end, he did sign a lot of false payrolls.

"Everyone in the school knew what was up, and for a long time nobody tried to interfere. But there were some teachers who didn't like Dona Dora because she was so tough and because sometimes she would correct the teachers in public and humiliate them. She couldn't stand laziness, and some of the teachers were lazy. So a few of them got together and decided to denounce her. They went to the authorities in Recife and explained what Dora had been doing with the grants and the school lunch supplies.

"And so, finally, the law caught up with her. There was a lot of money to be accounted for, millions of cruzeiros had disappeared. Severino was brought into court because he had signed so many false papers. His name came out in the newspapers saying that he was accused of a serious crime. Forgery, I think. The newspapers said that if Severino were convicted, he could go to prison for many years. We were hysterical. What would we do now? Severino would lose his job and our home, and he would go to jail, while I would be left with a gang of homeless children to feed.

"Our salvation came to us in the form of Dr. Urbano Neto, the state deputy and the older brother of Seu Félix. I went myself to Dr. Urbano, and I begged him to use his political connections to help us out. He agreed, and he got a lawyer for Severino who was so good that Severino got off with a fifteen-day suspended sentence. Of course, he still has this blemish on his record. But our good luck, our *felicidade*, was Severino's ignorance! Despite everything, Severino was still a *matuto*, and he didn't really understand a lot about the laws and the state. And that is what the lawyer kept repeating again and again in the courtroom: 'This simple man, this simple, ignorant, and backward man.' And so for once in my life I was grateful that Severino was so backward! The judge wanted to exile Severino, to send him deep into the *sertão* far away from his 'bad' influences so that he could start his life all over again. But Dr. Urbano Neto interceded for us again. He said it would be cruelty to send a poor, simple *matuto* from the *zona da mata* into the backlands of the *sertão*, where he had no family, no friends, and no knowledge of the *sertanejos* and their ways of life. And so that part of the sentence was removed, and Severino was sent to work in another school in Bom Jesus."

Biu de Ninguem

Later that afternoon I tried to find Biu in her smokey lean-to on the dirt path called the Third Crossing of the Indians. She was cooking outside on a small table using a little clay charcoal burner. It was next to impossible to get Biu to be still long enough for an interview, let alone a life history. Her hands and legs were always in motion. She talked incessantly and almost always with a hand-rolled cigarette between her lips. She liked a pipe even better, but older Alto women had taken their pipes "underground," smoking them only in the privacy of the outhouse or late at night outside after everyone else was quite asleep. Pipe smoking had gone the way of squatting, comfortable bodily customs that were now rejected as "primitive" by the younger generation. Instead of squatting, women now sat on the ground or the floor with their legs stretched out straight in front of them, but I missed the conviviality of the old position.

Biu was cutting up tripe in a bowl of water, and she laughed explosively at her own jokes. A prankster who was agile at ducking my questions and directing the talk elsewhere, Biu the clown, like the proverbial Pagliacci, was wounded and vulnerable. It was just that soft core of vulnerability that I was about to probe, and so she was responding with an appropriate evasiveness. The interview was complicated, too, by the surroundings: her tiny single room where she and four (sometimes five) of her several children lived, more outside than in, spilling over onto the concrete doorstep sitting and resting or stretching out at midday for siesta or in the back showering under a makeshift shelter of patched blankets with an upside-down bucket for a shower head or cooking on a portable table in the backyard *quintal*, dangerously close to the open latrine. The smells of burning charcoal, salted fish, trash, and backed-up sewage were indistinguishably mixed. No wonder Xoxa, the middle child, so often complained of nausea when it was time to eat. There were no chairs. Inside one sat on the edge of the single mattress in a room where it was always too dark to take notes, or one sat outside on the doorstep or on the ground.

Of the three half-sisters, Biu is my agemate. Sandwiched between Antonieta and Lordes, Biu was once the most beautiful of the three. Now, in 1989, at forty-five years, she could easily be mistaken for a woman twenty years older. Her one remaining vanity, her long, thick, brown-black hair, remained uncut, although she generally wore it modestly pulled back and pinned into a roll at the nape of her neck. I remembered how in the old days, when Biu was still in her early twenties, she would shake her hair down in the evening and brush it forward over her face so as to frighten the children of the Travessa de Bernardo Vieira where we lived. It was my role to sound the alarm, warning the children that a "wild beast from Africa" or a "hairy Russian bear" was on the loose, and the children would scream and take cover in a state of terrified delight as Biu would stage her mock attacks, her hair bristling and flying out in all directions.

At that time Biu was still living with Valdimar, a large, gangly black man many years older than herself. Valdimar was a quiet man, troubled by inner demons. A facial paralysis (a *susto*, his family called it) had left his mouth twisted into a fearful grimace, a few of his teeth permanently exposed. When I first moved onto the hillside niche occupied by the three sisters and their companions, I was afraid of Valdimar, and I avoided him as much as I could. My fear dissolved into shame, however, when one night I found myself stranded on my way home, halfway up the main street of the Alto. The Rua da Cruzeiro was illuminated by a few street lamps, and these were suddenly extinguished during a power failure. I began to tremble. How would I ever find my way to the small turnoff that led to the cliff, with its small compound of houses formed by Tonieta, her two sisters, their mother, Tia Josefa, and their neighbors Nailza and Zé Antônio? I do not know how long I stood there frozen in my tracks until I heard my name called softly. I wheeled around, and in the intense light of a kerosene lamp held high in his hand was Valdimar, with his menacing, involuntary smile. I stifled a scream. "Don't be afraid, Dona Nancí," he said quickly. "Biu sent me to help you find your way home in this blackness. Don't mind my ugly face. I would never hurt you." Some months later I was able to repay the favor by helping Biu to deliver her first surviving child, a daughter named Edilese, who later grew up a thief and a disreputable "marginal" living in the stigmatized prostitution *zonas* of Recife.

Biu's life is like a roller coaster gone haywire, its ups and downs colliding, sometimes jerking the cars off the tracks entirely. She seems buffeted by fate, her life a tangle of events over which she is powerless. And yet Biu projects an image of strength and hardiness, if not resilience. Only those who know her very well indeed have ever seen the facade crumble and Biu reduced to a hysterical despair. The hardest working of the three sisters, Biu has worked in fields and factories, in streams, and on hillsides. She has cleared plantation lands, stacked cut cane, fished, hunted for small game, collected grasses for animal feed and kindling for resale. She has worked in the infested river digging up sand for construction sites and washing pack animals. She has washed, starched, and ironed clothes for wealthy and particular families, all outdoors and without the help of electricity.

Severina is also the most uncompromising of the three sisters. She refuses to marry, saying, "I was born a spinster, and God willing I will die the same." Nor will Biu work inside the "houses of others," for that, she says, is as good as slavery. She wants no long-term contracts, no dependent relations with a husband or a "boss," good or bad, *bom patrão* or *mau*. She is the only one of the sisters who has not been rescued by a wealthy sponsor or patron at one time or another in her life. "In the end, the price is always too high," she explained. The advice she gives her own teenage daughters as they go out to make their way on their own is "Don't trust anyone more than yourself."

Although Biu is not ashamed to beg, she refuses to do anything that will make her feel "beholden" to anyone. Like her mother before her, Biu believes that those who have more in life have a moral obligation to share with those who have less or who are needy. She prefers to ask for help, quite directly, when she needs it. She does not ask to "borrow" money or food or bus fare or cigarettes, nor does she promise to give anything in return. "Can you spare a few smokes?" she is likely to ask. "Or have you got a good pair of shoes I could fit into?" But Biu will not steal or "trick" others into sharing with her against their will. Biu prefers fieldwork to domestic service, but she will take in wash as long as she is free to take the laundry down to the river. She will not wash clothes, as her sister Lordes does, in the patio of a local big house. Nor will she work in the kitchens of the wealthy, as Antonieta sometimes does. "Before long," Biu says, "people start calling you Lordes *de* Carminha [Lordes who belongs to Dona Carminha, the wealthy widow]." Biu will not be anyone's property. "I am Biu de Ninguem [Nobody's Biu]," she likes to say.

It was hard for Biu to focus for any length of time on her past, so preoccupied was she with the struggles of the present. I had to catch her story on the run and in small, disconnected fragments. These I have patched together into the semblance of a single, seamless narrative from several short conversations during the four days of Brazilian *carnaval* in 1988.

"I was born on the Engenho Bela Vista in 1944. There isn't much to tell about those early years. When I was little my situation was *triste*. I had to beg as soon as I could walk because my father left my mother soon after I was born. His name was Antônio Gonçalvez—at least that's what people say. Tonieta says that he was a rich man, but if he was, I don't know anything about it, and he certainly hasn't left any of it to me! After my father left us, Mãe had to go out to work, so she gave me and Antonieta to Tia Josefa to raise. Often Tia sent the two of us out begging to help things along. Once we went as far as Mocos [a *vila* several kilometers from Bela Vista], and a man jumped out of some bushes with a knife, and he chased us away, calling us little thieves. After that we never had to beg again, as long as we lived with our aunt. 'From now on we will have to put our faith in God,' she said.

"Tia washed clothes and ironed them for a living, and we helped her with that work, and that's how we got by. She used a heavy old iron with a lid that opened and that you filled up with burning charcoal. It was hard work, and your arms would ache dragging that iron across men's shirts and pants and women's dresses. You had to be very careful not to burn a hole or to rip anything, or the *patroa* would really give it to Tia. Sometimes Tonieta and I would dry the clothes by hanging them on barbed wire, and it would leave a tiny hole in a shirt, or some rust would come off onto a white blouse. We would get walloped by Auntie whenever that happened! We had to starch and iron little girls' underpants with lace trim and crochet on them, while we were often naked under our skirts! Tonieta would sometimes try the little lace clothes on herself, but I would laugh at the children who had to be dressed like that—God deliver me!

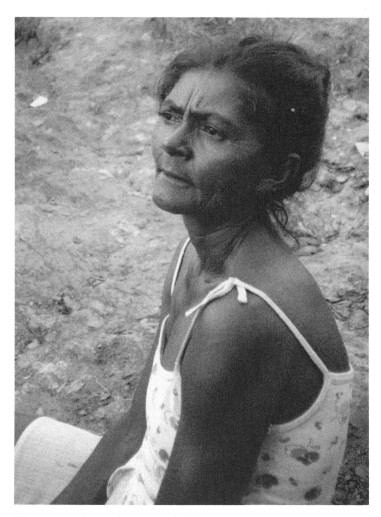

Biu, caught off guard at a thoughtful moment.

"With all this work we had we still went hungry many times. In those days when you were hungry and there was nothing to eat, country people were forced to eat the *mata*—wild greens and grasses, even *catinga* [a cactus]. These were the same herbs and plants that the goats and cows ate, and sometimes we grazed right alongside them. That was how we killed our hunger then! Compared to this kind of suffering, life today is much better. Today you can always show up in the house of a neighbor, and your *comadre* will never deny you a piece of bread or some cornmeal to take home or even just a cup of black coffee. God save my children from ever having to eat the *mata* in their life!

"When I was about eight years old we moved to Tia's house on the Alto do Cruzeiro, and Mama and Auntie tried to put me into school. But it wasn't for me. I was always into mischief; I even tore up all the schoolbooks. The teachers said that I was *malcriada* [poorly raised]. Finally, they sent me home for good. I left without learning how to sign my name, and to this day I am an *analfabeta pura* [pure, unadulterated illiterate]!

"At the age of fifteen I ran off with Valdimar, the older brother of our neighbor Sebastiana, who lived on the Indians' Road. Valdimar was old, almost fifty, and he was a widower. My family tried to prevent us from getting together. They raised every objection. Mama and Auntie said that Valdimar was too old for me, that he was 'finished' [sterile and/or impotent], and that he was ugly and too dark. They said he would blacken our race. They said that Valdimar was a drunkard and that he ran around with other women. But I just laughed and I wouldn't listen to a thing. I was determined to have that old *nego* [black man] no matter what! So we hatched a plan. Valdimar and I ran off together on Good Friday afternoon when everyone was in the *praça* for the procession. We knew that no one would even notice that we were missing. When we came home the next day, Holy Saturday, it was done. We had spent the night together. No one could say anything now. It was too late. They had to accept us as a couple.

"So I was a mother by the age of sixteen. They were wrong about one thing. Valdimar was good in bed, and I had six pregnancies by him. My firstborn, Sonia, lived to be a year and four months, and then she died of *gasto*, the diarrhea that has no cure. By the time she died she was so wasted, and so was I. After that I had a miscarriage. Then came another living child, a son named Severino, but he lasted only eight months. I began to have some luck, finally, when Edilese was born. You remember because you were her *mamãe de umbigo* [godmother of her navel], the one who cut her cord.

"I never much liked being a 'wife,' but I loved being pregnant. I adored it when I was huge with a pregnant belly! I always felt so beautiful. Pregnancy was my form of riches. Any woman who doesn't want babies shouldn't take a man in the first place. As for me, I had fifteen pregnancies in my life, and if I hadn't gotten so disgusted with men, I would have had fifteen more. But as it was, after Mercea was born, I told the doctor to tie my tubes. I was willing to call it quits. The truth is I never wanted a husband under my roof, and getting pregnant always involved men. Although I've lived with men, I never took one for a husband. It was my choice. I am single today, and God willing, I will die the same.

"Valdimar *wanted* to marry me. In those days when I was living with him, a rich woman, a *senhora de engenho*, the wife of my boss, took an interest in me. She thought I was too beautiful to be working in the cane fields. So she took me aside, and she offered to arrange my marriage with Valdimar. She wanted to pay for everything, to be the main sponsor of the wedding. She would have arranged all the paperwork and purchased the wedding clothes and the flowers, everything. But I refused her offer; I preferred to remain single. But I had to pay dearly for my stubbornness. After Valdimar killed himself, the children and I were totally abandoned. As the 'widow' of a man to whom I was never married, I wasn't entitled to anything, not me or the children. I hadn't registered the children in their father's name, only in mine. So when the time came, there was no proof of our relationship. His death brought me nothing, not even the smallest widow's pension.

"Life with Valdimar was pretty awful. Soon I even lost my taste for sex with him. I left Valdimar seven times. Six of those times I came back to him. I would put up with a lot, and then one day I would come home from work, dog-tired, and I'd take one look at him sleeping on the floor or in a hammock, dead drunk, and I would say to myself, 'This is no head of house; this is a worthless bum.' And when he would come to, I'd put him out the door. If he refused to leave, I would pack up a few things and leave myself. 'Now *you* can take care of the kids,' I would tell him.

"What kept me coming back? I'd begin to worry about the children. Or I'd think about getting old and skinny and worn out. I was beautiful once, but I was losing all the good looks I had. In the whole world Valdimar was really the only person I had. And I would look in the mirror and say, 'Who would ever want you now?' I began to think of Valdimar as my 'fate' in life, and so I would decide to make the best of it. But no sooner would I come back than he would do something to disappoint or annoy me, and I would leave him again. And that's how it happened that we were living apart when Valdimar hung himself. It was his sister, Sebastiana, not me, who cut him loose. Valdimar's end didn't surprise me. He was never right in his head. He would brood and brood and go for days without talking to anyone, and then suddenly he would fly into a rage. I once had him locked up in the 'hospital for crazies' in Recife, but it didn't do him any good at all. He was a rum drinker, and in the end it was the *cachaça* that turned his head for good.

"After Valdimar died I had nowhere to turn. My family had all turned against me because I always did what I wanted. I never took their advice. So I did the only thing a woman in my situation could do. I'm not ashamed of it. I took the children with me by bus to Recife, and I lived in the center of the city begging on the sidewalk. I would lay out a large piece of cardboard and set up my little clay burner, and that was how we lived, in the street up against a building next to the bridge. There was always a lot of action there, and I could catch people coming and going across the bridge. But it was during this time that my firstborn daughter, Edilese, went bad on me. She ran away and became a street *moleque*. I lost her to the streets of Recife. Then my baby, my little son, died. His nervous system was too fragile for life on the street. He couldn't take all the noise and the fights and the violence. All I had left then was Edilene, my middle child, and I could see that she wasn't going to last too long either. I was killing the last of my children off, one by one, but it was not from ill-will toward them, no! Word of my situation got back to Tonieta, and she took pity on me. She told me to come back to Bom Jesus and to give her my Edilene to raise. I did, and that was the girl's only salvation. It's because of Tonieta that Edilene is alive and well today and a mother herself.

"After I returned to Bom Jesus I found myself a job on the plantation Votas. It was hard fieldwork, but I was happy again. I adore life in the country! I like to work without anyone on my back telling me every minute what needs to be done. I can see that for myself! When you work in the country you get paid by the amount of land you clear or weed, and the time you put in is up to you. I am a woman who was never afraid of work. Tonieta and Lordes were always ashamed to see me set off before dawn with a rag wrapped around my head and a pair of men's trousers covering my legs and held up with a piece of rope for a belt! 'What a beauty!' they would say. But shame is for those who cheat and steal. Shame is for those who do violence to others. There is no shame in walking down the hill with a hoe across your back!

"It was while working in Votas that I met Oscar. I was assigned to a field where he was working, and we started joking with each other, calling each other names, and it didn't take long before we got together. And so I took up with another man after telling myself that I was completely through with men. I certainly wasn't out looking to find another one. But it was a good arrangement at first, and I wound up living with Oscar for fourteen years. I had nine pregnancies with him. But I am still alone and single.

"Look, I won't speak badly about Oscar. He treated me and the children well at first. He didn't drink and he was faithful to me. He never abused me or the children. At first we lived in a little mud hut near the top of the Alto do Cruzeiro. After a few years Antonieta helped us to get a good COHAB [state-subsidized] house close to hers on the Alto de Independência. Those were good times for us. They were never better, and we might have been living there still if Oscar hadn't gotten it into his head to try making an even better life for us in São Paulo. Tia and Mama and Antonieta tried to talk us out of it, but Oscar was determined. He had a brother living in São Paulo, and this brother sent word for us to come and join him there. His brother said that there was good work at high wages and a better place to live and bring up our children. He said that we could make our way in São Paulo and that it was where everything was happening. Bom Jesus was a backward place, a place for *matutos*. The future, he said, was in São Paulo.

"So against everyone's objections, we sold our COHAB house, and we took up a collection for our bus fare. But what misery lay waiting for us in São Paulo! We had been completely deceived by Oscar's brother. We arrived exhausted and hungry after days riding the bus only to find that his brother lived in a filthy, crowded hovel far, far outside the city. His neighborhood was an ugly and violent shantytown. The local police were killing people at liberty. There was no protection for the poor. The buses into the city were crowded and dangerous. There was no room for us to live and no work to be found. The children became sick with fevers and flus. I thought we would all die of the cold. At night our teeth rattled in our heads from such cold that I never knew existed in this world, let alone in our Brazil.

"I started to lose my mind. I suffered from a nervous attack that almost cost me my life. I finally had to send word to Mama begging her to forgive me and asking her to arrange the money for our return bus fare, or else we would all be dead within the month. Tonieta sent the money for me and the children. After I came home, Oscar soon followed me. We tried to put our life back together again on the Alto do Cruzeiro, but it was never the same. We had lost so much, and neither one of us had the energy to start over again. Oscar started to drink, and everything began to go downhill. He took up with another woman. Before long Oscar had two families on the Alto do Cruzeiro. This went on for a long time. He had four more children by his little *neguinha* [darling], and there were seven still left from our nine. He tried to support all of us on his single minimum wage [about a dollar and a quarter a day].

"This continued for several years, with each of us complaining about the other woman and insisting that he let one or the other go. And finally he did. On the night of São João in 1986, the night of the barn fires and square dances, Oscar came home early and in a bad mood. He ordered me to pack up his belongings in a satchel because he was finally leaving me for his other woman. Then he took his pick of the children, our two healthy sons, to help him in the fields and our beautiful, fat Patricia. He left me with the rest, the two, worthless older girls, Xoxa and Pelzinha, Carolina, the skinny middle girl, and Mercea, my hopeless last born, who has never been well a day in her life.

"I became hysterical, and I yelled, 'Why are you doing this to me now?' He said to my face, 'Because you have turned into a *coroa*, a toothless old hag. You are used up, and you're not good for anything anymore.' I was so revolted by him and by what he did to me that I began to take it out on the children. I told them that I hated them because they were his and that looking at their faces reminded me of the abuse I had suffered at his hands. But the more I abused the children, the more they stuck fast to me.

"There are times, Nancí, when I think I can't stand it anymore. I tell the children, 'If you bother me, if you ask me for one more thing that I can't possibly give you, I am going to pack up your clothes in a tight little bundle and send you off to live with your papa and his other woman. Let him take care of the whole lot of you!' But they are so attached to me. The little one never lets me out of her sight. Mercea hangs onto my skirts, and she cries whenever I leave the house. I can't take a step without her. What kind of children are these, so afraid to move without their mama? So I yell at them to toughen them up. I say, 'Hell, you are eating me up alive! When I die they are going to have to make me a very large coffin so I can carry you all along with me!'

"What does the future hold? My life will be more of the same. My only fear is that I will die a pauper on the streets, neglected and abandoned [à míngua], with no one to bury me. That would be a fitting end to the life of Severina, Biu de Ninguem!"

The tears had begun to form at the corner of Biu's eyes. But just as suddenly as they came, Biu banished them away. She roughly wiped her eyes with her charcoal-sooted hands, making herself look for all the world like a coal miner. Reflecting suddenly on the days of *carnaval* ahead, Biu jumped up, hitched up her skirt, and showed the crowd of small children gathered in front of her door a lively *frevo* step. Soon her antics—sticking out her tongue, shaking her behind, pushing her false teeth out of her mouth—had the children splitting their sides with laughter. Pagliacci emerged once again, and there would be no turning back. She gave me a wide and mischievous grin.

Jeitos *and* Malandragem

Although I have occasionally used the word *strategy* with reference to the daily practices of the women and men of the Alto, perhaps the time has now come to disown the term with all its biologic and militaristic overtones. For the people of the Alto do not really strategize, though they do imagine, invent, dream, and play. Michel de Certeau (1980, 1984) made a useful distinction between "strategy" and "tactic" that I take up here.

The strategic metaphor (see de Certeau 1984:35–39) implies that people are consciously organized and prepared for action. It suggests that they have a clear-sighted vision of the lay of the land and a certain knowledge of the "enemy," that they can look (optimistically) to the future, and that they can plan toward an upset victory. But this is not the reality in which the *moradores* of the Alto do Cruzeiro find themselves. Their daily lives are circumscribed by an immensely powerful state and by local economic and political interests that are openly hostile to them. The power that constrains them is so encompassing and, given the international dimensions of Brazilian economics, so "englobing" that it has obscured their field of vision.

A strategy implies a "base," a starting point, a specific location, one that is also a locus of power. None of these is available to the *moradores* of the shantytown, who live instead with the shadow of the death squads falling across their doorsteps, so that even speech is suppressed for fear of being "overheard" and thereby marked. Suspicion is rampant: "No one is innocent here" is a popular expression of general mistrust. It is too much to expect the people of the Alto to organize collectively when chronic scarcity makes individually negotiated relations of dependency on myriad political and personal bosses in town a necessary survival tactic.

Following Michel de Certeau, we can substitute "tactics" for "strategy" as a better description of the everyday, oppositional survival practices of the poor. Tactics are not autonomous acts; they are defined in the absence of real power:

> The space of a tactic is the space of the other. It must play on and with a terrain imposed on it. . . . It does not have the means to keep to itself, at a distance, in a position of withdrawal, foresight, and self-collection: it is a maneuver "within the enemy's field of vision" . . . and within enemy territory. . . . It operates in isolated actions, blow by blow. It takes advantage of opportunities and depends on them, being without any base where it could stockpile its winnings, build up its own position, and plan raids. What it wins, it cannot keep. . . . In short, a tactic is an art of the weak." (de Certeau 1984:37)

Tactics are defensive and individual, not aggressive and collective, practices. They should not be confused or conflated with the domain of "resistance," as James Scott (1985) and his colleagues (see Colburn 1989) and even de Certeau have done from time to time. Although tactics may temporarily divert the more organized power plays of the *patrão* and planter class of the Northeast, they do not challenge the definition of the political-economic situation.

When my Alto friends refer to finding a *jeito* or a *jeitinho*—that is, a quick solution to a problem or a way out of a dilemma—they are speaking the language of tactics. *Jeitos* entail all the mundane tricks for getting by and making do within the linear, time-constrained, everyday, uphill struggle along the suffering *caminho*. The Brazilian *jeitoso* is an ideal personality type connoting one who is attractive, cunning, deft, handy, and smooth. When the word *jeito* is invoked to imply a "getting away with murder" or a "taking advantage" of a situation at someone else's expense, it is closely related to *malandragem*, a term without an English equivalent, although "swindling" comes close. *Malandragem* is the art of the scoundrel and the rascal: a "badness" that entails an enviable display of strength, charm, sexual allure, charisma, street smarts, and wit (see also da Matta 1979, 1989:95–105).

The *malandro* (rake) and the *jeitosa* (one who operates around and outside the law and who lives by her wits) are products of the clash of competing realities and social ethics in contemporary Brazil. As social personalities and distinct interactional styles, they are culturally derived defenses against the rigidity of the race-class system, the complexity of Brazilian laws, and the absurdity of an unwieldy, inflated, and corrupt state bureaucracy. *Jeitos* and *malandragem* are forms, wrote da Matta, of "national social navigation" (1989:101–102), and hence they are not tactical "weapons" of the poor alone. But where da Matta described the various social maneuvers used by middle-class Brazilians to "beat the system" by circumventing the law and the state bureaucracy, I am concerned with the daily improvisations and sleights of hand used by the poor of the Alto just to stay alive at all. Although among middle-class Brazilians *malandragem* is a characteristically male, sex-linked trait, in the rougher context of shantytown life, women, too, can survive as rakes and scoundrels. There was certainly something of the scoundrel in Tonieta's various schemes for getting by, while "sweet" Lordes with her four "husbands" was something of a rake. Meanwhile, Mãe was a little of each. Only Biu played her hand openly and directly, and we can see how far that got her on the Alto do Cruzeiro.

Staying alive in the shantytown demands a certain "selfishness" that pits individuals against each other and that rewards those who take advantage of those even weaker. *Moradores* admire toughness and strength, and they point with pride to those who show a knack for life, including a seductive charm and a "way" with words that can move, motivate, and fool others. And they pity those who are *sem jeito*—that is, weak, hopeless, without the "right stuff," altogether graceless and deficient beings.

And so *moradores* try, like Tonieta, to work the traditional *patrão* system to their advantage. They try to make alliances with the strong, the beautiful, and the powerful. As *eleitors* they will vote for the local, regional, and national candidates who are most likely to win, and they will avoid association with likely losers, even if the "weaker" candidate has expressed solidarity with their class. As Tonieta qualified her support of local political leaders, "If you're going up, I'll tag along with you. If you're going down, *adeus*, you can go without me." Some *moradores* rejected Lula, the Socialist

Workers Party presidential candidate, not only because he was unlikely to win but because he was too *ugly*: "Lula is too much like us: weak and defective [referring to his injured fingers], and his speech is rough, not beautiful." Biu drew large imaginary circles around her underarms. "He *sweats*, Nancí, and he leaves stains on his work shirts. Oh what a *homem sem jeito*, what a graceless, hopeless man to be our president!"

Moradores treat their spiritual patrons with a similarly undisguised pragmatics. As folk Catholics they "work" the spirit world using the familiar, everyday tactics of barter, blackmail, debt, and shifting loyalties. An ineffective patron saint is of no more use than a drunken, unemployed husband, and he or she is just as easily dismissed or exchanged for another. Not all patron saints are equally *jeitoso*.

"Do you really believe in the power of Padre Cícero?" Biu challenged Black Irene, who had just returned from a costly and difficult pilgrimage to Juàzeiro do Norte to pay a "promise" that she owed to the large ceramic image of her spiritual patron and "godfather."

"I do, of course," Irene replied.

"I don't," Biu the skeptic replied. "Who knows if he is a *real* saint or just an ordinary padre no different from our priest. I prefer to put my faith in Nossa Senhora das Dores because she is the *real* mother of Jesus, and with her behind you, you *can't* go wrong."

"Well, maybe Our Lady works for you," broke in Zulaide, "but she hasn't done much good for me. When I lost my two-year-old I lit a candle at her altar, but I didn't pray to her. I 'gave it' to her instead. I said, 'Lady, this is your last chance. If you don't start paying me some attention, you're finished [fired].' "

"I myself prefer Nossa Senhora Aparecida [Our Lady of Apparitions]," broke in the old praying woman Dona Carminha. "Tell me, who has ever *seen* Our Lady of Sorrows, except as a plaster saint over the altar of the church? With Our Lady of Apparitions you are more secure because she appeared to a lot of people. That's how she got her name."

But where faith in patrons, material or spiritual, is weak or lacking, there are always alcohol and drugs: *cachaça*, marijuana, and glue sniffing. When all else is blocked or fails, the body is enlisted as a final outpost of self-destructive protest, rage, and defiance. The weekend "drunks" following the frustrations of Friday payday and Saturday marketing on the Alto do Cruzeiro are a case in point. These escapes into the oblivion of drugged stupor also constitute ways of getting by and making do on the Alto do Cruzeiro. Biu was given to glue sniffing and to the more than occasional "toke" of marijuana during the period when she and Oscar were feuding over his second wife. *"Mas é, Dona Nancí, mas é um jeito,"* Biu said, not denying Oscar's accusation of her addictions. "The drugs had made her crazy, a real *doida*," Oscar explained in defense of his walking out on her in 1986. "Well, what can I say?" replied Biu. "That's the way it was. The dope was a little *jeito*, just a way of getting by."

Love and Family Life: Bricolage

Today is Father's Day—what a joke!

Carolina Maria de Jesus (1962:96)

The people of the Alto work their *jeitos* vertically through alliances with the rich and powerful and laterally through instrumental friendships and sexual relationships. Consequently, personal loyalties are often necessarily "shallow," and they may follow a trail of gifts and favors. Love is often conflated with material favors. "*Of course*, my mother loves me," insisted the little nine-year-old beggar Giomar, an all but abandoned street child who sometimes slept in our doorway when it rained. "She *has* to love me," he reasoned with the indisputable logic of the survivor: "I bring her money and food to eat." Similarly, Lordes described Nelson as her "husband" during the months that he visited her on Saturday nights, bringing her a *feira* basket of groceries. When the groceries ended, so did the relationship.

I recall how Xoxa once broke down in a fit of convulsive sobbing because Biu had given a cheap pair of plastic hair clips to each of her two younger girls but not to the overly sensitive then-fifteen-year-old. "Mama doesn't love me" was all that the inconsolable girl-woman could say, despite my shaky insistence to the contrary, for I feared that Xoxa, the family scapegoat, might be right. "Give me yellow hair ribbons and five hundred cruzados, *madrinha* Nancí," Xoxa finally demanded, in between sobbing and sucking her thumb, her larger than child's head heavy on my lap. And I laughed in spite of myself, seeing how the young girl had managed to bamboozle me again. In the absence of a mother, a hastily fabulated "godmother" would do in a pinch. And when I laughed, she laughed, too.

People of the Alto form households and families through an inventive bricolage, fashioning and making up relations as they go along, following a structured improvisation. Women do sometimes fashion husbands, like Lordes, of weekend visitors, just as later on they may replace their own mortally neglected and dead infants with *filhos de criação*. On the Alto do Cruzeiro a mother and her surviving children form the stable core of the household and, as I suggested in Chapter 7, fragile infants, casual "husbands," and weekend "fathers" are best thought of as detachable, exchangeable, and circulating units.

Alto men, like Oscar, often engage in an informal practice of polygyny, often referring to two (or more) women and offspring as their "wife and children" while married to neither woman and often not the natural father of all their many children. Seu Biu de Caboclos, the winsome and charismatic head of an organized *carnaval* "school" on the Alto do Cruzeiro, managed to keep the secret of his second Alto wife and children from me for a very long time, until the Saturday afternoon that I inquired of a group of men playing dominoes at the top of the Alto whether Biu had returned home from *feira*.

"Which home?" one of the men answered, laughing.

"Why, the home of Caboclo Biu and White Gabriela," I replied. "Is there any other?"

"You had better ask Biu for yourself."

"Look, I'll tell you," Ferreirinho the transvestite offered somewhat maliciously. "Your good friend, Biu de Caboclos, has a *mulher branca* but also a little *neguinha* who lives along the Rua dos Índios.

"Who told you?" Seu Biu accosted me, when I tracked him down to his second little hut and family on the Alto that same afternoon. "I bet it was that dirty little *viado* [queer] Ferreirinho, wasn't it?"

"It's common knowledge," I lied to protect the accused.

"Well, yes, it is true," Biu replied, calming down. "I have had three wives in my life."

"At the same time?"

"I never intended to live with more than one woman. I am a good Catholic. I lived with my first woman for ten years, and she died before I had a chance to marry her as we had intended. We never had any children. She had a terrible sickness that wasted her flesh and made her old, old. Just before she died I arranged a little *neguinha* on the side. It was a small consolation for me, and it meant a great deal to her, for the poor woman had a gang of hungry kids. No, not by me, not any one of them! But I felt sorry for her and her children, and I began to visit her and help her out. I never intended to live with her because the woman didn't come free; she came burdened down with all those children.

"So, instead, as soon as I had a chance [that is, after his first wife died], I got together with my little *galega*, Gabriela. She was a child of fourteen, a virgin, and she came to me from the *mata* innocent and free! And it was with her that I had eight children in our nine years together. But I couldn't just walk out on the other woman all at once. She had come to depend on me, and her children knew only *me* as their father. They even call me *pai-inho* [little daddy]. I have such pity for them! But Gabriela is jealous—she resents every little thing I give to them. She begrudges the crusts of bread I put in their mouths."

"But Seu Biu Caboclo, *any* woman would be jealous. How can you possibly divide your earnings [about nine and a half dollars a week] among so many mouths?"

"I can't! If I were to *divide* what I earn, *everyone* would starve. I give every penny of my earnings to Gabriela. I give her no reason to complain. What I manage to give to the 'other' is only what I can arrange on the side: the little I win from gambling or a few *cruzados* I borrow from friends or a package of spaghetti or a box of powdered milk that I buy on credit. And she, at least, never complains. She is grateful for whatever little I bring into her hut."

Caboclo Biu's other woman, a tall, thin, and fine-featured woman, her face striking for its high cheekbones and smooth, jet black skin, stood in the doorway that led to her outdoor kitchen. She said nothing.

These loosely constructed, improvisational families are sustained consensually and continue only for as long as they are "useful" or gratifying. Alto women readily dislodge alcoholic or unemployed husbands from their huts, as did Biu with Valdimar and Little Irene with her much younger companion, Manoel, and with sentiments of "good riddance." Similarly, Alto men, when forced to choose among their wives and households, will walk out on a woman and her young children with the chilling words that their relationship was only, after all, a temporary arrangement, a little piece of *malandragem* that the man had entertained on the side. Oscar used words similar to these in walking out on Biu, although his conjugal situation was complicated by the fact that he had fathered children by both women, so that each could claim him as her "legitimate" spouse. In the Alto context, "legitimacy" refers to biological paternity, with or without marriage, as distinguished from more "fictive" social relations, as for example, Biu de Caboclos's relationship to his *neguinha* and her children by other men.

There is a parallel in the often fragile relations between women and their informally adopted foster children, *filhos de criação*. Although grandmothers on the Alto frequently rear their daughters' children for indefinite periods of informal fosterage, many of the older women are explicit about the ground rules. "I will keep them only as long as they are virgins" is a common stipulation, one that puts adolescent girls and their unwanted babies at great risk. But almost as quickly as one woman will spurn or cast off a disappointing husband or a spoiled adult daughter or granddaughter, other *moradores* will come forward to claim them and bring them into their own household for an indefinite period of time. Flexibility is a prerequisite of survival. So is the ability to dance spitefully in the face of death.

In concluding the account of her life history, Biu refused to let it end on a sorrowful or desperate note. She came close up to my face, so close I could smell the faint aftertaste of dried fish and *celantro*, as salty and bitter as tears. But Biu would not have it that way.

Xoxa with sick-to-death Mercea a few days before *carnaval*.

"No, Nancí, I *won't* cry," she said. "And I won't waste my life thinking about it from morning to night. My life is hard enough. One husband hung himself, and another walked out on me. I work hard all day in the cane fields. What good would it do me to lie awake at night crying about my fate? Can I argue with God for the state that I'm in? No! So I'll dance and I'll jump and I'll play *carnaval!* And yes, I'll laugh, and people will wonder at a *pobre* like me who can have such a good time. But if I don't enjoy myself, if I can't amuse myself a little bit, well, then, I would rather be dead."

Meanwhile, we all tried to ignore the hacking, convulsive coughing of Biu's miserable three-year-old daughter, Mercea. As Biu and I made tentative plans to meet again later that evening in the *praça* to greet the first organized *carnaval* group, O Grilo, Mercea whined pitifully. Her breathing was shallow and rapid, and her tiny, bony chest jumped along with the fast beat of the *frevo* music that blasted from every transistor radio on the Alto. "And what will be your *carnaval* costume?" I bent down to ask Mercea, trying to divert her attention. But as I touched the child, she whined more loudly and crawled away from me, dragging her wasted legs behind. Her skin was hot and dry as parchment. The excitement was too much for the sick little girl, and she began to cough violently; she threw up into the eroded and rocky ravine that separated the two sides of her hillside niche.

Reluctantly, Biu took a wrinkled wad of precious cruzados from her pocket—*feira* money for the next day—and she dispensed one of the older children to Feliciano's pharmacy for another useless cough medicine and an aspirin for the girl's fever. The local hospital clinic was closed for the days and nights of *carnaval*.

"Who will stay with Mercea tonight while we follow the revelers?" I asked Biu, looking around for Xoxa, Mercea's usual baby-sitter, who was noticeably absent. "Xoxa has just gone to work for a woman on her *sítio*," replied Biu. "She won't be home for a week. Pelzinha will have to take care of Mercea," she continued, pointing to her eldest, sixteen-year-old daughter, who said nothing but smiled to herself as she carefully painted her toenails in preparation for the evening. She did not look like a very likely baby-sitter to me.

I could begin to see the *carnaval* crowds gathering in the town below. There was no more time to waste if I was to get home and change my clothes.

11 *Carnaval*
The Dance Against Death

"And now," cried Max, "let the wild rumpus start!"
Maurice Sendak (1963:8)

"It is impossible," wrote Roberto da Matta, "to have a funeral without sadness or a Carnival without joy" (1983:163). For da Matta, as for a generation of scholarly observers, the bacchanalian pre-Lenten celebration is a spontaneous explosion of the collective social body, a festival of license, liminality, and laughter. The essential ingredient of all *carnaval* play is that it offers a privileged "space of forgetting" where the bothersome problems of the mundane world are banished. "What explains the style of *carnaval* is the necessity of inventing a celebration where things that must be forgotten can be forgotten if the celebration is to be experienced as a social utopia" (da Matta 1984:232).

The anthropologist continued that there could be no *carnaval* at all "if Brazilians insisted upon thinking about the secular and problematic aspects of their lives, such as the country's formidable external debt, the high rates of both infant mortality and illiteracy, the chronic absence of civil and political liberties, and the shocking socioeconomic contrasts" (231). These issues are present, of course, but only as the invisible background of everyday life against which the carnivalesque reacts and responds with its characteristic ritual abandon and with the necessary forgetting. In other words, there would be no need of *carnaval* in the first place if there were not monstrous things that needed to be banished and forgotten.

This interpretation of the Brazilian festival follows a long tradition in the writings of Johann Huizinga (1950) on the ludic moments of social life, Victor Turner (1969, 1979, 1983) on liminality and process, and Natalie Zemon Davis (1978) on symbolic inversions of the social order. But da Matta owes his greatest debt to Mikhail Bakhtin (1984:80), who saw in European carnivals the fullest and purest expression of a folk, or popular, culture.

480

Hence, da Matta's emphasis on the ribald sexuality (*sacanagem*) and the mocking laughter of *carnaval*, which stand in defiant opposition to the humorless "official" culture, specifically the repressive military dictatorship that dominated the Brazil of da Matta's day. *Carnaval* is about freedom; it is naturally subversive.

Carnaval players spin on an axis of inversions and reversals of high and low, order and disorder, male and female, inside and outside, public and private, freedom and repression, life and death. *Carnaval* dissolves order and rationality into chaos and nonsense; it tumbles the lofty as it celebrates the humble, absurd, and grotesque. Both the erotic and the maudlin, sexuality and death, are present in *carnaval,* so that destruction and regeneration are merged in the absurd *carnaval* cry "*Viva a morte!* Long live death!"

If the everyday world is structured by the metaphor of the *luta* in which suffering (*sofrimento*), pain (*dor*), and sickness (*doença*) mark one's passage through time and space along the path that leads inevitably to death, then once a year *carnaval* ruptures this linear and tragic trajectory. The relentless, punishing straight line of the everyday is symbolically and actually breached by the dizzying, dancing circle of samba revelers, who spin round and round in their wide skirts, and by *frevo* dancers, who leap up and down going nowhere at all. The everyday struggle evaporates in the wide open, enfolding embrace of the *carnaval* ball dancers, who, arms outstretched, call all things to the center and to themselves.

The ideology of *carnaval* hints at a brave new world, a world of pleasures and many different freedoms. The "vale of tears" gives way to a world of laughter and forgetting, a world of happiness (*felicidade*) and joy (*alegria*). The workaday, adult world of *trabalho* gives way to the child's world of fantasy and play. And so one "plays" and one "jumps" *carnaval,* just as an unfettered child jumps, unable to contain her excitement. *Carnaval* is about permissible regression and the return of the repressed, often in "grotesque" shapes and forms. One "plays" and "toys" with the body and its many eroticized parts—genitals, breasts, mouth and lips, hips and legs, buttocks and anus (see Parker 1990: chap. 6). Sucking is a predominant *carnaval* mode as men attach huge, pendulous breasts (or, alternatively, penises) to themselves and offer their exaggerated body parts to passersby while singing the most popular *carnaval* refrain of all times: "*Mamãe, eu quero; mamãe, eu quero; mamãe, eu quero mamar* [Mama, I want to suck]!" But hips and buttocks are also privileged in *carnaval* costume and dance, and men and boys sometimes play a game of "counting coup" that entails touching, fondling, squeezing, and roughly swatting each other's buttocks. Above all, *carnaval* is "dirty," mixing above and below, front and behind, inside and outside, water and mud, motor oil and honey, semen and excreta. And it is full of surprises.

Every *carnaval* has its jesters and its clowns, the little, mocking voices from the sidelines ridiculing the pretenders and the pretentious, pulling at loose threads. And so in the spirit of the *carnavalesco* I am playing the fool in tumbling the official and sanctimonious theory of *carnaval* so as to view it from a topsy-turvy position. I argue that in Bom Jesus da Mata at least, *carnaval*, while containing the lewd and ludic elements of the official description, is something else besides. If Brazilian *carnaval* creates a privileged space of forgetting and a dream world where anything is possible, the marginals' *carnaval* of Bom Jesus also provides a space for *remembering* and is as much a ritual of intensification as a ritual of reversal.

What the poor of the Alto do Cruzeiro, women especially, keep most before their eyes during *carnaval* time are scenes of their own exclusion, marginality, sickness, and debt. The opening day of *carnaval* is the Saturday before Ash Wednesday, and Saturday is also *feira*, market day, in Bom Jesus. The *carnaval* image of the abundant, overflowing cornucopia and of the banquet table is mocked by the empty *cesta* basket used for marketing. While cheap bootleg rum from the surrounding sugar mills flows in abundance during *carnaval* time, many among the poor dance on an empty stomach during the four days and five nights of the festival. And so *carnaval* and Ash Wednesday, feasting and fasting, are prematurely joined.

Meanwhile, the *fantasias* (meaning both the masks and costumes *and* the private fantasies) of Alto revelers project images of the fantastically real that emphasize ordinary and everyday social realities. Even while throwing themselves into the spontaneous joy and abandon of the festival, their *carnaval* "play" can also do the dirty work of class, gender, and sexual divisions, which by means of grotesque exaggeration are etched even more deeply into the individual and collective bodies. And here "dirty" takes on more sinister and less playful connotations.

My point is not that the libertine *carnaval* of Bakhtin and da Matta does not exist in Bom Jesus da Mata, for it does indeed reign as the official public sentiment of the festival. Rather, I wish to explore the more peripheral and marginal expressions of a celebration that is heterogeneous, open, and polysemic, full of ambiguities and contradictions. Real-life *carnavals* can be as egalitarian and emancipatory as Bakhtin, da Matta (1979, 1981, 1986), and Davis (1978) wish them to be, as oppressive and hierarchical as the Marxist and clerical critics of *carnaval* play can *only* see them to be, or both simultaneously. For "*carnaval*, with its wide smile and its grand sensuality, is a rite without a center and without an owner" (da Matta 1986:2).

I have noted the ambivalence of the Brazilian state toward *carnaval* over the past few decades. There is no single, unifying policy because there is no single, unified *carnaval*. *Carnaval* is both the opiate (or the metaphorical "speed" or "crack") of the popular classes *and* their symbolic Molotov cocktails. *Carnaval* crowds are unpredictable; they can explode and turn from revelry to mass protest. That this so rarely happens is remarkable.[1] *Carnaval* in Recife in 1965, the year after the military coup, was an eerie experience. One jumped and danced in the streets, along the beaches, and in the back of open trucks and jeeps under the watchful eye of armed military police officers. Their rifles and ammunition were not *fantasias*. Nudity was prohibited, and costumes could not mock or satirize public officials, the military, or the police. Political themes were banned in *carnaval* songs and in the floats and parades of the organized samba schools of Rio. In short, one played *carnaval* at one's risk. On the last night of *carnaval* that year I was lifted onto the back of a truck circling the main streets of downtown Recife, while the revelers, high on canisters of intoxicating ether-laced perfume that they inhaled to enhance *carnaval* play, chanted, "Viva Miguel Arraes! Viva Miguel Arraes!" They were calling for the return of the then recently imprisoned, later exiled, populist, and vaguely left-leaning ex-governor of the state of Pernambuco. We were chased by military police officers on foot, who fortunately chose not to shoot at the rebel truck. The subversive potential of *carnaval* play was recognized by the nervous, young military government.

As the years passed, however, and military power and presence were routinized, restrictions on *carnaval* play were gradually lifted, and the city of Rio de Janeiro sponsored the building of its giant *carnaval* dome, where the samba schools now parade and flaunt their exotic and erotic costumes and dances as though under the circus "big top." Local governments as well as commerce and industry financially back and "sponsor" local *carnaval* "schools," *blocos* (small groups of revelers who dress and dance in unison according to a prearranged theme), and *carnaval* balls. The poor, who are the main *carnaval* street performers and entertainers, now expect their local political bosses and patrons to underwrite their organized play. In subverting the potential subverters, the state recognizes the usefulness of *carnaval*. But the truce between the state and the disorderly popular classes of Brazil is always tentative and unstable. It can shift at any moment.

The Carnivalesque in Bom Jesus da Mata

We might expect that Bom Jesus, with its multiple social realities of *casa*, *rua*, and *mata*, would provide an ideal setting for the carnivalesque tumbling and reversal of roles, statuses, and hierarchies. Alternatively, it should offer a space where these competing and colliding social worlds might merge in a momentary egalitarian utopia where everything is possible and nothing is forbidden. Victor Turner wrote that during *carnaval* in Rio, the very centers of Brazilian hierarchy—the house, office, and factory—are emptied, and the entire city is transformed into a home, a unifying symbol of Brazilianity. The everyday distinctions between public and private, *rua* and *casa*, are breached: "Carnaval may, indeed, invade the sacred homestead, itself, as masked revelers swarm through it and out again" (1987:82).

But what I saw that first evening (and for each subsequent evening) after leaving Biu's house and after catching up with the street dancers was a highly segregated and segmented *carnaval* where rich and poor, white and black, male and female, adult and child, loose "street" children and pampered "house" children, knew their "proper" places and kept to them. The wealthy families of the big houses played *carnaval* in the privacy of their vacation homes on the coast or in elite social clubs in Recife. They never showed their faces for the duration of the festivities. The middle classes emerged briefly on the street on Friday night, the eve of the official start of the festival. Then they, too, left town.

Organized around the *carnaval bloco* named Grilo (Cricket), the middle-class revelers (middle-aged businessmen, bankers, small landowners, professionals) danced briefly in the town *praça* for the enjoyment of the "little people," the poor and the *matutos*, of Bom Jesus. And they seized the moment to advance their own class-based agendas. Dressed as the chirping gadfly Jiminy Cricket, the Grilo revelers protested in song and political slogans taped to their backs the old plantation families and the wealth that had dominated local politics and economics since the nineteenth century. Their slogans read "More commerce in Bom Jesus," "We demand better terms of credit," "We need a university in Bom Jesus," and "We want a modern shopping center." They also demanded an end to the political reign of the Barbosa family in Bom Jesus and in the entire region so as to make way for a more "progressive" and "modern" local government, one that looked away from the big houses and their stagnating sugar plantations and toward the "street," with its banks and new commercial ventures.

The poor who had descended from their hillside shantytowns danced to the music of the bourgeois Grilo musicians, but they understood little of the protest. The demands of the Grilo revelers were alien to them. "What about clean water?" asked Little Irene, sidling up to me in the crowd. "Are they saying anything about water?" "It doesn't look like it," I replied. Then, just as suddenly as they appeared, the Grilo dancers rode off in the back of a new and brightly painted truck, forming part of the parade of decorated luxury cars carrying the costumed middle-class families to the safety of their private social club outside town, where they could play freely and unobserved by the more ragged and "overheated" popular classes.

By the next day, Saturday, the real start of the festival, virtually every wealthy and middle-class family had left Bom Jesus da Mata, taking their *frevo* bands, their elaborate *fantasias*, and (as Little Irene wryly put it) "their prestige" with them. The only concession to the poor, who were left behind, was an old, teetering, wooden sugarcane transporting truck that was left out in the main *praça* of town with a single loudspeaker. The mayor agreed to furnish the town with a small *carnaval* band that would play, using the back of the truck for a stage, three hours each evening of *carnaval*. But the town itself was boarded up, as the departing middle-class shopowners made sure to leave their vulnerable storefront windows protected during their absence from the chaotic press of poor revelers. No special lights or festive decorations adorned buildings, lampposts, or Nossa Senhora das Dores Church. The town looked as if it had been quickly abandoned following an emergency.

The result was disappointment and dejection in downtown Bom Jesus. For even though the town now "belonged" to the poor and marginal classes of Bom Jesus, it seemed to them as if they had arrived late, just as the party was over. "Where is everyone?" the people asked, dependent as they were on the more affluent residents of Bom Jesus to provide financial support and an appreciative audience. The traditional *carnaval* reversal was meant to put the poor and their organized *blocos* and samba schools in the "center" of the street and the rich on the sidelines, admiring and clapping wildly for their favorite dancers and costumed performers. But here the rich had disappeared. Pointing to the still empty crucifix at the top of Alto do Cruzeiro, the *moradores* complained bitterly, "Look, even Jesus Himself has gone off to the beach to play *carnaval* with the rich!"

"What do you suppose is the cause of the exodus?" I asked Luciano.

"Today all the wealthy of Bom Jesus own cars, and the road to the coast is paved. It is easy for the rich to leave town and to spend *carnaval* away from us. They do not appreciate us or our *carnaval* play. They do not want to lend their prestige to our festival. And so they show their disrespect, their contempt for us, in this way."

Several days later I visited Seu Félix at his official office in the *prefeitura* to ask him about *carnaval* in Bom Jesus and the local government's responsibility for it. He explained, "The *carnaval* of the interior of Pernambuco is very lively [*animado*] in those towns where local businesses take an interest in popular celebrations, and they sponsor *carnaval* preparations in the poor communities. But here in Bom Jesus it is different. *Carnaval* groups expect all their support to come from the local government. They have no initiative to do things on their own. A month before *carnaval* people come to me saying that they want to organize a *carnaval bloco* in their neighborhood. In Rio de Janeiro samba school parades cost millions of cruzados, and yet even the very poorest people in the shantytowns there manage to organize these extravaganzas. Why? Because they start early. The day after one *carnaval* is over, the leaders of the samba schools are already thinking about next year's *carnaval*. That's the right way to do it. And so naturally they are supported. They get help from big business and organized gambling. Here, the businesses aren't interested and nobody cooperates. They want to leave everything to me, to the local government. The mayor is supposed to pay for the *carnaval* bands, for the costumes, for the streetlights and decorations. Meanwhile, the rich, those who could most support the festival here, leave town during *carnaval*."

"What did you do during *carnaval* this year?"

"Me? I'm too old for *carnaval*. I went to the beach with my family."

As the poor of the Alto do Cruzeiro descended from the hill to dance in the streets without a samba band or a single *trio elétrico* (a lively amplified band that plays a combination of samba, lambada, and rock from a platform raised on a huge, modern rolling van), the *rua* merged with and was then swallowed by the *mata*. At last the poor had the town to themselves, but theirs was an angry and a solitary celebration. Men dressed in ragged, makeshift costumes as street beggars and as abandoned women holding sick and hungry infants, while abandoned street children "organized" themselves into *blocos de sujos* (dirty ones), their ripped clothing and faces smeared with ashes and motor oil. The costumes offered a cruel parody of the way the poor were already viewed by the *gente fina* of Bom Jesus. A few souped-up jalopies zoomed loudly around and around the main streets, and several groups of traditionally costumed "bulls" charged and raced down the deserted city streets in search, or so it seemed, of a target that had already left town. A steady downpour of rain dampened spirits, and one had to dodge the hoards of aggressive *meninos da rua*, who were given *carnaval* license to aim water hoses and throw buckets of motor oil, tar, honey, and mud on passersby in the traditional *carnaval* play called the *mela-mela* (messymessy). But ragged street children disguised as dirty ones did not create a world of fantasy, escape, and forgetting. Rather, their costumes seemed a hideous caricature of "everyone's" worst fears about these loose and "dangerous" children. And it struck me immediately how much this was a *carnaval* for men and boys.

Later in the day two large organized *blocos* were promised to appear—the Ciganas Revoltosas (Disgusting Gypsies) and the Vedetes (transvestite Dames). In the interim I climbed the Alto to see what kind of *carnaval* play, if any, was happening on the *morro*. The main roads of the Alto were quiet, and most *moradores* were enjoying the prospect of a four-day holiday. Many men were sleeping. The few residents on the main, paved street who were

Carnaval play: "Give my some money for my hungry baby."

wealthy enough to own a TV set were watching the *carnaval* parades in Rio televised directly from the festival dome. In contrast to their parents, Alto children were in high spirits, jumping, dancing, and spinning in delight. No matter that they had no costumes.

I finally went to the home of Seu Biu de Caboclos, the leader of the only organized *bloco* on the Alto, named the Caboclos Tupinambá. Seu Biu and his "band" of sixteen male *caboclos*, his four drummers, two flutists, six "queens," one *porta-bandeira* (banner carrier), and six child *caboclos*, three of each sex, were preparing to descend the Alto and parade through the

Carnaval play: the "Dirty-Dirties" out to get unsuspecting adults.

town. Biu's *bloco* was *bem alinhada*, "beautifully turned out," in matching satin shirts, sashes, and Indian skirts, with elaborate headdresses sporting real peacock feathers. No corners were cut. The group had been practicing twice a week since the feast of São João at the end of June, and the costume materials had been purchased at great personal sacrifice to Seu Biu. He reported using his *bom de menino* (a small state subsidy for the children of poor workers), his mother-in-law's retirement pension, and his *décimo* (the extra month's salary paid to workers at Christmastime) to finance his *carnaval* group.

Seu Biu took a few moments away from his elaborate ritual of face painting to explain, "I started to play *carnaval* from the time I was twelve years old. I joined other people's groups. Then, four years ago I started my own *bloco*. Today there are thirty-eight people in my *carnaval* 'game.' I have to pay something to each one because I am the boss, the *dono*, of the group. I am responsible for the costumes, the feathers, the paint, the bows and

The Caboclos on the Alto do Cruzeiro.

arrows, the bells, the drums, and the flags. Without me, nothing happens. I will play only beautifully adorned and well practiced. To play in an ugly or disorganized way isn't worth the bother. I won't do it. If people won't come to practice, or if they arrive late and already drunk, they are out of my game. No exceptions. That is why I have such a beautiful *bloco*. People say that my *bloco* is really 'it' during *carnaval*. Without my game there would be no *carnaval* in Bom Jesus. Every year I have to buy material for new skirts and new shirts. So I have to begin my preparations early. I am already imagining next year's costume. It will be a blue satin jacket with sequins, a red sash, and a yellow skirt made of shredded crepe paper. Maybe you would like to sponsor my game for next year? I will dedicate a song to you!"

"Who else is supporting you?"

"This year the *prefeito*, Seu Félix, gave me ten cruzados. And with these lousy cruzados I could never have organized my *carnaval*. That's why I have to use my social security and the children's stipend. If it weren't for *carnaval*, I could use the money to buy clothing and shoes for my children. But because of my *bloco*, I have to use their money for *carnaval* instead. But I don't let my children suffer because of it. I am training the boys to be *caboclos*, too. Soon they will be ready to go out with my group. The *bloco* is a kind of school for my children, and they will benefit from my *carnaval* game."

Seu Biu's wife, Gabriela, pregnant with her ninth child, listened to her husband's explanation with a pained smile on her face. "Do you play *carnaval*?" I asked her in jest. The shy young woman found this an impossibly funny question, and she laughed, shaking her head.

Outside Biu's house the Caboclos Tupinambá were warming up, and a small crowd of curious neighbors formed around them. The Caboclos danced an Amerindian step in unison to the music of drums, tambourines, rattles, whistles, and flutes. If the dancing and costume were inspired by the native cultures of Brazil, the music and the responsorial style of singing were of decidedly African origins. I recognized one of the drummers, who also played for Xangô rituals on the Alto. "Yes," he replied to my question, "I like all kinds of *brincadeiras* [games]—Xangô as well as Caboclos. I am a folklorist." The Caboclos were going very strong, indeed, when they began their descent to the street below, and yet when they arrived, they danced and sang unappreciated, for there was no line of spectators, and the streets of Bom Jesus were mostly deserted.

Sexual Abandon or Abandonment?

It was the women, however, in whom I was especially interested, particularly their place in the festival. For *carnaval* is said not only to liberate the body but the female body in particular. "Women," Victor Turner wrote, "become the very soul of the samba in street and club. In a sense the whole city worships Aphrodite on the half-shell" (1987:82). With da Matta, the reification is total: "Woman is the mother of *carnaval*. . . . It is as if her body were the epicenter toward which everything gravitates and from which everything comes" (1984:235). It is in the realm of the sexual that the *carnaval* reversal is near perfect, da Matta argued, for it is women who are permitted to express and create a cornucopia of pleasure and abundance so that the entire social world is feminized.

In Bom Jesus I saw, to the contrary, a *carnaval* largely designed for the pleasure of men and boys. The "female" was liberated but only in male bodies or for the purpose of titillating male fantasies of sexual abundance and erotic abandon. I cannot say how wealthy and middle-class women of Bom Jesus played *carnaval* once they left Bom Jesus to dance in their private beach homes and social clubs on the coast, but I do know that on the eve of *carnaval*, when the middle-class revelers made their brief appearance in town, all but one of the small, informal, spur of the moment *blocos* were made up of male revelers. Middle-class women and girls did not participate in the street dancing at all. Rather, they observed the organized chaos from their latticed verandahs and open windows or from inside the family car.

One small group of middle-class women, all neighbors from the same elegant street of Bom Jesus, organized themselves into a *bloco* of clowns. They met in the home of Dona Ines to paint their faces and adjust their wild red wigs. Meanwhile, their husbands sat quietly outside by the family pool waiting to accompany their wives to the central plaza to observe O Grilo inaugurate *carnaval* festivities in Bom Jesus. The women clowns descended rapidly from their family cars for a brief presentation of themselves on the street; then they were rushed back into the vehicles, and they, too, joined the exodus, the motorcade of the bourgeoisie headed for the private "sport club" outside town.

Meanwhile, my presence and that of my research assistant, Cecilia de Mello, both of us married women and in Bom Jesus for the duration of *carnaval* without our husbands, threw the community into considerable turmoil. The situation we had put ourselves in was scandalous, even though we were personally considered above reproach. The hurried solution was to offer us "hospitality" for the days and nights of *carnaval* downtown, where we would be "closer" to all the activity. The pleasant and airy room that was offered us, however, was in the cloistered Franciscan convent, the most secure, chaste, and physically impenetrable institution in the entire community! Imprisoned, without a key, by high gates and ferocious German shepherd dogs kept in the courtyard, Cecilia and I had to leave and reenter the convent surreptitiously with the assistance of a sympathetic novice, who lent us her own ring of keys and who kept the dogs tied and at bay during the four nights of *carnaval*. And we were not the only local women, married or single, whose movements were severely curtailed during this great festival of "license" and laughter.

On Saturday afternoon two large *blocos* finally made their appearance in downtown Bom Jesus, and both were organized around sexual and gender themes. The first was formed by the prostitutes of the *zona*. Town women kept a respectful distance. They waited and watched for the group to appear from along the elevated railroad tracks several streets away from the *zona*. Meanwhile, men and boys excitedly stalked the *zona*, waiting in front of the cabarets from which the prostitute *bloco* was to emerge. The bosses of the *bloco*, as well as the financial sponsors, were a few wealthy male patrons of the *zona*. Finally, the prostitutes emerged, dressed as sexually alluring Gypsies, and they lined up behind their rhinestone-studded and embroidered felt banner with its legend "The Disgusting Gypsies." Whistles and catcalls accompanied their appearance. Even in the fantasy play of *carnaval*, these "street" women were paraded to be diminished and scorned. The Gypsies' *bloco* offered no reversal and certainly no threat to the everyday violence of sexual politics in Bom Jesus da Mata. Nonetheless, once the seductive music and dancing began, the Gypsies led a charismatic *bloco de arrastão* (dragnet) that attracted a large and enthusiastic crowd, which, unable to resist the call to revelry, was "pulled" and "dragged" into the net to become one with the *bloco*, "dirty," "disgusting," or otherwise.

The second *bloco*, made up of working-class men, some single, some married, some heterosexual, others gay or bisexual, paraded as transvestites calling themselves the Vedetes. Male cross-dressing *blocos* are a central component of *carnaval* play. Jorge Amado's novel *Dona Flor and Her Two Husbands* opens, for example, with the death of Flor's first husband from a fatal heart attack after dancing in a transvestite *carnaval bloco*. In these transvestite games the elements of fantasy play and reversal are prominent. But the fantasy is one-sided. Women rarely, if ever, cross-dress in *carnaval*. The role of those women who do participate in *carnaval* play is to undress, not to cross-dress, as the colorful and erotic photos of nude women in all the major Brazilian *carnaval* magazines readily testify. Moreover, the representation of female gender and sexuality in the male transvestite *blocos* is a projection of male sexual fantasies. It offers only a travesty of female gender and sexuality.

In Bom Jesus the transvestite Dames offered a counterpoint to the public sexuality of the Disgusting Gypsies. The Dames presented themselves as female coquettes, coy, demure, modest, and shy. Dressed in wide-brimmed

Vedetes, the Dames: "It makes me feel so feminine!"

hats, veils, and long-hooped skirts with wide petticoats, the Vedetes bobbed, curtseyed, and tiptoed before their spectators. They giggled and batted their false eyelashes. They allowed themselves to be touched, their "breasts" and behinds to be squeezed, and their lips to be kissed by male spectators, who demonstrated their prowess by "taking advantage" of the "broads." *Carnaval* custom prevented the Dames from defending themselves against unwanted sexual advances. They were expected to behave as perfectly docile and receptive sexual objects. When asked why they enjoyed cross-dressing, members of the Dames gave various responses.

"I love to play *carnaval* dressed as a woman. I adore my dress, my hat, and my makeup."

"Why?"

"They make me feel so feminine!"

"Who designs the costume?"

"I select everything. I dream it up in my own head, everything—the cut of the dress, the kind of fabrics to be used, the colors, the hairstyle, even the earrings. I want to be truly beautiful. I want to turn myself into my ideal."

Another Vedete offered, "We are celebrating women. Women are our country's national treasure. Women are Brazil's *patrimônio*, our natural birthright."

A short, heavy-set man in a yellow dress explained, "I dress as a woman because it is a family tradition. My father did it for eight years. He was a

'Virgin,' one of the founding members of the oldest transvestite *blocos* in Bom Jesus. Now he has left it to me, his oldest son."

A man in a red dress with a lace bodice added, "All year round we have to prove that we are real men, but in *carnaval* we can play at being women. During these three days it is okay to be passive and soft."

In a way these working-class men can have it all: macho and dominant at home and demure and strutting at *carnaval*. Those of the Vedetes who were married said that their spouses did not mind the travesty, but no wives or girlfriends accompanied these *carnaval* dancers. And in one case a young school teacher prevailed upon her fiancé to drop out of the *bloco* in respect for their engagement.

"What do you find offensive in it?" I asked the teacher.

"It is not a very elevated entertainment," she replied. "It may be about women, but it has nothing to do with me. All my fiancé has to show for it at the end of the festival is a bad hangover and a ridiculous, sweat-stained dress."

Two young liberation theology seminarians, Chico and Luciano, were following the transvestite *bloco* from a safe distance, holding up the rear, but they took a few tentative *frevo* jumps from time to time.

"What is this *bloco* all about?" I asked them.

"It's nothing, just a game that we Brazilians enjoy playing," replied Chico a little defensively.

"But it's not *just* a game," disagreed Luciano. "It's a social critique as well."

"A critique of what? Of women?"

"No," Luciano replied, after a pause. "Of homosexuality in Brazil. We have too much of it and of AIDS, too."

"But some of the dancers *are* homosexuals," I replied.

Later on in the week after *carnaval* was over, I pursued the *chefe*, the "leader," of the Vedetes and finally found him at home. A tall, good looking, young married man and doting father to his two small children, Hiberão was also the most beautiful of the transvestites, his bright green gown offering just the right contrast to his long dark hair and bright, dark eyes. If anyone should know what the Vedetes meant to represent, it should be the leader and organizer of the game. And Hiberão readily offered his interpretation of the *bloco*: "The Vedetes is a critique. It is a critique of those men in Brazil who are no longer men, and it is a critique of those women who are *mulher chamosa*, women who have lost their sweetness and their sex and want to be the boss. Because the women of Brazil have forgotten how to be *real* women, the men of Brazil have forgotten how to be chivalrous. We are setting ourselves up as a model of how we want women to behave. We want them all to be Vedetes like us—sweet, demure, pleasing, and teasing. Our *bloco* is a kind of school, and we, the dames, are teachers."

Overall, *carnaval* participation was highly selective in Bom Jesus. Not everyone took part. Although "the female" emerged as a unifying erotic image that was central to the festival, most "women" were peripheral to the celebrations. Those who did not leave town simply remained at home, leaving the streets, as usual, to the men. Walking up and down the Alto do Cruzeiro during the days of *carnaval*, I found most of my Alto women friends engaged, as usual, in household tasks and child care. Their attitude toward the *folia* (madness) in the streets below was generally dismissive. Some threw up their hands and said, "*Carnaval?* I hate it. I don't want any part of it." Another woman said, "I'm too busy for this nonsense. How can I entertain myself when I have a house full of sick children? *Carnaval* is for men and cows [meaning the traditional parade of the bulls]."

Yet another woman offered, "*Mela-brinca-pula-razga* [Mess it up, play it up, jump it up, rip it up]—that's entertainment for men and for children. The woman who participates in this madness is *doida* [meaning both crazy and sex crazed].

"What do I do during *carnaval?* I don't do anything! I don't like it. When I was a child I played, but now? God forbid!"

"Do I like to play *carnaval?* No, I prefer to play with my grandchildren."

But at last there was Ninha, the attractive young mother of four children who liked to have a good time. She was wearing a decorated headband and a short, satin *carnaval* skirt and was about to descend the hill. But even Ninha was lukewarm about *carnaval:* "I play," she said, "but only a little bit. I follow the *blocos* in town and the cow parades. But I could do without it. There are too many hotheads in the crowd and too much confusion."

It is the actual and symbolic abuse of women during *carnaval*—when license and rape are sometimes confused—that makes the Catholic clergy nervous and ambivalent about this folk festival. On the one hand, the clergy praises the *carnaval* spirit as an expression of the Catholic, as opposed to the dour Protestant, "mentality" in Brazil. Protestants constitute one social group that does not participate in *carnaval* at all, which Evangelical sects in particular view as the Antichrist. On the other hand, priests and nuns are uncomfortable with the public expressions of nudity and eroticism that are especially pronounced in the urban *carnavals* of cosmopolitan centers such as Rio, Recife-Olinda, and Salvador, scenes of which are directly transmitted locally via television.

At the home of the local padre of Bom Jesus, his mother, Dona Elena, sat in a rocking chair crocheting fringes on dishcloths and hand towels, while the samba schools of Rio, each with their bare-breasted and bikini-clad erotic dancers, flashed across the priest's television screen. "Shameless!" his mother commented, her eyes glued to the screen. Padre Agostino Leal, however, expressed considerably more ambivalence, which he conveyed in the following excerpts from a long, taped interview.

"*Carnaval* is a preparation for Lent. It is a festive and a noisy time, a preparation for Lenten silence. One can release what is inside, express one's desires, and eat meat. Here is where the 'carnal' comes into *carnaval*. In the fantasy of the masks and the disguises people can express what is normally hidden. It is a kind of psychotherapy for the popular classes. *Carnaval* is a means of popular expression. It is a form of communication.

"As Christians we should not have a negative attitude toward *carnaval*. It is true that within *carnaval* there is some exploitation, but we should not just condemn it the way the Protestants do. We have to ask ourselves what kind of *carnaval* we are talking about, for there are many different *carnavals* in Brazil. The *carnavals* of Rio and Bahia that we see on the TV screen are very different from the *carnaval* of small interior towns like Bom Jesus. But even in Rio the people are expressing, through their costumes and songs, what is happening to us today in Brazil. They are commenting on social and economic realities, inflation, foreign debt, AIDS, dengue fever, the new constitution. What are this year's *carnaval* songs? They are singing 'Bye, Bye Brazil, good-bye to corruption, good-bye to the cruzeiro, good riddance to violence, to *marginals*, and to street crime.' So *carnaval* is also a moment of critical reflection for the poor.

"There are also excesses in *carnaval*. Sexuality, which is a gift of God, is often degraded and disrespected, especially in the form of female nudity. People can lose their sense of shame in *carnaval*. But *carnaval* is also an anesthesia for the people. It deadens the pain of so many problems and crises, all the hardships that our country is going through today. *Carnaval* is, so to speak, the opiate of the people. But that is not to condemn it. For people *need* to play. It is a time of great joy and of movement. People want to be happy. You can see that most of the people who are dancing in the *blocos* and samba schools are from the poorest classes. This is their one time during the year when they can stand out and be valorized for themselves. *Carnaval* is their heritage, and they have a right to it.

"As Catholic priests we should not criticize the people. We should help the people to feel happy and to express themselves. What is wrong with playing and jumping? I like to do it myself! To jump in the streets, to play without nastiness or dirtiness, it is a beautiful thing! *Carnaval* should be understood as a time of great joy and as a time when people can say good-bye to the pleasures of the flesh before the start of Lent. When it is practiced like this, *carnaval* is a great 'club,' a community of all the faithful."

The Death of Mercy: Farewell to the Flesh

Remember, man, you are ashes and into ashes you will return.
                    Traditional Catholic blessing for Ash Wednesday

Of my three closest women friends, Antonieta, Lordes, and Biu, only Biu made any effort to play *carnaval*. Antonieta spent the days of *carnaval* at home taking advantage of the holiday to clean house. Her husband, Severino, took a rather dim view of *carnaval* and used the free time to make extra money at odd jobs. Lordes spent the four days of *carnaval* running back and forth between her home and the local hospital, where her unlucky and accident-prone husband, Jaime, was recuperating from a fall from a ladder that had broken both his legs. The hospital workers were on strike and were not expected to return to work until after Ash Wednesday. Seu Jaime's broken bones would have to await the end of the festivities. Lordes, looking pale and drawn, wondered aloud whether God was still angry at them because of their sin. "When do you think our accounts with Jesus will ever be clear?" she asked no one in particular.

But Biu did join the revelers, though I did not meet up with her in the streets. Like Biu, I soon got lost, swallowed up in the crush of bodies that followed the Gypsies and the Vedetes up and down and around the length and breadth of Bom Jesus.

The next time we met, *carnaval* was over, and we were hurriedly assembled at the home of Antonieta to prepare little Mercea's body for burial. Mercea had died of pneumonia on her way to the hospital the night before. Now it was the morning of Ash Wednesday, and I had been planning to film the aftermath of *carnaval* 1988. This was not what I had in mind. Still photos took the place of the video camera, which I hastily tucked behind a bed in Tonieta and Severino's bedroom.

Biu was in shock. She barely had time to change out of her makeshift costume. Pelzinha had eloped, run off (*fugindo*) with her fifteen-year-old boyfriend, João, taking advantage of the chaos of the festival, just as her own mother had once done during Holy Week many years before. The new couple was still hiding out in the *mata* at a friend's house. Xoxa, Mercea's older sister and surrogate mother, was still away working on a banana plantation. Neither of the two older girls yet knew what had befallen their little sister during their absence. Lordes was too preoccupied with her husband's accident to respond to the call to her niece's wake. A few of her children were sent in her place.

Mercea's wake: "I don't know if you were called or just thrown out of this world."

Antonieta took over the preparations of the wake, carefully washing and dressing Mercea's wasted little body. She had suffered so much, everyone said; surely she was already a little saint in heaven, more than an angel, more like a little martyr. At Antonieta's insistence there would be no pauper coffin for their little saint. I went with Antonieta to select the coffin from the display of children's coffins hanging on the wall in the *casa funerária* owned by Seu Chico, someone with whom Antonieta had personal "connections." Seu Chico was kindly to Antonieta, and arrangements were made so that the cost of the coffin and the hired "taxi" that had been rented from the *funerária* to bring home Biu, Tonieta, and Mercea's body from the hospital the night before could be repaid in small monthly installments over the next year. The municipal ambulance refused to make the return trip once the child was pronounced dead in the waiting room of the *pronto socorro*, the "emergency clinic." "The municipal ambulance is not a hearse," the driver repeated, standing on some notion of propriety that escaped us. From the coffin maker we went to the *cartório civil* to register Mercea's death, the second child that day, I noted. Ash Wednesday was living up to its name.

By the time we returned from the *funerária*, Biu's estranged husband, Oscar, had arrived with Biu's other children. He sat in a corner, quiet and shamefaced, his head down and his thin arms folded across his chest. He could not get himself to gaze at the dead child. Antonieta fussed with Mercea in her coffin, while the children and I arranged a wreath from wild flowers picked earlier in the day.

The question that was foremost on everyone's mind that day was "Why did Mercea die?" Was it because Xoxa was away from her small charge? Was it because Oscar had abandoned part of his family? Was it because the child was never "well attended" in the local hospital and municipal clinic? Was it because the prayers of the *rezadeira* were "weak" or because the *remédios* purchased at Feliciano's pharmacy were the wrong ones? Was it because the municipal ambulance was just a little too late, the driver still groggy from playing *carnaval* the night before? Or was it because Mercea, as old as she was, never really had a knack or a taste for life?

But at least no one blamed Biu for dancing in the streets during *carnaval*. They affirmed her right to *brincar* and *gozar*, to take some small pleasure in the life of the festival. The family members would spend the next several months puzzling over this death, Xoxa in particular. Xoxa knew that much of the blame would be laid on her young shoulders, and she carried it as best she could.

Severino, Mercea's uncle and designated godfather at Mercea's wake-baptism, sprinkled holy water over the still little body, as somber in death as in life, while he prayed, "Mercea, I don't know whether you were called [*chamada*], taken [*tirada*], or thrown out [*jogada*] of this world. But look down on us from your heavenly home with tenderness, with pity, and with mercy. Amen."

Mercea's siblings, cousins, and playmates gathered outside to carry Mercea's coffin in procession to the municipal graveyard. At the cemetery

Leonardo handed Valdimar, the clubfooted gravedigger, the slip of paper documenting the death of Mercea earlier that morning. The gravedigger chided Leonardo for leaving the coffin untacked. "The ants will soon get to your sister," he told the boy angrily, and the boy reflected on this as he stood over his sister's open grave.

As for Biu, like Faulkner's Dilsey, "she endured." Later that evening following Mercea's burial, Biu shouted and gestured to me from a distance along a high path of the Alto. Biu's grief and rage earlier in the day over the death of her favorite daughter had been real and exhausting to us all. Antonieta forced a strong tranquilizer on Biu, and finally she fell into a fitful sleep. But here she was, a few hours later, back on her feet and ready to make some new demand. I waved her away, wanting some peace. But Biu caught up to me, and I could see the old mischievous twinkle in her tired eyes. "Don't try to slip away [to the United States], Nancí, without giving me a *special* going away present. I want something *really valuable* this time, understand?"

I believe I did. She was suggesting that a beautiful, memorable gift just might begin to compensate for a very great loss, indeed. But this was only because material objects often outlasted the more fragile human relationships they came to represent. Biu once surprised me by pulling from a box stacked away in a corner of her overcrowded lean-to a white silk party dress of mine that she had taken a fancy to several years earlier and that I had left her as a going away present. I thought she would have long since sold it. "*Sold* it, Nancí? What an idea!" Biu scolded. "And what if you had never come back?" This kind of symbolic substitution was part of the resilience of Alto life.

But where was Biu going now in such a hurry? "I'll tell you about it later," she shouted over her shoulder as she scampered down the rocky path of the Alto. She was already several yards ahead. "Oscar," she added with evident delight and pride in her voice, "has just sent for me."

When I visited the reunited Biu and Oscar the next day, they were holding hands like newlyweds. Biu smiled coyly into her recently estranged husband's face. Her long brown hair was shaken loose and hung fully and thickly around her thin face, neck, and shoulders. Oscar seemed a changed man from the day before when he was so cowed and laid low by his daughter's death. On this day he was verbal, forceful, philosophical, in control. Biu, too, was changed. She was quiet, almost restful, a Biu I hadn't seen before.

"Life is hard, brutal," said Oscar. "It is over for Mercea. Who dies never comes back. But for us still living on this earth, it is a case of *bota para frente*—go forward, straight ahead, and never look back. We have to believe there was a reason for Mercea's death. Perhaps she died to bring us back to our senses, to make us a united family again."

But what about Oscar's other woman and children?

"The whore counts for nothing," Oscar snapped defensively. "She is rubbish [*lixo*]. She always knew that I would return to my real wife and legitimate children [though Oscar was legally married to neither]."

But Oscar was to use similarly harsh words when once again he walked out on Biu a few weeks later. Although both had tried to patch things up "to make some good come out of Mercea's death," Biu said, they found that neither could forgive the other. The resentments were too old, the wounds too deep. But this time when Oscar left, Biu hardly cared. She was having too hard a time "snapping out" of her dejection over Mercea's death.

With Oscar, Pelzinha, and Mercea gone from her life, Biu fell onto particularly hard times. She began to drink and she stopped eating. Food "tasted like dust," she complained. She spent some time hospitalized with a severe attack of *nervoso*. Finally, in June 1989 during the *festas juninas*, Biu cut her long hair, trimmed and painted her fingernails, and took a job as a live-in domestic in Recife. The decision was out of character for Biu, but Antonieta said that there really was no other *jeito* and that in any case the regular job and meals suited her sister well. "She finally has some flesh on her bones," Tonieta commented.

Biu's runaway daughter, Pelzinha, eventually came home to the Alto do Cruzeiro and gave birth that next summer to a beautiful little baby girl with straight, dark hair. I put a gold *figa* around her wrist for protection. Pelzinha's young husband, João, left Bom Jesus soon after the birth of his daughter to find work in São Paulo. After five months he still had not sent word of his whereabouts, and Pelzinha settled in, as best she could, to the life of a single mother living in a rented hovel on the Alto do Cruzeiro.

When Xoxa returned home from the plantation where she had been working during *carnaval* to learn that her little sister had died in her absence, she grieved deeply. It especially bothered Xoxa that her sister was buried without stockings, and for several weeks Xoxa was awakened by apparitions of Mercea hovering over her cot pointing to her bare feet.

"She can't speak," said Xoxa, "because like all angel-babies she is mute." Some time later Xoxa purchased a pretty pair of white stockings from a stall at the open-air market, but when we reached the cemetery we could no longer locate Mercea's grave. It had been cleared and the space reused by an unlucky pair of twin infants. Mercea's remains were thrown into the bone depository at the west wall of the cemetery. I comforted the weeping Xoxa, reminding her that Mercea was now a spirit-child and that Xoxa could bury

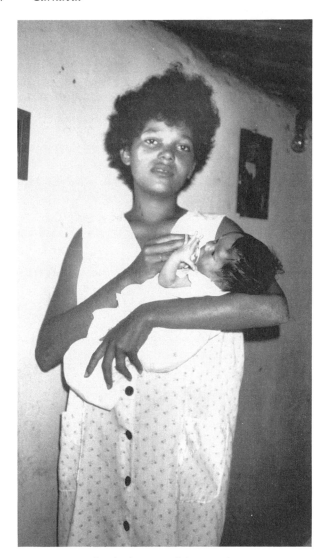

A repentent Pelzinha home with her newborn.

the stockings in a small mound next to the bone depository where Mercea could easily find them.

A year later Xoxa was much recovered. She was living alone in a small room attached to a shop just a few yards from the crucifix of O Cruzeiro. Mercea continued to appear to Xoxa every Thursday night. "She still wants something," Xoxa said, "but she is mute, and I don't know what it is." There is one thing, however, that Xoxa knew for certain: she would never marry or

Xoxa: "Mercea, may these stockings cover your bare feet and allow you to complete your journey. Amen."

have a child of her own. "I want no part of it," she said, and I believed her when she told me that she was as "untouched" as the Virgin Mary.

Carnaval: *The Travesty of Forgetting*

Nothing is really forgotten in carnaval. "The awful thing is that *nothing* is *ever* forgotten." The face and the image of death are never very far from the frenzied animation of *carnaval*. Death's presence, immortalized in the film *Black Orpheus*, hovers in the background of all *carnaval* play. The seductive, mesmerizing steps of the samba and the great bounding leaps of the *Nordestino frevo* are played to, and danced against, death. *Carnaval* is both a celebration of the flesh and a *farewell* to the flesh, as it is in the original Latin *carne vale*. And *carnaval* is followed liturgically by Ash Wednesday, with its cautionary "Unto dust thou shalt return." As the famous *carnaval* song ends: "Happiness is fleeting. Sadness is forever. And playfulness comes to an end on *quarta-feira* [Ash Wednesday]."

12 *De Profundis*
Out of the Depths

When I think of heaven, what do I see? For me, Nancí,
heaven will be a great *mutirão*, a *festa da gente* [people's
fiesta], in the sky.
> João Mariano, political *orientador*, UPAC

They endure and they get by, the women and men of the Alto, "making do"
as best they can, relying on their wits, playing the odds, and engaging in the
occasional *malandragem* of deceit and white lies, gossip and rumor, feigned
loyalty, theft, and trickery. But can we speak of resistance, defiance, opposition—themes that are so privileged in critical circles today? My friends on
the Alto do Cruzeiro do not deceive themselves anymore than do the few,
discouraged members of the surviving radical left in Bom Jesus, who now
speak only with irony and bitterness of when, "come the revolution," things
will be different.

The people of the Northeast have suffered a long history of popular
uprisings, armed struggles, messianic movements, anarchist fantasies, social
banditry, and Peasant Leagues, all of them crushed. And two decades of
military government have driven the point home and taken a toll on people
who can now be depended on to police, silence, and check themselves.
"Silence is protection," the people of the Alto are wont to say, often adding,
"Whoever says nothing has nothing to fear." As for resistance, the leaders of
UPAC often counsel each other to "take the path of *least* resistance" each
time they confront the unreasonable opposition of *os grandes* to their modest plans for improving the shantytown.

The traveling *repentista* singers of the marketplace keep alive the memory
of the heroic bandits of the *sertão*, Lampião and his Maria Bonita, Antônio
Conselheiro of Canudos, and Padre Cícero of Juàzeiro, among other rebel
priests, defiant cowhands, and utopian mystics and visionaries of the *Nordestino* backlands. But even as they sing the praises of the traditional folk
heroes, the *repentistas* usually strike a note of caution, warning against acts
of open defiance. And as for the popular heroes themselves, these generous
bandits, passionate visionaries, and charismatic miracle workers imagined

505

at best a new Brazil, a kingdom of God on earth, made up of a multitude of small subsistence-based peasant and herding communities independent of the state and secular authority and free of hunger, money, civil marriage, and the tyranny of landlords, political bosses, bureaucrats, and tax collectors.

The traditional social movements of Northeast Brazil were, in E. J. Hobsbawn's (1959) sense of the terms, "primitive" or "archaic," for while they contained the germ of class-based consciousness and the impulse of resistance, they for the most part remained "politically inarticulate" expressions of endemic protest against poverty and oppression. The social banditry of Lampião and his *cangaçeiro* outlaws (see Lewin 1979; Joseph 1990) was a cry of vengeance against the rich and greedy *latifundiários*, but beyond immediate redistribution their angry raids on particularly hated landlords lacked any sustainable political vision. The *cangaçeiros* often enlisted the help of impoverished rural workers in what were personal vendettas against rich and powerful men and local civil authorities with whom the head outlaw, himself often another kind of local big man, was feuding. The utopian, communitarian, pilgrim community founded by Antônio Conselheiro at Canudos in the 1890s (see da Cunha 1944 and, in novelized form, Llosa 1985) was perhaps more revolutionary in its absolute negation of class distinctions, money, and private property and in its defiance of the right of the state to interfere in its affairs. But the counselor's ideology, contained within a messianic, Catholic anarchism, could not hold out indefinitely against an increasingly centralized and militarized Brazilian state, and in October 1897 Canudos fell in a final and brutal massacre that left almost no survivors.

Equally devastating, however, were the capitulations by compromised and coopted popular leaders. In 1926 Lampião accepted a commission in the Brazilian Army that gave his ragtag band of rebel outlaws access to federal arms and monies. But Lampião's mission was to attack a dissident column of army officers and troops marching through the backlands of the Northeast led by Luis Carlos Prestes, who later became a leader of the Brazilian Communist Party (Forman 1975:223). In fact, however, Lampião avoided that confrontation and joined forces instead with the charismatic miracle worker, Padre Cícero, who was forming his alternative pilgrim community in Juàzeiro do Norte in the state of Ceará (see Della Cava 1970; C. Slater 1986). The followers of Padre Cícero were drawn from among the displaced rural workers and fleeing drought victims of the backlands in a region dominated by large plantations, feuding oligarchs, and insurrectionist stirrings among impoverished workers. Padre Cícero's fame as an advocate and a wise counselor to the rural poor as well as a miraculous healer of the sick brought migrants from surrounding regions and states teeming into little Juàzeiro do Norte, which grew during the height of the priest's spiritual and political influence (1872–1934) into the commercial and agricultural center of the *sertão*. Although silenced by the church's hierarchy and officially stripped of his clerical duties as a Catholic priest, Padre Cícero continued to celebrate mass and to preach to the throngs of pilgrims who revered him as their persecuted Christ figure. But Padre Cícero, too, eventually made his peace with the church hierarchy, and he eventually formed alliances with the ruling oligarchs and *latifundistas* of the backlands so as to become the first mayor of Juàzeiro do Norte and later the third vice-president of the state of Ceará.

The local branches of the Peasant Leagues active in the Northeast and in Bom Jesus during the 1950s and early 1960s (see chapter 1) were brutally suppressed by the military government, and local leaders and activists were imprisoned and physically abused. One of these, the retired cane cutter Zé de Mello of the Alto do Cruzeiro, remains perplexed, disillusioned, and embittered, convinced that he and his *companheiros* in the Leagues had been duped by that "devil" of a Francisco Julião. "In the end," Zé offered sadly, shaking his bowed head under his broad-rimmed straw hat, "our heroes always desert us." Perhaps so, for when Francisco Julião, the Marxist-inspired leader of the Peasant Leagues, returned to Brazil in 1980, following his years of exile in Mexico and Europe and during the first phase of the democratic reopening of Brazil, he was rumored to have become a legal counsel for the sugar mill and plantation owners of the *zona da mata* of Pernambuco.

Even the beloved, barefoot, and itinerant mystic-saint of the *Nordestino* backlands, Frei Damião, believed by many of the rural poor to be the living reincarnation of Padre Cícero and a powerful miracle worker in his own right, accepted the patronage of Fernando Collor de Mello during his presidential election campaign in 1989. And so the ragged little Italian Capuchin friar posed shyly and uncomfortably in front-page newspaper photos next to the aggressive and wealthy *latifundista* candidate who was running against Lula, the trade union leader and socialist candidate.

The people of the Alto, like rural poor of the Northeast more generally, understand human nature to be flawed and inclined toward treachery. They expect their popular leaders to turn against them if the rewards for doing so are great enough, and they are not self-righteously indignant or outraged on discovering self-serving political deception. Such events only confirm their worst suspicions and reinforce a well-grounded pessimism. Far from rebels or revolutionaries, the rural workers of the Northeast are by social temperament patient, long-suffering, and nonviolent people. They generally keep their peace despite the everyday violence of drought, hunger, sickness, and unnecessary death. And they are gentle in the face of the aggression of local bosses and big men, with their hired thugs and gunmen. The history of the Northeast calls to mind Eric Wolf's (1969:275) observation that it is primitive capitalism, not socialism, that is the revolutionary economic system and capitalists, not Marxists, who are truly "radical" in their destruction of traditional social forms, particularly kinship and reciprocity.

The people of the Alto swallow and deflect their anger by means of an ironic, absurdist black humor. "Don't fret, Dona Nancí," Seu Biu once tried to console me after a few dozen Alto families had dug huge pits in their backyards on the basis of an empty promise I had extracted from the Pernambucan secretary of sanitation of free cement slabs and other construction materials in support of the shantytown's "self-help" latrine project. Months had passed, and the winter rains had begun in earnest, filling the abandoned pits with rainwater, posing a grave risk to Alto toddlers and young children. Nevertheless, Seu Biu tried to cheer me up. "It's all right," he told me, his thin arm draped around my disappointed shoulders. "We don't eat enough to fill those holes, anyway."

Their nonviolence, humor, display of compliance do not mean, however, that the poor of the Alto are passively accepting of the situation in which they are trapped. The *moradores* understand and freely comment on the evils of the local political economy in the traditional, folk Catholic idiom of the seven deadly sins. Little escapes their devastating, running critique of human culpability, in particular the greed, pride, lust, and sloth of their political bosses and of the planter class. It is a tradition that has been greatly expanded in the work of liberation theology and its humanistic Marxism, as dramatized in "workers' Masses," popular missions, politicized Stations of the Cross, and celebratory and purifying bonfires. These ritualized enactments of the social sources of human suffering belie any generalized notion of "false consciousness" in the sick-poor of the Alto, though one can always point to specific instances of mystification and alienated thinking and practice.

Nonetheless, despite their understanding of the social sources of their collective misery, the people of the Alto remain skeptical of radical and revolutionary proposals and do their best to survive in the cracks and crevices of daily life in Bom Jesus da Mata through the charade of "learned helplessness," breached only by their biting humor and by the occasional, sometimes quite daring, act of trickery or cunning. And in these latter instances their silence and feigned ignorance serve as their cover. Nor shall I blow that cover here by giving specific illustrations of what I am alluding to! For the clerk of the records must also know when to keep silent.

Perhaps now we are in a better position to understand why more direct, overt, and collective instances of redress and resistance are rare in the Alto do Cruzeiro and why the few actual attempts at mobilization within the shantytown have been plagued with conflict and contradiction, assaulted equally by enemies from within and from without. I return now to complete the story of UPAC that I began in the Introduction.

UPAC: O Povo Desunido, *the People Divided*

The attempt to revive the shantytown association during the hopeful period of democratization in the 1980s was stymied by a number of seemingly insurmountable problems. For one, the younger generation of Alto residents had grown up and come of age during the military years, and accustomed as they were to living by the seat of their pants and "blow by blow," in the apt words of de Certeau, they had no experience of open, democratic, or collectivist ways of thinking and acting. One cannot underestimate the savagery of hunger and scarcity or the brutality of police terror in diminishing all possibilities for collective action. It did not help that the main impetus for the revival of UPAC came from among the original leaders of the creche, most of them now middle-aged and elderly women.

In 1985 several of these women sought the help and guidance of the new parish priest, Padre Agostino Leal, who was busily engaged in establishing ecclesiastical base communities in a dozen poor *bairros* and rural *vilas* of the *município*. These base communities, informed by the theology of liberation, extended the social activities of the "new church" through the work of indoctrinated and politicized local leaders in peripheral and poor communities; these leaders initiated Bible study classes that served as the basis for literacy training, critical reflection, and political action.[1] The padre's plans for social and political evangelization did not, however, include the Alto do Cruzeiro, which even he viewed with some suspicion as a dangerous, marginal, even criminal *bairro*, one ruled by *maconha* (marijuana), violence, and small-time "mafia" bosses and one in which the formal presence of the Catholic church was negligible. Nevertheless, Dona Zefina, a native of the Alto who had spent several years working in São Paulo and had returned with stories of base communities in urban shantytowns far worse than the Alto do Cruzeiro, convinced the padre to "give a little force" to her struggling and stigmatized hillside *bairro*. The priest assigned Irmã Juliana, a young Franciscan sister, to work in the shantytown as a liberation theology vanguard in an attempt to resurrect UPAC as an ecclesiastical base community. Her first assignment was to identify a cohort of local leaders by calling for an election in the *bairro*.

The election to form a new *diretoria* of UPAC was held almost immediately, with little preparation or orientation, in the spring of 1986. Zezinho
Barbeira, an emotionally unstable factory worker, emerged as the new
president of the association. Zezinho had several advantages over his com-
petitor, João Preto, a soft-spoken older black man who was an agricultural
worker on the local plantations. Zezinho, though unpolished and inarticulate, was considered a fearless big man, and he owned a gun, rather than just
a crude machete. He was a "progressive" *operário* who worked with powerful machines in the streets of town, rather than a "backward" *trabalhador*
who worked with a *foice* in the cane fields. Zezinho was *bem branco* (almost
white), and he was the founder and *chefe* of a local soccer team. But most
important, Zezinho's two-room house was located at the very top of the Alto
just a few yards from the creche building and from the Cruzeiro, the large
crucifix. The significance of the house's location requires some explaining.

The Alto do Cruzeiro is defined by the natural geography of the hillside,
which is subdivided by a symbolic cross that marks the "head" and the
"feet," the left and the right "arms" of the hill. The head represents the real
or true Alto do Cruzeiro, and those who live on the very top of the hill and in
the shadow of the cross, either on its left arm looking out to the *mata* and the
plantations or (like Zezinho) on its right arm looking out to the *rua* and the
paved streets of Bom Jesus, can claim an almost natural prerogative to
represent and lead the community. The *moradores* tend to reject a candidate
(like João) coming from the base, from the foot of the Alto, whispering
among themselves, "But he comes from down there 'below'; he is not really
of the Cruzeiro." And Zezinho defended his "right," once elected, to remain
the president of UPAC and the legitimate *dono* of the Alto, with the oft-
repeated words "Haven't I lived these thirty-two years on *top* of this Alto,
not twenty yards from the cross?" This defense was received with tolerance
by some *moradores*, accustomed as they were to the *machismo* and bravado
of big men, even those like Zezinho who arise from within their own *bairro*.

Zezinho proved himself a leader of limited political vision. Nonetheless,
he and his *diretoria* of several close associates initially sought to address the
chronic problems of insufficient and polluted drinking water; the absence of
street lights and the lack of electrification in Alto homes, many of which
were still lit by kerosene lamp; sewage and garbage disposal; and the general
illiteracy of the Alto population. "I myself am an illiterate donkey," Zezinho
would say, though after his election he took to wearing a pair of eyeglasses
and carrying a portfolio with the official documents of the association.
Zezinho did manage to regain control of the public *chafariz*, and he com-
manded his post at the water tank each morning and evening with the
seriousness of a border guard. The few pennies collected for each large can of

water paid the association's utility bills, and what remained was to be deposited in the treasury of UPAC.

Despite good intentions, the new *diretoria* of UPAC never looked for solutions that went beyond soliciting the support and patronage of local politicians and wealthy patrons in Bom Jesus. The extension of universal suffrage to the illiterate masses of Brazil had suddenly made populous shantytowns like the Alto do Cruzeiro of interest to local politicians wanting to gain an electoral foothold, and the inexperienced leaders of UPAC were easily flattered and manipulated by suddenly interested parties.

By 1987, a year following the election of the new *diretoria,* UPAC was in disarray, and little of anything concrete had been accomplished. In all, it appeared to the *moradores* of the Alto that their only reward for the attempt to reorganize the association had led to naught. They had regained, and then just as quickly they had lost, the creche building and their control over the public water pump and spigot, which quickly became the private property of Zezinho's household.

Worse, the initial attempts of the *diretoria* to "clean up" the Alto and to rid it of its unwanted glue sniffers, vagabonds, and prostitutes led to a historic, yet altogether unfortunate, agreement between the priest and the mayor of Bom Jesus. A committee of UPAC members approached Padre Agostino Leal and Seu Félix in 1987, inviting them to attend a meeting to discuss the problem of disorder and "sacrilegious behavior" on the Alto. The *moradores* explained to the priest and the mayor how their lives had been made miserable by the "indecencies" performed on the outdoor altar under the gaze of the Cristo by the "low-life marginals, perverts, and prostitutes" who congregated on weekend nights on the steps and base of the crucifix.

"The problem with that crucifix," offered Seu Félix, "is that it is poorly positioned on the top of the Alto. It needs to be pushed back further and a gate built around its altar and steps. We need to modernize the monument and to make it safe."

The *colégio* teacher, João Mariano, disagreed: "The problem is not with the crucifix but with the poverty of the Alto that has lead to a general 'demoralization' of the population. Moving the Cristo back a few yards is not going to prevent people using the altar to turn their tricks or to make their drug deals. And putting a gate around their crucifix would rob the people of their 'saint' and of its historical significance in the town."

"Nonetheless," broke in Padre Agostino Leal, "the Cristo *is* in bad shape. Its paint is peeling, and the electric wires that light Him up at night give shocks to the street children who like to stand on the altar. Sooner or later, one of the *moleques* will be electrocuted."

It was finally resolved that the priest would remove the Cristo and repaint

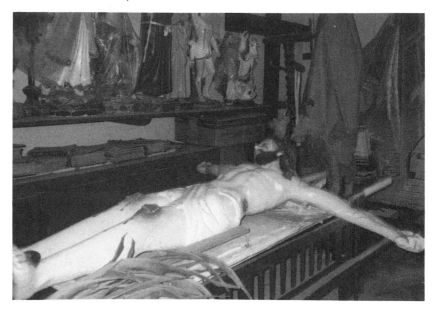

The Missing Cristo of the Alto do Cruzeiro.

and restore the long-"abused" body of Christ. For his part, the mayor agreed to have the town architect, Seu Virgílio, a longtime member of the Brazilian Communist Party, design a new base for the monument, one with a cast-iron gate that would discourage "riffraff" from using the Cristo as a meeting place. But the months passed into a year, and the huge cross of O Cruzeiro remained empty; no work was done on the base or the proposed gate for the monument. The agreement had fallen apart, and the people of the Alto were left without their beloved *santo*. Nothing had been explained to them. "Where is Our Lord?" the *moradores* would sometimes ask me out of the blue. "Do you have any idea who has taken Him?"

In fact, the body of the Christ of the Alto lay freshly painted but forgotten in a locked storeroom at the back of the Church of Our Lady of Sorrows. I implored the padre to return the Cristo to the people of the Alto, but he stubbornly refused to do so until the mayor had fulfilled his side of the agreement. Another meeting was called. Seu Félix, under the influence of Seu Virgílio, now balked. The mayor argued that restoring the old crucifix, stone steps, and pedestal was a waste of public money. The Cristo, he said was *meio-feio*, sort of ugly and baroque. It was hardly a fitting symbol of the Alto, or of the town itself, because the hillside and its huge cross dominated the vista as one approached the town of Bom Jesus from the highway. "The Cristo should be altered," the mayor concluded, "to make way for progress." He proposed the construction of a secular and patriotic monument, to be designed by Seu Virgílio, commemorating the establishment of the First Republic in Brazil.

Padre Agostino was livid at this suggestion. He argued that the Cristo was a historical monument, predating the town of Bom Jesus itself: "The Cristo came to Bom Jesus with the first colonists."

"Then why does it have 1927 inscribed on its base?" asked Seu Félix.

"It was put there later," the padre insisted.

"What a joke," laughed the mayor. "If it had come from Portugal, the *santo* would be made of wood. It would be a real piece of art. The piece of rubbish we are talking about is made of plaster. It came from the back of some João Pequeno's workshop in Caruaru." The meeting resolved nothing, and the matter remained deadlocked in a standoff between the forces of church and state in Bom Jesus. Meanwhile, the devout people of the Alto continued to mourn the disappearance of their *santo*.

Before long, the *diretoria* of UPAC, the vice-president, secretary, treasurer, and various fiscals and overseers, tried to enlist my support in an attempt to remove Zezinho, although he had not yet completed his term of office as president of the association. They complained that Zezinho was lazy and dishonest, and they described him as a brutal and temperamental "dictator" with a violent streak who understood nothing about democracy or community service. Zezinho refused to call general meetings of UPAC, and he used the creche building for private parties. They accused him of stealing money from the community *chafariz* and his wife of washing the family laundry, "even her menstrual rags," in the public water tank, which, they claimed, had made a number of *moradores* violently ill. Zezinho's "filth" had poisoned the *chafariz* water, making it unfit to drink. At an open meeting called to address some of these charges, Zezinho packed the creche with his supporters, many of them soccer players from his team, and he did his best to clear his good name. Tempers flared and knives and revolvers briefly appeared, but the brave little Franciscan nun, Juliana, put her body directly between the disputing men and their weapons and shamed them back into their places. But nothing was resolved.

Other obstacles to the success of UPAC were external to the shantytown and were largely bureaucratic. No federal or state entity would grant funds or otherwise support an association without current documentation of its official registration. The old and outdated bylaws were finally dug up and new ones were drafted with the help of João Mariano. Soon he assumed my old role of "political adviser" to the newly revived UPAC. But João Mariano's political activities on behalf of the Socialist Workers Party of Brazil meant that UPAC was again tainted by association with the left, and the newly drafted bylaws lay "imprisoned" in a bottom "drawer" at the civil registry office, unsigned by the conservative lawyer, Dr. Ricardo. He "desked" (*engavetou*) the bylaws, members of the *diretoria* complained, referring to a well-known strategy used by the rich against the poor of Bom Jesus. Meanwhile, the original title to the creche lands, hard won in 1965, was pronounced null and void by the judge of Bom Jesus. When the law was signed into effect, the *município* had failed to register the lands under its jurisdiction, so the town council was without any title to give. Foot-dragging, lies, and false compliance are not only the tactics of the oppressed and the weapons of the weak, as James Scott's (1985) analysis would seem to imply; they are also of strategic importance to politicians and bureaucrats, like those in Bom Jesus, hostile to the demands of the poor and popular classes.

Another common "tactic" of the rich and powerful—the creation of a new, parallel organization—was also used at this time to throw UPAC and its members into utter confusion. Dr. Urbano, the older brother of Seu Félix and a conservative political chief of the sugarcane region, sent flunkies into the shantytown to announce a new and better residents' association to rival UPAC. The new association, also called UPAC, was financially backed by Dr. Urbano himself, and those residents who agreed to become members received free sacks of cement, bleached flour, and powdered milk. But first they had to denounce any connections to the "old" UPAC. Fraudulent copies of UPAC membership cards, carrying Dr. Urbano's easily recognized signature, were distributed, and many residents, fearful of running afoul of the powerful Urbano-Barbosa family, accepted the new membership cards and destroyed their old ones, "signed" by Zezinho with his X and thumbprint, the visible stigmata of the humiliated illiterate.

Rather than sitting out this period of confusion or waiting for the next UPAC elections in 1988, a few dozen active members of the association (including members of the *diretoria*) met regularly without their president. And in this roundabout way the revived association actually *did* begin to function as a base community. Irmã Juliana, Padre Agostino Leal, João Mariano, and I served as political advisers and facilitators at the meetings. We tried to reintroduce Freirian notions of critical thinking and consciousness-raising to the mostly elderly, still faithful members of UPAC. But I understood from my daily encounters with *moradores* in their homes and in the fields how terrified many of the younger people were of the "radical" rhetoric of Sister Juliana and João Mariano, who frequently wore his blood-red "Che" T-shirt to the evening meetings.

At first the *moradores* sat attentively, though silently, through long meetings that sometimes degenerated into "lectures" about collective action and solidarity. "Do you have any questions?" João Mariano or Irmã Juliana would ask in an attempt to engage the silent group. And then a hand might be raised and an elderly woman would ask, "Are we going to pray soon?" much to the dismay of even Sister Juliana, who would reply, "Who can pray to Our Father in Heaven with an empty stomach? Let us try to find ways to fill our stomachs first, and the prayers will come more easily later." But to the humble people of the Alto this was a strange message to come from a nun in her full habit and sandals, even a nun who had ragged fingernails and whose heavy, long skirts were often held together, like their own, with large and unseemly safety pins.

In time the UPAC meetings finally began to take on the character of dialogues, but it was really only in the few tangible projects of the members—the collective *mutirão* to build new homes for various members who had become homeless during winter rains and the collective effort to restore the creche building itself—that the old spirit of UPAC, at once festive, noisy, and outrageous, arose. The Rabelaisian image of the banquet table was never far from Alto people's notions of "the good community," and any grassroots organizing that failed to take account of the playful spirit of merrymaking never got very far on the Alto do Cruzeiro.

When the time finally arrived for the new UPAC elections in 1988, Zezinho, simply refused to "allow" them to take place. Modeling himself after Sarney, the last military president of Brazil, Zezinho announced that he would be president of UPAC "for life." To prove his point and to show that he had the *força* to command the community, Zezinho locked up the creche and turned off the electric pump and the public water spigot of the *chafariz* for several days. To protect himself, Zezinho took to carrying his gun sticking visibly out of the top of his trousers. *Moradores* were afraid to cross him. Zezinho made new alliances with the police of Bom Jesus and with various powerful, if unsavory, wealthy patrons. The local *delegacia* announced that Zezinho had struck up a "deal" to give the creche building to the *município* to be used as a new police precinct. Meanwhile, the secretary of health, Dr. Francisco, announced that Zezinho had promised *him* the creche building to be used for an outpatient injection clinic. When I returned for the last time in 1989, the creche was still locked up, though various homeless men and street children had taken to sleeping there at night.

A second attempt to hold UPAC elections in August of that year was again blocked by Zezinho, who came to be seen as useful to the wealthy of Bom Jesus as a little big man who could be counted on (i.e., easily bought). Zezinho was able to enlist the support of the local district attorney of Bom Jesus in prohibiting the elections on the grounds of chaos within the shantytown (e.g., the multiple membership cards, accusations of "false" and "true" members of the association, and so on), a confusion that had of course been provoked by Zezinho and by the political *malandragem* of Dr. Urbano Neto. But Zezinho did not stop there. He circulated the story that he had gone to a neighboring *vila* to enlist the help of a renowned and powerful sorcerer of Umbanda to rain down harm on any of the *moradores* who tried to "remove" Zezinho from his "rightful" position.

Not surprisingly, the contesting UPAC candidates failed to assemble on the designated night of the election. They were sorely afraid. Instead, they met in private to dream aloud of their revenge. They would secretly change the locks of the creche and reoccupy the building. They would collectively storm the little home of Zezinho (while he was away at work) and demand of his wife that she hand over the keys and documents belonging to UPAC. They would have a mass said in the open air on the steps of the Cruzeiro, and the padre would "condemn" Zezinho as a sinner against the community.

They would . . . they would . . . but soon it was midnight and eyelids began to grow heavy. Seu Neginho, the alternative candidate for the new president of UPAC, was the last to speak, and he spoke well (they agreed) and with great wisdom and authority. "My friends," he said, "what you have proposed tonight is violence, and we, the legitimate wing of UPAC, do not want any part of violence. Instead, we will let Zezinho have his creche, his keys, his official documents and papers. But he cannot accomplish anything without the support of the people. We will do nothing, but we will have nothing to do with Zezinho. In the end he will come to us, for he will be isolated; we will have frozen him out." And there the wobbly future of UPAC rested.

How do we explain the failures of UPAC? Obviously, many of the everyday, highly individualist tactics of "making do" and "getting by" that I described earlier get in the way of collective action. We can see the adverse effects of the culture of fear and silence on the *moradores* and of the social psychology of patronage in the tendency of *moradores* to put themselves at the service of those unworthy of their fragile trust. And so they *would* choose Zezinho, the light-skinned "modern" man of the *rua* over black João, the rural worker. Above all, I point to the lack of basic trust that has its origins in an experience of insecurity that occurs so early that it is "naturalized" and is part of the habitus of the *moradores*. Their fundamental mistrust of the world is taken in hungrily with their first water and scanty *mingau*, and it is later reinforced by the structured relations of inequality, dependency, and police violence that rule the adult lives of *moradores*.

Liberation Theology: The Festive Community

"Viva Frei Damião! Viva, o povo de Deus!"

"Long live Brother Damian! Long live the people of God!"
Popular chant during the Holy Missions,
August 1989, Alto do Cruzeiro

But I will not end on so hopeless and cheerless a note. For though there is much that separates and divides them, the people of the Alto are still united by a common destiny and a shared social identity in the shadow of their Cruzeiro, their monumental cross. They see themselves as a *bairro sofredor*, a patient and long-suffering community of sinners, and they make daily reference to the Alto as their "Calvary," their hill of penance as well as their hill of redemption. And so the shantytown is also called *meu Alto do amor*, the "hill of my affections," my beloved hill. And in addition to their individualized *jeitos* and *malandragem*, there is also the *Nordestino* festive spirit—the parties, the revelries, and the often spontaneous gatherings on the Alto do Cruzeiro that are the transcendent, transgressive, and sometimes transformative celebrations of the collective, social body.

The word *festa* has a multiplicity of meanings and uses in Bom Jesus. Its origin is in the Catholic liturgical cycle, in the holy "feasts" of the saints' days and other days that mark off and call to mind the sacred in human life and the presence of God, the Virgin Mary, and the saints in the human community. But a *festa* is also a party, a celebration of any significant event: a christening, birthday, name day, graduation, or wedding. And the more of these there are, the better. For the people of the Alto *do* make merry as often as they can, and their little ones need hardly any provocation to jump into the air demanding a *"festa! festa!"* for no reason at all. And all it may take to do so on a lazy Sunday afternoon is a borrowed phonograph or transistor radio, a few bottles of Coca-Cola, a daub of cologne, and one's sandals kicked off to the side, all the better to *forró*. *Festas* connote the popular cultural tradition within which people play *carnaval*; dance their *cirrandas*, *forrós*, and *quadrillas*; and light their fireworks and bonfires.

But *festas* have political connotations as well, emphasizing the deep social and economic cleavages in the community, as do the private *festas* and *carnaval* celebrations held in the exclusive social clubs of Bom Jesus, which the poor of the Alto can observe only from outside through latticed windows. But I am also thinking of the huge street parties thrown by the newly elected "socialist" mayor, Gil, the *prefeito carnavalesco*, to amuse the poor and divert their attention from the everyday violence and misery of their lives. On a more positive note, the odd juxtaposition of politics and revelry is captured in local demonstrations for clean water, land reform, or (less frequently) human rights. These popular demonstrations are referred to as *festas da gente*, "people's parties." UPAC itself was founded in the wake of a neighborhood party, a street dance in celebration of São João's day on the Alto do Cruzeiro in 1965. And the image of the *festa* was carried through during the months of collective work building the creche, which was referred to as a year-long *festa de tijolos*, "brick party."

Popular Catholicism has always provided tools and materials for conviviality, both the old church, with its elaborate public pageants recalling the lives (and deaths) of the saints and celebrating the heroic in human life, and the new church, with its dramatic public rituals honoring ordinary men and women, the heroes of everyday life, in its expressed "preferential option" for the poor (see Comblin 1985; Gutiérrez 1980). When Padre Agostino Leal arrived in Bom Jesus in 1981 to replace the elderly and ailing Monsignor Marcos, a traditional cleric who had put his spiritual and material resources at the service of the *casas grandes* of Bom Jesus, the new priest initiated some radical changes. He closed the modern and tastefully appointed chapel of the Franciscan convent, which was open for private meditation and exclusive liturgies held for the wealthy families of Bom Jesus, whose daughters attended the nuns' finishing school. Henceforth, all masses were public and celebrated in the baroque and dilapidated mother church of Bom Jesus, Our Lady of Sorrows. *All* parishioners—landowners and *bóias-frias*—would be expected to share the same pews. Meanwhile, Padre Agostino invited the Franciscan sisters to leave behind the sheltered and cloistered gardens of their convent school and join the new "social ministry" in the poor *vilas*, *bairros*, and shantytowns of the *município*. And all but the most frail and elderly nuns readily did so.

The Mass itself was transformed: the liturgy was presented in the simple dialect and idiom of the rural workers, and the hymns addressed Our Lady of the Oppressed and Our Lord of the Workers. The Offertory and thanksgiving prayers asked for clean water, fair wages, food to fill hungry stomachs, and rain to soak the traditional squatters' remaining small *roçados*. God was spoken of as Our Papa here on earth, accompanying the *moradores* in their daily round of activities, while the magisterial and distant Father in Heaven receded far into the background of peasant consciousness.

At smaller, more intimate masses held in the new base community chapels in each of the poor neighborhoods, rural *vilas*, and shantytowns of Bom Jesus, unemployed cane cutters, the sick and elderly, *curandeiras* and practitioners of Afro-Brazilian spiritism, washerwomen, young marginals (petty criminals), and abandoned street children were recognized, and their needs were addressed collectively.[2] At each mass members of a previously stigma-tized or marginalized group were invited to join the priest at the altar and to coconsecrate with him the host so that together priest and peasant, priest and *catimbeiro* spirit medium, or priest and washerwoman would call on Jesus to descend and be "possessed," claimed, and contained within the altar bread and wine. The reception of Holy Communion took on the appearance of a common feast, even if only a simple banquet of bread and wine. But the bread was now thick and leavened, and the wine was rich and sweet. "There are so many hungry people among us," prayed Padre Andreas, the visiting liberation theology missionary, as he held the consecrated loaves in his hands, "that God would only dare to appear to us in the form of bread."

The priests' sermons, too, had changed: "Blessed are those who steal," a priest opened his homily on Sunday, July 23, 1989. And he continued, "Blessed are the thieves among us, for they, too, hunger and thirst after justice. . . . A person of deep moral convictions once told me that he was capable of assisting a group of hungry people in making an assault. Can it be that God could bless such behavior? I think so, my dear people. God is always challenging and disrupting our ordinary perspectives on things. In the book of Exodus, God freed a group of slaves and made them into His own chosen people. He subverted a social system that had robbed people of their freedom. If we can understand this biblical story, then we can imagine that God could forgive theft and robbery by the poor and by street children. Is not robbery a denunciation of injustice? Is not theft a desperate search for the equality that God wants? Let us be slow to call out, 'Thief! Criminal!' and to rush out to find the police, who will only beat the poor boy senseless with clubs. Perhaps the boy only wanted some cheap rum to warm his body. So small a theft for so harsh a punishment! So for this reason I say blessed are those who steal and blessed are those who hunger and thirst after justice! In the name of the Father and of the Son and of the Holy Spirit."

"Amen," answered the somewhat perplexed congregation. Such is the radical rhetoric of the new church. And such is the hostility of the wealthy and middle classes of Bom Jesus to these changes that they have largely left the church and its local clergy, who no longer represent their interests.

"We don't go to Mass anymore," boasted Rosália, the granddaughter of the recently deposed mayor, Seu Félix, one evening in 1989 as we sat around the family dinner table. "Not since the priests started preaching commu-nism and land reform," Jacita said, trying to soften her daughter's state-ment, but the thirteen-year-old girl refused to be quieted.

"Mother, the priests were even collecting votes against Grandpa in the confessional!"

Her younger brother chimed in, "And they were holding political rallies in the *praça* against us. Grandpa said it was *bruxaria* [witchcraft], not religion. Isn't that right, little grandpa?"

My old friend, Seu Félix, smiled wryly and threw up his hands, saying, "The church wants to give away everybody's land but their own. It has become a political party in Brazil and an enemy of the *fazendeiros*."

The political rallies that Seu Félix and his grandchildren were referring to are religious "missions"—several days of dawn-to-dusk processions, Stations of the Cross, public prayer and singing, and passionate and emotional sermons—that are held periodically in Bom Jesus, as in other *Nordestino* communities. Some of the missions are traditional and folkloric, held to honor a popular saint, living or dead, while others are informed by the new theology and practice of liberation, and these do sometimes take on a frankly political character. Although the old and the new style of missions reveal a Catholic church in transition and very much in contention among the clergy and the hierarchy, among the popular classes of Bom Jesus there is no contradiction. The faithful have simply added the new theology and rituals to their older practices of a popular Catholicism that was always isolated from official and mainstream theology.

And so in 1989 a popular mission honoring a visit to Bom Jesus of Frei Damião, the elderly and saintly Italian Capuchin friar and poor people's counselor, confessor, and prophet, was followed a week later by a liberation theology mission led by Padre Andreas, a Paulist priest from Salvador, Bahia, accompanied by a team of radicalized nuns and seminarians. Although wildly divergent in their messages and practices of folk spirituality, both missions provided the poor of Bom Jesus with a public forum.

On the day that Frei Damião arrived, several hundred of his local followers gathered at the small bridge that serves as the entrance to Bom Jesus to greet their saint. When Damião finally arrived, several hours late and perched precariously on the back of a huge, new, bright red truck with enormous tires, the people cheered, jumping and leaping, punching the air with their closed fists. "Long live Brother Damião! Long live the people of God!" they cheered for themselves as well as for their little friar, so old, so small, and so frightened by the noise and jostling of his truck that he clutched onto the large, decorated statue of Our Lady of Sorrows that accompanied him. Brother Damião seemed no larger than a seven-year-old child and as ancient and otherworldly as Yoda. The people chased behind the truck as it made its way through the town, and several young men tried to jump into the back to be with Brother Damião. Everyone wanted to touch him.

Each morning the mission began with Brother Damião rising long before dawn to walk the streets of town ringing his large bell to awaken the faithful and call them to prayer. By dawn hundreds of the poor gathered at a predetermined spot, and a procession through Bom Jesus, up the hills and down, followed. All were fasting, many were barefoot, and some performed little penances along the way. Frei Damião led the procession, walking so fast that he seemed almost to glide above the ground and across the sometimes steep and rough terrain. From time to time the procession would stop, and Frei Damião would be lifted onto a straight-backed chair or onto a ledge to preach his austere message: repent and turn away from the forces of evil and from the Antichrist; reject all forms of material seduction; fast, do penance, return to celibacy; prepare for the end of the world, which was imminent and would come on the heels of a great world war that would erase all signs of human habitation from the earth. Damião preached against "giving scandal" to the young and against popular music, nudity, and all forms of sensuality. "The kiss," he told an amused group of young people, "*é um horror* [it is ghastly]!"

Few seemed to pay attention to the friar's words, which were taken with a grain of salt. People would talk, move about, and make quite a bit of noise during the sermons. "*Silêncio!*" the funny little saint would finally explode with impotent rage, but the people laughed and continued going about their business. Frei Damião, unlike themselves, was not of this world, and his words were naturally somewhat strange and irrelevant. "Tsk! Tsk!" older women would say, with pity in their voice, "*Hein! Hein! Bichinho* [poor little creature]!" And they would come up very close to the friar, who was often standing above them, and they might tug affectionately on his brown robe or pat his swollen and gnarled bare feet. But most of all, they liked to approach him from behind and pat the top of his head, for that was considered very lucky, indeed.

The power of Frei Damião had nothing to do with his harsh, abstract, and disembodied words. Rather, it resided in his own person, his strange little, hunchbacked, corporeal self. He was a miracle worker, one who transcended the ordinary boundaries of everyday life. "We know something about our saint, but we cannot speak of it aloud," a woman whispered harshly in my ear. "Did you know about the little girl who tugged on his robes and whispered the secret in his ear? Brother Damião was so angry that he stamped his foot on the ground. In less than a week the little girl was dead. You see, she *knew*, and she told Brother Damião that she had seen him fly!"

It is in the idiom of their popular religion that the poor of Bom Jesus dare to criticize their oppressors and dare to dream of a utopia, a new world, where wrongs will be righted and where the "first shall be last, and the last shall be first." In this utopian space all the faithful will learn the art of celestial navigation, gliding, like Brother Damião, above their troubles, skimming the rocks and brambles and the stinging nettles of the *mata*, untouched

Brother Damião and the mission cross.

by earthly pain. It is in this "miraculous imagination" of the foresters and *moradores*—so much at odds with the language and discourse of modern sociology and anthropology, with their analysis of socioeconomic and political relations—that the "hope" of liberation is stored, nurtured, and savored. The revolutionary impulse is contained in the folk tradition, in the pious belief "that the vanquished of history—the body on which the victories of the rich and their allies is continually inscribed—may well (in the 'person' of their humiliated saint, Brother Damião) rise again as a result of the blows rained down on their adversaries from on high" (de Certeau 1984:17).

Frei Damião is an embodiment of the wrath of God, a God who (the poor imagine) is angry *for* them, on their behalf ("Wasn't it the *senhores latifundiários* of His day that put Our Lord Jesus up on that cross?"). The Antichrist of which Damião speaks could only be the godless *fazendeiro*, the selfish and greedy *senhor de engenho*, or the cruel *patroa*. And so it did not seem so strange, after all, when on the final day of his mission, Frei Damião was asked to bless the large, plain cross that would serve as the generative symbol of the liberation theology mission to be held on the Alto do Cruzeiro during the following week.

Padre Andreas, the peasant-worker priest from Salvador who would be leading that mission, received the cross from Brother Damião. But as a liberation theology missionary, Padre Andreas declined the invitation to sleep in the priest's rectory; he spent each night in a different hovel of the Alto listening to the stories of the *moradores*, recording oral histories, mapping the obscure paths and hillside ledges of the Alto in an attempt to recover "the lost history and the secret geography" of the shantytown. This was his way of preparing for the Alto mission.

The liberation mission itself seemed inspired by Brechtian and Basagliani tactics of symbolic inversion, parody, dramatization, and transgressive rituals of protest.[3] Many of the subversive tactics were spontaneously invented in festive meetings on the Alto during or following participatory liberation masses. Traditional devotional customs such as the Stations of the Cross, the procession calling to mind fourteen steps and events surroundings the passion and death of Jesus, were creatively reworked so as to serve as the basis for a radical reflection on oppression and human suffering. The folk traditions of lighting bonfires to honor Saint John or the blessing of automobiles on the feast day of Saint Christopher set the stage for public denunciations of capitalist greed, police violence, and worker exploitation, the new evils and "social sins" that required collective exorcisms.

Padre Andreas called the first procession to begin at dawn in front of the straw hut of Zé de Mello, one of the oldest *moradores* and cane cutters of the Alto; the cross was firmly planted in the pile of garbage at his door in which pigs and goats foraged. The priest called on the cane cutters to be the first group to "accept" the cross on their shoulders and lead the community in procession along a new *via sacra*, Stations of the Cross. As one group grew weary another group—street cleaners, single mothers, *curandeiras*, street children—was called and came forward to take up the cross in procession. At

All the rural workers carry the cross.

each designated "station" in the town below, the procession paused while Padre Andreas reflected on a common human dilemma. At the manioc market he spoke of food shortages and of the "crisis of the *roçados*," and he explained the laws that did exist to protect the rights of traditional peasants and rural squatters. At the door of the police precinct the priest reflected on police brutality; at the prison he talked about the social conditions that forced the poor into criminal acts; on the steps of the town hall he spoke of political deception, fraud, and indifference; and at the hospital he reflected on the lack of care and fraternity toward the abandoned sick-poor, who died unattended, without even the help of a Simon of Cyrene or a Good Samaritan to wipe the sweat from a fevered brow or to offer a taste of water or wine to fevered lips.

"These Stations of the Cross represent *your* Calvary," Padre Andreas took the microphone to explain. "They recall the steps of your own crucifixion, suffering, and death in Bom Jesus da Mata." Later, the procession moved indoors toward the main altar of Nossa Senhora das Dores, and it paused at the feet of Our Lady of Sorrows. A nun came forward to reflect on the Pietà, traditionally the thirteenth Station of the Cross, the dead Jesus taken down from the cross and laid in the arms of His mother.

"What is before our eyes?" she began. "Here is Mary, our Mother, receiving the lifeless body of Her Son. What torture! The same hands that received Him at birth, full of life, full of grace and love. Now lifeless, dead. What uncanny silence in a life that could never die. What mother here has not felt those same daggers stab at her own heart? In the days in which we are living, motherhood has become a burden, a punishment, even a curse, for like the Holy Mother, the poor women of Bom Jesus all know the sorrowful weight of a dead son or daughter in their arms."

Finally, the procession ended at the municipal cemetery to reflect on the fourteenth and last traditional Station of the Cross, Jesus being laid in his tomb. "If Jesus died today in Bom Jesus," Padre Andreas reflected, "what rich man, what Joseph of Arimathea, would come forward to offer Him a catacomb? More likely Jesus would be wrapped in a sheet and dumped in a common grave with the marginals and paupers of Bom Jesus, the anonymous dead of Bom Jesus da Mata." On the return to the Alto do Cruzeiro Padre Andreas called for a miracle: "Yes, I want a miracle. I want all the sick of Bom Jesus, all the blind and the lame, to come forward and carry the cross home to the very top of the Alto." And they did so amid cheers and wild applause.

Following the morning procession and Stations of the Cross Padre Andreas and his team spent the day in small meetings with the people of the Alto, attempting to organize the washerwomen into a collective, discussing plans with the *curandeiras* for a community pharmacy that would dispense herbal medications and natural cures, listening to the street children's complaints against the police and the "social workers" of the local FEBEM reform school.

The approach taken was Freirian and dialectical—critical discussion, spontaneous dramatization, and transgressive rituals. When several Alto women were invited to discuss their needs, one mother shyly said that women and children were often "poorly treated" at the public clinics. "Indeed" replied Padre Andreas. "Can you show me what this is like so that we can all see it?" And in a few minutes a skit was enacted between a very pregnant woman and a bored clinic doctor who never looked up once but continued to write in her appointment book while the woman tried to explain that she had begun to hemorrhage. "Umm," said the doctor, "here is a free sample of a new medication. It is very good for cleaning out the liver." The Alto people roared with laughter. The playful skit had struck home.

Padre Andreas used the moment to address one of his primary concerns. "There is a new sickness," he said, "a sickness that is as common and as serious as hunger, and we must all learn how to escape it. It is the sickness of medication, of unnecessary drugs dispensed without conscience by the clinic doctors and the pharmacists. Many people are killing themselves with these medications. Many of the drugs are toxic, they are poisonous, and they are given out to the poor without regard for their side effects. Be vigilant; wait before you run to the doctor or to the pharmacy or the hospital. Don't put your faith in doctors and in drugs. This woman who was hemorrhaging, what good did the doctor do for her? She would have been better off going to a local midwife, a *parteira* or *curiosa*. Put your trust in our *curandeiras*, in our popular healers who understand the powers of the herbs in God's pharmacy. We can begin to cure ourselves with the healing herbs that are free for the taking. We need to protect our forests and our healing herbs and not allow greed and the sugar plantations to choke them into oblivion." Then the priest called on all the midwives, healing women, and praying women of the Alto to come forward, and he led the people in a rousing hymn of praise to traditional healers.

The feast of St. Christopher coincided with the liberation theology mission, and Padre Andreas invited the Alto *curandeiras* to take his place in blessing the automobiles and trucks of the rich during the traditional car procession in the town plaza. Instead of holy water, however, the women would "bless" the shiny cars with dirty river water and polluted water from the public *chafariz*. On the evening of the procession, the praying women of the Alto descended from the hill carrying their large tins of water on their heads and singing a liberation theology hymn. They climbed onto the parade reviewing stand set up in front of the mother church next to Padre Agostino Leal and Padre Andreas. As the parade of luxury cars began to roll slowly by the reviewing stand, Padre Andreas took the microphone to retell the myth of Saint Christopher. He told of this patron saint of travelers, who, like the people of the Alto, walked long distances by foot. Once Saint Christopher carried the baby Jesus and the sins of the world across a wide river on his broad shoulders, just as the people of the Alto often had to cross the infected rivers that ran through plantation lands while carrying heavy loads on their heads and across their tired shoulders. "The sins of the world rest on the backs of our workers!" he exhorted the crowds.

Meanwhile, the old women of the Alto doused the cars with their dirty water, much to the angry surprise of the drivers, who had to roll up their windows to avoid the spray. Padre Andreas smiled benevolently over the procession, commenting delightedly in a soft voice, "Now you are all truly baptized!" When the sugarcane trucks passed by in their turn, it was too late for the drivers to turn back, and each was thoroughly splashed by the women, while their *padre-companheiro* commented on the daily suffering of the *bóias-frias*, who were packed into the backs of the trucks and dropped off at great distances from where they had to work for the day.

Finally, on the last night of the liberation theology mission, Padre Andreas announced a procession to be led by the *bóias-frias* to an empty field just outside the borders of Bom Jesus. There, the mission cross would be planted for the last time, and a celebratory bonfire would be lit to close the mission. He asked every man, woman, and child to bring a stick, including sticks of dried sugarcane, to add to the roaring fire that would cleanse the community of its social sins. Each stick would represent a social ill—hunger, sickness, unemployment, illiteracy, exploitation, the minimum wage, contaminated drinking water, greed, paternalism, racism—"everything that is contaminating and polluting."

The bonfire: cleansing Bom Jesus of its social sins.

That night one by one the people of the Alto came forward, some of them breaking sticks of sugarcane and tossing them into the fire, saying, "Let's give it to the sugar bosses!" Others said, "These sticks of cane are sucking the blood of the workers!" Still others, emboldened by their *companheiros*, came forward and named their boss, their landowner, their work crew manager, their mill manager, and the engineers of the *usina*, and in the name of each one they broke a stick of cane and added it to the pyre. Others came forward to throw into the flames their half-used bottles of medicines and glucose injection syringes, saying that they had been "fooled" by the doctors and the pharmacists of Bom Jesus, and schoolchildren burned the blank pages of copybooks from local schools where the children of the poor were taught nothing at all.

"Who are the chosen people of God?" asked Padre Andreas.

"We are," answered the crowd, "the poor and the humble!"

"Who are the sinners?"

"The landowners, the mill owners, the *fazendeiros!*"

"What shall we do with them?"

"Throw them into the fire!"

The traditional ritual St. John's Day bonfire had been turned upside down and against the plantation and mill owners, following the logic of the new theology. It is in rituals like these, perhaps rightfully described by the wealthy classes of Bom Jesus as "clerical witchcraft," that the *moradores'* culture of silence begins to be breached. For it is through liberation theology that the "witches"—the Afro-Brazilian priestesses and the elderly *curandeiras* and healing women of the Alto—have found a new form of public legitimacy.

Useless Suffering

Thus, the very least one can say about suffering is that in its own phenomenality, it is useless, "for nothing."
Emmanuel Levinas (1986:157–158)

But it is here that I must enter with a critique. For despite its radical praxis, liberation theology has still failed to respond to the useless suffering of mothers and infants, two social groups abandoned by the rhetoric of empowerment and by the "good news" of the social gospel of Jesus. On questions of sexuality and reproduction, it is the new church that is mute.

"I cannot speak with great authority on birth control, abortion, and sterilization," wavered Padre Agostino Leal, "for these are subjects that I, as a celibate male priest, have had no personal experience with and very little training about. There was no course on human sexuality taught at the seminary I attended in Rio de Janeiro. The best I can do is to try to give comfort in the confessional to those women and men who have sinned. I do not scold women who have taken drastic measures to avoid pregnancy, but it is my priestly duty to explain that the church still teaches that these practices are sinful, even though they are understandable, sometimes even necessary, evils. Our faith is in social and collective solutions to the needs of mothers and children so that we do not fall into the quagmire of godless, secular thought that views the birth of any one child as unnecessary. Even the popular expression *to avoid* [*evitar*] pregnancy is ugly. Why would anyone want to avoid children? This is an alien, secular philosophy, a philosophy of despair."

Although the breath of fresh air from the open window of liberation theology has blown away some of the old cobwebs of baroque religious traditions affecting mothers and infants, in particular those concerning the wake celebrations of angel-babies, it has left nothing in their place. The new priests view the death of infants and small babies as a human tragedy, and they discourage mothers from falling into the old, comfortable religious consolations. These are spurned as the archaic survivals of a "primitive" folk Catholicism. "Jesus never intended that the innocent should suffer and die for our sins," Sister Juliana now tells the bereaved mothers of the Alto do Cruzeiro. "He wants your babies to live." But they die all the same.

When I asked Padre Agostino about the lack of church ceremony surrounding infant death today as compared to earlier decades, the priest replied, "In the old days child death was richly celebrated [*muito festejada*], but those were the baroque customs of a conservative church that wallowed in death and misery. The new church is a church of hope and of joy. It is wrong to celebrate the death of child-angels. We try to tell the mothers that Jesus doesn't want all the babies that *they* send him."

But even if Jesus doesn't want them, Alto mothers cannot possibly raise all the babies Jesus does send to them. It is an odd sort of kula ring, played with a valuable token of exchange that the players try to pass along rather quickly so as not to be the one left holding the baby.

The mothers of the Alto have been thrown into moral and theological confusion. The old Catholic tradition that held that angel-babies decorated the throne of God was, at the very least, consoling to the parents of a little dead *anjinho*. It rendered the suffering and death meaningful. The new theology of liberation has challenged the conventional, folk Catholic wisdom on the spiritual meanings of human suffering, on theodicy, but it has not offered an alternative. If Jesus does not want their little angels, why *were* they born, and what is the meaning of their suffering? It appears to some women of the Alto that now even the church has turned away from them, denying their dead *anjinhos* their rightful place in the communion of saints and denying the women the comfort of their once serene faith and conformity to God's will.

Indeed, the contemporary Brazilian church is caught in the clutches of a moral double bind. The theology of liberation imagines a kingdom of God on earth, one based on justice and equality, a world without hunger, sickness, or child mortality. But at the same time the church, even under the new guise of liberation theology, has not modified its hostility toward female sexuality and reproduction, and so it remains mute on the theological sources of gender oppression and on the church's historical contribution to the useless suffering of mothers and infants.

In the writings of the Jewish philosopher Emmanuel Levinas one finds a moral sensibility that, even while it is no more personally consoling than the contemporary teachings of the Catholic church, at least refuses to turn away from the meaninglessness of human suffering. As a modality, suffering is all passivity, Levinas wrote (1986:157). It is pure undergoing, a blow against freedom, an "impasse of life and being." It is unambiguously evil and absurd. His intent was to deny theodicy, all attempts, whether theological, philosophical, or anthropological, to imbue suffering with meaning. The search for meaning in suffering has allowed humans to blame themselves and others for their own sickness, pain, and death, to rationalize suffering as penance for sin, as a means to an end, as the price of reason, or as the path of martyrs and saints.

We can see this human impulse, for example, in Oscar and Biu's willingness to assign a cause, an ultimate "meaning" to Mercea's death: "Perhaps she died to bring us to our senses, to make us a united family again." Xoxa was more theological and more ambivalent in her quest for the meaning of her sister's death. She explained, "I think that God was, in part, good because He took Mercea away from her life of misery. He ended her constant begging for things that we didn't have to give her. He put an end to her talk [*fala*] and her longing [*desejo*] for things that were an impossibility. So, in part, it was good of God to take her away from never having enough food to eat or clothes to cover her, from having to cry all day and all night. It was better in a way for us, too, so that we could end our humiliating hunting down of Oscar after he had left us, begging him for money, for medicines, for food, everything for Mercea. But I think that, in part, God was not so good because He did not really put an end to Mercea's suffering or our own. Mercea is still hovering around us, still begging for things, but now she is a hungry, sick, broken spirit, a wandering soul, an *alma penanda*. And she cannot even speak to us. She only whimpers and points to her feet, which are cold and blistered. But now Mercea is no longer with us or in a place where we can try to sort out and resolve some of her problems. And so we continue to suffer for her."

The justification of another human being's pain and suffering is, according to Levinas, the source of immorality. A more ethical way to think about suffering is to envision it as "meaningful in me, but useless in the other." One may blame oneself for suffering; but one may never blame the other, nor allow her suffering to be seen as serving any purpose. Following from this, the only ethical way to view the death of Mercea is to see her suffering as useless and her death as irretrievably tragic and purposeless. And yet who would deny Biu, Oscar, Tonieta, and Xoxa (or even the useless anthropologist, Dona Nancí) their endless search to derive some earthly meaning from Mercea's cold and hungry angel-body?

Silence in the Dialogue with the Oppressed

If speaking means existence with others, making use of our
body as in a kind of reciprocal mingling on common ground,
what creates this reciprocal bond is the silence that precedes it,
the silence in which the two partners take stock of one
another, reciprocally recognizing their own place, their own
space, their own body.

Franco Basaglia (1969:99)

I have made much of silence throughout this text, the culture of silence that is the obvious correlate of the culture of violence and terror in the shantytown but also the silences of less than courageous complicity and the failures of nerve that can present themselves as the love of harmony and nonviolence. But in addition to the seething silence of coerced compliance is the maddening, bureaucratic stone wall of silence toward the suffering of the anonymous marginals of the Alto do Cruzeiro. There is also the unexpected silence of the church bells of Our Lady of Sorrows that no longer toll for the hungry, felled angels of the shantytown or for the mutilated bodies of Nego De and other young men who run afoul of the forces of law and disorder in Bom Jesus. And finally there is the silence of Mercea, the angel-baby, who reappears only to gesture, to "sign" her continued suffering.

I end, then, with a few reflections on the meanings of silence in Bom Jesus, particularly the silence of the poor and the oppressed. Paulo Freire's (1970) analysis of the "muteness" of the rural classes of the Nordeste and of their "culture of silence," which contributes to but is not seen as the *cause* of their oppression, has been taken to task by some younger scholars. Roger Lancaster (1988:199), for example, saw Freire's analysis as a kind of "orientalism" that casts the poor as inanimate and inert, almost prereflexive, predialogic "things" devoid of all subjectivity.

Freire proposed literacy as the vehicle for establishing creative dialogue, insofar as the illiteracy of rural Brazilians in the modern state was a source and symbol of their "muteness." The irony (or the final "insult") was Freire's suggestion that the silent oppressed had to be "taught" to surrender their passivity and their fear of taking direct action. Freire's radical pedagogy was marred, Lancaster suggested, by a false notion of dialogue, insofar as it depends on the role of the "teacher-vanguard" to enter the imprisoned community from without to initiate reflexive speech, to rupture the silence of the oppressed, and to release the long-trapped flow and exchange of ideas, language, and critical thinking.

The metaphor of the "imprisoned" and "silent" community, so central to Freire's analysis, bears some resemblance to the radical critique of the debilitating effects of total and violent institutions on hospitalized mental patients made by Franco Basaglia and his radical *equipe* in Gorizia, Italy (see Scheper-Hughes & Lovell 1987). The attempts of the Gorizia psychiatric team to establish an "open-door" policy and a "therapeutic community" among chronic mental patients institutionalized in traditional Italian asylums were thwarted by the effects of imprisonment on the patients' mortified humanity, buried histories, and lost subjectivities. The open door, which was the terror of Italian legislators, who viewed the insane as dangerous public enemies, merely reminded the mental patients of their condition as the involuntarily confined. The newly "liberated" patients responded to the open door passively, sitting quietly by and waiting for their psychiatrist-liberator to tell them "what to do next, to decide for them, because they no longer knew how to appeal to their own efforts, freedom, and responsibilities" (Basaglia 1987a:19). The released inmates remained imprisoned by an internalized image of the asylum. Locked doors and barred windows were no longer necessary. They had lived so long as wards and dependents of the "total institution" (see also Goffman 1961) that their only choice was to live as undialectically as they were able.

The violence of the institution, where "treatment" was difficult to distinguish from punishment, had surpassed ordinary powers of endurance. Consequently, the open-door policy produced a paradox: the great quagmire of patient gratitude to their benevolent doctor-father. Basaglia's immediate solution to prevent the therapeutic community from deteriorating into a "cheerful haven for grateful slaves" was to engage the patient-inmates in a relationship of reciprocal tension, challenging their mortified humanity by calling forth long-suppressed feelings of anger and aggressivity. If a patient suggested at one of the open community meetings that the living conditions of a certain back ward were deplorable, Basaglia and his staff would agree and suggest to the man that he and his fellow inmates dismantle and destroy the hateful space and in so doing begin to dismantle and destroy the passivity and years of silent acquiescence that had gradually eroded the inmates' sense of free will and choice.

Having worked in both contexts, with long-term psychiatric patients in traditional mental asylums in Ireland and the United States and with marginalized squatters in the nervous-hungry and terrorized shantytowns of Northeast Brazil, I find the analogy between Freire's and Basaglia's radicalizing practices striking. The hostile paternalism of traditional doctor-patient and boss-worker relations reproduces the violence of the asylum and of the *casa grande,* where dependency, silence, and passivity are rewarded and where loyalty to the doctor-jailer or the patron-boss is the most valuable token of economic exchange for survival. The shantytown, like the mental asylum, exists as a "total institution," a satellite of the sugar plantation and sugar mills, and anonymity, depersonalization, and surveillance are used, as in the hospital, to create a climate of fear, suspiciousness, and hopelessness.

We could compare the open-door policy implemented by Basaglia and his coworkers in the Democratic Psychiatry Movement in the 1960s in Italy to the Brazilian policy of *abertura,* the open-door politics of democracy and free society. The recent history of both experiences indicates that before "silenced" and "imprisoned" people can begin to recognize themselves as autonomous, reflexive, and dialogical beings, they need to relearn, slowly and gradually, the everyday practices of personal (and later of political) freedom. Such was the case in the asylum at Gorizia, and such is the case in the shantytown of Alto do Cruzeiro.

"Today I spoke up at the women's circle in the creche," an elderly Alto woman commented. "Later in the day I realized that this was the first time I had ever spoken out in public. I was always somebody who kept quiet and accepted whatever was said. But I learned today that I *did* have an opinion, although I was raised *para não ser pessoa* [not to be a person]."

In writing against cultures and institutions of fear and domination, the critical thinker falls into a classic double bind. Either one attributes great explanatory power to the fact of oppression (but in so doing one can reduce the subjectivity and agency of subjects to a discourse on victimization) or one can try to locate the everyday forms of resistance in the mundane tactics and practices of the oppressed, the weapons of the weak, described by Michel de Certeau (1980), James Scott (1985), and others. Here one runs the risk of romanticizing human suffering or trivializing its effects on the human spirit, consciousness, and will.

In this regard I would contrast Carol Stack's (1974) description of the cunning and lively "survival strategies" of poor urban ghetto residents of the "Flats" with the writings of her mentor, Oscar Lewis (1958, 1963, 1965, 1966), who emphasized the oppressive weight and destructive effects of poverty on the lives of Mexican peasants and New York City slum dwellers. Or I would contrast Paulo Freire's pessimism with the optimism of Frantz Fanon (1963, 1967). If Paulo Freire erred in his unidimensional view of *Nordestino* peasants as mere objects of the rich and powerful so that their knowledge and experience of themselves as self-reflexive humans was all but destroyed, Frantz Fanon erred in his belief that the victims of colonialist oppression could remain strong throughout their torment and emerge altogether unscathed from cultural and economic enslavement, with their subjectivity and culture intact. Moreover, in granting power, agency, choice, and efficacy to the oppressed subject, one must begin to hold the oppressed morally accountable for their collusions, collaborations, rationalizations, "false consciousness," and more than occasional paralyses of will. With agency begin responsibility and accountability.

In these pages I have tried to argue a middle ground, one that acknowledges the destructive signature of poverty and oppression on the individual and the social bodies, for Freire's "culture of silence" is recognizable on the Alto do Cruzeiro, but one that also acknowledges the creative, if often contradictory, means the people of the Alto use to stay alive and even to thrive with their wit and their wits intact. The goal of the *moradores* of the Alto do Cruzeiro is not *resistance* but simply *existence*. And in the context of these besieged lives I find human resilience enough to celebrate with them, joyfully and hopefully, if always tentatively.

Epilogue
Acknowledgments and Then Some

Ethnographic fieldwork and writing take a long time. They depend on intimate ties and attachments, and they entail a good deal of traveling. And so they are costly. The work of putting together this book required four periods of fieldwork between 1982 and 1989 and two additional teaching leaves for analysis and writing. Fieldwork in 1982 was supported by small grants from the Southeast Consortium for International Development, Washington, D.C., and an R. J. Reynolds Faculty Research Award from the University of North Carolina, Chapel Hill. In other words, "development" and "tobacco," two social ills, put me in the field and in their debt, but each did so graciously and without strings, even though I accepted their patronage with considerably less grace. Fieldwork in Brazil during 1987 and 1988 was supported by a John Simon Guggenheim Fellowship, supplemented by a travel award from the Center for Latin American Studies at the University of California, Berkeley. A book publication advance and a small faculty research grant from the University of California, Berkeley, allowed me to return to Brazil for a final fieldwork season in 1989.

The months of quiet contemplation necessary to writing were provided by the Center for Advanced Study in the Behavioral Sciences at Stanford (and a grant from the John D. and Catherine T. MacArthur Foundation) during 1987–1988; the Rockefeller Foundation Bellagio Study and Conference Center in Italy during November–December 1989; and the National Humanities Center (and a grant from the National Endowment for the Humanities) in Research Triangle Park, North Carolina, during the spring and summer of 1990. Each study center offered just the right balance of solitude and conviviality, and my work and life were enriched by the many social scientists, humanists, artists, and fellow writers I met in each place and with whom I shared many meals and continual late night and early morning discussion and debates on writing projects as diverse (taking just Bellagio as an example) as Tim Halliday's book on courtship and mating in animals; Valeria Vasilevski, Stuart Wallace, and Bill T. Jones's collaborative operatic work, *Allos Maker (happy in a different way) OK;* Denise Levertov's collection of new poems; and David Slavitt's parody of the death of Mussolini.

Within Brazil and Bom Jesus da Mata the personal debts and intimacies span a twenty-five-year period, and I cannot do justice to them here. I single out only a few individuals, beginning with Nailza de Arruda da Silva, an Indian migrant from Mato Grosso to the Brazilian Nordeste with whom I lived in the close quarters of a mud shack on the Alto do Cruzeiro in 1965–1966 and with whom I coparented our adopted son, Marcelinho, who is today, to my dismay but no less in my affections, a soldier in the Brazilian military. The late Jacques Ferreira Lima (the "Seu Félix" of this book), the long-reigning mayor of Bom Jesus, was my first introduction to the world of *Nordestino* plantation society, politics, and *parentela.* Despite our many differences, I loved Seu Jacques and his absurd sense of humor dearly. I hope I have not done violence to his memory in these pages. Betsey Rubin Rosenbaum, Jude Peterson, and Steve Hettenbach were fellow Peace Corps workers in Brazil in the 1960s who remain dear and important friends. Antonieta and Severino Ferreira Nascimento have been family in Bom Jesus since I first lived next door to them in the 1960s, and their lives, and those of their ten children, are an example of generosity and faith. My *comadres,* Biu and Lordes, are like sisters to me, and I offer their life histories and narratives as a small attempt to bring their lives, hopes, and dreams to the public. Doutor Claudio José da Silva has been an exacting teacher of *Nordestino* culture and tradition as well as a dear friend. In Josímario ("João Mariano") and Marcelo the long-suppressed radical tradition of the Brazilian Northeast is again ablaze. Greetings, *companheiros!* Padre Orlando (i.e., Padre "Agostino Leal"), Padre Andreas, Padre Raimundo, Irmã Juliana, and the hopeful seminarians Chico and Luciano exemplify the passionate commitment to justice and equality of the new church in Brazil. Dom Helder Câmara, spiritual leader of the poor and dispossessed of the Brazilian Nordeste, intervened once on my behalf during the military investigation of the shantytown association of the Alto do Cruzeiro in 1966, and he warmly received me and my family in Recife on our arrival in 1982. There is a way in which Dom Helder is always in the wings, his impish eyes twinkling; his head bobbing in agreement; his small, expressive hands darting the air; his warm smile enfolding and accepting of outsiders of goodwill, despite the egregious economic assaults by a greedy, interfering First World on his hungry part of the Third World. "Yes," he assured me, "if you write about the hunger of the Northeast, you will have my blessing." Well, then, *bênção*, Padrinho? "Your blessing, Godfather?"

I am of course indebted to many Brazilian anthropologists, social scientists, writers, and scholars, beginning with one passionate son of the Brazilian Northeast whom I never met, the late Josué de Castro, whose book *Death in the Northeast* inspired this "sequel." Naomar de Almeida, Roberto da Matta, Fátima Quintas, Juarandir Freire Costa, Ondina Leal, Sonia Corrêa, Luis Fernando Dias, Teresa Caldeira, and Clarice Mota have each been important in different ways.

Without colleagues and collaborators this odd scholarly life and profession would be, as one colleague put it, "a lonely little office with a shelf of books and a telephone." Colleagues and collaborators are our lifeblood as writers. So, in particular, I mention Gail Kligman, who has made Berkeley, California, a home for the heart as well as the mind. For several years Margaret Lock and I have collaborated in an effort to create a critical, reflexive medical anthropology. To Anne Lovell I am grateful for making our collaborative work on Franco Basaglia, radical phenomenology, and Italian democratic psychiatry come alive so that Basaglia's thinking now infuses the way in which I experience, reflect on, and write about the world. I had the great good fortune to share a memorable year of fellowship with Carol Stack (as well as a less memorable damp and dingy garage apartment) while at the Center for Advanced Study in Stanford. To Mick Taussig, who has been a steadfast friend and source of inspiration and from whom I have borrowed a great deal over the years, I am grateful for his dark and brooding, yet carnivalesque, view of the human condition and for his poetic vision of what anthropology could be. David Daube has long been a mentor, a wise spiritual and intellectual guide, and in the example of his life and work, he has given me the stamina to face the "black hole" in my own choice of difficult questions to ponder.

My colleagues in the Department of Anthropology at Berkeley, but especially Paul Rabinow, Aihwa Ong, Laura Nader, Gerald Berreman, Bill Simmons, and Stanley Brandes, have turned Kroeber Hall into a lively intellectual community and more than just the perennial resting ground for the Ishi exhibit. In Chapel Hill, my former colleagues in the Anthropology Department of the University of North Carolina, especially T. M. S. Evens, Lee Schlessinger, and Sue Estroff, have often forced me to think more deeply and write more responsibly while reminding me to live more congenially. Former students who have produced dissertations, articles, and books that have corrected the deficiencies of my own anthropological education and whose good company and advice I have sought include Roger Nelson Lancaster, Richard Parker, Thomas Ward, Marie Boutte, Vincanne Adams, Lynn Morgan, Linda Green, Donna Goldstein, and Lesley Sharp. To Cecilia de Mello I have a special relationship: she spent several weeks in Bom Jesus da Mata as my research assistant, and we "played" and studied *carnaval* together in 1988. I am grateful for her intelligence, good humor, and intuitive understandings of her native Brazil.

Joanne Wyckoff encouraged me to write this book and Naomi Schneider brought me back to the University of California Press and as intellectual midwife and kindred spirit guided a long project to its conclusion. Betsey Scheiner kindly withstood my ill-humored response to her reasonable request that I cut some hundred pages from the original manuscript, thus rescuing my readers from further eye strain.

Many individuals read and commented on portions of the original text or responded to oral presentations of my findings. In particular I want to acknowledge the help I received from Gilles Bibeau, Teresa Caldeira, Nancy Chodorow, Naomar de Almeida, David Eaton, T. M. S. Evens, Ronnie Frankenberg, Gene Hammel, Peter Homans, Gail Kligman, Charles Leslie, Catherine Lutz, Gananath Obeyesekere, Linda-Anne Rebhun, the late Paul Riesman, Lee Schlessinger, Rick Shweder, Candace Slater, Carol Stack, Judith Stacey, Marcelo Suarez-Orozco, and Michael Taussig. Sara Ruddick's most careful reading and critical response to earlier versions of chapters 7, 8, and 9 resulted in significant changes for which I am most grateful.

Sharon Ray and Karen Carroll typed beautiful copy during the transitional period when I was still computer illiterate, or nearly so.

More personal debts are owed. My husband, Michael Hughes, and our three now very nearly grown children, Jennifer, Sarah, and Nathanael, have been part of this project from its inception to its protracted conclusion. We have been an "anthropological" family as long as we have been together, and we tend to count the years and recall the significant events of our lives in terms of field sites. That happened, we are likely to say, in the "year of the Irish" (1974–1975), during the first Taos Pueblo pow-wow (1980), on Saint Patrick's Day in South Boston (1979–1980), and so on. We recall that Nathanael took his first steps on Irish soil, that our three-year-old Sarah stopped speaking altogether when we put her in a bilingual day care center in Texas in preparation for fieldwork in northern New Mexico, and that Jennifer (who suffered more than her share of lumps) had a broken arm in both Ireland and in Brazil and was knocked unconscious in a rough-and-tumble fray in a playground in Ranchos de Taos, New Mexico.

Most of all, however, we recall the rough time that all the children had during our first fieldtrip to Bom Jesus da Mata in 1982, when Sarah suffered a profound form of culture shock and then fell so gravely ill that we all feared briefly for *her* life. The children were still too much children themselves to understand my research on child mortality as anything other than personally threatening. Nathanael wrote in large, eight-year-old scrawling magic marker script on the cover of the diary that he faithfully kept throughout our stay in 1982, *"BRAZIL 1982 by NATE HUGHES.* WHY WE WENT: Trying to find out Why the CHILDREN are DYING. Main Idea." On an early page of the diary he recorded, "We went up to the Alto where Mom is interviewing the women. One of the mothers had 17 children and 11 of them died. One had 5 and 4 of them died. One had 11 and 6 of them died."

Perhaps this is how Rudolf Virchow's career in social medicine began, but it was a lot to ask of a small boy coming from a protected and relatively affluent community in the United States. Jennifer's twelve-year-old response was a nurturing one; she wanted to "rescue" the sick babies on the Alto do Cruzeiro. When she heard that our friend Antonieta had found an abandoned infant in a basket on her doorstep, Jennifer developed a fantasy that we might acquire a baby in the same way.

Eventually, Michael and I learned to create some distance and private space for the children apart from my often disturbing work on the Alto do Cruzeiro. And we often took weekend trips into Recife and to the beautiful beaches of Boa Viagem. These thoroughly enjoyed excursions, however, made the many returns and necessary readjustments to life in Bom Jesus all the more taxing. "We got on a bus and went back to Bom Jesus," wrote Nate in his diary on July 15, 1982. "Tired and sad looking at our little house. I went inside upsetly. Sarah was upset, too. Sitting on a hammock with mosquitoes biting us. I said, 'Did we have to come here to do this research?' Well, with the look on Mom's face I think we had to. After that one question we all fell down and went to sleep."

I had my own doubts, of course, about the wisdom and the fairness of bringing my family so far afield, especially to a demanding living situation with so little that was comfortable or familiar. When Sarah became very ill with an undiagnosed fever, my worst fears for the health and safety of the children were confirmed. Nate, our faithful field diarist, recorded his own feelings (sentiments and anxieties that each of us shared):

> August 6, 1982. In the middle of the night Sarah had three terrible fevers. One was 102, one was 103, and the other was 104. In the morning it was raining and Sarah was sick again. 103. She was sick while cuddling up in my bed under the mosquito net. The doctor came to see what was the matter. She was sick all right, the doctor said. She had to have some medicine quick. So Dad and I ran out to get it. While we were rushing back to the house I was thinking that

Sarah would die if we don't treat her. Worst of all, it was her birthday [her tenth], and I would die if she had to die on her birthday.

It would be ironic, indeed, if a book dealing with maternal threats to child
survival did not mention the risks that anthropological parents take each
time they bring their small children to the field with them. But, thankfully,
Sarah did recover with a powerful course of antibiotics, though she never did
overcome her initial "resistance" to Brazil on that first expedition, and
subsequent field research was postponed for another five years until I felt
that the children could make informed decisions as to whether to stay at
home or join me in a return to the field.

With the announcement of my Guggenheim award in 1987, which made
a longer return trip to Brazil feasible, all three children decided to return to
Bom Jesus. Sarah, in particular, was determined to make a better go at
learning Portuguese and at appreciating Brazilian life. Arriving in Bom Jesus
with three adolescents aged thirteen, fifteen, and seventeen was an entirely
different experience. The children were amazed at how much Bom Jesus and
the Alto do Cruzeiro had changed. I was amazed at how much the children
had changed, while Bom Jesus seemed hardly changed at all. Sarah forced
herself to speak Portuguese, took to wearing her skirts considerably shorter,
and discovered a passion for Brazilian music and dance. Nate found his way
among the various bands of street *moleques* that gathered near our house,
and he played soccer to his heart's content.

Jennifer, my eldest, deserves special mention because, beginning in 1987,
she became my research assistant and occasional project photographer, producing many of the photos reprinted in this book. She worked in the
archives of the local *cartório civil* painstakingly recording the data on infant
and child deaths for several selected years. The work was tedious in the
extreme, and she was both careful and uncomplaining. Jennifer often accompanied me in my daily visits to households on the Alto do Cruzeiro, and she
often entertained small children so that their mothers or both parents could
be free to talk and visit with me. At home in the United States Jennifer
helped me to assemble data and to transcribe audiotapes. After several false
starts, Jennifer was able to help me overcome my strong, native resistance to
the computer and its ugly screen. On the last fieldtrip to Brazil in 1989,
Jennifer worked actively with the shantytown association and with the base
community movement of Bom Jesus. When I left Brazil to return to teaching, Jennifer remained in Brazil to observe the first presidential elections in
more than twenty years and to assist in a liberation theology mission held in
Bom Jesus just before the elections. Jennifer's contribution to the analysis of

the role of the New Church in Chapter 12 is formidable. Jennifer is today a serious student of Latin American, especially Brazilian, history, but Brazil is very much a part of the lives of all three children.

Finally, Michael has, on two occasions, taken a leave of absence from his work as a clinical social worker to accompany me and our children to Bom Jesus da Mata. Although we share many similar concerns, especially those bearing on the health and survival of women and children in our society as well as in the Third World, Michael is not a collaborator in the research, nor would he ever want to be an anthropologist or an ethnographer. Moreover, he does not often read what I write. He is far too gentle an observer of human life to appreciate anthropology; and there is no hint of cunning or guile in him. The kinds of interactional jujitsu that anthropologists must sometimes engage in are thoroughly alien to him. He has, moreover, a natural gift for "fraternity and recognition" that is undiluted by the desire or the need to analyze. He is able to take people in, fully and deeply, and he radiates both unconditional acceptance and warmth in the company of others. Michael has been with me at virtually every field site, actively participating in the communities in which we have lived, volunteering for collective tasks, whether "haying" in western Ireland, teaching school, organizing youth groups in Bom Jesus, or simply patiently responding to endless questions about ourselves and our life in the United States. In short, Michael makes himself available, unstintingly so. There is no doubt that I have been tolerated in some field situations (Ireland, I suspect, was one of these) only because of the community's real affection for him as well as for our children. Michael, both at home and in the field, is my *companheiro* and my *conselheiro*, and I would be a good deal more in the dark without his company, his wise counsel, and his example.

Notes

1. The "negative worker" is a species of class traitor, usually a "technician of practical knowledge" (doctor, teacher, lawyer, social worker, manager, or supervisor) who colludes with the powerless to identify their needs *against* the interests of the bourgeois institution. I am talking about hospital-based psychiatrists or nurses who side with their resistant or "noncompliant" patients; grade school teachers who side with their "hyperactive" students; jailers, with their petty thieves; store managers, with their angry consumers; social workers, with their welfare "cheats"; and so on. I once knew a psychiatric nurse who, following from her close reading of Franco Basaglia (see Scheper-Hughes & Lovell 1987) assumed the role of "negative worker" on her ward. She would "lose" or dispose of the massive tranquilizers that several of her "schizophrenic" patients generally had to be forced to swallow. The concept of the "negative worker" or the "negative intellectual" was developed by René Lorau, a French sociologist and leader in the "institutional analysis" movement that grew out of the "May events" of 1968. Institutional analysis entailed making symbolic gestures within traditional institutions to expose or to subvert their "true" social controlling functions. (See Lorau 1975.)

1. O NORDESTE

1. See Hirschman 1963; Robock 1965; T. Smith 1965; de Andrade 1980; Furtado 1965; N. Aguiar 1979.

2. "Secretaria Registra 69 Casos de Tifo," *Diário de Pernambuco*, July 15, 1982; "Combate a Doença de Chagas na Área Rural Prossegue," *Diário de Pernambuco*, July 12, 1982; "Febre," *Diário de Pernambuco*, July 16, 1982; "Desnutrição Está Cada Vez Mais Alarmante na Região," *Diário de Pernambuco*, July 15, 1987; Simons 1987.

3. See "Clima Tropical: Risco para Saúde?" *Diário de Pernambuco*, July 19, 1982.

4. Although some physical anthropologists believe that a "taste" for sugar and an aversion to bitterness are most likely evolutionarily adaptive responses that protected our foraging ancestors from consuming poisonous plants, recent studies at the

French National Scientific Research Center suggested that a taste for sugar is, at least in part, a learned response. See Gordon 1987.

5. The Jesuits were the first to agitate on behalf of the rights of Brazilian Indians. They sought to Christianize (and also to protect) the indigenous seminomadic hunting and gathering peoples of Brazil by settling them into missions, called *adeias*, where they were taught European languages and culture as well as colonial trades. See Burns 1962.

6. Slave traffic was ended in 1850. In 1871 the Law of the Free Womb (Ventre Livre) declared free all children born to slaves. Final emancipation followed in 1888.

7. A seventeenth-century English traveler described his visit to a traditional sugar mill in the Northeast: "In these mills they work both day and night, the work of immediately applying the cane into the mill being so perilous as if through drowsiness or heedlessness a finger's end be but engaged betwixt the posts, their whole body inevitably follows, to prevent which, the next Negro has always a hatchet ready to chop off his arm, if any such misfortune should arrive" (Flecknoe 1654:80).

8. Also see "Brazil: Black Sheep—Or Red?" *Newsweek*, February 27, 1961, p. 51; "Brazil: Reform or Revolution?" *Newsweek*, July 3, 1961, p. 41.

9. The rural syndicate movement was mobilized by local priests in Pernambuco who were fearful of communist infiltration in the Peasant League movement. Less politically threatening than the Peasant Leagues, the rural trade unions survived the period of military repression. In recent years, with the democratization of Brazilian society, the rural unions have become stronger and the Catholic clergy involved in the syndicate movement more bold.

10. In the debate about the effects of "modernization" and wage labor on women's status (see Illich 1983; Boserup 1970), it seems that the case of Northeast Brazil supports the argument of those who see women as doubly exploited "shadow workers" once they leave the autonomy and independence of subsistence work for wage labor.

11. The Rural Labor Statute (1963) extended to rural workers many of the same rights and benefits that were earlier guaranteed the urban worker, including minimum wage, paid holidays, severance pay, and the *décima*, an extra month's salary paid each year during the Christmas–New Year season.

12. I am using the term *female worker in the cane* advisedly. It is meant to complement Sidney Mintz's vivid portrait of the life of Anastacio Zayas Alvarado, a Puerto Rican worker in the cane. Don Taso, as Mintz's informant was called, was meant to typify the life of the traditional rural worker in Puerto Rico. Although Don Taso's wife appeared to have been a worker in the cane at times as well (1960:179), her life history was treated only in passing. As in so many traditional ethnographies, women's work and their contributions to household and family subsistence were either left unexamined or simply taken for granted.

13. This "piecemeal" system of wage labor first came into general use in the 1940s (Palmeira 1979:81). Originally, weeding was paid by measures called *tarefas* (tasks), a square area almost an acre on each side, that required the labor of one man for two or four days. Later, weeding was paid by a new measure, a *conta* (bill) measuring 22 by 22 meters and requiring the work of one man in a day or less. This measure— although referred to as a *quadro*—is supposed to be the same one that is in existence today. Ideally, one should be able to complete the work on one's *quadro* in a single day's labor. That few workers, male or female, are unable to do so today leads to charges of *preguiça* (laziness) by the landowner and countercharges of fraud by the

workers, who are convinced that they are being cheated by the *cabo*, who represents the interests of the *senhor de engenho* or the *usineiro*.

14. Rural syndicate leaders have long suspected that the prohibition of alcohol and the absence of bars and cantinas on *usina* property are also motivated by the desire to suppress conviviality among workers and common meeting grounds where political organizing can take place.

2. BOM JESUS

1. In Brazil a *município* is a local administrative unit that includes both a central township and outlying rural lands, villas, plantations, and *fazendas*. It corresponds roughly to a county in the United States. Bom Jesus da Mata, then, refers *both* to the town itself *and* to the surrounding rural area. One learns from the context of the discussion which meaning is implied. The entire *município* is governed by an elected *prefeito*, a "mayor," and a dozen or more town councilmen called *vereadores*. Local elections were suspended during the military years, and the first municipal elections were resumed in 1982 after a hiatus of more than fifteen years.

2. In James L. Taylor's (1970) *Portuguese-English Dictionary*, *matuto* is translated as "backwoodsman, shy, suspicious . . . a simple-minded person, especially one from the country." In the southern part of Brazil the word *caipira* is used in the same way to describe a rustic or a country yokel.

3. As first alluded to in chapter 1, the myth of Brazil's racial democracy, or "racial paradise," was proposed by Gilberto Freyre in his *Casa-Grande e Senzala* (especially chapters 4 and 5). There and in his numerous other publications, Freyre developed the thesis that widespread "miscegenation" among masters and slaves on the colonial sugar plantations led to a racial harmony, and to a notion of "black" and "white" in Brazil not as a polarized dichotomy but as "fraternizing halves" so that even up through the present day the expressions *meu nego*, *neguinha*, and *pikininho* are terms of endearment rather than of hostility. Freyre suggested that the mixed offspring of white Europeans and their black slaves produced a multicolored society in which, even today, the more than one hundred different racial terms confound the best efforts of the IBGE, the Brazilian census bureau, to define the racial composition of the population. In the 1980 census, for example, Brazilians volunteered more than 130 definitions of their color (and it is their color, their *cor*, not their race, *raça*, or their ethnicity that Brazilians are asked to identify on the official census), including "silvery brown," "pale mulatto," "corn colored," "dirty white," "dappled," and "quasi-Negro." Although such a rich popular culture of racial diversity gives an appearance of racial democracy (or at least of racial anarchy), it means little or nothing to wealthy and upper-middle-class white households, where there is no ambiguity on the color issue and where mulattos and blacks are easily recognized, labeled, and treated as social inferiors.

In fact, according to the 1980 census, approximately 44 percent of Brazil's sixty million people are black or mulatto, but of Brazilians earning more than five hundred dollars a month, fewer than 10 percent are nonwhites. As in the United States, race is an economic issue in Brazil, where racial "democracy" exists only at the bottom rungs of the social-economic pyramid. Of the 559 members of Brazil's congress, only 7 are black, while there are currently no black generals in the Brazilian army, no black *latifundistas* in the Northeast, and there is at best a flimsy black middle class. Black

Brazilians account for two-thirds of families surviving on fifty dollars a month or less. Even in the capital city of Salvador, Bahia, where 80 percent of the two million residents are black, the city has never had a black mayor, although the black singer Gilberto Gil was a candidate for that office in 1988. And Bahian "society" is still controlled by a tiny Euro-Brazilian white elite. In all, racial discrimination is wide-spread in Brazil.

4. I use the term *anomic anarchism* advisedly insofar as a libertarian variant of anarchism is strong among a small but significant segment of the intelligentsia of Bom Jesus. These largely middle-class individuals are thoroughly disenchanted with the Brazilian government and with the state generally. In their pursuit of life free of state or government control, they represent an extremist backlash to the years of military dictatorship and political repression. Although some of Bom Jesus' intellectuals have read and cite Proudhon and Kropotkin, their own interpretive slant smacks more of North American libertarianism and "rugged individualism." Absent in their political philosophy is any socialist or collectivist alternatives to the state. Hence I use the qualifying term *anomic*. Among the poor and desperate men and women of the Alto do Cruzeiro, a strong anarchist impulse also exists, expressed mainly in the negative statement that nothing in the democratic or party-based system represents their interests. "The only time I will ever work in a political campaign in Bom Jesus," stated an ex-president of UPAC, "it would have to be to convince the people of the Alto to stay away from the elections." See also Drummond 1986.

5. The local elections held in 1988 overturned this local dynasty and put into place a young *prefeito* from the working class of Bom Jesus, a self-made man of new wealth earned through commercial interests and, in particular, ownership of the main local radio station of Bom Jesus. The new *prefeito* is a self-described socialist whose primary commitments to date have been in the area of various "modernization" projects and street parties, earning him the pet name *o prefeito carnavalesco*—"the carnavalesque mayor," but it doesn't translate well.

3. RECIPROCITY AND DEPENDENCY

1. The subject of patron-client relations has been treated exhaustively by anthropologists working in peasant communities in Mexico, Central America, and South America as well as elsewhere. George Foster's (1961) article, "The Dyadic Contract," remains an early but classic description of patron-client relations. Foster, like many social anthropologists following him, emphasized the utilitarian and voluntaristic nature of the exchanges between equals as well as those between patrons and their dependent clients where the question of free choice is debatable. Patron-dependent and patron-client relations in Brazilian society have been examined by, among others, Wagley 1971; Harris 1952; Greenfield 1979; Forman 1975; Forman and Riegelhaupt 1979; Johnson 1971. James Scott (1972) has discussed patron-client relations in the context of political ferment among peasants in Southeast Asia.

2. My reservations concerned whether in so doing I was participating in just the kind of patron-client relations that were ultimately detrimental to the foresters in their dealings with oppressive bosses and social superiors. Short of open rebellion, however, dependence on various intermediaries remains one of the squatters' only effective resources against those who control their lives. In fact, Roberto da Matta (1979:144–168) might argue to the contrary that the role of *despachante* is an

organic Brazilian gesture, one that mediates the perennial tensions between equality and hierarchy in modern Brazil, so that the *despachante* can meet the seemingly imperviously "neutral" (but powerful) public official with influence and status claims of his or her own that can equalize the relationship to the benefit of the "client."

Perhaps now I ought to explain just how I fit into this local dynamic as an outsider, yet one who lived in close proximity with the people of the Alto for relatively long stretches of time. During the first period of my stay in the mid-1960s, I was young, single, and far from affluent. My unstylish clothes and the few possessions I brought with me to Brazil revealed a working-class background that made me the envy of few, and not even the poor of the Alto expected me to assume the role of a mighty benefactor to the community. To the contrary, it was more often the reverse as I sought "patronage," or at least a place to shower and eat, from time to time among the more affluent families of Bom Jesus.

On the Alto I was "adopted" into a small, extended family formed by a mother (whom to this day I still know only as Mãe), her sister (Tia), and her three adult daughters, Antonieta, Biu, and Lordes, and their families. During those early years I was godmother to several Alto children, and I did my best to help my *comadres* in raising them, although the financial support I offered was minimal. I tried to save what I could from my monthly Peace Corps stipend of fifty dollars to initiate or rescue small community projects on the Alto. My relations with the people of the Alto were relatively easy and equitable, although I had my share of enemies as well as good friends. There was, however, one exception to the rule of equity—it was the courtesy title of *dona* that was put before my name, a term usually reserved for older, or at least married, women. The affectionate but vexing and anachronistic title, which has stuck with me to this day, helped to put a little distance between myself and the young men of the Alto, thus allowing me more freedom of movement and action than most single women of my age enjoyed. But it did not put so much distance that I did not seriously entertain a marriage proposal from the handsome, eldest son of Seu Tavares, the water carrier.

I lived in several households on the Alto for varying periods of time, and I accepted hospitality and meals from people who had little to share, especially the water that an extra body required, endlessly it seemed. In exchange I gave my waking hours to the shantytown association, UPAC. My Alto neighbors and I borrowed freely from each other, sometimes without asking, a feature of Alto reciprocity that I misunderstood at first but that I learned to participate in with some enjoyment. During these early years I came to know the residents of the Alto as destitute but still relatively independent people who survived through patterns of mutual exchange and codependency not dissimilar to the patterns of reciprocity that Carol Stack (1974) described for the poor, urban, black community in her classic, *All Our Kin.*

When I returned in 1982 as a *doutora, professora,* and wife and mother to an apparently affluent family, my relations with the people of the Alto changed accordingly, though I did my best to call on our old ties of friendship, coresidency, and coparenthood. Because I was able to, I offered a small gratuity to the women who participated in my reproductive history sample of seventy-four households. And so I became a *patroa* of sorts, and dozens of women in the sample besieged me with requests for much needed assistance in their daily lives. Initially I tried to "collectiv-ize" the gifts that I made, offering to purchase tools and supplies for the renovation of the community creche, fix the ailing public water pump, and host a community *festa* in celebration of the twentieth anniversary of UPAC. But the requests for individual help continued, and like everyone else in the community, I had to make choices about which requests I would honor and which I would dismiss. Triage played a part in these decisions, just as it did for the women and mothers of the Alto. In all, the constant barrage of daily requests from *moradores* was something of a game, a bit of a diversion not unlike numbers games such as the ever-popular *bichos*. The failure to "deliver" never meant the end of a relationship, just as the occasional "coming through" with a request never meant more than that the lines of communication, friendship, and mutual dependencies were open. In 1987 I began keeping a list of the items most frequently requested:

—Medications: especially those that could not be easily gotten at the free dispensaries, especially various expensive antibiotics, worm medications, painkillers, tonics, and nerve pills, including requests for phenothiazines
—Food: especially craved "luxury" items such as sweet breads and cakes, soft drinks, cheese, and hot dogs to tempt appetites that were often described as "turned off" or "fed up" with the staples of beans, cornmeal, rice, and manioc
—Four-hundred-gram cans of Nestlé's Nestogeno powdered milk "formula" for the current baby of the household
—Cigarettes
—Bus fares to the capital city or as far away as Rio or São Paulo for *moradores* in search of work
—Sacks of cement and house tiles for the construction of an outhouse or for the repair of a house damaged by floods
—Soccer balls and soccer T-shirts
—Sponsorships: first birthday parties and baptismal celebrations; wedding parties; wakes and burial arrangements; Xangô festivals (Afro-Brazilian possession religion), which includes the purchase of special fabrics for the appropriate vestments honoring a particular saint or *orixá* as well as ropes of tobacco, marijuana, alcohol, candy, incense, perfume, and special ritual foods, depending on the particular "tastes" of the *orixá* to be honored; costumes for a small *carnaval bloco*, an organized group of dancers
—Clothing: a special dress to present oneself to a potential employer, whether a *senhor de engenho* (a plantation owner) or the local dona of a wealthy household in Bom Jesus; work clothes, especially for women working for the first time in sugarcane; shoes, shirts, shorts, or skirts for new schoolchildren (also pencils and notebooks); requests for any (and all) items from my or my family's personal wardrobe, including even our few rings and watches, but also articles of clothing that, unlaundered, still carried our own *cheirinho*, distinctive body scent, so that the memory of ourselves and of our time together could be preserved
—False teeth: partial, plastic, and very inexpensive dentures, requested especially by teenage girls who had come to think of their missing teeth as unattractive

In turn, the people of the Alto would try to find ways to be "useful," as, for example, in generously "lending" me their children. The children, whom I didn't know quite what to do with at first, turned out to be very useful indeed as messengers, carrying information back and forth between distant homes and to workers in the fields whom I wished to visit or interview. Often my Alto friends would surprise me with touching (and far too expensive) going away presents that took into account my own special "tastes" and preferences, which they had carefully noted. In all, reciprocity and even just talk about reciprocity made life more bearable and more secure-feeling for everyone, myself included. It was, after all, how social life was constructed in the *mata* before these men and women had been transformed into wage earners totally dependent on money to satisfy all their basic needs as well as their newly acquired "addictions."

But, now that I have said all this, did it make me nervous? Yes, at times I had my doubts, especially following an argument with my radical friend, João Mariano, who once taunted me, "Did you ever think, Dona Nancí, that some of the people on the Alto only like you because you give them things?" "And have you ever thought," I taunted in return, "that they only tolerate you, *despite* your politics, because you are so tall and *bonito?*"

For what is human interaction based on, after all, if not on the circulation and exchange of our small personal gifts, such as they are?

3. Breast-feeding has almost vanished on the Alto do Cruzeiro. Nailza, who is part Guarani Indian, took great pleasure in so doing.

4. In a familistically patriarchal world such as that of rural Northeast Brazil, the model for all authority is the paterfamilias, who rules absolutely and often arbitrarily over the lives of his wife (or wives), concubines, and children. The woman to whom he may delegate some household authority—his *senhora* or *dona da casa*—rules her children or servants in the name of her husband's authority and charisma. And so it is still appropriate to refer to a female *patroa* and her relations to her dependents as an aspect of patriarchal familism. In teaching literacy and engaging in critical consciousness raising at an UPAC meeting in the 1960s, I took the words *pãe, padre, patrão*, and so on to teach about a stem word and to open a critical discussion about the branching social system of paternalism in the Northeast.

4. DELÍRIO DE FOME

1. *Doença de cão* may also refer to any unholy or tainted sickness, a sickness from the devil (the *cão*, in this instance) rather than a natural sickness, meaning to the *moradores* a sickness sent from God in the sense that *all* events are ordained by God.

2. The Jewish community in Warsaw was the first population to suffer starvation at the hands of the Germans. The medical aspects of this prolonged "natural experiment" in human starvation were recorded in a volume edited by Apfelbaum-Kowalski 1946. The German blockade of Leningrad during World War II produced a famine there during the winter and spring of 1941–1942, documented with respect to conditions found in the local hospitals (see Brozek, Chapman, & Keyes 1948). Medical observations and reports on the physical and physiological conditions of those unfortunates interned in European prison and concentration camps during World War II are many (see, for example, those by Zimmer, Weill, & Dubois 1944; Lipscomb 1945; Nirenberski 1946; Dols & Van Arcken 1946).

3. In *The Nuer*, E. E. Evans-Pritchard's classic, he commented on the role of food scarcity in shaping economic and ritual activities among those African pastoralists.

4. Nevertheless, there are excellent social historical accounts of the experience of famine in Africa in the twentieth century. See McCann 1987; Vaughan 1987.

5. See Birenbaum 1971; E. Cohen 1954; Frankel 1959; Hardman 1958; Levi 1969; Poller 1961.

6. This list represents the normal Saturday *sesta básica* for the family, based on

several marketing trips with Seu Manoel during 1987–1988. The variation from week to week and month to month was small, with the exception of June–August, when corn replaced rice and *macarrão* (spaghetti). Fruit entered the diet when Terezinha's mother sent some from her *roçado* in the country.

7. See the Bibliography for a partial list of Nelson Chaves's publications.

8. At a recent Rockefeller Foundation–sponsored conference, Overcoming Hunger in the 1990s (Rockefeller Foundation Bellagio Study and Conference Center, Villa Serbelloni, Italy, November 13–17, 1989), a distinction was drawn between "actual" hunger and "medical" hunger. Actual, virtual, or "true" hunger was taken to refer to hunger from insufficient food. "Medical" hunger was used to refer to all those intervening medical conditions (parasites and worm infestations, in particular) that interfere with the body's ability to utilize the food nutrients that are ingested. It was argued by some of the participants (representing UNICEF, the Carter Presidential Center, the World Hunger Program, the International Food Policy Research Institute, and the World Bank) that "medical hunger" should not be included within "world hunger" programs because the condition is independent of the availability of food resources. It is a view that is hard to defend in light of the experience of hunger, both actual and medical, in Northeast Brazil.

9. The preference for foods served in a mixture, rather than eaten separately or in small, measured "courses," was shared by affluent residents of Bom Jesus da Mata. Seu Reinaldo, for example, a local sugar baron who in 1987 had recently returned from a holiday in Europe, amused house visitors with the story of how he had bullied a waiter in the south of France, telling him to bring out all the food ordered at one time so that Reinaldo could eat them properly mixed up on the same plate. Roberto da Matta also has something to say on this aspect of Brazilian popular culture:

> Actually, *farinha* serves as a kind of cement to link all of the dishes and foods [in a typical meal]. While the English and French use sauces specific to each dish, we [Brazilians] have foods that are multiplied into a variety of dishes each with its own blend of broths, sauces and juices. It's important to emphasize that food which is a mixture is a kind of perfect image of its own making in that it is the blend of foods that brings out and adds to its flavor. This itself is one of the most important patterns that transforms the ordinary act of eating into a Brazilian gesture. (1989:63)

5. NERVOSO

1. Biu is a common nickname for both men and women among the dozens of Severinas and Severinos of the Alto, including several couples whose members are both named Biu.

2. The TAT consists of a series of standardized pictures that reflect everyday characters in a variety of poses, situations, and moods. The individual is asked to make up a story for each picture and to tell what each character in the picture is thinking and feeling. The TAT is a straightforward projective test, relatively free of cultural bias and requires no depth-psychological analysis. One can read the responses to the pictures for their manifest content; themes, dilemmas, and emotions emerge right on the surface.

3. Foster's much maligned model of the "limited good" worldview of Mexican peasants who acted *as if* all material and psychological "goods" were in short supply so that one man or woman's gain was seen as another's loss is deficient only in its failure to analyze the social relations of production that make this worldview an

accurate assessment of the social reality in which most contemporary peasants live. More important, however, is the precapitalist orientation to "goods" valued for use and not for surplus that is encoded in this peasant philosophy, a philosophy that is antagonistic to capitalist relations of work and production. Limited good thinking can be seen as a healthy antidote to the industrial capitalist fantasy of "unlimited goods." It is only a negative view if one sees the world through the lens of the Protestant work ethic and all that it entails.

4. In 1968 in Medellín the Catholic bishops of Latin America recommended the formation of ecclesiastical base communities through which a new "popular church" dedicated to a "preferential option for the poor" could be put into direct practice. These base communities are usually neighborhood organizations where people gather to reflect on the scriptures in light of their everyday practical problems in living. The Brazilian theologian of liberation, Clodovis Boff (1978), called for a grounded, down-to-earth theology, a *teologia-pé-no-chão* in which priests would serve as Gramscian organic intellectuals directly connected with popular struggles for liberation.

5. "All men are intellectuals," wrote Gramsci, "but all men do not have the function of intellectuals in society" (1957:121). "Organic" intellectuals are those who arise out of, and are clearly identified with, a specific class. An impoverished or a working class is as capable of producing its own intellectuals as is the bourgeoisie.

6. Marina Cardoso similarly reported the generalized use of major tranquilizers by clinic doctors in Rio de Janeiro for cases of neurosis, organic diseases, and for chronic pain. Young and inexperienced doctors working in public clinics and treating mainly poor and working-class patients tended to "experiment" with drugs. One doctor explained, "I started to practice 'psychiatry' after I began to see how often patients' complaints had no observable organic basis. Since psychotropic drugs were much in vogue and were giving good results, and following the advice of M [a senior practitioner], I adopted the practice, too" (1987:107, my translation). Other doctors in Cardoso's study had a pragmatic attitude toward Haldol, a major antipsychotic drug with powerful and dangerous side effects, which they used for neurotic (as well as psychotic) patients though using a smaller dosage. One doctor reported using Haldol in a case of "incurable" diarrhea: "In principle, of course, I was opposed to the idea," he said. "But I ended up accepting it. There was no other solution than to tranquilize the patient. I'm not going to be stuck with a patient for whom there is no cure" (108, my translation).

6. EVERYDAY VIOLENCE

1. The *papa-figos* of Brazilian folklore are the "liver-eating" monsters that are used throughout Brazil to frighten badly behaved children, especially those who refuse to go to sleep at night. Papa-Figo comes by stealth and grabs the child away to devour in secret her tasty liver. This is obviously a traditional form of the organ-stealing rumor. Freyre (1986a:339) recounted the widespread Papa-Figo story in Pernambuco told of a certain rich man who could eat nothing but children's livers. He had his black servants go out everywhere with gunny sacks to look for young, fat ones.

2. In May 1990 Anthony Zielinski (*New York Times*, July 19, 1990 [AP]), a young member of the Milwaukee County Board of Supervisors, proposed that the county government sell the organs of dead welfare recipients to private medical companies, without their prior consent, as a way of reducing the county's public burial expenses.

The supervisor introduced his bill by saying, "If these people can't help society while they're alive, maybe they can help it when they're dead." Criticism from welfare rights and homeless organizations forced Zielinski to drop the proposed bill and to apologize. Nevertheless, another proposal—that welfare recipients be invited to sign forms permitting the county to donate their organs after death—is still under consideration.

3. "Until recently," wrote Emmanuel Thorne and Gilah Lagner, "it was possible to joke that the value of the body, based on its chemical constituents, was about $1.98. Now its value exceeds $200,000 and is rising. Tissue is being harvested for transplantation, research and diagnostic and therapeutic products. . . . However repugnant the idea, the body now has economic value that cannot be wished away or ignored" (1986:23).

4. See also Kligman (1988), for a fascinating discussion of virginity and death in Transylvania.

7. TWO FEET UNDER AND A CARDBOARD COFFIN

1. The German psychoanalyst Heinz Hartmann developed the concept of the "average expectable environment of the child" in his *Ego Psychology and the Problem of Adaptation*. The term refers to the role of biological and social adaptation in the survival of the infant during the first critical months of its life. Under normal situations, Hartmann wrote, "the newborn human and his average expectable environment are adapted to each other from the very first moment. That no infant can survive under certain atypical (on the average, not expectable) conditions and that traumata certainly are integral to typical development do not contradict this proposition" (1958:51). One problem for the anthropologist concerns the ill-defined notions of what is to be considered "average" and "expectable" in the given environment. Here I am suggesting, not without a certain amount of irony, that the "average expectable environment" for the neonate of the Alto do Cruzeiro is one that is filled with risk and danger so that "death" is the most "average and expectable" outcome for these infants.

2. The great epidemiologic transition refers to that period in modern European social history when an earlier mortality pattern characterized by a very high rate of infant mortality, with an additional scattering of deaths over all other age groups, came to be replaced by the "modern" clustering of deaths at the higher age groups, so that death became relatively "standardized" at old age and consequently seemed less "chaotic" and unpredictable. This transformation began in Europe around 1825 and was "completed" by the first decades of the twentieth century.

3. The word *kwashiorkor* first appears in the 1976 *A Supplement to the Oxford English Dictionary*, vol. 2 (H–N), edited by R. W. Burchfield, p. 561. The dictionary traces the word's introduction to the English-speaking world to a physician, C. D. Williams, writing in *The Lancet* on November 16, 1935, who noted its uses in Africa. In 1951 G. C. Shattuck included kwashiorkor in his *Diseases of the Tropics*. The pediatric disease first gained real currency, however, through the writings of D. B. Jelliffe in his second edition of *The Diseases of Children in the Subtropics and Tropics* (1970:vii). Before the "discovery" of tropical and subtropical kwashiorkor, there were only infantile and childhood wasting diseases of "uncertain seat" (Wright 1988:306).

4. This is a reference to the UNICEF-sponsored "child survival" campaign, which has attempted not only to decrease rates of child mortality worldwide but to establish a universal and "fundamental principle which UNICEF believes should affect the course of political, social, and economic progress in all nations over the next decade." This "principle of first call" proposes that the lives and normal development of children should have "first call" on a society's concerns, resources, and capacities. It establishes that "the child should be able to depend on that commitment in good times and in bad, in normal times and in times of emergency, in times of peace as in times of war, in prosperity and in times of economic recession" (Grant 1990:7). These are pretty words, indeed, but so out of touch with the realities in which most of the world's children (in advanced industrial as well as "developing" nations) live out their often brief and battered existences that they strike me as meaningless . . . as meaningless as the WHO slogan calling for "Health for All by the Year Two Thousand."

5. Brazil's national system of vital statistics was established in 1974, although data for the municipalities of state capitals and large towns are often available for earlier dates. Although vital statistics for São Paulo and a few other states are reasonably complete and consistent with estimates from the census, they still fall short of the reliability and completeness one would want for an analysis of national trends and differentials (see Altman & Ferreira 1979:55). A thorough assessment of the available data on Brazilian fertility and mortality during 1950–1976 was carried out by the National Academy of Sciences Committee on Population and Demography 1983.

6. It has been well documented that preterm and low-birth-weight infants are at a considerably higher risk for mortality in the early months of life. F. C. Barros, C. G. Victoria, J. P. Vaughn, and A. M. B. Teixeira (1987) examined the causes of 215 infant deaths in a population-based cohort of 5,914 infants from southern Brazil: 87 percent of the deaths occurred in the first six months of life, and 53 percent of the infants who died were of low birth weight as compared to just 7.9 percent of the survivors.

7. It is curious that some American anthropologists have been seduced by the commerciocentric values of the international business community into objecting to the Nestlé boycott on the grounds of "freedom of choice" for the women consumers (see Walters 1986; Raphael & Davis 1985). James Walters descried the "scapegoating" of the Nestlé company, which "saw its products avoided, its ethics attacked, its employees demoralized and its executives often vilified" (1986:21) because of the international "scandal" and boycott related to that company's infant formula advertising and marketing tactics in the developing world. He referred to the "social activism" and "moral concerns" of those Westerners involved in the boycott as self-serving, "arrogant," and harmful, even if well intentioned. He denied the relationship between the marketing of infant and baby formulas and the decline in the practice of breast-feeding in the Third World and suggested that the critics and advocates sought to "save babies" not only from "self-interested formula producers, but also . . . from Third World women who opted to use substitutes." Infant formulas, he maintained, "can free mothers to contribute more directly to the well-being of the community and family while maintaining the well-being of children" (21). Walters cited research showing that in the transition from subsistence to cash economies, fewer women worldwide initiate breast-feeding, while those who do terminate it sooner. Rather than critique the economic forces that have forced poor women into exploitative relations of wage labor, Walters argued that the critics of

Nestlé are interfering with the "freedom" of choice and "economic development" of women in the Third World, who are playing an "increasingly vital role in providing incomes for their family." This assumes that when women were involved in subsistence production, they were not playing a similarly "vital" role in the maintenance of their families and communities.

Along the same lines Dana Raphael and Flora Davis argued on behalf of women's right to choose whatever patterns of infant feeding "feel right" to them. Raphael and Davis wrote that women "should have the right to make their own choices about how to feed their infants—just as we do—and most will act wisely, just as we would" (1985:147). The authors argued for a traditional scientific "neutrality" that is "neither pro- nor anti-industry, pro- nor anti-advocacy" (135), and they cautioned that political advocacy that in any way "limits the choices" available to women (such as the regulation and control of infant formulas) "wrongly foist[s] our biases onto others" (147).

The idea of women's right to choose is, of course, a powerful ideological tool that has been used both for and against women, especially poor women for whom little choice of any kind exists. Representatives of the Upjohn Company, the manufacturer of the "morning after" contraceptive injection Depo-Provera (that was linked with cases of uterine cancer) likewise opposed Food and Drug Administration regulation of the sale of the product on the principle of "free choice" for the individual consumer. Those social scientists and anthropologists advocating free choice in the question of infant formulas are neither neutral nor objective observers; they are promoting a bourgeois notion of freedom that neglects the extent to which women's lives (and "choices") are constrained by external social and economic contingencies. Saying this is not to deny women agency or free will but rather to suggest that choices do not exist in a kind of free-market vacuum; the larger context of "necessity" and human needs must always be considered.

8. A statistical survey published by the Fundação Oswaldo Cruz (1986) reported that only 35 percent of *rural* Pernambucan women (aged fifteen to forty-four) used any form of contraception. Of these, 12.3 percent were using the birth control pill, 12.6 percent were sterilized, and 10.1 percent were using other methods.

9. During the period of slavery, however, the African priests did not forbid abortion. Instead, voluntary abortion, effected through mixtures of esoteric poisons from toxic plants, were used to "cause wombs big with future slaves to abort" (Bastide 1978:67). Bastide noted that although whites "encouraged slaves to breed," the slave birthrate remained quite low in *Nordestino* plantation society, at least in part because both contraception and abortion were practiced, with the help of Afro-Brazilian religious leaders, as a gesture of resistance (1978:421, n. 40).

8. (M)OTHER LOVE

1. The thesis of this preliminary article was challenged in a detailed and thoughtful critique by Nations and Rebhun 1988. The controversy occasioned by that piece was also discussed in Brazil; see Bonalume Neto 1989. Controversy of a more heated and popular nature followed the publication of my 1989 article.

2. I am indebted to Gail Kligman for this felicitous phrase.

3. See, in particular, the writings of Scrimshaw 1978 and Cassidy 1980, 1987 for rural Guatemala; B. Miller 1981, 1987 for rural northern India; and deVries 1987 for

Kenya. For correlates in our own war-torn inner-city neighborhoods and neglected rural zones, see Halperin and Morrow 1989.

4. See Haraway 1985. In place of a dichotomous, universal gender modeled on binary sex, Donna Haraway and other radical feminists have substituted a "cyborg heteroglossia."

5. Judith Ungar 1988 revealed her own chaotic and infanticidal impulses toward her crying infant, Ethan: "Every mother has tried to quiet a crying baby. A woman who quiets her baby permanently raises a mirror that we 'good' mothers are reluctant to face, lest someone resembling us stare back."

6. Traditional, or folk, Catholicism provides many instances of infanticidal practices related to spiritual beliefs among the popular classes. Jean-Claude Schmitt in his social historical study of the thirteenth-century French cult to St. Guinefort, the holy greyhound, offered details of an infanticidal rite that persisted among the Catholic peasantry for several centuries up through the early modern period in rural France. A frail or ailing child, suspected of being a changeling or a devil child, was carried by his or her mother and a traditional healing woman (a "witch-woman") to the outdoor pilgrimage site dedicated to St. Guinefort. There various offerings were made to the dog saint, and the child's swaddling clothes were hung up on bushes. The mother and the healing woman stood on either side of two trees and tossed the naked infant back and forth while praying that the fairy spirits take back the sick "changeling" and return the healthy child that was stolen. The mother then left the infant alone and out of sight and earshot for as long as it took a candle to burn out. If the child was still alive when the woman returned, she assumed that the baby had passed the test and was a true human child. If it died, it was a changeling and had gone back to the fairies (1983:71–73). The author noted that this rite "must clearly have caused the deaths of a fair number of children" (82). The clergy tried to purge the countryside of these folk Catholic rituals, and Stephen of Bourbon, a holy inquisitor, accused the mothers of infanticide. To the mothers, however, the whole purpose of the rite was to identify their real infants and *save* them.

7. The principal manifestation of acute, unremedied infantile diarrhea is severe dehydration, which produces a metabolic electrolyte imbalance in the body. The normal water content of the body, 50–60 percent of body weight, can be reduced in severe pediatric diarrheas to a mere 10–15 percent of body weight. The chemical imbalance (metabolic acidosis) throws the tiny body into shock. Such infants often display prominent central nervous system disturbances that can include lethargy, coma, muscular rigidity, exaggerated reflexes, and convulsions. There may also be compensatory hyperventilation and subdural effusions (Silver, Kempe, & Bruyn 1983:78–79). With severe dehydration, one also encounters depression of the anterior fontanelle and skin discoloration (cyanosis) accompanying the electrolyte disorders (abnormalities of serum sodium, potassium, and bicarbonate) in infants and small babies (70–71). An excess of sodium in body fluids resulting from water loss can lead to convulsions and death. Potassium deficiency causes various neuromuscular disturbances, including a reflexic paralysis. (See also Weiner & Epstein 1970.) Obviously, Alto women are excellent observers of the key signs and symptoms of severe infant distress.

8. In cases of severe pediatric diarrhea with hypernatremia (an excess of sodium in body fluids resulting from radical loss of water), there can be serious, long-term complications, some of which mimic the symptoms of *Nordestino* child sickness. Such infants often display prominent central nervous system disturbances, including

lethargy, coma, muscular rigidity, exaggerated reflexes, convulsions, and elevated levels of cerebrospinal fluid protein. Intracranial bleeding and subdural effusions are also seen. In severe cases permanent central nervous system damage may occur (see Silver, Kempe, & Bruyn 1983:78–79). But it is also the case that convulsive seizures are relatively common in children, resulting from central nervous system and other infections (meningitis, encephalitis, and tetanus are the most common), high fever, trauma to the brain, certain drugs and food toxins, or unknown causes. Long-term studies indicate that about 65 percent of young children suffering a febrile seizure will have no subsequent seizures, 32 percent will have one or more further episodes, and only 2 percent will actually go on to develop epilepsy by age seven (488–489).

9. OUR LADY OF SORROWS

1. See Aries 1962, Badinter 1980, de Mause 1974, Dyhouse 1978, Fox and Quitt 1980, Laslett 1965, J. Lewis 1980, Ross 1986, Shorter 1975, Stone 1977, and Walvin 1982, among others.

2. See Klaus and Kennell 1976, 1982; Klaus, Jeraud, and Kreger 1972; Lozoff, Brittenham, and Trause 1977. The reductionist versions of the maternal bonding thesis have been critically examined and its scientific status reevaluated by a number of researchers, most forcefully by Michael Lamb (1982), in a series of critical review essays in pediatric journals in the United States that look at the generally inconclusive nature of the evidence characteristic of the bonding literature. Meanwhile, a number of longitudinal studies have failed to demonstrate any long-term effects of either negative or positive mother-infant bonding in the first weeks of life (Curry 1979; de Chateau 1980; Ali & Lowry 1981; Chess & Thomas 1982). In England Michael Rutter (1972) critically examined the extensive research on bonding, separation, and deprivation, as first outlined by John Bowlby, and found many of the premises regarding the long-term effects of disruptions and inadequacies of the maternal bond unsupported by longitudinal studies.

3. This leads me to question the bioevolutionary theory called the "infant schema," which refers to the neonate's presumed innate capacity to "attract" adults and elicit a nurturant response from caretakers. The visual characteristics of the newborn that are said to be so irresistibly "winsome" to mothers include the infant's fetal (almost amphibian) features: a high and bulging forehead, large eyes, round cheeks, full face, stubby limbs, and large head in proportion to the rest of the body. That these same characteristics in the unborn do little to dissuade women from abortion or to promote empathy with the fetus leads me to suspect the infant schema altogether. Most women seem to show more affection for infants the more human and less fetal-like they come to appear, especially when infants demonstrate an ability to smile and respond to caretakers.

4. Arthur Imhof described the change in *mentalités* that accompanied the demographic and epidemiologic transitions in Germany from the sixteenth to the twentieth centuries, especially those bearing on the value of individualism and the nature of childhood (which, Imhof argued, influenced by Aries, were "inventions" of the late nineteenth century). He noted the practice among Bavarian farmers in some cases naming all their children after the paterfamilias: "By means of this two-fold, three-fold, four-fold, or, in one extreme case, nine-fold [simultaneous] occupation of the name-place, it was guaranteed that, despite high infant and child mortality, there

was always a Johannes left over who would continue that management of the farm under the same name" (1985:20).

5. Repression refers to the pushing away from consciousness the unpleasant awareness of one's own (morally disallowed) aggressive or sexual impulses. Denial is a defense mechanism that concerns disturbing perceptions of the real world, of external reality. If allowed to permeate the consciousness, such perceptions cause unbearable anxiety or profound displeasure. Instead, the individual may reframe the experience as minor and inconsequential through a turning away from, or a denial of, the reality itself. It is a way of protecting the self. I am not denying the existence of individual defense mechanisms or neuroses. But I am uncomfortable when psycho-dynamic concepts are applied to normative, cultural institutions and to collective ways of thinking and feeling. I am as reluctant to label all the women of the Alto do Cruzeiro who "fail" to grieve the death of their infants as manifesting a psychological condition of "denial" or "shellshock" or "posttraumatic stress" as of labeling all those adults who easily enter into "dissociative" religious possession and trance (whether devotees of Xango or evangelical Protestantism) as "hysterics." Reliance on such psychological terminology diminishes the human condition. Moreover, it serves as a shortcut (or short-circuit) analysis that allows one to think that the task of under-standing is completed when it has only just begun.

6. I am not so radical as to suggest that there are no constituted human drives for sex, attachment, and so on; rather, I mean to say that as compared with other species, human instinctual rituals are remarkably insecure and transient. Humans are not social automatons; it is our freedom from specific behavior patterns—our biological as well as our cultural "openness"—that represents our evolutionary heritage. While we have instinctual needs, the "objects" of our drives and the timing of our desires are shaped by experience and culture.

11. CARNAVAL

1. But the first major blow against the Batista dictatorship in Cuba was struck on July 26, 1953, during *carnaval* celebrations in Santiago. Fidel Castro and some 125 followers used the *carnaval* festivities as a cover to attack the Moncada Garrison, Cuba's second largest. The attack failed, and many of the rebels were captured and subsequently tortured to death in prison. Fidel himself escaped death when the lieutenant who arrested him took him to a civilian, rather than a military, prison (McManus 1989:32).

12. DE PROFUNDIS

1. On the theory and practice of liberation theology, see Antoine 1973; Azevedo 1986; Berryman 1987; L. Boff 1984; Boff and Boff 1986; Comblin 1985; Echegaray 1984; Ferm 1986; Guitiérrez 1980; Krischke and Mainwaring 1986; Petrini 1984; Queiroz 1985.

2. After centuries of hostility toward the practice and the practitioners of Afro-Brazilian religion and spiritism, some segments of the Catholic church in Brazil have come to accept spirit possession as a powerful and legitimate form of religious expression and of ethnic identity and solidarity among many Brazilian Catholics, both black and white (see da Silva 1984).

3. This is a reference to Bertolt Brecht, the self-defined "scribbler of plays" whose dramas satirized the contradictions of modern life. Franco Basaglia, an Italian anti-institutional psychiatrist, used the traditional mental hospital as a special space to enact a social revolution in the ways humans respond to madness and irrationality. Many of his techniques for dramatizing the plight of the mentally ill are reminiscent of Brechtian theater.

Glossary

abertura—opening; democratization (in its political context)

abrigo—shelter, asylum; old folks' home

abusado—impertinent, presumptuous, fed up

acabada—finished, exhausted

agonia da morte—death throes

agreste—rural, wild, uninhabited; semiarid zone of Pernambuco where cotton is grown

alegria—joy, gladness, merriment, festivity

alijado—to push out, rid oneself of; slang for physically disabled, crippled

almas inválidas—weak, disabled souls

almas penadas—suffering, tormented souls

alto—high; top of a hill

amigado, -da—living together; illicit cohabitation

à míngua—for want of, for lack of; scarcity, neglect

amizade—friendship

analfabeto—illiterate

animação—vivacity, quickness, liveliness, expressiveness

animador, -ra do bairro—activist; one who brings community groups and activities to life

anjinho—cherub; child dressed as a little angel in a religious procession; dead infant

anjo querubim—cherub; deceased angel-baby

anojamento—nausea, deep mourning, grief

antropologia pé-no-chão—anthropology with one's feet on the ground; anthropology for everyday life; anthropological praxis

aperreado, -a—vexed, afflicted, anxious, worried

apodrecer—to spoil, rot, putrify, corrupt

assembléia geral—general assembly; large open community meeting

ataque de nervos/crise de nervos—attack or crisis of nerves

babá—nursemaid

bagaceira—shed on a sugar plantation where the bagasse, the cane trash, is stored

bagaço—refuse material of crushed sugarcane

557

Baiana—Afro-Brazilian street vendor in Salvador de Bahia

bairro—neighborhood, district, part of town

bandeja—tray, serving dish; borrowed municipal coffin made of tin and used for the bodies of the "unknown" or the murdered

baratas—cockroaches

barraca—makeshift annex to a house used for a small shop

bate-bate—to bang, thump, or knock oneself

bate-queixo—literally, "chin-knocker"; borrowed pauper's coffin

batendo papo—chat, friendly conversation; chewing the fat

beata—exceedingly devout woman, church spinster (i.e., a woman who is "married" to the church)

bêbado—to be drunk, intoxicated; a drunk or sot

belisca—to nibble

besteira—nonsense, stupidity, baloney

bloco—any organized *carnaval* group

bloco de arrastão—"dragnet" of *carnaval* dancers; dancers who hold onto a rope that separates the official *bloco* dancers from the free-spirited revelers who follow them

blocos de sujos—*carnaval blocos* made up of dancers who dirty themselves and others with ashes, motor oil, and molasses

bôbo, -a—simple, goofy, dumb; a buffoon or dunce

bóias-frias—cold vittles, grub, chow; rural wage laborers on the plantations who carry their tin lunch pans of cold beans to work

bom de menino—monthly allowance paid by the state to families with small children; children's subvention fund

bota para frente—go for it, get ahead, push onward

brabo, -a—fierce, wild

branco, -a—white, pale, fair complexioned; well-bred person, person of distinction, or European

brincadeira—game, trick; any organized fun during *carnaval*

brincar carnaval—to play, participate in *carnaval* street dancing

burocracia—bureaucracy, state; used popularly to refer to the ominous web of power that constrains, exploits, and terrorizes poor people without connections

caatinga—region of stunted vegetation or sparse forest found in the drought regions of the Northeast

caboclo, -a—copper colored; "civilized" or mestizoized Indian; person of mixed Indian and white ancestry

cabra—brave mestizo of mixed black, white, and Indian ancestry

cabra safado—scoundrel, bum, good-for-nothing man

caçula—youngest, most beloved, and indulged pet child in the family

cafezinho—small cup of strong, black, very sweet coffee (demitasse)

câmara municipal—official state room, governmental chamber

caminho—road, path

camponês, -a—peasant, rural person, rustic

cana de açúcar—sugarcane

cangaceiro—bandit, outlaw; one weighted down with the *cangaço*, or bundle of weapons, that bandits in Northeast Brazil carry

cão—dog, hound; the devil

capim—grass, hay, pasture

careca—bald; bald person

carnaval—pre-Lenten festival of license, laughter, and dance

carnavalesco—carnivalesque; anything reminiscent of the spirit of *carnaval*

carne de sol—sun-dried and salted beef

cartório civil—civil registry office

casa funerária—coffin shop

casa grande—sugar plantation big house or mansion

castigo—punishment, chastisement

catimbó—sorcery

catimbozeiro—derogatory term for a practitioner of Umbanda or Xangô

catinga—any rank or offensive smell; body odor

cesta—large reed basket used for shopping at the peasants' market and for storing food at home

chá de erva santa—tea made from the tobacco plant; the newborn infant's first liquid food in the shantytown

chafariz—public faucet or watering place; wall with projecting spouts for filling buckets

charque (or *xarque*)—beef or donkey meat jerky

chefe—boss, leader

cheiros—scent, fragrance, odor

chupar—to suck, absorb

chupeta—child's pacifier

clandestinos, -as—clandestine workers; those who work without official working papers

coitado—poor, wretched, miserable; common expression of pity

colégio—private school offering primary or secondary instruction or both

comadre—co-mother (godmother); friend; respectful term of address for midwives, healing women, and praying women, those entrusted with the well-being of children and other family members

como Deus quiser—as God wills or wishes; common expression of resignation

compadre—co-father (godfather); particularly close or intimate friend

companheiro, -ra—companion, comrade, dear friend ("in the struggle"); spouse, mate, or lover

conformação—resignation, compliance, acquiescence, acceptance

conscientização—consciousness raising, awareness raising; clarification-of-thought community meetings where class, gender, and power relations are discussed

conselheiro, -ra—counselor, adviser, wise person

coração santo—sacred heart

coronelismo—system of rule by local, despotic big "bosses" called "coronels" in the rural Northeast

creche—day care center

criança condenanda—condemned or doomed child

cruzados (cruzeiros)—Brazilian currency

cruzados novos—"new" Brazilian currency (in circulation in the mid-1980s)

culpa—fault, blame

cuscuz—popular Brazilian dish made of steamed cornmeal

de repente—suddenly

décimo—a tenth; end-of-the-year bonus Brazilian workers receive, usually a full month's salary

defeituoso—defective, imperfect, marred

delegacia—police headquarters, police station

delírio de fome—madness of hunger

delírio de sede—madness of thirst

dentes recluído—trapped teeth, teeth that fail to appear or that retreat into the gums; potentially fatal folk pediatric illness of delayed or interrupted teething, probably resulting from severe malnutrition

dentição—teething, teething illness

depósito de ossos—bone depository, ossuary; collective pile of anonymous bones in the municipal cemetery

depressão—depression, dejection, the blues

deprimido, -a—depressed, dejected, downcast, heartsick

desanimação—depression, passivity, spiritlessness

desaparecidos—the disappeared; those who are "made to" disappear by the forces of law and disorder in Brazil

desconhecido—unheard of, unknown; a stranger

desejo—desire, wish, longing, appetite

desfile—parade, review, procession

desgostos—displeasure, dislike, disappointment, sorrow, grief (but *not* disgust)

despachante—paid functionary who cuts through bureaucratic red tape to get things done

difícil de criar—child who is difficult to raise in the sense that she or he will more than likely die no matter what the parents do

direitinho—right away, straight ahead, quite correct, just right

doença de criança—child sickness; doomed child syndrome

doente—sick; sick person

doido, -a—crazy; crazy, wild person; extravagantly impassioned or "sex-crazed" woman

dona de casa—female head of household

dono—boss, owner, head or chief of anything

dor—pain, suffering, affliction, sorrow, grief

doutor—doctor; person with university degree; honorary title conferred by the poor on their patrons

eleitor—voter, constituent

empregada—maid, domestic, servant

encerrar—to adjourn, bring to a close

encostado de—leaning on, propped up on, hanging on; order in which one child follows another

enfrentar—to face, confront, brave some difficulty

enganar—to deceive, delude, hoodwink

engenho—small, old-fashioned sugar mill; plantation complex

enterro—burial; funeral procession

escolas de samba—samba schools; organized groups of *carnaval* dancers, which can include several thousand members, who practice and parade together following a specific *carnaval* theme

esmola—alms, handout

fado—fate, destiny; Portuguese song of love and lament
faltar—to want, lack, fall short of something
fantasias—costumes, fancy dresses, masks; imagination, personal fantasies
farinha—flour, meal, especially manioc flour
farinha de roça—coarse, rough, unrefined manioc flour; the cheapest quality of flour
faz pena—it makes you feel bad; common expression of pity, sometimes carrying a hint of disdain
fazenda—plantation, ranch, large estate
fazendeiro—owner of a *fazenda*
fazer feira—to do one's marketing
feijão—bean
feira—open-air public market
felicidade—joy, happiness, good fortune, success
festa—festive celebration, holy day, party, gathering, entertainment
festas juninas—festive celebrations during the month of June in honor of Saints Anthony (June 13), John (June 24), and Peter and Paul (June 29)
fidalgo—a "somebody"; son of "someone"; man of the leisured class; of or pertaining to nobility
filho de criação—foster child
filho eleito—favorite, "elect" son
flagelados—afflicted ones; those whose lives are disrupted by drought or floods
fofa—soft, fluffy, cute
fofoca—gossip
foice—scythe
fome—hunger
força—strength, power, force, might
foreiro—tenant farmer
fornecedor de cana—sugarcane supplier
forró—fast-paced two-step (from the English "for all"), also known as the *arrasta-pé* (drag your foot); any noisy dance party or outdoor shindig
forte—strong, fat, healthy
fortificante—tonic
fraqueza—weakness, frailty, shortcoming, helplessness
frevo—wild, jumping *carnaval* dance

galega—fair or light-skinned person; of European-Portuguese background
garapa—fresh sugarcane juice; any sweet, cooling drink; sugar water
gasto—spent, wasted, worn, exhausted
gema—egg yolk; essence, central or vital part of something
gente—people, family members, people like oneself
gente fina—refined people; upper-class people; gentry
ginásio—lower part of secondary school
gordinho—diminuitive of *gordo* (fat); term of endearment
gosto—taste, flavor, relish
gotas de sereno—evening dew; pediatric folk ailment caused by exposure to the elements
gozar—to enjoy, take pleasure in
grilo—cricket; (slang) a problem, a complaint

inútil—useless, worthless

jeito—a skillful method, knack, air
jeitoso, -a—skillful, graceful, adroit, dexterous, handsome, appropriate
juízo—common sense, intelligence, discernment, judgment

latifúndio—large landed estate
lavadeira—washerwoman
lembrança—remembrance, memento, souvenir, keepsake, gift
loucura—insanity, madness, foolishness
luta—struggle, fight
luto—mourning, bereavement, sorrow, grief
luxo—luxury, extravagance, excess

macarrão—spaghetti
maconha—marijuana, hemp
macumbeiro—love sorcerer
madrinha—godmother
mãe—mother
mal criada—badly or poorly raised
malandragem—rascality, badness, mischievousness
malandro—scoundrel, rascal, rake, playboy
mamadeira—baby bottle
mamãe de umbigo—godmother of the navel; the one who cuts the newborn infant's cord
mandioca—common cassav, sweet manioc, tapioca root
marginal—criminal, marginal person
mata, -o—woods, forest, jungle, bush, thicket
matadouro—slaughterhouse
matuto, -a—one who comes from the *mato*; rustic, country person; any shy, backward person
mau olhado—evil eye sickness
medo—fear, dread, fright
meio-fraco—a bit weak
mela-mela—dirty-dirty: *carnaval* play with mud, soot, and ashes
meninão—huge or giant baby or child
menino da rua—street child, abandoned child
menino de engenho—child born to the family owners of a sugar mill and sugar plantation
mentira—lie, falsehood
mingau—pap, soft baby food, mush, porridge, gruel
miséria morta—deadly misery
moça—girl, young woman, virgin
mocambos—shacks in the woods; fugitive slave settlements
mole—soft, limp, flabby, tender
moleques—street urchins, ragamuffins
monocultura—single cash crop farming; plantation agriculture
moradores—inhabitants, residents, dwellers, squatters, tenants
moradores de condição—traditional rural squatters on marginal plantation lands
morros—hills
mortalha—shroud, winding sheet

morte desastrada—disastrous, calamitous, hapless death
mulato, -a—mulatto, a brown-skinned person of mixed ancestry
mulher cão—tough, forceful woman
mulheres da vida—prostitutes
município—division of local government; town and its rural environs (similar to county and county seat)
mutirão—collective work group; especially used with respect to a house raising

não tem jeito—it's hopeless
negão—tall or large black person
nego—abbreviated form of *negro;* used as term of endearment
nenê—baby
nervos, nervoso, doença de nervos—state or condition of extreme nervousness; common and potentially fatal psychosomatic folk syndrome
nojo—nausea, disgust, loathing, mourning
Nordeste—Brazilian Northeast
Nordestino—person from the Northeast
Nossa Senhora das Dores—Our Lady of Sorrows

o chente (or *o xente*)—popular expression of surprise sometimes mixed with disdain
Orixás—Afro-Brazilian pagan deity

padre—father; Catholic priest
padrinho—godfather
pai/mãe de santo—father or mother of the saints; head priest or priestess of a Xangô or Umbanda chapel
Pai Nosso—Our Father (the Lord's Prayer)
papa d'água—weak water and starch gruel fed to babies when milk is lacking
papa-figo—Brazilian liver-eating bogeyman; goblin
pardo—brown, dark skinned, mulatto
parentela—kindred, kinsfolk
parteira—midwife
partidos—political parties; any other social faction
pasmo—magical fright or shock; folk syndrome
paternalismo—paternalism
patrão—boss, employer
patrimônio—patrimony, inheritance, assets
pau de arara—parrot's perch; a derogatory term for *Nordestino* migrants to the industrialized south of Brazil
pegar—to hold, stick, catch (as in contagious)
pereba—folk term for any seriously infected sores, usually from scabies; infected insect bites
péssimo—horrible, terrible, hopeless
picolé—popsicle
pistoleiros—bandits, hired gunmen
pobrezinhos—poor people, humble people
porcaria—filth, rubbish, shit
porta-bandeira—girl or young woman who carries the flag that is the emblem of a particular *carnaval* group

posseiros—traditional peasant squatters
praça—town square
prefeito—mayor, prefect
prefeitura—city hall
preto—black, African-Brazilian
promessa—vow to a saint in return for some favor
pronto socorro—first aid, emergency room
pular—to leap, jump

quadro—square; measurement of land
qualidades—varieties
quarenta—forty; colloquial for a cornmeal mush (possibly a corruption of *polenta*)
quilombos—colonies of escaped slaves
quintal—backyard

raiva—anger, rage; rabies
rapadura—brown-sugar candy
reclamar—to complain, protest, demand
rede—hammock
regras—rules; menstruation
reis—old Brazilian currency
remédios caseiros—home remedies
remédios populares—folk remedies
repentista—troubadour; *Nordestino* challenge-and-response singing
resguardo—food and behavior prohibitions surrounding certain illnesses and dangerous life cycle events
retirantes—people escaping drought; refugees from the countryside
rezadeira—traditional healing woman; praying woman
roçado—garden plot; leased field for planting subsistence crops

sabido—wise, cunning
sabor—flavor, taste
sacanagem—dirty talk or play; any foolery
samba—Brazilian dance of African origin
sangue ruim, fraco, sujo, estragado—sick, weak, dirty, wasted blood
saudades—memory imbued with longing, sadness, and nostalgia
saudável—healthy, wholesome
seca—drought
sede—thirst
Semana Santa—Holy Week
senhor, -a de engenho—owner, boss of a sugar estate and mill
senzala—rows of slave huts on the traditional colonial sugar plantation in the Northeast
sertanejo—person from the *sertão*
sertão—hinterland, back country; remote, dry interior of Northeast Brazil
sesmaria—land grant in colonial Brazil
sítio—small farm, country place
sofrimento—suffering, misery
solteirona—old maid

soro—serum used for rehydration
susto—fright; magical fright; folk ailment

tabela—chart or schedule; calendar method of natural birth control
taipa—mud walled hut made of sticks
tanto faz—it makes no difference
telenovela—TV soap opera
tia—aunt
tostão—Brazilian nickel (no longer in circulation)
trabalhadores rurais—rural workers
trio elétrico—electric band on a motorized caravan
tristeza—sorrow, unhappiness, sadness

Umbanda—highly syncretic Afro-Brazilian spiritist religion
união—union, unity, joining
urubu—common black Brazilian vulture
usina—sugar factory in the sugarcane fields
usineiro—owner of a modern sugar mill and refinery complex

veado—queer; derogatory term for homosexual
Vedetes—Dames, Broads
velório de anjinho—angel-baby wake
vergonha—shame, embarrassment
Via Sacra—holy way; traditional Catholic Stations of the Cross
vigia—hired guard, night watchman
vingar—to avenge, revenge, win out in the end
visitadora—door-to-door public health worker and paramedic
vontade—will, wish, desire

Xangô—Afro-Brazilian spirit possession religion; African god of thunder and fire
(equated with Saint John in parts of Northeast Brazil)

zona—red-light district of a town
zona da mata—humid plantation zone of Northeast Brazil that was once thickly
forested

Dona Amor, storyteller.
Died a pauper in September
1992.

Little Irene, research assistant.
Struck by cholera in summer
1992 but escaped death (her
husband did not).

Bibliography

Abu-Lughod, Lila. 1986. *Veiled Sentiments: Honor and Poetry in a Bedouin Society.* Berkeley and Los Angeles: University of California Press.

Aguiar, Fernando. 1987. "A Desnutricão Infantil no Nordeste." Paper presented at the Forum Nacional Sobre Desnutrição, sponsored by the Academia Nacional de Medicina, Rio de Janeiro, July 6–8.

Aguiar, Niuma, ed. 1979. *The Structure of Brazilian Development.* New Brunswick, N.J.: Transaction.

Albanez, Teresa, Eduardo Bastelo, Giovanni Andrea Cornia, and Eva Jespersen. 1989. *Economic Decline and Child Survival: The Plight of Latin America in the Eighties.* Innocenti Occasional Papers, no. 1. New York: UNICEF.

Ali, Z., and M. Lowry. 1981. "Early Maternal-Child Contact: Effect on Later Behavior." *Developmental Medicine and Child Neurology* 23:337–345.

Allsebrook, Annie, and Anthony Swift. 1989. *Broken Promises.* London: Headway, Hodder, and Stoughton.

Almeida, José Americo. [1928] 1954. *A Bagaceira.* 8th ed. Rio de Janeiro: Olympio.

———. 1937. *Paraíba e Seus Problemas.* 2d ed. Porto Alegre: Livraria do Globo, Barcellos, e Bertaso.

Altman, A. M. G., and C. E. Ferreira. 1979. "Evolução de Censo Demográfico e Registro Civil como Fontes de Dados para Análise de Fecundidade e Mortalidade no Brasil." *Boletim Demográfico* 10 (2):1–85.

Amado, Jorge. 1974. *Gabriela, Clove and Cinnamon.* New York: Avon.

———. 1977. *Dona Flor and her Two Husbands.* New York: Avon.

Amaral, Amadeu. 1948. *Tradições Populares.* Rio de Janeiro: Instituto Progresso Editoral, S.A.

Americas Watch. 1991. *Rural Violence in Brazil: An Americas Watch Report.* New York: Human Rights Watch.

Amnesty International. 1988. "Brazil: Killing with Impunity." Briefing, September. New York: Amnesty International.

———. 1990. "Brazil: Torture and Extrajudicial Execution in Urban Brazil." Briefing, June. New York: Amnesty International.

Antoine, Charles. 1973. *Church and Power in Brazil.* Maryknoll, N.Y.: Orbis.

Apfelbaum-Kowalski et al. 1946. "Recherches Cliniques sur la Patologie du Systeme

Circulatoire dans la Cachexie du Famine." In *Malade de Famine*, ed. Apfelbaum-Kowalski et al., 189–225. Warsaw: American Joint Distribution Committee.

Appaduri, Arjun. In press. "Number in the Colonial Imagination." In *Orientalism and the Post-Colonial Predicament*, eds. Carol Breckenridge and Peter van der Veer. Chicago: University of Chicago Press.

Aragão, Luiz Tartei de. 1983. "Em Nome de Mãe." *Perspectivas Antropológicas da Mulher* 3:111–145.

Araújo, Alceu Maynard. 1979. *Medicina Rústica*. São Paulo: Companhia Nacional.

Aries, Philippe. 1962. *Centuries of Childhood*. New York: Vintage.

———. 1974. *Western Attitudes Toward Death from the Middle Ages to the Present*. Baltimore, Md.: Johns Hopkins University Press.

Armstrong, David. 1983. *Political Anatomy of the Body*. Cambridge: Cambridge University Press.

———. 1986. "The Invention of Child Mortality." *Sociology of Health and Disease* 8 (3):211–232.

Azevedo, Marcello. 1986. *Comunidades Eclesiais de Base e Inculturação da Fé*. São Paulo: Edições Loyola.

Badinter, Elizabeth. 1980. *Mother Love: Myth and Reality*. New York: Macmillan.

Bakhtin, Mikhail. 1981. *The Dialogic Imagination*. Austin: University of Texas Press.

———. 1984. *Rabelais and His World*. Bloomington: Indiana University Press.

Barros, F. C., C. G. Victoria, J. P. Vaughn, and A. M. B. Teixeira. 1987. "Infant Mortality in Southern Brazil." *Archives of Disease in Childhood* 62:487–490.

Basaglia, Franco. 1969. "Silence in the Dialogue with the Psychotic." *Journal of Existentialism* 6 (21):99–102.

———. 1987a. "Institutions of Violence" and "The Disease and Its Double." In *Psychiatry Inside Out: Selected Writings of Franco Basaglia*, ed. Nancy Scheper-Hughes and Anne M. Lovell, 59–86, 101–134. New York: Columbia University Press.

———. 1987b. "Peacetime Crimes: Technicians of Practical Knowledge." In *Psychiatry Inside Out: Selected Writings of Franco Basaglia*, ed. Nancy Scheper-Hughes and Anne M. Lovell, 143–168. New York: Columbia University Press.

Bastide, Roger. 1958. "O Messianismo e a Fome." In *O Drama Universal da Fome*, ed. Miguel Herédia, 52–64. Rio de Janeiro: Livraria Francisco Alves.

———. 1964. *Brasil, Terra de Contrastes*. São Paulo: Difusão Européia do Livro.

———. 1978. *The African Religions in Brazil*. Baltimore, Md.: Johns Hopkins University Press.

Bastos, Eliade. 1984. *As Ligas Camponesas*. Petrópolis: Vozes.

Batista Filho, Malaquias. 1987. *Nutrição, Alimentação e Agricultura no Nordeste Brasileiro*. Recife: Embraer.

Belmonte, Thomas. 1979. *The Broken Fountain*. New York: Columbia University Press.

Belote, James, and Linda Belote. 1984. "Suffer the Little Children: Death, Autonomy, and Responsibility in a Changing Low Technology Environment." *Science, Technology and Human Values* 9 (4):35–48.

Berger, John. 1984. *And Our Faces, My Heart, Brief as Photos*. New York: Pantheon.

Berger, John, and Jean Mohr. 1976. *A Fortunate Man: The Story of a Country Doctor*. London: Writers and Readers Cooperative.

Berryman, Phillip. 1987. *Liberation Theology*. New York: Pantheon.

Berquó, Elza. 1986. "Sobre o Declinico da Fecundidade e Anticoncepção em São Paulo." Analise Preliminai, *Nucleo de Estudos de População*—NEPO—UNICAMP, May.

Bettelheim, Bruno. 1943. "Individual and Mass Behavior in Extreme Situations." *Journal of Abnormal Social Psychology* 38 (4):417–452.

———. 1960. *The Informed Heart: Autonomy in a Mass Age.* Glencoe, Ill.: Free Press.

Bilac, Olavo. 1940. *Carnavalescos Poesias.* 18th ed. Rio de Janeiro: Fernando Alves.

Binswanger, Ludwig. 1958. "The Case of Ellen West." In *Existence*, ed. Rollo May, Ernest Angel, and Henri Ellenberger, 237–264. New York: Simon and Schuster.

Birenbaum, Halina. 1971. *Hope Is the Last to Die.* New York: Twayne.

Blok, Anton. 1974. *The Mafia of a Sicilian Village, 1860–1960.* Oxford: Blackwell.

Boff, Clodovis. 1978. *Teologia Pé-no-Chão.* Petrópolis: Vozes.

———. 1984. *Teologia e Prática: Teologia do Político e suas Mediações.* Petrópolis: Vozes.

Boff, Leonardo. 1984. *Do Lugar do Pobre.* Petrópolis: Vozes.

Boff, Leonardo, and Clodovis Boff. 1986. *Como Fazer Teologia da Libertação.* Petrópolis: Vozes.

Boltanski, Luc. 1984. *As Classes Sociais e o Corpo.* Rio de Janeiro: Graal.

Bonalume Neto, Ricardo. 1989. "Para Antropóloga, Amor Maternal é Mito Burguês." *Folha de São Paulo.* November 10, H-4.

Boserup, Ester. 1970. *Woman's Role in Economic Development.* New York: St. Martin's.

Bourdieu, Pierre. 1977. *Outline of a Theory of Practice.* Cambridge: Cambridge University Press.

Bowlby, John. 1961a. "Childhood Mourning and Its Implications for Psychiatry." *Journal of American Psychiatry* 118:481–498.

———. 1961b. "Processes of Mourning." *International Journal of Psychoanalysis* 42:317–340.

———. 1969. *Attachment.* New York: Basic Books.

———. 1973. *Separation: Anxiety and Anger.* New York: Basic Books.

———. 1980. *Loss: Sadness and Depression.* New York: Basic Books.

Brozek, Josef. 1950. "Psychology of Human Starvation." *Scientific Monthly* 70 (4):270–274.

Brozek, J., C. Chapman, and A. Keyes. 1948. "Drastic Food Restriction: Effects on Cardiovascular Dynamics." *Journal of the American Medical Association* 137:1569–1574.

Buber, Martin. 1952. "On the Suspension of the Ethical." In *The Eclipse of God: Studies in the Relation Between Religion and Philosophy*, 147–156. New York: Harper and Row.

Burns, E. Bradford. 1962. "Introduction to the Brazilian Jesuit Letters." *Mid-America* (July):181–186.

Burns, E. Bradford, ed. 1966. "The Royal Letters Granting Pernambuco to Duarte Coelho." In *A Documentary History of Brazil*, 33–49. New York: Knopf.

Caldeira, Teresa Pires do Rio. 1990. "The Experience of Violence: Order, Disorder, and Social Discrimination in Brazil." Berkeley: Department of Anthropology, University of California. Manuscript.

———. In press. "Direitos Humanos ou Privilégios de Bandidos: Desventuras da Democratização Brasileira." *Novos Estudos.*

Callahan, Daniel. 1990. *What Kind of Life: The Limits of Medical Progress.* New York: Simon and Schuster.

Calvalcanti, Helnilda. 1986. "O Delírio de Fome." *Estudos Sociais* 2 (2):461–472.

Camus, Albert. 1955. *L'Étranger.* New York: Appleton-Century-Crofts.

Cannon, Walter B. 1942. "Voodoo Death." *American Anthropologist* 44 (2):169–179.

Cardoso, Marina D. 1987. "Médicos e Clientela: Sobre a Assistência Psiquiátrica a Coletividade." Masters thesis, Universidade Federal de Rio de Janeiro, Museu Nacional.

Cassidy, Claire. 1980. "Benign Neglect and Toddler Malnutrition." In *Social and Biological Predictors of Nutritional Status, Growth, and Neurological Development,* ed. L. S. Greene and F. Johnson, 109–139. New York: Academic.

———. 1982. "Protein Energy Malnutrition as a Culture-Bound Syndrome." *Culture, Medicine, and Psychiatry* 6:325–345.

———. 1987. "Child Malnutrition and Worldview Conflict." In *Child Survival: Anthropological Approaches to the Treatment and Maltreatment of Children,* ed. Nancy Scheper-Hughes, 293–324. Dordrecht: Reidel.

Chahard, J. P., and R. Cevini, eds. 1988. *Crise e Infancia no Brasil: O Impacto das Politicas de Ajustamento Economico.* Brasília: UNICEF.

Chaves, Nelson. 1946. *O Problema Alimentar do Nordeste Brasileiro.* Recife: Livraria Editora Médica-Científica.

———. 1948. *A Subalimentação no Nordeste Brasileiro.* Recife: Imprensa Oficial.

———. 1955. *A Mata, a Terra, e o Homen no Nordeste.* Recife: Instituto do Açúcar e Alcool.

———. 1968. *Sexo, Nutrição, e Vida.* Recife: Editora Massangana, Fundação Joaquím Nabuco.

———. 1969. *O Açúcar na Nutrição.* Recife: Universidade Federal de Pernambuco.

———. 1973. *A Nutrição, o Cérebro e a Mente.* Recife: Universidade Federal de Pernambuco.

———. 1974. *Sistema Nervoso, Nutrição e Educação.* Recife: Universidade Federal de Pernambuco.

———. 1982. *Fome, Criança e Vida.* Recife: Editora Massangana, Fundação Joaquím Nabuco.

Chengappa, Raj. 1990. "The Organs Bazaar." *India Today,* July 31, 30–37.

Chess, Stella, and Alexander Thomas. 1982. "Infant Bonding: Mystique and Reality." *American Journal of Orthopsychiatry* 52 (2):213–222.

Chodorow, Nancy. 1978. *The Reproduction of Mothering.* Berkeley and Los Angeles: University of California Press.

Chomsky, Noam. 1985. *Turning the Tide: United States Intervention in Central America and the Struggle for Peace.* Boston: South End.

Choudhury, A., A. Khan, and L. Chen. 1976. "The Effects of Childhood Mortality Experiences on Subsequent Fertility." *Population Studies* 30:249–261.

Clements, Charles. 1987. Introduction, p. ix. *A Peasant of El Salvador* by Peter Gould and Stephen Stearns. Brattleboro, Vt.: Whetstone Books.

Clifford, James. 1988a. "On Ethnographic Authority." In *The Predicament of Culture: Twentieth Century Ethnography, Literature and Art,* 21–54. Cambridge, Mass.: Harvard University Press.

———. 1988b. "On Ethnographic Surrealism." In *The Predicament of Culture: Twentieth Century Ethnography, Literature, and Art,* 117–151. Cambridge, Mass.: Harvard University Press.

Clifford, James, and George E. Marcus, eds. 1986. *Writing Culture: The Poetics and the Politics of Ethnography.* Berkeley and Los Angeles: University of California Press.

Cohen, Elsie. 1954. *A Human Behavior in the Concentration Camp.* New York: Norton.

Cohen, Mark Nathan. 1989. *Health and the Rise of Civilization.* New Haven, Conn.: Yale University Press.

Cohen, Yehudi A. 1961. "Food and Its Vicissitudes: A Cross-Cultural Study of Sharing and Nonsharing." In *Social Structure and Personality,* ed. Yehudi Cohen, 312–346. New York: Holt, Rinehart, and Winston.

Cohn, Carol. 1987. "Sex and Death in the Rational World of Defense Intellectuals." *Signs* 12 (4):687–718.

Colburn, Forrest D., ed. 1989. *Everyday Forms of Peasant Resistance.* Armonk, N.Y.: Sharpe.

Comblin, José. 1985. *Jesus e a Preferência Pelos Pobres.* São Paulo: Edições Paulinas.

Connell, Kenneth Hugh. 1955. "Marriage in Ireland After the Famine." *Journal of Statistical and Social Inquiry* 19:82–103.

———. 1968. "Catholicism and Marriage in the Century After the Famine." In *Irish Peasant Society,* ed. Kenneth Hugh Connell, 113–163. Oxford: Clarendon.

Cornia, Giovanni Andrea, Richard Jolly, and Frances Stewart, eds. 1987. *Adjustment with a Human Face,* vol. 1. Oxford: Oxford University Press.

Crapanzano, Vincent. 1977. "The Writing of Ethnography." *Dialectical Anthropology* 2 (1):69–73.

———. 1985. *Waiting: The Whites of South Africa.* London: Granada.

Curry, M. A. H. 1979. "Contact During the First Hour with Wrapped or Naked Newborn." *Birth and Family Journal* 6:227–235.

Da Cunha, Euclides. 1944. *Rebellion in the Backlands.* Chicago: University of Chicago Press. (Translation of 1904. *Os Sertões.* Rio de Janeiro: Livraria Francisco Alves.)

Da Matta, Roberto. 1979. *Carnavals, Malandros, e Herois.* 3d ed. Rio de Janeiro: Zahar.

———. 1981. *Universo do Carnaval: Imagens e Reflexões.* Rio de Janeiro: Edições Pinakotheke.

———. 1983. "An Interpretation of Carnaval." *Sub/stance,* nos. 37–38:162–170.

———. 1984. "On Carnaval, Informality, and Magic: A Point of View from Brazil." In *Text, Play and Story: The Construction and Reconstruction of Self and Society,* ed. Edward M. Bruner, 230–246. Washington, D.C.: American Ethnological Society.

———. 1986. *Carnaval as a Cultural Problem: Towards a Theory of Formal Events and Their Magic.* Working Paper, no. 79. Notre Dame, Ind.: Kellogg Institute, University of Notre Dame.

———. 1987. *A Casa & a Rua.* Rio de Janeiro: Editora Guanabara.

———. 1989. *O Que Faz o Brasil, Brasil?* Rio de Janeiro: Rocco.

Da Silva, Antônio Aparecida. 1984. *Quando os Atabaques Batem.* Publicação Popular, no. 2. São Paulo: Edições Paulinas.

Dassin, Joan, ed. 1986. *Torture in Brazil: A Report by the Archdiocese of São Paulo.* New York: Random House. (Translation of 1985. *Brasil: Nunca Mais.* Petrópolis: Vozes.)

Daube, David. 1983. "Black Hole." *Rechtshistorisches Journal* (Frankfurt) 2:177–193.

———. 1987. *Appeasement or Resistance and Other Essays on New Testament Judaism.* Berkeley and Los Angeles: University of California Press.

Davies, James. 1983. *Human Nature and Politics.* Westport, Conn.: Greenwood.

Davis, Dona. 1963. *Blood and Nerves.* St. John's Institute of Social and Economic Research, Memorial University of Newfoundland.

Davis, Natalie Zemon. 1978. "Women on Top: Symbolic Sexual Inversion and Political Disorder in Early Modern Europe." In *Symbolic Inversion in Art and Society,* ed. Barbara Babcock, 147–190. Ithaca, N.Y.: Cornell University Press.

De Andrade, Manoel Correia. 1980. *The Land and People of Northeast Brazil.* Albuquerque: University of New Mexico Press.

De Andrade, Mário. 1941. "O Movimento Modernista." In *Aspectos da Literatura Brasileira,* 231–255. São Paulo: Martins.

De Castro, Josué. 1952. *The Geography of Hunger.* Boston: Little, Brown.

———. 1969. *Death in the Northeast.* New York: Random House.

———. 1983. *Fome, a Tema Proibido: Ultimos Escritos de Josué de Castro,* ed. Anna Maria de Castro. Petrópolis: Vozes.

De Certeau, Michel. 1980. "On the Oppositional Practices of Everyday Life." *Social Text* 3:3–43.

———. 1984. *The Practice of Everyday Life.* Berkeley and Los Angeles: University of California Press.

De Chateau, Paul. 1980. "Parent-Neonate Interaction and Its Long-Term Effects." In *Early Experience and Early Behavior,* ed. E. G. Simmel, 109–181. New York: Academic.

De Jesus, Carolina Maria. 1962. *Child of the Dark.* New York: Dutton. (Translation of 1960. *Quarto de Despejo.* Rio de Janeiro: Livraria Francisco Alves.)

De Léry, Jean. [1558] 1880. *Histoire d'une Voyage Fait en la Terre du Brésil.* Paris: Lemerre.

Della Cava, Ralph. 1970. *Miracle at Juazeiro.* New York: Columbia University Press.

De Mause, Lloyd. 1974. *The History of Childhood.* New York: Harper and Row.

De Mello, Cecilia, and Nancy Scheper-Hughes. 1988. *O Carnaval Marginal.* Department of Anthropology, University of California, Berkeley. Videotape.

De Melo Filho, Talvarez. 1984. *Stories That My Father Told Me.* Recife: Published privately.

Des Pres, Terrence. 1976. *The Survivor: An Anatomy of Life in the Death Camps.* New York: Oxford University Press.

Deutsch, Helene. 1937. "Absence of Grief." *Psychoanalytic Quarterly* 6:12–22.

Devereux, George. 1967. *From Anxiety to Method in the Behavioral Sciences.* New York: Humanities.

DeVries, Martin W. 1987. "Cry Babies, Culture, and Catastrophe: Infant Temperament Among the Masai." In *Child Survival: Anthropological Approaches to the Treatment and Maltreatment of Children,* ed. Nancy Scheper-Hughes, 165–186. Dordrecht: Reidel.

Didion, Joan. 1982. *Salvador.* New York: Pocket Books.

Dols, M. J., and D. J. M. Van Arcken. 1946. "Food Supply and Nutrition in the Netherlands During and After World War II." *Milbank Memorial Fund Quarterly* 24:319–355.

Dominguez, Luis Arturo. 1960. *Velorio de Angelito.* 2d ed. Caracas: Ediciones del Ejecutivo del Estado Trujillo, Imprenta Oficial Estado Trujillo.

Douglas, Mary. 1970. *Natural Symbol.* New York: Vintage.

Doyal, Lesley, with Imogen Pennell. 1981. *The Political Economy of Health.* Boston: South End.

Drummond, Jack Cecil. 1947. "Nutritional Requirements of Man in the Light of Wartime Experience." Eleventh Glukstein Memorial Lecture, London.

Drummond, José Augusto. 1986. "Elementos de uma Análise Política Anarquista." *Estudos Sociais* 2 (2):485–504.

Duarte, Luíz Fernando. 1986. *Da Vida Nervosa.* Rio de Janeiro: Vozes.

DuBois, Cora. 1941. "Food and Hunger in Alor." In *Language, Culture and Personality: Essays in Memory of Edward Sapir,* ed. L. Spier, A. I. Halowell, and S. S. Newman, 272–281. Menasha, Wisc.: Spier Memorial Publication Fund.

———. 1944. *The People of Alor: A Social-Psychological Study of an East Indian Island.* Minneapolis: University of Minnesota Press.

Dubos, Rene J. 1960. *The Mirage of Health: Utopias, Progress and Biological Change.* London: Allen and Unwin.

Dumont, Louis. 1970. *Homo Hierarchicus.* Chicago: University of Chicago Press.

Durkheim, Emile. 1915. *The Elementary Forms of the Religious Life.* New York: Macmillan.

Dyhouse, Carol. 1978. "Working-Class Mothers and Infant Mortality in England, 1895–1914." *Journal of Social History* 12 (2):248–267.

Eastwell, Harry D. 1982. "Voodoo Death and the Mechanism for the Dispatch of the Dying in East Arnhem, Australia." *American Anthropologist* 84 (1):5–18.

Ebelot, Alfredo. 1943. *La Pampa: Costumbres Argentinas.* Buenos Aires: Alfer and Vays.

Eberly, S. S. 1988. "Fairies and the Folklore of Disability: Changelings, Hybrids, and the Solitary Fairy." *Folklore* 99:59–77.

Echegaray, Hugo. 1984. *The Practice of Jesus.* Maryknoll, N.Y.: Orbis.

Engel, George. 1986. "A Life Setting Conducive to Illness: The Giving Up–Given Up Complex." *Annals of Internal Medicine* 69 (2):293–300.

Engels, Friedrich. [1845] 1958. *The Condition of the Working Class in England.* Stanford, Calif.: Stanford University Press.

Erikson, Erik. 1950. *Childhood and Society.* New York: Norton.

Evans-Pritchard, Edward Evan. 1937. *Witchcraft, Oracles and Magic Among the Azande.* Oxford: Oxford University Press.

———. 1940. *The Nuer.* Oxford: Oxford University Press.

———. 1956. *Nuer Religion.* Oxford: Oxford University Press.

Fanon, Frantz. 1963. *The Wretched of the Earth.* New York: Grove.

———. 1967. *Black Skin, White Masks.* New York: Grove.

Faria, Vilmar Evangelista. 1989. *Ciencías Sociais Hoje.* São Paulo: Vertice/Anpocs.

Ferm, Deane William, ed. 1986. *Third World Liberation Theologies.* Maryknoll, N.Y.: Orbis.

Fernandez, Renate Lellep. 1979. "The Decline of Breastfeeding: Interplay of Images and Policies." In *Breastfeeding and Food Policy in a Hungry World,* ed. Dana Raphael, 67–74. New York: Academic.

Figueiredo, Eurico. 1988. *Saudade e Depressão.* Lisbon: University of Lisbon Medical School. Manuscript.

Fildes, Valerie A. 1986. *Breasts, Bottles and Babies: A History of Infant Feeding.* Edinburgh: Edinburgh University Press.

Flax, Jane. 1980. "Mother-Daughter Relationships: Psycho-dynamics, Politics, and

Philosophy." In *The Future of Difference*, ed. Hester Eisenstein and Alice Jardine. Boston: Hall.

Flecknoe, Richard. 1654. *A Relation of 10 Years Travells in Europe, Asia, Affrique, and America*. London.

Fonseca, Claúdia. 1987. "O Internato do Pobre: Febem e a Organização Doméstica em um Grupo Porto-Alegrense de Baixa Renda." *Temos Imesc* 4 (1):21–39.

Forman, Shepard. 1970. *The Raft Fishermen: Tradition and Change in the Brazilian Peasant Economy*. Bloomington: Indiana University Press.

———. 1975. *The Brazilian Peasantry*. New York: Columbia University Press.

Forman, Shepard, and Joyce F. Riegelhaupt. 1979. "The Political Economy of Patron-Clientship: Brazil and Portugal Compared." In *Brazil: Anthropological Perspectives*, ed. Maxine Margolis and William E. Carter, 379–400. New York: Columbia University Press.

Foster, George M. 1960. "The Ritual of Death in Spanish America." In *Culture and Conquest: America's Spanish Heritage*, 143–166. New York: Viking Fund.

———. 1961. "The Dyadic Contract: A Model for the Social Structure of a Mexican Peasant Village." *American Anthropologist* 63:1173–1192.

———. 1965. "Peasant Society and the Image of the Limited Good." *American Anthropologist* 67 (2):293–315.

Foucault, Michel. 1975. *The Birth of the Clinic: An Archaeology of Medical Perception*. New York: Vintage/Random House.

———. 1979. *Discipline and Punish*. New York: Vintage/Random House.

———. 1980. *The History of Sexuality*, vol. 1. New York: Vintage/Random House.

———. 1982. "The Subject and Power." In *Michel Foucault: Beyond Structuralism and Hermeneutics*, ed. Hubert Dryfus and Paul Rabinow, 208–226. Chicago: University of Chicago Press.

Fox-Keller, Evelyn. 1983. *A Feeling for the Organism*. San Francisco: Freeman.

———. 1985. *Reflections on Gender and Science*. New Haven, Conn.: Yale University Press.

Fox, Vivian, and Martin Quitt, eds. 1980. *Loving, Parenting, and Dying*. New York: Psychohistory Press.

Fraginals, Manuel Moreno. 1976. *The Sugar Mill: The Socio-Economic Complex of Sugar in Cuba, 1879–1960*. New York: Monthly Review.

Frankel, Victor. 1959. *From Death Camp to Existentialism*. Boston: Beacon.

Frankenberg, Ronald. 1988. "Gramsci, Culture, and Medical Anthropology." *Medical Anthropology Quarterly* 2 (4):324–337.

Freire, Paulo, 1970. *Pedagogy of the Oppressed*. New York: Seabury.

———. 1973. *Education for Critical Consciousness*. New York: Seabury.

Freiro, Eduardo. 1957. *O Brasileiro Não é Triste*. Rio de Janeiro: Instituto Nacional do Livro.

Freud, Sigmund. 1957. "Mourning and Melancholia." In *The Standard Edition of the Complete Psychological Works of Sigmund Freud*, vol. 14, 243–258. London: Hogarth.

Freyre, Gilberto. 1945. *Brazil, an Interpretation*. New York: Knopf.

———. 1986a. *The Mansions and the Shanties: The Making of Modern Brazil*. Berkeley and Los Angeles: University of California Press. (Translation of 1936. *Sobrados e Macombos*. São Paulo: Companhia Editora Nacional.)

———. 1986b. *The Masters and the Slaves: A Study in the Development of Brazilian*

Civilization. Berkeley and Los Angeles: University of California Press. (Translation of 1933. *Casa-Grande e Senzala*. Rio de Janeiro: Maia and Schmidt.)

———. 1987. *Açúcar*. Recife: Fundação Joaquím Nabuco.

Fry, Peter. 1982. *Para Inglês Ver: Identidade e Política na Cultura Brasileira*. Rio de Janeiro: Zahar.

Fundaçao Oswaldo Cruz. 1986. *Dados: A Mulher Brasileira, Estatísticas de Saúde*. 1V (Outubro).

Furtado, Celso. 1965. *The Economic Growth of Brazil*. Berkeley and Los Angeles: University of California Press.

Galeano, Eduardo. 1975. *Open Veins of Latin America: Five Centuries of the Pillage of a Continent*. New York: Monthly Review.

Galloway, James H. 1968. "The Sugar Industry of Pernambuco During the Nineteenth Century." *Annals of the Association of American Geographers* 58 (3):285–303.

———. 1989. *The Sugar Cane Industry: An Historical Geography from Its Origins to 1914*. New York: Cambridge University Press.

Gama, Fernandes. 1844. *Memórias Históricas de Pernambuco*. Recife.

Garmezy, Norman, and K. Neuchterlain. 1972. "Invulnerable Children: The Fact and Fiction of Competence and Disadvantage." *American Journal of Orthopsychiatry* 42:328–329.

———. 1976. *Vulnerable and Invulnerable Children: Theory, Research and Intervention*. Washington, D.C.: American Psychological Association.

Geertz, Clifford. 1974. *The Interpretation of Cultures*. New York: Basic Books.

———. 1988. *Works and Lives: The Anthropologist as Author*. Stanford, Calif.: Stanford University Press.

Genovese, Eugene D. 1971. *The World the Slaveholders Made*. New York: Vintage.

Geuss, Raymond. 1981. *The Idea of Critical Theory*. Cambridge: Cambridge University Press.

Gilligan, Carol. 1982. *In a Different Voice: Psychological Theory and Women's Development*. Cambridge, Mass.: Harvard University Press.

Ginsberg, Carlo. 1988. "The Inquisitorial Interview." Paper presented at the annual meeting of the American Anthropological Association, Phoenix, Arizona, November 21–24.

Girard, René. 1987a. "Generative Scapegoating." In *Violent Origins: Ritual Killing and Cultural Formation*, ed. Robert Hamerton-Kelly, 73–105. Stanford, Calif.: Stanford University Press.

———. 1987b. "A Non-Sacrificial Reading of the Gospel Text." In *Things Hidden Since the Foundation of the World*, 180–223. Stanford, Calif.: Stanford University Press.

Glick, Ira, Roster Weiss, and Murray Parkes. 1974. *The First Year of Bereavement*. New York: Wiley.

Goffman, Erving. 1961. *Asylums: Essays on the Social Situation of Mental Patients and Other Inmates*. Garden City, N.J.: Anchor.

———. 1963. *Stigma: Notes on the Management of Spoiled Identity*. Englewood Cliffs, N.J.: Prentice-Hall.

Goldberger, Joseph, and Sydentricker, Edgar. 1944. "Pellegra in the Mississippi Flood Area." *Public Health Reports* 42 (44):33–47.

Gordon, Elisabeth. 1987. "Anthropologists Take to the Taste Trail." *Manchester Guardian*, March 15, 12.

Graham, Maria Dundes. 1824. *Journal of a Voyage to Brazil and Residence There During Part of the Years 1821, 1822, 1823.* London: Longman.

Gramsci, Antonio. 1957. *The Modern Prince and Other Writings.* New York: International Publishers.

———. 1971. *Selections from the Prison Notebooks of Antonio Gramsci,* ed. Q. Hoare and G. N. Smith. New York: International Publishers.

———. 1978. *Selections from Political Writings, 1910–1920,* ed. Q. Hoare. New York: International Publishers.

Grant, James P. 1983. *The State of the World's Children, 1983.* UNICEF Annual Report. Oxford: Oxford University Press.

———. 1990. *The State of the World's Children, 1990.* UNICEF Annual Report. Oxford: Oxford University Press.

Green, Linda. 1989. "The Realities of Survival: Mayan Widows and Development Aid in Rural Guatemala." Paper presented at the meeting of the American Anthropological Association, Washington, D.C., November 15.

Greene, Lawrence S., ed. 1977. *Malnutrition, Behavior and Social Organization.* New York: Academic.

Greenfield, Sidney M. 1979. "Charwomen, Cesspools, and Road Building: An Examination of Patronage, Clientage, and Political Power in Southeastern Minas Gerais." In *Structure and Process in Latin America: Patronage, Clientage and Power Systems,* ed. Arnold Strickon and Sidney Greenfield, 71–100. Albuquerque: University of New Mexico Press.

Gregor, Thomas. 1988. "Infants Are Not Precious to Us: The Psychological Impact of Infanticide Among the Mehinaku Indians." The 1988 Stirling Prize paper recipient, annual meeting of the American Anthropological Association, Phoenix, Arizona, November 16–20.

Gussler, Judith, and Linda H. Briesemeister. 1980. "The Insufficient Milk Syndrome." *Medical Anthropology* 4 (2):146–174.

Gutiérrez, Gustavo. 1980. *Pobres e Libertação em Puebla.* São Paulo: Edições Paulinas.

Haffter, Carole. 1968. "The Changeling: History and the Psychodynamics of Attitudes to Handicapped Children in European Folklore." *Journal of the History of the Behavioral Sciences* 4:55–61.

Halperin, E. C., and S. T. Morrow. 1989. "Reducing Infant Mortality in North Carolina." *North Carolina Medical Journal* 50 (8):419–420.

Hamsun, Knut. 1967. *Hunger.* New York: Farrar, Straus, and Giroux.

Haraway, Donna. 1985. "Manifesto for Cyborgs: Science, Technology, and Socialist Feminism in the 1980s." *Socialist Review* 80:65–108.

Hardin, Garrett. 1974. "Living on a Lifeboat." *BioScience* 24 (10):561–568.

Hardman, Leslie. 1958. *The Survivors: The Story of the Belsen Remnant.* London: Vallentine, Mitchell.

Harris, Marvin. 1952. "Race Relations in Minhas Velhas." In *Race and Class in Rural Brazil,* ed. Charles Wagley et al. New York: UNESCO.

———. 1985. *Good to Eat: Riddles of Food and Culture.* New York: Simon and Schuster.

Hartmann, Heinz. 1958. *Ego Psychology and the Problem of Adaptation.* New York: International Universities Press.

Helman, Cecil G. 1981. " 'Tonic,' 'Fuel,' and 'Food': Social and Symbolic Aspects of the Long-Term Use of Psychotropic Drugs." *Social Science and Medicine* 153:521–533.

Herzfeld, Michael. 1991. *The Social Production of Indifference: Exploring the Symbolic Roots of Western Bureaucracy.* Oxford: Berg.

Hirschman, Alberto O. 1963. *Journeys Toward Progress.* New York: Twentieth Century Fund.

Hobsbawn, Eric J. 1959. *Primitive Rebels: Studies in Archaic Forms of Social Movement in the 19th and 20th Centuries.* New York: Norton.

Hochschild, Arlie. 1979. "Emotion Work, Feeling Rules, and Social Structure." *American Journal of Sociology* 85:551–575.

———. 1983. *The Managed Heart: Commercialization of Human Feeling.* Berkeley and Los Angeles: University of California Press.

Holmberg, Alan R. 1950. *Nomads of the Long Bow: The Sirino of Eastern Bolivia.* Washington, D.C.: GPO.

Homans, Peter. 1987. Comments on Nancy Scheper-Hughes's "Mother Love and Child Death." Chicago Symposium on Culture and Human Development, Chicago, Illinois, November 6.

———. 1988. "Disappointment and the Inability to Mourn." In *Freud: Appraisals and Reappraisals, Contributions to Freud Studies,* ed. P. Stepansky, vol. 2, 3–101. Hillsdale, N.J.: Analytic Press.

Horowitz, Irving Louis. 1964. *Revolution in Brazil.* New York: Dutton.

Howard, Richard Baron. 1839. *An Inquiry into the Morbid Effects of Deficiency of Food: Chiefly with Reference to Their Occurrence Amongst Destitute Poor.* London: Simpkin, Marshall.

Huizinga, Johann. 1950. *Homo Ludens: A Study of the Play-Element in Culture.* New York: Roy.

Hunt, Gary, Linda Hunt, and Nancy Scheper. 1970. "Hunger in the Welfare State." In *Divided We Stand,* ed. Ramparts, 112–118. San Francisco: Canefield.

IBGE (Instituto Brasileiro de Geografia e Estatística). 1986. *Perfil Estatístico de Criaças e Mães no Brasil.* Rio de Janeiro: IBGE.

Illich, Ivan. 1976. *Medical Nemesis.* New York: Pantheon.

———. 1983. *Gender.* New York: Pantheon.

Imbert, J. B. M. 1843. *Guia Médico das Mães de Família, ou a Infância Considerada na Sua Higiene, Suas Moléstias, e Tratamento.* Rio de Janeiro.

———. 1847. *Ensaio Higiênico e Médico sobre o Clima do Rio de Janeiro e o Regime Alimentar de Seus Habitantes.* Rio de Janeiro.

Imhof, Arthur E. 1985. "From the Old Mortality Pattern to the New: Implications of a Radical Change from the Sixteenth to the Twentieth Century." *Bulletin of the History of Medicine* 59:1–29.

James, O. W. 1980. "Diminished Maternal Anthropomorphization of Infant Behaviors in a Society with a High Infant Mortality Rate: Patterns of Mother-Infant Interaction in Northwest Ecuador." London. Photocopy.

Janowitz, Barbara, et al. 1982. "Cesarean Section in Brazil." *Social Science and Medicine* 16:19–25.

Jelliffe, D. B. 1970. *The Diseases of Children in the Subtropics and the Tropics.* London: Edward Arnold.

Johnson, Allen. 1971. *Sharecroppers of the Sertão.* Stanford, Calif.: Stanford University Press.

Johnson, J., and M. J. Cunningham, S. Ewing, D. Hatcher, and C. Dannen. 1982. *Newborn Death*. Omaha: Centering Corp.

Joseph, Gilbert. 1990. "On the Trail of Latin American Bandits: A Reexamination of Peasant Resistance." *Latin American Research Review* 25 (3):7–53.

Julião, Francisco. 1962. "A Alforria do Camponês." In *Que São as Ligas Camponesas?*, 11–18. Rio de Janeiro: Editora Civilização Brasileira.

———. 1963. "Brazil, a Christian Country." In *Whither Latin America*, ed. C. Fuentes, 11–18. New York: Monthly Review.

———. 1964a. "Carta de Ouro Preto." In *Revolution in Brazil*, ed. Irving L. Horowitz, 55–62. New York: Dutton.

———. 1964b. "Listen, Peasant: Letter from Pernambuco." In *Revolution in Brazil*, ed. Irving L. Horowitz, 34–55. New York: Dutton.

Kafka, Franz. 1971. *The Complete Stories*, ed. Nahum Glazer. New York: Schocken.

Kahn, Miriam. 1986. *Always Hungry, Never Greedy: Food and the Expression of Gender in a Melanesian Society*. Cambridge: Cambridge University Press.

Kant, Roberto de Lima. 1990. "Criminal Justice: A Comparative Approach, Brazil and the United States." Notre Dame, Ind.: Kellogg Institute, University of Notre Dame. Manuscript.

Keys, Ancel, et al. 1950. *The Biology of Human Starvation*. 2 vols. Minneapolis: University of Minnesota Press.

Klaus, Marshall, R. Jeraud, and N. C. Kreger. 1972. "Maternal Attachment: Importance of the First Postpartum Days." *New England Journal of Medicine* 286:460–463.

Klaus, Marshall, and John Kennell, eds. 1976. *Maternal-Infant Bonding*. St. Louis: Mosby.

———. 1982. *Parent-Infant Bonding*. Rev. ed. St. Louis: Mosby.

Kleinman, Arthur, and Joan Kleinman. 1986. "Somatization: The Interconnections Among Culture, Depressive Experience, and Meanings of Pain." In *Culture and Depression*, ed. Arthur Kleinman and Bryon J. Good, 429–490. Berkeley and Los Angeles: University of California Press.

Kligman, Gail. 1988. *The Wedding of the Dead*. Berkeley and Los Angeles: University of California Press.

———. 1990. "Reclaiming the Public: A Reflection on Creating Civil Society in Romania." *East European Politics and Societies* 4 (3):393–438.

Kohlberg, Lawrence. 1981. *The Philosophy of Moral Development: Moral Stages and the Idea of Justice*. San Francisco: Harper and Row.

Kretschmer, Ernest. 1927. *Theorie et Pratique de Psychologie Medicale*. Paris: Payot.

Krischke, Paulo, and Scott Mainwaring. 1986. *A Igreja nas Bases em Tempo de Transição (1974–1985)*. Porto Alegre: CECEC.

Kristeva, Julia. 1977. "Julia Kristeva: A Quoi Servent les Intellectuels?" *La Nouvel Observateur*, June 20, 99.

———. 1980. "Motherhood According to Giovanni Bellini." In *Desire and Language: A Semiotic Approach to Literature and Art*, ed. Leon S. Rowdiez, 237–270. New York: Columbia University Press.

Kübler-Ross, Elisabeth. 1969. *On Death and Dying*. New York: Macmillan.

LaFontaine, Jean. 1985. "Person and Individual." In *The Category of the Person*, ed. Michael Carrithers, Steven Collins, and Steven Lukes, 123–140. Cambridge: Cambridge University Press.

Lamb, Michael. 1982. "Maternal Attachment and Mother-Neonate Bonding: A

Critical Review." In *Advances in Developmental Psychology*, ed. Michael Lamb and Anne L. Brown, vol. 2, 1–39. Hillsdale, N.J.: Erlbaum.

Lancaster, Roger Nelson. 1988. *Thanks to God and the Revolution: Popular Religion and Class Consciousness in the New Nicaragua*. New York: Columbia University Press.

Langer, William. 1974. "Infanticide: A Historical Survey." *History of Childhood Quarterly* 1:353–365.

Laqueur, Thomas. 1983. "Bodies, Death and Pauper Funerals." *Representations* 1 (1):109–131.

Laslett, Peter. 1965. *The World We Have Lost*. London: Methuen.

Leite, Dante Moreira. 1976. *O Caráter Nacional Brasileiro*. São Paulo: Livraria Pioneira Editora.

Lenz, Rodolfo. 1953. "Velorio de Angelito." In *Antologiá Ibérica Americana del Folklore*, ed. Félix Coluccio, 115–118. Buenos Aires: Guillermo Kraft.

Lepowsky, Maria. 1985. "Food Taboos, Malaria, and Dietary Change: Infant Feeding and Cultural Adaption on a Papua New Guinea Island." *Ecology of Food and Nutrition* 16 (2):105–126.

Leser, William. 1972. "Relacionamento de Certas Características com a Mortalidade Infantil no Município de São Paulo." *Saúde Pública* 6 (1):45–55.

Levertov, Denise. 1987. "What Were They Like?" In *Poems, 1968–1972*, 123. New York: New Directions.

Levi, Primo. 1969. *If This Man Is a Man*. New York: Orion.

Levinas, Emmanuel. 1986. "Useless Suffering." In *Face to Face with Levinas*, ed. Richard Cohn, 156–167. Albany: State University of New York Press.

———. 1987. "Meaning and Sense." In *Collected Philosophical Papers*, 75–107. Dordrecht: Martinus Nijhoff.

LeVine, Robert. 1990. "Infant Environments in Psychoanalysis: A Cross-Cultural View." In *Cultural Psychology: Essays on Comparative Human Development*, ed. James Stigler, Richard Shweder, and Gilbert Herdt, 454–476. Cambridge: Cambridge University Press.

Levi-Strauss, Claude. 1961. *A World on the Wane*. New York: Criterion.

———. 1964. *Mythologiques I: The Raw and the Cooked: Introduction to a Science of Mythology*. New York: Harper and Row.

———. 1965. "The Culinary Triangle." *Partisan Review* 33:586–595.

———. [1955] 1973. *Tristes Tropiques*. New York: Washington Square.

Lewin, Linda. 1979. "Oral Tradition and Elite Myth: The Legend of Antônio Silvino in Brazilian Popular Culture." *Journal of Latin American Lore* 2:157–204.

———. 1987. *Politics and Parentela in Paraíba*. Princeton, N.J.: Princeton University Press.

Lewis, Jane. 1980. *The Politics of Motherhood*. Montreal: McGill–Queens University Press.

Lewis, Oscar. 1958. *Five Families*. New York: Random House.

———. 1963. *The Children of Sanchez*. New York: Vintage.

———. 1965. *La Vida: A Puerto Rican Family in the Culture of Poverty—San Juan and New York*. New York: Random House.

———. 1966. "The Culture of Poverty." *Scientific American* 215 (4):3–10.

Lifton, Robert Jay. 1967. *Death in Life*. New York: Touchstone.

———. 1975. "Preface." In *The Inability to Mourn*, by Alexander Mitscherlich and Margarete Mitscherlich, vii–xv. New York: Grove.

―――. 1979. *The Broken Connection: On Death and the Continuity of Life.* New York: Simon and Schuster.

Lillo, Baldomero. 1942. "El Angelito." In *Relatos Populares,* 219–234. Santiago de Chile: Nascimento.

Lindburgh, Peter. 1975. "Tyburn Riot Against the Surgeons." In *Albion's Fatal Tree: Crime and Society in Eighteenth-Century England,* ed. Douglas Hay et al., 65–82. New York: Pantheon.

Linhares, E. D. R., J. M. Round, and D. A. Jones. 1986. "Growth, Bone Maturation, and Biochemical Changes in Brazilian Children from Two Different Socioeconomic Groups." *American Journal of Clinical Nutrition* 44:552–558.

Lipscomb, F. M. 1945. "Medical Aspects of the Belsen Concentration Camp." *The Lancet* 2 (10):313–315. September 8.

Lispector, Clarice. 1977. *A Hora da Estrela.* Rio de Janeiro: Livraria J. Olympia Editora.

Llosa, Mario Vargas. 1985. *The War at the End of the World.* New York: Avon.

―――. 1986. *The Real Life of Alejandro Mayta.* New York: Vintage.

Lock, Margaret, and Pamela Dunk. 1987. "My Nerves Are Broken: The Communication of Suffering in a Greek Canadian Community." In *Health in Canadian Society,* ed. D. Coburn et al., 295–313. Toronto: Fitzhenry and Whiteside.

Lorau, René. 1975. "Lavoratori del Negativo, Unitevi! (Negative Workers, Unite!)." In *Crimini di Pace,* ed. Franco Basaglia and Franca Ongaro Basaglia, 191–212. Turin: Einaudi.

Low, Setha. 1981. "The Meaning of Nervios." *Culture, Medicine, and Psychiatry* 5:350–357.

Loyola, Maria Andréa. 1984. "Medicina Popular." In *Saúde e Medicina no Brasil: Contribuição para um Debate,* ed. Reinaldo Guimarães, 225–251. 4th ed. Rio de Janeiro: Edições Grall.

Lozoff, Barbara, Thomas G. Brittenham, and Mary Anne Trause. 1977. "The Mother-Infant Relationship: Limits of Adaptability." *Journal of Pediatrics* 91:1–12.

Lutz, Catherine. 1988. *Unnatural Emotions.* Chicago: University of Chicago Press.

―――. 1990. "Emotion, Discourse, and the Politics of Everyday Life." In *Language and the Politics of Emotion,* ed. C. Lutz and L. Abu-Lughod, 1–23. Cambridge: Cambridge University Press.

Macedo, Roberto. 1988. "Brazilian Children and the Economic Crisis." In *Adjustment with a Human Face,* ed. Giovanni Andrea Cornia, Richard Jolly, and Frances Stewart, vol. 11, 35–68. Oxford: Clarendon.

Maior, Mário Santo. 1986. *Remédios Populares do Nordeste.* Recife: Fundação Joaquím Nabuco.

Marcus, George, and Dick Cushman. 1982. "Ethnographies as Texts." *Annual Review of Anthropology* 11:25–69.

Martí, José. 1975. *Inside the Monster: Writings on the United States and American Imperialism.* New York: Monthly Review.

Marx, Karl, and Friedrich Engels. 1964. *On Religion.* New York: Schocken.

Mauss, Marcel. [1938] 1985. "A Category of the Human Mind: The Notion of the Person, the Notion of the Self." In *The Category of the Person,* ed. Michael Carrithers, Steven Collins, and Steven Lukes, 1–25. Cambridge: Cambridge University Press.

———. 1950. "The Notion of Body Techniques." In *Sociology and Psychology: Essays*, 97–119. London: Routledge and Kegan Paul.

McCann, James. 1987. *From Poverty to Famine in Northeast Ethiopia: A Rural History, 1900–1935*. Philadelphia: University of Pennsylvania Press.

McKeown, Thomas. 1976. *The Modern Rise of Population*. London: Arnold.

McManus, Jane. 1989. *Getting to Know Cuba*. New York: St. Martin's.

Medical Society of Rio de Janeiro, Commission on Public Health. 1832. *Causes of Infection of the Atmosphere of the Court*. Rio de Janeiro: Medical Society of Rio de Janeiro.

Memmi, Albert. 1984. *Dependency*. Boston: Beacon.

Messer, Ellen. 1989. "Small But Healthy? Some Considerations." *Human Organization* 48 (1):39–51.

Miller, Barbara D. 1981. *The Endangered Sex: Neglect of Female Children in Rural North India*. Ithaca, N.Y.: Cornell University Press.

———. 1987. "Female Infanticide and Child Neglect in Rural North India." In *Child Survival: Anthropological Approaches to the Treatment and Maltreatment of Children*, ed. Nancy Scheper-Hughes, 95–112. Dordrecht: Reidel.

Miller, Henry. 1961. *Tropic of Cancer*. New York: Grove.

Mills, C. Wright. 1959. *The Sociological Imagination*. London: Oxford University Press.

Mintz, Sidney. 1960. *Worker in the Cane: A Puerto Rican Life History*. New Haven, Conn.: Yale University Press.

———. 1985. *Sweetness and Power: The Place of Sugar in Modern History*. New York: Penguin.

———. 1987. "Choosing Freely." Paper presented at a meeting of the American Anthropological Association, Chicago, Illinois, November 21.

Mohanty, S. P. 1989. "Us and Them: On the Philosophical Bases of Political Criticism." *Yale Journal of Criticism* 2 (2):1–31.

Mull, Dorothy S., and J. Dennis Mull. 1987. "Infanticide Among the Tarahumara of the Mexican Sierra Madre." In *Child Survival: Anthropological Approaches to the Treatment and Maltreatment of Children*, ed. Nancy Scheper-Hughes, 113–134. Dordrecht: Reidel.

National Research Council, Food and Nutrition Board. 1943. *Inadequate Diets and Nutritional Deficiencies in the U.S.* Bulletin no. 109. Washington, D.C.: GPO.

Nations, Marilyn, and Linda-Anne Rebhun. 1988. "Angels with Wet Wings Can't Fly: Maternal Sentiment in Brazil and the Image of Neglect." *Culture, Medicine, and Psychiatry* 12:141–200.

Neruda, Pablo. 1991. *Canto General*. Berkeley and Los Angeles: University of California Press. (Translation of 1976. *Canto General*. Caracas: Biblioteca Ayacucho.)

Nirenberski, Martin. 1946. "Psychological Investigations of a Group of Internees at Belsen Camp." *Journal of Mental Science* 92:60–74.

Noonan, John T. 1965. *Contraception: A History of Its Treatment by Catholic Theologians*. Cambridge, Mass.: Harvard University Press.

Oliver-Smith, Anthony. 1969. "The Pishtaco: Institutionalized Fear in Highland Peru." *Journal of American Folklore* 82 (326):363–368.

Paim, Jairnilson Silva, Silvia Netto Dias, and José Duarte de Araújo. 1980. "Influencia de Fatores Socias e Ambientais na Mortalidade Infantil." *Boletim de la Oficina Sanitaria Panamericana* 88 (4):327–341.

Palmeira, Moacir. 1979. "The Aftermath of Peasant Mobilization: Rural Conflicts in the Brazilian Northeast Since 1964." In *The Structure of Brazilian Development*, ed. Neuma Aguiar, 71–97. New Brunswick, N.J.: Transaction.

Pan American Health Organization. 1990. *Health Conditions in The Americas*. Washington, D.C.: PAHO (Pan Am. Health Org.).

Parker, Richard. 1990. *Bodies, Pleasures, and Passions*. Boston: Beacon.

Parsons, Talcott. 1972. "Definition of Health and Illness in the Light of American Values and Social Structure." In *Patients, Physicians, and Illness*, ed. E. Gartly Jaco, 107–127. Glencoe, Ill.: Free Press.

Parsons, Talcott, and Renée Fox. 1952. "Illness, Therapy, and the Modern Urban American Family." *Journal of Social Issues* 8:31–44.

Parsons, Talcott, Renée Fox, and Victor M. Lidz. 1972. "The Gift of Life and Its Reciprocation." *Death in the American Experience* (special issue of *Social Research*) (Autumn):367–415.

Patel, C. T. 1988. "Live Renal Donation: A Viewpoint." *Transplant Proceedings* 20 (supplement 1):1068–1070.

Paul, Benjamin. 1988. "The Operation of a Death Squad in a Lake Atitlan Community." In *Harvest of Violence: The Mayan Indians and the Guatemalan Crisis*, ed. Robert M. Carmack, 119–155. Norman: University of Oklahoma Press.

Pelto, Gretel, and Pertti J. Pelto. 1983. "Diet and Delocalization: Dietary Changes Since 1750." In *Hunger and History: The Impact of Changing Food Production and Consumption Patterns on Society*, ed. R. Rotberg and T. Rabb, 309–330. Cambridge: Cambridge University Press.

Pelto, Gretel, and Pertti J. Pelto, eds. 1989. "Small But Healthy Symposium Papers." *Human Organization* 48 (1).

Pereira, Alfonso Cézar B. 1986. "Sim, Não Temos Despachantes." *Estudos Sociais* 1 (3):315–328.

Petchesky, Rosalind. 1984. *Abortion and Woman's Choice*. Boston: Northeastern University Press.

Peters, Edward. 1985. *Torture*. London: Blackwell.

Petrini, João Carlos. 1984. *CEB's: Un Novo Sujeito Popular*. Rio de Janeiro: Paz e Terra.

Phillips, Virginia. 1978. "Children in Early Victorian England: Infant Feeding in Literature and Society, 1837–1857." *Tropical Pediatrics and Environmental Child Health* (August):158–166.

Piers, Maria. 1978. *Infanticide*. New York: Wiley.

Pires, Cecilia. 1986. *A Violencia no Brasil*. São Paulo: Editora Moderna.

Poller, Walter. 1961. *Medical Block, Buchenwald*. London: Souvenir.

Power, Jonathan. 1989. "Bringing the Children Off the Streets." *International Herald Tribune*, November 18–19, 1, 7.

Prado, Paulo. 1931. *Retrato do Brasil: Ensaio Sobre a Tristeza Brasileira*. 4th ed. Rio de Janeiro: Briguiet.

Puffer, Ruth R., and Carlos V. Serrano. 1973. *Patterns of Mortality in Childhood*. Scientific Publication, no. 262. Washington, D.C.: PAHO/WHO.

Queiroz, José. 1985. *A Educação Popular nas Comunidades Eclesias de Base*. São Paulo: Edições Paulinas.

Quintas, Fátima. 1986. *Sexo e Marginalidade*. Petrópolis: Vozes.

Rabinow, Paul. 1977. *Reflections on Fieldwork in Morocco*. Berkeley and Los Angeles: University of California Press.

Radcliffe-Brown, A. R. 1940. "On Social Structure." In *Structure and Function in Primitive Society*. London: Cohen and West.

Ramos, Gracíliano. 1984. *Barren Lives*. Austin: University of Texas Press. (Translation of 1938. *Vidas Secas*. Rio de Janeiro: Editora Record.)

Raphael, Dana, and Flora Davis. 1985. *Only Mothers Know: Patterns of Infant Feeding in Traditional Cultures*. Westport, Conn.: Greenwood.

Raymond, Janice. 1989. "At Issue: Children for Organ Export?" *Reproductive and Genetic Engineering* 2 (3):237–245.

Reddy, K. C., et al. 1990. "Unconventional Renal Transplantation in India: To Buy or Let Die." *Transplant Proceedings* 22 (3):910–911.

Rich, Adrienne. 1976. *Of Woman Born: Motherhood as Experience and Institution*. New York: Norton.

———. 1977. "Conditions for Work: The Common World of Women." In *Working It Out*, ed. Sara Ruddick and Pamela Daniels. New York: Pantheon.

Richards, Audrey. 1932. *Hunger and Work in a Savage Tribe: A Function Study of Nutrition Among the Southern Bantu*. London: Routledge.

———. 1939. *Land, Labor, and Diet in Northern Rhodesia*. London: Oxford University Press.

Richet, C. N. 1945. "Medicales sur le Camp de Buchenwald en 1944–45." *Bulletin Acad. Med.* (Paris) 129:377–388.

Riding, Alan. 1988. "In Brazil's Northeast Misery Molded by Man and Nature." *New York Times*, May 3, 1, A-4.

Robock, Stefan. 1965. *Brazil's Developing Northeast*. Washington, D.C.: Brookings Institution.

Robson, K. M., and R. Kumar. 1980. "Delayed Onset of Maternal Affections After Childbirth." *British Journal of Psychiatry* 136:347–353.

Rodrigues, José Carlos. 1983. *Tabu da Morte*. Rio de Janeiro: ACHIAME.

Rosaldo, Michelle. 1984. "Toward an Anthropology of Self and Feeling." In *Culture Theory*, ed. Richard Shweder and Robert LeVine, 137–157. Cambridge: Cambridge University Press.

Rosaldo, Renato. 1980. *Ilongot Headhunting, 1883–1974: A Study in Society and History*. Stanford, Calif.: Stanford University Press.

———. 1983. "Grief and a Headhunter's Rage: On the Cultural Force of Emotion." In *Text, Play, and Story*, ed. Steven Plathner and Edward Bruner, 78–195. Washington, D.C.: American Ethnological Society.

———. 1989. *Culture and Truth: The Remaking of Social Analysis*. Boston: Beacon.

Rosenblatt, Paul, Patricia Walsh, and Douglas Jackson. 1976. *Grief and Mourning in Cross-Cultural Perspective*. New Haven, Conn.: HRAF Press.

Ross, Ellen. 1986. "Working-Class Mothers and Their Children: London, 1870–1918." Paper presented at the meeting of the American Ethnological Society, Wrightsville Beach, North Carolina, April 15–18.

Rossi, Alice. 1977. "A Biosocial Perspective on Parenting." *Daedalus* 106 (2):1–32.

Ruddick, Sara. 1980. "Maternal Thinking." *Feminist Studies* 6:342–364.

———. 1989. *Maternal Thinking: Toward a Politics of Peace*. Boston: Beacon.

Rutter, Michael. 1972. *Maternal Deprivation Reassessed*. London: Penguin.

———. 1985. "Resilience in the Face of Adversity." *British Journal of Psychiatry* 147:598–611.

Sacks, Oliver. 1984. *A Leg to Stand On*. New York: Summit.

————. 1985. *The Man Who Mistook His Wife for a Hat.* New York: Simon and Schuster.

Salahudeen, A. K., et al. 1990. "High Mortality Among Recipients of Bought Living-Unrelated Donor Kidneys." *The Lancet,* 8717:725–728.

Sargent, Carolyn F. 1987. "Born to Die: The Fate of Extraordinary Children in Bariba Culture." *Ethnology* 23:79–96.

Sartre, Jean-Paul. 1956. *Being and Nothingness.* London: Methuen.

Scarry, Elaine. 1985. *The Body in Pain: The Making and Unmaking of the World.* New York: Oxford University Press.

Schecter, John. 1983. "Corona y Baile: Music in the Child's Wake of Ecuador and Hispanic America, Past and Present." *Revista de Músicia Latino America* 4 (1):1–80.

————. 1988. *Velorio de Angelito/Baquiné/Wawa Velorio: The Emblematic Nature of the Transcultural, Yet Local, Latin American Child's Wake.* Latin American Studies Working Papers, no. 3. Santa Cruz: University of California.

Scheff, Thomas. 1979. *Catharsis in Healing, Ritual and Drama.* Berkeley and Los Angeles: University of California Press.

Scheper-Hughes, Nancy. 1979. *Saints, Scholars and Schizophrenics: Mental Illness in Rural Ireland.* Berkeley and Los Angeles: University of California Press.

————. 1984. "Infant Mortality and Infant Care: Cultural and Economic Constraints on Nurturing in Northeast Brazil." *Social Science & Medicine* 19 (5):535–546.

————. 1985. "Culture, Scarcity, and Maternal Thinking: Maternal Detachment and Infant Survival in a Brazilian Shantytown." *Ethos* 13 (4):291–317.

————. 1989. "The Human Strategy: Death Without Weeping." *Natural History Magazine* (October):8–16.

————. 1990. "To Be a Child, Fair-Haired, Fair-Skinned, and Poor in Brazil: Baby Trade." *Los Angeles Times,* Sunday, April 1. *The Nation,* M3.

Scheper-Hughes, Nancy, and Margaret Lock. 1987. "The Mindful Body: A Prolegomenon to Future Work in Medical Anthropology." *Medical Anthropology Quarterly* 1 (1):6–41.

Scheper-Hughes, Nancy, and Anne M. Lovell, eds. 1987. *Psychiatry Inside Out: Selected Writings of Franco Basaglia.* New York: Columbia University Press.

Schmitt, Jean-Claude. 1983. *The Holy Greyhound: Guinefort, Healer of Children Since the Thirteenth Century.* Cambridge: Cambridge University Press.

Schwartz, Tomás. 1977. *Ao Vencador as Batatas—Forma Literária e Processo Social nos Inícios do Romance Brasileiro.* São Paulo: Duas Cidades.

Scott, James C. 1972. "Patron-Client Politics and Political Change in Southeast Asia." *American Political Science Review* 66:91–113.

————. 1985. *Weapons of the Weak.* New Haven, Conn.: Yale University Press.

————. 1989. "Everyday Forms of Resistance." In *Everyday Forms of Peasant Resistance,* ed. Forrest Colburn, 3–33. Armonk, N.Y.: Sharpe.

Scrimshaw, Susan. 1978. "Infant Mortality and Behavior in the Regulation of Family Size." *Population Development Review* 4:383–403.

Seckler, David. 1982. "Small But Healthy: A Basic Hypothesis in the Theory, Measurement, and Policy of Malnutrition." In *New Concepts in Nutrition and Their Implication for Policy,* ed. P. U. Sukhatme, 127–137. Pune: Maharashtra Association for the Cultivation of Science Research Institute.

Sendack, Maurice. 1963. *Where the Wild Things Are.* New York: Harper and Row.

Shack, Dorothy N. 1969. "Nutritional Processes and Personality Development Amongst the Gurage in Ethiopia." *Ethnology* 8:292–300.

Shack, William. 1971. "Hunger, Anxiety, and Ritual: Deprivation and Spirit Possession Among the Gurage of Ethiopia." *Man* 6:30–43.

Shattuck, George Cheever. 1951. *Diseases of the Tropics.* New York: Appleton-Century-Crofts.

Sheehy, Gail. 1986. *Spirit of Survival.* New York: Morrow.

Shorter, Edward. 1975. *The Making of the Modern Family.* New York: Basic Books.

Silver, Henry K., C. Henry Kempe, and Henry B. Bruyn. 1983. *Handbook of Pediatrics.* Los Altos, Calif.: Lange.

Silverman, Milton. 1976. *The Drugging of the Americas: How Multinational Drug Companies Say One Thing About Their Products to Physicians in the United States and Another Thing to Physicians in Latin America.* Berkeley and Los Angeles: University of California Press.

Simons, Marlise. 1987. "Brazil's Health Crisis: The Plague Is Just One Part." *New York Times*, February 15, 4.

Singer, Peter. 1972. *O Milagre Brasileiro: Causas e Consequencias.* Caderno 6 São Paulo: CEBRAP.

Slater, Candace. 1986. *Trail of Miracles: Stories from a Pilgrimage in Northeast Brazil.* Berkeley and Los Angeles: University of California Press.

Smith, Robert. 1989. "The Trafficking of Central American Children." *Report on Guatemala* 10 (3):4–5.

Smith, Thomas Lynn. 1965. *Agrarian Reform in Latin America.* New York: Knopf.

Sontag, Susan. 1979. *Illness as Metaphor.* New York: Farrar, Straus, and Giroux.

Stack, Carol. 1974. *All Our Kin.* New York: Harper and Row.

Steele, Branat F. 1986. "Notes on the Lasting Effects of Early Child Abuse." *Child Abuse and Neglect* 10:283–291.

Stigler, James, Richard Shweder, and Gilbert Herdt, eds. 1990. *Cultural Psychology: Essays on Comparative Human Development.* Cambridge: Cambridge University Press.

Stini, William. 1971. "Evolutionary Implications of Changing Nutritional Patterns in Human Populations." *American Anthropologist* 73:1019.

———. 1975. *Ecology and Human Adaption.* Dubuque, Iowa: Brown.

Stone, Laurence. 1977. *The Family, Sexuality, and Marriage in England, 1500–1800.* New York: Harper and Row.

Strauss, Erwin. 1966. "Upright Posture." In *Phenomenological Psychology: The Selected Papers of Erwin W. Strauss*, 137–165. New York: Basic Books.

Suarez-Orozco, Marcelo. 1987. "The Treatment of Children in the 'Dirty War': Ideology, State Terrorism, and the Abuse of Children in Argentina." In *Child Survival: Anthropological Approaches to the Treatment and Maltreatment of Children*, ed. Nancy Scheper-Hughes, 227–246. Dordrecht: Reidel.

———. 1990. "Speaking of the Unspeakable: Toward a Psychosocial Understanding of Responses to Terror." *Ethos* 18 (3):353–383.

Szulc, Tad. 1960. "Marxists Organizing Peasants in Brazil." *New York Times*, October 31, 1.

———. 1961. "Brazil in Transition." *Foreign Policy Bulletin*, March 1, 7–12.

Tambiah, Stanley J. 1968. "The Magical Power of Words." *Man* (n.s.) 3:175–208.

———. 1969. "Animals Are Good to Think and Good to Prohibit." *Ethnology* 8 (4):423–459.

———. 1990. *Magic, Science, Religion and the Scope of Rationality.* Cambridge: Cambridge University Press.

Taussig, Michael. 1978. "Nutrition, Development, and Foreign Aid." *International Journal of Health Services* 8 (1):101–121.

———. 1987a. "History as Commodity in Some Recent American (Anthropological) Literature." *Food and Foodways* 2:151–169.

———. 1987b. *Shamanism, Colonialism, and the Wild Man: A Study in Terror and Healing.* Chicago: University of Chicago Press.

———. 1989a. "The Nervous System, Part I: Homesickness and Dada." *Kroeber Anthropological Society Papers,* nos. 69–70:32–61.

———. 1989b. "Terror as Usual." *Social Text* (Fall–Winter):3–20.

Taylor, James L. 1970. *A Portuguese-English Dictionary.* Rev. ed. Stanford, Calif.: Stanford University Press.

Teixeira, José Maria. 1887. *Causas da Mortalidade das Crianças no Rio de Janeiro.* Rio de Janeiro.

Thompson, Edward Palmer. 1967. "Time, Work Discipline and Industrial Capitalism." *Past and Present* 38:56–97.

Thorne, Emmanuel, and Gilah Lagner. 1986. "The Body's Value Has Gone Up." *New York Times,* September 8, 23.

Trexler, Robert. 1973. "Infants in Florence: New Sources and First Results." *History of Childhood Quarterly* 1:98–116.

Turnbull, Colin. 1972. *The Mountain People.* New York: Simon and Schuster.

Turner, Victor. 1969. *The Ritual Process: Structure and Anti-Structure.* Chicago: Aldine.

———. 1979. *Process, Performance, and Pilgrimage: A Study in Comparative Symbology.* New Delhi: Concept.

———. 1983. "Carnaval in Rio: Dionysian Drama in Industrializing Society." In *The Celebration of Society,* ed. Frank E. Manning, 103–124. Bowling Green, Ohio: Bowling Green University Popular Press.

———. 1987. "Carnaval, Ritual, and Play in Rio de Janeiro." In *Time Out of Time: Essays on the Festival,* ed. Alessandro Falassi, 74–92. Albuquerque: University of New Mexico Press.

Ungar, Judith. 1988. "Good Mothers Feel Dark Urges." *New York Times,* May 10, A-19.

Urbain, Jean-Didier. 1978. *La Societé de Conservation: Etude Sémiologique des Cimetiéres de l'Occident.* Paris: Payot.

Valliant, George. 1977. *Adaptation to Life.* Boston: Little, Brown.

Vaughan, Megan. 1987. *The Story of an African Famine: Gender and Famine in Twentieth-Century Malawi.* New York: Cambridge University Press.

Victora, J. P., et al. 1989. "Effects of Bottle Feeding on Infant Survival." *Archives of Disease in Childhood* 66:102–109.

Wagley, Charles. 1971. *An Introduction to Brazil.* New York: Columbia University Press.

Waldron, I. 1983. "Sex Differences in Human Mortality: The Role of Genetic Factors." *Social Science and Medicine* 17:321–333.

Walters, James M. 1986. "Perspectives on the Nestle Boycott: Problems in Cross-Cultural Commerce." *Practicing Anthropology* 7 (4):21.

Walvin, James. 1982. *A Child's World: A Social History of English Childhood, 1800–1914.* London: Penguin.

Ware, Helen. 1977. "The Relationship Between Infant Mortality and Fertility: Replacement and Insurance Effects." *Proceedings of the International Population Conference,* vol. 1, 119–132. Brussels, Belgium: International Union for the Scientific Study of Population.

Warner, W. Lloyd. 1959. *A Black Civilization: A Social Study of an Australian Tribe.* New York: Harper and Row.

Weber, Max. 1944. "Charismatic Authority" and "Routinization of Charisma." In *Max Weber: The Theory of Social and Economic Organization,* ed. A. M. Henderson and Talcott Parsons, 358–386. New York: Oxford University Press.

Weiner, M., and F. H. L. Epstein. 1970. "Signs and Symptoms of Electrolyte Disorder." *Yale Journal of Biological Medicine* 43:76–77.

Wiesel, Elie. 1969. *Night.* New York: Avon.

———. 1990. *From the Kingdom of Memory: Reminiscences.* New York: Summit Books.

Williams, C. D. 1935. "Kwashiorkor: A Nutritional Disease of Children." *Lancet* ii:1151–1152.

Winnicott, Donald Woods. 1953. "Transitional Objects and Transitional Phenomena. *International Journal of Psycho-analysis* 34:89–97.

———. 1964. *The Child, the Family, and the Outside World.* London: Penguin.

———. 1986. *Home Is Where We Start from: Essays by a Psychoanalyst.* New York: Norton.

———. 1987. *Babies and Mothers.* Reading, Mass.: Addison-Wesley.

Wittengenstein, Ludwig. 1969. *On Certainty.* New York: Harper and Row.

Wolf, Eric. 1969. *Peasant Wars of the Twentieth Century.* New York: Harper and Row.

———. 1982. *Europe and the People Without History.* Berkeley and Los Angeles: University of California Press.

Wood, Charles. 1977. "Infant Mortality Trends and Capitalist Development in Brazil: The Case of São Paulo and Belo Horizonte." *Latin American Perspectives* 4 (4):56–65.

Woodham-Smith, Cecil. 1962. *The Great Hunger: Ireland, 1845–1849.* New York: Harper and Row.

World Bank. 1991. *Brazil: Women's Reproductive Health.* Population and Human Resources Division. Latin American and Caribbean Regional Office.

World Health Organization. 1980. *Infant and Early Childhood Mortality in Relation to Fertility.* Geneva: World Health Organization.

———. 1991. *Statistics Annual, 1990.* Geneva, Switzerland: WHO.

Wright, Peter G. 1988. "Babyhood: The Social Construction of Infant Care as a Medical Problem in England in the Years Around 1900." In *Biomedicine Examined,* ed. Margaret Lock and Deborah Gordon, 299–330. Dordrecht: Kluwer.

Young, Michael. 1971. *Fighting with Food.* Cambridge: Cambridge University Press.

Zaluar, Alba. 1982. "As Mulheres e a Direção de Consumo Doméstico." *Colcha de Retalhos: Estudos Sobre a Família no Brasil,* 161–184. São Paulo: Editora Brasiliense.

Zawadzki, B., and Paul Lazarsfeld. 1935. "The Psychological Consequences of Unemployment." *Journal of Social Psychology* 6:224–251.

Zimmer, Richard, Joseph Weill, and Marcel DuBois. 1944. "The Nutritional Situation in the Camps of the Unoccupied Zone of France in 1941 and 1942 and Its Consequences." *New England Journal of Medicine* 230:303–314.

Xoxa, child-woman. Pregnant, summer 1992.

Antonieta, the Invincible, 1993.

Like Dilsey, they endure. . . .

Index

Compositor:	Keystone Typesetting, Inc.
Text:	10/13 Aldus
Display:	Aldus
Printer:	Malloy Lithographing, Inc.
Binder:	John H. Dekker & Sons